LIABILITY
IN
NEGLIGENCE

by

J. C. SMITH

Professor
Faculty of Law
University of British Columbia

1984

CARSWELL LEGAL PUBLICATIONS
Toronto   Calgary   Vancouver

SWEET & MAXWELL
London

Canadian Cataloguing in Publication Data

Smith, J. C. (Joseph Carman), 1930-
   Liability in negligence

Includes index.
ISBN 0-459-36590-8 (bound). — ISBN
   0-459-36600-9 (pbk.)

1. Negligence.   2. Liability (Law)   3. I. Title.
   K938.S65 1984   346.03'2   C84-091275-7

TO
LOIS

INTRODUCTION

In May 1982 the common law world celebrated the Golden Jubilee of the decision in *Donoghue v. Stevenson*. The Faculty of Law of the University of British Columbia organized a noteworthy conference on the theme, a report of which later appeared in the Law Review published by that University. Some of the ideas there advanced were developed at greater length in (1983), 46 M.L.R. 147, and are now to be found in the following pages treated with the depth of analysis and clarity of exposition for which Professor J.C. Smith is well known.

There is a distinct need in legal scholarship for monographs which will investigate in more depth than either an article in a periodical or a textbook some subject of topical importance. What subject is more suitable for such treatment than the tort of negligence? It is twenty years since Dr. R.B. Stevens (no timid conservative) complained that the Law Lords in *Hedley Byrne* had led people out into the wilderness and left them there. Since then the Law Lords have led the caravan even further into the desert: the decisions in *Anns* and *Junior Books* have left us staring out over a featureless plain in which all the traditional landmarks have been obliterated. All concerned with the exposition and development of civil liability, whether judges, practitioners or teachers, are anxiously seeking someone who will lead us back to sanity and clarity. Professor Smith puts himself forward as such a leader. He will surely find many followers — his arguments are firmly based on the reported judgments, and are put forward in calm and rational language. If he has to point out the errors of others, whether judges or academics, this is done in a way which is not abrasive; it is all very different from the tone adopted by many writers of case-notes in periodicals.

The starting point can only be *Donoghue v. Stevenson* and Lord Atkin's neighbour principle. Although in one place Professor Smith wishes that the case could be forgotten, he concedes elsewhere that this is unlikely to happen, and that for many years to come we shall be speaking the language of duty and foreseeability. This is sensible, for what has been decided has been decided and we should not wish to be deceived. But we can also hope that the traditional language will be our servant and not our master. So there is a full investigation of the meaning and value of the duty concept. This seems to me to lead to two conclusions.

First, there is a significant legal and moral difference between causing harm and failing to prevent harm from happening. If you have

$100, and fail to give it to a relief agency, and a child in an under-developed country dies, it is plain that you have not killed the child. You ought to have given the money to the agency, but you were under no obligation to do so. To put it in terms of the decision in *Anns*, the housing inspector did not cause the damage but merely failed to prevent it from happening. So the much-cited Wilberforce judgment in *Anns* is criticised for failing to make this distinction (which in the older language of common lawyers was that between misfeasance and nonfeasance). It is suggested that *Anns* can be limited to public authorities acting under statutory powers. In the light of the more recent English cases on breach of statutory duty, which accept that not every foreseeable consequence of a breach of such duty is remediable in tort, this suggestion may soon become the accepted orthodoxy. Another way of looking at this may be to assert that there is real value in the *Hedley Byrne* emphasis on voluntary undertaking and reliance. In this light the decision in *Ross v. Caunters* looks almost untenable: the plaintiff recovered although he had lost only a *spes*, or chance of an economic gain, and that although he had in no way changed his position in reliance on anything said or done by the defendant. The apparent judicial abolition of the distinction between tort and contract, which has been part of the intellectual framework of the common law from time whereof the memory of man runneth not to the contrary, is open to similar criticism. As Sir Owen Dixon was fond of saying, the doctrine of consideration cannot be abolished either by parliament or the courts.

A second major consequence is the demonstration (Chapter 8) that there is a real difference, inherent in the nature of things as well as in the intellectual structure of the law, between the problems of risk and the problems of remoteness. The concept of reasonable foreseeability is re-stated in such a way as to combine the requirements of probability (for the class of events) and possibility (which is sufficient for particular events falling within that class). The practitioner who wants a clear rule to enable him to give a clear answer to a client, as distinct from an argument which might attract an appellate tribunal, will be delighted to read that this analysis is compatible with the decisions in 92 per cent of the reported cases. (A similar analysis is applied both to the rescue cases and to those on nervous shock, with a success rate of over 80 per cent.) I hope that by now I shall have convinced my readers that they have before them a book which combines intellectual distinction with real practical value.

R.F.V. Heuston
March 1984

PREFACE

The aim of this book is to set out in a clear fashion the foundations of liability in the law of negligence. It does not attempt to cover areas such as standard of care and problems of proof, etc. which are adequately dealt with in many of the excellent standard texts on tort law. Rather, it concentrates on that network of concepts such as "duty of care," "risk," "proximity," "direct cause," and "remoteness of damages" which lie at the centre of so many of the difficult and frustrating problems of the law of negligence, such as the limits of liability for the causing of pure economic loss, or for a failure to act. The book is an attempt to develop a coherent theory of negligence which allows us to understand the function of these concepts and to recognize the shifts in meaning which they often undergo in judicial reasoning.

The first chapter sets out the conceptual steps through which an analysis of a negligence problem must proceed before a conclusion can be reached that a particular person is liable to another for a specified amount of damages. The various concepts which have evolved in the jurisprudence of negligence are then explained in terms of these steps. The balance of the book attempts to clarify the more difficult problem areas of the law of negligence in terms of this framework of analysis.

The book represents the culmination of 23 years of teaching, research, and writing in the area of the law of negligence. Consequently it incorporates substantial parts of previously published articles. I am especially grateful to the Butterworths publishing company, the Canadian Bar Review, the Modern Law Review, and the University of British Columbia Law Review for permission to reproduce in revised and altered form material which they have previously published.

Several of the prior published pieces were co-authored, and I would like to express my gratitude to Dean Peter Burns of the Faculty of Law of the University of British Columbia, Professor S.C. Coval of the Department of Philosophy of the University of British Columbia, and Joan Rush of the British Columbia Bar, who were collaborators with me on three of these articles. I am also most grateful to Professor W.V.H. Rogers for his helpful comments and suggestions regarding the manuscript, and to Joan Rush and Anna Fung who helped in the research and preparation of the appendices.

I am indebted to the Social Sciences and Humanities Research Council of Canada for a research time stipend and to the University of Sydney, Faculty of Law, for allowing me to spend the time with them in the preparation of the manuscript.

J.C. Smith
Vancouver, 1984

TABLE OF CONTENTS

TABLE OF CASES

[Note: Boldface numbers refer to cases mentioned or digested in the Appendices.]

1

THE MYSTERY OF DUTY

I. INTRODUCTION

Lawyers, judges, and academics generally take one of two approaches to the concept of duty of care in the law of negligence. There are those whom one would call "the true believers."[1] They take the concept seriously. This is to say that they believe that the concept of duty of care is a meaningful doctrine of the law of negligence. It has three aspects: foreseeability, limitation in regard to the scope of the law of negligence, and limitation to the scope of recovery. Somehow these three are aspects of one unity — duty of care. Like the mystery of the Holy Trinity, three in one, yet not one but three. This is a confused position which leads to ambiguity in the law.

Then there are those whom one would term "the sceptics." For them, duty of care is so much jargon which can cover a variety of different policy issues and is resorted to by judges when they are unable to clearly articulate the policies at stake or the reasons for taking one alternative rather than another in decision-making.[2] This approach leads to uncertainty in the law, and prediction of decisions becomes impossible. Some sceptics such as Lord Denning M.R. recommend banishing the term altogether from the language of negligence. In dealing with the difficult question of recovery for economic loss he writes:

> "The more I think about these cases, the more difficult I find it to put each into its proper pigeon-hole. Sometimes I say: 'There was no duty.' In others I say: 'The damage was too remote.' So much so that I think the time has come to discard those tests which have proved so elusive."[3]

The concept of duty is far too firmly entrenched in the jurisprudence of the law of negligence to be jettisoned.[4] Nor should it be so long as the

---

[1] See, e.g., Millner, *Negligence in Modern Law* (1967), at 24-89.

[2] See, e.g., Prosser, *Selected Topics on the Law of Torts* (1953), at 213-14, who states, "Duty is only a word with which we state our conclusion that there is or is not to be liability."

[3] *Spartan Steel & Alloys Ltd. v. Martin & Co. (Contractors) Ltd.*, [1973] 1 Q.B. 27 at 37, [1972] 3 W.L.R. 502, [1972] 3 All E.R. 557 at 562 (C.A.).

[4] In 1934 Winfield stated: "as to the usefulness of the idea [of duty], in theory it might well

concepts of legal rights and obligations furnish the conceptual foundations for recovery of losses through awards of damage. Our path of
action, therefore, should be to dispel the mystery with careful analysis.

There are certain ideas or notions which are basic to the concept of
negligence, whether within or without the law. It is said of a person that
he or she is negligent when they act without due care and attention in
regard to harmful consequences of their actions. The concept of negligence thus assumes the notion of risk, and the notion of risk entails the
idea of foreseeable harm. When we say that a person has been negligent
we are passing a normative judgment on or about them. We are saying
that they acted in a way that they ought not to have acted. This assumes
that we know how they ought to have acted. The way in which we
consider that they ought to have acted is the norm or standard which
entitles us to condemn them for being negligent when they fail to comply
with it. When a person complies with the norm or standard of care
expected of them, they cannot be judged to be at fault or found to be
negligent.

Where a person's actions do not comply with the standard of care
expected of them and injury to others results, we say of the person at
fault that he or she "caused" the damage. When a person causes injury
to someone else through the doing of an act which he or she ought not to
have done, we consider that person to blame or responsible for the
damage. This responsibility is the basis of justification for the law
requiring the person at fault to compensate the other party for this loss.

There are also certain steps which must be taken before we can reach
the conclusion that a person has been negligent, and decide what legal
consequences ought therefore to result. To begin with, a decision must
be made as to whether the law of negligence even covers or applies to a
particular kind of situation. It must then be ascertained whether the
defendant has created a risk of harm which would be recognized as
negligence in the legal sense. Next, it must be determined whether or not
the negligence was the cause of the loss. Finally, it must be decided
whether the particular kind of loss suffered is recoverable under the law,
and if so, how the loss is to be measured in monetary terms. Each of
these steps raises particular kinds of legal problems, and most are
closely interrelated with the basic ideas or notions which are a constitutive part of the concept of negligence.

---

be eliminated from the tort of negligence, for it got there only by a historical accident and it
seems to be superfluous." "Duty in Tortious Negligence" (1934), 34 Col. L. Rev. 41 at 66.
He states at p. 58, however, that "whether the idea of duty in negligence is useful or
useless, it is now too deeply embedded in English law to remove it."

Certain ideas or notions have been identified above such as "risk," "foreseeability," "standard of care," "causation" and "responsibility," which are entailed in, are a constitutive part of, or are related to the concept of negligence. A number of steps have also been enumerated which must be followed before it can be decided that a particular person is liable in the law of negligence to pay another person a specified amount in damages. Is the concept of "duty" equivalent to any of these ideas or notions? If not, is it an independent idea or concept in its own right which is entailed in or related to the concept of negligence? If so, how is it to be explained? Does it refer to a particular step in an action of negligence? If so, which one?

The fact that an answer to these questions is not obvious indicates that the concept of "duty of care" can be confusing and ambiguous. It is so because it is often used as equivalent to a number of the notions or ideas related to the concept of negligence, and as well is used to refer to several of the different steps in a negligence action.

If the confusion stemming from the use of the ambiguous concept "duty of care" is to be clarified and not perpetuated, the problem must be tackled in terms of categories and concepts which are independent of duty language. In Part II, such an analysis will be set out. In Part III, representative examples will be used to show the courts' use of the concept of duty of care to refer to several different aspects of a case in negligence, thus producing confusion.

Later chapters will show how this confusion can be dispelled by attacking several of the difficult problems of the law of negligence in terms of an analysis independent of duty language.

It is not advocated that lawyers argue cases without resort to duty language. If a judge wants to know whether or not the defendant owed the plaintiff a duty of care, then counsel must be prepared to argue the case in those terms; but at least we need not be prisoners of our own concepts. If we are able to pierce the mystery of duty of care and have our own analogies and understanding of the problems at issue, we can use the right cases and make the right arguments, dressing them in duty language if need be.

II.   THE ANATOMY OF A NEGLIGENCE ACTION

The following analysis of a case in negligence is offered.

a) Will the Courts Impose a Standard of Care?

There are certain kinds of activities in regard to which the courts will not impose any standard of care whatsoever upon those who carry them out, even though they may result in inadvertently caused harm. The law will not require such persons to take care and there will be no legal liability if they fail to do so. In certain situations the outcome of not imposing legal liability is of a higher value or of more importance than the outcome of imposing legal liability. This arises where the policies which would be served by not imposing a standard of care have a higher priority than the policies served by deterring and preventing harm-causing conduct, and by requiring the person at fault to compensate his or her victim. In other cases, although the conduct of one person might result in a loss to another, the law imposes no duty of care because the action is legitimate in that no wrong is committed.

The courts will not apply the law of negligence to participants in the judicial process within the courtroom, because of the value of being able to judge, testify or act independently without fear of legal liability, outweighing the value of giving recovery for damage suffered, even though fault may be involved.[5] Other advantages also weigh on the side of not extending the law of negligence to adjudicative processes. If we did allow such actions they would often require a retrial of the case, thus resulting in a loss of many important values such as speedy justice, certainty and economy.[6] The law of negligence imposes no standard of care on university examiners in evaluating examinations, because the expense and time involved in courts hearing what would in effect be appeals of an evaluative judgment requiring special skills outweigh the value of allowing recovery for negligence.[7] Unless a person has a special relationship to a person in danger the courts will impose no liability in negligence for a failure to rescue. For many years no action could be maintained between spouses because it had been believed (at least until the advent of motor cars and automobile liability insurance) that the

---

[5]*Rondel v. Worsley*, [1969] 1 A.C. 191, [1967] 3 W.L.R. 1666, [1967] 3 All E.R. 993 (H.L.); *Anderson v. Gorrie*, [1895] 1 Q.B. 668 (C.A.); *Marrinan v. Vibart*, [1963] 1 Q.B. 234, [1962] 2 W.L.R. 1224, [1962] 1 All E.R. 689, affirmed [1963] 1 Q.B. 528, [1962] 3 W.L.R. 912, [1962] 3 All E.R. 380 (C.A.). The above cases, plus all those decisions which established an absolute privilege in the law of defamation in regard to the courts, illustrate that on grounds of public policy the law will allow no causes of action, whether in negligence or as an international tort, to arise when people are participating in the judicial process within a court of law. The immunity from tort liability recognized by the British courts has been rejected by Krever J. in *Demarco v. Ungaro* (1979), 21 O.R. (2d) 673, 8 C.C.L.T. 207, 27 Chitty's L.J. 23, 95 D.L.R. (3d) 385 (H.C.).

[6]For a full discussion of these policy factors, see the judgments of the members of the House of Lords in *Rondel v. Worsley, supra*, note 5.

[7]*Thorne v. University of London*, [1966] 2 Q.B. 237, [1966] 2 W.L.R. 1080, [1966] 2 All E.R. 338 (C.A.).

damage to the marriage relationship resulting from spouses litigating outweighed the value of having a spouse financially compensate the other for damage caused.[8] A person is free in the normal course of business to inflict certain kinds of economic loss on competitors.

The first issue which the courts must decide in a negligence action is whether any standard of care at all should be imposed on the defendant. We might refer to the above kind of questions as raising an "issue of extension" because the question which the court must face is whether the law of negligence extends to cover the particular kind of activity out of which the damage arose. Issues of extension deal with the limits of the law of negligence. The development of negligence in recent years has been in the direction of extending its limits, so much so that now in most negligence actions this first step presents no problem for the courts.

b) Is There a Reasonably Foreseeable Risk of Harm?

Given that the activity which caused the damage or injury is one to which the law of negligence will extend in that the courts will impose a standard of care on the particular kind of conduct, the next question which must be answered is whether there is any justification for imposing a standard of care on the defendant in the particular circumstances of the case. One is not expected to take due care unless one can reasonably foresee that if one does not, damage can occur. There must, in other words, be a foreseeable risk of harm before there can be a finding of negligence. To query whether or not a reasonably foreseeable risk of harm exists is equivalent to asking whether the degree of experience and understanding of the ordinary person in regard to the relationships between causes and effects should lead one to anticipate or expect harm to occur in given circumstances.

c) What is the Standard Which the Courts Will Impose?

i) What kind of action would have been needed to avoid the harm?

ii) Can the defendant reasonably be expected to have taken this action?

Some of the relevant factors which the courts will take into account in deciding questions of the standard of care are:

---

[8]The various Married Women's Property Acts of most Commonwealth jurisdictions provide that husbands and wives are not entitled to sue each other in tort. Whatever undesirable side effects there are of not allowing spouses to do battle in the courts, these have no relevance in regard to motor vehicle accidents where the traditional bar allows insurance companies to avoid paying under a policy where one spouse is injured as the result of the negligence of the other. The trend now is to remove or substantially diminish this bar. See *e.g.*, The Law Reform (Husband and Wife) Act, 1962 (Imp.), c. 48, s. 1.

(a)   What was the probability of the damage happening?

(b)   What would be the expense of avoiding the risk?

(c)   How serious is the likely damage or injury?

(d)   What is the social value of the conduct causing the risk?

(e)   Who is in the best position to avoid the risk?

(f)   Who gets the most benefit from the risk-creating activity?

(g)   What is the standard of care generally taken by other people in similar circumstances in regard to similar risks?

(h)   Does any statute require a particular standard of care under these circumstances?

d) Is the Actual Conduct of the Defendant a Departure from the Standard of Care?

  i) What did the defendant do or fail to do?

 ii) Does his actual conduct conform to the standard of care?

e) Is There a Cause-Effect Relationship?

Would the plaintiff have suffered this same loss if the defendant had not been negligent?

f) The Remoteness Issue

To require a defendant to pay compensation for all losses resulting from his or her negligent acts to any persons whatsoever does not strike us as being just or fair. Unless some limits are placed on the potential liability of people for the results of their acts, freedom of action will be seriously impaired. The issue of remoteness deals with the question of how far down the chain of causation liability is allowed to run. The courts will not always shift onto a negligent defendant all the damage which bears a cause-effect relationship with his fault. Such damages may be too crippling, giving rise to numerous suits against a single person, and also may require defendants to pay damages out of all proportion to their actual fault. The degree of fault ought to bear some proportionate relationship to the amount of damages which can be recovered.

g) What Principles Will the Courts Use to Assess the Damages?

After a court decides that a certain loss is recoverable, it must then decide how the loss is to be measured, and if it is not economic, how it is to be translated into monetary terms.

III. THE AMBIGUITY OF THE DUTY CONCEPT

There are at least four different kinds of questions which can be isolated in terms of the analysis of an action in negligence set out in the previous section, each of which can be, and often is, phrased in terms of duty of care language. One kind of question raises issues of extension or of the limits to the law of negligence. Another raises the issue of the presence of a foreseeable risk of harm. A third raises the issue of what standard of care ought to be taken in regard to the risk and a fourth raises the issue of remoteness.

When the issues in the law of negligence are framed in duty of care language, problems of extension, foreseeability of harm, standard of care, and remoteness often become muddled. The failure to distinguish the basic kinds of problems leads to the use of tests and policy considerations which are not appropriate to the real issue before the court. Thus considerations relevant only to problems of risk are used to solve remoteness issues, and problems of remoteness are dealt with in terms of policies and considerations relevant only to questions of extension. Much of the conceptual confusion in the law of negligence can be traced to this failure to distinguish between these various basic problems. Once these questions are separated, an examination of the relevant policies can then be made.

The reason that duty of care language has been used to refer to at least four different kinds of problems (with the result that we fail to distinguish between them) lies in the distinction which the common law historically has made between questions of fact and questions of law. Under the traditional common law theory regarding the distinction between the role of the judge and that of the jury, questions of law were to be decided by the judge and questions of fact by the jury. If, however, the judge wished to take from or keep a case from being put to the jury, he or she could do so by framing the issue in terms of a question of law which was then conceived to be appropriate only for the judge to decide. This way of conceiving of legal problems has remained, although for all practical purposes the jury system has nearly ceased to exist as far as civil actions are concerned. This historical pattern, plus the fact that psychologically a question of law appears to be susceptible of a more decisive and certain answer than does a question of fact, has led the common law judge to express decisions, wherever possible, in terms of responses to issues of law rather than to issues of fact. The presence or absence of a duty of care has always been considered to be a matter of law; consequently, any issue which can be phrased as a matter of duty of care becomes a question of law.[9]

a) Duty Language used to Deal With Issues of Extension

There are, as pointed out in Part II, certain areas of human activity with which the courts will not interfere either on grounds of public policy or because the imposition of a duty would be inconsistent with existing rights. That is, they will not impose any standard of care on a person in regard to a particular kind of activity or a particular kind of loss. Where the judge feels that no standard of care ought to be imposed on a particular kind of activity, the court will rule that, as a matter of law (and this is a true question of law and not of fact) no duty of care is owed by the defendant. Thus, duty of care language is used to deal with problems of extension, or the limits of the law of negligence. For example, public bodies such as municipalities and public officials or employees were generally not held liable for damages caused by a failure to act. The English courts radically departed from the old line of precedents in *Dutton v. Bognor Regis Urban Dist. Council* and *Anns v. Merton London Borough Council,*[11] when they held municipal bodies liable for damages resulting from the failure of municipal building inspectors to inspect properly the foundations of houses. When members of the courts raised and dealt with the issue of whether municipalities and the inspectors owed a duty of care to subsequent purchasers of houses the courts were grappling with a problem of extension, and their finding that a duty exists means no more than that the law of negligence now extends to such bodies and persons in the sense that the law will impose a standard of care upon them not only in regard to risks arising from their actions, but for risks which they did not create but failed to remove. A similar issue of extension was raised in *Home Office v. Dorset Yacht Co. Ltd.*[12] where the House of Lords ruled that the Home Office was liable for damage to a yacht caused by inmates of a Borstal institution when supervision became lax. Lord Diplock first stated the issue in terms of duty of care language, then interpreted the question as a problem as to the perimeters or limits of the law of negligence.

---

[9]For a history of how duty language developed in the law of negligence, and whence it came, see Winfield, *supra*, note 4. See also Fleming, "Remoteness and Duty: The Control Devices in Liability for Negligence" (1953), 31 Can. Bar Rev. 471.

[10]*East Suffolk Rivers Catchment Board v. Kent*, [1941] A.C. 74, [1940] 4 E.R. 527 (H.L.).

[11][1972] 1 Q.B. 373, [1972] 2 W.L.R. 299, [1972] 1 All E.R. 462 (C.A.), and [1978] A.C. 728, [1977] 2 W.L.R. 1024, [1977] 2 All E.R. 492 (H.L.).

[12][1970] A.C. 1004, [1970] 2 W.L.R. 1140, [1970] 2 All E.R. 294 (H.L.).

"The specific question of law raised in this appeal may therefore be stated as: Is any duty of care to prevent the escape of a Borstal trainee from custody owed by the Home Office to persons whose property would be likely to be damaged by the tortious acts of the Borstal trainee if he escaped?

"This is the first time this specific question has been posed at a higher judicial level than that of a county court. Your Lordships in answering it will be performing a judicial function similar to that performed in *Donoghue v. Stevenson* [1932] A.C. 562 and more recently in *Hedley Byrne & Co. Ltd. v. Heller & Partners Ltd.* [1964] A.C. 465 of deciding whether the English law of civil wrongs should be extended to impose legal liability to make reparation for the loss caused to another by conduct of a kind which has not hitherto been recognised by the courts as entailing any such liability.

"This function, which judges hesitate to acknowledge as law-making, plays at most a minor role in the decision of the great majority of cases, and little conscious thought has been given to analysing its methodology. Outstanding exceptions are to be found in the speeches of Lord Atkin in *Donoghue v. Stevenson* and of Lord Devlin in *Hedley Byrne & Co. Ltd. v. Heller & Partners Ltd.* It was because the former was the first authoritative attempt at such an analysis that it has had so seminal an effect upon the modern development of the law of negligence.

"It will be apparent that I agree with the Master of the Rolls that what we are concerned with in this appeal 'is . . . at bottom a matter of public policy which we, as judges, must resolve.' "[13]

b) Duty Language Used To Deal With Issues of Risk

Given that the case deals with conduct where the courts will impose a standard of care, the next question is whether or not a reasonable person would have foreseen a risk of harm. If the judge believes that a reasonable person would not, he or she will often express this conclusion by saying that the defendant owes no duty of care to the plaintiff. This would be the case, not because the defendant's conduct was the kind for which courts will not impose any standard of care, but because the court believes there was in fact no foreseeable risk of harm. Equally, if the judge concludes that there was a reasonably foreseeable risk of harm, he or she often expresses this by saying that the defendant owed the plaintiff a duty of care.

This use of duty language may be illustrated by the judgment of *Nova Mink Ltd. v. T.C.A.*[14] where the court held that a pilot was not negligent in causing female mink to eat their young as the result of the noise of the aircraft which he flew overhead, because he did not know and could not reasonably have foreseen that there were mink farms in the district. The issue of whether there was a foreseeable risk of harm was stated and

---

[13]*Ibid.*, at 1057-58. Lord Reid's judgment, on the other hand, is a prime example of the confusion of the concepts of "extension" and "risk."

[14]26 M.P.R. 389, [1951] 2 D.L.R. 241, 66 C.R.T.C. 316 (N.S.C.A.).

answered in duty language. MacDonald J. first asks, "Does the evidence establish that the defendant was under a legal duty to use care to avoid injury to the plaintiff's business as a mink ranch operator?"[15] He frames the test of the existence of a duty in the following words:

> "The common law yields the conclusion that there is such a duty only where the circumstances of time, place and person would create in the mind of a reasonable man in those circumstances such a probability of harm resulting to other persons as to require him to take care to avert that probable result."[16]

He states further:

> "Many attempts have been made to generalize the circumstances which create a legal duty of care . . . What is common . . . is the idea of a *relationship between parties attended by a foreseeable risk of harm* . . . That relationship may arise out of circumstance of physical proximity; but it is not that circumstance per se which gives rise to duty but the probability of harm inhering in the relationship of parties, spatial or otherwise. If such a relationship does exist in fact, or in contemplation, and is fraught with the likelihood of harm to another in that relationship, the basis of duty exists; and it is immaterial that the locus or date of the occurrence of the apprehended harm be unknown."[17]

Lord Atkin's famous dictum in *Donoghue v. Stevenson* is the classic formulation of the risk issue in terms of duty language:

> "At present I content myself with pointing out that in English law there must be, and is, some general conception of relations giving rise to a duty of care, of which the particular cases found in the books are but instances . . . You must take reasonable care to avoid acts or omissions which you can reasonably foresee would be likely to injure your neighbour."[18]

c) Duty Language Used to Deal With Issues of Standard of Care

Even though there may be a reasonably foreseeable risk of harm, the judge may believe that on the facts the defendant did all that could reasonably be expected to prevent the harm. This conclusion is often expressed in the form of a ruling that the defendant did not have a duty to take the particular action which would have prevented the risk of harm from materializing. If, on the other hand, the court is of the opinion that it is reasonable to expect the defendant to guard against the risk, the conclusion could be expressed as a finding that the defendant owed a duty of care.

Bolton v. Stone[19] furnishes us with a paradigmatic case of this kind of

---

[15]*Ibid.*, at 253-54.
[16]*Supra*, note 14, at 254.
[17]*Supra*, note 14, at 256.
[18][1932] A.C. 562 at 580 (H.L.).
[19][1951] A.C. 850, [1951] 1 All E.R. 1078 (H.L.).

usage. That case dealt with the issue of whether the operators of a cricket field were liable to a person standing on an adjacent highway who was struck by a cricket ball. It was clear that such an accident was a foreseeable risk, as cricket balls had been struck over the fence on a few occasions over the preceding years. The probability of a ball being struck over the fence and hitting someone, however, was very small. The basic issue in the case was whether the cricket club could be expected to move the cricket pitch to a different position, or build the seven-foot fence even higher to prevent such an occurrence from happening at all. This problem was discussed as follows by Lord Oaksey:

> "In such circumstances was it the duty of the appellants, who are the committee of the club, to take some special precautions other than those they did take to prevent such an accident as happened? The standard of care in the law of negligence is the standard of an ordinarily careful man, but in my opinion an ordinarily careful man does not take precautions against every foreseeable risk. He can, of course, foresee the possibility of many risks, but life would be almost impossible if he were to attempt to take precautions against every risk which he can foresee. He takes precautions against risks which are reasonably likely to happen."[20]

Lord Reid dealt with the issue in a similar fashion, stating:

> "This case, therefore raises sharply the question what is the nature and extent of the duty of a person who promotes on his land operations which may cause damage to persons on an adjoining highway. Is it that he must not carry out or permit an operation which he knows or ought to know clearly can cause such damage, however improbable that result may be, or is it that he is only bound to take into account the possibility of such damage if such damage is a likely or probable consequence of what he does or permits, or if the risk of damage is such that a reasonable man, careful of the safety of his neighbour, would regard that risk as material?"[21]

Or, in other words, ought the court to impose a sufficiently high standard of care on the defendants so as to require them to remove the risk?

d) Duty Language Used to Deal With Issues of Remoteness

We judge persons negligent when, as a result of failing to take due care in their actions, they create a foreseeable risk of harm. But as it is so often pointed out, negligence and risk are terms of relation.[22] The relation is between an act and its foreseeable consequences in terms of a particular kind of harm happening to particular persons. Often, however, other things happen than those which are entailed within the ambit of the

---

[20]*Ibid.*, at 863.

[21]*Supra*, note 19, at 864.

[22]*Palsgraf v. Long Island Railroad Co.* (1928), 248 N.Y. 339, 162 N.E. 99 at 101, 59 A.L.R. 1253 (C.A.).

risk. A different kind of harm may result. Thus A., by his or her action, creates a risk of harm x. to B., but B. may suffer harm y. as well as or in place of harm x. Or harm may result to someone other than or as well as the person who is the subject of the risk; as well as or instead of B., C. may suffer either harm x. or harm y. The courts will not always give full damages to all injuries or losses resulting from the acts of a negligent person as obvious policy reasons dictate that there must be some limits placed on a person's legal liability. Where a judge feels that a particular loss falls outside these limits, he or she can express this conclusion by holding that the defendant did not owe a duty of care in regard to the particular kind of harm or to the particular person where the judge considers that either the harm or the person who suffers it, or both, fall outside the limits which must be placed on the defendant's legal liability. Duty language in such instances is thus used to deal with problems of remoteness.

Applications of the so-called foreseeability test of remoteness often furnish us with a classic example of the confusion which can arise from multiple uses of "duty" language. The issue of whether a particular injury to a particular person is too remote is stated in terms of whether or not the defendant owed a duty of care to that person in regard to the particular loss. The judge or court then surreptitiously shifts to a usage of the term "duty" appropriate for the issue of the presence of a reasonably foreseeable risk of harm. The test of foreseeability of harm, appropriate for dealing with an issue of risk, is then introduced as a test of remoteness.

This pattern appears in several of the judgments of members of the House of Lords in *Hay (or Bourhill) v. Young*.[23] In that case a cyclist, through his negligence, caused an accident which resulted in nervous shock to the plaintiff. There was no question of the defendant's negligence; consequently, no issue in regard to standard of care arose. The court clearly saw the issue as one of remoteness and dealt with it in terms of duty language.

Each member of the court discussed the question of the limits of liability for damages resulting from the defendant's negligence (this is what is at stake in a true remoteness issue) in terms of a duty of care in the sense of the creation of a risk of harm. Lord Porter, for example, states:

"In the case of a civil action there is no such thing as negligence in the abstract. There must be neglect of the use of care towards a person towards whom the defendant owes

---

[23][1943] A.C. 92, [1942] 2 All E.R. 396 (H.L.)

the duty of observing care, and I am content to take the statement of Lord Atkin in *Donoghue v. Stevenson* as indicating the extent of the duty."[24]

He then quotes the passage from Lord Atkin's judgment which has been quoted above and applies that definition of duty in terms of risk to the problem of remoteness, explaining:

> "Is the result of this view that all persons in or near the street down which the negligent driver is progressing are potential victims of his negligence? Though from their position it is quite impossible that any injury should happen to them and though they have no relatives or even friends who might be endangered, is a duty of care to them owed and broken because they might have been but were not in a spot exposed to the errant driving of the peccant car? I cannot think so. The duty is not to the world at large. It must be tested by asking with reference to each several complainant: Was a duty owed to him or her? If no one of them was in such a position that direct physical injury could reasonably be anticipated to them or their relations or friends normally I think no duty would be owed, and if, in addition, no shock was reasonably to be anticipated to them as a result of the defender's negligence, the defender might, indeed, be guilty of actionable negligence to others but not of negligence towards them."[25]

IV. CONCLUSION

It is doubted whether, in the foreseeable future, the legal profession will give up the use of duty language in negligence cases. Judges like to use it because with it they can turn a factual question or a difficult policy problem into the legal issue, "Did the defendant owe the plaintiff a duty of care?" Such a question can be answered with a decisive "Yes!" or "No!" and the conclusion, whatever it is, has the appearance of being reached by an inevitable pattern of legal logic. Even though a judge may realize that it is circular reasoning to conclude that there is no liability because the defendant did not owe the plaintiff a duty of care, or that there is because he or she does, it is easier for the judge to sneak in his or her conclusion in the guise of a premise about the existence of duty than to attempt to articulate some of the policy premises which were the actual bases of the decision. In any case, the duty language is so ingrained in the jurisprudence of negligence that it is unlikely that a precedent-oriented conservative profession such as ours will make such a change lightly. And as long as the judge asks counsel, "Did the defendant owe the plaintiff a duty of care?", then the lawyer must be prepared to deal with the case in that manner. In consequence, those who teach torts to budding lawyers must equip them to deal with a problem in duty language. The issue is not whether or not we continue to use duty language, but whether we are to be masters of the language or be caught up in the morass.

---

[24]*Ibid.*, at 116-17.

[25]*Supra*, note 23, at 117.

The purpose of this analysis is to enable one to recognize the separate fundamental steps or problems in a negligence action and the basic policies which are at stake in each, and to deal with them clearly. Then it does not matter whether or not the conclusion is stated in terms of the existence of duty of care. Presumably both judge and counsel can better serve justice and the ends of the law if they recognize the basic issues and can muster the right precedents and policies. Surely a lawyer will be more effective if he or she is able to distinguish among questions about the perimeters of the law of negligence, questions of risk of harm, questions of standard of care, and questions about remoteness. Judges have to be more competent or proficient if they focus their attention on the policy which leads the law to favour recovery for rescuers than they do if they are trying to decide whether or not the rescuer is foreseeable.

Judges and practitioners who function within the law of negligence are continually going to be faced with shocked mothers, pre-natally injured infants, explosions, cricket balls hitting heads, snails in bottles, toes in chewing tobacco,[26] weird chains of events, and simple crushing, breaking, burning and cutting of the human body. A decision must be reached and given as to whether a loss will be shifted from the person suffering the loss to the actor who may have caused it. That decision must be justified in terms of "the law." If that justification is to be meaningful and not merely empty words, we must at least have a theory about "duty of care." The above is offered for that purpose.

Since it is unlikely that either judge or academic will exorcize the "spirit" or "ghost" of duty from the law, we must be satisfied with attempting to banish the mystery surrounding the concept and the way it functions in the law.

---

[26]*Pillars v. R.J. Reynolds Tobacco Co.* (1918), 117 Miss. 490, 78 So. 365 (S.C.).

2
DUTY AND RISK

I. INTRODUCTION

If one were to ask a recent graduate of an English, Canadian, Australian or New Zealand law school what was the most important decision in all the common law, he or she would likely and without hesitation say *Donoghue v. Stevenson*.[1] The reason would probably be that no other case has had to carry the burden of such a broad area of law as has this decision. It would appear to underpin the entire law of negligence or it at least seems to be the starting point of judicial reasoning in every negligence action.

We may well ask why the entire law of negligence should rest on a decision regarding the potential liability of a manufacturer of ginger beer who distributes it in opaque bottles, one of which also contains a decomposed snail which makes a woman sick when she consumes the contents. It seems rather obvious that a manufacturer who puts on the market such a mixture of beverage and protein is clearly negligent.

The point has nowhere been stated more simply and clearly than in the judgment of Cook P.J. in the case of *Pillars v. R.J. Reynolds Tobacco Co.*[2] The Reynolds Tobacco Company were manufacturers of "Brown Mule Chewing Tobacco." In the words of the judge:

> "It seems that appellant consumed one plug of his purchase, which measured up to representations, that it was tobacco unmixed with human flesh, but when appellant tackled the second plug it made him sick, but, not suspecting the tobacco, he tried another chew, and still another, until he bit into some foreign substance, which crumbled like dry bread, and caused him to foam at the mouth, while he was getting 'sicker and sicker.' Finally, his teeth struck something hard; he could not bite through it. After an examination he discovered a human toe, with flesh and nail intact. We refrain from detailing the further harrowing and nauseating details. The appellant consulted a physician, who testified that appellant exhibited all of the characteristic symptoms of ptomaine poison. The physician examined the toe and identified it as a

---

[1] [1932] A.C. 562 (H.L.).

[2] (1918), 117 Miss. 490, 78 So. 365 (S.C.).

human toe in a state of putrefaction, and said, in effect, that his condition was caused by the poison generated by the rotten toe."[3]

After a very short judgment, Mr. Justice Cook concisely concluded:

> "We can imagine no reason why, with ordinary care, human toes could not be left out of chewing tobacco. and if toes are found in chewing tobacco, it seems to us that somebody has been very careless."[4]

Why is *Donoghue v. Stevenson* not a simple case or example of the application of the principle of *res ipsa loquitur*, "the thing speaks for itself?" What is it that makes *Donoghue v. Stevenson*, to quote Mr. Justice Linden of the Supreme Court of Ontario, "a source of inspiration, a beacon of hope, a fountain of sparkling wisdom, the seed of an oak tree, a sky rocket bursting in the midnight sun?"[5] The abrogation of the immunity of manufacturers for liability for damages caused by negligence, independent of a breach of contract, although an important advancement in the law of negligence, is not in and of itself a change of sufficient magnitude to justify the prominence given this case.

The importance of this case, in part, lies in its correction of a serious error made by judges in their reasoning during the early period of the development of the law of negligence. The courts had taken a wrong trail, an unfortunate detour, and that mistake was the failure to make a very fundamental distinction, the distinction between misfeasance and nonfeasance, or, to put it in the terms of ordinary language, between doing something and failing to prevent something from happening.

There is a significant moral difference between causing harm and merely failing to prevent harm from happening: if one person takes another person's food, one commits theft, but if one merely fails to share food with the other person, that is only being uncharitable. One has a right that one's food not be taken, but one does not generally have a right to the food belonging to someone else.

The distinction between misfeasance and nonfeasance was at one time clearly recognized in the law, as is evidenced by the 19th century decision of *Winterbottom v. Wright*.[6] The plaintiff in that case was an employee of a contractor who provided horses and drivers to the postal service. The defendant had a contract with the postal service to provide

---

[3]*Ibid.*, at 365-66.

[4]*Supra*, note 2, at 366.

[5]Linden, "The Good Neighbour on Trial: A Fountain of Sparkling Wisdom" (1983), 17 U.B.C.L. Rev. 67.

[6](1842), 10 M. & W. 109, 152 E.R. 402 (Exch.).

carriages and to keep that contract in that the carriages were allowed to get into a state of disrepair resulting in an injury to the plaintiff. The plaintiff brought an action against the people who should have made the repairs, and the court found no liability because there was no contractual relationship between the parties. The decision reflects the well known principle of the law of contract that third party beneficiaries of a contract have no cause of action against a contracting party in breach of such contract. The defendant had not caused the harm, but had merely failed to prevent it from happening. There was no liability because the plaintiff was unable to establish that the defendant owed him a duty to carry out the repairs.

Later courts failed to realize that *Winterbottom v. Wright* was applicable only to cases of nonfeasance, and had no application to misfeasance, where liability is based on the negligent causing of harm. They applied *Winterbottom v. Wright* to cases of misfeasance, to the actual causing of harm through one's actions. The result was that if a negligent act which caused harm to someone also constituted a breach of contract to someone else, there would be no liability because there was no contractual nexus between the plaintiff and the defendant. What these courts presumably failed to realize was that it did not follow from the absence of contractual grounds for liability that there could not be other grounds for liability, namely the negligent causing of harm.

This misapplication of *Winterbottom v. Wright* became institutionalized in at least two areas of the law. The first was in regard to the liability of manufacturers for damage arising from negligently manufactured products. The existence of the contract between the manufacturer and the distributor of the product became a bar to the recovery of damages which might be suffered by the eventual user of the product. This misapplication was corrected by the House of Lords in *Donoghue v. Stevenson.*

From the trial through to the final appeal in the House of Lords, the relevance of the distinction between misfeasance and nonfeasance was extensively argued. In their brief to the House of Lords, counsel for the defendant specifically attacked the reasoning of the Lord Ordinary, Lord Moncrieff, whose judgment rested principally on the validity of this distinction. The brief reads:

> "The Lord Ordinary also founds strongly upon certain criticisms in *Salmond on Torts* upon the line of authorities relied on by the Respondent, and uses these criticisms as a basis for doubting the validity of these decisions. The ground of that learned author's criticisms of these cases, and the ground upon which he professes to find them 'unsatisfactory' and 'inconsistent' depends, however, upon a distinction which he seeks to make between nonfeasance and misfeasance — a distinction which forms no part of the decision in any of them, and which, it is humbly submitted, in no way impairs

their authority. Indeed it only enables the learned author to justify some of the decisions upon grounds upon which the cases were either neither argued nor decided . . .''

After the decision in the House of Lords of *Donoghue v. Stevenson* there should have been no further justification in principle or in precedent for failing to distinguish between misfeasance and nonfeasance. Unfortunately, however, courts limited this decision to chattels, failing to see its implications for realty, the other major area where the misapplication of *Winterbottom v. Wright* had become institutionalized. Where a contract existed, for example, between a landlord and tenant, or between a builder and the person who contracts these services, the courts by misapplying *Winterbottom v. Wright* would find no liability against the landlord or builder for making the premises dangerous through their actions.[7]

A classic example of the law in this regard prior to *Donoghue v. Stevenson* was the case of *Malone v. Laskey*.[8] In that case the plaintiff, the wife of the tenant, was in the bathroom sitting on the toilet. The plaintiff was injured when the overhead water closet, or cistern, and two heavy iron brackets which the landlord had negligently erected to hold up the cistern, came away from the wall and fell on her head. Even though this was a case of negligent action, no recovery was given.

Malone v. Laskey, although wrongly decided in principle, was at least consistent with the decisions which found no liability on the part of manufacturers for damage caused to non-contracting parties by the negligent manufacture of goods. There was absolutely no justification, however, for the decision in *Davis v. Foots*,[9] which was decided after *Donoghue v. Stevenson*. The defendant landlord rented premises to the plaintiff's husband, and offered to leave in a gas heater installed in a fireplace, for a further amount to be added to the agreed rent. The plaintiff's husband declined and the defendant then removed the gas fixture but did not close or seal the open gas pipe, and when the gas was turned on by the gas company after the plaintiff and her husband took possession, the plaintiff and her husband were gassed, resulting in injury to her and death to her husband. The court found no liability to the plaintiff because the landlord owed her no duty of care, since she was not a party to the rental agreement. The independent ground of liability, the negligent causing of harm through the defendant's action, was totally

---

[7]See, *e.g.*, *Cavalier v. Pope*, [1906] A.C. 428 (H.L.); *Bottomley v. Bannister*, [1932] 1 K.B. 458, 459 (C.A.); *Otto v. Bolton & Norris*, [1936] 2 K.B. 46, [1936] 1 All E.R. 960.

[8][1907] 2 K.B. 141 (C.A.).

[9][1940] 1 K.B. 116, [1939] 4 All E.R. 4 (C.A.).

ignored, and *Donoghue v. Stevenson* was distinguished on the ground that it did not apply to realty. Both *Malone v. Laskey* and *Davis v. Foot* and a number of other similarly decided decisions were expressly or implicitly overruled by the House of Lords in the case of *A.C. Billings & Sons v. Riden*[10] when the House of Lords ruled that the principle of *Donoghue v. Stevenson* applied equally to realty as well as to chattels.

II.   THE EVOLUTION OF THE PRINCIPLE OF *DONOGHUE v. STEVENSON*

If the restoration to the law of negligence of the distinction between misfeasance and nonfeasance was the only matter of import for the case, there would be little point in referring to it after 1958, the year in which the decision of the House of Lords in *A.C. Billings & Sons v. Riden* was decided. The importance of *Donoghue v. Stevenson* today, however, rests on other grounds. It is taken as having set out the foundation principle of the law of negligence. The most famous statement of the principle, and the one most often referred to, is to be found in a passage in the judgment of Lord Atkin, often referred to as the "good neighbour principle." Lord Atkin there states:

"At present I content myself with pointing out that in English law there must be, and is, some general conception of relations giving rise to a duty of care, of which the particular cases found in the books are but instances. The liability for negligence, whether you style it such or treat it as in other systems as a species of 'culpa' is no doubt based upon a general public sentiment of moral wrongdoing for which the offender must pay. But acts or omissions which any moral code would censure cannot in a practical world be treated so as to give a right to every person injured by them to demand relief. In this way rules of law arise which limit the range of complainants and the extent of their remedy. The rule that you are to love your neighbour becomes in law, you must not injure your neighbour; and the lawyer's question, Who is my neighbour? receives a restricted reply. You must take reasonable care to avoid acts or omissions which you can reasonably foresee would be likely to injure your neighbour. Who, then, in law is my neighbour? The answer seems to be — persons who are so closely and directly affected by my act that I ought reasonably to have them in contemplation as being so affected when I am directing my mind to the acts or omissions which are called in question."[11]

On the 25th anniversary of the decision of the House of Lords in *Donoghue v. Stevenson*, Professor Robert F. V. Heuston wrote:

"[T]he significance of the neighbour principle has been over-emphasised by both its supporters and its opponents. It was not intended to be, and cannot properly be treated as being, a general formula which will explain all conceivable cases of negligence. Even

---

[10][1958] A.C. 240, [1957] 3 W.L.R. 496, [1957] 3 All E.R. 1 (H.L.).
[11]*Donoghue v. Stevenson*, [1932] A.C. 562 at 580 (H.L.).

at a fairly high level of abstraction it needs considerable qualifications and reservations before it can be accepted. It is indeed a sign of the poverty of thought about the law of torts in this country that the proposition should have been called upon to bear a weight so manifestly greater than it could support."[12]

In the time since that thoughtful piece was written, the "neighbour principle" has not merely been over-emphasized, but has been canonized and made the very foundation of the law of negligence. Seldom in the history of the common law has a single statement of a single judge in a single case had such a profound effect on the development of the law. It is ironic, therefore, that Lord Atkin probably did not intend his now famous "neighbour principle" to be the theoretical foundation of his judgment. It is almost certainly now being viewed differently from the way in which he meant it to be, and is being given a meaning that is inconsistent with the rest of his judgment and that of the other law lords in that case.

From an historical perspective the *ratio decidendi* of a case can usefully be viewed in three stages. The first occurred in the period immediately following the decision, when the case tended to be viewed only in the light of its own facts. The second occurred when the case had been widely followed and applied, and an attempt was made to state the *ratio* in terms of a legal principle that would encompass the cases that had purported to have followed the initial decision. The third stage began when a final court of appeal gave a more or less final and authoritative formulation of the rule of the initial case.

It is proposed here to trace briefly the evolution of the principle of *Donoghue v. Stevenson* through these three stages, and to show that in the final stage Lord Atkin's passing analogy to Christian theology, probably added as a mere rhetorical flourish or by way of literary licence, has been taken out of context and turned into a fundamental source of civil obligation for the entire law of negligence.

Reference to the risk, neighbour principle, or proximity test, however it is referred to, has taken the place of hard, careful judicial reasoning. Indeed, "the poverty of thought about the law of torts," which Professor Heuston decried 25 years ago, is even more evident today.

Causation is the principal ingredient necessary for a finding of liability in the law of torts.[13] In general, people are held legally responsible for

---

[12]Heuston, "*Donoghue v. Stevenson* in Retrospect" (1957), 12 M.L.R. 1 at 23.

[13]Epstein, "A Theory of Strict Liability" (1973), 2 Journal of Legal Studies 151; Hack, "Bad Samaritanism and the Causation of Harm" (1979/80), 9 Philosophy and Public Affairs 230.

the damage they do only where there is fault, although in a narrow range of cases of strict liability they may be held responsible even without fault. Fault may be found because of an intention to cause harm, or because of negligence — that is, a failure to maintain a reasonable standard of care in one's conduct.

An action for an intentionally caused harm is generally brought within the confines of a number of nominate torts, such as assault, battery, false imprisonment, malicious prosecution, fraudulent misrepresentation, and the like. There is an overriding general principle which explains most of the intentional torts. That principle, stated by·Mr. Justice Wright in *Wilkinson v. Downton* as the wilful doing of an act calculated to cause and causing physical harm, is applicable where no justification can be alleged for the act.[14] The principle is limited to physical harm to persons and property and does not extend to cover purely economic loss. The class of intentional torts is not closed. If an intentionally caused physical harm does not fit within any of the existing categories and there is no good reason to justify the causing of the harm, then the courts may use this general principle to generate new torts, as is exemplified by the case of *Wilkinson v. Downton* itself.

One might wonder why it would be necessary to continue the separate categories once the general principle has been recognized and formulated. Why not have a general tort of the intentional causing of all kinds of harm, physical as well as non-physical? The reason is that there are many important policy considerations involving different interests in the context of different kinds of conduct that could not all be accommodated and taken into account in the context of a general principle. For example, a mere affront to dignity can be actionable in assault and battery, while the most damaging and intentional attack on reputation and character is not actionable in defamation, providing that the allegation is true. Physical contact, or the threat of it, are treated very differently from damaging words, and for good reason. Obnoxious physical contact, or the threat of it, can lead to violent retaliation for which there is no justification. Defamation, too, may be provocative, but the importance of freedom to communicate true information counterbalances the harm that may ensue. The relative simplicity of the action of trespass to land reflects the high value placed by society on private space.[15] By contrast, the many necessary conditions for a successful action in malicious prosecution incorporate into the law a policy of effective law enforcement by not

---

[14][1897] 2 Q.B. 57 at 58-59.

Only an unjustified direct interference with land need be shown.

discouraging people from invoking the legal process when they believe a crime has been committed.[16] In regard to the nominate torts, the advantages of the simplicity achievable by working under a single general principle would be far outweighed by the complexity and variety of exceptions that would be necessary to accommodate the various relevant policy considerations at stake. This, however, does not prevent the courts from falling back on general principles when the existing categories prove inadequate.

A close parallel can be drawn between the law of the nominate torts and the law of negligence as it was prior to 1932, and between *Wilkinson v. Downton* and *Donoghue v. Stevenson* in particular. Prior to, and for some time after, the House of Lords' decision in *Donoghue v. Stevenson*, different duties of care were owed with respect to different kinds of activities. Different duties of care were required of, for example, persons on the highway, users of dangerous objects, and professionals in the course of their employment. Lord Atkin, in *Donoghue v. Stevenson*, expounded a general principle purported to underlie most negligence cases in a similar fashion to the way in which Mr. Justice Wright in *Wilkinson v. Downton* laid down a general principle from which new causes of action could be treated.

For many years the pattern of reasoning used in negligence was not markedly different from that used in regard to the nominate torts. In the case of the latter it was first asked whether the causing of the harm fell within one of the existing categories of torts, and if not, whether it would fall under the general principle articulated in *Wilkinson v. Downton*. In a case of negligence it was asked whether the causing of harm constituted a breach of a legally recognized duty of care, and if not, whether it fell under the general principle of *Donoghue v. Stevenson*. The principle of *Donoghue v. Stevenson* was gradually used to cover more and more situations where liability did not lie at common law.

III.   THE *PRIMA FACIE* DUTY OF CARE DOCTRINE

Over the ensuing years the courts have gradually shifted their approach from that of ascertaining a specific duty of care for each kind of situation or class of relationships, to that of starting from the position of the general duty of care as enunciated in *Donoghue v. Stevenson*, and in particular Lord Atkin's formulation in the "neighbour principle." Even

---

[16]One must prove (a) the institution of criminal proceedings which are (b) terminated in favour of the plaintiffs, and which were (c) instituted without reasonable cause and with (d) malice and (e) damage.

statutory law reform, as in the occupier's liability legislation adopted by many common law jurisdictions, has contributed to the shift.[17] The process of change has culminated in the House of Lord's authoritative statement of the approach now to be taken, and first expounded by Lord Reid in *Home Office v. Dorset Yacht Co. Ltd.* where he stated:

> "About the beginning of this century most eminent lawyers thought that there were a number of separate torts involving negligence, each with its own rules, and they were most unwilling to add more . . .
>
> "In later years there has been a steady trend towards regarding the law of negligence as depending on principle so that, when a new point emerges, one should ask not whether it is covered by authority but whether recognised principles apply to it. *Donoghue v. Stevenson* [1932] A.C. 562 may be regarded as a milestone, and the well-known passage in Lord Atkin's speech should I think be regarded as a statement of principle. It is not to be treated as if it were a statutory definition. It will require qualification in new circumstances. But I think that the time has come when we can and should say that it ought to apply unless there is some justification or valid explanation for its exclusion."[18]

It would appear then that the state of the law of negligence today is that the onus is on the plaintiff to prove a negligent causing of harm, and that the defendant will then have to pay damages unless he or she can show that the situation falls under one of the exceptions where the law of negligence does not apply.

Lord Wilberforce in *Anns v. Merton London Borough Council* gave the following formulation of the doctrine of the *prima facie* duty to take care:

> "Through the trilogy of cases in this House — *Donoghue v. Stevenson* — *Hedley Byrne & Co. Ltd. v. Heller & Partners Ltd.*, and *Dorset Yacht Co. Ltd., v. Home Office* . . . the position has now been reached that in order to establish that a duty of care arises in a particular situation, it is not necessary to bring the facts of that situation within those of previous situations in which a duty of care has been held to exist. Rather the question has to be approached in two stages. First one has to ask whether, as between the alleged wrongdoer and the person who has suffered damage there is a sufficient relationship of proximity or neighbourhood such that, in the reasonable contemplation of the former, carelessness on his part may be likely to cause damage to the latter — in which case a prima facie duty of care arises. Secondly, if the first question is answered affirmatively, it is necessary to consider whether there are any considerations which ought to negative, or to reduce or limit the scope of the duty or the class of person to whom it is owed or the damages to which a breach of it may give rise . . ."[19]

---

[17]In British Columbia, *e.g.*, the statutory duty owned by an occupier to an entrant is a general duty of care without regard to the nature of the entry: the Occupiers Liability Act, R.S.B.C. 1979, c. 303, s. 3.

[18][1970] A.C. 1004 at 1026-27, [1970] 2 W.L.R. 1140, [1970] 2 All E.R. 294 (H.L.).

[19][1978] A.C. 728 at 751-52, [1977] 2 W.L.R. 1024, [1977] 2 All E.R. 492 (H.L.).

The *prima facie* duty of care doctrine is based on Lord Atkin's formulation of his good neighbour principle, which in turn cites the dictum of Brett M.R. in *Heaven v. Pender*.[20] In that case the defendant dock owner supplied under a contract with the shipowner defective scaffolding which resulted in the plaintiff suffering physical injury. The issue to be decided was whether or not the defendant owed a duty to take any care at all. This was in issue because the contract between the shipowner and the dockowner made this case similar to the line of cases which misapplied *Winterbottom v. Wright* to cases of misfeasance.

After discussing two cases where the courts did impose a standard of care, Brett M.R. went on to say:

> "It follows, as it seems to me, that there must be some larger proposition which involves and covers both sets of circumstances. The logic of inductive reasoning requires that where two major propositions lead to exactly similar minor premisses, there must be a more remote and larger premisse which embraces both of the major propositions. That, in the present consideration, is, as it seems to me, the same proposition which will cover the similar legal liability inferred in the cases of collision and carriage. The proposition which these recognised cases suggest, and which is, therefore, to be deduced from them, is that whenever one person is by circumstances placed in such a position with regard to another that every one of ordinary sense who did think would at once recognise that if he did not use ordinary care and skill in his own conduct with regard to those circumstances he would cause danger of injury to the person or property of the other, a duty arises to use ordinary care and skill to avoid such danger."[21]

The underlying structure of this reasoning of Brett M.R. is somewhat as follows:

1. There is a set of cases where courts have found liability for failing to take care.

2. In these cases the courts imposed a duty to take care — in the sense of a standard of care.

3. In these situations we can infer from the fact that the law imposes a duty (standard of care) that the law imposes a duty to take care — the law of negligence extends to this kind of activity.

4. The individual cases are instances of a more general principle — the law imposes a duty to act in such a way so as not to cause a risk of physical harm to persons or property.

5. The case in question is one where the defendants created a risk of physical harm, therefore it falls under the general principle and is an instance of a situation where the law does impose a duty to take care.

---

[20](1883), 11 Q.B.D. 503 at 509 (C.A.).

[21]*Ibid.*

The same structure underlies the reasoning of Lord Atkin.

The first logical step in any negligent action is to ask whether the law imposes a duty to take care. If it does not, the fact that a particular defendant did not take care, created a risk of harm, or was in other words negligent is irrelevant. The action must end at this point. This issue is a question of law. It is what is called in Chapter One the issue or problem of extension.

If the answer to this first question is yes, the next logical step is to ask whether there was a breach of that duty, or what is the same thing, whether the defendant was negligent in not taking care. Then we must define the foreseeable risk, the standard of care that might have been maintained to avoid the foreseeable harm, and whether the actual conduct in issue met this standard. We can then conclude that the defendant was negligent — that he or she was in breach of a duty to take care. The standard of care determines the context of the duty under the specific circumstances. The foreseeable risk determines the standard of care. The foreseeable risk or "proximity" is relevant to the issue of standard of care, that is, what care a defendant has a duty to take. Risk or proximity, however, has nothing to do with the question of whether the law will or will not impose a duty to take care, irrespective of the particular content of the duty. The duty to take any care at all, therefore, cannot be derived from risk or proximity. If, however, there is a duty to take care imposed by law, the risk or proximity will determine the content of that duty, or, in other words, the standard of care in the particular circumstances, or in light of the risk. There is no possible way, however, that it can be inferred from the fact that in a particular instance a defendant created a foreseeable risk of harm that the law imposes a duty in that instance to take care to avoid the harm. The existence of the particular risk is relevant to that question.

The only way to establish whether or not the law will impose a duty to take care in a particular instance is to show that the particular facts instance a general principle of liability. After his famous "good neighbour" passage, Lord Atkin goes on to state what that general principle is. The law imposes on people a duty to take care in their actions so as to not cause a risk of physical harm to persons or chattels.

---

[22]The circular nature of the reasoning in the risk of proximity test (the use of the neighbour principle to decide whether under the law a duty of care is owed) has long been recongized and often pointed out. See e.g., Millner, *Negligence in Modern Law* (1967), at 25-29; Buckland, "The Duty to Take Care" (1935), 51 L.Q.R. 637; Winfield, "Duty in Tortious Negligence" (1934), 34 Columbia L. Rev. 41 at 43; Stone, *Legal System and Lawyers' Reasonings* (1964), at 258-60.

If a case does not fall under that principle where, for example, a person creates a risk of harm which is not of a physical nature, or which is a result of non-action rather than action, one cannot conclude that the law imposes a duty to avoid the risk from the fact that a risk was created. If so, then how can proximity determine the presence of a duty to take care?

Courts have, however, in recent years been following a line of reasoning which has the following structure:

1. If there is proximity (a reasonably foreseeable risk of harm), then there must be a duty to take care.

2. If there is a duty to take care, then the law must impose a duty to take care.

The first premise is only true if the risk is of a kind where the law does impose a duty to take care. The reasoning becomes circular in any other situation because the very thing in issue or which needs to be decided is arbitrarily assumed.

IV.   CONCLUSION

The proximity doctrine, or the use of risk to establish the existence of a duty to take some kind of care therefore must assume that the foundations of liability are the same for all actions in negligence or that the law of negligence can be derived from a single principle. Lord Atkin might be taken to imply as much when he states that ''[a]t present I content myself with pointing out that in English law there must be, and is, some general conception of relations giving rise to a duty of care, of which the particular cases found in the books are but instances.''[23] He meant this, however, in the context of action causing risk of physical harm. If the principle of liability which is referred to in *Heaven v. Pender and Donoghue v. Stevenson* is so limited, then any line of reasoning which purports to decide a question of duty in regard to risks of non-physical harm, or in cases of failure to act, will be fallacious and circular because it must assume the very thing to be decided.

In subsequent chapters it will be argued that the entire law of negligence cannot be reduced to a single principle of liability, and that the *prima facie* duty doctrine has application only to risks of physical harm arising out of action. The House of Lords has, in authoritatively expounding the principle of *Donoghue v. Stevenson*, expanded the case far beyond

---

[23]*Donoghue v. Stevenson*, [1932] A.C. 562 at 580 (H.L.).

the limits of the principle of law underlying the decision. It has been able to do so with an appearance of logicality by being able to surreptitiously shift meaning between "duty of care" in terms of the issue of extension and "duty of care" in terms of issues of risk and standard of care. Thus a duty to take care is fallaciously inferred from the existence of a risk.

3

MISFEASANCE AND NONFEASANCE

I. INTRODUCTION

The *prima facie* duty of care doctrine assumes that the entire law of negligence can be brought within the confines of a single principle, or, which is the same thing, that the source of the obligation to take care is common for all actions in negligence. This is not the case, nor is there any good reason why it should be so. In particular, the source of our obligation to take care not to create risks of harm when we act is totally different from the source of our obligations to take care to remove risks of harm which we did not create, wherever such duties exist, when they exist at all.

This reflects the basic difference between doing something and merely letting something happen. If a person who has a hundred dollars knows that if he or she donates it to U.N.E.S.C.O. the life of an African child, who otherwise would die, will be saved, but does not donate the sum, it cannot be said that he or she killed the child. It can only be said that he or she let the child die. The difference is fundamental when it comes to questions of culpability and responsibility.

There is also a clear difference between what we "ought" to do and what we have an "obligation" to do.[1] Although we ought to do that which we are obligated to do, we are not obligated to do everything which we ought to do. It may be the case that one ought to share what

---

[1] Some moral theorists still claim that no meaningful distinction can be drawn between what we ought to do and what we have an obligation to do. See, *e.g.*, Stoljar, *Moral and Legal Reasoning* (1980), at 131-32. The prevailing philosophical view, however, is that there is a difference. As put by J.G. Urmson in "Saints and Heroes," in A.I. Melden (ed.), *Essays in Moral Philosophy* (1968), at 13. "A line must be drawn between what we can expect and demand from others and what we can merely hope for and receive with gratitude when we get it; duty falls on one side of this line, and other acts with moral value on the other, and rightly so." While it may be the case that if we have an obligation to do x. then we ought to do x. but it certainly does not follow that if we ought to do x. (in a moral sense) we have an obligation to do x. See J.C. Smith, *Legal Obligation* (1976), Chapters 3, 4 and 5.

one has earned with someone less fortunate, but it does not follow from this that one is obligated or bound to share, or that the less fortunate person has a right to a portion of one's earnings. The failure to make a fundamental distinction between causing harm and failing to prevent harm reflects a confusion between what one "ought" to do and what one has an "obligation" to do. The obligation not to cause harm is universal, and a breach of that duty creates a duty to compensate the persons harmed for the harm they have suffered. One *ought* to prevent harm but one does not have an *obligation* to prevent it, outside of special circumstances that furnish grounds for a duty.

Given no duty to prevent harm, there can be no duty to compensate a person for failure to prevent harm. Thus the fact that one ought to rescue a person in danger *might* be sufficient grounds for a "Good Samaritan" law providing punishment for failing to rescue, but certainly it cannot alone furnish a justification for requiring a person to pay damages to another whom he or she fails to rescue. Arguments which *might* be sufficient to justify making a failure to rescue an offence are not necessarily sufficient to make it a tort. The grounds for punishment are not co-extensive with the grounds for compensation.[2] Much of the literature advocating a civil duty to rescue fails to draw this distinction. The authors argue for a duty to rescue in terms of reasons which might justify punishment, but certainly do not justify a duty to compensate.[3]

Let us assume, for example, the following hypothetical set of facts. A very rich man, A., falls off a wharf into deep, cold water, in sight of B. B. is sane and more or less normal in that he would not deliberately stand by and watch A. drown. B. panics, fails to notice a rope and lifebuoy nearby, fails to notice a telephone nearby or it does not occur to him to use it, and he fails to run and get help which is available close by. Rather, B. mindlessly shouts for help. Let us also assume that if B. had thrown in the lifebuoy and rope, or telephoned an emergency number clearly shown on the telephone, or gone into a nearby building, any one of these actions would have saved A.'s life. On the basis of these facts let us assume that B. has not maintained the standard of care of a reasonable man in his attempt to rescue.

---

[2]See Fletcher's article, "Punishment and Compensation" (1981), 14 Creighton L. Rev. 691, for a clear discussion of the distinction between punishment and compensation, and the implications of the distinction for the law of torts. See also T.M. Benditt, "Liability to Rescue", in Bayles and and Chapman, *Justice, Rights, and Tort Law* (1983), at 211.

[3]See *e.g.*, Weinrib, "The Case for a Duty to Rescue" (1980), 90 Yale L.J. 247; Shapo, *The Duty to Act; Tort Law, Power and Public Policy* (1977); Ratcliffe (ed.), *The Good Samaritan and the Law* (1966).

We can clearly say that B. ought to have thrown the lifebuoy to A. and/or telephoned for help, or run into the building for assistance. If there was a penal "Good Samaritan" law in effect we might well say that B. deserved to be fined for its breach. Can we say, however, that B. has an obligation to compensate A.'s wife and family the same $100,000 that he would have had to pay if he had negligently run over A. with his motor car rather than merely negligently failed to rescue him?

Let us assume that a relatively similar set of circumstances takes place on another wharf, where a poor man, Y., falls into the water and Z. negligently fails to rescue him. Let us assume that the loss to Y.'s wife and family is $10,00 rather than $100,0000. The fault of B. and Z. is the same so the penal sanction each should receive should be similar if they were subject to a "Good Samaritan" law. Could we, however, justify the different results which would arise from the imposition of civil liability?

It is self-evident that duties and rights are correlative in the sense that, if one person owes a duty to another to do or refrain from doing a particular act, then the person to whom the duty is owed has a right that the act be done or not done against the person who has the duty. The statement that X. owes a duty to Y. to do act c. is semantically equivalent to the statement that Y. has a right against X. that X. do act c. If statements about duties can be rephrased into semantically equivalent statements about rights, we should be able to state the doctrine of a *prima facie* duty of care in terms of a *prima facie* right that care be taken. If we limit such a statement to misfeasance only, a statement such as the following can be formulated: "Your neighbours *prima facie* have a right that you take reasonable care in your actions so as to avoid acts or omissions which you can reasonably foresee would injure them." If, however, we expand the statement of a *prima facie* right to include nonfeasance as well, we would have to add a further provision such as "and that you take such action as you can reasonably foresee will prevent harm from happening to them."

The statement of a *prima facie* right not to be harmed is consistent with well recognized principles of morality and law. The addition of a provision applying to nonfeasance clearly is not. Consider the following examples:

1. Your neighbours' crops are threatened by a fungus which will result in a serious total loss if they are not sprayed. They do not have the money to pay for the spraying of their crops but you do.

2. Someone has left your neighbour's gate open and it is obvious that if you do not go over and close it, livestock will wander off and some could be injured or lost.

3. Your neighbour's house has burned down. You are leaving the same day for a lengthy vacation. If you do not allow your neighbour to occupy your house he will incur expensive hotel bills which he can ill afford.

One could with little effort set out a long list of similar examples, each of which would fall under a *prima facie* duty to take positive action to prevent harm if proximity or foreseeability were the measure of duty. Yet in none of these cases could we say that your neighbours have either a moral or a legal right that you give them or lend them the money so that they can spray their crops, or a right that you close their gate for them, or a right that you give them possession of your house, such that if you fail to do so they have a right that you compensate them for the damages which you could have prevented, if you had acted.

One could say of the above examples that you ought to give or lend your neighbours the money so they can spray their crops, or that you ought too close the gate for them, or that you ought to give them possession of your house. The things which we have a duty or obligation to do cover a much narrower range than those things which we ought to do. This is particularly the case in regard to taking positive action to prevent harm from happening to others.

One could argue that cases such as the above are exceptions to the *prima facie* duty to take positive action to prevent harm. If so, then the list of exceptions would be almost endless, and we would find the rule applying in only exceptional cases. A rule where the exceptions outnumber the cases where the rule would apply is useless for practical purposes.

II.   PRINCIPLES OF LIABILITY FOR A FAILURE TO ACT

A general rule establishing a positive duty to take action to prevent harm from happening should be founded on a general underlying principle applicable to all the cases which fall under the rule. But no such general principles can be found which will explain all those cases where the law has recognized a duty to take positive action. For example, the voluntary undertaking of an obligation plus reliance on the undertaking will explain the foundations of liability for damages for breaching a non-contractual promise,[4] but will not apply to justify the positive duties

---

[4]*Baxter & Co. v. Jones* (1903), 6 O.L.R. 360 (C.A.); *Myers v. Thompson*, [1967] 2 O.R. 335, 63 D.L.R. (2d) 476, affirmed [1967] 2 O.R. 335n, 63 D.L.R. (2d) 476n (C.A.); *Kostiuk v. Union Accept. Corp.*, 66 D.L.R. (2d) 430, [1969] I.L.R. 1-239 (Sask. Q.B.).

of the occupier of land to take positive action to keep his premises safe.[5] If different grounds for kinds of liability underlie the different areas of the law where liability lies for nonfeasance, then nonfeasance is not amenable to being brought under one single general principle.

The grounds of liability for nonfeasance are different from the grounds of liability for action.[6] While it is sometimes difficult to decide in a particular case whether something is nonfeasance or misfeasance, the distinction is nevertheless fundamental. It does not follow merely because a distinction has a grey area that it is not an important one or that it should not be made in appropriate cases. Liability for nonfeasance is exceptional. In a case where a person negligently causes damage through his or her action, there is a *prima facie* presumption of responsibility unless it can be excused or justified. Consequently, all cases of causing damage through action can fall under a single principle of obligation. It is exceptional for people to be considered responsible for failing to act. There is, therefore, a *prima facie* presumption of no responsibility for a failure to act. There must first be shown an obligation or duty to act before there can be a duty to compensate for damages which could have been prevented had there not been a failure to act. The reasons for the existence of a duty to act will be of a kind different from those for the existence of a duty to take care when acting. Consequently both misfeasance and nonfeasance cannot possibly be dealt with adequately in terms of a single principle.

A breach of a legal duty or obligation is both a necessary and a sufficient condition for a court to order the payment of compensation for damage resulting from the act which constitutes a breach. A legal obligation is the converse of a liberty to act; thus the imposition of a duty must be justified, since it constitutes a limitation on the right of freedom of action or the free agency of individuals. The voluntary assumption of a legal obligation is a sufficient justification for an obligation because it is a free exercise of agency, and is thus consistent with the liberty of the subject. When a legal obligation is assumed voluntarily, it makes no difference whether the duty is to refrain from acting or to act positively.

Obligations which protect the right to freedom of action, which will include all of the fundamental liberties such as freedom of speech,

---

[5]*Goldman v. Hargrave*, [1967] 1 A.C. 645, [1966] 3 W.L.R. 513, [1966] 3 W.L.R. 513, [1966] 2 All E.R. 989 (P.C.); *Leakey v. Nat. Trust for Places of Historical Interest or Natural Beauty*, [1980] 1 Q.B. 485, [1980] 2 W.L.R. 65, [1980] 1 All E.R. 17 (C.A.).

[6]McNiece and Thornton, "Affirmative Duties in Tort" (1949), 58 Yale L.J. 1272; Shapo, *The Duty to Act: Tort Law, Power and Public Policy* (1977); Atiyah, *Accidents, Compensation and the Law*, 3rd ed. (1980), at 95-112.

assembly, movement, etc., guarantee and protect the agency of individuals from interference. Obligations to refrain from causing harm, like obligations which we voluntarily assume, are consistent with freedom of action. Obligations to refrain from causing harm are consistent with human agency in that they furnish a necessary condition (freedom from interference) for the function of agency. Thus, particular duties to refrain from harmful acts (misfeasance) need no specific justification. Rather, specific justification is required for harm causing acts if they are not to constitute a breach of duty.

The duties of non-interference represent a minimum limitation on agency which is more than compensated for by the maximization of freedom of action which such protection makes possible. The burden of such duties falls reciprocally on all persons as do the benefits. One cannot claim the rights of freedom of action in the sense of protection from interference with others without accepting the duties which such rights entail.

Duties to act positively to prevent harm (nonfeasance) are not necessary for the free functioning of agency, and since they constitute a limitation on freedom of action or agency, they must be specifically justified.

The sorts of relationships that have traditionally been held by the courts to give rise to a duty of preventing harm are as follows:

1. contractual relationships;

2. non-contractual undertakings where reliance gives rise to a foreseeable risk of harm;[7]

3. fiduciary relationships;[8]

4. special relationships of dependency (such as those between pupils and teachers);[9] and

5. relationships between occupiers of adjacent land.[10]

The obligations to take positive action arising from the first four kinds of relationships are derived from a specific voluntary commitment, or they are a part of the duties of a role, function, or position which has been voluntarily assumed. Thus they need no justification in terms of the limitation that they place on the freedom of action of individuals.

---

[7]*Supra*, note 4.

[8]*Nocton v. Lord Ashburton*, [1914] A.C. 932 (H.L.).

[9]*Rich v. London County Council*, [1953] 1 W.L.R. 895, [1953] 2 All E.R. 376 (C.A.).

[10]*Supra*, note 5.

The duties of occupiers of land to keep their premises safe from risks of harm to adjoining land-owners require a different sort of justification. The negative duties to refrain from using one's land in such a way that physical damage is *caused* to adjoining land, or persons or property thereon, need not be specifically justified, since the justification will be much the same as that for refraining from injuring others through any particular kind of action. The justification for a duty on the occupier to remove risks to adjoining land, which he did not create nor which he is even responsible for creating, must be specifically justified. The justification is fairly clear. The occupier is in the best position to recognize and remove the risk, while the occupiers of adjoining land would be trespassers if they went on the aforementioned occupier's land to prevent damage to their own. Secondly, while an occupier's duty to take positive action to make his land safe in regard to the use and enjoyment of neighbouring occupiers is an infringement on his liberty, the benefits are reciprocal in that the occupier enjoys the rights which are correlative to similar duties resting on his neighbours. Given that positive duties to remove risks such as putting out fires caused by lightning[11], pruning trees, clearing drains,[12] etc. are generally not onerous, but that the benefits are great, and that these risks can arise on any piece of land, the mutual assumption of such duties enhances the agency of the occupier in the use and enjoyment of his land, rather than diminishes it. Since duties to take positive action are justifiable in regard to occupiers of land, there is little point in making a distinction between misfeasance and nonfeasance in regard to the law of occupier's liability.

The *prima facie* duty doctrine of *Donoghue v. Stevenson*[13] is valid for misfeasance because the justification for taking care in not causing harm when acting applies similarly to all examples or kinds of actions. The general duty can be stated in the form of a single proposition such as, "Everyone is under an obligation to take care in their action to avoid causing harm to others without proper justification." There is no *prima facie* duty to prevent harm by taking positive action to remove risks, because there is no single justification applicable to all cases where action by one person could prevent or alleviate harm happening to someone else.

The critical test should be whether it is possible to state a similar workable principle for nonfeasance, which would have a general application. Such a principle would have to be of some form such as,

---

[11]*Goldman v. Hargrave, supra*, note 5.

[12]*Sedleigh-Denfield v. O'Callaghan*, [1940] A.C. 880, [1940] 3 All E.R. 349 (H.L.).

[13][1932] A.C. 562 (H.L.).

"Everyone is under an obligation to take positive action to prevent harm from happening to others."

Taking care in acting is totally different from taking positive action to prevent or relieve harm. Risks of harm can arise in a wide variety of ways, and the costs of removing the risk or giving relief to suffering can range from little to a great deal. The costs to individuals of meeting such a widely drawn duty would be so great as to severely interfere with the pursuit of their own goals. Such duties as we have to prevent or alleviate harm must be justified on a more individual or specific basis.

If the "neighbour principle" is interpreted to mean simply that a *prima facie* duty of care lies whenever it can reasonably be foreseen that damage will follow an act or a failure to act, then a duty to prevent harm would no longer have to be justified and the defendant would have to show that he or she fell under an exception. But since in the past there has been no general duty to take positive action, there has been no basis for developing a list of exceptions. Instead, the imposition of duties of positive action are the exceptions to a general rule that one is not to be held responsible for risks which he or she never created. The application of the *prima facie* duty doctrine to nonfeasance, in the absence of a well-developed set of exceptions, would thus result in a radical change in the law.

The situation prior to *Donoghue v. Stevenson* was that relationships between employers and employees, occupiers of land and passers-by, occupiers of land and persons coming onto the land, occupiers of land and adjoining occupiers, users of the highway, manufacturers and subsequent consumers, etc. were all treated as being covered by separate duties of care. Once the distinction is recognized between misfeasance and nonfeasance, however, specific duties need only be established in the case of nonfeasance, but not in the case of misfeasance. In the case of actions, as contrasted with non-action, a *prima facie* duty of care can be assumed, and then concern focuses on the policy-grounded exceptions to that duty. Once the House of Lords, in *A.C. Billings & Sons v. Riden*,[14] declared the distinction between chattels and realty to be irrelevant so far as negligent action is concerned, it was only a matter of time before the courts developed a doctrine of a *prima facie* duty of care.

Such a doctrine was articulated by Lord Reid in *Home Office v. Dorset Yacht Co.*[15] where the defendant was held liable to the plaintiff for damage caused to its yacht by Borstal inmates under the control and

---

[14][1958] A.C. 240, [1957] 3 W.L.R. 496, [1957] 3 All E.R. 1.
[15][1970] A.C. 1004, [1970] 2 W.L.R. 1140, [1970] 2 All E.R. 294 (H.L.).

supervision of a servant of the defendant. This was a case of misfeasance in that the damage was caused by the action of the defendant's servants in bringing the Borstal inmates to the vicinity of the plaintiff's property and then not supervising them, when it was reasonably foreseeable that, if they were not supervised, they would cause damage to the plaintiff's property. While failing to supervise is in itself a failure to act, it is in the context of an overall act, in the same way that, while failing to put one's foot on the brakes of a car constitutes a failure to act, running over a person is still a case of misfeasance, since the damage is caused by the action of driving the car. In this case Lord Reid, after setting out the doctrine of a *prima facie* duty of care, then went on to list some of the exceptions to the neighbour principle and included the absence of liability for a failure to rescue. Thus it would appear that he also believed that the neighbour principle underlies the whole of the law of negligence.

If one looks carefully at Lord Atkin's judgment in *Donoghue v. Stevenson* and at the decision of *Heaven v. Pender*[16] upon which he partly relied, one will see that Lord Atkin is talking throughout about conduct or action, and when in his statement of the ''neighbour principle'' he refers to ''acts or omissions which are called in question'' the omissions are in the context of actions, such as the failure to take precautions when acting in such a way that a risk of harm is created. The ''acts or omissions which are called in question'' must be taken to refer to the specific allegations of negligence in the context of the conduct which caused the harm. This would cover omissions such as failing to unload a gun which is placed in the vicinity of children, or failing adequately to inspect a product that is negligently manufactured and placed on the market. The word ''omissions'' in the context of the ''neighbour principle'' refers to omissions as part of an action, and not to merely letting something happen.[17]

The causing of harm through negligent action is the foundation of liability in *Donoghue v. Stevenson* and so this case can be the source of a general principle for all negligent causing of harm. The law of negligence, however, does not include just the causing of harm. There are certain narrow areas where the law will impose a duty to act positively indepen-

---

[16](1883), 11 Q.B.D. 503 at 509 (C.A.).

[17]Brett M.R.'s statement of the underlying principle of the law of negligence refers to misfeasance only in that he speaks about causing injury by failing to use ordinary care and skill in conduct. Lord Atkin clearly draws no distinction between this formulation of the principle of liability in negligence and that of his ''neighbour principle'' in that he refers to Brett M.R.'s statement in *Heaven v. Pender* just prior to and just following the statement of his ''neighbour principle.''

dent of a contractual obligation, and since traditionally these areas have been considered to constitute a part of the law of negligence, the principle in *Donoghue v. Stevenson* cannot possibly furnish a foundation for the entire law of negligence. Nonfeasance, or failing to act, cannot be considered even an exception to the principle of *Donoghue v. Stevenson* because it does not fall under the general rule. Something must *prima facie* fall under a rule before it can be said to constitute an exception to the rule.

III.   THE IMPACT OF THE *ANNS* DECISION

Although Lord Reid, in his statement of the *prima facie* duty of care doctrine, in the *Dorset Yacht Case* seems to imply that the "neighbour principle" from which it is derived underlies the whole of the law of negligence, he in fact applies it to a case of misfeasance. Unfortunately, the House of Lords, in the decision of *Anns v. Merton London Borough Council*[18] has specifically applied the *prima facie* duty of care doctrine to a clear case of nonfeasance, in holding a municipality liable to a subsequent purchaser of a house for damages resulting from the subsidence of the building due to improper installation of foundations by the builder. The ground of liability was the failure of the defendant municipality's servant to inspect the foundations, a clear case of a failure to prevent harm from happening rather than causing it to happen. While it is true that the inspectors may have carelessly *approved* the inadequate foundations,[19] they did not cause the damage to happen through their actions. Rather, they allowed it to happen, or failed to prevent it from happening.

It would appear that the courts have again made a serious error, again taken a wrong turn, an unfortunate detour. In applying the doctrine of a *prima facie* duty of care to both cases of action and non-action, the law has come full circle. The distinction between nonfeasance and misfeasance has again been eliminated and the irony is that is has been eliminated on the basis of the authority of the very case which had restored or established it. The historical error which was eradicated by *Donoghue v. Stevenson* was a failure to distinguish between misfeasance and nonfeasance. After *Winterbottom v. Wright*[20] the courts held that if the conduct of the

---

[18][1978] A.C. 728, [1977] 2 W.L.R. 1024, [1977] 2 All E.R. 492 (H.L.).

[19]In *Dutton* it was so found as a fact, the defendant council not calling any evidence, whereas *Anns* involved a preliminary point whereby, for the purposes of the motion, it was presumed that the foundations of the maisonettes had been carelessly inspected. This last matter could only be factually resolved by either an admission by the defendant or at a trial.

[20](1842), 10 M. & W. 109, 152 E.R. 402 (Exch.).

defendant constituted a breach of contract, a third person who was not a party to the contract could not recover for damages which he or she suffered as a result of the breach. The conduct in question in *Winterbottom v. Wright* was nonfeasance — a failure to repair a carriage. Later courts were wrong in applying the principle of *Winterbottom v. Wright* to cases of misfeasance.[21] *Donoghue v. Stevenson* merely held that the fact that actions which cause damage also happen to constitute a breach of contract is no reason for not allowing recovery. It did not, however, overrule *Winterbottom v. Wright*. Now, as a result of the *prima facie* duty doctrine of Lord Wilberforce in *Anns v. Merton London Borough Council*, the error of failing to distinguish between misfeasance and nonfeasance corrected by *Donoghue v. Stevenson* is again being made, but this time on the authority of *Donoghue v. Stevenson*.

The *prima facie* duty of care doctrine places the onus on the plaintiff to show that the necessary conditions for a *prime facie* duty of care are present, and that the defendant is in breach of that duty. At this point the onus then shifts onto the defendant to show that he or she falls under an exception to the rule based on legally recognized grounds of policy. In regard to misfeasance, the plaintiff must show that the defendant by actions created a reasonably foreseeable risk of harm by failure to take care, which risk materialized resulting in the plaintiff's suffering damages. If, however, it is assumed that the *prima facie* duty of care doctrine also applies to nonfeasance, the plaintiff, in regard to nonfeasance, need show only proximity, that the defendant was in a position in which he or she could by acting have prevented the plaintiff's suffering a loss and that the defendant was aware of that position or ought reasonably to have foreseen that if he failed to act the plaintiff would suffer a loss.

The application of a *prima facie* duty of care doctrine to nonfeasance, however, avoids the necessity of finding some reasoned basis for a legal obligation and consequent liability. The grounds of liability are assumed to be self-evident in the neighbour principle of *Donoghue v. Stevenson*. As has been shown, however, the rationale of the neighbour principle is derived from the right which people have not to be injured or harmed by the action of others, which is the correlative of the obligation which people have to take responsibility for their actions and to act with care. It has nothing to do with non-action, and consequently cannot furnish a theoretical foundation for a *prima facie* duty in regard to nonfeasance. The result will be that the grounds of liability will be assumed without ever having been established.

---

[21]*E.g., Davis v. Foots,* [1940] 1 K.B. 116, [1939] 4 All E.R. 4 (C.A.), and *Malone v. Laskey,* [1907] 2 K.B. 141 (C.A.). *Malone* was overruled in this regard by the House of Lords in A.C. *Billings & Sons v. Riden, supra,* note 14.

If the positive action which the defendant failed to take to prevent harm from happening to the plaintiff was an action which the defendant ought to have taken from a moral point of view, it will be even more difficult to show that he or she falls under an exception. If the *prima facie* duty doctrine is applied to nonfeasance, a case cannot be made for conduct which morally ought to be pursued as being an exception without attacking the *prima facie* duty to act positively itself, something which cannot be done if the duty to act positively is assumed to be the law.

Given that there is no well developed set of policy exceptions to a *prima facie* duty which applies to nonfeasance, and given that, assuming such a rule, an argument cannot be made for an exception where one morally ought to have acted positively to prevent harm from happening to another, a distinction between law and morality will be very difficult to maintain. Yet such a distinction was considered fundamental by Lord Atkin, the author of the neighbour principle. He stated in his decision in *Donoghue v. Stevenson* that:

> ". . . acts or omissions which any moral code would censure cannot in a practical world be treated so as to give a right to every person injured by them to demand relief. In this way rules of law arise which limit the range of complainants and the extent of their remedy. The rule that you are to love your neighbour becomes in law, you must not injure your neighbour . . ."[22]

Elimination of the distinction between not injuring your neighbour and taking positive action to prevent harm from happening to your neighbour collapses important distinctions between law and morality; so such a law would now force us all to become Good Samaritans by making us pay damages if we are not.

It is not the case that the courts will immediately start finding liability in all cases where action could have prevented loss. Rather, the courts will probably examine a broad range of factors in the context of establishing the standard of care to be applied. Such things as ease of opportunity, risk, amount of cost, financial ability of the defendant to bear the cost, etc. will affect a court's decision. These factors, however, are matters of fact which differ radically from case to case. If the courts follow such a path, then predicting the outcome of decisions will become much more difficult, and litigation will consequently increase.

The *Anns* decision itself illustrates the degree to which the application of the *prima facie* duty of care doctrine to nonfeasance brings a high degree of indeterminacy into the law. In this case a public authority was

---

[22]*Supra*, note 13, at 580.

sued in negligence based on the failure of its servants properly to inspect the foundation of some maisonettes as they were being constructed. Under by-laws enacted pursuant to public health legislation,[23] the public authority was empowered to inspect, and the issue in the House of Lords was whether or not it was under a duty to inspect and, if so, whether such a duty enured to the benefit of the owners and occupiers of the apartments. The matter was raised on a preliminary objection, so that the facts were assumed for the purpose of resolving the issue.

After adopting the *prima facie* duty of care test as an initial point of enquiry in any negligence action,[24] Lord Wilberforce, for the House, moved on to adopt an exceptional mode of analysis for public authorities exercising statutory powers. He noted that in such cases public authorities are inevitably granted a wide area of discretion both as to the initial exercise of the power and the way in which such power is in fact exercised.

In order to give effect to this wide area of residual power granted to public authorities by duly constituted legislative assemblies, Lord Wilberforce set out a formula whereby a duty to take care in either choosing to exercise it or in fact exercising it would be imposed. In short, no duty of care exists at the point of deciding to exercise or not exercise such power.[25] This is an area of discretion residing solely within the function of the public authority. The only duty is to *bona fide* consider the question whether or not such a power should be exercised at all.[26]

---

[23]Public Health Act, 1936 (26 Geo. 5 & 1 Edw. 8), c. 49, s. 1; Bylaws [sic] 6, 18, and 19 of the Borough of Mitcham, 1953.

[24]*Anns v. Merton London Borough Council, supra,* note 18, at 751-52: "First one has to ask whether, as between the alleged wrongdoer and the person who has suffered damage there is a sufficient relationship of proximity or neighbourhood such that, in the reasonable contemplation of the former, carelessness on his part may be likely to cause damage to the latter — in which case a prima facie duty of care arises. Secondly, if the first question is answered affirmatively, it is necessary to consider whether there are any considerations which ought to negative, or to reduce or limit the scope of the duty or the class of person to whom it is owed or the damages to which a breach of it may give rise . . ."

[25]*Ibid.,* at 754-55. See also the following articles: Banakas, "Defective Premises — Shall the Ratepayer Foot the Bill?" (1977), 36 Camb. L.J. 245; Uxton, "Built Upon Sand" (1978), 41 M.L.R. 85; Phagan, "Damages for Improper Exercise of Statutory Powers" (1980), 9 Sydney L. Rev. 93; Stanton, "Negligence and Local Authorities" (1977), 93 L.Q.R. 488.

[26]*Supra,* note 24, at 755. "Thus, to say that councils are under no duty to inspect, is not a sufficient statement of the position. They are under a duty to give proper consideration to the question whether they should inspect or not. Their immunity from attack, in the event of failure to inspect, in other words, though great is not absolute. And because it is not absolute, the necessary premise for the proposition 'if no duty to inspect, then no duty to take care in inspection' vanishes."

Once the decision to exercise the power has been made, however, the case is governed by a different subset of legal imperatives. Although, in principle, there should be a duty to take care in implementing the public authorities' functions, the statutory power may still grant the authority another ongoing area of discretion uncontrolled by the courts:

> "There may be a discretionary element in its exercise — discretionary as to time and manner of inspection, and the techniques to be used. A plaintiff complaining of negligence must prove, the burden being on him, that action taken was not within the limits of a discretion bona fide exercised, before he can begin to rely upon a common law duty of care. But if he can do this, he should, in principle, be able to sue."[27]

Having already described the two legally relevant functions of a public authority (relevant, that is, in cases of alleged negligence, namely, discretionary functions where no duty of care is imposed, and operational functions where a duty of care *may* be imposed), Wilberforce L. J. held that the facts in *Anns*, if established, may give rise to an action in negligence.[28]

In this case the borough had a statutory power to inspect but in legislative terms was under no positive duty to inspect. This is, then, a classic case of what was formerly regarded as nonfeasance and, it is submitted, is parallel in every material respect to *East Suffolk River Catchment Bd. v. Kent.*[29] In dealing with the effects of the legally critical

---

[27]*Supra*, note 24, at 755.

[28]*Supra*, note 24, at 760.

[29][1941] A.C. 74, [1940] 4 All E.R. 527 (H.L.). In *Anns v. Merton London Borough Council*, [1978] A.C. 728 at 755-56, [1977] 2 W.L.R. 1024, [1977] 2 All E.R. 492 (H.L.), Lord Wilberforce distinguishes this case: "It is said that there is an absolute distinction in the law between statutory duty and statutory power — the former giving rise to possible liability, the latter not . . . My Lords, I do not believe any such absolute rule exists: or perhaps, more accurately, that such rules as exist in relation to powers and duties existing under particular statutes, provide sufficient definition of the rights of individuals affected by their exercise, or indeed their non-exercise, unless they take account of the possibility that, parallel with public law duties there may coexist those duties which persons — private or public — are under at common law to avoid causing damage to others in sufficient proximity to them. This is, I think, the key to understanding of the main authority relied upon by the appellants . . ." Lord Wilberforce continued at 757-58: ". . . the law, as stated in some of the speeches in *East Suffolk Rivers Catchment Board v. Kent* . . . requires at the present time to be understood and applied with the recognition that, quite apart from such consequences as may flow from an examination of the duties laid down by the particular statute, there may be room, once one is outside the area of legitimate discretion or policy, for a duty of care at common law. It is irrelevant to the existence of this duty of care whether what is created by the statute is a duty or a power: the duty of care may exist in either case. The difference between the two lies in this, that, in the case of a power, liability cannot exist unless the act complained of lies outside the ambit of the power." Uxton, *supra*, note 25, points out one distinguishing feature between the two cases: in *East Suffolk* the damage had already been sustained when the

characterization of a public authority's functions as either discretionary or operational, Lord Wilberforce noted that many operational functions "have in them some element of 'discretion.' It can safely be said that the more 'operational' a power or duty may be, the easier it is to superimpose upon it a common law duty of care."[30]

How then could the court dispose of its own decision in *East Suffolk*? The plaintiff in that case was the occupier of marshland pasture and kept in repair earthen walls which prevented inundation by tides. Legislation was passed empowering the Board to maintain the walls. After an exceptionally high tide carried the walls away the Board sent inexperienced workmen with poor equipment who took 178 days to do what should have been done in 14 days. The House of Lords found no liability for the damage suffered by the plaintiff as a result of this excessive delay. The *East Suffolk* case was distinguished on two grounds. The first was that it was quite consistent with the new legal analysis in that the defendant catchment board's conduct had not moved from the area of discretion into the operational area and thus it was proper not to impose a duty to take care. If this was correct, it is difficult to see what meaning can be granted to the term "operational" in any other set of facts. What could be more operational than having inexperienced workers futilely attempting to drain farmland for 178 days?

The second point of distinction is largely precatory. It turns on the fact that the pervasive effect of *Donoghue v. Stevenson's* general duty of care was fully realized only in the Dorset Yacht case and was certainly not given its proper weight by the majority in the *East Suffolk* case. This last ground has two features. By post hoc analysis the general duty of care has become the fountain-head of all duty/non-duty relationships. As well, had the majority in the *East Suffolk* case taken the general duty of care into account and applied it properly, then the result in that case would have been the same.

What then is the result of the *Anns* case? Apart from removing characterizations of "misfeasance" and "nonfeasance" from the public authority class of cases, and replacing them with characterizations of "discretionary" and "operational" functions, it has created even greater uncertainty in an already uncertain branch of negligence. The courts make the distinction between discretionary and operational functions,

---

catchment board became involved, whereas in *Anns* the damage could possibly have been prevented by a stop work order if the defects in the foundations had been observed and acted on. The distinction drawn is one that goes to causation rather than the issue of duty of care or no duty of care.

[30]*Supra*, note 24, at 754.

advising, in terms of how it will be made, that the more operational a function is, the easier it will be to superimpose a duty of care. Since this will always be a question of degree, there is no principled way in which any party can predict how a court will characterize a particular function and, because we are also told that even if a function is operational there may be a discretionary element in its exercise as to "time and manner," there is no principled way of predicting how such a function has been exercised. If this is true, what are the unstated factors that will influence courts in deciding whether such function is one subject to a duty of care or not — the capacity of the victim to bear the loss, the resources of the local authority, analogies with private undertakings of similar functions, or efficiency in expending public moneys?[31]

If these are indeed the unstated policy issues underlying the "discretionary-operational function" dichotomy, then courts must move to reveal them and systemize rules that recognize them. As it is, the *Anns* formulation grants courts the capacity to characterize conduct of public authorities on an *ad hoc* basis without really having to ground it in principle. Trial courts in particular will find this an attractive approach, since it certainly enables them to effect justice as between the parties, at least as perceived by that court. But the ordering function of the law is lost, including the capacity for broad predictability. Cases will be litigated merely because counsel know that trial courts now have a wide area of discretion in controlling outcomes by characterization. Until a clear and authoritative statement of the principle or principles that govern such characterization is made by the highest appeal courts this branch of the law will remain in a most unsatisfactory state.

It is not suggested that the *Anns* decision is wrongly decided, nor that a governmental body should not be liable where it is empowered by statute to carry out certain functions, and as a result of its failure to do so citizens suffer a loss. In Chapter Six a legal principle of civil obligation which would justify the result in the *Anns* case will be suggested. However, the House of Lords has failed clearly to express grounds which would justify such liability, nor has it provided us with a test which would allow us to distinguish cases where liability should lie from those cases where it should not be imposed. This absence of a theoretical foundation to the decision is obscured in part by reliance on the *prima facie* duty of care doctrine of *Home Office v. Dorset Yacht Co.*, which, it is submitted, is totally inapplicable to a case of nonfeasance. This absence of clearly stated grounds for civil liability will inevitably lead to a greater reliance

---

[31]For an attempt at predicting the line between duty and no-duty situations see Uxton, *supra*, note 25, at 286-91.

by courts on contingent factors such as the size of the body, the financial resources available to it at the particular time, the practices of similar bodies in similar situations, etc. The resulting indeterminacy in regard to potential liability may well act as a deterrent to the provision of services, and governments may even insert clauses in empowering legislation exempting statutory bodies from civil liability.

The *Anns* decision is, of course, a binding authority for the abolition of the distinction between misfeasance and nonfeasance only with regard to public authorities acting under statutory powers. By justifying its decision in terms of the *prima facie* duty doctrine, however, the judgment implies that cases of nonfeasance fall within the *prima facie* duty test. Thus the *prima facie* duty test itself on Lord Wilberforce's interpretation draws no distinction between misfeasance and nonfeasance. While it is open for courts to distinguish the *Anns* decision as only applicable to public bodies, the case nevertheless furnishes a precedent and an open invitation to the courts to apply the *prima facie* duty doctrine to situations of nonfeasance outside the realm of public bodies.

IV. CONCLUSION

The *prima facie* duty doctrine created from Lord Atkin's "neighbour principle," first authoritatively pronounced by Lord Reid in *Dorset Yacht v. Home Office Co.* and restated and applied to nonfeasance by Lord Wilberforce in the *Anns* case, enacts a fundamental change in the basis of tort liability which inevitably will have important economic, social, and political consequences. It marks a shift from formalistic law to "ad hoc balancing of interests."[32] It is a device whereby courts are enabled to exercise a discretion as to the creation of legal liability, in that the existence of a duty, since it is assumed, need not be justified in terms of precedent or principle relating to well recognized grounds of civil obligation. Instead, the ultimate cost-bearing issue is shifted from the legal question of the existence of a duty to the factual questions of standard of care. This is because only the most overwhelming argument in terms of such *prima facie* duty of care being negated by policy will persuade a court to reject the plaintiff's case at this point. It is much easier from a judicial standpoint to admit the duty (unless negated by statute or precedent) and go to the factual merits. At the fact-finding stage a court is not compelled to justify its conclusions (assuming the evidentiary burden is met) and its fact-finding discretion is virtually unchallengeable.

Factors such as the financial capacity of a defendant to forestall harm, the ease with which an individual defendant could have prevented harm

---

[32]Unger, *Law in Modern Society: Toward a Criticism of Social Theory* (1976), at 192.

that he did not cause, will all become important determinants of liability whenever the *prima facie* duty doctrine is followed. The judicial tendency favouring the shift of the focus of liability in negligence from the duty issue to the issue of fact is seen in the creation of the standard of the humane occupier in occupier-trespasser cases.[33] This, in turn, will make predictability of the legal outcome of disputes more difficult, and will probably lead to an increase in litigation. While the reasons for the separation of legal from factual issues may be less compelling in Great Britain, the separation is still critical in other jurisdictions, including Canada, where the jury trial is still retained for some civil cases.[34]

The pendulum has now swung from over-particularization to the other extreme of over-generalization. In retrospect, it is possible to conclude that the decision of *Donoghue v. Stevenson* has not been entirely beneficial for the law of negligence. Although it has permitted cases to be brought under the umbrella of negligence where there are good grounds for a legal obligation in terms of the causing of damage through action, the law of negligence would probably have developed to cover these cases without that particular decision. It can now be used, however, to impose liability where there are no good grounds to support a civil obligation, or in place of articulating those grounds if they do exist. A grave injustice will result if a person is forced to pay damages by way of compensation for a failure to act, where there are no proper grounds for a duty to act. The requirement to act under those circumstances will result in a deprivation of liberty. Finally, the application of the *prima facie* duty doctrine will take the place of sound reasons for judgment. The decision as to liability or no liability will be shifted from the legal question of the existence of a duty to a factual question of standard of care. Judgment, therefore, will become more discretionary and the outcome of an action will be even less predictable than it already is.

What is happening is that reference to the single case of *Donoghue v. Stevenson* is being allowed to replace the careful theoretical analysis that any area of law requires if it is to remain viable and healthy. Thus, *Donoghue v. Stevenson* is now a liability to the law of negligence. It is time the case was laid gracefully to rest in the tombs of the law reports alongside the myriad of other cases which are no longer relevant in the

---

[33]*Br. Ry. Bd. v. Herrington*, [1972] A.C. 87, [1972] 2 W.L.R. 537, [1972] 1 All E.R. 749 (H.L.).

[34]One reason why the duty issue is one of law is to enable the court to control the nature of cases actually put to a jury if one is sitting. Thus where the court is persuaded that policy dictates or statute or precedent compels no duty to be found, it may non-suit the plaintiff at the outset of the proceedings. Formerly, the burden of establishing the whole duty was on the plaintiff and extensions of liability tended to be conservatively applied.

last two decades of the 20th century because their unique contributions have long since been incorporated into the law. The only service to the law it can now perform is to remain as a warning to judges of the dangers of relying on judicial platitudes such as Lord Atkin's "neighbour principle," rather than on careful analysis and sound reasoning. Even as Lord Atkin stated the principle he was concerned with this risk when he enjoined:

> "I venture to say that in the branch of the law which deals with civil wrongs, dependent in England at any rate entirely upon the application by judges of general principles also formulated by judges, it is of particular importance to guard against the danger of stating propositions of law in wider terms than is necessary lest essential factors be omitted in the wider survey . . ."[35]

It would appear that Lord Atkin's fears have been realized and his warning ignored.

---

[35]*Donoghue v. Stevenson*, [1932] A.C. 562 at 583-84 (H.L.).

4

THE PROBLEM OF ECONOMIC LOSS

I. INTRODUCTION

The one thing which is clear about the topic of economic loss is that the principles regarding recovery are obscure. Consequently, it is often difficult to predict in any particular case whether or not recovery for a purely economic loss is likely. The law should, as much as possible, be decisive, consistent and allow for prediction of outcome. The fact that the law is not decisive, consistent and predictable regarding economic loss would indicate that there has been a basic confusion in our approach to the subject. This confusion, it is submitted, stems from the use of the concept "duty of care." If so, some of the distinctions drawn in Chapter One regarding the variety of uses made of the term "duty" or "duty of care" may help to clarify this area of the law of negligence.

(a) Extension — will the courts impose any standard of care at all in regard to a particular kind of situation?

(b) Risk — is there a reasonably foreseeable risk of harm which would require the imposition of a standard of care?

(c) The standard of care — what is the standard which the courts will impose in regard to the foreseeable risk?

(d) The presence of negligence — is the actual conduct of the defendant a departure from the standard of care?

(e) Cause-effect — is there a cause-effect relationship between the conduct of the defendant, which was a departure from the standard of care, and the loss of the plaintiff?

(f) Remoteness — how far down the chain of causal consequences of the negligent act is liability to run?

(g) Damages — according to what principle will the courts assess the damages?

It has been shown that duty language is frequently used to deal with issues of (a) extension, (b) risk, (c) standard of care, and (f) remoteness, with the result that they often become confused. Because economic loss has traditionally been dealt with in terms of "duty" language, it is often not clear which of the four issues are involved in such problems. Since it is fairly clear that economic loss does not raise any particular or special problems in regard to standard of care, we can narrow the field to three — extension, risk and remoteness.

It is particularly important to keep a sharp distinction between problems or issues of extension, risk and remoteness, as the failure to distinguish between these three essential steps or questions is probably one of the greatest sources of confusion in the law of negligence. The problem of extension deals with *the limitations on the law of negligence itself*, the problem of risk deals with *the harm foreseeable if care is not taken in acting*, and the problem of remoteness deals with *the limitations on the liability of particular defendants* within the boundaries of the law of negligence. In (a) we are concerned with the limits of the law. In (b) we are concerned with the nature of the potentially harm-causing action. In (f) we are concerned with the limits of liability within that law. In (a) we ask, "Does the law apply at all?" In (b) we ask, "What is the harm foreseeable resulting from the action if care is not taken?" In (f) we ask, "What are the limitations on personal liability when the law has been infringed?"

II.   THE NATURE OF THE PROBLEM

Does economic loss raise an issue of extension (will the courts impose a standard of care in regard to activities which can result in pure economic loss) or does it raise an issue of remoteness (under what circumstances does economic loss fall beyond the limits of legal liability)? If economic loss is an issue of extension, then the proposition that there is a general rule that liability in negligence does not extend to purely economic loss except in limited circumstances is substantially correct. If, however, economic loss raises an issue of remoteness, then we must start from the basic assumption that as far as the extent or perimeters of the law of negligence is concerned, there is no basis or reason for distinguishing between physical damage and pure economic loss. Economic loss is recoverable unless it is too remote. This is to say that non-recovery for economic loss is the exception rather than the rule.

Which position is the correct one is certainly not clear from the cases. Two decisions of the English Court of Appeal on the question of economic loss are particularly illustrative of the divergent views found running throughout the cases on this subject. In *S.C.M. v. W.J. Whittall & Son*,[1] the defendant contractors negligently cut into an electric cable

---

[1] [1971] 1 Q.B. 337, [1970] 3 W.L.R. 694, [1970] 3 All E.R. 245 (C.A.).

causing a loss of power over a seven-hour period. As a result, molten material solidified in the plaintiff manufacturer's machines. It took the plaintiff practically until the power came on again to clean and repair its equipment. As well as claiming for the damaged machines and products, the plaintiffs sought the lost profits from one full day's production. The court held unanimously that the economic loss was recoverable because the economic loss was consequent on the physical damage. Both Lord Denning M.R. and Winn L.J. dealt with the question of recovery for economic loss in general. Lord Denning M.R. treated it as a question of remoteness,[2] while Winn L.J. took the position "that apart from the special case of imposition of liability for negligently uttered false statements, there is no liability for unintentional negligent infliction of any form of economic loss which is not itself consequential upon foreseeable physical injury or damage to property,"[3] thus treating it as an issue of duty in the sense of the extension of the law of negligence. Buckley L.J. considered it unnecessary to deal with the question of economic loss in general as the loss in this particular case was directly consequential on physical damage.

In *Spartan Steel & Alloys v. Martin & Co. (Contractors)*[4] the English Court of Appeal dealt with a similar set of facts except that in addition to loss of profits resulting from damage to the manufactured product, the plaintiff sought to recover the loss of profits which resulted merely from the fact that production had to cease until the power was restored. Lord Denning M.R., two years after his judgment in *S.C.M. v. W.J. Whittall & Son*, after stating that he was unable to decide whether economic loss cases raise an issue of duty (extension) or remoteness, held that this kind of economic loss was not recoverable on grounds of public policy. It is not at all helpful, however, to say that an issue is a matter of policy unless one knows precisely the nature of the legal issues and which policies are relevant. Policies relating to issues of extension are generally of a different kind than those relating to questions of remoteness. It does make a great deal of difference whether we treat economic loss as an issue of extension and start with a rule prohibiting recovery except within a limited number of exceptions, or start with a rule allowing recovery except where the loss is too remote. Recovery should be broader if the second position is the proper one, as one starts with a presumption of recoverability of economic loss rather than non-recoverability.

---

[2]*Ibid.*, at 344.
[3]*Supra*, note 1, at 352.
[4][1973] Q.B. 27, [1972] 3 W.L.R. 502, [1972] 3 All E.R. 557 (C.A.).

Lawton L.J. in *Spartan Steel* took the position that *Cattle v. Stockton Waterworks Co.*[5] instances a general rule that economic loss is not recoverable, and concurred with Lord Denning in finding no liability as the losses suffered did not fall within any of the recognized exceptions, thus treating the question of economic loss as one of duty in the sense of the extension of the law.[6]

Edmund Davies L.J., on the other hand, took the position that the authorities lay down no such rule. Rather he started from the assumption that economic loss is generally recoverable, and on being unable to draw a distinction between loss of profits resulting from being unable to complete the processing of materials and loss of profits resulting from being unable to carry out the process at all, dissented from the majority, holding that such economic loss could be recovered. In reaching this conclusion he used tests normally associated with issues of remoteness.[7]

Probably the most thorough canvassing in recent years of the legal issues raised by pure economic loss is that by the High Court of Australia in *Caltex Oil (Aust.) Pty. Ltd. v. The Dredge Willemstad.*[8] As a result in part of negligent navigation, the dredge Willemstad fractured a pipeline laid on the sea-bed in a bay, running between the plaintiff's terminal and a refinery. Both the pipeline and refinery were owned by Australian Oil Refining Proprietary Limited. Although the oil in the pipeline was owned by the plaintiff Caltex, the agreement between Caltex and Australian Oil Refining provided that the risk of damage or loss of the oil rested with the oil refinery. As a result of the damage to the pipeline caused by the negligent dredging operations of the barge, the plaintiff Caltex suffered financial loss in having to provide alternative methods for transporting the oil until the pipeline was repaired. The action brought by Caltex was dismissed at trial on the ground that only pure economic loss had been suffered. The High Court of Australia allowed the appeal and imposed liability for the purely economic loss.

The opening sentence of the judgment of Mr. Justice Murphy that "there is no satisfactory general principle governing the recovery of economic loss caused by negligence"[9] expressed a sentiment implicitly reflected in the judgments of the other members of the court. The various judges discussed and rejected a variety of approaches taken by other judges in the past. The approach of Lord Denning in *Spartan Steel &*

---

[5](1875), L.R. 10 Q.B. 453.

[6]*Supra*, note 4, at 47.

[7]*Supra*, note 4, at 46.

[8](1976), 11 A.L.R. 227, 51 A.L.J.R. 270 (H.C.).

[9]*Ibid.*, at 285.

Alloys v. Martin & Co. of treating each individual case as a matter of policy was rejected as leading "to great uncertainty in the law,"[10] if the sole criterion. The court followed the English Court of Appeal in *S.C.M. v. W.J. Whittal & Sons* and in *Spartan Steel* in rejecting the "parasitic" damage doctrine propounded by the Ontario Court of Appeal in *Seaway Hotels Ltd. v. Consumers' Gas Co.*[11] which would allow for recovery of pure economic loss provided some physical damage had taken place. The foreseeability of economic loss under a test such as that of *Wagon Mound (No. 1)*[12] was rejected as not sufficiently limiting recovery for economic loss as many kinds of economic loss for which one cannot recover are, in fact, reasonably foreseeable; thus the net is cast too widely. That economic loss can only be recovered provided it was directly consequential on physical damage to persons or property was rejected as casting the net too narrowly in that it would leave too many exceptions such as that of the cases falling under the rule in *Hedley Byrne & Co. v. Heller & Partners*[13] which could not be rationally justified in terms of relevant criteria.

Most of the judges recognized the problem which pure economic loss raises, as what Cardozo C.J. aptly described as that of "liability in an indeterminate amount for an indeterminate time to an indeterminate class,"[14] thus raising the kinds of considerations normally dealt with in issues of remoteness. Most recognized that a duty of care was not generally owed in regard to pure economic loss arising out of injury to persons or property. Most justified liability in the particular case, in terms of proximity, in that the particular loss to the particular plaintiff was foreseeable in a way which other kinds of economic loss to a general class would not be. Thus extension, risk and remoteness are blended together.

Mr. Justice Gibbs, for example, in dealing with the line of cases on economic loss, stemming from *Cattle v. Stockton Waterworks Co.*, stated:

"The simplest explanation of these decisions appears to be that it was thought that the wrongdoer owed the plaintiff no duty to take care to avoid causing him loss which was purely economic, although in some cases the reason given was that the damage was too

---

[10]*Supra*, note 8, at 253, *per* Stephen J.

[11][1959] O.R. 581, 21 D.L.R. (2d) 264 (C.A.).

[12]*Overseas Tankship (U.K.) v. Morts Dock & Enrg. Co. (The Wagon Mound)*, [1961] A.C. 388, [1961] 2 W.L.R. 126, [1961] 1 All E.R. 404 (P.C.).

[13][1964] A.C. 465, [1963] 3 W.L.R. 101, [1963] 2 All E.R. 575 (H.L.).

[14]*Ultramares Corp. v. Touche* (1931), 255 N.Y. 170, 174 N.E. 441 at 444, 74 A.L.R. 1139 (C.A.).

remote, for in this as well as in other branches of the law of negligence questions of duty of care and remoteness of damage are difficult to disentangle."[15]

After extensive discussion of the cases and criticism of various formulations of the problem, he drew the conclusion that:

> "In my opinion it is still right to say that as a general rule damages are not recoverable for economic loss which is not consequential upon injury to the plaintiff's person or property. The fact that the loss was foreseeable is not enough to make it recoverable. However, there are exceptional cases in which the defendant has knowledge or means of knowledge that the plaintiff individually, and not merely as a member of an unascertained class, will be likely to suffer economic loss as a consequence of his negligence, and owes the plaintiff a duty to take care not to cause him such damage by his negligent act."[16]

Thus Mr. Justice Gibbs categorizes the problem as one of remoteness because of the possibility of unlimited liability, then states his conclusion in terms of extension, that is, in terms of whether the law will impose a duty to take care, and finally prescribes a test in terms of the particularity of the foreseeable risk. Thus the blend of extension, risk, and remoteness so characteristic of the use of the language of "duty" in the jurisprudence of negligence.

III.   A SUGGESTED SOLUTION

If we separate the issues of extension, risk, and remoteness we should be able to clarify the principles which should be applied to decide issues related to economic loss. In some situations economic loss raises problems of extension — will the courts impose a standard of care — and in other situations economic loss raises problems of remoteness — does the economic loss fall within or outside the cut-off point of recovery on the chain of causation. It is also quite possible for a factual situation to give rise to both kinds of issues. If the law does impose a standard of care in regard to particular types of economic loss, there still can arise an issue as to whether or not some are too remote.

Economic loss cases can be divided into two kinds. The first category contains cases where the economic loss results from an act which is negligent because it creates a risk of physical harm to persons or property. The economic loss suffered in the *Caltex* case is a good example as it was caused by physical damage to a pipeline. The second class of cases are those where the act is deemed to be negligent because it creates a risk of economic loss rather than physical damage. The loss suffered by the plaintiff in *Hedley Byrne & Co. v. Heller & Partners* falls into this category.

---

[15]*Supra*, note 8, at 237.

[16]*Supra*, note 8, at 245.

The subject of the risk, the creation of which was the basis of the finding of negligence, was the economic loss itself. The law clearly does impose a standard of care on persons to avoid creating a risk of physical harm to persons or property. If economic loss results from a breach of the duty to take care, there will be no issue of extension because the existence of the duty to avoid causing physical harm or injury is the basis of the imposition of a duty to take care, the breach of which constitutes the negligence. The economic loss suffered follows on the causal chain of effects resulting from the negligent action. The question of whether liability will extend that far down the causal chain is one of remoteness.

Clearly, economic loss often poses a problem of remoteness because it is often so widespread. In *Cattle v. Stockton Waterworks Co.*, Blackburn J. gives the example of a flooded mine:

". . . the defendant would be liable, not only to an action by the owner of the drowned mine, and by such of his workmen as had their tools or clothes destroyed, but also to an action by every workman and person employed in the mine, who in consequence of its stoppage made less wages than he would otherwise have done."[17]

Widgery J. in *Weller & Co. v. Foot and Mouth Disease Research Institute* makes the same point in regard to economic loss resulting from the escape of foot and mouth virus:

"It may be observed that if this argument is sound, the defendants' liability is likely to extend far beyond the loss suffered by the auctioneers, for in an agricultural community the escape of foot and mouth disease virus is a tragedy which can foreseeably affect almost all businesses in that area. The affected beasts must be slaughtered, as must others to whom the disease may conceivably have spread. Other farmers are prohibited from moving their cattle and may be unable to bring them to market at the most profitable time; transport contractors who make their living by the transport of animals are out of work, dairymen may go short of milk, and sellers of cattle feed suffer loss of business. The magnitude of these consequences must not be allowed to deprive the plaintiffs of their rights, but it emphasises the importance of this case."[18]

In regard to remoteness, the problem is not that the loss is economic. In the final analysis the law measures all loss including bodily injury in terms of money. The problem is that economic losses can often be widespread and trigger other economic loss in a chain of causation. Recovery for economic loss has never presented a problem for the law of contract because the ambit of the agreement always limits the degree of recovery.

Economic loss which is not caused by an action which creates a risk of physical harm to persons or property raises issues of extension because

---

[17]*Supra*, note 5, at 457.
[18][1966] 1 Q.B., [1965] 3 W.L.R. 1082, [1965] 3 All E.R. 560 at 563.

there are a vast number of situations where our actions do create foreseeable risks of economic loss to other people where the law will not impose a duty to take care.

The problem of extension regarding economic loss which is created by an action which does not create a risk of physical harm to persons or property arises precisely from the fact that the loss is economic. Given that there is no general duty to take care in regard to preventing pure economic loss being suffered by other people, recovery for such damages is exceptional. *Hedley Byrne & Co. v. Heller & Partners* set out the principles which can give rise to such a duty, and these will be discussed more fully in Chapters Five and Six.

The decision of the Supreme Court of Canada in *Rivtow Marine Ltd. v. Washington Iron Works*[19] is useful in helping to distinguish between economic loss which raises problems of remoteness — how far down the causal chain can one still recover from economic loss — and problems of extension — will the courts impose a duty to take care in regard to economic loss. The defendant manufacturer in this case negligently designed and manufactured a type of crane which was chartered to the plaintiff by the second defendants, who were distributors of the crane. Both defendants were aware of defects in the cranes but failed to warn the plaintiffs. When an identical crane chartered to another company had collapsed killing a workman, the plaintiff took the cranes out of service for repairs. The plaintiff sued for the loss of profits resulting from removing the cranes from his operation while they were being repaired, and for the actual cost of the repairs.

The trial judge awarded damages for the difference in what the loss of profits would have been if the cranes had been removed in the slow season when the defendants first became aware of the defects and the actual loss of profits which resulted from the cranes being removed in the busiest season at the time when the plaintiff first became aware of the defects.[20] Damages were not awarded for the cost of the repairs. The British Columbia Court of Appeal found no liability for any of the purely economic losses,[21] and an appeal was taken to the Supreme Court of Canada.

Mr. Justice Ritchie, in his judgment which was concurred in by four other judges, held that both defendants had a duty to warn.[22] That duty

---

[19][1974] S.C.R. 1189, [1973] 6 W.W.R. 692, 40 D.L.R. (3d) 530.

[20](1970), 74 W.W.R. 110 (B.C.S.C.).

[21][1972] 3 W.W.R. 735, 26 D.L.R. (3d) 559.

[22]*Supra*, note 19, at 536, 542.

was, of course, to prevent the risk of physical injury such as loss of life which had happened with the actual collapse of a crane in use by another company. The court next faced the issue of whether the plaintiff could recover for pure economic loss which was not consequent on physical damage to person or property. The court cited *Hedley Byrne & Co. v. Heller & Partners* as authority for the proposition that "where liability is based on negligence the recovery is not limited to physical damage but extends also to economic loss."[23] The court restored the judgment of the trial judge as to recovery for loss of profits but refused recovery for the cost of repairing the barge on the ground that *Donoghue v. Stevenson* does not apply to purely economic loss resulting from the diminished value of a manufactured article resulting from defective design or manufacturing. Such issues, according to the court, were better dealt with in contract.[24] If recovery were allowed in tort, a subsequent purchaser would often have a better remedy than would the original purchaser, as the original contract of purchase could contain contractual limitations on the liability of the manufacturer.

Laskin J., as he then was (with whom Mr. Justice Hall concurred), placed great stress on the fact that although the economic loss was not the consequence of physical damage to persons or property, it was caused by negligence which created a risk of such physical loss. He stated:

"This rationale embraces, in my opinion, threatened physical harm from a negligently-designed and manufactured product resulting in economic loss. I need not decide whether it extends to claims for economic loss where there is no threat of physical harm or to claims for damage, without more, to the defective product.

"It is foreseeable injury to person or to property which supports recovery for economic loss suffered by a consumer or user who is fortunate enough to avert such injury. If recovery for economic loss is allowed when such injury is suffered, I see no reason to deny it when the threatened injury is forestalled. Washington can be no better off in the latter case than in the former. On the admitted facts, a crane on another person's barge, of similar design to that installed on the appellant's barge, had collapsed, killing its operator. It was when this fact came to its notice that the appellant took its crane out of service. Its crane had the same cracks in it that were found in the collapsed crane, and they were due to the same faulty design in both cases. Here then was a piece of equipment whose use was fraught with danger to person and property because of negligence in its design and manufacture; one death had already resulted from the use of a similar piece of equipment that had been marketed by Washington."[25]

Laskin J. dissented from the majority regarding the cost of repairs and

---

[23]*Supra*, note 19, at 546.

[24]*Supra*, note 19, at 541-42.

[25]*Supra*, note 19, at 552.

would have also awarded those to the plaintiff, as against the negligent manufacturer, but not the distributor.[26]

This case is an interesting one because it furnishes us with an authority for the proposition that economic loss is recoverable even though it is not the consequence of physical harm to persons or property, if it is caused by an action which creates such a risk. The issue is really one of remoteness even though the court relies on *Hedley Byrne v. Heller* which is a case dealing with the problem of extension.

The issue of whether the cost of repairs is recoverable is a question of extension where the negligent design creates no risk of physical harm. Laskin J. , however, in pointing out the necessity of making repairs to prevent physical harm from happening by removing the risk, moves the question from one of extension to remoteness.

IV. CONCLUSION

Most courts, judges, and academic writers fail to make the distinction between economic loss arising from actions creating no risk of physical injury to persons or property from those which are caused by actions which do. Some distinguish between economic loss consequential on physical damage and economic loss which is not, and others distinguish between economic loss arising from a negligent misrepresentation and economic loss arising some other way. Some have said the above distinctions are important, while others have said there is no logical basis for them. Thus it is common to find *Hedley Byrne v. Heller* being cited as an authority to establish that a pure economic loss is not too remote, while *Caltex Oil v. The Dredge Willemstad* is cited to establish that a duty of care may be owed in regard to pure economic loss.

It is now at least clear from the decided cases that a duty to take care is owed regarding pure economic loss resulting from acts which create a risk of physical harm to persons or property. That economic loss may, however, be too remote for recovery if it raises the possibility of large losses to indeterminate numbers of persons. The remoteness problem regarding economic loss will be further discussed in Chapter Eleven. Economic loss not resulting from the creation of a risk of harm to persons or property raises an issue of extension. No duty is owed unless there is a right interfered with. While there is a general *prima facie* duty owed regarding physical injury to persons or property, there is no *prima facie* duty to take care in regard to pure economic loss caused by acts which create no risk of physical injury or harm. The defence of this thesis will be the subject matter of the next two chapters.

---

[26]*Supra*, note 19, at 552-53.

5

ECONOMIC LOSS AND THE CONVERGENCE OF CONTRACTS AND TORTS

I. INTRODUCTION

In the common law tradition from at least the latter part of the 19th century, contracts and torts have generally been considered to be separate areas of the law. Texts deal exclusively with one or the other, but seldom are both treated in the same volume in any significant way. Each is taught as a separate subject in the law school curriculum, and experts in one area are seldom knowledgeable authorities in the other. In the civil law tradition, on the other hand, the law of contracts and the law of delicts (the civil law equivalent of torts) are generally not segregated to anywhere near the same extent. Contract and delict form a part of the law of civil obligations which is generally treated by the same authorities in the same texts, and both are taught within the confines of the same course.

Donoghue v. Stevenson[1] provided for the co-existence of contractual and tortious liability. Prior to that decision, the very presence of a contract generally precluded liability in tort. If an act by A., causing harm to C., happened to also constitute a breach of a contract between A. and B., C. was precluded from recovering against A. Thus manufacturers owed no duty of care in tort to the ultimate consumer, builders owed no duty of care in tort to a subsequent purchaser, and landlords owed no duty of care in tort to a guest or spouse of a tenant. The absence of privity of contract precluded a person from recovering against a negligent actor who caused that person harm, wherever the negligent act constituted a breach of contract with someone else.[2] The House of

---

[1][1932] A.C. 562 (H.L.).

[2]This line of cases seems to stem from a misapplication *Winterbottom v. Wright* (1842), 10 M. & W. 109, 152 E.R. 402 (Exch.). In that case, however, the breach of contract was a failure to carry out a positive contractual duty. No concurrent action in negligence would lie because the defendant's breach was nonfeasance, a failure to prevent harm rather than a

Lords, in *Donoghue v. Stevenson*, ruled that manufacturers did owe a duty of care to the ultimate consumer in negligence not to create risks of harm through the manufacturing process. In reaching this conclusion the court generalized from specific kinds of duties which the law had imposed in a variety of situations, to state a general principle.

The principle of *Donoghue v. Stevenson* was gradually extended in the following years to cover negligent actions related to chattels. In 1957, in the decision of *A. C. Billings & Sons v. Riden*,[3] the House of Lords applied it to realty and buildings. There still remained, however, a number of areas where the law of negligence imposed no duty to take care. Two in particular became the focus of litigation: pure economic loss, and failures to carry out statutory duties or exercise statutory powers.

At this point we should shift the focus of our attention away from tort to contract, the other partner in this new nuptial union. The common law of contract has evolved with as many, if not more, restrictions than has the law of negligence. In particular:[4]

1. The ambit of the contract is more narrowly drawn within the common law tradition in that some representations are not deemed to be a part of the contract and are not enforceable at common law.

2. Promises or undertakings given without consideration are not enforceable at common law under the law of contract.

3. Third party beneficiaries have no right of action under a contract.

The Anglo-Commonwealth law of contract is even more restricted than that of the United States where judicial creativity and statutory law reform have given third party beneficiaries the right to enforce contractual obligations within certain limits. Paragraph 304 of the American Law Institute, *Restatement of the Law of Contract* (Second), "Creation of Duty to Beneficiary," provides that "A promise in a contract creates a duty in the promisor to any intended beneficiary to perform the promise, and the intended beneficiary may enforce the duty."

The law of contract in the civil law tradition is broader than that of the common law. The following provisions from several different civil codes

---

causing of it. The mistake of later courts was to apply *Winterbottom v. Wright* to cases of nonfeasance, as *e.g.* in *Malone v. Laskey*, [1907] 2 K.B. 141 (C.A.), or *Davis v. Foots*, [1940] 1 K.B. 116, [1939] 4 All E.R. 4 (C.A.).

[3][1958] A.C. 240, [1957] 3 W.L.R. 496, [1957] 3 All E.R. 1 (H.L.).

[4]See Swan, "Consideration and the Reasons for Enforcing Contracts", in Reiter and Swan, *Studies in Contract Law* (1980), at 23-59; Reiter, "Contracts, Torts, Relations and Reliance", in Reiter and Swan, *Studies in Contract Law, ibid.*, at 288 *et seq.*; MacNeil, *The New Social Contract* (1980).

are examples of where the civil law is likely to impose liability in situations where no liability would likely be imposed at common law. Article 1135 of the French Civil Code provides that, "Agreements obligate not only for what is expressed therein, but also for all the consequences which equity, usage or the law gives to an obligation according to its nature."[5] A similar provision is to be found in the Quebec Civil Code.[6] Book 2, Section II, Title 3 of the German Civil Code is entitled, "Promise of performance for the Benefit of a Third Party" and provides that, "A contract may stipulate performance for the benefit of a third party, so that the third party acquires the right directly to demand performance."[7] The latter part of the article goes on to declare that even where the contract does not specifically stipulate that a performance is for the benefit of a third party, a right of the third party to demand performance may be implied from the circumstances and object of the contract.[8] Article 1121 of the French Civil Code provides that he who makes a stipulation for the benefit of a third party may no longer revoke it if the third party has declared that he wishes to benefit thereby.[9] Article 537 of the Japanese Civil Code provides that, "Where a party to a contract has agreed therein to effect an act or performance in favour of a third person, such third person is entitled to demand such act or performance directly to the obligor."[10] Subsection 2 of article 537 provides that the third party beneficiary's rights under the contract come into existence as from the time when he declares to the obligor his intention to accept the benefit of the contract. Article 538 provides that once the third party beneficiary's rights have come into existence, neither of the contracting parties can alter or extinguish them.

Neither the French nor German, nor the Japanese law of contract require consideration as a necessary condition for a contractual obligation.[11]

---

[3]Crabb (trans.), *The French Civil Code* (1977), Book 3, Title III, c. III, s. I, at 221. The common law may, at least in part, achieve similar results through use of the concept of implied terms of the contract.

[6]Crepeau, Paul-A., *The Civil Code (1982)*, Book 3, Title III, c. 1, s. IV, art. 1024 at 221.

[7]Forrester, Goren, Ilgen (trans.), *The German Civil Code* (1975), art. 328 (1), at 54.

[8]*Ibid.*, art. 328(2).

[9]*Supra*, note 5, Book 3, c. II, s. 1, at 218.

[10]*The Civil Code of Japan* (1981), Book 3, c. II, s. 1, at 89.

[11]One of the four necessary conditions for a valid contract as prescribed by art. 1108 of Book 3, c. II of the French Civil Code, is a "*licit causa*". *Supra*, note 5, a 218. "Cause," however, does not mean the same thing as consideration in the common law of contracts. Article 984, of Book 3, Title III, s. I of the *Quebec Civil Code, supra*, note 6, at 215, contains a similar provision with the words "or consideration" following "cause," "Consideration", however, has always been interpreted as meaning the same thing as

Unilateral contracts are enforceable in all three civil law systems. The French Civil Code distinguishes not only between mutual and unilateral contracts,[12] but also between contracts and quasi-contracts,[13] as does the Civil Code of Quebec.[14] Article 423 of the Japanese Civil Code provides that, in order to protect his claim, an obligee may exercise the rights belonging to the obligor, thus enabling a party to one contract to directly sue a person such as a sub-contractor, with whom there is no privity of contract.[15]

Not only is the law of contract of civil law systems broader than that of the common law, the civil law of delict has not been plagued by the limitations on liability from which the common law of negligence has suffered. The French Civil Code provides that, "Any act whatever of man which causes damage to another obliges him by whose fault it occurred to make reparations."[16] The German Civil Code prescribes that, "A person who, wilfully of negligently, unlawfully injures the life, body, health, freedom, property or other right of another is bound to compensate him for any damage arising therefrom."[17] The Japanese Civil Code simply states that, "A person who violates intentionally or negligently the right of another is bound to make compensation for damage arising therefrom."[18] We should not conclude from these general provisions that the area of losses for which recovery is given in civil law systems is necessarily substantially broader than it is in the common law. For example, the recovery of pure economic loss unrelated to physical damage is the exception rather than the rule in civil law jurisdictions. Rather, the two systems approach these problems somewhat differently. In general while the common law has had to move in the direction of broadening the bases of liability by the extension of existing doctrines, the civil law has had to move in the direction of placing limits on liability grounded on extremely broad general principles.

"cause," so that in spite of this addition, the law of Quebec is taken to be much the same as the law of France in this regard. See Newman, "The Doctrine of Cause or, Consideration in the Civil Law" (1952), 30 Can. Bar Rev. 662, and Lee, "Cause and Consideration in the Quebec Civil Code" (1916), 25 Yale L.J. 536.

[12]Book 3, Title III, c. 1, arts. 1102 and 1103, *supra*, note 5, at 217.

[13]See Book 3, Title IV — Engagements Formed Without An Agreement, c. 1 — Quasi-Contracts, *supra*, note 5, at 252.

[14]Book 3, c. II, s. 1, *supra*, note 6, at 225.

[15]Book 3, c. I, s. 2, *supra*, note 10, at 70.

[16]Book 3, Title IV, c. II, art. 1382, *supra*, note 5, at 253.

[17]Book 2, s. VII, Title 25, *supra*, note 7, at 134.

[18]Book 3, c. V, art. 709, *supra*, note 10, at 116.

II. HEDLEY BYRNE v. HELLER

From 1932 until 1963 *Donoghue v. Stevenson* was recognized as applying only to actions causing a risk of physical harm to the person and to property. The cases which were brought under the umbrella of *Donoghue v. Stevenson* all fell within the ambit of the general principle upon which the decision in that case rested (people have a duty of care when acting to act so as not to create an unreasonable risk of harm to other persons or their property). *Donoghue v. Stevenson* was not considered to apply to cases of nonfeasance or to purely economic loss.

The case which opened the law of negligence to the recovery of pure economic loss caused by actions which created no risk of physical injury to persons or property, was *Hedley Byrne & Co. v. Heller & Partners Ltd.*[19] Up to this time the existing law was as set out in *Derry v. Peek* that there was no liability for purely economic loss resulting from a negligent misrepresentation.[20] The fact that the economic loss was as the result of a negligent misrepresentation was not as significant as the fact that it resulted from an action which created no risk of physical harm to persons or property.

A negligent misrepresentation creating a risk of physical harm to persons or property would, in fact, give rise to civil liability. The English Court of Appeal in *Le Lievre v. Gould*,[21] in following *Derry v. Peek*, ruled that the risk principle as expressed in *Heaven v. Pender*[22] did not apply to purely economic loss created by actions which created no risk of physical harm to persons or property. The rule of no recovery was not, however, absolute. The House of Lords in *Nocton v. Lord Ashburton* found liability for purely economic loss where there was no risk of physical damage where a fiduciary relationship existed between the parties,[23] and thus furnished a precedent upon which an argument could be made in *Hedley Byrne v. Heller* for adding a further exception to the general rule of no liability.

The plaintiff in *Hedley Byrne v. Heller* sought to recover damages for the pure economic loss it suffered when it relied on references as to credit-worthiness of a particular company, which references it had requested from the defendant bank and which the bank undertook to give in a letter which ended with a disclaimer of responsibility for the

---

[19][1964] A.C. 465, [1963] 3 W.L.R. 101, [1963] 2 All E.R. 575 (H.L.).

[20](1889), 14 App. Cas. 337 (H.L.).

[21][1893] 1 Q.B. 491.

[22](1883), 11 Q.B.D. 503 at 509 (C.A.).

[23][1914] A.C. 932 (H.L.).

information. The plaintiff alleged that it suffered loss by relying on the reference which had been negligently prepared. The issue which went from trial on to the final appeal before the House of Lords was whether or not under the circumstances the defendants owed a duty to take care. If they did not there could be no liability even though the defendants were negligent in creating a reasonably foreseeable risk of harm.

The House of Lords held that when banks or bankers undertook to give references as to credit-worthiness they had a duty to take care in doing so, and could be liable for purely economic loss resulting from their negligence, but in this particular case, by adding the disclaimer as to liability, the bank had made it clear that they were not undertaking such a duty and that the plaintiffs must accept the references at their own risk. The foundations or source of the duty to take care is clearly set out in the various judgments of the court.

The plaintiffs based their arguments on two grounds, one being the general duty of care, good neighbour, or proximity principle of Lord Atkin in *Donoghue v. Stevenson*, and the second being based on an analogy with contract and assumpsit in that by responding to the request the defendants voluntarily assumed a duty to take care. Lord Reid rejected the first argument and accepted the second. Of *Donoghue v. Stevenson* Lord Reid stated:

> "That [*Donoghue v. Stevenson*] is a very important decision, but I do not think that it has any direct bearing on this case. That decision may encourage us to develop existing lines of authority, but it cannot entitle us to disregard them. Apart altogether from authority, I would think that the law must treat negligent words differently from negligent acts."[24]

Lord Reid sets out two necessary conditions for a duty to take care, the breach of which could give rise to liability for pure economic loss. "The most natural requirement", he states, "would be that expressly or by implication from the circumstances the speaker or writer has undertaken some responsibility . . ."[25] The second necessary condition is a reasonable foreseeability of a loss as a result of relying on the undertaking being properly carried out. Lord Reid states,

> ". . . I can see no logical stopping place short of all those relationships where it is plain that the party seeking information or advice was trusting the other to exercise such a degree of care as the circumstances required, where it was reasonable for him to do that, and where the other gave the information or advice when he knew or ought to have known that the inquirer was relying on him."[26]

---

[24]*Supra*, note 19, at 482.

[25]*Ibid.*, at 483.

[26]*Ibid.*, at 486.

Lord Reid concluded, however, by pointing out that by making an adequate disclaimer the defendants made it clear to the plaintiffs that they were not undertaking any such duty, and that the plaintiffs relied on it being done properly, at their own risks.

Lord Morris of Borth-y-Gest accepted the argument made for the plaintiffs that a duty to take care could arise from a voluntary undertaking. After stating the issue he writes: "My Lords, it seems to me that if A assumes a responsibility to B to tender him deliberate advice, there could be a liability if the advice is negligently given."[27] Unlike Lord Reid, however, who found *Donoghue v. Stevenson* not relevant to the issue, Lord Morris went on to accept the argument based on *Donoghue v. Stevenson*, concluding that he could see no reason in logic "for distinguishing injury which is caused by a reliance upon words from injury which is caused by a reliance upon the safety of the staging to a ship or by a reliance upon the safety for use of the contents of a bottle of hair wash or a bottle of some consumable liquid."[28] Thus the difference between pure economic loss and physical injury, it would appear, was irrelevant in his opinion. He concluded his judgment, however, by ruling that by their disclaimer the banks made it clear that their reply was without responsibility or, in other words, they had not assumed a duty to take care.

Lord Devlin, while noting that he could find neither logic nor common sense to underlie the distinction between economic loss caused through physical injury and economic loss caused directly, felt that "the appellants in their argument tried to press *Donoghue v. Stevenson* too hard" and that the proximity principle, "does not get them very far."[29] "The real value of *Donoghue v. Stevenson* to the argument in this case", he went on to say, "is that it shows how the law can be developed to solve particular problems."[30] He stated further that if it were not for the requirement of consideration the case could be treated as a matter of contract. He writes:

> "A promise given without consideration to perform a service cannot be enforced as a contract by the promisee; but if the service is in fact performed and done negligently, the promisee can recover in an action in tort."[31]

After discussing the liability of a bailee who negligently carried out an undertaking Lord Devlin reasoned:

---

[27]*Ibid.*, at 494.

[28]*Ibid.*, at 496.

[29]*Ibid.*, at 525.

[30]*Ibid.*, at 525.

[31]*Ibid.*, at 526.

"I think, therefore, that there is ample authority to justify your Lordships in saying now that the categories of special relationships which may give rise to a duty to take care in word as well as in deed are not limited to contractual relationships or to relationships of fiduciary duty, but include also relationships which in the words of Lord Shaw in *Nocton v. Lord Ashburton* are 'equivalent to contract,' that is, where there is an assumption of responsibility in circumstances in which, but far the absence of consideration, there would be a contract."[32]

Lord Devlin draws the conclusion that "wherever there is a relationship equivalent to contract, there is a duty of care," but then follows by saying "I regard this proposition as an application of the general conception of proximity."[33] The final paragraph of his judgment, however, makes clear the true basis of the duty. He concludes:

"A man cannot be said voluntarily to be undertaking a responsibility if at the very moment when he is said to be accepting it he declares that in fact he is not. The problem of reconciling words of exemption with the existence of a duty arises only when a party is claiming exemption from a responsibility which he has already undertaken or which he is contracting to undertake. For this reason alone, I would dismiss the appeal "[34]

Lord Pearce finds a basis for a clear distinction between "negligent acts causing physical damage" and "negligence in word causing economic damage"[35] and limits the application of *Donoghue v. Stevenson* to only the former. After articulating the general principle that "if persons holding themselves out in a calling or situation or profession take on a task within that calling or situation or profession, they have a duty of skill and care,"[36] Lord Pearce went on to dismiss the appeal on the ground of the defendant's disclaimer.

Lord Hodson found the existence of a duty to take care in terms of both an undertaking and proximity,[37] but also dismissed the appeal because of the presence of the disclaimer.

Of the five judges, three found *Donoghue v. Stevenson* not applicable or not particularly relevant. All five, however, ruled that where a person undertook to give advice in such circumstances a duty of care arose, but that the disclaimer as to liability negated the undertaking. The reason why Lord Devlin was tempted to link relationships which are "equivalent to contract" with the proximity principle, and Lords Morris and Hodson were prepared to accept the proximity principle as one ground for their

---

[32]*Ibid.*, at 528-29.

[33]*Ibid.*, at 530.

[34]*Ibid.*, at 533.

[35]*Ibid.*, at 536.

[36]*Ibid.*, at 538.

[37]*Ibid.*, at 505 and 514.

decision, probably was because reasonable foreseeability is the foundation of risk, and risk is a necessary element of negligence, even where the duty to take care to avoid the risk arises as a result of an undertaking.

If a duty of care in the circumstances of *Hedley Byrne v. Heller* arose out of the risk of proximity, the disclaimer should not negate the duty unless it could be shown to diminish the risk. Disclaimers are not particularly relevant to the risk in that it is quite foreseeable that people will rely on the advice or information irrespective of the disclaimer. The fact that all five judges held for the defendant upon the basis of the disclaimer would indicate that the foundations of liability or civil obligation in *Hedley Byrne v. Heller* are based on a principle whereby a voluntary undertaking to carry out a service will give rise to a duty to take care, where one ought reasonably to foresee that a person will suffer economic loss by relying on the undertaking if care is not taken. The disclaimer sets limits on the undertaking.

This can be illustrated by the judgment of Barwick C.J. in the Australian High Court decision in *Mutual Life & Citizens Assur. Co. v. Evatt*[38] where the Chief Justice adopted the reasoning of the House of Lords in *Hedley Byrne v. Heller* as to their interpretation of the earlier decisions, but rather than locating the foundations of a duty of care in a principle of voluntary undertaking akin to contract, founded the basis of the duty in the application of the risk or proximity principle of *Donoghue v. Stevenson*. Since the duty "would be imposed by law and not arise out of any consensual or unilateral assumption of the duty,"[39] the Chief Justice went on to doubt that "the speaker may always except himself from the performance of the duty by some express reservation at the time of his utterance."[40] Thus a disclaimer would only be a defence if it negated the risk.

Since the disclaimer was a complete defence in *Hedley Byrne v. Heller* the only interpretation of the case which is consistent with the denial of liability is the one which bases the duty to take care on the voluntary undertaking of a task. Risk then becomes relevant only to the question of whether there has been negligence, that is, a breach of the duty.

Where a risk of physical harm to persons or property is created by the negligent carrying out of an undertaking, the undertaking is not the foundation of the duty to take care. The duty is there in regard to the

---

[38] 122 C.L.R. 556, 42 A.L.J.R. 316, reversed [1971] A.C. 793, [1971] 2 W.L.R. 23, [1971] 1 All E.R. 150 (P.C.).

[39] *Ibid.*, at 568.

[40] *Supra*, note 38, at 570.

action irrespective of whether or not it is done in fulfilment of an undertaking. Since in general there is no duty to take care in regard to purely financial loss, it must be in some way voluntarily assumed or created by an undertaking for it to come into existence.

III.   *JUNIOR BOOKS v. VEITCHI*

If *Hedley Byrne v. Heller* announced the engagement of contract and tort, it is *Junior Books v. The Veitchi Co.*[41] which has solemnized the union. In *Junior Books v. Veitchi*, the defendants were flooring contractors who were engaged as sub-contractors to lay a floor in a factory being constructed by the principal contractors for the plaintiffs. The plaintiffs alleged that as a result of the floor being improperly laid the surface of the floor began to crack and had to be relaid. The plaintiffs brought an action for the economic loss they suffered in removing the machinery and the surface of the old floor, the cost of putting down a new surface, and the loss of profits while the floor was being relaid. For some reason unknown to the court, the action was not brought against the principal contractor who, if the averments were true, would be in breach of contract, but rather the action was brought in negligence against the sub-contractors with whom there was no contractual relationship.

The principal hurdle which the plaintiffs had to overcome before they could argue that the defendant would be liable for negligence was to establish that the defendants owed to them a duty to take care, as the damage was not a physical injury to persons or property as a result of the floor being improperly constructed, but was purely economic, and in regard to a diminished value of the product. Traditionally, at least, it was considered that the principle of *Donoghue v. Stevenson* did not apply to the negligently manufactured product in regard to its diminished value, but that such issues fell exclusively under the law of contract. The plaintiffs thus relied heavily on the *prima facie* duty of care doctrine of Lord Wilberforce in the Anns decision,[42] which can be used to assume the very thing to be decided.

Lord Fraser of Tullybelton and Lord Roskill each accepted the reasoning of each other and Lord Russell of Killowen agreed with the reasoning of both.

Lord Roskill cited and applied the *prima facie* duty of care doctrine and proximity test of Lord Wilberforce. Thus the circular reasoning implicit

---

[41][1982] 3 W.L.R. 577, [1982] 3 All E.R. 201 (H.L.).

[42]*Anns v. Merton London Borough Council*, [1978] A.C. 728, [1977] 2 W.L.R. 1024, [1977] 2 All E.R. 429 (H.L.).

in using risk to establish a duty to take care was used to assume the answer to the question in issue. As well as *Anns v. Merton London Borough Council*, he also relied on the cases of *Hedley Byrne v. Heller, Dutton v. Bognor Regis Urban Dist. Council*,[43] *Batty v. Metro. Property Realisations*[44] and the dissenting judgment of Laskin J. (as he then was) in *Rivtow Marine Ltd. v. Washington Iron Works*,[45] all of which involved the question of recovery for costs related to the defect in the negligently constructed house or article itself rather than to costs resulting from damage caused by the defect.

Lord Fraser of Tullybelton dealt with the floodgate argument for refusing recovery for economic loss, and ruled that it had no application to the facts of this case as the loss suffered was restricted to a foreseeable amount in regard to a foreseeable plaintiff. There are, of course, no grounds for arguing that the loss in this case is too remote. The critical issue is one of extension — does the defendant owe a duty to the plaintiff independent of contract?

Lord Keith of Kinkel, in regard to the neighbour principle of *Donoghue v. Stevenson*, took the position that "the duty extended to the avoidance of acts or omissions which might reasonably have been anticipated as likely to cause physical injury to persons or property,"[46] but that the scope of the duty had been extended by *Hedley Byrne v. Heller*; therefore, it was not relevant to the issue before the court, "except in so far as it established that reasonable anticipation of physical injury to person or property is not a sine qua non for the existence of a duty of care."[47] He then concluded that:

> "They [the defendants] must have been aware of the nature of the respondents' business, the purpose for which the floor was required and the plan it was to play in their operations. The appellants accordingly owed the respondents a duty to take reasonable care to see that their workmanship was not faulty, and are liable for the foreseeable consequences, sounding in economic loss, of their failure to do so. These consequences may properly be held to include less profitable operation due to the heavy cost of maintenance."[48]

There is little substantive difference between the way that Lords Roskill, Fraser, and Russell, and the way that Lord Keith approach the duty issue (what I have called the problem of extension). The majority

---

[43][1972] 1 Q.B. 373, [1972] 2 W.L.R. 299, [1972] 1 All E.R. 462 (C.A.).

[44][1978] Q.B. 554, [1978] 2 W.L.R. 500, [1978] 2 All E.R. 445 (C.A.).

[45][1974] S.C.R. 1189, [1973] 6 W.W.R. 692, 40 D.L.R. (3d) 530.

[46]*Supra*, note 41, at 205.

[47]*Ibid.*, at 206.

[48]*Ibid.*, at 206.

judgment extends the principle of *Donoghue v. Stevenson* to pure economic loss arising from an action which creates no risk of physical injury to person or property exposed to the danger, and cites the dissenting judgment of Laskin J. in *Rivtow Marine Ltd. v. Washington Iron Works* cited with approval by Lord Wilberforce in *Anns v. Merton London Borough Council*. Any purely economic loss which did not arise from an action creating a risk of physical harm to persons or property must be recovered under the principle of *Hedley Byrne v. Heller*.

Lord Brandon raised a further bar to recovery. "It has further, until the present case," he writes, "never been doubted, so far as I know, that the relevant property for the purpose of the wider principle on which the decision in *Donoghue v. Stevenson* was based, was property other than the very property which gave rise to the danger of physical damage concerned."[49] To apply the principle of *Donoghue v. Stevenson* to the very defectively manufactured product itself, "would be, in substance, to create, as between two persons who are not in any contractual relationship with each other, obligations of one of those two persons to the other which are only really appropriate as between persons who do have such a relationship between them."[50]

The implications which Lord Brandon finds implicit in the view of the majority are worth setting out in full. He writes:

"In the case of a manufacturer or distributor of goods, the position would be that he warranted to the ultimate user or consumer of such goods that they were as well designed, as merchantable and as fit for their contemplated purpose as the exercise of reasonable care could make them.

"In the case of sub-contractors such as those concerned in the present case, the position would be that they warranted to the building owner that the flooring, when laid, would be as well designed, as free from defects of any kind and as fit for its contemplated purpose as the exercise of reasonable care could make it.

"In my view, the imposition of warranties of this kind on one person in favour of another when there is no contractual relationship between them, is contrary to any sound policy requirement.

"It is, I think, just worth while to consider the difficulties which would arise if the wider scope of the duty of care put forward by the pursuers were accepted. In any case where complaint was made by an ultimate consumer that a product made by some persons with whom he himself had no contract was defective, by what standard or standards of quality would the question of defectiveness fall to be decided? In the case of goods bought from a retailer, it could hardly be the standard prescribed by the contract between the retailer and the wholesaler, or between the wholesaler and the distributor, or between the distributor and the manufacturer, for the terms of such

---

[49]*Ibid.*, at 216.
[50]*Ibid.*, at 218.

contracts would not even be known to the ultimate buyer. In the case of sub-contractors such as the [appellants] in the present case, it could hardly be the standard prescribed by the contract between the sub-contractors and the main contractors, for, although the building owner would probably be aware of those terms, he could not, since he was not a party to such contract, rely on any standard or standards prescribed in it. It follows that the question by what standard or standards alleged defects in a product complained of by its ultimate user or consumer are to be judged remains entirely at large and cannot be given any just or satisfactory answer.

"If, contrary to the views expressed above, the relevant contract or contracts can be regarded in order to establish the standard or standards of quality by which the question of defectiveness falls to be judged, and if such contract or contracts happen to include provisions excluding or limiting liability for defective products or defective work, or for negligence generally, it seems that the party sued in delict should in justice be entitled to fly on such provisions. This illustrates with especial force the inherent difficulty of seeking to impose what are really contractual obligations by unprecedented and, as I think, wholly undesirable extensions of the existing law of delict.

"By contrast, if the scope of the duty of care contended for by the defenders is accepted, the standard of defectiveness presents no problem at all. The sole question is whether the product is so defective that, when used or consumed in the way in which it was intended to be, it gives rise to a danger of physical damage to persons or their property, other than the product concerned itself."[51]

Lord Keith of Kinkel expressed similar concerns and concurred in the decision of Lord Brandon in regard to this matter. He writes:

"To introduce a general liability covering such situations would be disruptive of commercial practice, under which manufacturers of products commonly provide the ultimate purchaser with limited guarantees, usually undertaking only to replace parts exhibiting defective workmanship and excluding any consequential loss. There being no contractual relationship between manufacturer and ultimate consumer, no room would exist, if the suggested principle were accepted, for limiting the manufacturer's liability. The policy considerations which would be involved in introducing such a state of affairs appear to me to be such as a court of law cannot properly assess, and the question whether or not it would be in the interests of commerce and the public generally is, in my view, much better left for the legislature. The purchaser of a defective product normally can proceed for breach of contract against the seller who can bring his own supplier into the proceedings by third party procedure, so it cannot be said that the present state of the law is unsatisfactory from the point of view of available remedies. I refer to *Young & Martin Ltd. v. McManus Childs Ltd.* [1968] 2 All E.R. 1169, [1969] 1 A.C. 454. In the second place, I can foresee that very considerable difficulties might arise in assessing the standards of quality by which the allegedly defective product is to be judged. This aspect is more filly developed in the speech to be delivered by my noble and learned friend Lord Brandon, with whose views on the matter I respectfully agree."[52]

He reconciles his concurrence with the finding of the majority of the existence of a duty of care with his concurrence in the reasoning of the

---

[51]*Ibid.*, at 218.

[52]*Ibid.*, at 207.

dissenting judgment of Lord Brandon, by limiting the duty to situations such as in the case in issue where the exact details of the risk of harm were foreseeable, a situation less likely to occur as between general manufacturers and ultimate consumers.

The majority decision of the Supreme Court of Canada in the earlier case of *Rivtow Marine Ltd. v. Washington Iron Works*[53] gave reasons similar to those of Lords Brandon and Keith of Kinkel for denying liability for the cost of repairs of the negligently created defective product itself and the economic loss arising therefrom. Laskin J.'s dissent was specifically cited and relied on by the majority judges in *Junior Books v. Veitchi*.[54] This raises an interesting problem for Canadian courts. Can *Junior Books v. Veitchi* be reconciled with *Rivtow*, since *Junior Books* assumes the correctness of the dissent in *Rivtow*? The British Columbia Court of Appeal in *Nicholls v. Richmond*[55] followed and applied *Junior Books* without making any reference to *Rivtow*, and the Supreme Court of Canada has since refused leave to appeal. Not only is *Rivtow* inconsistent with *Junior Books*, it is probably also inconsistent with both *Dutton v. Bognor Regis Urban Dist. Council*[56] and *Anns v. Merton London Borough Council*. We may conclude from the majority judgment in *Rivtow* that *Donoghue v. Stevenson* does not apply to the defective article itself, but only to damage to other persons and property caused by the deficit. Liability of the municipal inspector in both *Anns and Dutton* is based on the assumption that the negligent builder is primarily liable for failing to construct proper foundations. Lord Denning M.R., in the latter case, states: "I would agree that if the builder is not liable for the bad work the council ought not to be liable for passing it."[57] It would be outrageous if a plaintiff could recover against a negligent building inspector but not against the builder himself who is primarily responsible.

To hold the builder liable, however, is to apply *Donoghue v. Stevenson* to the very negligently manufactured article itself, a step the Supreme Court of Canada refused to take in *Rivtow*. Surely there can be no difference between the economic loss suffered in repairing a crane and that suffered in repairing a house. Lord Denning, however, was unaware that he was applying *Donoghue v. Stevenson* to allow recovery for the loss suffered as a result of the diminished value of a negligently built house,

---

[53] *Supra*, note 45.

[54] [1982] 3 WQ.L.R. 477, [1982] 3 All E.R. 201 at 212 (H.L.).

[55] [1983] 4 W.W.R. 169, 43 B.C.L.R. 162, 33 C.P.C. 310, 24 C.C.L.T. 253, 145 D.L.R. (3d) 362, 1 C.C.E.L. 188 (C.A.).

[56] [1972] 1 Q.B. 373, [1972] 2 W.L.R. 299, [1972] 1 All E.R. 462 (C.A.).

[57] *Ibid.*, at 392.

but assumed that the case was one of physical damage resulting from a negligently manufactured or constructed product, failing to note that in the standard case the physical damage was always in regard to property other than that manufactured or constructed negligently.[58]

The conflict between *Dutton and Anns* on the one hand and *Rivtow* on the other was addressed by the British Columbia Court of Appeal in *Kamloops v. Nielsen*,[59] decided before *Junior Books*, in which an action was brought by a subsequent purchaser of a house for loss due to faulty foundations, where the city failed to enforce a stop-work order. In the judgment of the court, Lambert J.A. distinguished Rivtow on the grounds that it dealt with a case of concurrent liabilities in contract and in tort, while in the *Anns* type of situations the duties of the municipalities had nothing to do with a chain of contractual relations.

In *Robert Simpson Co. v. Foundation Co. of Can.*[60] the Ontario Court of Appeal, in an action brought for the cost of repairs by lessees of a negligently constructed building against builders with whom they had no contractual relationship, also distinguished *Rivtow* on the grounds that the defendants "negligently misrepresented the materials and the method used for erecting the ceiling as being adequate for the weight and design of the ceiling and capable of suspending it, when they knew or ought to have known that the plaintiffs were relying upon them to provide proper materials and to use proper building methods."[61] Consequently if liability were to lie, it would be based on *Hedley Byrne v. Heller*, and since "the principles set out in *Rivtow* have no application to an action based upon negligent misrepresentation,"[62] *Rivtow* would not preclude recovery.

---

[58]The author raised this issue in a conversation with Lord Denning, who admitted that it had not occurred to him until the time of the discussion that *Dutton* was not just another case of physical damage, and that in writing the decision he was not conscious of the distinction discussed in *Rivtow* of applying *Donoghue v. Stevenson* to the cost of repairs of the article itself as in contrast to damage to other property caused by the defective product. Equally, the House of Lords in *Anns* seemed unaware of the fact that the defective foundations posed no risk to persons or other property.

[59][1982] 1 W.W.R. 461, 31 B.C.L.R. 311, 19 C.C.L.T. 146, 16 M.P.L.R. 221, 129 D.L.R. (3d) 111, leave to appeal to S.C.C. granted 41 N.R. 538 (S.C.C.).

[60](1982), 36 O.R. (2d) 97, 20 C.C.L.T. 179, 26 C.P.C. 51, 134 D.L.R. (3d) 458 (C.A.).

[61]*Ibid.*, at 200, *per* Cory J.A.

[62]*Supra*, note 60, at 201, *per* Cory J.A. Contrast this case with *Condominium Plan No. 7821918 v. Alldritt Dev. Ltd.* (1982), 24 Alta. L.R. (2d) 178, 44 A.R. 189 (Alta. Q.B.), where the trial judge struck out of the pleadings an allegation of negligence against a subcontractor who allegedly had caused the plaintiff owner of a condominium economic loss sustained in repairing badly laid pavement, on the grounds that under the law as set out by the Supreme Court of Canada in *Rivtow Marine and Washington* the pleadings disclosed no cause of action. No mention was made of the case of *Junior Books*.

IV. CONCLUSION

On the basis of the House of Lords decisions in *Hedley Byrne v. Heller*, and *Junior Books v. Veitchi*, we can draw the following conclusions:

1. Representations made between contracting parties, but which are not part of the contract, may be enforceable in tort.

2. Promises or undertakings for which there is no consideration may be enforceable in tort.

3. Third party beneficiaries under a contract may have a right of action in tort.

4. Some standards of fitness (warranties?) may be enforced in tort in the absence of privity of contract.

By way of summary we can conclude the following:

1. The common law of contract when compared with the law of contract of civil law systems will be found to be rigid and limited by the past practice of courts in defining the boundaries of contracts narrowly, the doctrine of consideration, the doctrine of strict privity of contract, and the absence of rights of third party beneficiaries under a contract.

2. The common law of negligence was equally narrow and restrictive in that manufacturers were immune from liability to the ultimate consumer for their negligence; landlords owed no duty of care outside of contract to the spouses or guests of tenants, builders owed no duty of care independent of contract, to the guests or spouses of the purchaser or to subsequent purchasers; no duty was owed by statutory bodies for damage suffered as a result of their failure to carry out their statutory duties or exercise statutory powers, or for carrying them out badly; and no duty of care was owed in regard to pure economic loss.

3. The law of contract failed to develop sufficient contractual principles for reforming the law and broadening the bases of liability.

4. The law of negligence developed the principle of risk or proximity by which it was able to extend liability.

5. The proximity or risk principle has turned out to be sufficiently flexible that courts have been able to use it to reform not only the law of negligence, but the law of contract as well. Hence the union of contract and tort.

6

RELIANCE AS A SOURCE OF DUTY TO TAKE CARE

I. INTRODUCTION

It is premature, however, to celebrate the nuptials. The marriage of contract and tort is beset with serious problems. The risk principle spreads liability far too widely. Third parties will probably end up with better remedies than the very parties to the contract. Contracting parties will not be able to limit their liability, and consequently adequate liability insurance will be extremely expensive.

The recent decision of the British Columbia Court of Appeal in *Nicholls v. Richmond*[1] furnishes us with a good example of the propensity of the risk principle to spread the net of liability too widely. In that case the plaintiff sued the defendant municipality for wrongful dismissal, and the mayor, several aldermen, and two municipal officials for conspiracy and negligently inducing a breach of contract by persuading the municipality to terminate the plaintiff's employment. The defendants sought to have the latter struck out of the pleadings on the grounds that there is no such cause of action as negligently inducing a breach of contract. The British Columbia Court of Appeal took the position that in the light of the *prima facie* duty of care doctrine of Lord Wilberforce in *Anns v. Merton London Borough Council*[2] and *Junior Books v. Veitchi Co.*,[3] cases such as *Cattle v. Stockton Waterworks Co.*,[4] and *Weller & Co. v. Foot and Mouth Disease Research Institute*,[5] "should be seen as specific examples of a denial of recovery on the basis of absence of proximity, or remoteness of damage, or both."[6] The court then overruled the decision on similar facts of

---

[1][1983] 4 W.W.R. 169, 43 B.C.L.R. 162, 33 C.P.C. 310, 24 C.C.L.T. 253, 145 D.L.R. (3d) 362, 1 C.C.E.L. 188 (C.A.).

[2][1978] A.C. 728, [1977] 2 W.L.R. 1024, [1977] 2 All E.R. 492 (H.L.).

[3][1982] 3 W.L.R. 477, [1982] 3 All E.R. 201 (H.L.).

[4](1875), L.R. 10 Q.B. 453.

[5][1966] 1 Q.B. 569, [1965] 3 W.L.R. 1082, [1965] 3 All E.R. 560.

[6]*Supra*, note 1, at 174, *per* Lambert J.A.

Taylor J. in *McLaren v. B.C. Institute of Technology*,[7] on the following grounds:

> "Suppose an airline has a policy of discharging pilots who suffer from a medical disability and requires its pilots to undergo a medical examination each year by a doctor, selected by the airline, who knows the purpose of the examination. Suppose the doctor carelessly and incorrectly diagnoses a disability and the pilot is discharged. Would the pilot, as a matter of legal policy, be denied a cause of action against the doctor? I do not think so. Yet the loss suffered by the pilot would be economic loss arising from the doctor's negligent interference with the pilot's contractual relations with the airline. I leave unanswered the question of what difference it would make, if any, if the doctor was a salaried employee of the airline.

> "And of course, the action for loss of services, when it lies, extends to an action arising from a negligent act which injures the employee and at the same time interferes with the contractual relations between the employee and the employer, and so causes economic loss to the employer. See *Nykorak v. A.G. Canada* [1962] S.C.R. 331, 37 W.W.R. 660, 33 D.L.R. (2d) 373.

> "So it is my opinion that in appropriate circumstances an action may be sustained by a former employee against another employee of his employer, or against a corporate or municipal officer, based on an act, omission or misstatement, in breach of a duty of care, that results in economic loss to the former employee through discharge from employment."[8]

The above hypothetical case of the airline pilot is an example of a negligently carried out undertaking, and could consequently be justified in terms of an expanded view of the principle of liability underlying *Hedley Byrne v. Heller*.[9] *Nykorak v. A.G. Can.* is an action of *per quod servitium amisit*, involving economic loss arising out of physical injury to the person.[10] Neither case justifies the recognition of a new cause of action for negligently interfering with contractual relations.

There is a wide variety of ways in which it is foreseeable that our actions can have adverse effects on the contractual relations of others. Social intercourse and commerce will be enormously expensive or impossible if liability is to follow risk. Risk or proximity may be a necessary condition for liability, but it should not be allowed to become a sufficient condition. Other factors such as a voluntary undertaking and reliance or a special relationship whether contractual, quasi-contractual or fiduciary should also be required in order to place reasonable limits on liability for pure economic loss where there has been no risk of physical harm to persons or property.

---

[7][1978] 6 W.W.R. 687, 7 C.C.L.T. 692, 94 D.L.R. (3d) 411 (B.C.S.C.).
[8]*Supra*, note 1, at 174-75.
[9][1964] A.C. 465, [1963] 3 W.L.R. 101, [1963] 2 All E.R. 575 (H.L.).
[10][1962] S.C.R. 331, 37 W.W.R. 660, 33 D.L.R. (2d) 373.

A necessary condition for the imposition by the law of a duty to take care is that the damage caused by the act, if intentional, would give rise to liability. It would indeed be strange if one were to be held liable for doing negligently that for which there would be no liability if done intentionally. One is less culpable for negligently caused harm than if one did the same thing intentionally because to show that harm was caused unintentionally is to offer an excuse or a partial defence. If damage was caused negligently, then it cannot be caused intentionally. One is not free from culpability altogether, however, unless one can show that one maintained a reasonable standard of care in trying to avoid harm.

One will nearly always be liable for the intentional causing of physical harm to persons or property unless a defence such as that of lawful authority or necessity applies. One will generally not be liable for the intentional causing of economic loss to others by acts which do not create a risk of physical harm to persons or property. In a world where demand far exceeds resources, it is inevitable that the actions of any one person in satisfying his or her needs or goals, or in pursuing his or her interests will have a negative impact on the economic interests of others, and in a good many situations it will be reasonably foreseeable.

One would not be liable for appropriating a competitor's supply of raw materials for one's own purposes by offering a higher price than one knows one's competitor can afford to pay, so long as there is no intentional inducing of a breach of contract. If one, on the other hand, intentionally or negligently physically damaged the materials after one's competitor achieved ownership, then there would be a breach of right and liability not just for the cost of replacement, but probably for loss of profits as well. If as a result of one's purchase of one's competitor's normal supply of raw materials the competitor was forced to lay off employees, there would be no liability to them for loss of income. If, however, as a result of one's negligent driving, one of them was physically injured then his or her loss of earnings would be recoverable.

People can be said to have a liberty or are at liberty to do that which is not expressly prohibited by the criminal law, statute, or implicitly prohibited by the civil law. Even after taking into account the legislation prohibiting various unfair trade practices, the laws of patents and copyright, and the various economic torts such as the intentional inducing of a breach of contract, or civil conspiracy, there is a vast range of actions and behaviour which although capable of causing foreseeable economic loss to others, are neither prohibited nor tortious.[11]

---

[11]*Victoria Park Racing & Recreation Grounds Co. Ltd. v. Taylor* (1937), 58 C.L.R. 479 at 509, [1937] A.L.R. 597, 11 A.L.J. 197, leave to appeal to P.C. refused [1938] W.N. (Eng.) 34.

The parameters of the area of conduct causing risk of economic loss which gives rise to civil liability have been set out by the courts in recent decisions such as *Dunlop v. Woollahra Mun. Council*,[12] *Lonrho v. Shell Petroleum Co.*,[13] *R.C.A. Corp. v. Pollard*,[14] as well as the earlier line of cases such as *Lumley v. Gye*,[15] *Mogul S.S. Co. v. McGregor Gow & Co.*,[16] *Crofter Hand Woven Harris Tweed Co. Ltd. v. Veitch*,[17] *Derry v. Peek*,[18] and many others. Not only is there a series of torts such as deceit, injurious falsehood, passing off, all dealing with conduct causing purely economic loss, but as well, most jurisdictions have statutes which regulate business behaviour.

There is absolutely no way these various causes of action can be brought under a single principle. The general principle articulated by Mr. Justice Wright in *Wilkinson v. Downton*[19] applies to physical and emotional injury only. There can be no general principle in regard to pure economic loss because all these various causes of action are exceptions in and of themselves — exceptions to the general position that one is not liable for causing purely economic loss to others by actions which create no risk of physical harm to persons or property.

If there is no *general* principle prohibiting the intentional causing of purely economic loss, then there can be no general principle prohibiting the negligent causing of purely economic loss, in which case there can be no general duty to take care to prevent purely economic loss to others where no risk of physical harm is involved.

Risks of purely economic loss are not exceptions to *Donoghue v. Stevenson* as they do not even fall under the principle. The grounds of liability for the negligent causing of pure economic loss, or the foundation of the duty to take care, must be and are different from those which relate to the causing of physical harm to persons and property.

If the above argument is sound, then economic loss arising from actions which create a risk of physical injury to persons or property must be treated separately and under different principles from purely economic loss which arises from actions which do not create a risk of

---

[12][1981] 2 W.L.R. 693, [1981] 1 All E.R. 1202.

[13][1981] 3 W.L.R. 33, [1981] 2 All E.R. 456.

[14][1982] 3 W.L.R. 1007, [1982] 3 All E.R. 771 (C.A.).

[15](1853), 2 E. & B. 216, 118 E.R. 749 (Q.B.).

[16]23 Q.B.D. 598, affirmed [1892] A.C. 25 (H.L.).

[17][1942] A.C. 435, [1942] 1 All E.R. 142 (H.L.).

[18](1889), 14 App. Cas. 337 (H.L.).

[19][1897] 2 Q.B. 57 at 58-59.

physical harm to persons or property. The first creates problems of remoteness of damage only. The latter generally do not create problems of remoteness but entail issues of extension — will courts impose any duty at all to take care.[20]

II.   RIGHTS AND THE LIMITS OF RECOVERY FOR PURE ECONOMIC LOSS

Hedley Byrne v. Heller[21] should not be seen as an application of *Donoghue v. Stevenson* nor as an extension to it as is implied by Lord Wilberforce in his statement of the *prima facie* duty principle of *Anns*; it should be recognized as an independent ground of civil obligation standing alongside of *Donoghue v. Stevenson*. *Donoghue v. Stevenson* then would apply only to actions creating a risk of physical harm to persons or property.

The distinctions between misfeasance and nonfeasance (action and failing to act), and between physical injury to persons or property and pure economic loss, are not particularly relevant in the law of contract given that the damage springs from a breach of contractual duty. In the common law tradition, if physical damage resulting from a breach of contract is caused intentionally or negligently liability will also lie in tort. Equally if damage arises from a non-contractual but nevertheless enforceable undertaking, these same distinctions should not matter. Liability under *Hedley Byrne v. Heller* should be like contract in this regard — a distinction between misfeasance and nonfeasance, physical damage and pure economic loss should not be relevant. If the damage constitutes physical injury to persons or property as a result of negligently carrying out an undertaking, liability should lie under both the principle of *Donoghue v. Stevenson* and that upon which *Hedley Byrne v. Heller* is based.

While many courts have in recent years dismissed *Hedley Byrne v. Heller* as if it were merely an extension of the proximity principle of Lord Atkin in *Donoghue v. Stevenson*, the view that best accords with a careful reading of the case was well expressed by the Chief Justice of the High Court of Australia. Mr. Chief Justice Gibbs, in *Shaddock & Associates Pty. Ltd. v. Parramatta*, stated, in speaking of the principle underlying the decisions of *Hedley Byrne v. Heller* and *Mutual Life and Citizens Assur. Co.*

---

[20]In an earlier article, "Clarification of Duty — Remoteness Problems Through a New Physiology of Negligence: Economic Loss, a Test Case" (1974), 9 U.B.C.L. Rev. 213, this writer expressed the opinion that economic loss raised issues of remoteness rather than duty. Insofar as pure economic loss not arising from actions creating a risk of physical harm to persons or property is concerned, this was incorrect and the error stemmed from the false assumption that the principles of *Donoghue v. Stevenson* underlay the whole of the law of negligence.

[21][1964] A.C. 465, [1963] 3 W.L.R. 101, [1963] 2 All E.R. 575 (H.L.).

v. Evatt:[22] "The courts in those cases rejected the view that the principle stated by Lord Atkin in *Donoghue v. Stevenson* . . . provided the basis of liability in the case of negligent mis-statements."[23] There is, however, no basis for a distinction between negligent acts and negligent words which create risks of physical harm to persons or property, nor for making a fundamental difference between physical damage and pure economic loss resulting from an act which has caused or created a risk of physical damage. The fundamental difference lies between acts which create risks of physical damage and acts which create risks of only pure financial loss.

Why this is so can be demonstrated by comparing two recent decisions involving economic loss. The first is *Ross v. Caunters*.[24] A testator, wishing to make certain alterations in his will, sent a letter to the defendant, his solicitor, containing the proposed changes, and the query, "Am I right in thinking that beneficiaries may not be witnesses?" The defendant sent the testator copies of the new will but left the testator's question unanswered. The testator signed the will in front of two witnesses, one of whom was the plaintiff's husband. The plaintiff was a beneficiary under the will and the gift to her failed because her husband signed the will as a witness. The defendants failed to notice this defect on receiving from the testator the signed copies of his new will. The plaintiff brought an action against the negligent solicitor for the amount she would have received under the will if it had been witnessed by someone other than her husband. The defendants' position was that they owed the plaintiff no duty of care.

Sir Robert Megarry V.C., applying the *prima facie* duty of care test as set out by Lord Reid in *Home Office v. Dorset Yacht Co.*[25] and Lord Wilberforce in *Anns v. Merton London Borough Council*, held that the defendant solicitor did owe the plaintiff, the potential beneficiary, a duty of care. Sir Robert writes: "If one approaches the present case in the manner indicated by Lord Wilberforce, I can see only one answer to the question that has to be asked at the first stage. Prima facie a duty of care was owed by the defendants to the plaintiff because it was obvious that carelessness on their part would be likely to cause damage to her." [26] He then went on to conclude that he could find no good policy reason for excluding liability. The case represents a classic example of the circular reasoning implicit in the *prima facie* duty of care doctrine.

---

[22][1971] A.C. 793, [1971] 2 W.L.R. 23, [1971] 1 All E.R. 150 (P.C.).

[23](1981), 36 A.L.R. 385 at 389, 55 A.L.J.R. 713 at 715.

[24][1980] Ch. 297, [1979] 3 W.L.R. 605, [1979] 3 All E.R. 580.

[25][1970] A.C. 1004 at 1026-1027, [1970] 2 W.L.R. 1140, [1970] 2 All E.R. 294 (H.L.).

[26]*Supra*, note 24, at 310.

The Full Court of the Supreme Court of Victoria, in *Seale v. Perry*,[27] a case where the facts were similar to those of *Ross v. Caunters*, refused to apply the *prima facie* duty of care doctrine and declined to follow *Ross v. Caunters*. Mr. Justice Lush at the commencement of his judgment rejects the idea that a duty to take care can be inferred from the presence of a foreseeable risk. He states: "In neither the general nor the particular statements [of Lord Atkin's neighbour principle] therefore, does it appear that the mere foresight of possible injury to some person or persons is sufficient of itself to give rise to a duty to take care to avoid that injury."[28]

Mr. Justice Lush then went on to distinguish *Hedley Byrne v. Heller* on the grounds that "the final definition of the liability which would have existed in the absence of the saving words imposes the requirement that there should be on the part of the defendant an express or implied acceptance of responsibility to the plaintiff or to a class of persons to which the plaintiff belonged."[29] The *prima facie* duty of care doctrine of the *Dorset Yacht* case and the *Anns* case were not, according to Mr. Justice Lush, applicable to a case of purely financial loss but in both cases "the plaintiff or plaintiffs owned property alleged to be damaged or adversely affected by the defendants' conduct . . ."[30]

The essence of the judgment of Mr. Justice Lush was that there could be no liability by the defendant solicitor to the plaintiff potential beneficiary because the defendant had infringed no right of the plaintiff. He writes:

"There is another approach which leads to the same conclusion. In the cases which I have cited, the speeches and judgments have been expressed in terms which concentrate on examining the question whether a duty exists. A duty, however, cannot exist by itself. To the duty seen as imposed on the defendant, there must be a correlative right in the plaintiff: for either to exist, both must be capable of being identified.

"It is possible that this proposition is at the root of the reluctance of the common law, evident for a long time, to recognize purely economic loss as a form of damage recoverable in an action for negligence. If person or property were damaged, it was not difficult to identify the plaintiff's right as a right to have care taken not to cause that damage. If the plaintiff suffered an economic loss, such as the loss of the profits of a business, it was less easy to identify anything in the nature of a right to be protected by an action for negligence . . .

"I venture to think that it is really the problem of identifying the right which the plaintiff is entitled to have protected which underlies the difficulties of allowing actions

---

[27][1982] V.R. 193 (S.C.).

[28]*Ibid*, at 194.

[29]*Ibid*, at 195.

[30]*Ibid*, at 198.

to be brought in cases where the plaintiff has suffered and suffered only economic loss
. . .

"In the present case, there is nothing in the position of the plaintiffs on which a right
can be founded. They had no form of right at law, by contract or otherwise, to the
benefaction, and there is nothing which can be treated as analogous to the enjoyment or
continuous enjoyment of a service . . .

"For my part, I do not regard the emphasis on property damage and personal injury
in decided cases . . . as either arbitrary or restrictive. I think a consideration of the right
which must be correlative to any suggested duty reveals the reason for this emphasis.
In broad terms, the common law of tort afforded protection by personal actions to
property rights and to integrity of the person."[31]

Mr. Justice Lush concluded: "No extension of the concept of right or
protected interest which has yet been made will suffice to sustain the
present plaintiffs' case."[32] His arguments for coming to that conclusion
included reference to the fact that the testator himself owed no duty to
the plaintiffs to either make the bequest or perfect the execution of his
intention to do so, and could have at any time changed his instructions to
the defendant. The defendant thus interfered with no right of the plaintiffs nor did he undertake any duty to them.

Mr. Justice Murphy argued similarly:

"I find it rather odd as a concept that this duty owed by a solicitor to a third party
arises only in circumstances where the client intends or desires to confer a 'benefit' on
a third party, and that if the intendment (or perhaps it is the effect) of the client's
instructions was not to confer a benefit but even to injure the interests of a third party,
then no duty to take care arises."[33]

He then went on to say:

"What I would think it surprising to find is that, although a testator himself owed no
duty of care to persons he proposed to benefit (because they have no rights apropo
him), and need not take care to see that his will is properly executed (whether
homemade or professionally drawn), yet if the testator employed a solicitor to do the
very same thing on his behalf, then that solicitor does owe a duty of care to persons
whom his client proposes to benefit."[34]

After discussing a number of cases Mr. Justice Murphy further concluded:

"The cases mentioned above reaffirm the fundamental rule of the common law that
the third party beneficiary cannot sue on the contract for damages or specific performance following a deliberate breach of or failure to perform a contract. It follows that

---

[31]*Ibid.*, at 200-202.

[32]*Ibid.*, at 202.

[33]*Ibid.*, at 206.

[34]*Ibid.*, at 208.

the third party beneficiary cannot sue on the contract for damages or specific performance following a negligent breach of or failure to perform a contract."[35]

Mr. Justice McGarvie reached the same conclusion following similar patterns of reasoning to those used by Mr. Justices Lush and Murphy. Throughout all three judgments a variety of hypothetical cases were suggested which should fall under *Ross v. Caunters*, if followed, but would lead to very unusual results. Where, for example, a testator wished to revoke a codicil making a specific gift to a particular person, and the solicitor negligently failed to do so, would the solicitor be in breach of a duty of care owed to the beneficiaries who would have benefited if the particular gift had been properly revoked?

A year prior to *Ross v. Caunters* Mr. Justice Aikins of the Supreme Court of British Columbia in *Whittingham v. Crease & Co.*[36] found a solicitor liable to an intended beneficiary when the gift under the will failed because the plaintiff's wife was allowed to witness the will on the ground that the case fell under the principle of *Hedley Byrne v. Heller*. Chief Justice Burt of the Supreme Court of Western Australia in *Watts v. Pub. Trustee* followed *Ross v. Caunters* stating that, "the basis of the solicitor's liability to others is either an extension of the *Hedley Byrne* principle, or, more probably, a direct application of the principle of *Donoghue v. Stevenson*."[37] On the other hand, Mr. Justice Thorp of the New Zealand High Court, in *Gartside v. Sheffield, Young & Ellis* struck out the statement of claim on the grounds that it disclosed no cause of action where it was alleged that the solicitors had negligently procrastinated the carrying out of the 89-year-old hospitalized testatrix's instructions to draw up a new will, until her death precluded the drafting of the will. *Thorp J. declined to follow Ross v. Caunters* on the grounds that "the consequences would include providing, through tort, a right equivalent to a jus quaesitum tertio in contract, without any consideration of the complex factors involved in such a step . . ."[38] He held further that the plaintiff was unable to establish the necessary reliance to fall under the principle of *Hedley Byrne v. Heller*.

The problem which the courts in the above cases attempted to solve through the use of the law of negligence arises, not from the inflexibility of the law of contract, but rather from the rigidity of the formal requirements for a valid will. A far better solution would be to reform the law of

---

[35]*Ibid.*, at 210.
[36][1978] 5 W.W.R. 45, 6 C.C.L.T. 1, 3 E.T.R. 97, 88 D.L.R. (3d) 353 (B.C.S.C.).
[37][1980] W.A.R. 97 at 101 (S.C.).
[38][1981] 2 N.Z.L.R. 547 at 564 (H.C.).

succession along the lines adopted regarding the rule against perpetuities to give judges a discretion to waive the formal requirements where the intent of the testator is clear and no improper influence has been brought to bear.[39]

Recovery for pure economic loss has never presented a problem for the civil law, because the civil law approaches such problem in terms of the existence of rights rather than duties. The civil law systems all either expressly or implicitly recognize a general right of persons not to have their person or property physically injured. No such general right, however, is recognized in regard to purely economic interests. Where the law does afford such protection, it is in terms of specific limited rights.[40] Common law judges, on the other hand, have distinguished between physical damage and economic loss, negligent words and other kinds of actions, but seldom expressly in terms of negligence which creates risks of physical harm to persons or property and negligence which creates risks of only purely economic loss.[41] Consequently questions of duty have been confused with questions of remoteness, The proposed analysis, implicit in civil law systems, is as follows:

ISSUES OF REMOTENESS	ISSUES OF DUTY
actions which create	actions which create
risks of physical injury	risks of only pure
to persons or property, and	economic loss.
economic loss also or	
instead of follows.	

III. VOLUNTARY UNDERTAKINGS

There is a further reason why pure economic loss has never posed a particular problem for the civil law. Most civil law systems implicitly or

---

[39]Luntz, "Solicitors' Liability to Third Parties" (1983), 3 Oxford Journal of Legal Studies 284 at 289. See also *Gartside v. Sheffield, Young & Ellis, ibid.*, at 565.

[40]Each of the civil codes of Germany, France, Japan and Quebec contains an extensive set of articles *regulating* the law of contract, followed by a set of specific grounds of civil obligations such as mandate, unjust enrichment, quasi-contracts, most of which would be concerned with mainly economic loss, and a very broad provision requiring compensation for the causing of damage by fault or by breach of right. While only the German Code (art. 823) is specific about physical damage, the specific articles following the general delict provision seem mostly applicable to only physical damage and economic loss consequential thereto.

[41]Mr. Justice Widgery in *Weller & Co. v. Foot and Mouth Disease Research Institute*, [1966] 1 Q.B. 569, [1965] 3 W.L.R. 1082, [1965] 3 All E.R. 560, comes closest to drawing this distinction. He distinguishes between direct injury and loss consequential thereon, and indirect injury, and defines direct in terms of physical injury and indirect in terms of economic loss. See pp. 585 and 587.

expressly recognize at least three rather than two grounds for civil obligation: delict (tort), contract, and quasi-contract and special undertakings. Recovery for pure economic loss is generally only given in contract, quasi-contract, and where there has been a voluntary assumption of responsibility for a task or a special relationship. In 1891 Joseph H. Beale in an article in the Harvard Law Review entitled "Gratuitous Undertakings," argued that three rather than two kinds of rights are to be found in the common law. He stated:

> "A contract is a right which A has (*in personam*) against B, because B has consented, for a consideration, or in some formal manner, to assume the correlative duty. A tort is a violation of a right which A has (*in rem*) against B, equally with all others, because society has decreed that the corresponding duty should be laid upon every member of it. Between these classes of rights exists a third; which, unlike a tort, depends upon some voluntary act by B, by which he undertakes a duty, and, unlike a contract, does not depend upon any promise of B, but only upon the mutual relations of A and B. In other words, B assumes a duty merely by voluntarily entering into a new relation towards A."[42]

Professor Beale, at the end of the last century, pointed out that at old common law "there seems at one time to have been a three-fold division of personal actions into (1) trespass, and trespass on the case; (2) case induced by assumpsit; (3) covenant."[43] The middle ground of *assumpsit* seems to have been swallowed up by the law of negligence on the one hand and contract on the other.[44] Yet it was to cases drawn from this middle ground that Lord Denning in his famous dissent in *Candler v. Crane, Christmas & Co.*[45] which was adopted by the House of Lords in *Hedley Byrne v. Heller*, turned to find a basis of civil obligation in regard to negligently made representations resulting in purely economic loss.

Professor B.J. Reiter has argued that recent developments in the law of torts and contract "have made contract indistinguishable from tort in many relational contexts,"[46] and that underlying both is a common set of principles relating to the creation of "reasonable reliance and expectations,"[47] which are the foundation of civil obligation. He further argues that today, nothing should turn on whether an action based on reliance is brought in contract or in tort.

---

[42]*Beale*, "Gratuitous Undertakings" (1891-1892), 5 Harvard L. Rev. 222.

[43]*Ibid.*, at 225.

[44]Baker, "The Establishment of Assumpsit for Nonfeasance," *The Reports of Sir John Spellman* (1977), vol. 2, 94 Seldon Society; Alice Erh-Soon Tay, "The Essence of a Bailment: Contract, Agreement or Possession?" (1966), 5 Sydney L. Rev. 239.

[45][1951] 2 K.B. 164, [1951] 1 All E.R. 426 (C.A.).

[46]Reiter, "Contracts, Torts, Relations and Reliance" in Reiter and Swan, *Studies in Contract Law* (1980), at 310.

[47]*Ibid.*, at 248.

Reliance relationships are also protected and enforced through promissory estoppel.[48] "The underlying basis of equitable estoppel", according to Mr. M.P. Thompson, "is to allow a court to fulfill, either wholly or in part, an expectation that has been acted upon."[49] Thompson argues that while in the initial stages of its development it was viewed as a defence against rights being enforced, it now can be argued that it has evolved to the point that it can be said to give rise to a cause of action.[50]

At least four kinds of reliance relationships which can give rise to liability in tort, can be differentiated:

(1) Undertakings made in the context of contractual relations.

(a) What Professor Reiter calls "pre-contractual torts."[51]

In *Esso Petroleum Co. v. Mardon*,[52] for example, the defendant company was held liable in fact for damages suffered by the plaintiff as a result of his reliance on a negligently made inaccurate representation as to the potential gasoline sales of a service station site, made to induce the plaintiff to enter into a contract with the defendant. Many other cases *where liability is based on the principle of Hedley Byrne v. Heller* would fall into the category of pre-contractual torts.

(b) Concurrent liability in contract and tort.

The kind of mutual exclusivity of tortious and contractual liability which the Supreme Court of Canada tried to maintain in *J. Nunes Diamonds v. Dom. Elec. Protection Co.*[53] and in *Rivtow* will no longer be tenable if *Junior Books v. Veitchi* is conceived to be the law.[54]

Post-contractual torts.

In *Baxter & Co. v. Jones*,[55] a 1903 decision of the Ontario Court of

---

[48]*Central London Property Trust v. High Trees House*, [1947] 1 K.B. 130, [1956] 1 All E.R. 256.

[49]M.P. Thompson, "From Representation to Expectation; Estoppel as a Cause of Action" (1983), 42 Cambridge L.J. 257.

[50]*Ibid.*, at 266. See M.A. Hickling, "Labouring with Promissory Estoppel: A Well-Worked Doctrine Working Well?" (1983), 17 U.B.C.L. Rev. 183; *Chitty on Contracts*, 25th ed. (1983), at 236-37.

[51]*Supra*, note 46, at 259.

[52][1976] Q.B. 801, [1976] 2 W.L.R. 583, [1976] 2 All E.R. 5 (C.A.).

[53][1972] S.C.R. 769, 26 D.L.R. (3d) 699.

[54]See, *e.g.*, *N.B. Telephone Co. v. John Maryon Int. Ltd.* (1982), 24 C.C.L.T. 146, 141 D.L.R. (3d) 193, 43 N.B.R. (2d) 469, 113 A.P.R. 469, leave to appeal to S.C.C. refused 43 N.B.R. (2d) 468, 113 A.P.R. 468, 46 N.R. 262 (S.C.C.); see also Rafferty, "The Tortious Liability of Professionals to Their Contractual Clients", in Steel and Rodgers-Magnet, *Issues in Tort Law* (1983), at 243-63.

[55](1903), 6 O.L.R. 360.

Appeal, the court unanimously held the defendant insurance agent liable in tort for losses suffered by the plaintiff as a result of the defendant's failure to carry out a gratuitous undertaking to notify other insurance companies of the existence of the additional insurance purchased from the defendants. The courts relied principally on *Coggs v. Bernard*[56] which was later cited by Lord Devlin in *Hedley Byrne v. Heller*[57] in reaching the conclusion that a person who enters upon the performance of a mandate or gratuitous undertaking on behalf of another can be held liable in negligence not only for what he might do, but also for what he might leave undone. *Baxter v. Jones* was followed and applied, along with *Hedley Byrne v. Heller*, in *Myers v. Thompson*[58] and in *Kostiuk v. Union Accept. Corp.*[59]

(d) Tort claims by third persons who are not a party to the contract.

Junior Books v. Veitchi, and the set of cases where named beneficiaries fail to take under an improperly witnessed, drafted, or executed will, are examples of this fourth kind of claim.

2. Undertakings independent of contract.

(a) Some forms of bailment.[60]

(b) Non-contractual undertakings made in a professional capacity.[61]

3. The undertaking of special relationships such as fiduciary relationships which entail a set of duties.[62]

4. Undertakings entailed in the exercise of statutory powers.

Although Lord Wilberforce does state in his decision in *Anns* that:

> "1 do not think that a description of the council's duty can be based upon the 'neighbourhood' principle alone or upon merely any such factual relationship as 'control' as suggested by the Court of Appeal. So to base it would be to neglect an essential factor which is that the local authority is a public body, discharging functions under statute: its powers and duties are definable in terms of public not private law."[63]

---

[56](1703), 2 Ld. Raym. 909, 92 E.R. 107.

[57][1964] A.C. 465 at 526, [1963] 3 W.L.R. 101, [1963] 2 All E.R. 575 (H.L.).

[58][1967] 2 O.R. 335, 63 D.L.R. (2d) 476, affirmed [1967] 2 O.R. 335n, 63 D.L.R. (2d) 476n (C.A.).

[59]66 D.L.R. (2d) 430, [1969] I.L.R. 1-239 (Sask. Q.B.).

[60]*Coggs v. Bernard, supra,* note 56.

[61]See, *e.g., Cann v. Willson* (1888), 39 Ch. D. 39; *Dodds v. Millman* (1964), 47 W.W.R. 690, 45 D.L.R. (2d) 472 (B.C.S.C.).

[62]See, *e.g., Nocton v. Lord Ashburton*, [1914] A.C. 932 (H.L.); *Elderkin v. Merrill Lynch Royal Securities Ltd.* (1977), 80 D.L.R. (3d) 313, 22 N.S.R. (2d) 218, 31 A.P.R. 218 (C.A.).

[63][1978] A.C. 728 at 754 (H.L.).

The *Anns* line of cases does have something in common with the *Hedley Byrne v. Heller* line of cases: that in both situations where parties undertake to carry out a particular task, a duty to take care arises where it is foreseeable that someone will suffer loss if care is not taken in carrying out the task.[64] While Lord Salmon in his judgment in *Anns* thought that reliance was not even remotely relevant to the issue in *Anns*,[65] we do have public bodies undertaking to render a service in situations where they know that the public will take for granted that the service will be rendered, and it will not be considered necessary to make their own independent investigations. The only difference between the *Anns* line of decisions and a case such as *Windsor Motors Ltd. v. Powell River*[66] where a municipality was held liable under *Hedley Byrne v. Heller* for the negligence of their licence inspector who issued a licence for a used car lot in an area not zoned for such businesses is that in the latter the servant of the municipality knew that a particular person was relying on the representation while in the *Anns* kind of case the reliance is more general. The principles applying to public bodies undertaking to offer services need not be identical for those applying to people undertaking to act in the course of their professions, in regard to a particular calling or in regard to a specific undertaking. Where the exercise of a statutory power becomes a standard practice, the reliance of a particular plaintiff should not be required. It should only be necessary to show that the existence of the practice makes it no longer necessary for people to make their own enquiries or find substitute services.

IV. CONCLUSION

In conclusion, it is argued that there are, and have always been, at least two, not one, sources of a duty to take care in negligence. The first arises from people's rights of non-interference in regard to their persons and property. *Donoghue v. Stevenson* is the leading authority for the existence of a duty to take care to prevent physical harm to persons or property by our actions.

The second arises from voluntary undertakings where it is foreseeable that damage may be suffered by persons relying on the undertaking

---

[64] For an early application of this principle, see *Wilkinson v. Coverdale* (1793), 1 Esp. 75, 170 E.R. 284.

[65] *Ibid.*, at 768-69.

[66] (1969), 68 W.W.R. 173, 4 D.L.R. (3d) 155 (B.C.C.A.). See also *Welbridge Holdings Ltd. v. Winnipeg*, [1971] S.C.R. 957, [1972] 3 W.W.R. 433, 22 D.L.R. (3d) 470; *H.L. & M. Shoppers Ltd. v. Berwick* (1977), 3 M.P.L.R. 241, 82 D.L.R. (3d) 23, 28 N.S.R. (2d) 229, 43 A.P.R. 229 (T.D.); *Jung v. Burnaby*, [1978] 6 W.W.R. 670, 7 C.C.L.T. 113, 91 D.L.R. (3d) 592 (B.C.S.C.); *Shaddock & Associates Pty. Ltd. v. Parrametta* (1981), 36 A.L.R. 385, 55 A.L.J.R. 713 (H.C.).

being carried out properly. Although a combination of the rule in *Derry v. Peek*[67] and a line of cases such as *Cattle v. Stockton Water Works*, raising issues of remoteness regarding economic loss, for many years blocked recovery for pure economic loss arising from a negligent misrepresentation, *Hedley Byrne v. Heller*, *Anns v. Merton London Borough Council*, and *Junior Books Ltd. v. Veitchi*, have now removed these barriers, restoring a continuity in the law, reaching back to the old action of assumpsit. Where a duty of care arises from undertakings which create reliance, it should make little difference if the action is found in contract or tort; whether the damage is physical or purely economic; and whether the damage is a result of misfeasance or nonfeasance.

After a long and tortious history the common law of civil obligations has now evolved closer to the equivalent areas of law in civil law systems. On the other hand, since World War II, civil law systems have grown closer in spirit to the common law through relying on precedents for interpreting, filling in gaps, or limiting broad general principals in their civil codes. If we are to make sense of the recent developments in the law of negligence we need to understand why we have had the conceptual problems we have had in the past, the nature of the gaps in our law which have led to the present developments, and the fundamental principles of civil liability underlying it all.

The task which our courts should now undertake is to gradually separate *Hedley Byrne v. Helter*, *Anns* and *Junior Books* from *Donoghue v. Stevenson* and the doctrine of a *prima facie* duty of care, and develop and refine a set of principles based on reliance, and which should result in a law of civil obligation which will include equitable estoppel, and will fill the gap between the traditional law of negligence and the traditional law of contract.[68]

---

[67](1889), 14 App. Cas. 337 (H.L.).

[68]For in-depth discussions of the factors which should underlie liability for the causing of pure economic loss and for the creation of a duty of care by voluntary undertaking see Reiter, "Contracts, Torts, Relations and Reliance", *supra*, note 46, at 236-311; Feldthusen, "Negligent Misrepresentation: A Closer Look at the Basis of the Defendant's Duty of Care", in Steel and Rodgers-Magnet, *Issues in Tort Law* (1983), at 179-217; Bishop, "Economic Loss in Tort" (1982), 2 Oxford Journal of Legal Studies 1-29.

7

THE REMOTENESS PROBLEM

I. INTRODUCTION

"Once upon a time" is the phrase that starts fairy tales and the case of *Falkenham v. Zwicker*[1] is so much like a fairy tale that it seemed quite appropriate, and so this is how I will commence Chapter Seven. Once upon a time a lady was driving along the highway when a cat ran across the road. She negligently lost control of her vehicle when she slammed on her brakes to avoid hitting the cat. Her car ran off the road and into a wire fence with the impact popping out the staples for a fair distance in either direction. This all happened on the first of February. In the middle of May, the farmer noticed the missing staples and found several on the ground. About two weeks later he put dairy cows into the field to pasture. The cows eventually ate some of the staples and contracted "reticulitis" or what is more commonly known to those to whom such things are common knowledge, as "hardware disease," with the result that several valuable milking cows ended up at the meat-packing plant rather than contentedly producing milk as was their habit. Thereafter, according to the facts of the case, cattle pastured in this field had to have magnets placed in their stomachs to protect them from the lack of discretion in the selection of their food.

Those familiar with the law of negligence will not be overly shocked to know that the judge found that "the damage was of the type of kind which a reasonable person might foresee,"[2] even though the farmer himself did not foresee it, having had two weeks to think about it before putting the cows in the pasture, unlike the defendant who had only a split second between the time she first saw the cat and the time she slammed on the brakes on the car.

It is no news to practitioners, judges, academics, and law students who sometimes have to struggle with the niceties and fine distinctions of remoteness cases that often what judges say about foreseeability bears

---

[1](1978), 93 D.L.R. (3d) 289, 32 N.S.R. (2d) 199, 54 A.P.R. 199 (T.D.).
[2]*Ibid.*, at 292.

little resemblance to the reality of ordinary people. Not because judges do not know what they are doing. In fact in general they do know, because most remoteness cases are correctly decided. Rather the difficulty lies with the set of concepts available to justify the decision.[3]

Ascertaining a rational basis for prediction of judicial decisions in remoteness cases continues to be a problem which plagues negligence practitioners. Judges have agonized over the problem. Their frustration has been poignantly articulated by Watkins L.J. in *Lamb v. Camden London Borough Council* where he states:

> " 'This doctrine of remoteness of damage is one of very considerable obscurity and difficulty.' So wrote the editor of Salmond on the Law of Torts (17th Edn, 1977, p 38). If I did not consciously share that opinion previously from a fairly long acquaintance with the subject, I have, since hearing the able submissions made to this court, to confess to feelings of apprehension of never emerging out of the maze of authorities on the subject of remoteness into the light of a clear understanding of it. On my way to providing an answer to the question raised in this appeal I have sometimes felt like Sir Winston Churchill must have done when he wrote:
>
>> " 'I had a feeling once about mathematics — that I saw it all. Depth beyond depth was revealed to me — the byss and abyss. I saw — as one might see the transit of Venus or the Lord Mayor's Show — a quantity passing through an infinity and changing its sign from plus to minus. I saw exactly how it happened, and why the tergiversation was inevitable — but it was after dinner and I let it go.' "

Noted academics have registered dismay that despite the pronouncement of a definitive "test" for determining recovery by the Privy Council in *Wagon Mound (No.1).*,[4] no sound rules have emerged to guide us in this area. The foreseeability test set out in *Wagon Mound (No. 1)* has been whittled, varied, and even gutted. Do courts follow a set of rules in determining when and whether damage is too remote to place liability for it on a negligent defendant, and if so, what are these rules? On what basis are such decisions made?

In Chapter Ten a test for remoteness will be proposed which can account for the outcome of approximately 90 per cent of all decided remoteness cases irrespective of whether the court purported to use a foreseeability or a direct causation test. The 10 per cent it cannot explain is assumed to be wrongly decided in terms of the test and in terms of consistency with the majority of decided cases. Assuming that judges continue to decide remoteness issues in much the same way as in the

---

[3][1981] Q.B. 625, [1981] 2 W.L.R. 1038, [1981] 2 All E.R. 408 at 419 (C.A.).

[4]*Overseas Tankship (U.K.) v. Morts Dock & Enrg. Co. (The Wagon Mound)*, [1961] A.C. 388, [1961] 2 W.L.R. 126, [1961] 1 All E.R. 404 (P.C.), hereinafter referred to as *Wagon Mound (No. 1).*

past, the test should allow us to predict the outcome of remoteness issues in new cases with about the same degree of accuracy. Further, the proposed test can be shown to be consistent with the jurisprudence of the recent authoritative decisions in this area of the law of negligence.

II. THE REASON FOR "THE CONSIDERABLE OBSCURITY AND DIFFICULTY"

It will be helpful to first briefly review the landmark decisions on, and tests for, remoteness in the law of negligence to examine why they failed to resolve the issue and the result of this failure. The keynote cases of *Polemis*[5] and *Wagon Mound (No.1)* display the classic moral dichotomy intrinsic to the issue of remoteness. The first school of thought, represented by *Polemis*, is that of broad liability based on causation; once an actor is found culpable of negligence he or she is then liable for all of the consequences which flow from his or her negligent act, for it is more just that as between the innocent plaintiff and the negligent defendant, the loss should fall on the shoulders of the person who committed the wrong.

The decision in *Polemis* arose from an arbitration in which the owners of a steamship claimed to recover from the charterers for the destruction of their ship by fire. The fire resulted from an explosion caused by the stevedores dropping a plank into the ship's hold which was filled with benzine or petrol vapour. The three arbitrators held that the fire arose from a spark caused by the falling board striking against something, that the stevedores were negligent in dropping the board, since it created a risk of some damage to the ship, but that it was not foreseeable that the board would cause the spark and the ensuing explosion. The question facing the Court of Appeal was whether on the facts as found by the arbitrator, they were justified in law in shifting the loss to the charterers.

Lord Justices Bankes, Warrington, and Scrutton drew a distinction between culpability and liability, and stated further that foreseeability was clearly relevant in establishing culpability, fault or negligence, but was not necessarily relevant to the question of whether having once found culpability on the part of the defendant, he or she ought to stand the loss. *Smith v. London & South Western Ry. Co.*[6] and *Weld-Blundell v. Stephens*[7] were cited as authority for this proposition. The court then

---

[5] *Re Polemis and Furness, Withy & Co. Ltd.*, [1921] 3 K.B. 560 (C.A.), hereinafter referred to as *Polemis*.
[6] (1870), L.R. 6 C.P. 14 (Ex. Ch.).
[7] [1920] A.C. 956 (H.L.).

suggested the test of directness of consequences in ascertaining whether, once negligence had been found, the loss ought to be shifted, and held the defendants liable on the ground that their servant's negligent act was the direct cause of the loss. The core of the reasoning in the case is succinctly expressed by Lord Justice Scrutton who stated:

> "To determine whether an act is negligent, it is relevant to determine whether any reasonable person would foresee that the act would cause damage; if he would not, the act is not negligent. But if the act would or might probably cause damage, the fact that the damage it in fact causes is not the exact kind of damage one would expect is immaterial, so long as the damage is in fact directly traceable to the negligent act, and not due to the operation of independent causes having no connection with the negligent act, except that they could not avoid its results. Once the act is negligent, the fact that its exact operation was not foreseen is immaterial."[8]

The *Polemis* test of direct causation gives absolutely no criterion for deciding whether loss should be shifted. The term "cause" as used in torts is extremely ambiguous. If the term is limited to the "cause-effect" relationship between an act and damage, then it is not a question of law, but is a question for the natural sciences to solve. The court would be faced with only evidentiary questions. The term, however, seldom is limited to this meaning in legal usage, but instead the courts and writers speak of "legal cause."

The concept of legal causation includes but has a wider reference than the mere cause-effect relationship. It usually refers at the same time to a normative judgment of blame or responsibility. Any concept which mixes together in this manner naturalistic factual with normative or evaluative content is bound to be ambiguous. Adjectives such as "direct" or "proximate" add nothing. They do not refer to the cause-effect relationship, since it either exists or does not exist. It equally refers to no normative or evaluative criteria.

Take, for example, the situation where chemist A. puts chemical x. in a beaker, and two days later chemist B., knowing of the presence of chemical x., adds chemical y., causing an explosion. Clearly, chemical x. is as much a cause in the naturalistic sense as is chemically. There is no factual basis for stating one to be more proximate or direct than the other. The time element is not the test, because in other situations the cause first in time sequence would be the one that was proximate. For example, A. puts a small amount of a highly poisonous white powder in H.'s teacup, and B., not knowing of the poison, adds tea and gives it to H. with the result that he drinks it and dies. A court would probably say that the act of putting in the poison was the proximate cause of H.'s

---

[8]Supra, note 5, at 577.

death. In these two situations the court would classify as proximate the act carried out by the person who had the highest degree of fault in relation to the injury.

Assuming a cause-effect relationship, and applying a direct cause test of remoteness, the issue of whether an injury is too remote can be formulated as whether the defendant was directly responsible for the injury. To say that the injury was not too remote because the defendant was directly responsible is to merely state the conclusion twice. Since direct causation or responsibility is the issue, it cannot also be the justification for the decision. The decision could only be justified in terms of *why* the defendant is directly responsible.

The decision of the Privy Council in *Overseas Tankship (U.K.) v. Morts Dock & Enrg. Co. Ltd.*, commonly known as *Wagon Mound (No. 1)*, is the leading authority for the foreseeability test of remoteness. On October 30, 1951 the vessel Wagon Mound, while taking on bunkering oil, was moored to a jetty of the Caltex Oil Company in Morts Bay, Sydney Harbour. Due to the carelessness of employees of the charterers, a large quantity of oil was allowed to spill into the harbour and was carried by the wind and tide to the proximity of the wharf owned by the Morts Dock and Engineering Company Limited, at which two vessels, the Corrimal and the Audrey D., were docked and undergoing repairs. When the works manager of the wharf company became aware of the oil, he immediately instructed their employees to refrain from using electric torches and oxyacetylene welding equipment. On being assured by the manager of the Caltex Oil Company that they could safely resume their operations, the works manager ordered the men to continue. On November 1, while work was in progress, the oil on the water suddenly became ignited and the fire spread, doing extensive damage to the wharf and both vessels.

Counsel for the plaintiff was faced with the difficulty that if he took the position that a risk of fire was foreseeable, contributory negligence would be found in that the plaintiff's works manager ordered work to proceed with full knowledge of the presence of the oil. As at this time New South Wales did not have contributory negligence legislation, the plaintiff would be either barred from recovery or at least could be said to have had the last clear chance to avoid the accident. The plaintiff's counsel, therefore, did not base his case on foreseeability of fire, but argued it in terms of causation. Relying on the authority of *Polemis*, he contended that it was foreseeable that the oil would be carried to the plaintiff's wharf where it would congeal on the slipways and intefere with their use, and that the ensuing fire was the direct consequence of this negligence. The trial judge, Mr. Justice Kinsella, held that the fire was caused by drops of molten metal from the welding and cutting operations that ignited some cotton waste or rag floating in the water which in turn acted as a wick igniting the oil, and further, that it was not reasonably foreseeable that furnace oil could be ignited upon water. He found, however, that the oil congealing on the plaintiff's slipways was foreseeable and that, applying the *Polemis* test, the negligent act of spilling the oil was the direct cause of the fire. This argument was accepted by the Full Court of the New South Wales Supreme Court,[9] whereupon the defendants appealed to the Privy Council which refused to follow *Polemis* and allowed the appeal. The court, after examining the case law supporting the alternative tests of "direct cause" and "foreseeability," concluded that the latter was better law.

The judgment of the Board is based on three fundamental assumptions. The first is that culpability and compensation are the same thing. The second is that risk as the test of the limits of liability logically follows from the fact that risk is the test of whether there is any fault or negligence. The third is that the test of risk gives results which conform to the community standards of morality. The validity of the *Wagon Mound (No. 1)* judgment depends on the correctness of these three assumptions.

That the Privy Council saw the question of liability and culpability as a single problem is evidenced by their statement that the proposition of Lord Summer in *Weld-Blundell v. Stephens* that "this, however, goes to culpability, not to compensation,"[10] is fundamentally false. The Privy Council goes on to say that:

"It is vain to isolate the liability from its context and to say that B is or is not liable, and then to ask for what damage he is liable. For his liability is in respect of that damage and no other. If, as admittedly it is, B's liability (culpability) depends on the reasonable foreseeability of the consequent damage, how is that to be determined except by the foreseeability of the damage which in fact happened — the damage in suit?"[11]

The problem as to what standard of care the courts will impose in given circumstances, and whether the defendant's conduct meets that standard, is made synonymous with the problem of how far down the causal chain of a negligent act liability is to extend. Thus, the problem of remoteness disappears. As stated by Professor Glanville Williams:

"In future, broadly speaking, there will not be two questions in the tort of negligence, a question of initial responsibility and one of 'proximity,' but only one question — was the defendant negligent as regards this damage?"[12]

---

[9]*Mort's Dock & Enrg. Co. Ltd. v. Overseas Tank Ships (U.K.) Ltd.*, [1961] S.R. (N.S.W.) 688.

[10]*Supra*, note 7, at 984.

[11]*Supra*, note 4, at 425.

[12]Williams, "The Risk Principle" (1961), 77 L.Q.R. 179.

Culpability, however, is a normative judgment that a person is at fault. Liability, on the other hand, is a decision on the part of a court that damages will be awarded. Culpability in the tort of negligence is a prerequisite to liability rather than identical with it. Historically and in ordinary usage these two words have been conceived as being quite different in meaning. For example, where, for various reasons of policy, courts refuse to protect a particular kind of interest to which a loss has been suffered, there may be culpability without liability.[13] The continued existence of the question of remoteness in negligence law requires a separation of these two concepts.

The second basic assumption, that risk as the test of the limits of liability logically follows from the fact that the foreseeable risk is the test of whether there is any fault or negligence, although not expressly stated, is implicit in the judgment. According to Professor Williams:

"If we say that a defendant in breach of a duty of care because he should have foreseen and guarded against a particular risk, it seems a logical corollary to say that he is not liable for a consequence outside the risk altogether — a consequence in respect of which the defendant was not negligent."[14]

This position, however, can only be justified when no distinction is drawn between culpability and liability.

The third assumption that the test of foreseeability produces results which conform to the community standards of morality is to be found in the following passage from the judgment of the Privy Council:

"For it does not seem consonant with current ideas of justice or morality that for an act of negligence, however slight or venial, which results in some trivial foreseeable damage the actor should be liable for all consequences however unforeseeable and however grave, so long as they can be said to be "direct". It is a principle of civil liability, subject only to qualifications which have no present relevance, that a man must be considered to be responsible for the probable consequences of his act. To demand more of him is too harsh a rule, to demand less is to ignore that civilized order requires the observance of a minimum standard of behaviour."[15]

Even though it probably is not in accord with the current ideas of justice or morality that a person should be held liable for serious unforeseeable damages resulting from a trivial act of negligence, it does not follow that where an individual creates a very serious risk of harm and something unforeseeable develops, that he or she should not be made

---

[13]See Prosser, *Handbook of the Law of Torts*, 4th ed. (1971), at 244; Fleming, *The Law of Torts*, 6th ed. (1983), at 170; Salmond and Heuston, *The Law of Torts*, 18th ed. (1981), at 186; Hart and Honore, *Causation in the Law* (1959).

[14]*Supra*, note 12, at 179.

[15]*Supra*, note 4, at 422.

liable. It could equally be argued that, as between an innocent victim and the person who causes injury, the latter ought to bear the loss if some fault is found on his or her part. It is probably more accurate to state that the test of reasonable foreseeability as a test for remoteness does not accord with the current ideas of justice or morality because, as between a person guilty of no fault and a person guilty of some fault, this test would sometimes lead to an innocent person bearing the loss.

The *Polemis* decision and the test of direct causation is oriented toward recovery for the plaintiff. The *Wagon Mound (No. 1)* decision and the test of foreseeability, on the other hand, is defendant-oriented. Although the rule of *Polemis* was capable of being carried to unjust extremes; it was within the historical stream of widening liability. The decision of *Wagon Mound (No. 1)*, however, runs counter to this trend. In cases of physical injury to persons, risk is an inadequate test because it spreads the net too narrowly. If, on the other hand, the loss is of an economic nature, foreseeability often spreads the net too widely. Furthermore, when the damage is nervous shock, foreseeability furnishes little guide as to where the line of recovery ought to be drawn.

The direct cause test was attacked because it furnished no guidelines for monitoring liability once negligence was proved. There is no apparent attempt in the statement of the test to tie the nature of the risk of harm created by the negligent actor to the type of consequence which results from the act. It is irrelevant, according to the direct cause test, that the loss is totally outside of a class of possible damage which might be foreseen as a risk of harm created by the actor. If negligence is proven, and the loss directly follows, then liability as well follows. But without a clear criterion of directness the limits to be placed on liability are purely arbitrary.

The foreseeability test as propounded in *Wagon Mound (No. 1)*, on the other hand, creates more confusion than it resolves. When are remote consequences foreseeable to the reasonable man? Almost by definition the remote consequence is one which is weird, unexpected, unpredictable, or in sum, unforeseeable. In explaining the foreseeability test, ''the word consequence might be qualified by any description from 'almost certain' to 'remotely possible'.'' Many other problems were left unsolved by the foreseeability test defined in *Wagon Mound (No. 1)* which almost at once the courts began to address. The effect of dealing with the short-comings of the decision was to considerably weaken the impact of the foreseeability test.

III.   CONCLUSION

The three basic assumptions which are the foundation of the decision in *Wagon Mound (No. 1)* have all been expressly or implicitly rejected by the courts. The fallacy in the claim that culpability and compensation are the same thing may be illustrated by the facts of the South African case of *Alston v. Marine & Trade Ins. Co. Ltd.*[16] The defendant in this case, through his operation of a motor vehicle, caused injuries to the plaintiff which resulted in the plaintiff suffering from manic depressions. A part of the medical treatment for this mental condition consisted of taking a drug called parstellin. As the result of eating cheese at the same time as taking the drug, the plaintiff suffered a stroke which was caused by the effects of these two substances in the body at the same time.

Clearly the first issue a court would have to decide on these facts is whether the defendant was negligent in regard to the driving of his motor vehicle. The answer to this question depends not upon whether the particular damages resulting from the accident were foreseeable, but whether a risk of some harm was created. If no harm was foreseeable then the defendant is not negligent or culpable and that is an end to the matter. If he or she is found to be negligent, then the question arises as to what damages he or she is liable for.

In the above case the defendants admitted negligence and liability for everything but the stroke. Although holding that this damage was too remote, the trial judge, Mr. Justice Hiemstra, pointed out the above mentioned fallacy in the Privy Council's decision in *Wagon Mound (No. 1)*. He states:

> "This question, whether there can be a different criterion for determining culpability and compensation, so the Wagon Mound rightly says [at p. 409 in the All E.R. Report]. 'goes to the root of the matter.' The Wagon Mound sweeps away all difference, and here it immediately becomes unconvincing. An accident and some injury can be foreseeable but the form and the extent of the damage hardly ever. The escape from this truism is to say that the type of damage can be foreseen, namely, fire or bodily injury, and that the extent thereof was not meant to be included in the foreseeability test. The statement of Viscount Simmonds at p. 415 seems unconvincing:
>
> " 'But there can be no liability until the damage has been done. It is not the *act* but the consequences on which tortious liability is founded.' "[17]

Mr. Justice Hiemstra further states:

> "The first enquiry must be whether a delict has been committed. This depends on culpability . . . When that is established, the damage must be determined and the

---

[16][1964] 4 S.A. 112 (Witwaterstrand Local Div.).

[17]*Ibid.*, at 115.

question of remoteness is inescapable. The Wagon Mound has laid down a rule of thumb which will in most cases be easy to apply but is neither intellectually satisfying nor always just. It already breaks down upon the 'eggshell skull' cases. Or, differently put, it has to be lovingly accommodated before it will harmonise with the well-established rule. 'You must take your victim as you find him.' It is probably unforeseeable that you will run down a millionaare in a slum, but he is nevertheless entitled to his much higher compensation than the pauper. These considerations convince me that the dichotomy between culpability and compensation is not as fundamentally false as the *Wagon Mound* would make out."[18]

An examination of the remoteness decisions since *Wagon Mound (No. 1)* indicate that most courts use an entirely different test of foreseeability for the test of remoteness than is used to establish risk or culpability. The fact that these tests extend liability down the causal chain far more widely than if risk alone was used to limit liability indicate that the strict risk — foreseeability test of *Wagon Mound (No. 1)* does not conform with current ideas of justice or morality, but casts the net of recovery far too narrowly. The prediction of Professor J. G. Fleming, made shortly after the *Wagon Mound* decision had been handed down, that *Polemis* would probably survive the amputation of its accompanying opinion,[19] has been confirmed by the remoteness decisions since that time. *Wagon Mound (No. 1)* has abolished the causation test of remoteness without changing the outcome of hardly any cases. What we now have is the courts reaching the same conclusions as they did in applying *Polemis*, but justifying them in the language of risk or foreseeability.

---

[18]*Ibid.*

[19]Fleming, "The Passing of Polemis" (1961), 39 Can. Bar Rev. 489 at 528.

8

THE RETREAT FROM
WAGON MOUND (NO. 1)

I. THE THIN-SKULL RULE

The courts, while accepting the foreseeability test, have recognized or developed a number of qualifications and methods of paying lip service to it without actually applying it, the combined effect of which is to abrogate the rule to the point that it has become almost meaningless. The first was created by Lord Parker C.J. in *Smith v. Leech Brain & Co. Ltd.*,[1] when he held that a defendant who created a risk of a small burn should be liable for the unforeseeable death of a cancer-prone plaintiff from a malignancy resulting from the minor injury. Lord Parker relied upon the thin-skull rule, that a tortfeasor must take his victim as he finds him, contending that it was an exception to the foreseeability test which the Privy Council had no intention of affecting when they rendered their judgment in *Wagon Mound (No. 1)*.[2] This means that not only is a tortfeasor liable for foreseeable injury to a person, but also for unforeseeable damage resulting from an unusual or special susceptibility or weakness on the part of the victim.

The thin-skull rule, even where applicable may not be a satisfactory alternative to *Wagon Mound (No. 1)* because its application may result in the awarding of a large sum of damages where there is only a small degree of fault. In situations where the fault is sufficient that the judge intuitively feels that the defendant ought not to escape some liability, but not sufficient to justify the shifting of an extensive loss, the court may avoid an all or nothing decision by manipulating the size of damages.

The Ontario decision of *Bates v. Fraser* furnishes us with an excellent example of this technique. The plaintiff in this case in 1950 was found to be suffering from Parkinson's disease, resulting in uncontrollable tremor

---

[1][1962] 2 Q.B. 405, [1962] 2 W.L.R. 148, [1961] 3 All E.R. 1159.

[2]*Overseas Tankship (U.K.) v. Morts Dock & Enrg. Co. (The Wagon Mound)*, [1961] A.C. 388, [1961] 2 W.L.R. 126, [1961] 1 All E.R. 404 (P.C.), hereinafter referred to as *Wagon Mound (No. 1)*.

of the head and limbs, and muscular rigidity. The intensity of the disease, however, was closely related to certain emotional problems. As the result of the combined effect of the disease and her state of mind, she eventually became incapacitated. In 1957, however, she suffered a fall in which she struck her head. As a result she developed amnesia in regard to events after 1939, including all recollection of her husband, children or home. With her loss of memory her symptoms of Parkinson's disease disappeared to such an extent that only a medical expert would have been able to recognize the remaining organic basis of the malady. Since a restoration of her memory through psychiatric treatment would have caused a return of the emotional problems which again would have aggravated the Parkinson's disease, she decided to continue her life without her memory for the years between 1937 and 1957. From 1957 on she lived a normal happy life with her family, until 1960 at which time the defendant struck the car in which she was riding. The plaintiff only received a bump on the head, but as a result of this slight injury, her memory returned and with it all the old symptoms of her Parkinson's disease to the extent that she was again incapacitated.

The defendant admitted that he was negligent but denied liability for incapacitating the plaintiff on the grounds that such extensive damage was not foreseeable. If the trial judge applied the *Wagon Mound (No. 1)* decision, the plaintiff ought only to recover for the foreseeable damage, i.e., a bump on the head. If he applied the thin-skull rule, the defendant would be liable for a substantial amount of damages. Grant J. used the thin-skull rule for the purpose of distinguishing *Wagon Mound (No. 1)*. He then held that the plaintiff's condition was not "entirely due" to the collision![4] Other factors had contributed to her injuries. He therefore assessed damages for pain and suffering and loss of the pleasures of life at $3,000, a far smaller amount than if the thin-skull rule had been truly applied.

But in all cases where the thin-skull rule applies, a pre-existing condition of the plaintiff is a contributing factor to injury. What Mr. Justice Grant did, in fact, was to apportion the loss between the plaintiff and defendant through the assessment of damages. In this way the degree of fault bore a reasonably proportional relationship to the liability of the defendant.

II.   *HUGHES v. LORD ADVOCATE* AND THE MANIPULATION OF THE FORESEEABILITY TEST

The second major qualification to the *Wagon Mound (No. 1)* test is one

---

[3][1963] 1 O.R. 539, 38 D.L.R. (2d) 30 (H.C.).

[4]*Ibid.*, at 36.

of interpretation rather than an exception to the rule. The House of Lords in *Hughes v. Lord Advocate*[5] has held that neither the precise way in which the injury occurs nor the exact nature of the damage need be foreseeable. All that it is necessary to foresee is that the accident or damage is of a similar type or kind to that which could be anticipated as likely to happen. The servants of the defendants in that case had left four paraffin warning lamps burning near an open manhole covered by a shelter tent. When the plaintiff, a child, knocked one of these into the opening an explosion ensued causing him to fall into the hole where he received severe burns. The trial court and the First Division of the Court of Session on the appeal applied the *Wagon Mound (No. 1)* rule, finding no liability on the basis of expert testimony that it was unforeseeable that paraffin would explode in this manner. The five judges, two of whom were on the Board which heard the appeal in *Wagon Mound (No. 1)*, found the defendants liable, however, on the ground that it was foreseeable that little boys might suffer burns through playing with the lamp and dropping it, and that burns suffered as a result of an explosion were sufficiently similar to burns caused through merely breaking the lamp to justify liability being imposed.

This technique was used by the English Court of Appeal in *Stewart v. West African Terminals Ltd.*[6] The facts of this case were that the plaintiff boilermaker, while walking along the deck of a vessel, lifted with his right hand a slack preventer wire which was looped across the passageway, and steadied himself by placing his left hand on a stationary running wire. At that moment the running wire moved, pulling the plaintiff's hand into a block, resulting in the loss of the ends of his fingers. The trial judge found the defendant stevedores negligent in failing to shackle the preventer wire thus preventing it from obstructing the passageway. On appeal, the defendants argued in effect that it was not foreseeable that the obstructing of the passageway would result in the plaintiff getting his hand caught in a block. Lord Denning M.R. stated in answer to this defence:

> "It has been argued before us that this consequence was not reasonably foreseeable. It is said that since the case of *The Wagon Mound*, the old doctrine of *In re Polemis and Furness Withy & Co.* has gone and a person is not liable for the consequences of negligence except so far as they are reasonably foreseeable by him. That proposition must be taken subject to this qualification, that it is not necessary that the precise concatenation of circumstances should be envisaged. If the consequence was one which was within the general range which any reasonable person might foresee (and

---

[5][1963] A.C. 837, [1963] 2 W.L.R. 779, [1963] 1 All E.R. 705 (H.L.).

[6][1964] 2 Lloyd's Rep. 371 (C.A.). *Cf. Chapman v. Hearse* (1961), 106 C.L.R. 112 (H.C.); *Siwek v. Lambourn*, [1964] V.R. 337 (S.C.).

was not of an entirely different kind which no one could anticipate), then it is within the rule that a person who has been guilty of negligence is liable for the consequences. That appears not only from *Hughes v. Lord Advocate*, but also from the recent case of *Doughty v. Turner Manufacturing Company Ltd.* in this Court. Applying the principles to this case, it seems to me that the stevedores could have reasonably anticipated that if they left this preventer wire, so that it would obstruct the passageway of anyone going along the side of the ship, it might be that many kinds of accident might result; someone might trip up; or a man might strain himself in lifting it out of the way; or indeed he might, as in this present case, seize hold of something else so as to steady himself. It seems to me that this action of his was not of an entirely different kind which no one could anticipate. It was within the general range of contemplation and therefore within the consequences of negligence for which the defendants are liable."[7]

If stumbling over an obstruction or straining oneself in lifting a heavy line can be said to be the same kind of harm as catching one's hand in a block, then surely the foresight test becomes meaningless.

Before *The Wagon Mound (No. 1)* decision, damages were awarded on the basis of *Polemis*[8] in situations where there was a foreseeable risk resulting in more extensive unforeseeable injury rather than finding no liability where there had been some degree of fault. Courts now tend to find all the damage to be foreseeable rather than finding no liability where there has been some degree of fault. An example of this kind of technique for avoiding the effects of *Wagon Mound (No. 1)* is furnished by the Ontario Court of Appeal decision in *Thiele v. Rod Service (Ottawa) Ltd.*[9] The defendant mail carrier's employee left his mail truck unlocked and unattended with the result that the plaintiff's business records, which were being sent through the mail, were stolen. Because of the theft, the plaintiff had to pay $1,200 in accounting fees to have them replaced. The Ontario Court of Appeal held that:

"We are of the view, if reasonable foreseeability is the test now to be applied in this jurisdiction, that the damages allowed upon the facts of the case were such as to be reasonably foreseeable by the carrier, consequent upon the loss of the registered article. It is common knowledge that a very wide variety, indeed, of articles are the subject-matter of carriage by registered mail and that the damages arising from the loss of many of such articles in a reasonably foreseeable manner may far exceed the intrinsic value of the actual articles insured."[10]

This is equivalent to saying that it is foreseeable that anything may be carried in the mail, and any kind of consequential damages could result from such a loss. Thus the test of foreseeability is made sufficiently wide

---

[7]*Supra*, note 6, at 375.

[8]*Re Polemis and Furness, Withy & Co. Ltd.*, [1921] 3 K.B. 560 (C.A.), hereinafter referred to as *Polemis*.

[9][1964] 2 O.R. 347, 45 D.L.R. (2d) 503 (C.A.).

[10]*Ibid.*, at 504-505.

to justify decisions which would previously have been decided on the basis of *Polemis*.

A further, but similar, technique to avoid the effects of *Wagon Mound (No. 1)* is to break the facts of a case up into a chain of individual events, then ask if each event is foreseeable. Thus a factual situation could be broken upon into events A., B., C., D., E. and F. The court would ask whether fact A. was foreseeable, whether fact B. was foreseeable and so forth down the chain, coming to the conclusion that each event could be foreseen. The difficulty with this procedure is that in a situation where every step in the chain of events must be present before damage could occur, it does not follow because each event is foreseeable as a single fact, that the particular chain of events in that particular sequence is foreseeable as a whole.

A somewhat similar technique was used by the Supreme Court of Canada in *Ayoub v. Beaupre; McMurtry v. Beaupre; Empire Wallpaper & Paint Ltd. v. Beaupre.*[11] This was an action brought by the owners and occupiers of premises surrounding the defendant's garage for damage by a fire which had started on and spread from the defendant's premises. The court broke down the facts into six separate events:

1. The defendant's servant, while working in a pit under the car in order to remove the gas tank, hung an extension lamp in an insecure place.

2. After draining the tank into a gasoline can which he lowered to the floor, he allowed a few drops of gasoline to fall.

3. He allowed a few more to fall when he removed the funnel from the tank and put on the lid.

4. He failed to wipe off the top of the can immediately.

5. He failed to move the lamp back from its insecure position before attempting to move in the confined area of the pit.

6. He bumped into the lamp causing it to fall.

The bulb was protected by a rubber guard with a wire mesh front, with one-inch spaces between the heavy wires. Witnesses testified that normally the bulb would not break if such lamps were dropped. The court therefore assumed that the lamp had fallen on the spout of the gasoline can, which penetrated through the one-inch wire mesh, and caused the bulb to break. The broken bulb ignited the small amount of gasoline vapour which in turn started the fire. No negligence was found at the trial level or by the Ontario Court of Appeal.

---

[11][1964] S.C.R. 448, 45 D.L.R. (2d) 411 at 418-19.

The Supreme Court of Canada, claiming to apply a high standard of care as gasoline is a dangerous substance, found each step to be an act of negligence. Each individual action, however, created no risk without the presence or foreseeability of the other steps. Thus, to hang a lamp insecurely creates no risk of fire unless it is foreseeable that it will break if it falls, and that gasoline vapour will be present. It is foreseeable that the lamp will break only if it is foreseeable that the lamp will fall on the spout of the can. Equally, allowing a few drops of gasoline to vapourize creates a foreseeable risk only when a method of igniting it is equally foreseeable. By isolating the events and taking them one at a time, the uniqueness of the particular sequence necessary for damage is masked.

By using this technique one could make a plausible argument for the foreseeability of the fire in *Wagon Mound (No. 1)*. It may be foreseeable that the oil would reach the wharf; that a piece of cotton waste could fall from a ship being overhauled and outfitted; that the waste could fall on a piece of floating wood; that the waste could be ignited by a drop of molten metal from welding operations carried out above; it may be foreseeable that the burning waste could ignite what it was floating on, or an oil-covered pile; that a burning pile or piece of wood could reach 170 degrees fahrenheit, the flash point of furnace oil, and thus ignite it. But such a combination of events taken as a whole may not be reasonably foreseeable.

III. *WAGON MOUND (NO. 2)* AND THE FORESEEABLE AS POSSIBLE TEST

It is somewhat ironic that the most important qualification of the foreseeability rule arose from the very same set of facts which gave it birth. In *Overseas Tankship (U.K.) v. Miller S.S. Co. Pty.*,[12] now designated as *Wagon Mound (No. 2)*, the Privy Council held that a tortfeasor will be liable for the results of the acts in regard to which he is negligent even though the damage is highly improbable, if it is foreseeable as possible, and there is no justification for not taking care. The owners of the Corrimal and the Audrey D. waited until the action brought by the owners of the wharf was finally disposed of before proceeding to trial. The case was argued in nuisance and negligence before Mr. Justice Walsh, who made the following findings of fact:

"(1) Reasonable people in the position of the officers of the Wagon Mound would regard furnace oil as very difficult to ignite upon water.

"(2) Their personal experience would probably have been that this had very rarely happened.

"(3) If they had given attention to the risk of fire from the spillage, they would have

---

[12][1967] 1 A.C. 617, [1966] 3 W.L.R. 498, [1966] 2 All E.R. 709, reversing [1963] 1 Lloyd's Rep. 402 (P.C.).

regarded it as a possibility, but one which could become an actuality only in very exceptional circumstances.

"(4) They would have considered the chances of the required exceptional circumstances happening while the oil remained spread on the harbour waters, as being remote.

"(5) I find that the occurrence of damage to the plaintiff's property as a result of the spillage, was not reasonably foreseeable by those for whose acts the defendant would be responsible.

"(6) I find that the spillage of oil was brought about by the careless conduct of persons for whose acts the defendant would be responsible.

"(7) I find that the spillage of oil was a cause of damage to the property of each of the plaintiffs.

"(8) Having regard to those findings, and because of finding (5), I hold that the claim of each of the plaintiffs, framed in negligence, fails."[13]

Mr. Justice Walsh found the defendants liable in nuisance, however, on the grounds that nuisance was a different cause of action to which the foreseeability test of remoteness did not apply. The defendants appealed from this judgment directly to the Privy Council, and after the passage of 15 years from the time of the fire, the wheels of swift justice finally resolved the dispute.

In *Wagon Mound (No. 1)*, Mr. Justice Kinsella found it necessary to consider the question of nuisance because he found that there was liability in negligence,[14] and the Privy Council remitted the case to the Full Court to be dealt with on the issue of nuisance, but the wharf owners proceeded no further with this aspect of their action, probably preferring to await the outcome of the action brought by the shipowners. The basis of one of the plaintiff's arguments in *Wagon Mound (No. 2)* was that, as negligence was not an essential element for liability in nuisance, it would be illogical to limit recovery to only those damages which were foreseeable. The Board considered a number of cases in nuisance and concluded that, although they were not conclusive on the issue, they pointed strongly to the conclusion that there is no difference as to the measure of damages between nuisance and negligence. The court then examined the issue from the point of view of principle and concluded that the limits of liability should be the same in both torts.

After disposing of the issue of nuisance in this manner, the court then went on to deal with the case as an action in negligence. The decision of principal concern to the court was that of *Bolton v. Stone*,[15] where the plaintiff had been struck on the head by a cricket ball driven out of the defendant's grounds. The ball, according to the evidence, had been

---

[13][1963] 1 Lloyd's Rep. 402 at 426.

[14][1961] A.C. 388, [1961] 2 W.L.R. 126, [1961] 1 All E.R. 404 (P.C.).

[15][1951] A.C. 850, [1951] 1 All E.R. 1078 (H.L.).

driven over the fence only about six times in the preceding 28 years. The House of Lords held that the chances of the ball hitting a passerby, although foreseeable, were so fantastically small that a reasonable man would have been justified in disregarding such a risk. The Privy Council distinguished this case from the facts of *Wagon Mound* by pointing out that in the latter situation the activity was unlawful while in the situation of *Bolton v. Stone*, the activity was justifiable. The court argued:

> "But it does not follow that, no matter what the circumstances may be, it is justifiable to neglect a risk of such a small magnitude. A reasonable man would only neglect such a risk if he had some valid reason for doing so, e.g., that it would involve considerable expense to eliminate the risk. He would weigh the risk against the difficulty of eliminating it. If the activity which caused the injury to Miss Stone had been an unlawful activity, there can be little doubt but that *Bolton v. Stone* would have been decided differently. In their Lordships' judgment *Bolton v. Stone* did not alter the general principle that a person must be regarded as negligent if he does not take steps to eliminate a risk which he knows or ought to know is a real risk and not a mere possibility which would never influence the mind of a reasonable man. What that decision did was to recognise and give effect to the qualification that it is justifiable not to take steps to eliminate a real risk if it is small and if the circumstances are such that a reasonable man, careful of the safety of his neighbour, would think it right to neglect it.

> "In the present case there was no justification whatever for discharging the oil into Sydney Harbour. Not only was it an offence to do so, but it involved considerable loss financially. If the ship's engineer had thought about the matter, there could have been no question of balancing the advantages and disadvantages. From every point of view it was both his duty and his interest to stop the discharge immediately."[16]

It is implicit in the above statement that the Privy Council based liability on more factors than mere foreseeability; it also assessed the following considerations: the size of the risk, the social utility and legality of the risk-creating activity, the degree to which the defendant is felt to be at fault, and the cost of eliminating the risk. It is also implicit in this quote that the court, contrary to *Wagon Mound (No. 1)*, drew a distinction between culpability and liability. By distinguishing *Bolton v. Stone* on the grounds that the activity of the defendant in that case was lawful while the activity of the engineer was an offence and unjustifiable carelessness, the court is saying in effect that the defendant is liable because he is culpable. The court found liability on the ground that, although the reasonable man would find the risk of fire highly improbable, the possibility of it was foreseeable. The effect of this judgment is that, while the actual damage may not be reasonably foreseeable, a defendant may still be liable if there is a mere possibility of that damage, and the defendant was negligent in doing the act which caused it. Where, in other words, a defendant causes a risk to a plaintiff who is without fault, and there is some fault in regard to the defendant, the defendant ought to

---

[16]*Supra*, note 12, at 642-43.

bear the loss. This makes a substantial change in the *Wagon Mound (No. 1)* rule in that it extends the application of the test of foreseeability of damage to possibility rather than to probability. The law now, therefore, is little different than it was under *Polemis*, since almost any kind of damage can be foreseeable as possible.

The Privy Council justified this decision on the grounds that Mr. Justice Walsh came to a different conclusion as to foreseeability on the facts than did Mr. Justice Kinsella in *Wagon Mound (No. 1)*.[17] Mr. Justice Walsh found that "if they had given attention to the risk of fire from the spillage, they would have regarded it as a possibility, but one which could become an actuality only in very exceptional circumstances."[18] Mr. Justice Kinsella, on the other hand, found that "the defendant did not know, and could not reasonably be expected to have known, that it was capable of being set on fire when spread on water."[19] A comparison of these two sentences alone would lead one to conclude that the courts came to different factual conclusions. An examination, however, of other statements of both judges, and the evidence upon which they principally relied, discloses no essential difference in the finding of fact. Mr. Justice Kinsella based his decision primarily upon the evidence of the expert witness, Professor Hunter, a chemical engineer at the University of Sydney, and in particular on the following testimony:

"Q.: As you indicated, prior to doing the tests you would not have thought that this oil was a fire hazard? A.: Not a serious hazard.

"Q.: I suppose you would say now in the light of what you know that if you had a quantity of furnace oil of flash point 150° F. to 190° F. beneath a wharf in circumstances where it was of a depth on the water of more than 1/16th of an inch that it would, in your opinion, constitute a fire hazard? A.: I think I can best answer that by putting it this way: the fire hazard under those circumstances depends on the habits of the people working on the wharf rather than the oil itself . . . Q.: If there is fuel oil not more than 1/16th of an inch then you don't have to consider fire risk, whatever they are doing on the wharf? A.: That is right. Q.: What I suggest is, if you increase the height of it above 1/16th of an inch, there is then something under the wharf that is a fire danger that was not there before? A.: If the oil is there entirely by itself, it does not constitute a fire danger but if it is oil plus floating wicks it is then a fire danger."[20]

Mr. Justice Kinsella drew from this the following conclusion:

"This evidence I interpret to mean that before he made his tests and, of course, before he knew of the subject fire, the Professor did not regard floating oil as a serious hazard in any circumstances; and that, in the light of knowledge gleaned from his tests,

---

[17]*Supra*, note 12, at 640.
[18]*Supra*, note 13.
[19][1961] S.R. (N.S.W.) 688 at 698.
[20]*Ibid.*, at 697.

he now regards it as not being dangerous in itself, but capable of being made dangerous by people who are working near it. These latter remarks throw no light on the problem, as they would apply equally to every substance which is capable of being set on fire. .

"I feel bound, on the evidence, to come to the conclusion that, prior to this fire, furnace oil in the open was *generally* regarded as safe, and that, in the light of knowledge at that time, the defendant's servants and agents reasonably so regarded it."[21]

The very use of the words "not a serious hazard" and "reasonably safe" indicates not that fire was impossible but that it was highly improbable, or as stated by Mr. Justice Walsh, the reasonable man "would not have thought of a wharf fire from this cause as anything but a remote possibility."[22] Six years previously in another Australian port a severe wharf fire occurred where oil spread on water was ignited by "a wick."[23] Although Mr. Justice Kinsella concluded that there was no evidence that the defendants or their agents were aware of that fire, nevertheless the principle of the wick can certainly be taken as common knowledge. It is evident that, taking the judgment as a whole, Mr. Justice Kinsella meant, when he stated that the defendants "could not reasonably be expected to have known that it was capable of being set on fire when spread on water," no more than that the risk was not reasonably foreseeable — the identical conclusion of Mr. Justice Walsh.

There is some dispute as to the real effect of the *Wagon Mound (No. 2)* decision. One theory is that it would "for all practical purposes restore the *Re Polemis* test, for surely all direct consequences must be regarded as possible if the ordinary man is not required to foresee how they are to eventuate."[24] It has been argued on the facts of the case that the *Wagon Mound (No. 2)* test is limited to conduct which is unlawful, unjustifiable and which lacks any social utility.[25] There is no doubt, however, that the courts have adopted the *Wagon Mound (No. 2)* test as a technique for avoiding the application of the strict foreseeability rule.[26]

The Manitoba Court of Appeal in *Assiniboine South S.D. v. Hoffer* held a father liable for an explosion which resulted from a rather unusual chain

---

[21]*Supra*, note 19, at 697 (italics mine).

[22]*Supra*, note 13, at 414.

[23]*Eastern Asia Navigation Co. Ltd. v. Fremantle Harbour Trust Commrs.* (1951), 83 C.L.R. 353 (H.C.).

[24]Glasbeek, "Wagon Mound II — Re Polemis Revived; Nuisance Revised" (1967), 6 Western Ont. L. Rev. 192 at 200.

[25]Green, "The Wagon Mound No. 2 — Foreseeability Revised" (1967), Utah L. Rev. 197.

[26]Fleming, in *The Law of Torts*, 6th ed. (1983), at 189, describes the position after *Wagon Mound (No. 2)* as "the hazard should not be defined with over much particularity, lest the unique features inherent in every case disqualify the injury from falling within the description of the apprehended risk. Nor should it be defined too broadly, lest a defendant be held liable for all resulting harm of which his default was a cause-in-fact."

of events.[27] The father was found to be negligent in that he gave his 14-year-old son a snowmobile which the boy, because of his age, was not large or strong enough to properly operate. The machine shot forward when the boy started it, and struck a gas-rise pipe with the result that gas escaped, entered the boiler room of a school through a fresh air inlet duct situated in the wall of the school, where it mixed with the air and was ignited by a flame, thus exploding and doing extensive damage to the school. The court, on the basis of *Wagon Mound (No. 2)* stated: "The test of foreseeability of damage becomes a question of what is possible rather that what is probable."[28] The Supreme Court of Canada upheld the judgment without reasons.[29] Presumably they were prepared to accept the reasoning of the Manitoba Court of Appeal, and, if this is so, then the "foreseeable as possible" test can be accepted as the law of Canada regarding remoteness until the Supreme Court states differently.

IV. CONCLUSION

The situation now seems to be this. If a court wishes for whatever reason to find a particular loss or damage too remote, it will find the damage not to be reasonably foreseeable and will cite *Wagon Mound (No. 1)*. If the court wishes to find the damage not too remote, it will cite *Wagon Mound (No.2)* and apply the foreseeable as possible version of the test of remoteness. No one will be disturbed very much by the fact that the two tests are inconsistent with one another.

The result of the assaults made on the foreseeability test is that no clearly defined or definable test now seems to exist. The current confused state of the law is vividly shown in the obfuscation presented by this paragraph from Halsbury's Laws of England:

> "In the tort of negligence the degree of likelihood relevant to the measure of damages is the same as the degree of likelihood relevant to the existence of a duty. A plaintiff recovers damages in respect of a foreseeable accident, even though only an accident of that type and not the precise circumstances were foreseeable, for an unforeseeable form of a foreseeable type of injury, and for unforeseeable consequences of a foreseeable type of injury."[30]

Lord Upjohn, in *Koufos v. C. Czarnikow Ltd.* combined the *Wagon Mound (No. 1)* and *(No.2)* versions of the foreseeability test into the proposition that "the tortfeasor is liable for any damage which he can reasonably

---

[27][1971] 4 W.W.R. 746, 21 D.L.R. (3d) 608 (Man. C.A.).

[28]*Ibid.*, at 751, *per* Dickson J.A.

[29][1973] 6 W.W.R. 765, 40 D.L.R. (3d) 480 (S.C.C.).

[30]12 Hals. (4th) 1139.

foresee may happen as a result of the breach however unlikely it may be, unless it can be brushed aside as far fetched."[31]

The irritation felt by legal writers at the apparent lack of a clear set of guidelines has led to a stream of argument that remoteness decisions are necessarily based on policy considerations. By "policy" it is ostensibly meant that the courts have (and should have) broad discretionary powers to consider a variety of moral, social, and economic factors to aid in the decision-making process.[32] One author submits that *Wagon Mound (No. 1)* was a policy decision in itself motivated by the courts' desire to lay down a just, clear and defensible decision as well as an ongoing rule.[33] Another states "that however stable and predictable we may wish the law to be in this area the realities of the problems posed by injury-bearing activity in an increasingly complex society work in the opposite direction[34] . . . the court has not only to decide whether a person is guilty of negligent conduct but also whether the case is ripe for the imposition of negligence liability . . . This particular question clearly involves an ought; it is within the realm of legal policy."[35] A third suggests that the court must be left "sufficient discretionary powers"[36] to "control the findings of liability by a jury."[37] and notes that this means the correct determination of policy "for the circumstances" will be left "to our trial judges."[38] Yet another argues that courts should approach each remoteness case with a view to deciding the issue based on a number of policy considerations, including the nature of the injury, the entity of the defendant, i.e., whether a corporation or a person, the factors of insurance coverage and the potential for deterrence and education. He maintains that "it is hard to escape the conclusion that the best we can ever do is to rely on the common sense of the judge and jury"[39] and concludes that "all future attempts to resolve these cases with an automatic formula are doomed."[40]

---

[31][1969] 1 A.C. 350 at 422, [1967] 3 W.L.R. 1491, [1967] 3 All E.R. 686 (sub nom. *The Heron II; Koufos v. C. Czarnikow Ltd.*) (H.L.).

[32]Linden, "Foreseeability in Negligence Law" (1973), Law Society of Upper Canada Special Lectures 55.

[33]Merrills, "Policy and Remoteness" (1973), 6 Ottawa L. Rev. 18 at 24-25.

[34]McLaren, "Negligence and Remoteness — The Aftermath of Wagon Mound" (1967), 32 Sask. Bar Rev. 45 at 46.

[35]*Ibid.*, at 47.

[36]Glasbeek, "Wagon Mound II — Re Polemis Revived; Nuisance Revised" (1967), Western Ont. L. Rev. 192 at 200.

[37]*Ibid.*, at 201.

[38]*Ibid.*

[39]*Supra*, note 32, at 68-69.

[40]*Supra*, note 32, at 66.

Undoubtedly, there is sufficient reason to warrant such argument, and that is the inadequacy of the tests offered by the courts to solve remoteness issues. The direct or proximate cause test for remoteness enunciated in *Polemis* came to mean a blunt and clumsy tool in a sophisticated society. The foreseeability test offered in *Wagon Mound (No. 1)* as a replacement for a modern community in order to be "consonant with current ideas of justice or morality"[41] proved unworkable or unjust in a number of instances and had to be manipulated to such an extent that it lost much of its validity.

It is not surprising then that argument arose to the effect that the decisions were, and perhaps had to be, based on policy. However, as many or perhaps more problems flow from a reliance on policy as a tool for decision making. If a finding of liability, once a remoteness issue is discerned, is left entirely to judicial discretion, similar cases will no doubt have dissimilar results. Policy considerations concerning the financial ability of defendants to pay damage, of their capacity for education or deterrence may lead to utterly different holdings depending on the nature of the defendant, regardless of the similarity of the negligence which gave rise to the injury in each case.

A variation in result based on considerations such as these can only lead to a distrust of, and disrespect for the legal process. Social order demands both a uniform application and an ongoing constancy in the application of the law. Without this continuity or uniformity we lack certainty, and a legal system cannot persist without some stability of expectations. We have to believe that the same set of legal rules will be applied to people in similar situations or our faith in the legal system itself is eroded. Policy, in truth meaning *public* policy, may be the underlying purpose or motive behind a particular rule, but cannot be a justification for discriminating judgments which may vary from case to case.

It is, of course, accepted that public policy does have a part to play in remoteness decisions as it does in all legal decisions. If an overturned lantern should result in the burning of all Chicago, no one would suggest that Mrs. Murphy who so carelessly placed the lantern too near her cow's hoof should be held liable for the loss of the city, and this conclusion is based on policy. There must be some limitation on the liability of defendants, or otherwise it would be impossible for people to insure against potential liability, and consequently to plan one's eco-

---

[41]*Overseas Tankship (U.K.) v. Morts Dock & Enrg. Co. (The Wagon Mound)*, [1961] A.C. 388 at 422, [1961] 2 W.L.R. 126, [1961] 1 All E.R. 404 (P.C.).

nomic affairs, or to prevent economic ruin. As a matter of policy courts avoid imposing "liability in an indeterminate amount for an indeterminate time to an indeterminate class."[42] A cut-off point may be arbitrary, but nevertheless necessary. Liability for economic loss and nervous shock are examples where arbitrary limitations have been evolved by the courts as a matter of policy. But it is submitted that the line where policy tools are needed is placed far distant from the initial question of liability in remoteness cases and exists only where the scope of damage is vastly beyond the ability of the ordinary person to compensate, or where certain other factors of scope must be considered.

---

[42]*Ultramares Corp. v. Touche* (1931), 255 N.Y. 170 at 179, 174 N.E. 441, 74 A.L.R. 1139 (C.A.), *per* Cardozo C.J.

9

RISK AND THE PRIVITY OF FAULT DOCTRINE

I. INTRODUCTION

The underlying assumption of *Wagon Mound (No. 1)*[1] that no distinction is to be made between culpability and liability stems from a failure to distinguish between problems of risk — is there a foreseeable risk of harm which would require the imposition of a standard of care — and problems of remoteness — how far down the chain of causal consequences of the negligent act is liability to run — just as the *prima facie* duty or proximity test of *Anns*[2] fails to distinguish between the issue of risk and the issue of extension — will the courts impose any standard of care at all in regard to a particular kind of situation. The ambiguity in both cases is possible because of the multiple ways we can use the concept of "duty," in particular:

1. Did the defendant owe a duty to take care — the problem of extension.

2. Did the defendant owe a duty to take care because it was reasonably foreseeable that if he or she did not, the plaintiff would suffer harm — the problem of risk.

3. Did the defendant owe a duty to do or not do the act which would have prevented or not caused the loss to happen — the problem of standard of care.

4. Did the defendant owe a duty to a particular person in regard to a particular kind of loss — the problem of remoteness.

According to Lord Atkin, in his judgment, in *Donoghue v. Stevenson*, "in English law there must be, and is, some general conception of

---

[1] *Overseas Tankship (U.K.) v. Morts Dock & Enrg. Co. (The Wagon Mound)*, [1961] A.C. 388, [1961] 2 W.L.R. 126, [1961] 1 All E.R. 404 (P.C.), hereinafter referred to as *Wagon Mound (No. 1)*.

[2] *Anns v. Merton London Borough Council*, [1978] A.C. 728, [1977] 2 W.L.R. 1024, [1977] 2 All E.R. 492 (H.L.).

relations giving rise to a duty of care, of which the particular cases found in the books are but instances.''[3] He defines that relationship as:

> "You must take reasonable care to avoid acts or omissions which you can reasonably foresee would be likely to injure . . . persons who are so closely and directly affected by [your] act that [you] ought reasonably to have them in contemplation as being so affected when [you are] directing [your] mind to the acts or omissions which are called in question.''[4]

The above risk principle furnishes the basis for a finding of negligence or culpability. It has nothing to do with the question of extension — whether or not the law will impose a duty to take care — and is far too narrow a principle to set limits on liability once negligence has been established. Yet it has been used both to extend the law of negligence into new areas of human conduct and, on the other hand, to limit the extent of liability given negligence. It is used to extend the law of negligence to areas of pure economic loss caused by an action, which creates liability for a failure to act by a line of reasoning which, as shown in Chapter Two, has the following underlying structure.

Assumption one: All persons are under a duty (in carrying out their actions) to take care to avoid acts or omissions which they can reasonably foresee would be likely to injure (physically the person or property of) their neighbour.

Assumption two: If a person (in carrying out his actions) creates an unreasonable risk of (physical) harm to (the person or property of) his neighbour, by his acts or omissions, then he is in breach of the duty to take care (to prevent physical harm to the person or property of his neighbour).

Assumption three: If a person was in breach of a duty to take care (in his actions to not create an unreasonable risk of physical harm to the person or property of his neighbour) then there must have been a duty owed to take care.

Assumption three tautologically follows from assumptions one and two. Assumption one is true only when the qualifications in brackets are included. Some courts, however, have left out those qualifications in their statements of the risk principle and thus have extended the law of negligence to cover instances of nonfeasance and pure economic loss. When the qualifications are omitted the line of reasoning becomes: if there is a risk of a particular harm to a particular person, then there is a duty to take care. Thus risk is used to extend the law of negligence.

---

[3][1932] A.C. 562 at 580 (H.L.).
[4]*Ibid.*

The risk or proximity principle as used to establish whether or not the law will impose a duty on a particular person in regard to a particular harm prescribes that there is a duty to take care to prevent a particular harm to a particular person if, and only if, there is a reasonably foreseeable risk of that harm. It logically follows from this that: if there is no reasonably foreseeable risk of a particular harm to a particular person then there is no duty to take care in regard to it. Thus risk can be used, framed in the language of duty, to limit the extent of one's liability, making risk, culpability, and liability synonymous. So if a person creates a risk of harm x. to another person, but harm y. is suffered instead of or as well as x., there would be no liability for harm y. because it did not fall within the risk and consequently there was no duty owed in regard to it. If there was no duty owed in regard to it, then there can be no liability for it, and thus the risk defines the limits of liability.

The need to distinguish between culpability and liability can further be demonstrated by imagining what would happen if the kind or degree of foreseeability used by courts to establish whether or not a particular damage was too remote, was used to establish risk, or whether or not there was negligence.

It has been described in Chapter Two how during the early period of the development of the law of negligence a serious error was made, and how the deviation was recognized and corrected in *Donoghue v. Stevenson*. It was the idea that if a particular negligent act happened to be a breach of contract, a third party injured as a result could not recover as he or she was not a party to the contract. This error arose from a misinterpretation of the old case of *Winterbottom v. Wright*,[5] where the court found the defendants, who had a contract with the Postmaster General to keep certain carriages repaired, not liable to the plaintiff, a driver injured as a result of the negligent failure to keep the carriage in good repair. The decision in the case is based upon the distinction between misfeasance and non-feasance, that is to say, the creation of a risk of harm and the failure to remove the risk which one did not create. The facts of *Winterbottom v. Wright* are a classic case of nonfeasance. The defendants were not responsible for the deterioration of the carriage. The breakdown was the result of wear and tear. The defendant's fault lay in failing to repair the carriage, thus removing the risk. This was a basis of liability in contract but not in negligence. If the defendants had created or extended the risk by repairing the carriage negligently, then presumably they would have been liable to the plaintiff for negligence as they would have created a risk of harm and thus furnished a basis of liability independent of contract.

---

[5](1842), 10 M. & W. 109, 152 E.R. 402 (Exch.).

Later courts, however, failed to recognize the distinction between creating a risk and legal responsibility for failing to remove it, and found no liability to a third party where the negligent act constituted a breach of contract even though the act created a risk. Manufacturers escaped liability for negligently manufactured products resulting in damage to the ultimate consumer,[6] landlords avoided liability for damage resulting from negligent repair of premises so long as the person injured was not the tenant,[7] and individuals injured as the result of a badly built building could not recover, outside of contract, against the builder.[8] The language that the courts used in reaching this conclusion of no liability was none other than that of duty of care. The defendant was not liable because there was no duty of care owed to the plaintiff (it is assumed that there was no contractual duty).

From the position that a lack of a (contractual) duty was a bar to liability, the courts moved to the position that the existence of a duty to the plaintiff was a necessary condition for liability. When the House of Lords exposed the error outlined above they further entrenched the concept of duty by finding its basis in foreseeable risk of harm. It was an easy move, then, for the courts to say that the duty must be owed to the plaintiff, and from there to reason that the risk must be a risk to the plaintiff. By this means the courts have created a doctrine of privity in the law of negligence. It is a privity of fault rather than of contract. The doctrine of privity has raised problems and difficulties in the law of contract. It is a freak, an aberration, in the law of torts. The doctrine of privity confuses questions of risk of harm with problems of remoteness, and the language of duty of care is the vehicle for this confusion.

Judges have said that there is no such thing as negligence in the abstract or in the air, and this is, of course, true. A risk of harm must be a risk to someone in order for it to be a risk of harm or negligence. It is often the case, however, that as a result of negligence persons who are not the prime subjects of the risk are harmed as well. It could be someone whose presence could not be anticipated. It might be a person who suffers a nervous shock as the result of witnessing the main or initial harm, or it might be a rescuer who is injured in trying to prevent the harm. These examples all raise questions of remoteness of damage because the legal issue is whether or not the defendant's liability extends

---

[6]*Bates v. Batey & Co. Ltd.*, [1913] 3 K.B. 351.

[7]See, *e.g.*, *Cavalier v. Pope*, [1906] A.C. 428 (H.L.); *Malone v. Laskey*, [1907] 2 K.B. 141 (C.A.); *Travers v. Gloucester Corp.*, [1947] K.B. 71, [1946] 2 All E.R. 506.

[8]See, *e.g.*, *Bottomley v. Bannister*, [1932] 1 K.B. 458 (C.A.); *Otto v. Bolton & Norris*, [1936] 2 K.B. 46, [1936] 1 All E.R. 960; *Travers v. Gloucester Corp.*, *supra*, note 7.

to these persons as well as the persons who were the prime subjects of the risk, or, to rephrase the issue, whether the damage suffered by these persons is too remote from the original risk which is the foundation of the finding of negligence. It is known that injuries to one person will often result in, or bear a causal connection to, damage to other people. No event stands in a causal isolation. Some limits must be placed, however, on just how much of this the defendant will be required to compensate. This issue will be examined in the context of the following situations: a) the unforeseen plaintiff, b) victims of nervous shock, and c) rescuers.

II. THE UNFORESEEN PLAINTIFF

One of the first full-fledged expositions of a doctrine of privity of fault was by Chief Justice Cardozo of the New York Court of Appeals in *Palsgraf v. Long Island Railroad Co.*[9] The plaintiff had been injured by scales which fell over on her as the result of a fireworks explosion. The fireworks were contained in a parcel which was negligently knocked from the hands of a passenger by the defendant, employed as a guard by the defendant railway company, when he helped the passenger onto the train. The explosion was probably caused when the package fell under the wheels of the train. The court held no liability because there was no breach of a duty to the plaintiff. "The conduct of the defendant's guard," states Cardozo C.J., "if a wrong in its relation to the holder of the package, was not a wrong in its relation to the plaintiff, standing far away. Relatively to her it was not negligence at all . . . What the plaintiff must show is 'a wrong' to herself; i.e., a violation of her own right . . . The risk reasonably to be perceived defines the duty to be obeyed . . ."[10]

Prosser and Smith wrote in 1952 that, to their knowledge, only one case had actually squarely applied and followed the *Palsgraf* decision.[11] The reason is that courts are not willing to limit the ambit of liability to the confines of the initial risk. The courts may pay lip service to a privity of fault doctrine, but they will then go on to find the damage to persons who would not fall within the initial risk, to be *reasonably foreseeable* if

---

[9](1928), 248 N.Y. 339, 162 N.E. 99, 59 A.L.R. 1253 (C.A.).

[10]*Ibid.*, at 99-100.

[11]Smith and Prosser, *Cases and Materials on Torts* at 231, *Palsgraf*, however, is still enshrined in the American Law Institute *Restatement of the Law of Tort* (Second) which provides, "The actor is liable for an invasion of an interest of another if . . . (b) the conduct of the actor is negligent with respect to the other, or a class of persons within which he is included . . ." As will be argued in Chapter 10, if the plaintiff falls into a foreseeable class of persons the damage will not be found to be too remote on any test of remoteness providing the damage falls into a foreseeable class of injury.

the court, for other unarticulated reasons, finds the damage not to be too remote. Even if the damage does fall within the risk, the courts will then conclude that it is *not* reasonably foreseeable if, for other unstated reasons, they consider the damage to be too remote. Foreseeability when so treated becomes the justification for a conclusion about remoteness, reached on other grounds, rather than the real test or basis of the decision. Prosser describes this kind of foreseeability as follows:

> "Such piecemeal foresight is a rope of sand, and offers neither certainty nor convenience, as the foundering in the cases seems to show. Here is Learned Hand, a great judge blandly assuring us that it is beyond reasonable anticipation that a barge with which the defendant collides will sink, and will be carrying insurance. Here is Pennsylvania, twice asserting that no reasonable man could foresee that any object struck by a speeding train or bus would fly off at an angle and hit a person not directly in its path. Here is Wisconsin, affirming that when a child is run down in the street there is no recognizable risk that its mother, in the vicinity, may suffer mental shock. Here is New York, solemnly declaring that the foreseeability of the spread of the fire ends at the first adjoining house. I do not believe these things, I think they are rubbish. At the other extreme is another New York case, finding it all foreseeable when a collision forced a taxicab over a sidewalk and into a building and loosened a stone, which fell on a bystander and killed her, while the taxicab was being removed twenty minutes later by a wrecking car. There is also Texas, which had no difficulty at all in foreseeing that a mudhole left by a defendant in a highway would stall a car, that a rescuer attempting to tow it out would get his wooden leg stuck in the mud and that a loop in the tow rope would lasso his good leg and break it. Illustrations might be multiplied, as every negligence lawyer knows, but surely these are enough."[12]

A good example is the way in which a recent Canadian court dealt with injuries to a baby caused by the negligent driving of the defendant when he struck the car in which the mother was a passenger while the baby was yet unborn. The court began in the traditional manner by stating that "there must be a duty to take care owed by the defendant to the plaintiff."[13] After discussing the authorities, the court concluded:

> "Ann's mother was plainly one of a class within the area of foreseeable risk and one to whom the defendants therefore owed a duty. Was Ann any the less so? I think not. Procreation is normal and necessary for the preservation of the race. If a driver drives on a highway without due care for other users it is foreseeable that some of the other users of the highway will be pregnant women and that a child en ventre sa mere may be injured. Such a child therefore falls well within the area of potential danger which the driver is required to foresee and take reasonable care to avoid."[14]

But why is it necessary to foresee that the unborn infant may be injured? What if a pregnant woman wearing a false beard dresses up as a fat man

---

[12]Prosser, *Selected Topics on the Law of Torts* (1953).

[13]*Duval v. Seguin; Seguin v. Duval; Blais v. Duval*, [1972] 2 O.R. 686, 26 D.L.R. (3d) 418 at 432, affirmed (sub nom. *Duval v. Blais*) 1 O.R. (2d) 482, 40 D.L.R. (3d) 666 (C.A.).

[14]*Ibid.*, at 433, *per* Fraser J.

for a costume ball and accepts a ride from a person who believes her to be a man? If, as a result of negligent driving, she is injured and the baby is later born suffering damage from pre-natal injury, surely the infant could equally recover. Why should it make any difference to the infant's recovery whether its presence en ventre sa mere is foreseeable?

Foreseeability is essential for a finding of negligence. It is the basis of responsibility. It is because the driver could foresee injury to the mother if he did not take care that we are entitled to find him negligent and thus responsible. The risk to the mother is the basis of the fault. Since we know that injuries to some persons can also trigger losses for others, we have to decide what the limits of liability are going to be. Infants en ventre sa mere generally fall within the limits of liability whether or not their particular presence is reasonably foreseeable.

One of the more critical factors in deciding remoteness issues is the degree of fault or the seriousness of the initial risk which is the basis of a finding of negligence. The greater the fault, the wider the range of liability. The injury to the plaintiff in the *Palsgraf* case was too remote because the initial risk was not serious, i.e. the loss of a package.

III.   VICTIMS OF NERVOUS SHOCK

Nowhere are the questions of the perimeters of the law of negligence, risk, and remoteness more likely to become confused than in the area of nervous shock. And it is because of the fact that all three of these issues are often dealt with in terms of "duty" language that this confusion takes place.

Nervous shock does not raise an issue of extension. The law of negligence does apply to the kinds of activities which can produce nervous shock. One would be hard pressed to think of any kind of activity that is capable of producing nervous shock which falls within one of the exceptions to the *Donoghue v. Stevenson* principle.

Nervous shock seldom raises problems of risk of harm. In almost every single case dealing with nervous shock, the nervous shock has been caused by some negligent action which created a risk of physical harm.[15] How else could the nervous shock have been caused? The plaintiff suffers nervous shock either because he or she has suffered physical harm, narrowly missed suffering physical harm, witnessed

---

[15]Even in cases of shock resulting from the seeing or eating of adulterated food there is a risk of physical harm in the sense of illness or from metal or glass in the food. See, *e.g.*, *Taylor v. Weston Bakeries Ltd.*, [1976] W.W.D. 165, 1 C.C.L.T. 158 (Sask. Dist. Ct.), and *Negro v. Pietro's Bread Co.*, [1933] O.R. 112, [1933] 1 D.L.R. 490 (C.A.).

someone else suffering physical harm, or is closely related and emotionally involved with someone suffering physical harm. Where the risk of physical harm was a reasonably foreseeable one and could have been avoided by taking care, then the creator of the risk can generally be judged to be negligent. Nervous shock, therefore, is generally a by-product of the risk of physical harm, the creation of which is the basis of the negligence.

In the nervous shock cases, there generally is no problem in regard to the defendant's liability for the physical harm which he or she has caused. The issue is whether his or her liability should also include the damage caused by the nervous shock. It is obvious that there must be some limits placed on the defendant's liability in this regard. If the defendant, through his or her negligence, causes a rather gruesome accident in a crowded area, it would extend liability too far if the defendant had to pay compensation for everyone who suffered nervous shock as the result of witnessing the accident. Equally, it is extending liability too far if the defendant is required, on top of the damage for physical injury which he or she must pay, to have to pay compensation for nervous shock caused to all the close relatives of the victim of his or her negligence. (One must also keep in mind the problems of proof which nervous shock can raise.) The problem of the limits of one's liability for negligence is precisely what is at stake in the remoteness issue. There can be no question, therefore, that nervous shock cases generally raise problems of remoteness.

The problem which the courts face in regard to nervous shock cases is how and where to place the limits on liability. The courts generally have used the "duty" concept in placing such limits. The argument generally proceeds as follows:

1. Did the defendant owe the plaintiff a duty of care in regard to the nervous shock?

2. A person owes a duty to take care where there is a foreseeable risk of harm. Could the defendant have foreseen that if he or she did not take care the plaintiff would have suffered the nervous shock?

Foreseeability of a particular harm to a particular person is only relevant, however, to establish negligence. Once we have a finding of negligence we have fault, which is the basis for liability. To use reasonable foreseeability of particular events as a test for remoteness is to confuse that issue with problems of risk.

To ask whether the nervous shock suffered by a particular person is foreseeable or not is a strange kind of question. When a person creates a risk of physical harm which results in nervous shock, he or she is negligent because of the risk of the physical harm. The nervous shock is merely a by-product. A man who negligently runs over a child in the presence of the mother is negligent because he struck the child. It is totally irrelevant whether or not he thought about or ought to have thought about the shock which the mother might suffer. That is a secondary factor. It just simply is not taken into account when the negligence issue is decided.

The effect of this pattern of reasoning is to require a foreseeable risk of harm to the plaintiff as a necessary condition for liability. The defendant must be at fault in regard to the plaintiff. Thus, there must be some kind of fault relationship between the plaintiff and the defendant. Wherever a court attempts to solve a remoteness issue in terms of whether or not a duty of care was owed to the particular plaintiff, and uses foreseeability as a test of duty, the court is making privity of fault a prerequisite of liability. The classic example of the privity of fault doctrine in English law is to be found in the "nervous shock" decision of *Hay* (or *Bourhill*) *v. Young*.[16] The plaintiff, as she was alighting from a tram, heard the impact of a motor-cyclist, who, as a result of negligent driving, struck a motor car and was killed. After the cyclist's body was removed the plaintiff approached the site of the accident and saw the blood left on the roadway. As a result of the fright and terror she felt, she suffered nervous shock which resulted in a miscarriage. She then brought an action against the estate of the dead motor-cyclist.

All of the members of the House of Lords hearing the appeal followed a similar pattern of reasoning by asking whether there was a duty of care, and answering the question by holding that it was not foreseeable that the plaintiff would have suffered these injuries. Lord Wright, for example, stated:

> "It [negligence] is . . . always relative to the individual affected. This raises a serious additional difficulty in the cases where it has to be determined, not merely whether the act itself is negligent against someone, but whether it is negligent vis-a-vis the plaintiff. This is a crucial point in cases of nervous shock. Thus, in the present case John Young was certainly negligent in an issue between himself and the owner of the car which he ran into, but it is another question whether he was negligent vis-a-vis the appellant . . . If, however, the appellant has a cause of action it is because of a wrong to herself. She cannot build on a wrong to someone else."[17]

It is not beyond the realm of foreseeability that bystanders and relatives can suffer nervous shock as the result of witnessing a particularly gruesome accident. It is precisely because such a possibility is foreseea-

---

[16][1943] A.C. 92, [1942] 2 All E.R. 396 (H.L.).

[17]*Ibid.*, at 108.

ble that the law ought to tread carefully in imposing liability, as it would place a further extensive financial burden on a defendant who already must pay compensation for the physical personal injury, economic loss, and the property damage which he or she has caused through his or her negligence.

We need only examine a few cases to see the contradictory and strange results which the risk-duty privity of fault doctrine has produced. In *King v. Phillips* the English Court of Appeal found no liability for the nervous shock suffered by a mother as the result of a taxicab backing into her child on a tricycle, because "the taxicab driver cannot reasonably be expected to have foreseen that his backing would terrify a mother 70 yards away."[18] The same court, however, in *Boardman v. Sanderson*, found a defendant who injured an infant while backing his car liable to the father for causing nervous shock because the defendant knew of the father's presence. [19] But why should recovery or non-recovery turn on that? In both cases the basis of negligence is the risk to the child. That, and that alone, is why the driver is at fault.

The problem of dealing with nervous shock cases in terms of privity of fault doctrine is best illustrated by the Saskatchewan Court of Appeal decision in *Abramzik v. Brenner* where the court found the defendant not liable for the nervous shock suffered by a mother on learning that two of her children had been killed and the third injured as a result of the defendant's negligent driving. The court reasoned:

> "The first question which arises is whether nervous shock is a substantive tort or whether a particular instance of damage flowing from a particular tort. If the latter, recovery depends upon the question of remoteness. If the former, recovery depends upon a breach of duty. Legal writers and commentators have expressed contrary views, but in my opinion the authoritative view is that nervous shock, other than that flowing from a physical injury suffered by a claimant as a result of a negligent act, is a substantive tort. This then poses the problem of what is the duty the breach of which gives rise to a claim for damages for nervous shock."[20]

The judgment of the court, given by Mr. Justice Culliton, concludes with this passage:

> "I think I have made it clear that, in my opinion, the plaintiff can only recover damages in nervous shock if it can be proved that the defendant ought, as a reasonable man, to have foreseen nervous shock (as opposed to physical injury) to the plaintiff as the result of his conduct. In the present case I am satisfied the plaintiff Ursula Abramzik did not prove that the shock which she experienced, resulting in her illness,

---

[18][1953] 1 Q.B. 429 at 442, [1953] 2 W.L.R. 526, [1953] 1 All E.R. 617 (C.A.), *per* Denning L.J.

[19][1964] 1 W.L.R. 1317 at 1322 (C.A.), *per* Ormrod L.J.

[20](1967), 62 W.W.R. 332 at 335, 65 D.L.R. (2d) 651 (Sask. C.A.), *per* Culliton C.J.S.

was one which the defendant Julia Brenner ought, as a reasonable person, to have foreseen as a result of her conduct."[21]

Is it not foreseeable that a mother would suffer nervous shock on hearing of the death of two children and serious injury to a third? The defendant in the *Abramzik v. Brenner* case was aware of the existence of the dead children's mother as she was a friend of the family. Why should knowledge of the parent's or spouse's presence at the scene of an accident make any difference? Why should nervous shock be treated as a substantive tort, separate from the negligence action for the personal injury when it was the creation of the risk of that personal injury which is the basis of the defendant's fault and responsibility to compensate?

We can see a clear pattern in the nervous shock decisions. Recovery from nervous shock has generally been given only to the person who is the subject of a risk of physical harm or to that person's very close relatives who are present at the time the physical harm is suffered. Since nervous shock is generally ancillary to a risk of physical injury, it presents a problem of remoteness. To ask whether the defendant ought to have foreseen that a particular person or persons will suffer nervous shock is irrelevant and not at all helpful.

IV.   RESCUERS

Rescuers who are injured as the result of attempting to aid a person in danger, or as the result of a defendant's negligent action, always recover. The reason they do is simply that it is the policy of the law that persons be encouraged to rescue or aid those in danger. Damages suffered by a rescuer are, therefore, never found to be too remote. The courts, of course, pay lip service to the doctrine of privity of fault by always suggesting that the particular rescuer is foreseeable. In *Videan v. Br. Tpt. Comm.*, the United Kingdom Court of Appeal held that a negligent driver of a railway trolley was not liable to a child trespasser to whom he caused injury as a result of travelling too fast, as "it could not reasonably be foreseen that a trespasser would be there,"[22] and then found liability to a rescuer killed in saving the child's life because the driver "ought reasonably to foresee that, if he did not take care, some emergency or other might arise, and that someone or other might be impelled to expose himself to danger in order to effect a rescue."[23] What nonsense to find the presence of the person in danger not foreseeable but the presence of

---

[21]*Ibid.*, at 340.

[22][1963] 2 Q.B. 650, [1963] 3 W.L.R. 374, [1963] 2 All E.R. 860 at 867, *per* Lord Denning M.R.

[23]*Ibid.*, at 868 *per* Lord Denning M.R.

the rescuer foreseeable. The real foundation of the decision is expressed in the statement, "Whoever comes to the rescue, the law should see that he does not suffer for it."[24]

In *Jones v. Wabigwan*, a trial judge held that it was not foreseeable that a person following a speeding car would be injured when the car went off the road, struck a power pole causing the wires to fall to the ground and give the defendant a serious electrical burn when he stumbled on them while going to the aid of the injured defendant.[25] The decision was reversed by the Ontario Court of Appeal which held that:

> "In our view a reasonable man in the position of the defendant should have antici-pated that if he negligently collided with the hydro pole it was a probable consequence that the pole and the live electric wires would fall to the ground; that persons travelling along the highway in proximity to this point might be attracted to the field where the damaged vehicle, with its lights burning, was visible, and that they might reasonably be expected to come in contact with the live wires attached to the broken hydro pole and sustain serious personal injury. If this conclusion be valid as to any person who might pass along the highway at the time that the danger created by the defendant materialized, whether that person entered the field moved by a natural curiosity or a desire to render needed assistance, then the defendant's conduct was a proximate cause of the plaintiff's injuries and damages in the sense that they were reasonably foreseeable and not too remote."[26]

Such foreseeability, as stated by Prosser, is indeed a "rope of sand."[27]

In *Chadwick v. Br. Ry. Bd.*, a rescuer who suffered nervous shock after rendering assistance to the survivors of a train wreck was allowed to recover. Mr. Justice Waller held that:

> "In my opinion, if the defendants had asked themselves the hypothetical question: 'If we ran one train into another at Lewisham in such circumstances that a large number of people are killed, may some persons who are physically unhurt suffer injury from shock?', I think that the answer must have been 'Yes.' "[28]

We can assume from this the conclusion to be drawn is that one there-fore ought not to run one train into another. Surely, however, the reason that one train should not be run into another is because people will likely be killed. In the light of that, what relevance is it that we can also foresee that someone might suffer shock? The only reason the plaintiff recov-ered was because he was a rescuer.

The unforeseeable plaintiffs, the victims of nervous shock, and rescu-ers are generally treated in the standard texts, either in a general chapter

---

[24]*Supra*, note 22, at 868.

[25][1968] 2 O.R. 837, 1 D.L.R. (3d) 40 (H.C.).

[26][1970] 1 O.R. 366 at 369-70, 8 D.L.R. (3d) 424 (C.A.), *per* Schroeder J.A.

[27]Prosser, *Selected Topics on the Law of Torts* (1953).

[28][1967] 1 W.L.R. 912, [1967] 2 All E.R. 945 at 951 (Q.B.).

which is entitled "Duty of Care" and which includes problems of whether or not the law of negligence applies to a failure to aid, to arbitrators or barristers etc., (thus confusing questions of the limits of the law of negligence with issues of remoteness which are concerned with the limits of liability of individual. defendants for negligent acts) or it deals with them in a chapter on "Risk of Harm" which confuses together the question of fault with the limits of compensation. Indeed, some authors have placed all three kinds of questions together in one chapter.

Every finding of negligence involves the creating of a risk of harm to someone. The injuries of the principal subject of the risk are generally never too remote. A remoteness problem arises when other persons also suffer a loss as a result of the negligence to the person who is the main subject of the risk. The use of duty language to deal with these secondary losses suffered by those people transfers their damage into separate torts isolated from the fundamental risk, the creation of which is the foundation of the defendant's negligence and, in the final analysis, the true and only basis of the responsibility to compensate anyone who has suffered a loss as a consequence of negligent action.

V. THE RISK-REMOTENESS CONFUSION AND THE PROBLEM OF UNFORESEEABLE DAMAGE

The privity of fault doctrine means that if the defendant negligently creates a risk of harm to A. and as a result B. suffers damage as well as or instead of A., B. can only recover if the defendant was negligent to him because there was also a foreseeable risk that he as well as A. would be harmed. B. can only recover if he has his own independent negligent action. Fault with regard to A. will not do for liability for B. This kind of reasoning can be taken one step further. It is sometimes the case that a risk of one kind of injury can result in a different kind of damage. The defendant could create a risk of harm x. to A. and A. could instead, or as well, suffer y. It could then be argued that not only must each plaintiff be treated as a separate action in negligence, but each specific kind of damage must be treated separately as well. A. can only recover for damage y. if there is a foreseeable risk of harm of y. A risk of harm of x. will not do for liability for y. The same arguments would apply.

(a) A defendant is liable in negligence only if he is in breach of a duty of care.

(b) In order for there to be a breach of a duty of care there must be a foreseeable risk of the harm.

(c) If the particular harm was not foreseeable, the defendant did not owe a duty of care in regard to it, and therefore cannot be liable for it.

Here again we have the confusion between problems of risk or culpability, i.e. , the existence of negligence, and the limits of liability, which is a problem of remoteness. Questions of risk relate to whether or not there has been negligence, which is quite a separate and different question from whether a particular loss caused by the negligence is recoverable or is too remote. When one uses "duty of care" as a test of remoteness these two separate issues are collapsed into one. For example, in *Woods v. Duncan*[28] an action was brought by the relatives of some of the men who perished in the submarine Thetis which sank during a diving trial because of a door to a torpedo tube being opened while the bow-cap was for some unknown reason not closed. Before the inside door could be opened a lever had to be raised which uncovered a small hole from which water would run if the torpedo tube was more than half way filled. The purpose of this apparatus was not to indicate whether the bow-cap was closed or open but whether the tube was filled with water which, unless pumped out, would spill onto the floor of the compartment. The small hole, however, had been painted over and not cleared, and no inspection of it had been made. There was clearly a cause-effect relationship between the sinking of the vessel and the failure to remove the paint in that, if the hole had been clear, the door to the tube would not have been opened without the tube first being emptied, which in turn would have led to the discovery of the open bow-cap. The risk created, however, was not that the submarine would sink that a quantity of water would spill on the compartment floor. The House of Lords agreed with the decision of the Court of Appeal that the builders and sub-contractors were negligent because they did not inspect properly and clear the hole, but they held that the negligence was not the "cause" of the accident. This case, unlike *Wagon Mound (No. 1)*, thus makes a clear distinction between culpability and compensation.

VI. CONCLUSION

If we refrain from using duty language to deal with remoteness issues the whole morass can be avoided. In the early history of the evolution of the law of negligence, courts and lawyers functioned quite well without the use of the concept of duty of care.[30] In *Blyth v. Birmingham Waterworks Co.* Alderson B. gave this definition of negligence:

---

[29][1946] A.C. 40, [1946] 1 All E.R. 420n, reversing in part [1944] 2 All E.R. 159n (C.A.).

[30]Teh, "Reasonable Foreseeability in Negligence (1833-1882)" (1975), 5 U. of Tasmania L. Rev. 45.

"Negligence is the omission to do something which a reasonable man, guided upon those considerations which ordinarily regulate the conduct of human affairs, would do, or doing something which a prudent and reasonable man would not do."[31]

To define negligence as a breach of a duty of care adds nothing.

The requirement that the defendant must owe to the plaintiff a duty to take care does not entail a doctrine of privity of fault. Contractual rights are *in personam* so naturally there must be a specific set of right-duty relationships between the contracting parties. The rights which we have in regard to our persons and property are *in rem*. They run against anyone in the legal system. Duties of non-interference do not arise out of risk, but out of the rights which every person has not to be interfered with or damaged in regard to their persons or property. The correlative duties to those rights, since they fall on everyone or anyone in the legal system, do not have to be specifically established as existing between a particular plaintiff and a particular defendant. Since the legal relations are *in rem*, a doctrine of privity is totally unnecessary for the law of torts. One need only establish:

1. that the law imposes a duty to take care in regard to a particular kind of activity and damage;

2. that there has been negligence and thus a breach of that duty to take care;

3. that the negligent act caused some harm; and

4. that the damage suffered is not too remote.

The proper test for establishing whether or not a particular damage or loss is too remote, will be the subject-matter of the next chapter.

---

[31](1856), 11 Ex. 781, 156 E.R. 1047 at 1049.

10

A RESTATEMENT OF THE FORESEEABILITY TEST

I. INTRODUCTION

It is argued in this chapter that a rational, systematic basis for predicting recovery in remoteness cases can be formulated which allows us not to have to swing between the poles of the direct causation and the foreseeability test, or between the poles of the "foreseeable as probable" test of *Wagon Mound (No. 1)*[1] and the "foreseeable as possible" tests of *Wagon Mound (No. 2)*.[2] What is needed is a development of a theoretical basis for legal liability from which a test can be formulated which will conform to the historical evolution of the law of remoteness in terms of explaining past decisions, and will also be consistent with the present leading authorities. The test which will be proposed can be described as a synthesis of the landmark decisions which have dealt with the shortcomings of *Wagon Mound (No. 1)*, including *Hughes v. Lord Advocate*[3] and *Wagon Mound (No. 2)*, together with the ruling case of *Wagon Mound (No. 1)* itself.

The fundamental principle upon which the law of torts rests is that agents are held to be responsible for the natural and probable consequences of their actions. "Natural and probable" are given meaning in terms of foreseeability. Foreseeability of harm is therefore a necessary condition for culpability and consequently for the liability derived therefrom.

The clearest case of foreseeability and therefore culpability is where the harm caused is the very intent of the actor. "Intent" might be defined as the state of mind which directs a person's actions toward a specific object and an "intentional act" may be described as a voluntary

---

[1] *Overseas Tankship (U.K.) v. Morts Dock & Co.*, [1961] A.C. 388, [1961] 2 W.L.R. 126, [1961] 1 All E.R. 40 (P.C.), hereinafter referred to as *Wagon Mound (No. 1)*.

[2] *Overseas Tankship (U.K.) v. Miller S.S. Co. Pty.*, [1967] 1 A.C. 617, [1966] 3 W.L.R. 498, [1966] 2 All E.R. 709 (P.C.), hereinafter referred to as *Wagon Mound (No.2)*.

[3] [1963] A.C. 837, [1963] 2 W.L.R. 779, [1963] 1 All E.R. 705 (H.L.).

act directed by the conscious mind with the desire to bring about certain consequences. Our law makes actors liable for the intentional causing of harm, and the intentional wrongdoer may well be held liable for unintended consequences. That is, remoteness is seldom a defence in the intentional torts. A party intending to cause harm is generally liable for all of the consequences.[4]

Absence of intention, however, is in itself a defence: lack of intention reduces or eliminates culpability. An actor can show that an act was not intentional by showing that what occurred was not matched in intention owing to an accident, mistake, inadvertence or carelessness.[5] An unintentional act might be a negligent act, however, and negligence assumes the defence of no intent. The element of negligence is introduced by considering what the actor ought to have foreseen as a result of his action, that is, he ought to have foreseen the intervening event which caused the accident, he ought to have known the true facts, he ought to have foreseen the consequences of his action, or he ought to have taken care in acting.

Even though harm has been caused by an actor's negligent act, it can be a defence to say that its consequences were not foreseeable, and therefore that in regard to them there can be no culpability, and consequently no liability.

For any negligent act there are certain harmful effects which are foreseeable. These effects constitute the risk and determine the standard of care to be applied. When these effects materialize as a result of an action, remoteness is not a defence. These effects cannot be too remote because they are the very things which the actor ought to have had in mind in acting.

There are other effects, however, which could not be said to be reasonably foreseeable. It is in regard to these that the defence of remoteness of damage might be raised. While these effects may not be reasonably foreseeable in and of themselves, they may, nevertheless, belong to a class of effects which is foreseeable. Foreseeability can exist in terms of a singular description of events, and in terms of a general description of events.

Take, for example, the category of highly dangerous or intrinsically dangerous activities such as the handling of highly inflammable or explosive chemicals, or highly toxic substances. While certain particu-

---

[4]*Wilkinson v. Downton*, [1897] 2 Q.B. 57.

[5]Coval, Smith, and Burns, "The Concept of Action and its Juridical Significance" (1980), 30 U.T.L.J. 199.

lar effects are reasonably foreseeable, there is a set of other effects of which any particular one is not reasonably foreseeable, although the class as such is reasonably foreseeable. Thus if a plank is negligently dropped into the hold of a loaded ship it is reasonably foreseeable that damage will be done to the cargo. It is the reasonable foreseeability of this particular risk which is the basis of judging the act to be negligent. There is, moreover, a set of other possible consequences, no particular one of which is foreseeable as probable. They may not even be nameable beforehand. The plank might hit a person working within the hold with the cargo, or the plank might strike a spark and cause an explosion if the cargo is inflammable, or the plank might dislodge cargo which later falls on a crewman passing by. It is specifically foreseeable that if oil is spilled on the water, damage will be caused to the foreshore. But there is a further set of "possible" ways in which the oil might cause damage, including its ignition by a series of improbable but possible events.

If a person drives while intoxicated at 90 miles an hour down the wrong side of the street and sideswipes an oncoming car, he or she will be found culpable and liable to pay for the damage. If the person strikes an oncoming car in a head-on collision and kills six passengers, we would find him or her equally culpable, and liable for the full amount of the damage. There is no difference in degrees of culpability in a case where the driver merely sideswiped an oncoming car, or destroyed it, killing a carload of passengers. The amount of damage done is a matter of bad or good luck. Equally if the intoxicated driver careened off the road, hit a fence and popped out the staples, which were then eaten by cattle resulting in their loss due to contracting hardware disease, that concatenation would also be a matter of chance. Whether or not a negligent dangerous act results in other "possible" damaging events which are not reasonably foreseeable in the particular, is purely a matter of luck. The culpability is the same because of the likelihood of a wide unspecified variety of similar events the set of which is foreseeable.

Thus a negligent action will have particular consequences which are foreseeable, and it may also have a set of other consequences which are foreseeable as a set, but no particular member of the set may be reasonably foreseeable. The latter consequences will not be too remote where the foreseeability condition is satisfied for the set. Only a particular consequence which is not foreseeable, and which does not belong to a reasonably foreseeable set would be too remote. The following diagram will illustrate a remoteness issue:

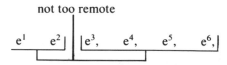

Particular damaging events which are reasonably foreseeable	Class of events which is reasonably foreseeable, while any one particular event may not be nameable beforehand.	Not foreseeable in the particular nor a member of a foreseeable class.

These distinctions can be illustrated by the following set of facts.[6] A city constructs in one of its parks a tower from which a flag is flown. The tower is made up of four pieces of angle iron joined by strips of metal, and coming together at the top to support a single metal pole from which the flag is flown. The construction of the tower at the particular site in the park is negligent because a particular damaging event is foreseeable, that is, young children will likely climb up the tower using the metal strips as a ladder, and some of them may fall and injure themselves.

There is a further set of risks, however, which are not nearly as foreseeable as an injury to a child as a result of a fall, but are foreseeable as a class. A child might fall and injure a person who might happen to be at the foot of the tower at the time. A mother might suffer nervous shock seeing her child in danger. A child may climb to the top of the tower and become too frightened of the height to come back down, and a rescuer may fall in trying to bring the child back down.

Let us assume, however, that a child climbs the tower and his weight causes the whole tower to fall over causing serious injury to a person underneath. Let us also assume that the tower was properly built but that the reason it fell was because the bolts holding it to the concrete were made of defective metal, and that there was no way the city could or should be aware of this defect. This particular damaging event would not be foreseeable either in the particular or as a member of a class.

The injury of a person by the falling of the tower would be too remote because it was not foreseeable in terms of either a singular or a general description. In regard to this kind of risk the city had met the standard of care. If the tower had been constructed in such a way that children could

---

[6]The example is drawn from the fact pattern of *Booth v. St. Catharines*, [1948] S.C.R. 564, [1948] 4 D.L.R. 686.

not climb it, it could still fall by other means such as a high wind, or a workman repairing or painting the tower, given the defective bolts. An injury from a child falling on a person below, however, would not be too remote because it would be preventable by complying with the standard of care regarding the safety of children.

In the case of *Gilchrist v. A. & R. Farms Ltd.*[7] the defendant employer company failed to repair the track and rehang a heavy barn door which had to be lifted or slid to open, and which from time to time blew over and had to be lifted and leaned against the barn in an upright position. The plaintiff employee suffered a severe back injury caused when he found the door lying on the ground and proceeded to lift it into an upright position. The plaintiff argued that the defendants were negligent in that the loose door created a risk of harm to children and others of injury which could be caused by the door falling on them. Counsel for the plaintiff invited the court to apply the direct causation test of *Polemis* and to reject the foreseeability test of *Wagon Mound (No. 1)*. The trial judge and a unanimous Court of Appeal declined this invitation and found the back injury too remote as it was not reasonably foreseeable.

That someone could be hurt by the door falling on them was reasonably foreseeable. The probability of someone being hurt by lifting the door was far less because, as it came out in evidence, lifting things of equal or greater weight such as bags of feed was a normal part of the plaintiff's job.

Negligent actions, however, can result in damage in a variety of ways. The fact that by chance the damage actually occurred in a less probable way should be no defence if the particular way in which the damage occurred is a part of a set of foreseeable possibilities of injury.

A back injury is not a part of the kinds of injuries or damage which could be caused by a door being blown over. If the negligence was the creation of a risk of injury from a falling door, an injury from lifting is too remote to that particular risk. There could be liability only if the risk from lifting was in itself reasonably foreseeable or was actually foreseen. If this is the case then there is no remoteness case at all, but the issue relates to standard of care. The Supreme Court of Canada upheld the appeal on the basis that the evidence disclosed that a conversation had taken place between the plaintiff and the defendant's manager in which the possibility of a person being hurt by lifting the door was specifically mentioned. Given this finding of facts, any risk of the door being blown over is irrelevant.

---

[7][1966] S.C.R. 122, 54 W.W.R. 595, 54 D.L.R. (2d) 707.

It is a fact of life that damage can materialize from dangerous or damaging events in a variety of ways, and that these damaging events can lead to other damaging events. The fact that an action is judged to be negligent in terms of the risks which have the highest probabilities should not be allowed to free negligent actors from liability for damage of a lower probability in the particular, if the class of which it is a member has a fair degree of probability in terms of foreseeability.

II.   EXAMPLES OF FORESEEABLE CLASSES OF INJURY

Some classes of injury are only foreseeable in regard to specific kinds of negligent actions, while others are foreseeable for any damage-causing event. The clearest example of the latter are the following.

a) The Thin-Skull Cases

It is clearly foreseeable that people have different susceptibilities to damaging events, both physically and mentally. These may be the result of genetic abnormalities, illness, physical handicaps, or disease. Although no particular susceptibility will be foreseeable, the reasonable possibility of some kind of susceptibility clearly is. Consequently the law provides that the negligent actor must "take his victim as he finds him". Damage due to the existence of a particular physical or mental susceptibility is thus not too remote.

b) Medical Complications

The potential for unforeseen medical complications as the result of an injury is clearly reasonably foreseeable. The complications may arise in the natural course of the illness. They might be the result of the treatment for the injury, whether or not the treatment itself was properly or negligently carried out. Complications also can arise as a result of further injury brought about by the initial damaging event, such as where a person who has his leg broken breaks his other leg because of the handicap of the first break. While no single such event may have been foreseeable, the possibility of complications of this nature are entailed by any risk of serious physical harm.

c) Rescue

Whenever any person is put into a dangerous situation as a result of a negligent act, it is reasonably foreseeable that people will come to their aid, if given the opportunity, and in doing so will put themselves under a risk of harm. It is not foreseeable that on a particular occasion a particular person may stop to render aid to people injured in a motor vehicle accident, but it is reasonably foreseeable that persons do come to the aid of others under such circumstances, and in doing so will be in danger of injury. Injury invites rescue, and some rescue invites injury.

d) Nervous Shock

The suffering of nervous shock as the result of witnessing an injury to another or arriving upon the aftermath of an injury is the kind of thing which is reasonably foreseeable in general, but not necessarily so in any particular case. It is not so frequent as can be said to be reasonably foreseeable in each particular case, but happens often enough so that it is a distinct foreseeable possibility in general.

III.   THE RESTATEMENT OF THE FORESEEABILITY TEST

The traditional foreseeability test for remoteness of damages, based on the privity of fault doctrine, draws no distinction between the foreseeability required to establish fault, or a departure from the standard of care of the reasonable man in regard to a particular action, and foreseeability necessary to establish responsibility for a particular effect of that action. Culpability is established in terms of the primary or more obvious risks foreseeable as a result of one's actions. When we assess culpability, we generally look at the obvious particular risks. These risks, however, are not the only foreseeable results of an action. There are actions which *predictably have harmful unpredictable consequences*, and there are therefore sets of ancillary risks entailed by primary or obvious particular risks.

Agents have a right not to be injured by the negligent actions of other agents, and all agents have a duty to other agents to meet certain minimum standards of care in their actions. Agents, therefore, owe not only a duty of care in regard to particular risks to particular people, but also in regard to classes of risks to classes of people. Privity of fault between the defendant and plaintiff, if it is deemed to be a necessary condition for liability, must be taken to include classes of kinds of risks to classes of people as well as particular risks to particular people. Defining culpability in these wider terms thus is consistent with a privity of fault doctrine.

The *Wagon Mound (No. 1)* test required each unique damage to be treated in terms of particular foreseeability. Once negligence has been established, the onus is on the negligent actor to show that the particular results were not foreseeable. It is not sufficient to show that it was not foreseeable in the particular; it must also be shown that it was not foreseeable in general in order to deny culpability.

The test proposed can be stated as follows: *Damage is not too remote when it is either foreseeable in the particular, or falls within a class of possible damages, which class satisfies the foreseeability condition, although any particular event falling within the class may not satisfy that condition.* This test for recovery uses the concept of reasonable foreseeability as expressed in *Wagon Mound (No. 1)*, that is, foreseeable as probable, but allows it to apply to a class with members of merely possibly foreseeable particular damaging events.

Of the negligence cases which raise issues of remoteness of damages, decided by the courts of England, Canada, Australia, and New Zealand from the latter part of the 19th century up to the present, the outcome of 92 per cent of the decisions is consistent with the above test whether or not the court has purported to use a direct or proximate cause, or a foreseeability test of remoteness. From the decisions which discuss remoteness of damages or cite cases relevant to this issue, those which were decided upon the bases of doctrines which are no longer relevant have been eliminated. Of the remaining cases those in which the presence or absence of negligence is in issue, or where the dispute relates to risk or standard of care have also been eliminated, since they do not raise a true problem of remoteness.[8] In some cases authorities for the foreseeability test of remoteness are cited as authority for the risk principle. When used as a statement of the risk principle, the foreseeability test of *Wagon Mound (No. 1)* becomes equivalent in meaning to the good neighbour principle of Lord Atkin in *Donoghue v. Stevenson*.[9] Cases where the damage has been found to be foreseeable in the particular, and where those foreseeable damages are the subject of the risk, the creation of which constitutes the negligence, do not raise true remoteness issues and have thus not been included in this study.[10] The damage can never

---

[8]In *Wood v. C.P.R.* (1879), 30 S.C.R. 110, the plaintiff became entangled in long grass while attempting to couple cars together and was seriously injured by another train when he fell. The injury was held not to be reasonably foreseeable. This constitutes a finding of no departure from the standard of care of the reasonable man, and consequently no negligence. It is a remoteness issue if in a hot and dry season the long grass constituted a risk of fire as in *Smith v. London & South Western Ry. Co.* (1870), L.R. 6 C.P. 14 (Ex. Ch.), and the plaintiff was injured not by fire, but by being hit by a train when he became entangled in the long grass and fell.

[9][1932] A.C. 562 at 580 (H.L.).

[10]*E.g.*, in *M'Kenna v. Stephens & Hull*, [1923] 2 I.R. 112 (K.B.), the defendant company negligently failed to construct a walkway around one of its construction sites. The plaintiff was forced to walk on the roadway where he was struck by a negligent motorist and injured. This was the very risk which the defendant ought to have foreseen and to have guarded against. The issue is one of whether or not the defendant was negligent. No remoteness issue is involved.

be too remote if it constitutes the risk which is the basis of a finding of negligence. A true remoteness issue arises when something else occurs as well as or instead of the risk of the particular foreseeable harm. For the same reason, the cases involving the intervening acts of third parties where those acts were the very particular risk, the creation of which is the basis of a finding of negligence, have been eliminated, while those cases where the intervening act of the third party was merely an ancillary risk, or a part of a wider class of risks which were created by the initial negligence, have been retained.

From the set of cases remaining which raise true remoteness issues, those classes of injury or risks which can follow from any damage-causing event are separated and divided into the categories of thin-skull, medical complications, rescuers, and nervous shock. On the above restatement of the foreseeability principle, any damage falling into the first three categories should never be too remote, since it is foreseeable that these kinds of damages can follow from almost any negligent act. Nervous shock, for policy reasons to be later elaborated, has to be treated differently. The remaining cases deal with negligence in regard to actions which create a wide range of possibilities for the causing of harm. In general such activities may be classified as dangerous precisely because they can give rise to a wide class of possible injuries. Particular damage arising from negligence in regard to such actions is not too remote even though it might not be reasonably foreseeable in the particular because the damage is a member of a reasonably foreseeable class of damaging events. Such damage is not foreseeable in particular because the nature of the negligence actions are such that it is foreseeable that damage can result in a wide variety of different ways. This latter category is divided into three sub-categories: *transportation*, including automobiles, trains, vessels, and horses and carts; *dangerous substances*, *objects*, and *activities*, which include energy sources such as electricity and fire, explosives, inflammatory, toxic and poisonous substances, knives, guns and machinery etc.; and *others*, for activities which can give rise to a wide variety of ways in which injury can happen, but which do not fit into the other two general categories. Any damage which is caused by a negligent action which gives rise to a risk of a wide range of possibilities for causing harm is not too remote so long as it falls within the range of the risk, that is, it is included in the class of the kind of things which are foreseeable. From this analysis the following chart can be reproduced.

	Total Cases	Held for Plaintiff	Held for Defendant	Correctly Decided	Wrongly Decided
Actions Which Create a Wide Range of Possibilities For Causing Harm					
Moving vehicles	64	57	7	61	3
Dangerous Substances Objects & Activities	39	33	6	33	6
Others	23	18	5	21	2
Classes of Damage Which Can Follow any Negligence					
Mental or Physical Susceptibilities (thin-skull)	88	84	4	84	4
Medical Complications	37	32	5	34	3
Rescuers	29	27	2	27	2
Nervous Shock Suffered By Third Party	54	32	22	48	6
Totals	334	283	51	308	26

Per cent Correctly Decided: 92%

IV. ACTIONS WHICH CREATE A WIDE RANGE OF POSSIBILITIES FOR CAUSING HARM

In the famous case of *Palsgraf v. Long Island Railroad Co.* Mr. Justice Andrews stated in his dissent that courts must draw the "uncertain and wavering line" of the limits of liability as best as they can, taking into account all the relevant factors in the circumstances.[11] He argued that out of a "rough sense of justice, the law arbitrarily declines to trace a series of events beyond a certain point."[12] In fact, the reasoning which in some cases will trace an extended and improbable series of events in order to impose liability, as we have seen in *Falkenham v. Zwicker*,[13] and which in other cases will not do so, is not actually arbitrary. The analysis of the cases shows that a clear relationship exists between the nature of the activity and the resulting decision regarding the imposition of liability.

Where an activity is highly dangerous, it is foreseeable that negligence may result in various kinds of damage. In other words, the foreseeable class of risks of harm surrounding negligence when engaged in danger-

---

[11](1928), 248 N.Y. 339, 162 N.E. 99 at 104, 59 A.L.R. 1253 (C.A.).

[12]*Ibid.*, at 103.

[13](1978), 93 D.L.R. (3d) 289, 32 N.S.R. (2d) 199, 54 A.P.R. 199 (T.D.).

ous activity is broad and varied. As a general rule, the more intrinsically dangerous the activity involved, the greater the likelihood of a finding that the damage is not too remote.

This result accords with the general principle of maintaining proportionality between the fault on the part of the defendant and the liability imposed for the resulting damage. Where a person is engaged in extremely dangerous activity, society exacts a very high standard of care. If the person is negligent in such a situation he or she is rightfully culpable for all of the harm emanating from the negligence, whether foreseeable or not, as long as the actual damage falls within a class of risks created by the negligence. The more dangerous the activity, the wider will be the class of risks. Where the person is engaged in reasonably non-dangerous activity then the standard of care governing behaviour is lower and negligence will attract a lesser degree of culpability and thus the range of consequences for which he will be liable will be much more narrow.

Driving a moving vehicle is an example of an activity which is highly dangerous and which requires the utmost standard of care to be exercised. One need only consider the appalling statistics on death and injury resulting from motor vehicle accidents to ascertain the truth of this premise. Because of the intrinsically dangerous nature of driving, the reasonably foreseeable class of risks created by negligent driving is extremely broad. Therefore, where causation is proven in a remoteness case involving a motor vehicle accident the defendant should, with few exceptions, be found liable for all of the damage which stems from his or her negligence. Damage should only be deemed to be too remote where it is clearly outside of the class of risks created by negligent driving. A few of the cases which held for the defendant will be used to demonstrate when such a situation might arise.

It is clear from the strange and varied series of events revealed in the cases that almost any form of damage can happen as a result of an accident caused by moving vehicles such as cars, trains, or vessels. Naturally, all of the particular categories of remote damage can happen — the victim may have a thin skull, medical complications may set in, a rescuer may intervene, and so forth. Aside from these, a wide variety of other unforeseeable consequences may arise out of negligent driving. The facts of *Zwicker* have already been cited as one example. But domestic animals have not only eaten staples after car accidents; also they have inadvertently been released onto the highway causing other drivers to hit them,[14] and they have been frightened by car accidents into

---

[14]*Buchanan v. Oulton* (1965), 51 D.L.R. (2d) 383 (N.B.C.A.).

running across railroad tracks where they have been hit by oncoming trains. Fowl, as well as beasts, have suffered unforeseeable damage through negligent driving. In *Heeney v. Best*[16] the defendants negligently backed their truck into hydroelectric wires, interrupting the flow of electricity to the plaintiffs farm. The loss of power cut off the oxygen supply to baby chicks, suffocating them.

Humans have experienced all manner of unexpected injury by reason of motor vehicle accidents. In *Lauritzen v. Barstead*[17] the intoxicated defendant negligently pulled at the steering wheel, forcing the car off the road, and later hopelessly mired it in a hole while attempting to drive it. The plaintiff was forced to walk to town for help, suffered frostbite, and ultimately had to have parts of both feet amputated. A similar injury was the fate of the plaintiff in *Bradford v. Robinson Rentals*[18] who was required by his employers to make a long journey in an unheated vehicle in severe weather conditions. The plaintiff in *Ichard v. Frangoulis*[19] recovered for loss of enjoyment of a holiday when injuries inflicted in a car accident prevented him from completing his vacation. All the above losses were found by courts to be not too remote.

Judges have found remarkable series of events arising out of car accidents to be foreseeable. In *Lynch v. Mitchell*[20] the Queensland District Court found it entirely foreseeable that a car collision would force open the trunk of a car and that the tools in the trunk would be thrown out, injuring the plaintiff who was standing on a nearby footpath. The decision is correct although the analysis is questionable. To say that the particular injury was foreseeable, in this case the injury caused by flying tools, is a fiction. But the injury does fall within a foreseeable broad class of damage. Where the defendant has been negligent in an activity which is dangerous in nature then any form of damage ensuing which is within the same large class of foreseeable injury is recoverable.[21]

Those cases concerning moving vehicle accidents in which the remote damage falls within one of the particular categories such as the "thin-

---

[15]*Sneesby v. Lancashire & Yorkshire Ry. Co.* (1875), 1 Q.B.D. 42 (C.A.).

[16](1978), 23 O.R. (2d) 19, 94 D.L.R. (3d) 451 (H.C.).

[17](1965), 53 W.W.R. 207, 53 D.L.R. (2d) 267 (Alta. S.C.).

[18][1967] 1 W.L.R. 337, [1967] 1 All E.R. 267.

[19][1977] 1 W.L.R. 556, [1977] 2 All E.R. 461 (Q.B.).

[20](1963), 57 Q.J.P.R. 125 (Dist. Ct.).

[21]A second policy is at work here as well. It is the usual case that drivers carry insurance. Where additional persons are negligent in a series of events following a motor vehicle accident, the fact that a driver has insurance where the second party may not becomes particularly important.

skull'' cases were analyzed separately from the balance of the moving vehicle negligence cases. Sixty-four cases were considered in which the facts did not designate the case as falling into one of the other noted categories and 57 of these cases held for the plaintiff.[22] Negligent driving or navigation has constantly attracted a far-reaching range of liability.

Of the 64 cases in which the remoteness of damages resulting from an accident involving a moving vehicle was in issue, only seven cases held for the defendant. *Seymour Sawmills Ltd. v. Singh*,[23] for example, is a clear counter-example to the revised foreseeability test, that is, in terms of the test, it is wrongly decided. In that case the defendant driver backed his truck into a power pole and caused a short circuit, destroying a switch box located several miles away. The court applied a *Wagon Mound (No. 1)* test, and found the damage too distant to be foreseeable. According to our test the fact of proximity to the scene of an accident should be irrelevant to the question of recovery if the damage falls within a class of foreseeable risks. In this case it seems a particularly narrow view to demand that damage resulting from negligence be in the immediate vicinity of the act in order to be foreseeable.

In four of the cases the motor vehicle accident led a third party to actually cause the loss. Another counter-example, *Knightley v. Johns*,[24] is a recent decision of the English Court of Appeal. The defendant negligently caused a car accident in a tunnel. A police inspector at the scene sent two police against the flow of traffic to avert oncoming cars. The plaintiff, one of the bike drivers, was hit by an approaching car. The trial judge held the defendant wholly liable for the second accident, but this decision was overturned by the Court of Appeal who found the inspector entirely liable since the order he gave to the plaintiff was contrary to standing policy on road accidents. The Court of Appeal took the position that the negligence of the inspector acted as an intervening event which broke the chain of causation between the defendant's negligence and the injury to the plaintiff. Such metaphysical abstractions, or subtleties of thought, should not really be a part of a rational approach to the subject of remoteness. The difficulty a court is faced with is that it does not want to subject the defendant to broad liability when a second person has through his negligence also contributed to the harm. This problem should be resolved by an apportionment of liability between the first defendant and the second defendant (who will have been joined as a third party by the first defendant). The court should have the opportu-

---

[22]See appendices to this book for a complete breakdown of the cases.

[23](1963), 48 W.W.R. 129 (B.C. Co. Ct.).

[24][1982] 1 W.L.R. 349, [1982] 1 All E.R. 851 (C.A.).

nity to determine which actor contributed most to the occurrence of the unforeseen consequences and be able to apportion liability accordingly.

In the other three cases[25] the plaintiffs failed to recover damages for loss of consortium when their spouses deserted them because of the injuries they had suffered as a result of the defendants' negligence. While the cases are not unanimous on this point,[26] the prevailing view is that such damages are too remote.

On the revised foreseeability test, if the intervening act of the third party is foreseeable in the particular, or if it is a member of a foreseeable class of events involving the causing of harm by third parties, then the damage is not too remote. It is not foreseeable that a spouse will leave his or her injured partner. While it does sometimes happen, it is generally a very rare occasion. In fact in nearly all the reported decisions the evidence shows that the marriage, in any case, was rather fragile, or the injury was not the primary cause of the marital break-up.

On the other hand, the probability of people who are present at or attending the scene of an accident being injured by a subsequent vehicle is sufficiently high as to constitute a foreseeable class of events because by their very presence at the scene and involvement in the accident, either as passenger, medical attendant, rescuer[27] or police officer, they are in an area of danger from other swiftly moving vehicles using the road. Contrast *Knightley v. John* with the case of *Patten v. Silberschein*[28] where the plaintiff was robbed of $80 while he was lying unconscious on the road after being struck by the defendant's car. On the revised foreseeability test this case would be wrongly decided because it was not foreseen in the particular, and in the place and time in which it occurred, too rare of an event to be said to be a member of a foreseeable class.

The seventh case holding for the defendant, *Laurie v. Godfrey*,[29] is a curious New Zealand case. The plaintiff was doing washing at the defendant's house. She had fastened a clothes-line across a laneway at right angles to a wire line fastened to a chimney. The defendant drove down the lane and, without waiting for the plaintiff to hoist up the line,

---

[25]*Antell v. Simons*, [1976] 6 W.W.R. 202, 26 R.F.L. 304 (B.C.); *Admiralski v. Stehbens*, [1960] Qd. R. 510 (S.C.); *Cameron v. Nottingham Ins. Co. Ltd.*, [1958] S.A.S.R. 174 (S.C.). See also *Lauritzen v. Barstead, supra*, note 17.

[26]*Lampert v. Eastern Nat. Omnibus Co. Ltd.*, [1974] 1 W.L.R. 1047, [1954] 2 All E.R. 719n (Q.B.); *Hird v. Gibson*, [1974] Qd. R. 14 (C.A.).

[27]*Chapman v. Hearse* (1961), 106 C.L.R. 112 (H.C.).

[28]51 B.C.R. 133, [1936] 3 W.W.R. 169 (S.C.).

[29][1920] N.Z.L.R. 231, [1920] G.L.R. 181 (S.C.).

he slowly drove through. The car pulled down the clothes-line, which in turn pulled down the wire line, which brought the chimney bricks down on the plaintiff. The Supreme Court of New Zealand found the injury unforeseeable. In this case the only apparent risk of harm of the plaintiff nudging his way past the clothes-line was that he might dirty the clothes. His driving presented no obviously dangerous risks. If he had careened through the clothes-line at 50 kilometres per hour he would probably have been liable for any injury he might have caused. Drivers, as a rule, are liable for extended consequences of negligence because driving at high speeds is dangerous. Where the driving presents no obvious risks, or is not dangerous according to any reasonable definition, then no broad class of risks exists, and liability for unforeseen consequences of negligence is confined to the narrow set of risks presented by the negligence. The damage caused in *Laurie v. Godfrey* was not reasonably foreseeable in the particular, nor did it belong to a class of reasonably foreseeable harm.

Apart from motor vehicle and train accidents, and the collision of vessels, which form the largest single category under the general heading of actions which create a wide range of possibilities for causing harm, a further set of cases was analyzed where the defendant was engaged in activities which involved the use of highly dangerous substances, such as inflammable liquids, toxics, poisons, or explosives or dangerous objects such as knives, guns, or machinery.

In this group of cases the specific concatenation of events which ended in the particular damage was not foreseeable, but what happened was the kind of thing which is likely to happen given negligence in that kind of activity. Thus in *Carmichael v. Mayo Lumber Ltd.*,[30] the defendant's negligent employee detonated explosives causing nearby houses to be shaken. The blast caused the plaintiff who, at the time of the explosion was about to sit down, to lose her balance and fall and injure her back. Such damage was found not to be too remote. Similarly, an injury from a shotgun which the defendant negligently kept loaded was found not to be too remote by the court in *Ry.Passenger Ins.Co.v. Brodeur*,[31] even though the gun went off in a rather unexpected way when a noise startled a horse throwing the defendant out of a rig in which he and the plaintiff were riding, with the result that the loaded gun which the defendant had been carrying on his lap discharged when it fell on the ground.

The six cases which held for the defendant are counter-examples to the revised foreseeability test; I would argue that they are wrongly

---

[30](1978), 85 D.L.R. (3d) 538 (B.C.S.C.).

[31][1920] 2 W.W.R. 924 (Man. K.B.).

decided. Generally these counter-examples are cases where the court has concluded that some intervening force, human or otherwise, has performed an intervening act, thereby breaking the chain of causation between negligence and damage. The fact of an intervening force should not be a reason in itself to withhold the imposition of liability on the defendant if the type of damage which ensues falls within a class of foreseeable damage. In *Bradford v. Kanellos*[33] the Supreme Court of Canada, Laskin J. (as he then was) and Spence J. dissenting, held for the defendant, a restaurant owner who had negligently caused a flash fire in the restaurant kitchen. A patron who heard the hiss of the fire extinguisher and mistakenly thought it was escaping gas shouted an alarm. In the stampede that followed the plaintiff was injured. The court decided that the action of the patron constituted an intervening act which was unforeseeable and not within the risk created by the defendant's negligence. Had the facts been only slightly different, however, the court would no doubt have reached the opposite conclusion. If the patron had seen the flames and shouted "fire" rather than "gas" it would be difficult to argue that such a reaction was unforeseeable. One risk of negligently causing a fire is that people will try to escape from it. Whether a patron is frightened by the fire itself or by the noise of the extinguisher makes no real difference, since the resulting injury falls within the same class of risks.

Employing the device of intervening act to place the burden of the unexpected onto the plaintiff rather than the defendant does seem inequitable in the case where the ultimate injury, regardless of what *causa finalis* provoked the denouement of the sequence of events, is within the class of risks created by the original negligence.[34]

Of a total of 103 cases considered under the major heading of actions which create a wide range of possibilities for causing harm, only nine are counterexamples to the proposed theory. Based on this analysis, over 90 per cent of the cases are correctly decided. These numbers indicate that, to a certain extent, judges do follow a set of guidelines when presented with remoteness cases. Despite the often propounded view that no clear means of decision-making exists for remoteness cases, it would appear that courts, for the most part, implicitly employ just such a theory as the foreseeable class test to reach their verdicts.

Actions which create a wide range of possibilities for causing harm, but do not involve moving vehicles or dangerous substances, objects, or

---

[32]*E.g.*, in *Macdonald v. David Macbrayne Ltd.*, [1915] S.C. 716, 52 S.L.R. 476, a roof unexpectedly collapsed under a man's weight.

[33](1973), 40 D.L.R. (3d) 578 (S.C.C.).

[34]*Weld-Blundell v. Stephens*, [1920] A.C. 956 (H.L.).

energy sources such as fire or electricity etc., are treated together in a single category. A number of these cases concern damage as the result of the negligent supervision or handling of animals, particularly horses. If, for example, a horse is left unattended, it is foreseeable that the horse could be frightened in a number of different ways and bolt, and cause a variety of possible injuries. In *Lynch v. Nurdin*[35] the horse was set in motion by a child, and another child who had jumped up on the cart was injured. In *Harris v. Mobbs*[36] the defendant left a horse and plow unattended on a road, which caused another horse to bolt and injure the plaintiff. In *Dorsett v. Adelaide Corp.*[37] an unattended horse and dray backed over the plaintiff tram conductor who was walking on a footpath alongside the tram car. In *Aldham v. United Dairies*[38] the defendant left a horse attached to a milk cart unattended. Rather than being frightened and bolting and running over someone, the horse bit and pawed the passing plaintiff. In all four cases the damage was found not to be too remote given the initial negligence in leaving the horse unattended. While any one of these injuries might not be sufficiently probable to be reasonably foreseeable, the class of such possible injuries is reasonably foreseeable.

In *Lathall v. Joyce & Son*,[39] a bullock being transported to a butcher was negligently allowed to escape. It was foreseeable that the frightened animal might run into or over someone in its escape. Rather, it attacked the plaintiff who was passing on a bicycle. The court held the injury to be too remote because it was unforeseeable that a bullock would attack someone. On our test, and when compared with the four cases involving horses, cited above, *Lathall v. Joyce & Son* is wrongly decided because while an attack on a person was not probable, it was clearly a member of a class of potential ways in which injury could be caused.

Another set of cases involved negligent ejectment. It is reasonably foreseeable that if intoxicated persons are ejected from a place of safety such as a train or a beverage room where their presence is not unlawful, they can get themselves into a situation where they can be injured by being hit by a car on a highway, by another train or by falling down stairs. In four such cases the injury was held not to be too remote.[40]

---

[35](1841), 1 Q.B. 29, 113 E.R. 1041.

[36](1878), 3 Ex. D. 268.

[37][1915] S.A.L.R. 71.

[38][1940] 1 K.B. 507, [1939] 4 All E.R. 522 (C.A.).

[39]55 T.L.R. 994, [1939] 3 All E.R. 854 (K.B.).

[40]*Can. Northern Ry. v. Diplock* (1916), 53 S.C.R. 376, 10 W.W.R. 986, 30 D.L.R. 240; *Howe v. Niagara, St. Catharines etc. Ry.*, 56 O.L.R. 202, 30 C.R.C. 95, [1925] 2 D.L.R. 115 (C.A.); *Menow v. Hornsberger*, [1970] 1 O.R. 54, 7 D.L.R. (3d) 494, affirmed [1971] 1 O.R. 129, 14

Contrast with these the case of *Glover v. London & South Western Ry. Co.*[41] The defendant was wrongfully ejected from a railway carriage and sued for the loss of a pair of racing glasses left behind. The loss was not recoverable, and rightly so, since it was not reasonably foreseeable in itself, nor did it belong to a reasonably foreseeable class of injury.

In *Mellish v. Campbell Storage*[42] a case decided consistent with the revised foreseeability test, the court held that where the defendant negligently damaged a piano, subsequent damage resulting from a fire where the piano was being stored in the warehouse of another company after being repaired was too remote. The decision was right because the damage by fire was not foreseeable in the particular, nor was it the kind of thing likely to happen from the negligent handling of the piano by the movers. In 23 cases of the above type, 21 were correctly decided according to the revised foreseeability test. Of those, 18 held for the plaintiff and three for the defendant.

V.   THIN-SKULL

No prior test for remoteness of damage has disturbed the general principle that the defendant takes his victim as he finds him. What is commonly known as the "thin-skull" principle is in accordance with this writer's test as well: the foreseeable class of risks flowing from a negligent act always encompasses the possibility that a plaintiff will have a predisposition to physical or mental frailty. In fact, recovery is almost invariably given in these cases, whether the precondition is heart disease,[43] haemophilia,[44] schizophrenia,[45] or even bad teeth.[46]

Altogether 90 thin-skull cases were analyzed. Included in this group are cases of physical as well as mental or nervous predisposition in the plaintiff who was exposed to the risk of harm. Cases where a second

---

D.L.R. (3d) 345, which was affirmed (sub nom. *Jordan House Ltd. v. Menow*) 38 D.L.R. (3d) 105 (S.C.C.); *Sherwood v. Hamilton Corp.* (1875), 37 U.C.Q.B. 410 (C.A.). In *Delahanty v. Michigan Central Ry.* (1905), 10 O.L.R. 388 (C.A.), the ejected intoxicated plaintiff wandered onto a bridge, fell off and drowned. The court found no negligence as the evidence disclosed that the plaintiff was not sufficiently intoxicated to be physically impaired. The finding of no negligence precludes a remoteness issue, and thus the case is not included in this analysis.

[41](1867), L.R. 3 Q.B. 25.

[42][1946] 3 W.W.R. 157 (B.C. Co. Ct.).

[43]*Barnaby v. O'Leary* (1956), 5 D.L.R. (2d) 41 (N.S.S.C.).

[44]*Bishop v. Arts & Letters Club of Toronto* (1978), 18 O.R. (2d) 471, 83 D.L.R. (3d) 107 (H.C.).

[45]*Elloway v. Boomars* (1968), 69 D.L.R. (2d) 605 (B.C.S.C.).

[46]*Smith v. Maximovitch* (1968), 68 D.L.R. (2d) 244 (Sask. Q.B.).

person suffers nervous shock on witnessing or learning of a threat to another are considered separately.

Four cases[47] were eliminated because a causal connection was not shown to exist between the negligence of the defendant and the injury suffered by the plaintiff. Evidence of causation is a necessary condition to recovery in the thin-skull cases. In *Foran v. Kapellas*[48] the plaintiff sought to have the damage award increased to compensate for deteriorating health after a car accident. The Supreme Court of Canada refused recovery for this head of damage on the basis that it had not been shown that the accident was the cause of the deteriorating health.

An anomaly in the older cases concerning nervous shock resulted from the decision of the Privy Council in *Victorian Ry. Commrs. v. Coultas*[49] which held there could be no recovery for nervous shock unless it was accompanied by physical injury. The case has long since been disapproved[50] and abandoned as a wrong decision, therefore older cases[51] which followed the *Coultas* decision have been eliminated from consideration.

Of the 88 cases examined, 84 held for the plaintiff and four held for the defendant. Regardless of which test for remoteness was used in the case, the courts have consistently found the possibility of particular abnormal physical and mental susceptibility to be reasonably foreseeable.

The four cases which found for the defendant reflect a predisposition on the part of the judges to discount injury of a psychological nature as an acceptable head of damages. For example, in *Swami v. Lo*[52] the plaintiff's husband was seriously injured in a car accident. He suffered unrelenting pain from which no medication gave him respite, and as a result became seriously depressed and ultimately committed suicide. The British Columbia Supreme Court found for the defendant on the basis that depression and death were not foreseeable eventualities.

---

[47]*Danjanovich v. Buma*, [1970] 3 O.R. 604, 13 D.L.R. (3d) 556 (C.A.); *Foran v. Kapellas*, [1975] 1 S.C.R. 46; *Negretto v. Sayers*, [1963] S.A.S.R. 313 (S.C.); *Strutz v. Ellingson* (1977), 2 A.R. 485 (T.D.).

[48]*Supra*, note 47.

[49](1888), 13 App. Cas. 222 (P.C.).

[50]*Coyle v. John Watson Ltd.*, [1915] A.C. 1 (H.L.), also not followed in *Delieu v. White & Sons*, [1901] 2 K.B. 669 (Div. Ct.).

[51]*Geiger v. G.T.R.* (1905), 10 O.L.R. 511 (Div. Ct.); *Henderson v. Can. Atlantic Ry.* (1898), 25 O.A.R. 437, affirmed 29 S.C.R. 632; *Miner v. C.P.R.* (1911), 18 W.L.R. 476, 3 Alta. L.R. 408 (C.A.); *Penman v. Winnipeg Elec. Ry.*, [1925] 1 W.W.R. 156, [1925] 1 D.L.R. 497 (Man. K.B.).

[52][1980] 1 W.W.R. 379, 11 C.C.L.T. 210, 105 D.L.R. (3d) 451 (B.C.S.C.).

Surely this decision is wrong. Clearly some people are more prone than others to nervous disorders just as some are more prone than others to arthritis. There is no rationale to support a differentiation between physical and mental preconditions. The cases which demand a higher degree of proof that the negligence caused a mental or nervous injury than if the predisposition was physical are anomalies and must be considered to be wrongly decided.

As a general rule, victims who suffer aggravated damage because of a physical or mental precondition will always recover, and their extended injuries will never be too remote, because the possibility of a predisposition to injury is foreseeable as a class of harm. The few counter-examples cannot be distinguished in any rational manner. The weight of authority confirms this argument, as the courts have followed this pattern in more than 95 per cent of the thin-skull cases.

Prima facie the strict application of the "thin-skull" rule might seem overly harsh in that a person responsible for very slight negligence, which would foreseeably bring about only minor damage, could be liable for enormous and unproportionate consequences. This result is contrary to the accepted principle that some degree of proportionality must be maintained between the fault of the defendant and the harm caused by his act. The courts have solved this problem through the assessment of damages. Where the plaintiff has a particular susceptibility which is likely to be triggered by a variety of causes the damage awarded will be decreased significantly on the basis that the same losses would likely be suffered in any event.

The leading case on this issue is *Smith v. Leech Brain & Co.* where a small burn on the lip of a man with a pre-malignant condition led to cancer, and ultimately death. The court considered the evidence that a burn was only one of the agents which could have promoted malignancy and, therefore, cancer to develop. Lord Parker C.J. wrote: "I am told that sunlight, heat and cold, weather, certainly scratches, certainly trauma, can be the promoting agent."[53] The court found that although the burn was in fact the agent, "there was a strong likelihood that at some stage in his life he would develop cancer."[54] Accordingly, there was a substantial reduction in the amount of damages awarded to the widow.

An interesting Canadian example is the case of *Bates v. Fraser*[55] discussed in Chapter Eight where the plaintiff suffered from Parkinson's

---

[53][1962] 2 Q.B. 405 at 412, [1962] 2 W.L.R. 148, [1961] 3 All E.R. 1159.

[54]*Ibid.*, at 413.

[55][1963] 1 O.R. 539, 38 D.L.R. (2d) 30 (H.C.).

disease, but was in a period of remission at the time of the accident, as the result of a loss of memory. She again fell victim to the symptoms of Parkinsonism after another small bump in a minor car accident, caused by the defendant's negligence, restored her memory. Although her physical injury from the accident was very slight, the returned symptoms were so severe as to once again render her an invalid. Mr. Justice Grant, in awarding a mere $3,000 damages, wrote: "If her condition were entirely due to the collision she would be entitled to very extensive compensation."[56] However, the plaintiff was "affected very readily" and "[t]he slightest reason might well have brought about emotional distress which would aggravate distresses and pains of her Parkinsonism."[57]

These cases show that while a strict adherence to the thin-skull rule might appear to work an injustice, in fact proportionality between the degree of wrong and the degree of liability imposed is maintained by the court's assessment of damages. Where it is legally correct to impose liability, but morally unjust to exact complete compensation, the courts can correct this imbalance through their ability to decrease the amount of damages by taking into account the probabilities of other events causing the same loss in the absence of negligence.

VI. MEDICAL COMPLICATIONS

In principle, there is no reason to distinguish the cases of medical complication from the thin-skull cases. As a general rule, all medical complications resulting from an injury are recoverable. This principle obtains regardless of whether the complication arises because of the former injury itself, as where one illness leads to another, or whether a second injury occurs because the plaintiff is rendered awkward by the first injury, or whether the plaintiff is forced to seek medical treatment which causes or creates further injury. Thus, recovery was granted where chronic asthmatic bronchitis developed after a lung injury,[58] where a woman who could not see properly over the neck brace she had to wear after the injury fell again,[59] where the plaintiff was using crutches after an accident and fell down the stairs,[60] and where the plaintiff's ulnar nerve was damaged when he was being treated in hospital for unrelated injuries suffered in a car accident.[61]

---

[56]*Ibid.*, at 36.

[57]*Ibid.*, at 37.

[58]*Lukasta v. Sawchuk*, [1975] W.W.D. 98 (Alta. Dist. Ct.).

[59]*Wieland v. Cyril Lord Carpets*, [1969] 3 All E.R. 1006 (Q.B.).

[60]*Goldhawke v. Harder* (1976), 74 D.L.R. (3d) 721 (B.C.S.C.).

[61]*Papp v. Leclerc* (1977), 16 O.R. (2d) 158, 77 D.L.R. (3d) 536 (C.A.).

Forty-two cases were analyzed where injury was aggravated due to medical complication.[62] Four of these[63] were eliminated from consideration because causation was not proved. Similarly with the thin-skull cases, a clear causal connection between negligence and injury is a necessary condition to recovery for medical complication. One other case was eliminated because it was based on a doctrine of law which has since been abandoned.[64] Out of the 37 remaining cases, 32 held for the plaintiff and five for the defendant. Two of the five cases finding for the defendant are correctly decided[65] and the other three, according to the writer's theory, are wrongly decided.

The three cases which provide counter-examples to the general rule are all based on a rationale of intervening cause. Some courts have accepted the argument that liability for medical complication should not be imposed where the defendant can show negligence on the part of the hospital staff, as this constitutes an intervening act which breaks the chain of causation.[66]

In the case of *David v. Toronto Transit Comm.*[67] the defendant, Toronto Transit Commission, was able to show negligence on the part of the surgeon and therefore liability for aggravated injuries was not imposed on the Commission. Arguably, the fact of negligence on the part of the physician should not influence a court to deny recovery to a plaintiff for aggravated injuries. If risks of medical complications are foreseeable generally, then medical negligence cannot be an unforeseeable possibility. In the case of medical malpractice which produces further injury the defendant should be made jointly and severally liable with the doctor or hospital, and the court can apportion liability.

---

[62]Not included among these is *Ostrowski v. Lotto*, [1973] S.C.R. 220, 31 D.L.R. (3d) 715, affirming [1971] 1 O.R. 372, 15 D.L.R. (3d) 402, which reversed [1969] 1 O.R. 341, 2 D.L.R. (3d) 440, where the Supreme Court of Canada found no negligence on the part of the doctor accused.

[63]*Gordon v. Can. Bank of Commerce*, 44 B.C.R. 213, [1931] 3 W.W.R. 185, 323, [1931] 4 D.L.R. 635 (C.A.); *Hawley v. Ottawa Gas Co.* (1919), 15 O.W.N. 454, affirmed 16 O.W.N. 106 (C.A.) *Oakes v. Spencer*, [1964] 1 O.R. 537, 43 D.L.R. (2d) 127 (C.A.); *Robinson v. Englot*, [1949] 2 W.W.R. 1137 (Man. K.B.).

[64]In *Walker v. Great Northern Ry. Co. of Ireland* (1891), 28 L.R. Ir. 69 (Q.B.), the plaintiff was *en ventre sa mere* and was injured by the defendant's negligence together with her mother who was a paying customer on the train. The court found no cause of action to exist as the only duty owed was to the mother.

[65]*Best v. Samuel Fox & Co.*, [1952] A.C. 716, [1952] 2 All E.R. 394 (H.L.). This is another case on the issue of partial loss of consortium. This is a form of damage which is unforeseeable in the particular or as part of a class of damage. A more complete discussion of the issue is found *supra* under *Dangerous Activity*.

[66]*Papp v. Leclerc, supra*, note 61.

[67](1976), 16 O.R. (2d) 248, 77 D.L.R. (3d) 717 (H.C.).

The class of foreseeable injury in the event of medical complication is defined by determining whether the further injury would have been possible but for the negligence of the defendant. If the accident had never occurred, the plaintiff would never have been exposed to the risk of further injury by medical treatment. In the case of *McKiernan v. Manhire*[68] a woman convalescing in hospital after a car injury fell off a step, further injuring herself. The court held for the defendant, endorsing even in 1977 the direct cause test of *Polemis*.[69] According to the writer's test, *McKieman* is wrongly decided. Owing to the negligence of the defendant, the plaintiff was necessarily hospitalized and subject to all the class of attendant risks which attach to hospitalization. She might have been exposed to a severe infection, such as staphylococcus, or undergone an unnecessary operation by some mistake. Liability should follow for any of these, since all fall within the class of foreseeable risks of medical complication created by the negligence of the defendant.

Intervening cause is not a proper rationale for denying recovery in these cases. Where a cause-effect relationship exists, no medical complication is too remote. The confirmation of this principle is again found in the weight of authority as almost 90 per cent of the cases have been decided in favour of the plaintiff.

VII.   RESCUER

The rescuer should always recover. When a person negligently imperils himself or another, the foreseeable class of risks created includes the possibility that a rescuer will intervene. The advent of a rescuer is foreseeable because, under normal circumstances, it is human nature to try to save others from harm.

At one time the courts, particularly the English courts, adhered to a harsher rule. Where a person voluntarily placed himself in the way of danger in order to rescue another the courts would invoke the doctrine of *volenti*. No recovery was granted to a volunteer. An example of this is the case of *Cutler v. United Dairies (London) Ltd.*[70] where the plaintiff was injured while attempting to arrest a runaway horse in response to cries for help from the driver. The dicta in *Cutler* was later questioned by the English Court of Appeal[71] and the principle applied in the case is now

---

[68](1977), 17 S.A.S.R. 571 (S.C.).

[69]*Ibid.*, at 576. See also Rowe, "The Demise of the Thin Skull Rule?" (1977), 40 M.L.R. 377.

[70][1933] 2 K.B. 297 (C.A.).

[71]*Haynes v. Harwood*, [1934] 2 K.B. 240, affirmed [1935] 1 K.B. 146 (C.A.).

considered to be wrong. The Canadian courts were not so strict in this regard, and very early Canadian decisions rejected the *volenti* doctrine in rescuer cases.[72] Four of the rescuer cases analyzed were based on the outmoded principle that a volunteer does not recover, and therefore these four have been eliminated from consideration.[73]

Of the remaining 29 rescuer cases,[74] 27 or 93 per cent held for the plaintiff. Rescuers of people, animals,[75] and even property[76] have recovered. In *Videan v. Br. Tpt. Comm.*[77] the rescuer of a young trespasser was awarded compensation although it was denied the child himself. Rescuers have recovered when the rescue attempt may have been unnecessary,[78] or was entirely mistaken,[79] if it was a natural reaction in the situation. The rescuer will recover for mental or nervous injury as well as for physical injury.[80] The maxim that rescuers always recover is valid for two reasons. Not only are rescuers foreseeable as a class, but also there is a strong policy consideration underlying the rule in that recovery to rescuers encourages rescue. In one of the two rescue cases decided in favour of the defendant, *Dupuis v. New Regina Trading Co.*,[81] this policy consideration is vividly illustrated. An employee of the defendant negligently imperiled herself, becoming pinned upside-down from an elevator. The plaintiff's husband went to the woman's rescue, fell down the elevator shaft, and was killed. The Saskatchewan Court of Appeal denied recovery to the widow, holding that there had not necessarily been any danger present in the rescue attempt, and notwithstanding the

---

[72]*Love v. New Fairview Corp.* (1904), 10 B.C.R. 330 (C.A.).

[73]*Anderson v. Northern Ry.* (1875), 25 U.C.C.P. 301 (C.A.); *Cutler v. United Dairies (London) Ltd.*, *supra*, note 70; *Kimball v. Butler Bros.* (1910), 15 O.W.R. 221 (C.A.); *The San Onofre*, [1922] P. 243 (C.A.).

[74]Not included with these is *Horsley v. MacLaren*, [1972] S.C.R. 441, 22 D.L.R. (3d) 545, affirming [1970] 2 O.R. 487, 11 D.L.R. (3d) 277, although the dicta in the case with respect to rescuers is frequently cited, because the Ontario Court of Appeal, in a decision affirmed by the Supreme Court of Canada, found no negligence in the defendant's handling of the boat.

[75]*Connell v. Prescott* (1893), 22 S.C.R. 147.

[76]*Hutterley v. Imperial Oil Ltd.*, [1956] O.W.N. 681, 3 D.L.R. (2d) 719 (H.C.); *Steel v. Glasgow Iron & Steel Co. Ltd.*, [1944] S.C. 237; *Hyett v. Great Western Ry.*, [1948] 1 K.B. 345, [1947] 2 All E.R. 264 (C.A.).

[77][1963] 2 Q.B. 650, [1963] 3 W.L.R. 374, [1963] 2 All E.R. 860 (C.A.).

[78]*Morgan v. Aylen*, [1942] 1 All E.R. 489 (K.B.).

[79]*Ould v. Butler's Wharf*, [1953] 2 Lloyd's Rep. 44 (Q.B.).

[80]In *Chadwick v. Br. Ry. Bd.*, [1967] 1 W.L.R. 912, [1967] 2 All E.R. 945 (sub nom. *Chadwock v. Br. Tpt. Comm.*) (Q.B.), the plaintiff recovered for an attack of anxiety suffered after he helped victims of a train wreck.

[81][1943] 2 W.W.R. 593, [1943] 4 D.L.R. 275 (Sask. C.A.).

danger, the company itself had not been negligent — only its employee had been negligent. The outcome of *Dupuis* would certainly tend to discourage rescue attempts! Undoubtedly the case is wrong. Rescuing a person from a possible fall down an elevator shaft is plainly a dangerous task, and companies are indeed liable for the negligent acts of their employees within company premises. Also, in terms of policy, it would be a sad comment on the legal system if a person had to consider the possible impairment of his legal position before endeavoring to rescue another.

In *Urbanski v. Patel; Firman v. Patel*[82] a father who volunteered a kidney for transplant, after the defendant doctors had negligently removed his daughter's only kidney by mistake, was compensated for the operation. Mr. Justice Wilson rejected the argument that the father had knowingly and wilfully accepted the risk by offering his kidney for transplant, or that the operation was unforeseeable. He found the father's act of donating his kidney to be a foreseeable consequence in accordance "with the principle developed in the many 'rescue' cases."[83] This principle is the view that, whatever the circumstances, a rescuer is always foreseeable and should never be denied recovery. It would be manifestly wrong to penalize a person for a selfless act of humanity.

VIII.   NERVOUS SHOCK

Recovery for nervous shock suffered by third parties has been an issue of extreme difficulty for courts. Judges from all jurisdictions have struggled with the determination of the outer limits of liability for nervous shock and have frequently insisted that an arbitrary cut-off point is necessary for reasons of policy. The history of the gradual broadening of recovery for nervous shock has been recently set out by the House of Lords in *McLoughlin v. O'Brian*[84] where the plaintiff's husband and children were injured, one child fatally so, in a car accident. On learning of the accident the plaintiff rushed to the hospital where she saw her husband and children begrimed and bloody and where she was told of her daughter's death. As a result of witnessing this calamity the plaintiff suffered severe nervous shock. The English Court of Appeal accepted the argument that it was foreseeable that the plaintiff would suffer nervous shock under these circumstances, but denied recovery to Mrs. McLoughlin. The court decided that, for reasons of policy, a limitation

---

[82](1978), 2 L.M.Q. 54, 84 D.L.R. (3d) 650 (Man. Q.B.).

[83]*Ibid.*, at 671.

[84][1982] 2 W.L.R. 982, [1982] 2 All E.R. 298, reversing [1981] 1 Q.B. 599, [1981] 2 W.L.R. 1014, [1981] 1 All E.R. 809 (H.L.).

on liability was necessary and the court chose presence at the scene of the accident as the limiting factor.

The House of Lords overturned the Court of Appeal decision and granted Mrs. McLoughlin damages for nervous shock. The court reasoned that justice is not served by allowing damages to the mother who witnesses her child's death and suffers shock, but withholding recovery from the mother who immediately after the accident comes upon the scene of destruction, or from the mother who, almost like a rescuer, rushes to hospital to attend her family and witnesses a more horrific scene than she had anticipated.

Lord Wilberforce and Lord Edmund-Davies agreed with the Court of Appeal that the defendant's liability must be limited to a certain class but ruled that the limit must not be arbitrarily set — it must emerge from the legal principles enunciated in the cases. Lord Wilberforce found three principles, or tests, to exist. A test of proximity should be used by the courts, but the test should not be restricted to actual presence at the scene of an accident. It should be expanded to include the relative who very soon after an accident comes upon its aftermath or consequences. A test of consanguinity should also be applied although the court has the ability to consider the nature of the relationship. A very dear friend will possibly be awarded damages for nervous shock, but a mere bystander will never recover. Finally, the way in which the shock occurs must be considered. The shock must be caused by the actual sight or sound of the accident or its aftermath and not by a communication from a third party. Lord Wilberforce concluded that this set of principles represented no new departure or arbitrary cut-off point for recovery, but rather was a statement of the existing law. The cases from all jurisdictions would appear, for the most part, to support his opinion.

Fifty-seven nervous shock cases were considered. Of the 32 cases which held for the plaintiffs, 28 are cases in which a close family relative was either present at the scene or came upon its immediate aftermath, and in another two cases recovery was given to close friends present at the scene. In the remaining two cases which held for the plaintiff, the nervous shock victim recovered despite not having been present at the scene of the accident.[85] Twenty-five cases were decided in favour of the defendant. Three of these were eliminated because they were decided at a time when nervous shock was not considered a proper head of damage, especially in the absence of any physical injury to the plaintiff.[86] In eight

---

[85]*Brown v. Mount Barker Soldiers' Hosp. Inc.*, [1934] S.A.S.R. 128 (S.C.); *McCarthy v. Walsh*, [1965] I.R. 246 (Ir. S.C.).

[86]*Baker v. Bolton* (1808), 1 Camp. 493, 170 E.R. 1033 (N.P.); *Campbell v. James Henderson Ltd.*, [1915] 1 S.L.T.R. 419 (Outer House); *Flemington v. Smithers* (1826), 2 C. & P. 292, 172 E.R. 131 (N.P.).

cases the plaintiff was not present at the scene, and in a further two the plaintiff did not actually witness the event but was informed of the injury later. In three cases the plaintiff was not a near family relative and in another the plaintiff suffered shock on reading an erroneous report of injury to her family. In one case a mother was denied recovery when she overreacted to her children's illness where the injury was neither permanent nor very serious. Altogether four cases are wrongly decided.[87] In these four the plaintiff was present at the accident or its immediate aftermath and witnessed the events but the court denied recovery for nervous shock. Forty-eight out of fifty-four cases, or 93 per cent, have been *decided according to the test prescribed in McLoughlin* by Lords Wilberforce and Edmund-Davies. In many of the judgments the courts have arrived at the proper conclusion either without fully stating the reasons for their decision or by justifying the decision in terms of policy. Clearly the same principles that Lord Wilberforce delineated have been at work at a subliminal level in other decisions.

Lord Russell of Killowen, Lord Scarman, and Lord Bridge of Harwick were prepared to go further in their decisions in *McLoughlin v. O'Brian* than Lord Wilberforce and Lord Edmund-Davies. They expressly rejected the placing of any limits on recovery on grounds of policy if the nervous shock was foreseeable. Thus being present at the scene of the accident or seeing the aftermath shortly thereafter was, for them, not a necessary condition for recovery. If the nervous shock is foreseeable then recovery should be given and it is the proper function of the legislature, not the judiciary, to place limits on the grounds of policy where the case falls within a legal principle such as that of foreseeability. Thus *Abramzik v. Brenner,*[88] where a mother failed to recover for nervous shock suffered after being informed of the death of two of her children and the serious injury of a third in a motor vehicle accident, would no longer be good law.

One risk of negligence which causes injury is that a near relative of the victim will be present and will suffer shock. The risk does not include every bystander who is without sufficient fortitude to endure the calamities that ordinarily occur in daily life or, as Lord Porter characterized the type in *Hay (or Bourhill) v. Young*, "who does not possess the customary phlegm."[89] Nor can the class of persons extend to every relative and

---

[87]*Chester v. Waverley Mun. Council* (1939), 62 C.L.R. 1 (H.C.); *Finbow v. Domino* (1957), 65 Man. R. 240, 23 W.W.R. 97, 11 D.L.R. (2d) 493 (Q.B.); *Griffiths v. C.P.R.* (1978), 6 B.C.L.R. 115 (C.A.); *Kernested v. Desorcy*, [1978] 3 W.W.R. 623, affirmed [1979] 1 W.W.R. 512 (Man. C.A.).

[88](1967), 62 W.W.R. 332, 65 D.L.R. (2d) 651 (Sask. C.A.).

[89][1943] A.C. 92 at 117, [1942] 2 All E.R. 396 (H.L.).

friend who is told of tragedy but does not witness it. Every grievor has no doubt suffered some shock due to the loss or injury of a loved one, but that tends to be less severe than the shock from actually witnessing the accident.

Nervous shock has been held in *McLoughlin v. O'Brian* to be recoverable providing it is foreseeable. The closer the familial or emotional relationship the greater will be the probability that shock will be suffered. As well, the closer the sufferer of shock is to actually witnessing the injuries of a loved one, the greater the likelihood of shock. While both consanguinity and proximity to the scene of an accident may no longer be a necessary condition for recovery, at least one or the other would have to be present before one could say that the shock was foreseeable. Of these two factors the family relationship seems to be the more important so far as foreseeability is concerned. The more serious or tragic the nature of the injury the less the need for some visual impact to trigger the shock. The effect of *McLoughlin v. O'Brian* is to allow courts to find liability with only one of what used to be two necessary conditions where there are special circumstances relating to the severity of the accident.

IX. CONCLUSION

It is proposed that the foreseeability test for remoteness be applied to classes of injury or damage rather than to the particulars of the specific cases. The recent decision of the English Court of Appeal in *Lamb v. Camden London Borough Council*[90] graphically demonstrates the problems which can arise when the test used is the foreseeability of the particular damaging event. The plaintiff in that case let her house to a tenant and moved to New York. The local council, while replacing a sewer, broke a water main close to the foundations of the plaintiff's house. The water washed out the soil from under the foundation causing subsidence and extensive damage to the structure, necessitating the termination of the lease and storage of the plaintiff's furniture. The plaintiff had the house secured and boarded up awaiting repairs. Squatters broke in and extensively damaged and vandalized the interior of the house. The council admitted liability for £50,000 damage to the structure arising from the subsidence. They disclaimed liability for a further £30,000 damage caused by the squatters on the grounds that this damage was too remote.

This case raises all the problems of distinguishing between degrees of foreseeability which are inherent in using the traditional forms of the foreseeability test, and can be used to demonstrate how these can be avoided by using our restatement.

---

[90][1981] Q.B. 625, [1981] 2 W.L.R. 1038, [1981] 2 All E.R. 408.

The official referee held that although squatting was at the time a reasonably foreseeable risk, it is not enough to demonstrate that the damage was reasonably foreseeable; it is necessary to go further and to show that the act was *likely* to occur. In this particular neighbourhood, according to the referee, squatting was not likely to occur, even though it was reasonably foreseeable that it could occur. Lord Denning M.R. rejected the various forms of the foreseeability test cited in argument and held the damage to be too remote on grounds of policy. Lord Justice Oliver found the damage to be not reasonably foreseeable, and Lord Justice Watkins found the damage to be too remote even though he said that he would regard "that damage or something like it as reasonably foreseeable in these times."[91]

All three judges of the Court of Appeal agreed that if the house had been in a different area of London, where there was a higher probability of squatters breaking in, this danger would not be too remote. In certain areas of a city, vacant premises are in danger of vandalism, not just from squatters, but a variety of people in a number of different ways. The plaintiff's house was not located in such an area and thus not subject to this class of risk.

The *Lamb* case is not a difficult one. The referee and all three judges of the Court of Appeal were in agreement that the damage was too remote. The difficulty came about when the judges attempted to justify their decision in terms of the reasonable foreseeability of this particular event.

Lord Justice Watkins clearly articulated what most judges feel when dealing with an issue of remoteness. He stated:

"A robust and sensible approach to this very important area of the study of remoteness will more often than not produce, I think, an instinctive feeling that the event or act being weighed in the balance is too remote to sound in damages for the plaintiff. I do not pretend that in all cases the answer will come easily to the inquirer. But that the question must be asked and answered in all these cases I have no doubt."[92]

It probably is the instinctive feeling of judges which is the bottom line in remoteness cases. The fact that, as has been shown, the instinctive feeling of judges has a 90 per cent conformity would indicate that some basic moral principles about responsibility and blame are at work at an unconscious level. The intention has been to articulate that principle in the form of the following restatement of the foreseeability rule: *Damages resulting from a negligent action are not too remote if they are reasonably*

---

[91]*Ibid.*, at 421.
[92]*Ibid.*

foreseeable in the particular, or are one of the reasonably foreseeable class of injuries.

In particular, it is reasonably foreseeable: 1) that dangerous activities when carried out negligently create a wide variety of particular kinds of risks of harm; 2) that injury to persons can also result in further damage from particular susceptibilities or medical complication to the injured person or to others: and 3) that the creation of a risk invites rescue.

Therefore it is concluded that as a general rule:

1. No physical injury or property damage caused by a motor vehicle accident is too remote.

2. No physical injury or property damage caused by a highly dangerous activity such as that involving the handling of explosives, highly inflammable or toxic substances, high-voltage electricity fire, or use of dangerous objects or machinery is too remote.

3. No increased physical or emotional injury resulting from an unusual or particular susceptibility of a person suffering damage as a result of a negligent act is too remote.

4. No medical complication resulting from an injury to a person whether or not the complications are due to an act of a third party, whether negligent or not, is too remote.

5. No physical or emotional injury suffered by a rescuer is too remote.

6. Nervous shock inflicted on a near family relative as a result of witnessing, coming upon the immediate aftermath, or being informed of an accident causing injury or death is not too remote.

Many of the situations encompassed by rules 1 to 6 will involve parties further than the person who causes the initial risk and the person to whom the risk is caused. Some third parties such as rescuers may be injured as well as the person who suffers as the result of the creation of the initial risk which is the foundation of the finding of negligence. Other third parties such as doctors who treat the plaintiff may increase the initial injury or cause subsequent damage of a different kind. In all such cases the damage in issue is not too remote if it is foreseeable in the particular, or is a member of a foreseeable class of persons or events. Thus the mere fact that injury or loss is a result of an intervening act will not make it too remote. On the other hand, even if the negligence which made the intervening act possible was in the context of driving a motor vehicle or in the use of a dangerous substance or instrument, the damage will be too remote if the intervening act was neither foreseeable in the particular, nor was a member of a foreseeable class. No test can avoid hard cases or difficult decisions, but at least we can be clear about our concepts. If we are unclear in the concepts and tests we apply to the facts then we will inevitably produce a high degree of indeterminacy in that area of the law. If we become clear about our concepts and tests we may never be able to accurately predict the outcome of every case, but we ought to be able to achieve at least a 90 per cent accuracy.

The revised foreseeability test is consistent with the existing leading authorities, *Wagon Mound (No. 1)*, *Wagon Mound (No. 2)* and *Hughes v. Lord Advocate*. In fact, it is the only interpretation of the foreseeability rule which allows us to reconcile *Wagon Mound (No. 1)*, which found the damage in issue too remote, and *Wagon Mound (No. 2)*, which found the same kind of damage arising out of the same accident not too remote. The test of foreseeability articulated and applied by the Privy Council in *Wagon Mound (No. 1)* is not the same as the test articulated and applied by the Privy Council in *Wagon Mound (No. 2)*. The version of the foreseeability test as applied to classes of events as well as to particular events is consistent with both versions.

Furthermore it is consistent with and similar to the version of the foreseeability test articulated by the House of Lords in *Hughes v. Lord Advocate* in which the test was stated in terms of similar kinds of damage. Kinds of damage is a class of similar damages. *Hughes v. Lord Advocate* is authority for using a class interpretation for the foreseeability test. A foreseeability test in terms of reasonably foreseeable classes of damaging events gives us a convergence of the three leading authorities. Thus there is a way of "emerging out of the maze of authorities on the subject of remoteness into the light of a clear understanding of it."[93]

---

[93]*Ibid.*, at 419, *per* Watkins L.J.

11

REMOTENESS AND ECONOMIC LOSS

I. INTRODUCTION

Where an action lies concurrently in both contract and tort, questions can arise as to which set of principles should govern where there is a difference, as, for example, where there is a divergence in the limitation periods or remedies available. At first glance the test for remoteness of damages in contract as set out in *Hadley v. Baxendale* as damage "such as may reasonably be supposed to have been in the contemplation of both parties . . . as the probable result of the breach,"[1] and the reasonable foreseeability test of *Wagon Mound (No. 1)* seem almost equivalent. In fact, one of the reasons the Privy Council gave for rejecting the *Polemis* test of remoteness was that it was inconsistent with *Hadley v. Baxendale* when "it had been universally accepted that the law in regard to damages for breach of contract and for tort was, generally speaking . . . the same."[2] There is a substantial difference between the test of *Hadley v. Baxendale* and that of the law of negligence when the qualifications on *Wagon Mound (No. 1)* in *Hughes v. Lord Advocate*,[3] *Wagon Mound*

---

[1] (1854), 9 Ex. 341, 156 E.R. 145 at 151. Although the test for remoteness of damage in *Hadley v. Baxendale* is traditionally referred to as containing two rules: (1) damages "as may fairly and reasonably be considered either arising naturally, i.e., according to the usual course of things, from such breach of contract itself" and (2) or such (damages) "as may reasonably be supposed to have been in the contemplation of both parties at the time they made the contract, as the probable result of the breach of it," they are both generally taken to form a part of the single principle that a person is liable for only those damages which are reasonably foreseeable as liable to result from the breach of contract: *Koufos v. C. Czarnikow Ltd.*, [1969] 1 A.C. 350 at 385 and 415, [1967] 3 W.L.R. 1491, [1967] 3 All E.R. 686 (sub nom. *The Heron II; Koufos v. C. Czarnikow Ltd.*) (H.L.), and *Victoria Laundry (Windsor) Ltd. v. Newman Indust. Ltd.*, [1949] 2 K.B. 528 at 539, [1949] 1 All E.R. 997 (C.A.). For a discussion of the issue of remoteness of damages in contract cases, see Swinton, "Foreseeability: Where should the Award of Contract Damages Cease?" in Reiter and Swan, *Studies in Contract Law* (1980), at 61-91.

[2] *Overseas Tankship (U.K.) v. Morts Dock & Enrg. Co. (The Wagon Mound)*, [1961] A.C. 388 at 419, [1961] 2 W.L.R. 126, [1961] 1 All E.R. 404 (P.C.).

[3] [1963] A.C. [1963] 2 W.L.R. 779, [1963] 1 All E.R. 705 (H.L.).

(No. 2),[4] and *Smith v. Leech Brain & Co. Ltd.*[5] (the thin-skull rule) are taken into account. Yet, on the other hand, in a number of recent decisions courts have taken the position that where a cause of action lies concurrently in contract and in tort there should be no disparity in regard to the issue or remoteness of damages.[6]

If the question of whether such damage in a particular case is or is not too remote is not to turn on whether or not the cause of action is brought in negligence or contract, then the test for remoteness must be the same for each of these two areas of the law. In *Koufos v. C. Czarnikow Ltd.*[7] the House of Lords rejected the use of the tort version of the foreseeability test of remoteness as unsuitable or unhelpful in the context of a breach of contract. Lord Upjohn stated: "But in tort a different test has been adopted in expanding the basic law of damages."[8]

In the case of *H. Parsons (Livestock) Ltd. v. Uttley Ingham & Co.*[9] the plaintiff sued the defendants for damages they suffered as a result of their pigs eating mouldy pig nuts. The pig nuts had become mouldy because the defendants had not properly installed the bulk food storage hopper which they built for the plaintiff, and were thus in breach of their contract. The English Court of Appeal, while accepting the declaration of the House of Lords in *Koufos v. C. Czarnikow Ltd.* that the test of remoteness of damages is different for tort than the one to be used for contract, at the same time were unanimous in holding that "the law must be such that, in a factual situation . . . the amount of damages recoverable does not depend upon whether, as a matter of legal classification, the plaintiff's cause of action is breach of contract or tort."[10]

Lord Denning M.R. attempted to resolve this apparent dichotomy by drawing a distinction between loss of profits and physical damages done to persons or their property, and/or for "ensuing expense."[11]

---

[4]*Overseas Tankship (U.K.) v. Miller S.S. Co. Pty.*, [1967] 1 A.C. 617, [1966] 3 W.L.R. 498, [1966] 2 All E.R. 709 (P.C.).

[5][1962] 2 Q.B. 405, [1962] 2 W.L.R. 148, [1961] 3 All E.R. 1159.

[6]See, e.g., *H. Parsons (Livestock) v. Uttley Ingham & Co.*, [1978] Q.B. 791, [1977] 3 W.L.R. 990, [1978] 1 All E.R. 525 (C.A.); *Baud Corp. N.V. v. Brook; Asamera Oil Corp. v. Sea Oil & Gen. Corp.*, [1979] 1 S.C.R. 633, [1978] 6 W.W.R. 301, 5 B.L.R. 225, 89 D.L.R. (3d) 1, 23 N.R. 181, 12 A.R. 271, varied [1979] 1 S.C.R. 677, [1979] 3 W.W.R. 93, 10 C.P.C. 166, 25 N.R. 451, 14 A.R. 407.

[7]*Supra*, note 1.

[8]*Ibid.*, at 422.

[9]*Supra*, note 6.

[10]*Ibid.*, at 536, *per* Scarman L.J.

[11]*Ibid.*, at 532.

Presumably the test of *Hadley v. Baxendale*, or an adoption thereof suitable for torts, would be applied to loss of profits irrespective of whether they arose from a breach of contract or a tortious act, while the test of remoteness in tort would be used for physical damage to person or property and ensuing expenses irrespective of whether the negligence constituted a breach of contract.

Lords Scarman and Orr, however, concluded that the cases do not support a distinction in law between loss of profit and physical damage, nor did they think such a distinction ought to be drawn.[12] They are right in this regard because often a loss of profits arises from physical damage. The distinction to be drawn should not be between different kinds of damages, but between different kinds of risks. If we draw a distinction between acts which create risks of physical injury to persons or property, and acts which create risks of only pure economic loss, the test for remoteness could be different for each, but within each of the two categories of contract and tort the test for remoteness should be the same.

The more narrow test of *Hadley v. Baxendale* is:

> "Now we think the proper rule in such a case as the present is this:— Where two parties have made a contract which one of them has broken, the damages which the other party ought to receive in respect of such breach of contract should be such as may fairly and reasonably be considered either arising naturally, i.e., according to the usual course of things, from such breach of contract itself, or such as may reasonably be supposed to have been in the contemplation of both parties at the time they made the contract, as the probable result of the breach of it."[13]

By substituting for the word "contract" other forms of relationships such as fiduciary or those arising in a *Hedley Byrne & Co. v. Heller & Partners* situation,[14] we have an adequate test for remoteness of damages for pure economic loss where no risks of physical injury are involved, whether or not liability is contractual, tortious, or both. Equally, the test of remoteness of damages for physical injury to persons and property, and for economic loss arising therefrom, *prima facie* at least should be the same whether or not the negligence constitutes a breach of contract.

II.   THE DUAL TESTS FOR BOTH CONTRACT AND TORT

An examination of the cases involving issues of remoteness of economic loss clearly shows that the courts have applied a different test to economic loss arising from physical injury to persons or damage to

---

[12]*Ibid.*, at 534 and 535.

[13](1859), 9 Ex. 341, 156 E.R. 145 at 151.

[14][1964] A.C. 465, [1963] 3 W.L.R. 101, [1963] 2 All E.R. 575 (H.L.).

property than they have to economic loss where no risk of physical damage is involved.

In those cases where recovery is given for pure economic loss arising from conduct which creates no risk of physical harm to either persons or property, the losses are those which fall precisely within the confines of the risk. Recovery in those cases falling under the *Hedley Byrne* rule *and not involving risk of physical harm* has been given for the difference between the actual value of the shares, a business or a building and the actual price paid as a result of negligent misstatements, but not for loss of potential or actual profits as a result of the investment, or other peripheral kinds of economic loss.[15] An examination, on the other hand, of the cases in which an issue of remoteness has arisen in regard to economic loss arising from physical injury to persons or damage to property will show that, except for one particular problem unique to economic loss, the test of remoteness for economic loss is the same as that used for the physical injury itself which gives rise to the economic loss.

One of the basic differences between physical injury to persons or property and economic loss arising therefrom is that the causal chains for physical damage tend to be much shorter than those for economic loss. The physical consequences of negligent actions tend to be much more limited than are the economic consequences.

In order that recovery for economic loss does not result in what Cardozo C.J. aptly describes as "liability in an indeterminate amount for an indeterminate time to an indeterminate class,"[16] there must be some limitations on the amount of recovery, the numbers of those who can recover, and the time within which the loss can arise. These limitations must be such that they form a part of the rule of the case when the

---

[15]See, *e.g., W.B. Anderson & Sons v. Rhodes (Liverpool)*, [1967] 2 All E.R. 850; *Bango v. Holt*, [1971] 5 W.W.R. 522, 21 D.L.R. (2d) 472 (B.C. S.C.); *Windsor Motors Ltd. v. Powell River* (1969), 68 W.W.R. 173, 4 D.L.R. (3d) 155 (B.C. C.A.). Contrast the above cases with *Sealand of the Pac. Ltd. v. Ocean Cement Ltd.*, [1973] 3 W.W.R. 60, 33 D.L.R. (3d) 625 (B.C. S.C.), where the court applied the *Hedley Byrne* rule to a negligent misstatement which resulted in physical damage to property, and gave damages for loss of profits. In *Esso Petroleum Co. v. Mardon*, [1976] Q.B. 801, at 821, [1976] 2 W.L.R. 583, [1976] 2 All E.R. 5 (C.A.), while Lord Denning M.R. declined to award the loss of profits which would have been made had the representation as to volume of sales been true, he nevertheless awarded a sum for loss of the profits which the plaintiff would have likely made had he not entered into the contract with the defendant, but instead had made it with someone else. Alternative opportunity costs were also awarded in *Wooldridge v. H.B. Nickerson & Sons Ltd.* (1980), 115 D.L.R. (3d) 97, 40 N.S.R. (2d) 388, 73 A.P.R. 388 (C.A.).

[16]*Ultramares Corp. v. Touche* (1931), 174 N.E. 441 at 444, 255 N.Y. 170 (C.A.).

particular decision is generalized; otherwise, there will be a remoteness problem.

The most common example of economic loss is loss of earnings or earning capacity as the result of negligently caused physical injury. Such losses raise no problem of remoteness because the amount is limited by prior earning capacity, the class who can recover is limited to those injured, and the damages are limited in regard to time by the date of loss of earnings or earning power and run to the time when earning power is restored or when one would anticipate earnings to cease in the normal event.

Economic loss suffered by the family or dependants of a person killed is recoverable under statute from the person negligently causing the death.[17] Such loss causes no problems of remoteness because the class that can recover is narrowly defined, the damages are limited in terms of amount by the dead person's earning record and capacity, and in regard to time by the estimated length of what his or her working career would have been if not interrupted by death.

Economic loss suffered as the result of a chattel being damaged is recoverable because such a loss is limited to the owner of the chattel, in amount by the nature of the chattel and its use, and in time by the period of its repair or replacement.[18]

A further line of cases allows recovery for economic loss where it can be directly related in some way to physical damage.[19] By relating economic loss to physical damage certain limitations can be placed on the class of people who can recover, the amount of loss, and the time within which the loss must arise. However, not just any kind of physical damage will do. It is hard to justify why a little property damage in itself should suddenly make a huge economic loss recoverable where it would not have been so in the absence of property damage. The English Court of Appeal was quite correct when in *S.C.M. v. W.J. Whittall & Son.*,[20] and

---

[17]Such acts are based on the English Fatal Accidents Act (Lord Campbell's Act), 1846 (9 & 10 Vict.), c. 93, as amended in 1864 (27 & 28 Vict.), c. 95, and again in 1905 (8 Edw. 7), c. 7.

[18]*H.M.S. London*, [1914] P. 72. In *Dredger Liesbosch v. S.S. Edison (Owners)*, [1933] A.C. 449 (H.L.), the capitalized value of insurance upon the dredger was allowed as an item of damage. See also *Morrison S.S. Co. v. Greystoke Castle (Cargo Owners)*, [1947] A.C. 265, [1946] 2 All E.R. 696 (H.L.).

[19]*Seaway Hotels Ltd. v. Gragg (Can.) Ltd.*, [1959] O.R. 177, 17 D.L.R. (2d) 292, affirmed [1959] O.R. 581, 21 D.L.R. (2d) 264 (Ont. C.A.); *British Celanese v. A.H. Hunt (Capacitors)*, [1969] 1 W.L.R. 959, [1969] 2 All E.R. 1252 (Q.B.); *Courtenay v. Knutson; Clausen v. Knutson* (1957), 32 W.W.R. 481, 26 D.L.R. (2d) 768 (B.C. S.C.).

[20][1971] 1 Q.B. 137 at 150-51, [1970] 3 W.L.R. 694, [1970] 3 All E.R. 245 (C.A.).

Spartan Steel & Alloys v. Martin & Co. (Contractors).[21] It rejected the "parasitic" damage doctrine (which would allow recovery for pure economic loss providing some physical damage had taken place) and refused to follow the decision of the Ontario Court of Appeal in *Seaway Hotels Ltd. v. Gragg (Can.) Ltd.*[22] In the latter case, the court held that a hotel could recover profits lost as a result of being unable to operate due to the defendant's negligent severing of the power lines. The justification for the recovery of the pure economic loss was that the hotel had also suffered physical damage in that some food spoilage had taken place because of the failure of the refrigeration equipment. Surely recovery for loss of profits could not be justly denied an adjoining hotel merely because it was not serving food and consequently had suffered no physical damage.

Some judges have attempted to limit economic loss to that which arises "directly" from or is consequential on physical damage, but they have produced no criteria for deciding when an economic loss is direct or when it is indirect, or when it is directly consequential.[23] Without such criteria, a statement that a particular damage is direct or indirect is only a conclusion, and not the reason for reaching it.

Physical damage can only be used to limit recovery of economic loss to a limited class, for a limited amount, arising within a specifiable time when the physical damage is a necessary condition for the suffering of the economic loss. If the economic loss is such that other people could suffer the same kind of economic loss as the result of the negligence, without the presence of any physical damage, then it cannot be a relevant factor in setting limits on recovery. This would explain the judgment in *Spartan Steel & Alloys v. Martin & Co. (Contractors)* where damages were given for the reduction in value of the oxygenated melt, and for the loss of profit on that melt, but not for the loss of profits in regard to any unprocessed melts which loss of profits would be in no different position than those suffered by any business which had to close down because it was unable to function without power.

It is difficult to see how pure economic loss arising from actions creating no risk of physical injury to persons or property can give rise to foreseeable economic loss "in an indeterminate amount for an indeterminate time to an indeterminate class." In regard to fiduciary and *Hedley*

---

[21][1973] 1 Q.B. 27 at 35 and 49, [1972] 3 W.L.R. 502, [1972] 3 All E.R. 557 (C.A.).

[22]*Supra*, note 19.

[23]*S.C.M.. v. W.J. Whittall & Son, supra*, note 20, at 352; *Spartan Steel & Alloys v. Martin & Co. (Contractors), supra*, note 21, at 46.

Byrne kinds of relationships the duty relationship itself furnishes the limits to recovery. In those limited cases where there is recovery in the law of torts for a breach of a promise, the ambit of the promise confines recovery in much the same way privity of contract generally limits recovery to the contacting parties, in regard to specific subjects and within a specified time. In the breach of promise case of *Baxter & Co. v. Jones*[24] which has been followed in *Myers v. Thompson*[25] and *Kostiuk v. Union Accept. Corp.*[26] the court perceived no problems at all in giving recovery for pure economic loss. We can conclude from a study of the cases where damages are awarded for pure economic loss in which there is no risk of physical injury or damage, that an economic loss will be too remote unless it is foreseeable in the particular with a fair degree of probability. An examination of about 125 cases where an issue of remoteness of economic loss was raised shows that in general, except for one qualification to be developed below, the test for remoteness of economic loss arising from physical injury or damage to property is the same as that used for the physical injury itself. In Chapter Ten that test was set out as follows: Damages resulting from a negligent action are not too remote if they are reasonably foreseeable in the particular, or are one of a reasonably foreseeable class of injuries.

Most damage awards for economic loss caused by an injury to the person are in the form of compensation for lost wages or salary, and most damage awards for economic loss caused by damage to property consist of compensation for the resulting loss of income or profits. Recovery is also given for a wide range of reasonably foreseeable ancillary classes of economic loss such as costs of renting substitutes for damaged property,[27] the reduction in value of property,[28] or clean-up

---

[24](1903), 6 O.L.R. 360 (C.A.).

[25][1967] 2 O.R. 335, 63 D.L.R. (2d) 476, affirmed [1967] 2 O.R. 335n, 63 D.L.R. (2d) 476n (C.A.).

[26][1969] I.L.R. 1-239, 66 D.L.R. (2d) 430 (Sask. Q.B.).

[27]See *e.g. Athabasca Airways Ltd. v. Sask. Govt. Airways* (1957), 23 W.W.R. 651, 77 C.R.T.C. 65, 12 D.L.R. (2d) 187, varied 25 W.W.R. 401, 78 C.R.T.C. 246, 14 D.L.R. (2d) 66 (Sask. C.A.); *Cammionneurs du Nord Ltée v. Sealy* (1982), 39 N.B.R. (2d) 272, 103 A.P.R. 272 (C.A.); *MacGillivray v. Ram* (1982), 52 N.S.R. (2d) 486, 106 A.P.R. 486 (T.D.); *Romano v. Smith* (1982), 41 N.B.R. (2d) 360, 107 A.P.R. 360 (Q.B.); *Smith v. Melancon*, [1976] 4 W.W.R. 9 (B.C. S.C.); *Summers v. March* (1982), 37 Nfld. & P.E.I.R. 437, 104 A.P.R. 437 (Nfld. Dist. Ct.); *Gardner v. R.*, [1983] N.Z.L.R. 730 (C.A.).

[28]See, *e.g., Black v. Keys, Rural Man. of Keys No. 303* (1981), 13 Sask. R. (2d) 286 (Q.B.); *Duce v. Rourke; Pearce v. Rourke* (1951), 1 W.W.R. (N.S.) 305 (Alta. S.C.); *Dutton v. Bognor Regis Urban Dist. Council*, [1972] 1 Q.B. 373, [1972] 2 W.L.R. 299, [1972] 1 Lloyd's Rep. 227, [1972] 1 All E.R. 462 (C.A.); *Gareau v. Montreal Street Ry.*, [1901] S.C.R. 463; *Batty v. Metro. Property Realisations*, [1978] Q.B. 554, [1978] 2 W.L.R. 500, [1978] 2 All E.R. 445

costs.[29] Out of 77 cases where plaintiffs who suffered physical injury to either their person or property also suffered economic loss, the plaintiffs recovered for the economic loss in 53 of the cases. Of the remaining 24 cases where recovery was not given, all involved some extra-causal factor for which the defendant was not responsible.

III.   MULTIPLE CAUSES

The leading case in the area of multiple causes for economic loss is the House of Lords decision in *Dredger Liesbosch v. S.S. Edison*.[30] The plaintiffs sued for both physical damage and pure economic loss suffered as a result of the defendant's negligent sinking of the plaintiff's dredger. Although there was another dredger readily available as a replacement, the plaintiff was not in a financial position to purchase it. Therefore, they had to make alternative arrangements which, in the long run, turned out to be more costly. The court allowed recovery for the pure economic loss suffered as a result of contract penalties for delay, but only up to the time within which another dredger could have been purchased and refitted. Penalties suffered from the hypothetical point of time until a replacement dredger was actually obtained, and the extra costs in obtaining it due to the plaintiffs' own indigency, were all held to be too remote.

The *Liesbosch* decision, in effect, rejects an analogue of the thin-skull rule as applicable to a plaintiff's financial condition. Thin-skull situations are cases of multiple causation, that is, cases where even given the defendant's negligent actions the particular damage would not have happened or would not have been as extensive without some further causal factor which is independent of the defendant's negligence (in thin-skull cases, a particular physical susceptibility of the plaintiff). Given that multiple causes meet the remoteness foreseeability test, there is no reason why there should be any distinctions drawn between

---

(C.A.); *Bowen v. Paramount Bldrs. (Hamilton) Ltd.*, [1977] 1 N.Z.L.R. 394, reversing [1975] 2 N.Z.L.R. 546 (C.A.).

[29]See, *e.g.*, *A.G. Ont. v. Crompton* (1976), 14 O.R. (2d) 659, 1 C.C.L.T. 81, 74 D.L.R. (3d) 345 (H.C.); *Hope Hardware & Bldg. Supply Co. v. Fields Stores Ltd.* (1978), 7 B.C.L.R. 321, 7 C.P.C. 253, 90 D.L.R. (3d) 49, varied 137 D.L.R. (3d) 58 (C.A.); *Poberznick v. Goldschmidt*, [1983] A.W.L.D. 117, 18 A.C.W.S. 193 (Q.B.); *Windsor Bldg. Supplies Ltd. v. Art Harrison Ltd.* (1980), 24 B.C.L.R. 145, 14 C.C.L.T. 120 (S.C.).

[30][1933] A.C. 449 (H.L.). A similar rule is applied in contract law that in damages suffered because of an inability to mitigate due to impecuniosity are not recoverable; *Freedhoff v. Pomalift Indust. Ltd.*, [1971] 2 O.R. 773, 19 D.L.R. (3d) 153 at 158 (C.A.). However, in contract those damages are recoverable where the defendant has express prior knowledge of the impecuniosity; *Wroth v. Tyler*, [1974] Ch. 30 [1973] 2 W.L.R. 405, [1973] 1 All E.R. 897 at 919.

them so far as liability is concerned. Generally, multiple causes are not foreseeable in the particular, but some general classes are foreseeable, and so far as physical damage to persons and property is concerned, recovery is given, as has been shown in Chapter Ten, for all damages resulting from multiple causes where the class of causes is foreseeable.

Conversely, if *Liesbosch* is taken as the law, and no recovery is to be given in regard to economic loss where the plaintiff's own pecuniary condition is also a cause of the loss, then there should in general be no recovery given for economic loss arising from multiple causes.

A distinction between "direct" and "indirect" causes is as meaningless in the area of economic loss as it is in the area of physical damage. Since most of the multiple cause cases in the area of economic loss fall within foreseeable categories, the refusal of courts to award such damages cannot be justified in terms of the foreseeability test. We can only conclude that physical damage arising from multiple causes is recoverable while economic loss resulting from multiple causes is not. This might be because the chances for multiple cause losses are much greater in regard to economic loss. Of the 125 economic loss cases examined, 28 involved multiple cause losses, and recovery was given only in three, all of which involved a strike as the additional causal factor. [31]

Where the physical damage is sufficient in and of itself to cause the economic loss, recovery has generally been given. If, however, the physical damage alone while necessary is not sufficient to cause the loss, recovery is generally denied. Thus in *Hellens v. Pederson*[32] the plaintiff was denied recovery for financial loss resulting from his inability to obtain employment after he had recovered from his injuries, where his lack of employment was no longer due to his physical incapacity but was caused by an economic recession which had set in during the period of his recovery, even though if he had not been injured it is likely he would still be working at his old job because of his seniority. His physical incapacity was a necessary and sufficient condition for his loss of earnings for the period in which he was unable to work and for his loss of seniority rights for which he was awarded $10,000. After he was able to work, a further causal factor was necessary for his lack of income, i.e. the recession. Thus the defendant's actions were a necessary, but not a sufficient, cause of the loss of wages following his recovery from the physical injury.

---

[31] *H.M.S. London*, [1914] P. 72; *Penman v. St. John Toyota Ltd.* (1972), 30 D.L.R. (3d) 88, 5 N.B.R. (2d) 140 (C.A.); *Shulhan v. Peterson, Howell & Heather (Can.) Ltd.* (1966), 57 W.W.R. 46, 57 D.L.R. (2d) 491 (Sask. Q.B.).

[32] [1977] 3 W.W.R. 372 (B.C. S.C.).

An examination of the cases reveals that whatever the justification, the *Liesbosch* case has been followed and applied.[33] When, however, judges find that a binding authority prevents them from applying a principle to a specific case which clearly falls within its ambit, and no good reason can be found for excluding the particular case, then the binding authority will be interpreted as narrowly as possible and distinguished whenever relevant differences can be found. It may well be that future courts will limit the *Liesbosch* just to pecuniosity and will give recovery for economic loss where a further causal event is necessary for it to be suffered, providing that the event and the loss is clearly foreseeable. Indeed recent decisions would indicate a trend in that direction.[34]

We should not conclude from the above, however, that where economic loss arises from actions which create a risk of physical injury to persons or property that the plaintiff who suffers the economic loss also needs to suffer some physical injury. Such a proposition was expressly rejected in *Caltex Oil (Aust.) Pty. Ltd. v. The Dredge Willemsted*.[35] In *Caltex* the defendant's dredge fractured a pipeline not owned by the plaintiff, but through which the plaintiff's oil flowed. The plaintiff was awarded recovery for the economic loss suffered as the result of having to make alternative arrangements for the transportation of its oil while the pipeline was being repaired. Mr. Justice Gibbs stated:

> "In my opinion it is still right to say that as a general rule damages are not recoverable for economic loss which is not consequential upon injury to the plaintiff's person or property. The fact that the loss was foreseeable is not enough to make it recoverable. However, there are exceptional cases in which the defendant has knowledge or means of knowledge that the plaintiff individually, and not merely as a member of an unascertained class, will be likely to suffer economic loss as a consequence of his negligence, and owes the plaintiff a duty to take care not to cause him such damage by his negligent act."[36]

His views were also shared by Mr. Justices Stephen and Mason.

The *Caltex* case is consistent with the decision of the Supreme Court of Canada in *Rivtow Marine Ltd. v. Washington Iron Works*.[37] Recovery was

---

[33]See, *e.g.*, *Burton v. Dom. Steel & Coal Corp.*, 14 M.P.R. 328, [1940] 1 D.L.R. 476 (N.S. C.A.); *Alta. Caterers Ltd. v. R. Vollan (Alta.) Ltd.* (1977), 5 Alta. L.R. (2d) 1, 5 C.P.C. 135, 81 D.L.R. (3d) 672, 10 A.R. 501, varied 11 A.R. 181 (T.D.); *Cammionneurs du Nord Ltée v. Sealy, supra*, note 27.

[34]See, *e.g.*, *Dodd Properties (Kent) v. Canterbury City Council*, [1980] 1 W.L.R. 433, [1980] 1 All E.R. 928 (C.A.); *Perry v. Sidney Phillips & Son*, [1982] 1 W.L.R. 1297, [1982] 3 All E.R. 705 (C.A.); and *Fox v. Wood* (1981), 35 A.L.R. 607 (H.C.).

[35](1976) 11 A.L.R. 227, 51 A.L.J.R. 270, 136 C.L.R. 529 (H.C.).

[36]*Ibid.*, at 555.

[37][1973] 6 W.W.R. 692, 40 D.L.R. (3d) 530 (S.C.C.).

given for the financial loss suffered as a result of having to take a negligently designed crane out of service in the busiest part of the season when the full danger of the structural defects finally became apparent as the result of the collapse of a similar crane killing a workman. The fact that the loss was economic posed no problem for the court, since it was limited to the charters, to a specific amount, within a given period of time. It would appear, therefore, from *Caltex* and *Rivtow* that a plaintiff can recover for economic loss without suffering any physical loss if the economic loss is foreseeable in the particular.

The one exception where damages for economic loss are awarded where the plaintiff is not the person who has suffered physical injury to the person or property, and the economic loss was not foreseeable in the particular, are the cases where an employer has suffered economic loss as a result of injuries to his or her employee. Damages are given only if the case comes within the old *actio per quod servitium amisit*. This old cause of action, however, is an historical anomaly dating from the period when masters were viewed as having a proprietary interest in their servants,[38] and therefore should be seen as an exception to the general rule. Unfortunately, while Great Britain[39] is narrowing the cause of action, Canada[40] and Australia[41] appear to be widening it. There were three other cases where damages for economic loss were awarded where

---

[38]David Cohen, "The Relationship of Contractual Remedies to Political and Social Status: A Preliminary Inquiry" (1982), 32 U.T.L.J. 31 at 68-69.

[39]See *e.g., Taylor v. Neri* (1795), 1 Esp. 386, 170 E.R. 393 (N.P.); *Inland Revenue Commrs. v. Hambrook*, [1956] 23 Q.B. 641, [1956] 3 W.L.R. 643, [1956] 3 All E.R. 338 (C.A.); contrast with *Lee v. Sheard*, [1956] 1 Q.B. 192, [1955] 3 W.L.R. 951, [1955] 3 All E.R. 777 (C.A.).

[40]See *e.g. R. v. Richardson*, [1948] S.C.R. 57, [1948] 2 D.L.R. 305; *Bermann v. Occhipinti*, [1953] O.R. 1035, [1954] 1 D.L.R. 560; *Nykorak v. A.G. Can.*, [1962] S.C.R. 331, 37 W.W.R. 660, 33 D.L.R. (2d) 373; *Kneeshaw v. Latendorff* (1965), 53 W.W.R. 672, 54 D.L.R. (2d) 84 (Alta. S.C.); *R. v. Murray*, [1967] S.C.R. 262, 59 W.W.R. 214, 60 D.L.R. (2d) 647; *Genereux v. Peterson, Howell & Heather (Can.) Ltd.*, [1973] 2 O.R. 558, 34 D.L.R. (3d) 614 (C.A.); *Racicot v. Saunders* (1979), 27 O.R. (2d) 15, 11 C.C.L.T. 228, 103 D.L.R. (3d) 567 (H.C.); contra, *A.G. Can. v. Jackson*, [1946] S.C.R. 489, 59 C.R.T.C. 273, [1946] 2 D.L.R. 481; *R. v. C.P.R.*, [1947] S.C.R. 185, 61 C.R.T.C. 24, [1947] 2 D.L.R. 1; *Swift Can. Co. v. Bolduc* (1961), 29 D.L.R. (2d) 651 (N.S. S.C.); *Pagan v. Leifer* (1969), 69 W.W.R. 247, 6 D.L.R. (3d) 714 (Man. Q.B.); *Schwartz v. Hotel Corp. of Amer. (Man.) Ltd.* (1970), 75 W.W.R. 664, 15 D.L.R. (3d) 764, affirmed (sub nom. *Alex E. Schwartz Agencies Ltd. v. Hotel Corp. of Amer. (Man.) Ltd.*) [1971] 3 W.W.R. 320, 20 D.L.R. (3d) 759 (Man. C.A.). For the latest pronouncement of the Supreme Court of Canada on the *per quod* action, see *R. v. Buchinsky*, [1983] 5 W.W.R. 577, 24 C.C.L.T. 266, 145 D.L.R. (3d) 1, 47 N.R. 208, 22 Man. R. (2d) 121, reversing [1981] 1 W.W.R. 88, 13 C.C.L.T. 298, 114 D.L.R. (3d) 721, 4 Man. R. (2d) 141.

[41]*Commr. for Rys. (N.S.W.) v. Scott*, 33 A.L.J.R. 126, [1959] A.L.R. 896 (H.C.); *Sydney City Council v. Bosnich*, 89 W.N. (Pt. 1) (N.S.W.) 168, [1968] 3 N.S.W.R. 725 (C.A.); contra, *A.G. N.S.W. v. Perpetual Trustee Co.*, [1955] 2 W.L.R. 707, [1955] 1 All E.R. 846 (P.C.).

the plaintiff had suffered no physical injury to the person or to property and where the loss was not foreseeable in the particular, and it is thus concluded that they are wrongly decided.[42]

IV. CONCLUSION

From an examination of the cases involving an issue of remoteness of economic loss arising from actions which create a risk of physical injury, the following conclusions can be drawn:

1. Like other kinds of damage for which recovery is given under the law, economic loss is recoverable providing it is not too remote.

2. In any given situation, economic loss will be too remote if the outcome of giving recovery, when generalized as a rule of law, will allow recovery by an indeterminate class, in regard to indeterminate amounts, arising within an indeterminate period of time.

3. Liability for economic loss can be limited in regard to the extent of the recovering class, the amount, and the time within which a loss can arise, by:

(a) The existence of a special relationship such as arises from a contract, a promise, an undertaking, a business transaction, or a fiduciary duty, or

(b) The existence of physical damage to persons or property without the presence of which the economic loss would not have occurred.

4. Except for cases of multiple causation, the test of remoteness of economic damage arising from physical damage is the same as that for physical injury to persons or damage to property.

The test for such economic loss can be stated as a variant of the general test for remoteness developed in Chapter Ten: Economic loss arising from actions which create a risk of physical injury to persons or damage to property is not too remote (a) if it is reasonably foreseeable in the particular, or (b) if it is a member of a reasonably foreseeable class of kinds of economic losses, *where the physical injury or damage is a necessary and sufficient condition for the economic loss.*

In spite of the more recent decisions such as *Rivtow, Caltex,* and *Junior Books v. The Veitchi Co.,*[43] the decision of Widgery J. in *Weller v.*

---

[42]*Dom. Tape of Can. Ltd. v. L.R. MacDonald & Sons Ltd.*, [1971] 3 O.R. 627, 21 D.L.R. (3d) 299; *Badham v. Williams*, [1968] N.Z.L.R. 729 (Auckland S.C.); *Smyth v. Hughes*, [1974] 2 N.Z.L.R. 573 (S.C.).

[43][1982] 3 W.L.R. 477, [1982] 3 All E.R. 201 (H.L.).

Foot and Mouth Disease Research Institute,[44] is still good law. In that case the plaintiff auctioneer was denied recovery for loss of income in his business as an auctioneer because of the death of cattle due to a virus having escaped from the defendant's laboratory. The plaintiff had suffered no physical damage to his property, and his particular loss was not foreseeable. In order to recover for economic loss, whatever the cause of action, that loss must be either foreseeable in the particular, or must be one of a number of foreseeable classes of damage for which the physical injury or property damage is both a necessary and a sufficient cause.

5. For economic loss arising from actions which create no risk of physical injury to persons or damage to property, but where the risk which is the foundation of a finding of negligence or breach of a special or a contractual duty is a risk of purely economic loss, the economic loss would be too remote unless it is foreseeable in the particular.

In regard to economic loss arising from actions which create no risk of physical harm to persons or property, there is little distinction to be drawn between culpability and compensation.[45] The test of foreseeability to establish the presence of negligence, culpability, or fault differs little from that used to establish remoteness.

The requirement that pure economic loss arising from actions or failures to act which create no risk of physical injury to persons or property must be foreseeable in the particular in order to be recoverable, provides an incentive to people to transfer information to one another. That which has been disclosed in the particular is foreseeable in the particular. When such information is disclosed pesons can tailor their undertakings accordingly.[46]

---

[44][1966] 1 Q.B. 569, [1965] 3 W.L.R. 1082, [1965] 3 All E.R. 560.

[45]*Overseas Tankship (U.K.) v. Morts Dock & Enrg. Co. (The Wagon Mound)*, [1961] A.C. 388 at 425, [1961] 2 W.L.R. 126, [1961] 1 All E.R. 404 (P.C.).

[46]W. Bishop, "The Contract-Tort Boundary and the Economics of Insurance" (1983), 12 Journal of Legal Studies 241 at 254-55.

APPENDIX I

NEGLIGENT MISREPRESENTATION
(*HEDLEY BYRNE*) CASES

AUSTRALIA

Held for Plaintiff

R.II. BROWN & CO. v. BANK OF NEW SOUTH WALES, [1971] W.A.R. 201 (S.C.)

Plaintiff firm sought information and advice from its bank as to the financial position of a company plaintiff wished to do business with. Plaintiff's bank obtained a report from another bank advising of the company's sound position financially and reported this to plaintiff. Plaintiff acted on the report and then failed to receive any payment from the company in respect of the goods plaintiff delivered. Plaintiff sued both banks for negligent advice and fraud. Held: Plaintiff's bank was neither negligent nor guilty of fraud. The second company's bank, however, was guilty of fraud, since the report was made with an intention to deceive. It was not liable for negligence, though, because of an express disclaimer in its report to plaintiff's bank.

O'LEARY v. LAMB (1973), 7 S.A.S.R. 159 (S.C.).

Plaintiff investors sought advice from defendant manager of finance company as to investment. Latter advised that the moneys could be safely invested in another finance company if secured by a second debenture on certain conditions. The manager failed to explain to plaintiffs terms on which money could be safely lent. The moneys were invested and lost. Plaintiffs sued defendant for negligent advice. Held: Defendant was liable to compensate plaintiffs for the sum of investment lost as a result of his negligent advice given in the capacity of a financial adviser (defendant had a financial interest in the brokerage he would receive on moneys invested).

SAN SEBASTIAN PTY. LTD. & ANOR v. THE MINISTER ADMINISTERING THE ENVIRONMENTAL PLANNING AND ASSESSMENT ACT, 1979 & ANOR, N.S.W.S.C., No. 6516, 12th May 1982 (unreported).

Defendant state planning authority and defendant city council prepared a study indicating extensive commercial development was possible in certain areas. The study was exhibited to the public. Plaintiff land developers bought property for development and invested large sums in it on the basis of the report. A subsequent change in government required development in the area to be residential. Plaintiffs suffered considerable loss as a result, and sued in tort. Held: Plaintiffs were entitled to recover on both *Hedley Byrne* and *Donoghue v. Stevenson* principles as the study was negligently prepared and published. *Shaddock* followed.

SHADDOCK & ASSOCIATES PTY. LTD. v. PARRAMATTA, 36 A.L.J.R. 385, 55 A.L J.R. 713, reversing [1979] 1 N.S.W.L.R. 566 (H.C.).

Plaintiffs made formal request to defendant municipal council for information as to road-widening proposals in relation to conveyancing transaction. The council gave an incorrect answer negligently. Loss was suffered by plaintiffs. The court held that there was no distinction between negligently supplied information and negligent advice. Defendant was liable for the expenses incurred on the basis of the incorrect information as well as the difference in value between the price paid by plaintiffs for the land, and its value as affected by the road-widening proposals. (Amount of recoverable damages for negligent misstatement is the amount of money necessary to restore plaintiff to position he was in before the statement, subject to such loss being foreseeable.)

STATE OF SOUTH AUSTRALIA v. JOHNSON (1982), 42 A.L.R. 161 (H.C. Full Ct.).

Plaintiff war veteran was granted a perpetual lease of property by state. State officers who earlier viewed property with plaintiff had described it as "suitable for fat lambs and wool production." Property in fact was subject to clover disease causing severe losses and infertility in sheep. Plaintiff had little success in 13 years of working the property, suffering severe losses of sheep and unprofitable venture into cattle and cropping, leading to ultimate cancellation of lease and forced sale of stock and plant. State officers were found negligent in making the statement and in failing to warn against clover disease (state had conceded that a duty of care existed). Plaintiff was awarded, for the years 1966-1970, direct costs attributable to clover disease, interest on increased debt to state resulting therefrom and some amount for lost opportunity of a more rapid and extensive development of property. No damages were awarded for cancellation of lease or forced sale as they were not causally linked to the misrepresentation.

TUCKEY v. BURROUGHTS LTD., [1980] 1 S.R. (W.A.) 201 (W.A. Dist. Ct.).

Defendant seller, holding itself out as an expert, negligently misrepresented the capacity of a computer system. Plaintiff prospective customer, relying on the misrepresentation, entered into a leasing contract with a finance company for a lease of the computer system. Plaintiff had to obtain another computer system upon discovering the true capacity of the one it had acquired. The court held that the plaintiffs were entitled to be compensated for the financial loss they suffered by having been induced to enter into the leasing contract through defendant's negligent misrepresentation.

Held for Defendant

DILLINGHAM CONST. PTY. LTD. v. DOWNS, [1972] 2 N.S.W.L.R. 49 (S.C.).

Plaintiff companies began work in deepening a harbour, but did not attain the planned rate of progress because blasting was ineffective. Plaintiffs had to adopt other methods of working, with attendant delay and increase in cost. Plaintiffs discovered that the government had known all along that there were disused coal workings under the harbour inhibiting blasting. Plaintiffs sued defendant for negligent misrepresentation inducing them to enter into a contract for deepening of the harbour with the government. Held: The relationship between plaintiff and defendant in the precontract period was not such that defendant was under a duty to plaintiffs to take reasonable care in gathering all material relevant to the site conditions and incorporate it into the specification and other tender documents.

DOM. FREEHOLDERS LTD. v. AIRD, 67 S.R. (N.S.W.) 150, 84 W.N. (Pt.2) 190, [1966] 2 N.S.W.R. 296 (C.A.)

Plaintiff public company sued defendant auditor for damages resulting from an erroneous report that the company's accounts were accurate. Defendant's report was based on information supplied by the company's accountant. Defendant joined the accountant for indemnity. On demurrer, held: No duty of care was owed by the accountant to the defendant auditor. (*Hedley Byrne* distinguished).

KOORAGANG INVT. PTY. LTD. v. RICHARDSON & WRENCH LTD., [1982] A.C. 462, [1981] 3 W.L.R. 493, [1981] 3 All E.R. 65 (P.C.).

A valuer employed by defendant estate agent to value property was told not to do any more valuations for plaintiff companies when they failed to pay their fees. The valuer continued to act for them despite this direction. The valuations proved to be negligently done, causing plaintiffs economic loss. Plaintiffs then sued defendant in negligence. Held: Defendant was not liable for valuer's negligence, since he had acted outside the scope of his employment with the defendants.

MAX GARNETT (DISTRIBUTORS) PTY. LTD. v. TOBLAS (1975), 50 A.L.J.R. 402 (H.C.).

Plaintiff client lent money to borrower on security of a second mortgage on borrower's property. Defendant solicitors failed to register the memorandum and lodge the caveat. The borrower then entered into a contract of sale for the property. The caveat was then lodged. Upon settlement of the sale, plaintiff failed to obtain full repayment of the money lent by him. Plaintiff sued defendants for negligent failure to give proper advice or negligent advice, and breach of contract. Held: There was no evidence that defendant had given any advice or that any negligently incorrect advice had been given.

MUTUAL LIFE & CITIZENS' ASSUR. CO. LTD. v. EVATT, [1971] A.C. 793, [1971] 2 W.L.R. 23, [1971] 1 All E.R. 150 (P.C.).

Plaintiff, policy holder in defendant insurance company, sued latter for negligence in giving gratuitous information and advice on the financial stability of an associated company knowing that plaintiff would invest in that company on that advice. Plaintiff lost his investments. Held: Plaintiff had no cause of action, since the company was not in the business of giving advice on investments and did not claim to have the skill and competence to give such advice. Its only duty was to answer honestly.

PRESSER v. CALDWELL ESTATES PTY. LTD., SOUTHERN ESTATES (WOL-LONGONG) PTY. LTD. (THIRD PARTY), [1971] 2 N.S.W.L.R. 471 (C.A.).

Plaintiffs relied on an antecedent innocent misrepresentation made to them by vendor's agent in deciding to buy a lot on the vendor's estate and build a house thereon. Cracks appeared in the house caused by subsidence of filling on the lot (the agent had assured plaintiffs there was no filling on the lot). Plaintiffs then sued the vendor in negligent misrepresentation. Held: The agent was only under a duty to give an honest answer based on the knowledge it possessed (which was that the lot was filled). Accordingly, the vendor was not vicariously liable for the failure of the agent to ensure that the answer he gave was correct regarding the filling of land.

CANADA

Held for Plaintiff

ATHANS v. CAN. ADVENTURE CAMPS LTD. (1977), 17 O.R. (2d) 425, 4 C.C.L,T 20, 34 C.P.R. (2d) 126, 80 D.L.R. (3d) 583 (H.C.).

Plaintiff, a professional water-skier, marketed his name for profit. Defendant C.A.C. Ltd. operated a summer camp featuring water-skiing. It hired I.D. Ltd. to prepare promotional material for the camp. Defendants failed to engage plaintiff to promote the camp, but I.D.

Ltd. nonetheless used a stylization of plaintiff's photograph for an ad for the camp which was approved by C.A.C. Ltd. Plaintiff succeeded in an action against C.A.C. Ltd. for wrongful misappropriation of personality. I.D Ltd. was held liable to indemnify C.A.C. Ltd. on the basis of *Hedley Byrne* as having negligently informed C.A.C. Ltd. that no release was required for the use of the drawings.

BABCOCK v. SERVACAR LTD., [1970] 1 O.R. 125 (Div. Ct.).

Plaintiff, a computer programmer with limited knowledge of automobiles and motor mechanics, sued to recover economic loss suffered as a result of careless diagnosis of the condition of a car by the defendant car clinic. Plaintiff, who had bought the car relying on defendant's written report, almost immediately incurred expensive repairs. Liability was imposed on the defendant on the basis of *Hedley Byrne*.

BEAVER LUMBER CO. LTD. v. McLENAGHAN (1982), 143 D.L.R. (3d) 139 (Sask. C.A.).

Defendant lumber company sold plaintiffs a package of components for a prefabricated house. Upon defendant recommending a third party as "the man for the job," plaintiffs hired him to assemble the components. The workmanship proved faulty and plaintiffs sued defendant for negligent misrepresentation. The court held for plaintiffs on the ground that defendant's negligent misrepresentation induced them to enter into a contract with the third party.

BREAN v. THORNE (1982), 52 N.S.R. (2d) 241, 106 A.P.R. 241 (T.D.).

In an action for trespass to land, landowners succeeded in obtaining a mandatory injunction requiring the removal of a house that the defendants had mistakenly built on plaintiff's land rather than their own. Held further: defendants were entitled to be indemnified by the real estate agent that negligently misdescribed the lot and the surveyor who prepared an erroneous report on the property lines.

BRUMER v. GUNN, [1983] 1 W.W.R. 424, 18 Man. R. (2d) 155 (Q.B.).

Defendant solicitor, acting as plaintiff's investment advisor, arranged for plaintiff to invest funds in a company. Plaintiff lost her investment when the security proved to be inadequate. Plaintiff then sued defendant to recover the money lost due to the negligent investment advice. Defendant was found to be both negligent and in breach of his contractual duty to the plaintiff when he permitted her to invest all of her money in the loans, approved of the inadequate security, and failed to advise her to discontinue the loans when the company was clearly in financial trouble.

BUDAI v. ONT. LOTTERY CORP. (1983), 24 C.C.L.T. 1, 142 D.L.R. (3d) 271 (Ont. Div. Ct.).

Defendant lottery operator incorrectly told plaintiff purchaser that he had won $835. Plaintiff thereon spent $480 in United States currency celebrating. He was later informed he had only won $5. Plaintiff succeeded in an action to recover the money squandered by him on reliance on defendant's information.

BURKE v. CORY, [1959] O.W.N. 129, 19 D.L.R. (2d) 252 (C.A.).

Defendant broker falsely told plaintiff customer that mine drilling had taken place with favourable results, thus inducing plaintiff to buy stock in the mine. The stock later became practically worthless. Defendant was held liable for negligent misrepresentation made in breach of his fiduciary duty to plaintiff.

BURMAN'S BEAUTY SUPPLIES LTD. v. KEMPSTER (1974), 4 O.R. (2d) 626, 48 D.L.R. (3d) 682 (Co. Ct.).

A client of defendant solicitor borrowed money on the security of a chattel mortgage to plaintiff lender. Defendant had prepared a document appearing to be a first mortgage to the plaintiff. The latter sued defendant for the loss suffered when the borrower defaulted and the chattels were seized by defendant as first mortgagee. Recovery was granted on the basis of *Hedley Byrne*: defendant owed plaintiff a duty of care, since he was aware plaintiff would not have advanced the money had he known the chattels were already mortgaged.

CANTWELL v. PETERSEN (1982), 25 R.P.R. 290, 139 D.L.R. (3d) 466 (B.C. S.C.).

Defendant appraiser negligently failed to detect dry rot and insect infestation in the foundations of a house while preparing an appraisal for a mortgage company that intended to make a mortgage loan to the purchasers of the property. Plaintiff purchaser relied on the appraisal in completing the purchase. Defendant was found liable for plaintiff's economic loss suffered in reliance on the negligent appraisal.

CARMAN CONST. LTD. v. C.P.R. (1980), 28 O.R. (2d) 232, 109 D.L.R. (3d) 288, affirmed 23 O.R. (2d) 472, 124 D.L.R. (3d) 680, which was affirmed [1982] 1 S.C.R. 958, 18 B.L.R. 65, 136 D.L.R. (3d) 193, 42 N.R. 147.

Plaintiff entered into a contract with defendant to excavate and remove a section of earth and rock on the basis of a negligent misrepresentation made by defendant's employee as to the quantity of rock to be removed. Plaintiff was put to extra expense in removing the extra rock. Plaintiff then sued defendant for negligent misrepresentation. The court held that as defendant knew or ought to have known it had the only information as to the quantity, it owed a duty to see that any representations made thereon were accurate. However, plaintiff's action failed by virtue of an exempting clause contained in the contract between the parties: *Hedley Byrne* applied.

CENTRAL B.C. PLANERS LTD. v. HOCKER, 72 W.W.R. 561, 10 D.L.R. (3d) 689, affirmed [1971] 5 W.W.R. 89, 16 D.L.R. (3d) 368n (S.C.C.).

Plaintiffs, relying on the advice of a salesman of a stockbroker firm, bought a large number of shares in a company. The salesman had made the representations based on information obtained from a salesman of another office. The representations proved inaccurate and plaintiffs suffered loss. The first salesman was found liable for breach of the duty of a stockbroker to a customer. The second salesman, however, was found not liable, since the representations made by the first salesman were substantially different from the information he had passed on.

CHAND v. SABO BROS. REALTY LTD. [1978] 1 W.W.R. 428, 81 D.L.R. (3d) 382, 10 A.R. 352, varied [1979] 2 W.W.R. 248, 14 A.R. 302 (C.A.)

Defendant real estate agent, hired by vendor accepted his statement that the land was jointly owned by himself and his wife. The agreement that the plaintiff purchaser entered into with the vendor proved unenforceable for failure of the wife to comply with the Dower Act. Plaintiff successfully sued defendant for negligent misstatement.

CREYKE v. ROYAL TRUST CORP. OF CAN. (1980), 17 R.P.R. 298 (Alta. Q.B.).

Plaintiff used defendant real estate agent's services in buying a house. Defendant knew plaintiff only had a very limited amount to spend on monthly mortgage payments. Defendant nonetheless relied on information supplied by the vendor to the multiple listing service in determining whether plaintiff could afford the house. In fact, the payments mentioned in the listing did not apply to plaintiff and she had to pay substantially more. Plaintiff recovered the extra payments from defendant as damages flowing from defendant's negligent misrepresentation. The court held that defendant should have checked the information in the listing and his failure to do so was negligence.

DEYONG v. WEEKS (1983), 25 Alta. L.R. (2d) 117, 43 A.R. 342 (Q.B.).

A lawyer agreed to act for a client who made a high-risk unsecured loan to a third party. The client had a silent partner who was also in contact with the lawyer even though the lawyer billed the client for the work resulting from the silent partner's suggestions. The lawyer failed to adequately check the legitimacy of the transaction for which the loan was required and relied upon the third party to confirm certain extraneous facts. The transaction proved illegitimate and the lawyer's client failed to recover most of the loan. The court found the lawyer to be liable to his client in both contract and tort and liable to the silent partner in negligence by applying *Hedley Byrne*, *Tracy v. Atkins* and *Whittingham v. Crease*.

DIXON v. BANK OF N.S. (1979), 13 B.C.L.R. 269, 10 C.C.L.T. 131 (Co. Ct.).

Plaintiff sued defendant bank and one of its bank managers, alleging that the latter had negligently misrepresented to him that the bank would back a company. Relying on this, plaintiff bought shares in the company which subsequently declined in value, causing loss to plaintiff. Defendant in fact had never given the company any financial support and did not endorse the company in any way. Both the bank and the bank manager were held liable for negligent misrepresentation.

DODDS v. MILLMAN (1964), 47 W.W.R. 690, 45 D.L.R. (2d) 472 (B.C. S.C.).

Plaintiff, an inexperienced buyer, relied on statements made by vendor's real estate agent in purchasing an apartment building. The statements, although not fraudulent, gave an entirely false impression of the building's capacity to produce a profit. The court held that plaintiff could recover damages in respect of the real estate agent's negligent misrepresentation on the basis of *Hedley Byrne* despite the absence of a contractual relationship.

DORNDORF v. HOETER (1981), 29 B.C.L.R. 71, 20 R.P.R. 99, 122 D.L.R. (3d) 758 (S.C.).

Plaintiffs, relying on representations from the city solicitor that their land would be expropriated, bought and improved new property. The expropriation plans fell through and plaintiffs sought to recover lost business income as a result of the move and the cost of acquiring new land. The court found the solicitor to be liable but that plaintiffs were contributorily negligent in failing to find out from the solicitor when it would he safe to act on the representation.

DUPUIS v. PAN AMER. MINES LTD. (1979), 7 B.L.R. 288 (Que. S.C.).

Defendant accountants were hired by a company to prepare financial statements intended to be shown to prospective investors. Plaintiffs invested in the company on the basis of the report, which was negligently done. Plaintiffs sued defendants in a *Hedley Byrne* action. The court held that the principles of *Hedley Byrne* extended to a non-specific class of beneficiaries and that the existence of a contract between the accountants and the company was not relevant to the consideration of the appropriate standard of care between plaintiffs and defendants.

EDSTRAND v. CREST REALTY LTD., [1977] 3 W.W.R. 310, 2 B.C.L.R. 186 (S.C.).

Plaintiff purchaser requested an inspection of a house by a third party before purchase. The real estate salesman suggested a contractor for the job. The contractor, who did not charge a fee for his inspection, pronounced the house to be sound. After completing the purchase, plaintiff found considerable dry rot and sued both defendants. The court found the contractor liable on the basis of *Hedley Byrne*, but dismissed the claim against the salesman on the grounds that plaintiff had not relied on the salesman's opinion as to the building's condition, and the salesman was not negligent in suggesting the contractor do the inspection.

ELDERKIN v. MERRILL LYNCH (1977), 22 N.S.R. (2d) 218, 80 D.L.R. (3d) 313 (C.A.).

Defendant stockbrokers negligently advised plaintiff clients to buy and hold shares in a certain company which collapsed. The shares became worthless and plaintiffs sued defendants to recover their loss. The court held that plaintiffs could recover on the basis of defendants' breach of fiduciary duty. Also, as a person possessed of a special skill, a stockbroker owes a duty of reasonable care to his clients. Where a stockbroker is negligent in the advice he gives or fails to give to his clients, thus causing them economic loss, he is liable for that loss.

ELLIOT v. RON DAWSON & ASSOC. (1972) LTD., 139 D.L.R. (3d) 323, [1982] I.L.R. 1-1564 (B.C. S.C.).

Plaintiff was advised by defendant insurance agent that separate baggage insurance for a proposed trip was unnecessary, loss being covered to the face value of plaintiff's existing tenants' policy. In fact, coverage under the policy was restricted. Loss having occurred, plaintiff sued for the uninsured loss. The court held defendant liable on the ground it was negligent in advising plaintiff. Plaintiff's failure to read his policy was held not to be contributory negligence, since he was entitled to rely on defendant's advice.

ESSELMONT v. HARKER APPRAISALS LTD., 14 B.C.L.R. 116, [1980] I.L.R. 91-589 (S.C.).

Plaintiff made a mortgage loan to the landowners on the basis of a negligent appraisal prepared by defendants on the landowners' instructions. Plaintiff sued defendants on the grounds that the negligent appraisal had induced him to make the loan when the landowners defaulted on the mortgage. Defendants were held liable.

FARISH v. NAT. TRUST CO., [1975] 3 W.W.R. 499, 54 D.L.R. (3d) 426 (B.C. S.C.).

Plaintiff, a contributor to a retirement savings plan, bought a plan from defendant trust company. The company failed to advise plaintiff of the possibility of a tax-free purchase of annuity. Plaintiff then sued defendant in respect of the tax liability incurred upon withdrawing the funds on retirement. The court held that in addition to a fiduciary relationship as a trustee of the plan, the trust company also owed a duty to plaintiff as an adviser giving advice to a layman whom he knew was relying upon it in a manner affecting his economic interest.

GADUTSIS v. MILNE, [1973] 2 O.R. 503, 34 D.L.R. 455 (H.C.).

Plaintiff, a prospective lessee of certain premises, inquired of the zoning department of the municipality as to whether they were permitted for use as a restaurant. An employee of the department negligently indicated that such use was permitted and issued a building permit. The permit was revoked after alterations on premises were begun. The court held that plaintiff could recover the loss suffered from entering into the lease and payments made in respect of alterations done in an action for negligent misrepresentation and negligence in issuing the permit.

GEN. MOTORS ACCEPT. CORP. OF CAN. v. FULTON INS. AGENCIES LTD., [1978] I.L.R. 1-981, 24 N.S.R. (2d) 114, 35 A.P.R. 114 (C.A.).

The seller of a truck required that the conditional buyer insure the truck with an endorsement for loss payable to seller. The seller called defendant insurance agent to ensure that the endorsement had been made. Defendant incorrectly confirmed that the endorsement had been made. The truck was destroyed by fire. The seller then successfully sued defendant for negligent misrepresentation causing him loss.

GRAND RESTAURANTS OF CAN. LTD. v. TORONTO; CHUZAR RESTAURANTS LTD. v. GRAND RESTAURANTS OF CAN. LTD. (1981), 32 O.R. (2d) 757, 123 D.L.R. (3d) 349, affirmed 39 O.R. (2d) 752, 140 D.L.R. (3d) 191 (C.A.).

A solicitor on behalf of a restaurant purchaser made written and telephone inquiries to the municipality prior to closing deal. The municipality failed to advise purchaser of outstanding work orders and of report describing building as unsafe. Plaintiff successfully sued the municipality for damages flowing from the negligent misstatement, but was found contributorily negligent as an experienced restaurateur in failing to make further inquiries.

H.L. & M. SHOPPERS LTD. v. BERWICK (1977), 3 M.P.L.R. 241, 82 D.L.R. (3d) 23, 28 N.S.R. (2d) 229, 43 A.P.R. 229 (T.D.).

Defendant town and building inspector negligently issued building permit to plaintiff, who began construction in reliance on it. Plaintiff suffered damages when it was forced to demolish the partially erected building because its construction was contrary to zoning by-laws. Plaintiff sued defendant in respect of the negligent issue of the building permit. The court held that defendant owed a duty to prospective builders to give correct information and to exercise care in issuing a permit.

HAIG v. BAMFORD, [1977] 1 S.C.R. 466, [1976] 3 W.W.R. 331, 27 C.P.R. (2d) 149, 72 D.L.R. (3d) 68, 9 N.R. 43, reversing [1974] 6 W.W.R. 236, 53 D.L.R. (3d) 85.

Plaintiff invested in a company on the basis of an audited financial statement prepared by defendant accountants. The statement was negligently prepared and plaintiff lost his investment. The court held that where defendants knew that the statement would be shown to potential investors, they owed a duty of care to and were liable for loss suffered by a person who invested in the company on the basis of the statement, even though he was not known to defendants at the time they prepared the statement or at the time it was shown to him.

HERRINGTON v. KENCO MTGE. & INVT. LTD. (1981), 29 B.C.L.R. 54, 125 D.L.R. (3d) 377 (S.C.).

An employee of an investment company made negligent misrepresentations regarding the value of some property, thus inducing plaintiffs to purchase a second mortgage executed in the employer's favour. The first mortgagor foreclosed and plaintiffs lost their security. Both the employee and the firm were found to have been negligent in failing to insure the information regarding the value of the property was correct.

JUNG v. BURNABY, [1978] 6 W.W.R. 670, 7 C.C.L.T. 113, 91 D.L.R. (3d) 592 (B.C. S.C.).

The municipal fire department negligently assured plaintiff prospective purchasers that a building complied with fire regulations. Plaintiffs bought the building only to find they were obliged to expend money to bring the building up to standards imposed by fire regulations. The court held that plaintiffs were entitled to reimbursement for the expenditures, since the relationship of the parties fell within the principles of *Hedley Byrne*.

KOCH v. NELSON LUMBER CO., [1980] 4 W.W.R. 715, 13 C.C.L.T. 201, 111 D.L.R. (3d) 140, 2 Sask. R. 303, affirmed [1980] 2 S.C.R. 598.

Plaintiff bought a prefabricated home from defendant manufacturer. The latter recommended a builder to put up the home but failed to disclose that he was an undischarged bankrupt. The builder abandoned the project before completion. Plaintiff succeeded in an action against the manufacturer in recovering the economic loss resulting from the negligent advice.

McBEAN v. BANK OF N.S., Ont. C.A., Nos. D.R.S. 90-216, D.R.S. 90-088, 30th November 1982 (not yet reported).

Plaintiff, a 60-year-old retired school teacher, was approached by an entrepreneur to invest in breeding and importation of exotic cattle. She went to defendant bank for a loan and advice regarding the proposed transaction. The bank manager told plaintiff the proposal was "a good deal — she couldn't lose money on it," and prepared a projection sheet showing profits over three years. Plaintiff invested on that advice and lost $27,000 as well as the money lent to her by the bank. In an action brought by plaintiff to recover her loss, the court held that a fiduciary relationship arose between the parties and that the bank was in a breach of its duty to exercise reasonable care in giving investment advice and its duty to disclose any information that might influence plaintiff's decision.

McLENAGHAN v. NIXON (1979), 1 Sask. R. 101 (Q.B.).

Plaintiff purchased a home from defendant manufacturer of prefabricated homes. Defendant recommended, without qualification, that plaintiff hire defendant N. to erect the home. The latter failed to erect the home in a workmanlike manner. Plaintiff successfully sued defendant manufacturer in respect of the negligent advice. Plaintiff was awarded damages for the cost of fixing and finishing the home to bring it into the condition of a home of comparable age. The manufacturer could not rely on a disclaimer contained in the contract of sale for the home, since the advice given to plaintiff regarding the builder was given without qualification.

MANUGE v. PRUDENTIAL ASSUR. CO. (1977), 81 D.L.R. (3d) 360 (N.S. T.D.).

Plaintiff sought pension information from defendant insurance company. Defendant stated in writing that plaintiff would receive over $11,000 per year at age 55, overstating the amount by more than $3,000 per year. Plaintiff, relying on this information, changed jobs, planning to retire at 55. Plaintiff later discovered the error and sued defendant in respect of the negligent misrepresentation. Judgment was granted in plaintiff's favour on the basis that defendant knew many of the requests for pension information were from people who intended to rely on that information in making their decisions.

MARKO v. PERRY, [1980] 3 W.W.R. 565, 18 B.C.L.R. 263 (sub nom. MARKO v. P.) (Co. Ct.).

By the terms of a settlement, a second mortgage was to be granted to plaintiff. Defendant R., mortgagor's solicitor, was to register the second mortgage but failed to do so. In the meantime defendant P., plaintiff's solicitor, delivered a copy of the second mortgage to plaintiff after the first filing, with the result plaintiff assumed it had been filed. Upon foreclosure by the first mortgagee, plaintiff sued the two solicitors for damages. Defendant P. was held liable for breach of his duty to his client and R. was held liable for negligence in not completing the registration once he had undertaken to register the mortgage (even though he was acting for mortgagor rather than for plaintiff).

NICHOLSON v. DUNLOP (1980), 3 A.C.W.S. (2d) 423 (N.S. C.A.).

Defendant salesman negligently represented that there were no liens against a car that he was selling to plaintiff purchaser whom he knew was relying upon the representation. Defendant was found liable to pay the lien on the car purchased by plaintiff.

NIELSEN v. WATSON (1981), 33 O.R. (2d) 515, 19 R.P.R. 253, 125 D.L.R. (3d) 326 (H.C.) (leave to appeal to C.A. granted).

Defendant real estate agents negligently advertised a property as a three-garage house. In fact, the garage was owned by someone else. Plaintiff buyers hired defendant solicitor to act for them in the purchase. The solicitor arranged for a survey of the property to be done but failed to note the discrepancy regarding the garage. Plaintiff then sued both defendants for damages. The real estate agent was held liable for negligent misrepresentation and the solicitor was found liable in contract.

NORTHRUP v. FREDERICTON (1979), 27 N.B.R. (2d) 373 (Q.B.).

Defendant municipality negligently issued a building permit for an apartment building on land that was not zoned for such use, and construction subsequently had to be abandoned. Municipality was held liable for the cost of construction and removal, legal fees connected with the purchase, and lost time. However, legal fees resulting from mechanic's lien were too remote. *Hedley Byrne* applied.

NORTHWESTERN MUT. INS. CO. v. J.T. O'BRYAN & CO., [1974] 5 W.W.R. 322, [1974] I.L.R. 1-639, 51 D.L.R. (3d) 693 (B.C. C.A.).

Plaintiff insurance company asked defendant brokerage firm to remove it from a pooled risk. Defendant failed to do so but its manager negligently assured plaintiff it was off the risk. Risk materialized and plaintiff had to pay. Plaintiff then sued defendant company for breach of contract and manager for negligence. Held: Both defendants were liable. Assurance was given in the course of business, and was relied on by plaintiff which would otherwise have dealt directly with the insured to cancel the risk.

OLSEN v. POIRIER (1978), 21 O.R. (2d) 642, 91 D.L.R. (3d) 123 (H.C.).

Vendor of dairy farm fraudulently told plaintiff purchaser the current milk quota without revealing it would be reduced upon sale of the farm. Plaintiff sued vendor for rescission of the land sale contract upon discovering the truck. Plaintiff also sued defendant real estate agent for negligent misrepresentation in respect of the milk quota. Held: Both defendants were liable, the vendor on the basis of contract, the real estate agent on the basis of negligence.

RAYLON INVT. LTD. v. BEAR REALTY LTD. (1981), 20 R.P.R. 288 (B.C. S.C.).

Defendant appraisers appraised property for its owner, who then showed appraisal to plaintiff mortgagee to buy a mortgage on the faith of the security of the land. The appraisal negligently over-valued property greatly. Mortgagor defaulted and plaintiff suffered loss after foreclosure. Plaintiff sued defendants for negligent appraisal. Held: Defendants knew appraisal was used for decision whether to advance money on mortgage. Appraiser owes duty of care not only to client, but also to those to whom it might be shown and who might be expected to rely on it in dealing with the security.

ROBERT SIMPSON CO. v. FOUNDATION CO. OF CAN. (1982), 36 O.R. (2d) 97, 20 C.C.L.T. 179, 26 C.P.C. 51, 134 D.L.R. (3d) 458 (C.A.).

Plaintiffs, through another company, had a retail store built for them. An inadequate suspension system for the store ceiling later discovered put the ceiling in danger of collapse. Plaintiffs sued the general contractor and builders in tort for costs in resuspending the ceiling and consequential disruption in business. Defendants moved to strike out plaintiffs' pleadings. Held: Action should proceed to trial. Where the defects are the direct result of defendants' alleged negligence in recommending this type of suspended ceiling, the authority against recovery in negligence for cost of repairing defects does not apply.

SODD CORP. v. TESSIS (1977), 17 O.R. (2d) 158, 25 C.B.R. (N.S.) 16, 2 C.C.L.T. 245, 79 D.L.R. (3d) 632 (C.A.).

Defendant chartered accountant and trustee in bankruptcy advertised stock of furniture business carried on by bankrupt for sale by tender. Plaintiff submitted tender after defendant negligently misrepresented quantity and value of stock. Plaintiff sued defendant for economic loss suffered as result of latter's misrepresentation. Held: A duty of care was created by the special relationship between plaintiff and defendant (defendant was a professional accountant and trustee in bankruptcy).

SPEED & SPEED LTD. v. FINANCE AMER. REALTY LTD. (1979), 12 C.C.L.T. 4, 11 R.P.R. 161, 38 N.S.R. (2d) 374, 69 A.P.R. 374 (C.A.).

A landowner approached plaintiffs for advancement of funds on a second mortgage on his property. Plaintiffs advanced funds on basis of negligent appraisal done by defendants which failed to mention absence of subdivision approval and represented the single parcel of land as eight lots. Plaintiffs' branch manager for some reason varied title search instructions to solicitors with the result that error was not discovered. Landowner then defaulted and plaintiffs suffered considerable loss on their loan. Held: Defendants were liable in contract and tort for professional negligence. Defendants were negligent in assessing property as consisting of eight lots, and in failing to warn plaintiffs of absence of subdivision approval (a fact *known* to the appraiser). Plaintiffs, however, were contributorily negligent in failing to conduct proper title-search.

SURREY v. CARROLL-HATCH & ASSOCIATES LTD., [1979] 6 W.W.R. 289, 14 B.C.L.R. 156, 10 C.C.L.T. 226, 101 D.L.R. (3d) 218 (C.A.). (Leave to appeal to S.C.C. granted 7th November 1979.)

Defendant architect, engineers and general contractors were hired to build new police station for Surrey. New building proved unstable due to lack of sufficient soil tests. Architect had requested only a few shallow "test holes" be done. Plaintiff's request for a "soils report" was forwarded to engineers who submitted reassuring estimates of the load-bearing capacity of the site. The engineer's certificate of conformity of building work to National Building Code was equally without foundation. Held: Although the general contractor was free from liability, both the architect and engineers were liable. Architect was liable in contract and tort, since he had a duty to give good advice and warn plaintiff of reliance on engineer's misleading report. Failure to so warn was negligence. The engineers were guilty of making negligent misrepresentations.

TOWER EQUIPMENT RENTAL LTD. v. JOINT VENTURE EQUIPMENT SALES (1975), 9 O.R. (2d) 453, 60 D.L.R. (3d) 621 (H.C.).

Manufacturer misrepresented the condition of a second-hand climbing crane to plaintiff purchaser in order to induce plaintiff to buy from third party and earn finder's fees. Plaintiff rejected the goods as not corresponding with the description and sued manufacturer for damages. Defendant was found guilty of negligent misrepresentation.

TRACY v. ATKINS (1979), 16 B.C.L.R. 223, 11 C.C.L.T. 57, 105 D.L.R. (3d) 632 (C.A.).

Through purchaser's fraudulent behaviour, plaintiff vendors lost a great deal of money on the sale of their property. The transaction, despite its obvious peculiarities, was completed by defendant, purchaser's solicitor. Defendant had failed to alert the vendors or verify the position with them prior to closing the transaction. Plaintiffs sought to recoup their losses from defendant solicitor. Held: Even in the absence of a contract between the parties, a solicitor may still come under a duty of care to a plaintiff by reason of proximity of relationship. This is especially true where the solicitor is the only one engaged in the transaction, or can foresee that the other party may rely on him for the protection of his interests. Liability here can fall within general principle of proximity of relationship or in more specific case of persons possessed of special skills: *Hedley Byrne*.

TRIDENT CONST. LTD. v. W.L. WARDROP & ASSOCIATES LTD., [1979] 6 W.W.R. 481, 1 Man. R. (2d) 268 (Q.B.).

Plaintiff general contractor signed contract with city of Winnipeg for construction of sewage disposal plant. City signed contract with engineer to supervise and approve contractor's work. Engineer was negligent in setting the elevations for the construction which were followed by the contractor. Faulty design had to be corrected and plaintiff was penalized for extensive delays according to its contract with the city. Plaintiff sued defendant for those costs. Held: Professional engineer had a duty of care towards the person who is to follow his design to ensure that the plans are workable.

VISCOUNT MACHINE & TOOL LTD. v. CLARKE (1981), 34 O.R. (2d) 752, 21 R.P.R. 293, 19 C.C.L.T. 53, 126 D.L.R. (2d) 160 (H.C.).

Defendant land surveyor negligently prepared a survey of plaintiff's land. As a result, plaintiff built a structure on adjoining lands and thereby suffered damages. Plaintiff sued defendant in contract and tort. Held: Although the contract action was statute-barred, plaintiff could recover in tort on basis of defendant's negligent misrepresentation. In negligence, the cause of action arises when damage is done, and not when the negligent act is performed.

WEST COAST FINANCE LTD. v. GUNDERSON, STOKES, WALTON & CO., [1975] 4 W.W.R. 501, 56 D.L.R. (3d) 460, varying [1974] 2 W.W.R. 428, 44 D.L.R. (3d) 232 (B.C. C.A.).

Auditors were liable in negligence to a director who invested in shares in the company based on an inaccurate, audited report. The measure of damages is the difference between the price paid and actual value of shares received.

WHITTINGHAM v. CREASE & CO., [1978] 5 W.W.R. 415, 6 C.C.L.T. 1, 3 E.T.R. 97, 88 D.L.R. (3d) 353 (B.C. S.C.).

Plaintiff was a beneficiary under his father's will and defendant solicitor was in charge of preparing the will and having it executed. Solicitor caused will to be witnessed by plaintiff's wife, making the bequest to plaintiff invalid under the Wills Act. Plaintiff sued defendant in negligence. Held: Plaintiff was entitled to recover difference between amount he would have received and amount he actually got. Solicitor had impliedly represented to beneficiary that the will would be legally effective if his directions were followed, and plaintiff's passive reliance on this representation satisfied requirements of liability for negligent misstatement. (Irrelevant that plaintiff himself did nothing in reliance on the implied representation.)

WINDSOR MOTORS LTD. v. POWELL RIVER (1968), 68 W.W.R. 173, 4 D.L.R. (3d) 155 (B.C. C.A.).

Plaintiff was contemplating leasing some land for a used car lot. Defendant municipality's officers negligently misinformed plaintiff as to uses permitted by zoning by-law in respect of the land. In reliance on representation, plaintiff leased land and set up business. He suffered financial loss when required to terminate land's use which was contrary to zoning by-law. Held: *Hedley Byrne* applied.

WOOLDRIDGE v. H.B. NICKERSON & SONS LTD. (1980), 115 D.L.R. (3d) 97, 40 N.S.R. (2d) 388, 73 A.P.R. 388 (C.A.).

Defendant employer negligently advised plaintiff prospective employee abroad that if he came to Canada he could easily obtain Canadian qualifications necessary for employment. Defendant failed to advise plaintiff of changes in regulations governing employment qualifications, requiring substantial Canadian experience. Plaintiff successfully sued defendant for negligent misrepresentation upon arrival in Canada. The court held plaintiff was entitled to damages in respect of the actual costs of locating and relocating his family and the amount he might otherwise have earned in the period between his arrival in Canada and the start of the action.

Held for Defendant

BANK OF N.S. v. LIENAUX (1982), 53 N.S.R. (2d) 541, 109 A.P.R. 541 (T.D.).

A bank prepared cash flow projections for a lawyer, who wanted a loan to open up his own law practice. The projections were an incorrect reflection of the financial position of the practice. Shortly after the opening of the practice, the lawyer experienced financial difficulties. The bank sued the lawyer for a sum owing on certain promissory notes. The lawyer in turn counter-claimed for damages for negligent misrepresentation. The court allowed plaintiff's claim and dismissed defendant's on the grounds that the bank did not anticipate that the lawyer would rely on the projections and that the lawyer did not rely on them to his detriment.

BEEBE v. ROBB (1977), 81 D.L.R. (3d) 349 (B.C. S.C.).

Plaintiff bought boat from defendant who told plaintiff the hull was sound when it was in fact in advanced stage of dry rot. Defendant relied on report of defendant marine surveyor that boat was sound. (Defendant surveyor was hired by vendor who told him the survey was for a bank loan.) Plaintiff sued both defendants for depreciation in value from sum paid and cost of repairs. Plaintiff succeeded in action for breach of contract against vendor. As for liability of defendant surveyor under *Hedley Byrne*, defendant would only be liable if he had known, or should reasonably have known, plaintiff would rely upon his report (not the case here).

BOWEN v. EDMONTON, [1977] 6 W.W.R. 344, 3 M.P.L.R. 129, 4 C.C.L.T. 105, 80 D.L.R. (3d) 501, 8 A.R. 336 (T.D.).

Plaintiffs bought lot in Edmonton intending to build on it. Due to soil instability plaintiffs discovered that it was imprudent to build on its lot. They asserted against city duties in respect of replotting of the subdivision which it failed to perform, with result that plaintiffs unknowingly bought lot. They sought damages from city in negligence for approving subdivision on ground that lot had no resale value. Held: Although city was negligent in approving the replotting scheme in view of Planning Act provisions directing that no land shall be subdivided unless it is suitable for its intended purposes, the fault lay within the city's legislative and quasi-judicial functions and accordingly did not give rise to a cause of action. *Welbridge* followed.

CARI-VAN HOTEL LTD. v. GLOBE ESTATES LTD., [1974] 6 W.W.R. 707 (B.C. S.C.).

Plaintiff bought farm through defendant real estate agent based on an appraisal done by defendant appraiser stating value of property greatly in excess of its true market value. Appraisal was given to defendant real estate agent. Plaintiff sued defendant agent for breach of contract and defendant appraiser for negligent misrepresentation in respect of loss suffered on resale of property. Held: Even if appraisal was defective, defendant agent could not be liable, since he neither guaranteed the accuracy of the appraisal, nor knew it was defective. With respect to the appraiser, although he owed duty of care not only to his client but to all who might be expected to rely on it (*Hedley Byrne*), he was not negligent in preparing the report, since his appraisal was based upon the highest and best use of the land. Negligence is not proved merely because the land proves to be saleable only at price substantially less than valuation.

CARMAN CONST. LTD. v. C.P.R., [1982] 1 S.C.R. 958, 18 B.L.R. 65, 136 D.L.R. (3d) 193, 42 N.R. 147, affirming 33 O.R. (2d) 472, 124 D.L.R. (3d) 680, which affirmed 28 O.R. (2d) 232, 109 D.L.R. (3d) 288.

Plaintiff contracted to excavate and remove earth and rock for defendant. A clause provided that plaintiff could not rely "upon any information given or statement made to him in relation to the work by the company." Plaintiff relied on a representation made by defendant's employee as to quantity in submitting its tender. The representation proved to have been negligently made. Plaintiff's action for negligent misrepresentation against defendant was dismissed on the ground that the clause clearly established that defendant was not assuming any duty of care to plaintiff.

DAVIS v. HALDIMAND-NORFOLK (1980), 12 R.P.R. 1 (Ont. H.C.).

Prior to entering into a contract with the government department to lease some property, plaintiff landlords asked a town official about the municipality's position on the property's permitted uses. A building inspector concluded later that plaintiffs' alteration work violated a zoning order and ordered work be stopped. Other officials later reached an opposite view. Plaintiffs then sued the municipality for the loss of rents occasioned by the delay in issuing a building permit as a result of the negligence and negligent misstatements of defendant's servants. The court refused to impose liability on the grounds that the building inspector exercised his duties honestly, and there was no evidence of any reliance on the town official's advice.

DESIDERATA BUSINESS PARKS LTD. v. ROYAL BANK OF CAN. (1983), 18 A.C.W.S. (2d) 238 (B.C. S.C.).

Plaintiff entered into agreement to buy goods from A. Ltd. Latter required deposit to complete transaction. Plaintiff inquired as to A. Ltd.'s financial position from its bank. Bank replied that company's financial position was satisfactory. Plaintiff then sent deposit to the company which went bankrupt three weeks later. Held: Bank did not make any negligent misrepresentation as it did not possess any information that would put into question A. Ltd.'s ability to provide goods. Also, plaintiff's reliance on bank's statement was unreasonable in the circumstances (plaintiff, a sophisticated businessman, waited 15 days before sending deposit).

T. EATON CO. v. TRANSCONA CREDIT UNION LTD. (1982), 13 Man. R. (2d) 79 (Q.B.).

Plaintiff contracted to do renovation work for country club. Before work began, plaintiff was told that necessary funds would come from defendant credit union. Plaintiff composed "letter of credit" outlining proposed loan from defendant to country club, signed by both defendant and country club representative. Not being paid after work was done, plaintiff sued defendant for negligent misrepresentation. Held: No misrepresentation or positive assurance was made by defendant to plaintiff that funds would be loaned to country club. Plaintiff relied on representations made in "letter of credit" which contained no misrepresentations and merely described the state of affairs between club and defendant.

GEORGE v. DOMINICK CORP., 70 W.W.R. 262, 8 D.L.R. (3d) 631, reversed [1971] 1 W.W.R. 110, 15 D.L.R. (3d) 596, which was affirmed [1973] S.C.R. 97, [1973] 3 W.W.R. 56, 28 D.L.R. (3d) 508.

Defendants acted as plaintiffs' stockbrokers and investment dealers in the sale of plaintiffs' shares on margin account. Plaintiffs had the power to close out their margin account whenever this was necessary for their protection. Defendants represented that shares were traded on a normal margin of 70 per cent, but in fact, 100 per cent margin was required by the exchange rules. Defendants then closed plaintiffs' accounts, resulting in a trading loss to plaintiffs. Plaintiffs sued defendants in negligent misstatement and for breach of its agreement. Held: Defendants were not liable for negligent misstatement, since the margin requirements were not a material "investment factor" influencing plaintiffs' decision to trade. Plaintiff's action against defendants for breach of contract also failed before the British Columbia Court of Appeal and the Supreme Court of Canada.

HODGINS v. HYDRO-ELEC. COMM. OF NEPEAN, [1976] 2 S.C.R. 501, 60 D.L.R. (3d) 1, 6 N.R. 451.

Defendant hydroelectric commission gave estimate of costs of heating electrically a proposed addition to a house based on generally accepted methods of calculation. The consumption of electricity exceeded the estimate and plaintiff house owner sued for the extra expense from his adoption of electric heating. Held: Commission acted reasonably in adopting generally accepted standards of calculation. Inaccuracy of the estimate was not conclusive of negligence.

LAKEX MINES LTD. v. MARATHON REALTY CO. (1980), 24 B.C.L.R. 332 (S.C.).

Plaintiff lost $350,000 in failing to convert a former ferry into a restaurant and commercial complex. Defendant realty company executed a deed of consent to a mortgage to it of the mooring site lease by way of sub-lease as security. The deed contained an incorrect acknowledgment that rental payments due under the mortgage bases had been made and that there had been no breach of any covenants contained in the leases. In fact, there were outstanding rent arrears and non-compliance with the by-laws. A stop-work order was posted by the city building inspector shortly after plaintiff made its advance. Plaintiff failed in its claim for damages in fraud and negligence against defendant. The court held that there was no evidence that plaintiff would rely on the acknowledgment as a statement of fact.

MONCTON PLUMBING & SUPPLY CO. v. ROYAL BANK (1982), 42 N.B.R. (2d) 232, 110 A.P.R. 232 (Q.B.).

Plaintiff plumbing contractor won sub-contract on large building project and approached its bank, defendant, which was financing the project, for assurance that funding was available for its sub-contract. Defendant affirmed that funding was available, but told plaintiff it would have to assess the risk itself. Subsequently, funding was cut off and plaintiff was not paid for its work. Held: Defendant bank was not liable to contractor for negligent advice, since it did not warrant plaintiff's account would be paid. Indeed, it only volunteered correct information and refrained from giving any opinion or advice.

J. NUNES DIAMONDS LTD. v. DOM. ELEC. PROTECTION CO., [1969] 2 O.R. 473, 5 D.L.R. (3d) 679, affirmed [1971] 1 O.R. 218, 15 D.L.R. (3d) 26, which was affirmed [1972] S.C.R. 769, 26 D.L.R. (3d) 699.

Plaintiff diamond merchant was protected by defendant's alarm system which was the best of its kind but capable of circumvention. Defendant failed to inform plaintiff of latter. An inspection of plaintiff's system was made after a burglary occurred at premises containing the same system, after which defendant's employees orally and in writing assured plaintiff of the efficiency of its system. Plaintiff's diamonds were stolen when system was circumvented. Plaintiff sued in contract and negligence. Held: Under the contract, defendant's liability was limited to $50 liquidated damages. As for tort liability in respect of defendant's representations, it could only be based on a tort unconnected with the performance of the contract which governed the parties' relations. (Per Spence and Laskin JJ. (dissenting): The contract established a relationship upon which a duty of care was established. Defendant was therefore liable in tort for plaintiff's loss.)

ORMINDALE HOLDINGS LTD. v. RAY, WOLFE, CONNELL, LIGHTBODY & REYNOLDS (1982), 36 B.C.L.R. 378, 135 D.L.R. (3d) 577 (C.A.).

Plaintiff owned rental accommodation which it wished to convert to long-term tenure. Conversion was restricted by legislation. Defendant law firm devised scheme to circumvent the legislation. Plaintiff lost great deal of money as result of implementing the scheme which proved unsuccessful. Held: Defendant was not guilty of breach of warranty or negligence. Although a lawyer might have to warn client of consequences that may flow from wrong advice, he is not normally required to warn experienced business clients of possibility that an opinion, however firmly held, may not in fact prevail.

SEALAND OF THE PAC. LTD. v. ROBERT C. McHAFFIE LTD., [1974] 6 W.W.R. 724, 51 D.L.R. (3d) 702 (B.C. C.A.).

Plaintiff had contracted with defendant corporation which employed the co-defendant naval architect to provide advice on use of materials for a floating oceanarium. Advice was bad and plaintiff incurred financial loss in replacing improperly specified materials. Plaintiff succeeded in contract against corporation but had his claims in tort dismissed against both the corporation and its employee.

SEMKULEY v. CLAY (1982), 140 D.L.R. (3d) 489, 39 A.R. 526 (Q.B.).

Vendor arranged to sell a building containing four rental suites. Municipal zoning permitted two rental suites only. Real estate agent told purchaser that the property could probably be rezoned without difficulty. Plaintiffs then completed the purchase but their application for rezoning was rejected. Plaintiffs sued agent for subsequent loss of revenue income. Held: Agent was not liable for fraud, since there was no intention to defraud; nor was she liable for negligent misrepresentation, since she did not profess to have any expertise in zoning law and plaintiffs could not reasonably rely on her statement.

SHARADAN BLDRS. INC. v. MAHLER (1978), 22 O.R. (2d) 122, 95 D.L.R. (3d) 480, reversing 17 O.R. (2d) 161, 79 D.L.R. (3d) 439 (C.A.)

Plaintiff inquired of municipality whether building permits would be issued for certain lands it wished to buy. Municipality advised plaintiff that permits would be available. Plaintiff then completed the transaction. Plaintiff then discovered permits were not available for some lots due to conservation restrictions. Held: Defendant was not liable for negligence. Plaintiff's inquiry was not directed to the existence of regulations imposed by the conservation authority. Also, defendant did not hold itself out as engaged in the business of or expert in advising upon requirements for permits other than those imposed by itself.

SILVA v. ATKINS (1978), 20 O.R. (2d) 570, 4 B.L.R. 209, 88 D.L.R. (3d) 558 (H.C.).

Plaintiff bought property from "H.R. & Ass. *Inc.* but requisitioned defendant sheriff for writs of execution in name of "H.R. & Ass. *Ltd.*" The practice in the sheriff's office was to show similar names for individuals but not corporations. Sheriff gave plaintiff a clear certificate. In fact, a writ of execution was filed under "H.R. & Ass. *Inc.*" Faced with prospect of losing the property, plaintiff sued defendant for negligence. Held: Plaintiff failed to show sheriff had a duty to provide information concerning similar names; nor was there any reliance by plaintiff on defendant to provide information concerning similar names.

SULZINGER v. C.K. ALEXANDER LTD., [1972] 1 O.R. 720, 24 D.L.R. (3d) 137 (C.A.).

Plaintiff incurred expenses in renting a replacement car during repairs, on the advice of an insurance adjuster retained by the insurer of the person who negligently damaged plaintiff's car. Plaintiff's claim against driver was lost by expiry of limitation period. Plaintiff then sued defendant insurance adjuster in negligence. Held: *Hedley Byrne* does not create cause of action here, since there was no relationship between the parties and defendant's advice was proper and not negligent. Plaintiff's expenses were recoverable from the wrongdoer rather than from the adjuster.

THE PAS v. PORKY PACKERS LTD., [1977] 1 S.C.R. 51, [1976] 3 W.W.R. 138, 65 D.L.R. (3d) 1, 7 N.R. 569.

Defendant municipality resolved to sell land to plaintiff for use which was prohibited by planning scheme and health by-law. Plaintiff continued to build after a ratepayer began an action to quash the resolution. The resolution was quashed by the court. Plaintiff then sued the town for the loss of its investment and loss of expectation of profits resulting from its negligent representation. Held: *Hedley Byrne* did not apply, since plaintiff did not seek advice or information from the town's officials, or rely on their skill or judgment.

VAN DER KUILEN v. TODD, [1979] 3 W.W.R. 165 (Sask. Q.B.).

Defendant car dealer introduced plaintiffs, who wanted to buy a used motor home, to a seller. Defendant told plaintiffs he had had previous dealings with the seller and was satisfied as to his honesty. Plaintiffs, after buying the motor home from the seller, discovered it was a stolen vehicle, plaintiffs then sued defendant for fraud and negligent misrepresentation. The court found there was no evidence of fraud. As for the claim based on *Hedley Byrne*, that was not established as plaintiffs had neither sought nor relied on defendant's advice, and it had not been shown that defendant failed to exercise care.

WELBRIDGE HOLDINGS LTD. v. WINNIPEG, 72 W.W.R. 705, 12 D.L.R. (3d) 470, affirmed [1971] S.C.R. 957, [1972] 3 W.W.R. 433, 22 D.L.R. (3d) 470.

Plaintiff builder spent money in reliance on a zoning by-law which was later declared invalid by the court. Plaintiff had to abandon plans for and work in progress on a multi-storey apartment building and suffered economic loss as a result. Plaintiff sued municipality in negligence. Held: No liability attaches to a municipality in negligence in exercising its legislative or quasi-judicial powers (here, the passing of a by-law which proves to be invalid).

WYNSTON v. MacDONALD (1979), 27 O.R. (2d) 67, 10 R.P.R. 113, 105 D.L.R. (3d) 527, affirmed 32 O.R. (2d) 108, 119 D.L.R. (3d) 256 (C.A.).

Defendant solicitor, who was acting for the mortgagor in a mortgage transaction, gave plaintiff's solicitor a statement of adjustments from the property sale indicating the mortgagor had paid $300,000. In fact the property was worth considerably less than $250,000 and when the mortgagor defaulted, the plaintiff mortgagee suffered loss. Plaintiff then sued the defendant for negligent misrepresentation. The court refused to impose liability on the defendant on the grounds that plaintiff did not rely on defendant's skill or judgment, but on his own solicitor, and defendant did not owe plaintiff a duty of care (*Hedley Byrne* distinguished).

GREAT BRITAIN

Held for Plaintiff

W.B. ANDERSON & SONS v. RHODES (LIVERPOOL), [1967] 2 All E.R. 850.

Plaintiff companies were fruit and vegetable wholesalers. Defendant firm was a wholesaler and commission agent buying for a third party. Defendant firm's buyer was not informed by its manager of the overdue state of account of the third party with the firm, and upon plaintiffs' inquiries, assured them of the party's credit-worthiness. Plaintiffs were not paid for the goods they delivered to the third party as the latter became insolvent. Plaintiffs then sued defendants in negligence. Held: Defendant's servant's representations concerned business transactions whose nature revealed the gravity of the inquiries and the importance attached to the answers. None of the plaintiffs would have sold to the third party on credit but for defendant's assurances as to its credit-worthiness.

ARENSON v. CASSON, BECKMAN, RUTLEY & CO., [1975] 3 W.L.R. 815, [1975] 3 All E.R. 901, reversing (sub nom. ARENSON v. ARENSON) [1973] Ch. 346, [1973] 2 W.L.R. 553, [1973] 2 All E.R. 235 (H.C.).

Plaintiff shareholder sold his shares to defendant company chairman at a price assessed to be the value of the shares by the company's auditors, the second defendants. The latter were stated to be "acting as experts and not as arbitrators." Plaintiff sued defendants in negligence upon discovering the shares were worth six times their assessed value. The second defendants sought to strike out plaintiff's claim. Held: The immunity of judges and arbitrators against an action in negligence does not extend to a "mutual" valuer who was not exercising any judicial function. Accordingly, the plaintiff has a cause of action against the second defendants.

ESSO PETROLEUM CO. v. MARDON, [1976] Q.B. 801, [1976] 2 W.L.R. 583, [1976] 2 All E.R. 5 (C.A.).

A petrol company, wishing to induce Mardon to take from them a tenancy of a garage, provided him with estimates of annual throughput that were negligently prepared. The estimates proved to be exaggerated and Mardon lost all his capital and incurred large bank overdraft in operating the garage. Esso then sued for the price of the petrol supplied. Mardon counter-claimed for breach of warranty and negligent misrepresentations. Held: Esso was liable for breach of warranty and for negligent misrepresentation inducing Mardon to enter into the contract. The petroleum company had held themselves out as having special expertise in the circumstances which gave rise to the duty to take reasonable care to ensure the representation was correct.

MIN. OF HOUSING & LOCAL GOVT. v. SHARP, [1970] 2 Q.B. 223, [1970] 2 W.L.R. 802, [1970], 1 All E.R. 1009 (C.A.).

Prospective land purchaser requested search of local land register maintained by county council (second defendant). Search was negligently made by clerk of council and a certificate issued omitting any reference to plaintiff ministry's registered charge on land. Purchaser completed purchase. Plaintiff was deprived by statute of any recourse against vendor or purchaser and sued county council for clerk's negligence. Held: Although plaintiff did not know of erroneous certificate and took no action in reliance upon it, clerk was in breach of common law duty of care and local authority was found liable. *Per* Lord Denning M.R.: *Hedley Byrne* doctrine extended in respect of the certificate "to any person whom [the clerk] knows, or ought to know, will be injuriously affected by a mistake" irrespective of knowledge and reliance.

OSMAN v. J. RALPH MOSS, [1970] 1 Lloyd's Rep. 313 (C.A.).

Defendant insurance brokers negligently advised plaintiff to insure with a car insurance company known to be in financial straits. Plaintiff paid the premium and was issued a 60-day cover note. The company then went insolvent, but the defendants assured plaintiff he was still insured. Plaintiff, fined and found civilly liable for driving while uninsured, sued defendants in negligence. Held: Defendants were negligent in recommending that plaintiff insure with a company known to be in financial straits, and were liable for all foreseeable consequences. Hence, plaintiff could recover not only the premium he had paid but also the costs of defending the civil and criminal proceedings, the fine imposed against him, and the amount paid by him in respect of repairs to the third party's car and the hiring of a replacement car.

PERRY v. SYDNEY PHILLIPS & SON (A FIRM), [1982] 1 W.L.R. 1297, [1982] 3 All E.R. 705 (C.A.).

Plaintiff purchased house in reliance on survey report prepared by defendant surveyors.

Report failed to disclose many defects in the house. Due to his financial position, plaintiff could not carry out repairs required. Plaintiff succeeded in claim based on contractual breach and negligence. The court held that it was reasonable for plaintiff not to carry out repairs in light of his financial position and the defendant's denial of liability: *Liesbosch* distinguished.

WOODS v. MARTINS BANK, [1959] 1 Q.B. 55, [1958] 1 W.L.R. 1018, [1958] 3 All E.R. 166.

Plaintiff, relying on the advice of the manager of defendant bank whom he had asked to be his financial adviser, invested in two companies which were also customers of the bank. It turned out that the manager had no grounds to believe that the companies were financially sound or that investments in these companies would be wise. Plaintiff sued for the loss in his investments, alleging fraud and negligence. Held: Although defendant was not liable for fraud, since he honestly believed the advice he gave, he was negligent in giving the advice he did in light of the fiduciary relationship that existed between plaintiff and defendants. The advice was neither careful nor skillful, and it induced plaintiff, who had no real business experience, to make the investments.

YIANNI v. EDWIN EVANS & SONS, [1982] Q.B. 438, [1981] 3 W.L.R. 843.

Plaintiffs applied to a building society for a mortgage on a house they wanted to buy. The society hired defendant surveyors to value the property. The survey, which was negligently carried out, was relied on by the society in its decision to advance the funds to plaintiffs. After plaintiffs purchased the house, cracks appeared that were caused by subsidence, entailing £18,000 in repairs. Plaintiffs sued defendants in negligence. Held: Defendants knew that their valuation would be passed on to plaintiffs, who would rely on its accuracy in deciding whether to buy the house. Accordingly, there was a sufficient relationship of proximity between the parties to warrant the imposition of liability for plaintiffs' loss.

Held for Defendant

ARGY TRADING DEV. CO. v. LAPID DEV., [1977] 1 W.L.R. 444, [1977] 3 All E.R. 785 (Q.B.).

Defendants, landlords, leased warehouse premises to plaintiffs who covenanted to insure against risk of fire. The landlords subsequently represented that they would insure the premises under a block indemnity policy. The insurance cover was duly effected. Defendants then cancelled the block policy without notifying plaintiffs. The premises were partially destroyed by fire. Plaintiffs sued defendants for the insurance moneys they would have received under the policy but for defendants' failure to continue the policy and their failure to notify them of its cancellation. Held: Although there was a duty not to give negligent advice arising from the special business relationship, the only information given by defendants related to their intention to insure at that time and was true then. Accordingly, no liability arose from their later decision not to renew the policy.

FORSTER v. OUTRED & CO. (A FIRM), [1982] 1 W.L.R. 86, [1982] 2 All E.R. 753 (C.A.).

Following defendant solicitor's negligent advice, plaintiff executed a mortgage on her property as a guarantor of her son's liabilities, with the result that she was subject to contingent liability to discharge her son's liability to the mortgagee company. Held: Plaintiff's action against defendant for negligent advice was complete when plaintiff relied on it and acted to her detriment by incurring a contingent liability that was capable of monetary assessment. However, plaintiff's action was struck out for want of prosecution (caused by inordinate and inexcusable delay).

HEDLEY BYRNE & CO. v. HELLER & PARTNERS, [1964] A.C. 465, [1963] 3 W.L.R. 101, [1963] 2 All E.R. 575 (H.L.).

Plaintiff advertising agents placed advertising orders for a company on terms according to which plaintiffs were personally liable for the orders. Plaintiffs asked their bankers to inquire into the company's stability. Latter asked the company's bankers who made favourable references but stated these were given "without responsibility." References were unwarranted and plaintiffs lost money relying on them. Plaintiffs sued company's bankers in negligence. Held: A negligent misrepresentation may give rise to an action for financial loss caused thereby, apart from any contract of fiduciary relationship. A duty of care arises where a party seeking information from a party having special skills relies on the latter to exercise due care, and where the second party knew or ought to have known of the reliance. Here, no such duty arises in the face of the express disclaimer of responsibility.

JEB FASTENERS LTD. v. MARKS BLOOM & CO. (A FIRM), [1983] 1 All E.R. 583, affirming [1981] 3 All E.R. 289 (C.A.).

Plaintiffs were negotiating to take over a company. The company auditors prepared the company accounts with the knowledge that the company required outside financial help. The auditors made the accounts available to plaintiffs. The accounts overstated the company's stock. Plaintiffs were aware of the inaccuracy but not the full extent of the inaccuracy. The takeover was unsuccessful and plaintiffs suffered a considerable loss. Plaintiffs then sued auditors for negligence in preparing the accounts leading plaintiffs to proceed with the takeover. Held: Although plaintiffs were aware of and had considered the accounts, they had not to any material degree affected plaintiffs' judgment in deciding to take over the company. Hence, defendants' negligence was not a cause of plaintiffs' loss.

McINERNEY v. LLOYDS BANK LTD., [1974] 1 Lloyd's Rep. 246 (C.A.).

A third party wished to buy some companies owned by plaintiff by way of a banker's commercial credit, allowing plaintiff to draw bills of exchange for payment of the price. The bank sent a telex message to plaintiff regarding the renewal of the period of credit. The third party subsequently failed to honour the bills of exchange. Plaintiff then sought to hold defendant bank liable for breach of contract or negligent misstatements contained in the telex. Held: No contract could be implied from the telex or the conduct between plaintiffs and defendants; nor did defendant proffer any advice to plaintiffs in the telex, which merely informed plaintiffs as to the method of credit it was to adopt in this matter.

WINRAM v. FINLAYSON, [1977] S.C. 19 (Outer House).

In a report it prepared for a prospective purchaser of land, defendant chartered surveyor erroneously calculated the acreage. Plaintiff alleged he bought the hotel in reliance on the report and that he only discovered the error when he later put the hotel up for sale. Plaintiff sued surveyor on the ground that he had been induced to pay a price he would not otherwise have paid for the hotel. The court held for defendant on the ground that plaintiff had failed to prove that a verbal report had been make to him about acreage before he entered into the purchase. (The written report was not tendered until after plaintiff had entered into the purchase of the land.) Furthermore, even if plaintiff had proved his case. he would not be entitled to damages as he had suffered no loss.

NEW ZEALAND

Held for Plaintiff

J. & J.C. ABRAMS LTD. v. ANCLIFFE, [1978] 2 N.Z.L.R. 420, affirmed [1981] 1 N.Z.L.R. 244 (C.A.).

Plaintiff builder estimated cost of building residential units for defendant at $30,500.

Defendant made frequent inquiries as to final price but construction had reached a stage where it would be impractical for him to withdraw before plaintiff told him price would be $57,000. Defendant could not sell the units upon completion. Plaintiff sued for amount owing on work done on construction and defendant counter-claimed for greater amount as loss in completing the uneconomic units. Held: Claim and counter-claim allowed. Plaintiff was negligent in failing to give defendant reliable information as to the final price of project as soon as he was in a position to do so and in time for defendant to withdraw.

BARRETT v. J.R. WEST LTD., [1970] N.Z.L.R. 789 (S.C.).

A real estate agent and director of the defendant firm of land agents, when asked by plaintiff prospective purchasers whether a mushroom-shaped object on the back lawn of house was a septic tank, answered that the house was now on mains sewerage, relying on listing particulars supplied to him. Plaintiffs bought the property and discovered that the only means of drainage was a septic tank. Plaintiffs sued defendant for negligent misrepresentation inducing them to buy the house. Held: Defendant was liable in failing to exercise reasonable care in answering the plaintiffs' inquiries. The specific inquiry made by plaintiffs as to the drainage of the property should have warned the agent the information on which he was relying might not be correct, but he chose to disregard that warning nonetheless.

CAPITAL MOTORS LTD. v. BEECHAM, [1975] 1 N.Z.L.R. 576 (S.C.).

Plaintiff, in purchasing a second-hand car from defendant car dealer, relied on defendant salesman's false representation that car only had two previous owners. The contract of sale contained a clause negativing oral representations. Plaintiff then sued defendant dealer for its servant's negligent misrepresentation causing economic loss when he discovered the car had five previous owners. Held: The measure of damages in tort for negligent misrepresentation inducing a sale is *prima facie* the difference between the price paid and the fair value at time of purchase.

DAY v. OST, [1973] 2 N.Z.L.R. 385 (S.C.).

Owners hired defendant architect. Plaintiff was a blocklaying and plastering sub-contractor. Plaintiff started work but stopped upon non-payment. Defendant asked plaintiff to resume work and assured him he would receive progress payment of $1000 and that ample funds were available to cover balance of price. Plaintiff completed work thereon but received only $1000 and his share of lien moneys. Plaintiff claimed damages for negligence on basis of *Hedley Byrne* (defendant was aware of financial position of head contract at time he gave the assurance.) Held: Defendant was in breach of his duty of care as an adviser. Plaintiff was entitled to recover loss suffered after recommencing the work.

GORDON v. MOEN, [1971] N.Z.L.R. 526.

Certificate prepared by marine surveyors upon vendor's request stated the launch to have no dry rot. Plaintiff purchased launch on basis of this certificate. Launch did have dry rot. Plaintiff sued defendants on basis of *Hedley Byrne*. Held: Plaintiff could recover cost of repairs and loss of value from defendants. Defendants were engaged in a calling requiring special knowledge and skill and owed vendor a duty to prepare the survey report with reasonable skill. Defendants knew vendor intended to raise financing on the launch, and issued an "open" survey report and were aware that persons receiving reports commonly disclosed them to others. The special relationship class to whom defendants owed duty of care extended to all those to whom knowledge of the report might reasonably come.

PHIL CLARK CONTRACTORS LTD. v. DREWET, [1977] 2 N.Z.L.R. 556 (S.C.).

Plaintiff, a machine operator, was sent out to drive a ditch-digging machine for defendant contractors. Plaintiff asked defendants' foreman if there were any underground cables before digging the trench and was told there were none. Plaintiff dug the trench and cut and damaged some Post Office cables. Plaintiff was ordered to make good the damage. Plaintiff then sued to recover that sum from defendants. Held: *Hedley Byrne* applied.

PORT UNDERWOOD FORESTS LTD. v. MARLBOROUGH COUNTY COUNCIL, [1982] 1 N.Z.L.R. 343 (H.C.).

Defendant council granted plaintiff company permission to plant a particular area of land in forest. In granting permission council had failed to follow the statutory procedure and the consent was later ruled invalid. Plaintiff had to remove the trees it planted. Plaintiff sued defendant for damages in negligence to recover the cost of planting and removing the trees. Held: The council owed plaintiff a duty of care to give it a valid, authorized permission under the statute.

R.A. CARLL & T.J. LTD. v. BERRY, [1981] 2 N.Z.L.R. 76 (H.C.).

Plaintiff purchasers of a restaurant business relied on advice from health inspector that he had recently inspected the premises and given them "a clean bill of health." Plaintiffs found the premises to be infested with cockroaches when they moved in. The premises were then closed by the health inspector. Plaintiffs successfully sued the health inspector for damages caused by his negligent advice.

RICHARDSON v. NORRIS SMITH REAL ESTATE LTD., [1977] 1 N.Z.L.R. 152 (S.C.).

Plaintiffs bought a property from defendant vendors relying on the vendors' land agents' representations as to boundaries of the property. Plaintiffs, after spending money on improving the area, discovered that portion of the property was part of the road reserve. Plaintiffs sued land agents for fraud or negligent misrepresentation, and the vendors for vicarious negligence. Held: The land agents were liable for negligent misrepresentation. The vendors, however, were not vicariously liable, since they had not authorized the land agent to make the representation; nor was the representation made within his apparent authority.

RUTHERFORD v. A.G., [1976] 1 N.Z.L.R. 403 (S.C.).

Plaintiff agreed to buy a heavy motor truck from defendant if the truck could get a certificate of fitness. Defendant then obtained a certificate of fitness from the Ministry of Transport. Plaintiff completed the purchase on the faith of the certificate, which turned out to have been negligently issued. The truck was actually in an unsafe or potentially unsafe condition, and required $1000 of work to be done before a certificate could be issued. Plaintiff claimed the amount from the vendor and the ministry. Held: Although the vendor was not liable, since he had not given any warranty, the ministry was liable to the purchaser for the negligent issue of the certificate. The duty to take care in exercising statutory powers extends to all road users including a purchaser purchasing on faith of the certificate. The claim for economic loss does not necessarily exclude liability in tort for negligence: *Dutton, Hedley Byrne* applied.

WALKER, HOBSON & HILL LTD. v. JOHNSON, [1981] 2 N.Z.L.R. 532 (H.C.).

Defendant doctor represented to plaintiff that he held an exclusive licence to mill timber on an island. Plaintiff entered into a contract of option and expended money on research. Option expired but plaintiff continued its research on the basis of defendant's assurances to renew. Defendant's licence was cancelled upon his default of conditions imposed on the licence which were unknown to plaintiff. Plaintiff sued defendant for economic loss suffered. Held: Plaintiff could recover in contract and tort in respect of damages suffered until expiry of the option. For losses suffered after expiry of the option, plaintiff could recover under *Hedley Byrne* (defendant had represented he was knowledgeable in matters pertaining to the island).

Held for Defendant

ALLIED FINANCE & INVT. LTD. v. HADDOW & CO., [1980] 2 N.Z.L.R. 428 (H.C.).

A company and its director were both clients of defendant solicitors. The director arranged for a loan from plaintiff ostensibly to finance his purchase of a yacht, signing security documents in his own name. Defendants returned the documents to plaintiff's solicitor with a letter certifying that the security was "fully binding" on the director. Defendant failed to tell plaintiff that the yacht was actually owned by the company and that the director was not, and would not, become its owner. The director declared bankruptcy and the loan was not repaid. Plaintiff recovered all but $7000 of his investment and sought to recover this from defendant for breach of a contractual undertaking as to the yacht's ownership, or negligence. Held: Defendant's letter did not constitute a contractual undertaking. They were also not liable in tort, since the solicitors, acting for different parties on opposite sides of a transaction, were not in a relationship of proximity/neighbourhood contemplated in *Hedley Byrne*.

DIMOND MFG. CO. LTD. v. HAMILTON, [1968] N.Z.L.R. 705, reversed [1969] N.Z.L.R. 609 (C.A.).

Accountants and auditors negligently prepared incorrect accounts for the information of company's shareholders and appended an unqualified certificate as to their correctness. A partner of the firm of accountants and auditors later showed balance sheet to plaintiff who bought shares relying on the incorrect accounts. Held: Although the firm was negligent in preparation and auditing of accounts, which constituted continuing misrepresentations of fact, plaintiffs failed to call evidence to establish extent of their loss and the true measure of damages. Hence, nonsuit judgment was the defendant.

GARTSIDE v. SHEFFIELD, YOUNG & ELLIS, [1981] 2 N.Z.L.R. 547 (H.C.).

Plaintiff beneficiary under a proposed will sued defendant solicitors for negligence in carrying out the 89-year-old hospitalized testatrix's instructions to draw up a new will, resulting in her death precluding the drafting of the new will. Defendants moved to strike out pleadings. Held: Defendants owed no duty of care to plaintiff in the circumstances (*Ross v. Cautners* not followed). Plaintiff was also unable to establish the necessary reliance to fall under *Hedley Byrne*.

HOLMAN CONST. LTD. v. DELTA TIMBER CO. LTD., [1972] N.Z.L.R. 1081 (S.C.).

Plaintiff building contractor was interested in tendering for a building contract. It required sub-contractors for doing specified work or supplying material. Defendant timber merchant quoted price for timber supply to plaintiff. Plaintiff, relying on that quote, successfully tendered for head contract. Defendant then revoked its offer to supply at quoted price and plaintiff had to take the next highest quote at a higher price. Plaintiff sued defendant for that sum. (Plaintiff had not accepted offer before defendant's revocation.) Held: There was no duty on the sub-contractor to make a careful estimate for the tender price. Plaintiff had no recourse to *Hedley Byrne* when it suffered loss by its own failure to accept defendant's offer before revocation.

JONES v. STILL, [1965] N.Z.L.R. 1071 (S.C.).

Plaintiff approached vendor's salesman, defendant, about buying a residential property. Defendant orally agreed to include in the sale carpets and drapes then in the house. Plaintiff alleged he accepted the offer in reliance on that oral term. Plaintiff failed to get the carpets and drapes and sued defendant for the cost of replacing them in an action for breach of warranty of authority or negligent misrepresentation. Held: A representation made by an agent on a matter not going to the question of his authority to act for his principal does not found an action for breach of warranty. *Hedley Byrne* does not apply unless the duty to take care arises from contract, a fiduciary relationship, or the representee's reliance on a special skill possessed by the representor.

MEATES v. A.G., [1979] 1 N.Z.L.R. 415 (S.C.).

Plaintiffs sued the New Zealand government for $1,000,000 on the basis of breach of contract and negligent misstatements made by the Prime Minister and other ministers on which plaintiffs relied to their financial detriment. Plaintiff company shareholders alleged defendants breached contract made for the supply of services and provision of development assistance to the company. Plaintiffs alleged they were led by defendants' negligent advice to establish the company to assist the government, and that they were assured that defendants would indemnify them should they get into financial difficulties. Held: There was no contract between the parties. In respect of the *Hedley Byrne* claim, there was no special relationship between plaintiffs and the minister, since the latter was not a person carrying on the business or profession of giving advice.

PLUMMER-ALLINSON v. SPENCER L. AYREY LTD., [1976] 2 N.Z.L.R. 254 (S.C.).

Plaintiffs owned a prosperous beauty salon business. Plaintiffs had insured with defendant insurance agents against risk of fire. Fire broke out in neighbouring premises and damaged plaintiffs' goods. Packets of perm solution were sent for testing. Defendant agents then told plaintiffs they were approved for use. Plaintiffs used the packets with unsatisfactory results and their clients had to have their hair redone without charge. Plaintiffs sued defendants for the pre-fire value of the packets and loss of profits through losing customers, on the basis of *Hedley Byrne*. Held: Defendant insurance company did not have sufficient financial interest to imply any special qualification, skill or competence regarding the usability of the packets. The essence of *Hedley Byrne* is the holding out by defendant that he has some special competence in the subject matter of his statement.

SCOTT GROUP LTD. v. McFARLANE, [1978] 1 N.Z.L.R. 553, affirming [1975] 1 N.Z.L.R. 582 (C.A.).

Plaintiff relied on the consolidated accounts of a holding company in making a takeover bid. The accounts had been negligently prepared by the company's auditors and overstated the company's assets. The error was discovered after plaintiff completed the takeover bid. Plaintiff then sued the auditors for negligent misrepresentation. Held: The principle of *Hedley Byrne* only applies in situations where defendant ought to have been aware that the information would be available to and was relied on by a particular person or group of persons for a particular transaction or a particular type of transaction. Furthermore, plaintiff did not suffer any loss, merely a reduction in the profit it could have made had the accounts been correct. Loss of profit, while recoverable in contract, cannot be recovered in tort.

APPENDIX II

UNDERTAKINGS CREATING RELIANCE IN PURE ECONOMIC LOSS WHERE *HEDLEY BYRNE v. HELLER* IS NOT RELIED UPON

AUSTRALIA

Held for Plaintiff

FRANKSTON & HASTINGS v. COHEN, 102 C.L.R. 607, 33 A.L.J.R. 427, [1960] A.L.R. 249 (H.C.).
Defendant was appointed auditor for a municipality by Governor in Council. He prepared the audit of the accounts of the municipality negligently with the result that a servant's theft and embezzlement of moneys escaped unnoticed and he was able to steal more moneys. The municipality then successfully sued defendant for the loss it sustained. Held: Defendant was guilty of breach of duty of care even in the absence of a contract between plaintiff and defendant.

PENNANT HILLS RESTAURANTS PTY LTD. v. BARRELL INS. PTY LTD. (1981), 145 C.L.R. 625, 55 A.L.J.R. 258, 81 A.T.C. 415 (H.C.).
Defendant insurance broker failed to arrange worker's compensation insurance for plaintiff employer with the result that the employer became liable to make periodic payments of compensation to an injured employee in respect of its liability under the Workers Compensation Act. Defendant insurance broker was found liable for negligence and breach of contract.

WATTS v. PUB. TRUSTEE, [1980] W.A.R. 97 (S.C.).
Defendant public trustee was asked by testator to draft a will with plaintiff as the residuary beneficiary. Defendant failed to notice that the beneficiary's wife was one of the parties who attested the will. The gift to the plaintiff failed. Plaintiff sued defendant for the loss of the benefit. Held: The liability of the public trustee is the same as that of a solicitor in an identical situation. Plaintiff owed a duty of care to ensure that in carrying out the testator's wishes he did not cause financial loss to an identified third party. "Loss" include a failure to receive an assured benefit: *Ross v. Caunters* applied.

Held for Defendant

SEALE V. PERRY, [1982] V.R. 193 (S.C. Full Ct.).
Deceased retained defendant solicitor to prepare will for him. Will was drawn according to deceased's instructions but was not executed according to Wills Act 1958. Plaintiffs, intended beneficiaries, failed to receive any interest in a house property as a result and

sued defendant in negligence. Held: The solicitor owed no duty of care to the intended beneficiaries (only to the deceased), because there was not a sufficient proximity of relationship between plaintiffs and defendant to give rise to a duty of care. In any event, no damage recognizable at law had been suffered by them (what was lost was only a *spes successionis*).

CANADA

Held for Plaintiff

BANKS v. REID (1977), 18 O.R. (2d) 148, 4 C.C.L.T. 1, 81 D.L.R. (3d) 730 (C.A.).
Plaintiffs, while being driven to their stalled car by service station employee A., were injured in a collision with a car driven by another person. A. was killed. Plaintiffs and A.'s father hired defendant lawyer to represent them in suit against second driver. Defendant did not advise plaintiffs of possible claim against A.'s estate and of their conflict of interest. Court held that accident was solely A.'s fault but by then the limitation period for bringing action against A.'s estate had expired. Plaintiffs then sued defendant for damages in negligence. Held: Plaintiffs would have succeeded against A.'s estate but for defendant's negligence. No immunity should be afforded in defendant in this case. If *Rondel v. Worsley* is applicable in Ontario, it should be confined to issues between a barrister and his client in the discharge of his duties before a court and is dependent upon consideration of barrister's duty to court and to client.

BAR-DON HOLDINGS LTD. v. REED STENHOUSE LTD., 24 Alta. L.R. (2d) 248, [1983] I.L.R. 1-1637, 44 A.R. 246 (Q.B.).
Plaintiff manufactured and transported mobile homes. It requested that defendant broker arrange for insurance on the homes. Defendant, who knew the nature and risks of plaintiff's business, acquired coverage for the mobile home while situated in specific locations but not while in transit. The home was destroyed at a location other than one of those specified in the policy. Plaintiff sued the broker for negligence in arranging for the insurance coverage. The court held for plaintiff on the ground that defendant should have protected plaintiff against "all foreseeable insurable risks." The broker's failure to provide the necessary coverage or inform plaintiff that it was not covered constituted negligence.

BAXTER & CO. v. JONES (1903), 6 O.L.R. 360 (C.A.).
Defendant general insurance agent gratuitously undertook to have additional policy placed on plaintiff's property, and to notify companies already holding policies of the additional insurance. Defendant failed to give such notice with result that when a loss occurred plaintiffs had to compromise claim at $1000 less than they would have recovered. Held: Defendant was liable for loss caused by negligence in performing the undertaking even though there was no consideration for the undertaking.

CAN. WESTERN NATURAL GAS CO. LTD. v. PATHFINDER SURVEYS LTD. (1980), 12 Alta. L.R. (2d) 135, 12 C.C.L.T. 211, 21 A.R. 459 (C.A.).
Plaintiff hired defendant to do survey of proposed natural gas pipeline. Pipeline was to be curved at one point. Defendant failed to complete last step of work and to stake the curve, resulting in a new line outside the easement area that conflicted with plans for a future water line. Plaintiff had to relay the wrong section and sued for cost of relaying. Held: Plaintiff could recover in contract and tort. Although plaintiff framed action in contract, he could have brought an action in contract or tort, since a duty of care arises where there is sufficient "proximity and neighbourhood" between the parties. If the latter is present, then courts will go on to consider whether scope of negligence is negatived by any policy considerations: *Anns* applied.

CLARENCE CONST. LTD. v. LAVALLEE, [1982] 2 W.W.R. 760, affirming 111 D.L.R. (3d) 582 (B.C.C.A.).

An interim agreement between plaintiff (vendor) and purchaser allowed for postponement of vendor's mortgage back to building loan mortgage. Defendant solicitor, acting for purchaser, prepared a second mortgage which allowed postponement to a *straight* first mortgage. When plaintiff vendor's security proved worthless, it sued defendant for negligence. Held: Despite the lack of a solicitor-client relationship between plaintiff and defendant, the change in the terms of the agreement gave rise to a day on the part of defendant solicitor to inform the vendor of the change or at least suggest that the vendor be independently advised. Defendant was liable for breach of this duty to plaintiff, who relied on him.

DEMARCO v. UNGARO (1979), 21 O.R. (2d) 673, 8 C.C.L.T. 207, 27 Chitty's L.J. 23, 95 D.L.R. (3d) 385 (H.C.).

Plaintiff hired defendant lawyer to represent him in suit for debt brought against him. Judgment was granted in favour of the claimant. Plaintiff then brought action against defendants alleging negligent conduct in pre-trial and trial work resulting in unfavourable judgment granted against plaintiff. Defendants sought to strike out action on basis of immunity from suit. Held: Motion denied. A lawyer in Ontario is not immune from action at the suit of a client for negligence in the conduct of the client's civil case in court: *Rondel v. Worsley* not followed.

DEYONG v. WEEKS (1983), 25 Alta. L.R. (2d) 117, 43 A.R. 342 (Q.B.).

Plaintiffs lent money to fraudulent borrowers, relying on advice of defendant solicitor retained by one plaintiff. Solicitor had failed to obey client's instructions to confirm delivery of goods by third party in accordance with letters of credit. Held: Defendant was in breach of contract for legal services to first plaintiff, and in breach of duty of care to plaintiff who was not a client but who was so closely affected by defendant's work that it was reasonably foreseeable he would be injured.

DORNDORF v. HOETER (1981), 29 B.C.L.R. 71, 20 R.P.R. 99, 122 D.L.R. (3d) 758 (S.C.).

Defendant notary public, acting for vendors in a real estate transaction, knew plaintiff purchasers were probably relying on him to protect their interests, but failed to caution plaintiffs that he was not looking after their interests. Plaintiffs sued defendant in negligence for damage suffered by proceeding with the transaction. Held: Defendant was liable for plaintiff's damages, since he owed them a duty of care, being aware of their reliance.

FINE'S FLOWERS LTD. v. GEN. ACCIDENT ASSUR. CO., 17 O.R. (2d) 529, 2 B.L.R. 257, [1978] I.L.R. 1-937, 81 D.L.R. (3d) 139 (C.A.).

Plaintiff asked and relied on defendant insurance agent to obtain "full coverage" for its large horticultural business. Defendant obtained coverage under a complex policy covering a number of business risks, but not that which occurred (damage in plants by freezing caused by failure of water pump). Held: Defendant was liable for breach of contractual undertaking and breach of duty imposed by parties' relationship to warn plaintiff of gap in coverage.

GROVE SERVICE LTD. v. LENHART AGENCIES LTD. (1979), 10 C.C.L.T. 101 (B.C. S.C.)

Defendant insurance agents had practice of automatically renewing plaintiff's policies since 1970. In 1974, plaintiff through defendants insured its boat with I.C.B.C. then advised defendant that coverage would cease after October 1975. Plaintiff agreed that defendants should seek to renew coverage with I.C.B.C. or get alternative coverage.

Defendants failed to do so. The boat was destroyed in 1976, at which time plaintiff discovered it was uninsured. Plaintiff sued defendant for agreed value of destroyed vessel for failure to give timely warning of non-continuance of insurance coverage. Held: Defendants were negligent in failing to obtain coverage or to give timely warning of inability to do so. This was a breach of duty of care arising out of history of dealings between the parties.

HELPARD v. ATKINSON MARINE & GEN. INS. LTD. (1980), 15 C.C.L.T. 241, 118 D.L.R (3d) 330, [1981] I.L.R. 1-1337, 43 N.S.R. (2d) 383, 81 A.P.R. 383 (T.D.).

Through defendant insurance company's negligence, plaintiff failed to obtain coverage for her new car, which was later involved in an accident. Although plaintiff recovered part of her losses from an out-of-court settlement with the authors of the accident, she sought the balance of her losses (including cost of proceedings against the municipality responsible for the accident) in a tort action against defendants. Held: Corporate defendant was liable in contract or tort. Since there was no contract between plaintiff and personal defendant, liability against latter must sound in tort. Although effect of allowing the claim is to disregard the corporate veil, the need to uphold the responsibilities of those possessing special skills toward those who relied on them is paramount.

HOFSTRAND FARMS LTD. v. R., [1982] 2 W.W.R. 492, 33 B.C.L.R. 251, 20 C.C.L.T. 146, 16 B.L.R. 302, 131 D.L.R. (3d) 464, reversing in part 22 B.C.L.R. 348, 114 D.L.R. (3d) 347 (C.A.).

A clerk in Department of Lands offered to arrange for courier delivery of Crown grants to be registered in another city two days later, knowing plaintiff's real estate transaction would be jeopardized if they were not delivered in time. Clerk hired plaintiff courier to provide one-day service. Due to courier's negligence, grants were not delivered in time and plaintiff could not close deal, resulting in substantial economic loss. Plaintiff sued Crown and courier. Held: Although the clerk did not owe plaintiff duty of care for which the Crown would be liable, the courier did owe plaintiff such a duty. It was within the reasonable contemplation of the courier that failure to make prompt delivery would result in loss to parties depending on the prompt delivery. Plaintiff was within the *limited class* to whom defendant owed duty of care, i.e., members of the public with business to be transacted at the receiving registry office who were directly concerned with contents of the envelope.

J & F TPT. LTD. v. MARKWART (1982), 136 D.L.R. (3d) 204 (Sask. Q.B.).

Plaintiff's bookkeeper fraudulently misappropriated cheques payable to plaintiff by opening account with defendant bank in plaintiff company's name. Bank did not inquire as to company's incorporation or names of signing officers. It failed to become suspicious even though bookkeeper gave home address and no business phone number. Plaintiff's action in negligence against defendant bank was allowed. Plaintiff's losses were caused solely by defendant in allowing bookkeeper to open bank account in which he could deposit and cash cheques payable to plaintiff.

JACOBSON FORD-MERCURY SALES LTD. v. SIVERTZ, [1980] 1 W.W.R. 141, 10 C.C.L.T. 274, 103 D.L.R. (3d) 480 (B.C.S.C.).

Plaintiff hired defendant solicitor to draw up a lease with option to purchase the property. Value of property rose steeply over the years. When plaintiff sought to exercise the option it was discovered that it was unenforceable. Plaintiff managed to buy the property, but at a price greatly in excess of that specified in option. Plaintiff sued defendant to recoup economic loss. Defendant claimed that action was only in contract and was statute barred. Held: In case of professionals, client can advance claim in tort or contract. Plaintiff could succeed here in negligence and recover from defendant difference between option price and price paid, difference between the respective mortgage rates, and fees incurred in seeking independent legal advice and in negotiating ultimate purchase.

KOSTIUK v. UNION ACCEPT. CORP., 66 D.L.R. (2d) 430, [1969] I.L.R. 1-239 (Sask. Q.B.).
Defendant finance corporation's manager undertook to get complete fire insurance coverage on goods being purchased by buyer on conditional sales contract. He reported to plaintiff buyer that insurance was placed. No insurance was ever completed and the interim cover orally extended by insurance agent was negligently allowed to lapse. Goods were destroyed by fire. Plaintiff sued defendant finance corporation for negligence.

McCANN v. WESTERN FARMERS MUT. INS. CO., 20 O.R. (2d) 210, 87 D.L.R. (3d) 135, [1978] I.L.R. 1-1022 (H.C.).
Plaintiffs bought property through defendant insurance agent for use as a residence and a business. Plaintiffs relied on defendant to obtain complete to coverage for building and contents. Defendant, knowing premises were used partly to carry on a business, still took out a policy excluding business use but failed to warn plaintiffs of lack of coverage. Premises were destroyed by fire. Plaintiffs sued defendant for the uninsured loss. Held: Defendant was negligent in failing to warn plaintiffs of lack of coverage on business portion (negligent in providing professional advice).

MacCULLOCH v. CORBETT (1982), 49 N.S.R. (2d) 663, 96 A.P.R. 663, reversing in part (sub nom. RHUDE v. CORBETT) 47 N.S.R. (2d) 472, 90 A.P.R. 472 (C.A.).
Defendant lawyer incorporated new company to take over financially troubled magazine with editor and plaintiff investors as directors. Defendant and two friends acted as provisional shareholders. Defendant issued no qualifying share to plaintiffs as directors and did not tell them they would be disqualified as directors if they did not hold shares within three months of appointment. Defendant transferred company control to editor when plaintiffs attempted to fire defendant. Plaintiffs attempted unsuccessfully to rectify share register and had to withdraw from venture. Held: Plaintiffs were entitled to recover cost of applying to rectify share register and had to withdraw from venture. Held: Plaintiffs were entitled to recover cost of applying to rectify share register as such costs arose directly from attempts to improve their position resulting from defendant's negligence and breach of fiduciary duty. But no award for loss of future profitability of magazine as this was too vague and speculative.

MAUGHAN v. INT. HARVESTER CO. OF CAN. (1980), 112 D.L.R (3d) 243, 38 N.S.R. (2d) 101, 69 A.P.R. 101 (C.A.).
Plaintiffs bought a backhoe from the manufacturer's dealer. A manufacturing defect appeared after six months. The dealer did defective repair work. The manufacturer assumed liability for the defect and the dealer's defective work. The machine continued to break down, causing plaintiffs loss of profits. The manufacturer was found liable for breach of warranty and for negligence causing plaintiffs' economic loss.

MEADWELL ENTERPRISES LTD. v. CLAY & CO., [1983] 3 W.W.R. 742, 44 B.C.L.R. 188, 27 R.P.R. 257 (S.C.).
Purchaser agreed to buy a motel from plaintiff vendor by way of substituting a new first mortgage by giving a second mortgage to vendor. Defendant, vendor's solicitor, failed to specify any limitation on the amount of the substituted first mortgage, or to notify plaintiff of the substantial increase in the amount of the substituted first mortgage given by the purchaser. The latter defaulted and plaintiff, upon foreclosure, lost the face value of the mortgage and interest payments. Plaintiff sued defendant in negligence. Defendant then

joined the purchaser's lawyer in third party notice. Held: Defendant was negligent in failing to set a maximum amount for the substituted first mortgage. The purchaser's lawyer, however, was not unethical in failing to bring defendant's attention to the amount of the substituted mortgage in the absence of any notice of fraud or knowledge that defendant had made a slip.

MISSISSAUGA v. HUB LEASEHOLDS LTD. (1981), 16 C.C.L.T. 1 (Ont. H.C.).

Plaintiff municipality entered into contract with defendants to build municipal office building on lands owned by defendants. Building was completed and lands were conveyed to plaintiff. The windows in the building were defectively installed by defendant sub-contractors. Plaintiff sued the latter in tort of negligence of cost of correcting defects. Defendants sought to strike out pleadings. Held: Application denied. No authority has applied *Rivtow* principle to cases not involving manufacturers' liability yet. While questions of law still remain, it would be inappropriate to strike out pleadings at this stage.

MORASH v. LOCKHART & RITCHIE LTD. (1978), 95 D.L.R. (3d) 647, 24 N.B.R. (2d) 180 (N.B.C.A.).

Defendant, plaintiff's insurance agent for 20 years, had invariably sent plaintiff a renewal of a fire policy and an invoice prior to expiry of each three-year term. In 1974, the insurance company decided not to renew three-year policies and defendant failed to notify plaintiff. In 1976, plaintiff's house was destroyed by fire without insurance cover. Held: Although the *Hedley Byrne* principle was confined to positive misstatements and did not extend to negligent omissions, defendant's past practice during course of its business relationship with plaintiff gave rise to a "self imposed duty in law" to renew policy or warn plaintiff it was not being renewed.

MYERS v. THOMPSON, [1976] 2 O.R. 335, 63 D.L.R. (2d) 476, affirmed [1967] 2 O.R. 335n, 63 D.L.R. (2d) 476n (C.A.).

Defendant insurance agent gratuitously undertook to change insured's life insurance policy to minimize estate taxes. He failed to act according to the insured's solicitor's instructions and did not inform insured or his solicitor of that failure. The executors of the estate sued the agent and the company for negligence. Defendant agent was held liable for the extra duties levied as a result of his negligent failure to follow plaintiff's instructions. Defendant insurance company, however, was not liable, since the agent's gratuitous undertaking was outside the scope of his proven authority.

PANKO v. SIMMONDS, [1983] 3 W.W.R. 158, 42 B.C.L.R. 50 (S.C.).

Defendant solicitor was instructed by plaintiff's son-in-law to transfer plaintiff's property to her daughter and son-in-law for no consideration. Plaintiff was an elderly unschooled widow. Defendant failed to explain the legal effect of the transfer to plaintiff, who believed that she was merely helping them to arrange for a loan at the time of the signing of the transfer at defendant's office. The couple then mortgaged the property without plaintiff's knowledge. An order *nisi* followed upon foreclosure. Plaintiff then sued defendant for negligence. Held: Defendant failed to observe the responsibilities of a solicitor when acting for both sides in a real estate transaction. He breached his duty of care to plaintiff, whom he should have known was relying on him to protect her interests.

POWER v. HALLEY (1978), 88 D.L.R. (3d) 381, 18 Nfld. & P.E.I.R. 531, 47 A.P.R. 531 (Nfld. T.D.).

Through defendant solicitor's alleged negligence, plaintiff client failed to get good title to certain land. In dealing with the question whether plaintiff's action against defendant was statute barred, held: The claim could be said to be equally founded in contract and in tort, and plaintiff can rely on whichever foundation gives him the more favourable position under the Statute of Limitations.

REARDON v. KINGS MUT. INS. CO. (1981), 15 C.C.L.T. 255, 44 N.S.R. (2d) 691, 83 A.P.R. 691 (T.D.).

Plaintiff requested his insurance agent to extend existing insurance coverage to protect newly-acquired barn. Agent forwarded request to defendant insurance company which sent inspectors to inspect barn. Inspectors decided barn was uninsurable and told the agent. Barn was destroyed by fire. Plaintiff did not know it was uninsured and sued agent and company for failure to advise him of rejection of application. Held: Although defendant insurance company owed no duty to advise plaintiff of rejection of his application, defendant agent was liable for his negligent failure to pass on information to his client. Although defendant insurance agent was arguably an agent of defendant company, the company was not vicariously liable as he was an independent contractor.

TABATA v. McWILLIAMS (1982), 40 O.R. (2d) 158, 140 D.L.R. (3d) 322, varying 33 O.R. (2d) 32, 19 R.P.R. 137, 123 D.L.R. (3d) 141 (C.A.).

Defendant solicitor acted for plaintiff purchaser in real estate transaction. Defendant was told by municipality that occupancy permit was required prior to plaintiff occupying the house. Defendant did not follow up requirement or notify purchaser. The house, built by vendors, had not been inspected during construction. The wall in the basement collapsed because of faulty design and construction after plaintiff moved in. Plaintiff sued defendant for breach of contract and negligence in failing to follow up requirement of occupancy permit or notify plaintiff. Had defendant followed up on the occupancy permit requirements, he would have discovered the reason vendors did not have one was because they failed to have house inspected during construction. Plaintiff would then have requested an inspection which would have revealed the defects. Plaintiffs recovered from defendant costs of rebuilding the wall and all related items in relation thereto.

WESTCOAST TRANSMISSION CO. LTD. v. CULLEN DETROIT DIESEL ALLISON LTD.; KATO ENRG. IND. INC. THIRD PARTIES (1983), 18 A.C.W.S. (2d) 485 (B.C. S.C.).

Plaintiff brought action to recover economic loss resulting from malfunctioning machines purchased from defendant. Plaintiff then applied to add manufacturer as a defendant upon discovering damages resulted from design incapacity known to manufacturer at time of installation. Held: Application granted. The law was not clear that there was no liability for economic loss arising from non-contracting manufacturer's tort.

TRAPPA HOLDINGS LTD. v. SURREY, [1978] 6 W.W.R. 545, 95 D.L.R. (3d) 107 (B.C. S.C.).

Plaintiff suffered loss of business as a result of defendant municipality and defendant contractor negligently failing to provide reasonable and adequate access to plaintiff's place of business while road work was going on. Held: Plaintiff's economic loss was not too remote. Defendants were aware of plaintiff's position and its dependence on ready access to its premises. (Defendants stated their aims to prevent loss of access arising from any actions on their part.)

Held for Defendant

C.T. INDUST. LTD. v. M & T RENTALS LTD. (1982), 41 B.C.L.R. 22 (Co. Ct.).

Purchasers' solicitor failed to discover arrears of taxes for two previous years on a home. The vendor, sued by the purchasers for the tax arrears, joined the solicitor as a third party, claiming latter was in breach of his duty to the vendor in failing to make a proper tax search. The court allowed the purchasers' action against the vendor, but dismissed the latter's third party action against the solicitor on the basis that it was not reasonable for the solicitor to assume that his carelessness could cause damage to the vendor. Furthermore, no duty of care was owed by the solicitor to the vendor, who was not his client.

GERLOCK v. SAFETY MART FOODS LTD., [1983] 2 W.W.R. 569, 42 B.C.L.R. 137 (C.A.).

Defendant, an employee of the company, indicated he wished to obtain some company shares and was referred to the defendant company's solicitor. The solicitor advised the employee to obtain independent legal and accounting advice regarding the purchase before completion. Plaintiff completed the purchase without obtaining independent advice and lost money on the investment. He then sued the solicitor in a negligence action. The court held for defendant on the ground that although he had a duty of care to advise plaintiff to obtain independent legal and accounting advice before entering the transaction, that duty did not extend to ensuring that plaintiff did in fact obtain that advice.

MUTUAL MTGE. CORP. LTD. v. BANK OF MONTREAL (1965), 53 W.W.R. 724, 55 D.L.R. (2d) 164 (B.C. C.A.).

Plaintiff mortgage company was approached by defendant bank manager to extend a loan to one of bank's customers. A letter from the branch manager's superintendent stating that the customer's efforts to expand were unwarranted and that its fixed assets were encumbered was not made known to plaintiff. After loan was given to customer, the business failed and defendant bank put it into receivership. Plaintiff was not repaid and sued bank and its manager for negligence. Held: Bank manager was not negligent, since plaintiff was experienced in lending money at high rates of interest on risk security whereas bank was not. No evidence that plaintiff would have been influenced by superintendent's letter or knowledge of customer's overdraft position. There was no failure to communicate information of enough import as to contribute to plaintiff's loss.

REMPEL v. PARKS, [1981] 3 W.W.R. 670, 34 B.C.L.R. 253 (S.C.).

Failure by a sheriff to serve a writ resulted in its lapse. Efforts to extend the time for renewal proved unsuccessful. The solicitor admitted liability to the client, but claimed over against the sheriff and his deputy, to whom the writ had been given for service. The court held the solicitor and the sheriff's deputy equally liable. The latter was negligent in failing to serve the writ on time or notify the solicitor before expiry of the time allowed for serving of the writ, thereby causing foreseeable damage to the solicitor.

SOURSOS v. C.I.B.C., [1983] 3 W.W.R. 176, 44 B.C.L.R. 66 (S.C.).

Plaintiff arranged with defendant bank for the mortgage of his home to finance purchase of another property. Defendant bank manager volunteered to alert the law firm handling the mortgage of plaintiff's needs. The law firm never received the manager's letter or a copy of the interim agreement sent by the manager. The conveyance and the property transaction fell through as a result. Plaintiff sued in negligence for economic loss against the bank, the manager, and the law firm. Plaintiff sued for loss of windfall profits. Held: The bank and its manager were not liable for plaintiff's lost entrepreneurial profits, since an offer to perform a gratuitous courtesy, arising from a commercial but not a contractual relationship, does not give rise to any duty of care in respect of a speculative profit opportunity. The law firm was also not liable since, in the absence of actual awareness of plaintiff's needs, no duty of care could arise.

GREAT BRITAIN

Held for Plaintiff

CANN v. WILLSON (1888), 39 Ch. D. 39.

Plaintiff prospective mortgagee requested a valuation of the property proposed to be mortgaged from mortgagors. Latter applied to defendant valuers for a valuation. Mortgage was completed on the basis of defendant's valuation. Plaintiff suffered a loss when mortgagor defaulted, and sued defendants in negligence and misrepresentation. Held: Defendants owed a duty to plaintiff, independently of contract, which they had failed to discharge. They made reckless statements on which plaintiff had acted.

JUNIOR BOOKS v. VEITCHI CO. LTD., [1982] 3 W.L.R. 477, [1982] 3 All E.R. 201 (H.L.).

Plaintiffs hired contractors to build factory. Contractors sub-contracted with defendants to carry out flooring work. Floor was defective and required continual maintenance costs to remain usable. Plaintiffs sued defendants for cost of replacing floor and consequential economic loss arising out of replacement. (N.B.: Floor did not create risk to persons or to property). Held: Plaintiffs' claim disclosed good cause of action. Duty not only to prevent harm being done by faulty product, but also to *avoid faults in the article itself.* Defendants liable for cost of remedying the defects or replacing the product and for any consequential economic loss (despite absence of any contractual relationship between the producer and the ultimate owner).

MIDLAND BANK TRUST CO. v. HETT, STUBBS & KEMP (A FIRM), [1979] Ch. 384, [1978] 3 W.L.R. 167, [1978] 3 All E.R. 571.

W. agreed to grant an option to purchase his farm to plaintiff, his son. Defendant solicitor was hired to draw up the option, but omitted to register option as a land charge or advise plaintiff of the need to do so. The option was defeated by the sale of land to a third party. Plaintiff then sued defendant in contract and negligence. Defendant was held liable in contract and tort. Although the negligence relied upon was not the giving of wrong and negligent advice but a simple nonfeasance, defendants were negligent in omitting to register the option before a third party acquired an adverse interest.

ROSS v. CAUNTERS, [1980] Ch. 297, [1979] 3 W.L.R. 605, [1979] 3 All E.R. 580.

Solicitor negligently drew up will with result that a bequest to plaintiff failed. The disappointed beneficiary was allowed to recover the value of the bequest in negligence (recovery of loss of a prospective gain). Liability was based on "neighbour principle" of *Donoghue v. Stevenson* rather than on "special relationship" of *Hedley Byrne.* A defective will is more like a defective product than a misstatement.

SAIF ALI v. SYDNEY MITCHELL & CO. (A FIRM), [1980] A.C. 198, [1978] 3 W.L.R. 849, [1978] 3 All E.R. 1033, reversing [1978] Q.B. 95, [1977] 3 W.L.R. 421, [1977] 3 All E.R. 744 (H.L.).

Plaintiff passenger in a van driven by A. was injured in a collision with a car driven by Mrs. S. and owned by Mr. S. Plaintiff contacted defendant solicitors, who turned to defendant barrister P. for advice. P. sued Mr. S. only despite being told by defendant solicitors that Mr. S.'s lawyers were alleging no agency relationship between husband and wife, and that A. was contributorily negligent. Plaintiff then abandoned suit against Mr. S. and lost any right to sue A. or Mrs. S. Plaintiff sued defendants for negligence. Defendants filed third party claim against barrister for indemnity. Held: Third party claim was good. A barrister's immunity from suit in the conduct of a trial extends only to those aspects of pre-trial work that were so immediately connected with the conduct of the case in court that they would affect the way the case was to be conducted.

CANDLER v. CRANE, CHRISTMAS & CO., [1951] 2 K.B. 164, [1951] 1 All E.R. 426 (C.A.) (Overruled by House of Lords in *Hedley Byrne*).

Defendant firm of accountants and auditors was instructed to prepare the accounts of a company required to be shown to a prospective investor. Relying on the accuracy of the accounts, plaintiff invested money in the company. The accounts were negligently done and the plaintiff lost the money he invested. Plaintiff sued defendants in negligence. Held: In the absence of a contractual or fiduciary relationship between the parties, defendants owed no duty of care to plaintiffs to exercise care in preparing the accounts.

FISH v. KELLY (1864), 17 C.B.N.S. 194, 144 E.R. 78.

Plaintiff employee inquired of employers' solicitor whether he would receive some money under a deed if he were to give notice to quit. Defendant told him "yes". Plaintiff then gave notice to quit but discovered that the deed stipulated the money invested for him by employer could only be paid to his executors upon his death. Plaintiff sued defendant for negligence. Held: Plaintiff could not recover his loss incurred upon relying on defendant's mistaken information in the absence of a solicitor-client relationship between the two.

LE LIEVRE v. GOULD, [1893] 1 Q.B. 491 (C.A.) (Overruled by House of Lords in *Hedley Byrne*.)

Plaintiff mortgagees of a builder's interest under a building agreement advanced money to him periodically on the strength of certificates given by defendant surveyor that specified stages of construction had been reached. The certificates negligently contained false statements as to the progress of the buildings. Plaintiffs sued defendant for their loss. Held: The surveyor, in the absence of a contract with plaintiffs, owed no duty to the mortgagees to exercise care in giving his certificates.

LOW v. BOUVERIE, [1891] 3 Ch. 82 (C.A.).

B., holder of life interest in a trust fund, asked plaintiff for a loan on that security. Plaintiff inquired of defendant, trustee of the fund, as to the security. Defendant replied that B.'s interest was subject to certain encumbrances, failing to mention others he had forgotten about. Plaintiff then advanced money to B. on the security of a mortgage on the life interest. Plaintiff then discovered several encumbrances prior to his own and sued defendant for the amount due on the security, alleging the advance was made upon the faith of defendant's written representations. Held: Defendant owed no duty other than to answer honestly to the inquiries of a stranger.

MOSS v. SOLOMON (1858), 1 F. and F. 342, 175 E.R. 756.

Plaintiff, holder of a bill, put it into the hands of an attorney to sue upon it in third party's name. That third party was really trusted by the attorney for his costs and was regarded as his client. Plaintiff sued attorney for negligence in proceeding with the action on the bill of exchange, resulting in loss to plaintiff. Held: Plaintiff was not entitled to sue defendant in negligence in the absence of any employment relationship between the parties.

OLD GATE ESTATES LTD. v. TAPLIS & HARDING & RUSSELL, [1939] 3 All E.R. 209 (K.B.).

Promoters of plaintiff company bought a block of flats and in promoting the company, which had not been formed yet, hired defendant firm to value the property. The evaluation turned out to be £14,000 too high and estimated the maintainable income from the property to be £1,100 greater than it should have been. Plaintiff company sued in negligence for the capitalized value of the defendant's error. Held: The doctrine in *Donoghue v. Stevenson* is confined to negligence causing physical risk of injury, and does not extend to the valuation of property.

RAE v. MEEK (1889), 14 App. Cas. 558 (H.L.).

Defendant, trustee of some funds, lent the trust fund on the security of an unfinished house under a building speculation. Defendant consulted their law agent and was told that there was no objection to the investment. The fund was lost by the failure of the speculation. Plaintiffs, ultimate beneficiaries of the fund, sued defendant and their law agent for the loss. Held: Defendant trustee was in breach of a positive duty owed to plaintiffs and was liable to restore the trust fund. The law agent, however, was not liable, since he was not employed by plaintiffs.

WILKINSON v. COVERDALE (1973), 1 Esp. 75, 170 E.R. 284.

Plaintiff brought premises from defendant which had a subsisting fire insurance policy. Defendant renewed the policy but failed to endorse the assignment of the policy to plaintiff, with the result that plaintiff failed to have any remedy on the policy when the premises were totally destroyed by fire. Plaintiff sued defendant vendor unsuccessfully in negligence.

NEW ZEALAND

Held for Plaintiff

BEVAN INVTS. LTD. v. BLACKHALL & STRUTHERS (NO. 2), [1973] 2 N.Z.L.R. 45 (S.C.).

Plaintiff hired architect to design and supervise construction of a building. Latter hired engineer to design and supervise the structural aspects. Plaintiff then entered into a building contract with a contractor. Latter abandoned the completion of the building when it found the design was structurally inadequate and unsafe. Plaintiff sued the architect and engineer for damages. Architect was found liable in contract and engineer liable in tort.

Held for Defendant

SUTHERLAND v. PUB. TRUSTEE, [1980] 2 N.Z.L.R. 536 (S.C.).

A testator left an entire substantial estate to his wife but the wife predeceased the testator and the estate on intestacy passed to the testator's nieces and nephews. Plaintiffs, the wife's children by a previous marriage, sued the public trustee for alleged negligence in not ensuring that the will contained a gift over to plaintiffs, even though plaintiffs had been residual beneficiaries under earlier wills. The suit was dismissed. Defendant had raised the possibility of intestacy with the deceased but the latter refused to consider a gift over.

APPENDIX III

FAILURE TO EXERCISE STATUTORY POWER (POST-*DUTTON* DECISIONS)

AUSTRALIA

Held for Plaintiff

SUTHERLAND SHIRE COUNCIL v. HEYMAN, [1982] 2 N.S.W.L.R. 618 (N.S.W.C.A.). Defendant council, which approved a building application for a dwelling house to be situated on a steep slope with supported footings, failed to inspect the footings and/or failed to detect what a reasonable inspection would have shown, that is, the footings were inadequately constructed. Defendant was held liable to the subsequent purchaser of the dwelling for the cost of remedial work caused by the footings which did not comply with the approved plans and specifications: *Anns* applied.

Held for Defendant

DUNLOP v. WOOLLAHRA MUN. COUNCIL, [1982] A.C. 158, [1981] 2 W.L.R. 693, [1981] 1 All E.R. 1202, affirming 2 N.S.W.L.R. 446 (P.C.).
Plaintiff incurred bank overdraft in buying land for the building of flats more than three storeys high. Defendant council, acting on solicitor's advice, passed resolutions fixing a building line for land and imposing a three-storey height restriction. Plaintiff paid architect to develop plans complying with these regulations. Resolutions were later declared void. Plaintiff sued for financial loss in respect of interest and charges on his overdraft during the period the void resolutions were in effect, rates and taxes for the same period and the architect's fee. Held for Defendants: 1. The claim under the *Beaudesert* principle failed since a void resolution is not in itself an unlawful act; 2. Defendant council was not negligent in failing to give notice of its intention to pass the one resolution; 3. Nor was it negligent in respect of the passing of the other resolution, which proved to be *ultra vires*, since it acted reasonably in taking the solicitor's advice.

CANADA

Held for Plaintiff

KAMLOOPS v. NIELSEN, [1982] 1 W.W.R. 461, 31 B.C.L.R. 311, 19 C.C.L.T. 146, 16 M.P.L.R. 221, 129 D.L.R. (3d) 111, leave to appeal to S.C.C. granted 1st February 1982.
Contractor, hired to build a house, failed to lay down foundations according to approved plan. Municipal building inspectors issued stop-work orders but failed to enforce them. House was sold to ultimate purchaser, plaintiff, who discovered foundations had subsided.

Plaintiff sued city and seller for costs of repairs and reconstruction. Held: Both defendants were liable. Cost of repairing the defective house was recoverable: *Rivtow* distinguished and *Anns* followed. City was carrying out an operation function in issuing the stop-work order and failing to enforce it.

ORDOG v. MISSION (1980), 31 B.C.L.R. 371, 110 D.L.R. (3d) 718 (S.C.).

Defendant building contractor constructed a house on his property that was inspected by defendant building inspector during construction. Plaintiff bought the house from the contractor who assured plaintiff the house was in good condition. Plaintiff then discovered a defective overhang that had not been constructed according to the plan filed with the municipality or according to the building code. The inspector had not noticed the defect during his inspection. Plaintiff sued the contractor and the building inspector for the cost of repairing the defect to prevent the wall from collapsing. The contractor was held liable in negligence for damages flowing from his negligent construction, and the building inspector was found liable for his negligent inspection under the principle in *Anns*.

Held for Defendant

BAIRD v. R. (1982), 135 D.L.R. (3d) 371 (Fed. Ct.).

Plaintiffs alleged economic loss resulting from the negligence of the Minister of Finance and Superintendent of Insurance in performing statutory duties in the licensing and inspection of a trust company. The plaintiffs' statement of claim was struck out on the basis that the claim to compensation for economic loss was not within the scope of Crown liability when the statutory duties were imposed and there was nothing in the legislation indicating an intention of Parliament to create a category of Crown liability which was previously unknown.

CAN. PAC. AIRLINES LTD. v. R., [1979] 1 F.C. 39, 87 D.L.R. (3d) 511, 21 N.R. 340, affirming [1977] 1 F.C. 715, 71 D.L.R. (3d) 421 (C.A.).

Plaintiff airline sought damages against Crown on the basis of a breach of statutory duty by Ministry of Transport in its failure to maintain the runways of its airports free of snow. Defendant, faced with a strike, had hired only certain designated employees who were prohibited from striking to maintain essential services. Plaintiff suffered economic loss as a result of the cancellation of certain scheduled commercial flights due to the forced closure of the runways. Held; Defendant's conduct was not negligent having regard to the public interest in maintaining harmonious labour relations. The duty also, being only a public duty imposed by the statute, did not give rise to a private action.

LAMPOLIER MFG. CO. LTD. v. GOVT. OF MAN. (1967), 60 W.W.R. 459, 51 C.P.R. 209, 36 Fox Pat. C. 144, 62 D.L.R. (2d) 425 (Man. Q.B.).

Defendant government official issued letters patent for new incorporation to plaintiff company under name which infringed another's registered trademark. Plaintiff sued defendant for losses and damage flowing from their being granted the name and then being compelled to change it. Held: Defendant was not negligent, since he had no personal knowledge of the objectionability of the proposed name. Duty lies on plaintiff to ensure the proposed name is unobjectionable (defendant had checked local records before approving the name).

McCREA v. WHITE ROCK, [1975] 2 W.W.R. 593, 56 D.L.R. (3d) 525, reversing [1973] 1 W.W.R. 542, 34 D.L.R. (3d) 227 (B.C.C.A.).

The owner of a building caused certain alterations to be done, including removing a wall supporting the roof and substituting a beam. After the plaintiff tenants moved in, the roof collapsed as a result of the defective alterations. The plaintiffs sued the building inspector and the city for failure to inspect. The defendants were found not liable on the grounds that the municipal by-laws merely provided that inspection was to take place on the request of the owner. Since no such request had been made, the defendants were not liable for the property loss and business loss suffered by the tenants.

GREAT BRITAIN

Held for Plaintiff

ACREREST LTD. v. S. W. HATTRELL & PARTNERS (A FIRM), [1982] 3 W.L.R. 1076, [1983] 1 All E.R. 17 (C.A.).

Plaintiffs hired defendant architects to design a block of flats. Defendants incorrectly specified a depth of 3½ feet for foundations. Local authority inspector, inspecting the foundations, also gave instructions regarding their depth. These instructions, which did not comply with building regulations, were carried out. Subsequent damage was caused to the building after it had been let to tenants, when the foundations proved inadequate. Plaintiffs sued defendants to recover the cost of remedying the damage and all sums that they might have to pay their tenants. Defendants admitted liability in contract and negligence, but sought indemnification from local authority. Held: Defendants were entitled to 25 per cent contribution from the local authority for its negligence in exercising its statutory power of inspection in failing to ensure that the foundations complied with building regulations.

ANNS v. MERTON LONDON BOROUGH COUNCIL, [1978] A.C. 728, [1977] 2 W.L.R. 1024, [1977] 2 All E.R. 492 (H.L.) (*Dutton* explained and followed).

A block of maisonettes was built with latent defects in its foundations. Plaintiff subsequent occupiers suffered damage from structural movements in the building. Plaintiffs sought to hold local authority liable in negligence for failure to inspect the building or make a proper inspection of the foundation before approving the plans. Held: An action could arise against the local authority on the ground it was under a duty to give proper consideration to the question whether there should be an inspection or not. Defendants, however, would not be liable for breach of duty unless (a) they did not properly exercise their discretion as to the making of inspections, and (b) they failed to exercise reasonable care to ensure that the by-laws applicable to the foundations were complied with in their acts or omissions.

DENNIS v. CHARNWOOD BOROUGH COUNCIL, [1982] 3 W.L.R. 1064, [1982] 3 All E.R. 486 (C.A.). (Leave to appeal to House of Lords granted).

Plaintiffs commissioned local builder to build a house on site of a former sand pit. Plans disclosing that house was to be supported by concrete raft were duly approved by defendant local authority. After completion of house, cracks appeared in the brickwork. Plaintiff sued defendant for loss and expense caused by defendant's negligence in approving plan. Held: Defendant was negligent in passing the plan because the known danger of building on made-up ground cast laid on defendant the duty to consider (and not merely assume) whether the raft would be adequate as a foundation.

DUTTON v. BOGNOR REGIS URBAN DIST. COUNCIL, [1972] 1 Q.B. 373, [1972] 2 W.L.R. 299, [1972] 1 All E.R. 462 (C.A.).

Builder constructed house on old rubbish dump without providing a sufficient foundation and a municipal inspector negligently approved the work. Builder sold house to third party who then sold to plaintiff. House began to shift and the walls cracked. Plaintiff sued municipal council employing inspector for repair costs and loss of market value. Held:

Plaintiff's claim was recoverable because it was precisely the kind of loss that the statutory inspection was supposed to prevent. The existence of a duty did not depend on whether the loss was physical or economic. (Lord Denning notes, however, that there was physical damage to the house.)

FELLOWES v. ROTHER DIST. COUNCIL, [1983] 1 All E.R. 513 (Q.B.).

Defendant protection authority exercised its statutory power to repair a groyne on a beach adjoining plaintiff's property. In the course of the work, the height of the groyne was lowered. Part of plaintiff's land adjoining the groyne was later washed away. Plaintiff sued defendant for loss of land due to defendant's negligence. In deciding a preliminary issue, held: Assuming that plaintiff could establish the lowering of the groyne was not within the area of the discretionary power conferred on defendant, there was a sufficient relationship of proximity between the parties to create a duty of care, and no policy factors against it. Plaintiff must still prove defendant's act was reasonably foreseeable to cause plaintiff's land to be washed away, although it was not necessary to show defendant caused fresh or additional damage to base liability: *Anns* applied.

SHARADAN BLDRS. INC. v. MAHLER (1977), 17 O.R. (2d) 161, 79 D.L.R. (3d) 439, reversed 22 O.R. (2d) 122, 93 D.L.R. (3d) 480 (C.A.).

Plaintiff inquired of municipality whether building permits would be issued for certain lands he wished to buy. Municipality advised plaintiff that permits would be available. Plaintiff completed transaction, then discovered permits were not available for some lots due to conservation restrictions. Held (High Court): Town liable for negligence of its officials in advising plaintiff building permits were available: *Dutton* followed. The Ontario Court of Appeal held defendant was not liable. Plaintiff's inquiry was not directed to the existence of regulations imposed by the conservation authority. Also, defendant did not hold itself out as engaged in the business of or expert in advising upon requirements for permits other than those imposed by municipality.

NEW ZEALAND

Held for Plaintiff

BRUCE v. HOUSING CORP. OF NEW ZEALAND, [1982] N.Z.L.R. 28 (H.C.).

Plaintiff built a house according to a design and materials approved by defendant housing corporation for the purpose of mortgage loan. The design and materials were unsuitable for the particular location and the house deteriorated beyond repair. The builders had become insolvent so plaintiff sued the defendant corporation. The court held that defendants were negligent in approving the design and the materials for the particular location and found a duty of care existed on the basis of the *Anns* decision.

GABOLINSCY v. HAMILTON CITY CORP., [1975] 1 N.Z.L.R. 150 (S.C.).

Defendant owner-subdivider (city corporation) offered plaintiff land for building purposes and granted a lease in perpetuity requiring the erection of a dwelling house on it. Defendant was negligent in preparing the land for sub-division. When house was built, plaintiff lessees discovered fractures caused by settling of the land. Plaintiff sued defendant for cost of repairs and consulting fees paid to engineers in an action for negligence. Held: *Dutton* applied: the principle of *Donoghue v. Stevenson* applies to realty and an action lies in respect of the city's negligence causing economic loss.

J.W. HARRIS & SON LTD. v. DEMOLITION & ROADING CONTRACTORS (N.Z.) LTD., [1979] 2 N.Z.L.R. 166 (S.C.).

Plaintiff hired defendant to build a crib wall for him to make a garden (wall was not required for the safety of the house). During construction, the wall was inspected by council's inspector who wrongly but honestly assumed the building permit requirements were complied with. In fact, defendant failed to comply with the permit. The wall collapsed. Plaintiff sued defendant for cost of replacing the wall. Defendant joined council as third party. Although defendant was liable for breach of contract, the council owed no duty of care to defendant and was not liable to indemnify defendant, despite the fact it had issued the building permit and inspected the property.

MOUNT ALBERT BOROUGH COUNCIL v. JOHNSON, [1979] 2 N.Z.L.R. 234 (C.A.).

Defendant council granted a building permit to defendant development company to build a block of flats. The foundations were inspected by the council before the concrete was poured. The building work was carried out negligently by the company's independent contractor. The subsequent purchaser suffered economic loss caused by subsidence of the flat due to inadequate foundations. Plaintiff sued the company and the council in negligence. Held: The development company had a duty to see that proper care and skill was exercised in the building of the flats. That duty cannot be avoided by delegation to an independent contractor. The company was therefore liable for the cost of the remedial work to be done. Since a builder was required under by-law to go down to a solid bottom, the council's initial failure to check adequately what the builder did, or to insist on something more, made the council liable in negligence also.

PORT UNDERWOOD FORESTS LTD. v. MARLBOROUGH COUNTY COUNCIL, [1982] 1 N.Z.L.R. 343 (H.C.).

Defendant council granted plaintiff company permission to plant a particular area of land in forest. In granting permission council had failed to follow the statutory procedure and the consent was later ruled invalid. Plaintiff had to remove the trees it planted. Plaintiff sued defendant for damages in negligence to recover the cost of planting and removing the trees. Held: The council owed plaintiff a duty of care to give it a valid, authorized permission under the statute.

APPENDIX IV

REMOTENESS AND PHYSICAL DAMAGE TO PERSONS AND PROPERTY

A. ACTIONS WHICH CREATE A WIDE RANGE OF POSSIBILITIES FOR CAUSING HARM

1. Moving Vehicles, Automobiles, Trains, Vessels

AUSTRALIA

Held for Plaintiff

KEALLEY v. JONES, [1979] 1 N.S.W.L.R. 723 (C.A.).
Plaintiff husband and wife were injured in a car accident caused by defendant's negligence. In addition to damages for their physical injuries, the husband also recovered damages for the loss of consortium and diminution of the services of his wife.

LYNCH v. MITCHELL (1963), 57 Q.J.P.R. 125 (Dist. Ct.).
A car collision caused the trunk of the car to fly open and the tools in the trunk to be thrown out. They hit the plaintiff who was standing on a footpath.

PARKER v. DZUNDZA, [1979] Qd. R. 55 (S.C.).
As a result of defendant's negligence, a wife was rendered tetraplegic. Her marriage broke up because of her injuries and a business which she had conducted and in which her husband was employed was sold. The husband then sought damages for loss of his wife's service and consortium. The court held that plaintiff could only recover for loss of consortium for the period before the dissolution of the marriage.

PARRY v. YATES, [1963] W.A.R. 42 (S.C.).
Elderly plaintiff was frightened by a nearby car collision and thinking she might be injured she ran, fell and injured herself.

TREZISE v. STEPHENSON, [1968] S.A.S.R. 174 (S.C.).
Plaintiff suffered injuries in a car accident, but despite them he insisted on moving his damaged vehicle to the curb. In doing so he sustained further injuries.

VERSIC v. CONNERS, [1969] 1 N.S.W.R. 481 (C.A.).
Plaintiff's husband drowned when his head acted as a dam in the road after a car accident overturned his truck.

Held for Defendant

ADMIRALSKI v. STEHBENS, [1960] Qd. R 510 (S.C.).

Plaintiff sustained injuries in a car accident causing sexual incapacity. Plaintiff could not recover damages for loss of consortium from wife's desertion.

CAMERON v. NOTTINGHAM INS. CO., [1958] S.A.S.R. 174 (S.C.).

After injuries received in a car accident, plaintiff believed he was incapable of sexual intercourse and communicated this belief to his wife who then deserted him.

CANADA

Held for Plaintiff

ABBOTT v. KASZA, [1976] 4 W.W.R. 20, 71 D.L.R. (3d) 581 (Alta. C.A.).

The defendant parked his tractor-trailer on a highway facing oncoming traffic. the plaintiff rolled his vehicle into a ditch in an unsuccessful attempt to get around the tractor-trailer.

ASSINIBOINE SOUTH S.D. v. GREATER WINNIPEG GAS CO., [1971] 4 W.W.R. 746, 21 D.L.R. (3d) 608, affirmed (sub nom. HOFFER v. ASSINIBOINE SOUTH S.D.) [1973] 6 W.W.R. 765, 40 D.L.R. (3d) 480n, 1 N.R. 32 (S.C.C.).

Father gave his 14-year-old son a snowmobile which he was too young to properly operate. The machine went out of control and struck a gas pipe. Gas seeped into the boiler room of a school and caused an explosion.

ATHONAS v. OTTAWA ELEC. RY., [1931] S.C.R. 139, 38 C.R.C. 341, [1931] 2 D.L.R. 473.

Defendant's railcar collided with an automobile which then struck and injured plaintiff. Defendant's failure to slow down the railcar was held to be the effective cause of the accident.

BOHLEN v. PERDUE, [1976] 1 W.W.R. 364 (Alta. S.C.).

Plaintiff was injured when her elbow, which she had stuck out through an open window of a city bus, hit a power pole as the bus pulled away from a curb on which the pole stood.

BUCHANAN v. OULTON (1965), 51 D.L.R. (2d) 283 (N.B.C.A.).

Defendant's cow escaped from his truck when he negligently ran into another vehicle. The cow wandered back on to the highway and plaintiff's car sustained damage when it struck the cow.

CARTER v. VAN CAMP, [1930] S.C.R. 156, [1929] 1 D.L.R. 429.

Defendant negligently struck another car and this car then injured plaintiff who was on the sidewalk. Defendant was held to have caused the collision and hence liable to plaintiffs.

DAVIES v. HARRINGTON (1981), 44 N.S.R. (2d) 384, 83 A.P.R. 384 (T.D.).

Defendant driver negligently hit and broke a power pole, disrupting the power source to plaintiff's barn. Live wires fell to the ground, starting a fire that partially destroyed the barn.

EMBREE v. BROWN; ARBUCKLE v. EMBREE; KRAUSE v. ARBUCKLE (1978), 30 N.S.R. (2d) 1, 49 A.P.R. 1 (T.D.).

Defendant driver negligently collided with two approaching vehicles. Moments later a driver following defendant, faced with the accident, failed to avoid hitting one of the wrecked vehicles. The court held that defendant's negligence in causing the initial collisions directly caused the last collision.

ERKAMPS v. B.C. HYDRO (1968), 64 W.W.R. 632 (B.C.C.A.).

Defendant driver cut in front of a bus in order to turn into a parking lot. The bus stopped quickly causing the passenger to fall.

FALKENHAM v. ZWICKER (1978), 93 D.L.R. (3d) 289, 32 N.S.R. (2d) 199, 54 A.P.R. 199 (T.D.).

Defendant through negligence lost control of her car and hit a fence, knocking metal staples into a field. Plaintiff's cows ate the staples and developed hardware disease.

FOSTER v. REG. OF MOTOR VEHICLES, [1961] O.R. 551, 28 D.L.R. (2d) 561 (C.A.).

Damages were sought under the Ontario Highway Traffic Act for injury caused by a piece of metal left by a prior collision on the road, when an unknown driver ran over it causing it to fly into plaintiff's mouth.

FRASZ v. JANZEN (1981), 10 Sask. R. 443 (Q.B.).

Plaintiff's wife was killed in a motor vehicle accident caused by defendant's negligence. Plaintiff recovered as part of damages under the Fatal Accidents Act damages for loss of consortium.

GEALL v. DOM. CREOSOTING CO., 55 S.C.R. 587, [1918] 1 W.W.R. 280, 39 D.L.R. 242.

Employees of a railway company had placed cars on the tracks, set the brakes and blocked the wheels. Defendant's men moved the railcars, but did not block the wheels. Some school boys set the cars in motion and they collided at the foot of a hill with a passenger coach.

GENEREUX v. PETERSON HOWELL & HEATHER (CAN.) LTD., [1973] 2 O.R. 558, 34 D.L.R. (3d) 614 (C.A.).

Solicitor claimed for loss of services of his wife whom he employed as his law clerk, and for loss of profits while she was incapacitated by injuries caused by defendant in a car accident. The court allowed recovery for loss of services only.

GOODYEAR TIRE & RUBBER CO. OF CAN. LTD. v. MacDONALD (1975), 51 D.L.R. (3d) 623, 9 N.S.R. (2d) 114 (C.A.).

Due to defendant's negligence in loading his truck a highway sign fell on the road in front of traffic. The first car was able to stop but the second car skidded in oily tar and ran into the first car.

HARRIS v. TORONTO TRANSIT COMM., [1967] S.C.R. 460, 63 D.L.R. (2d) 450.

A child fractured his arm, which was sticking out of a bus window, when the bus collided with a pole.

HASTINGS v. CLINTON, [1924] S.C.R. 195, [1924] 2 D.L.R. 217.

Plaintiff had intended to become a professional musician but due to a car accident was unable to follow that career.

HEENEY v. BEST (1978), 23 O.R. (2d) 19, 94 D.L.R. (3d) 451, reversed in part 20 O.R. (2d) 71, 11 C.C.L.T. 66, 108 D.L.R. (3d) 366 (C.A.).

Defendants negligently backed their truck into hydroelectric wires, interrupting the flow of electricity to plaintiff's farm. The power loss cut off the oxygen supply to baby chicks that subsequently died.

KENNEDY v. HUGHES DRUG (1969) INC. (1974), 5 Nfld. & P.E.I.R. 435, 47 D.L.R. (3d) 277 (P.E.I. S.C.).

Defendant's car hit a fire hydrant, and nearly three hours elapsed before employees of the water commission were able to shut off the water. The result was that plaintiff's basement was flooded and his property and furniture damaged.

LAPOINTE v. CHAMPAGNE (1921), 50 O.L.R. 477, 64 D.L.R. 520 (S.C.).

Plaintiff was involved in a collision. She sustained no bodily injury but shortly thereafter suffered a miscarriage.

LAURITZEN v. BARSTEAD (1965), 53 W.W.R. 207, 53 D.L.R. (2d) 267 (Alta. S.C.).

Plaintiff refused to stop defendant's car to buy liquor. Defendant, already intoxicated, pulled at the steering wheel forcing the car off the road and getting it stuck in a hole. Plaintiff attempted to walk to town for help and got frostbite with the result that parts of both feet had to be amputated.

McMARTIN v. TUCEK (1962), 40 W.W.R. 195 (Alta. S.C.).

Plaintiff's additional injuries gave rise to recovery for damages despite the fact that they were not discovered until four weeks after the car accident.

NAT. THEATRES LTD. v. MACDONALDS CONSOL. LTD., [1940] 1 W.W.R. 168 (Alta. Dist. Ct.).

Through the negligence of defendant driver, a fire escape on plaintiff's building was damaged. The cost of repairs was increased because plaintiff had to comply with a city by-law.

OGAWA v. FUJIWARA, [1937] 1 W.W.R. 364, 51 B.C.R. 388, [1937] 2 D.L.R. 133, affirmed (sub nom. FUJIWARA v. OSAWA) [1938] 1 W.W.R. 670, [1938] 3 D.L.R. 375.

Defendant cut in sharply in front of plaintiff's car immediately after passing it. In the emergency plaintiff stepped on the accelerator instead of the brake.

PATTEN v. SILBERSCHEIN, [1936] 3 W.W.R. 169, 51 B.C.R. 133 (S.C.).

Defendant motorist negligently struck a pedestrian, rendering him unconscious. He later discovered that during his unconscious period he had lost $80 which he had in his pocket.

R. v. COTE; MILLETTE v. KALOGEROPOULOS (1974), 51 D.L.R. (3d) 244, 3 N.R. 341 (sub nom. KALEGEROPOULOS v. COTE) (S.C.C.).

Defendant realized he could not overtake the vehicle in front, since another car was approaching. He therefore pulled in behind the car but touched its bumper. The highway being slick with ice, the forward car solid across the road into the path of the oncoming car.

REINHART v. REGINA (CITY), [1944] 2 W.W.R. 313, [1944] 4 D.L.R. at 569, affirmed [1944] 3 W.W.R. 452, [1945] 1 D.L.R. 43 (Sask. C.A.).

The brakeman on a streetcar started the car with a sudden jerk throwing a passenger off balance. As he fell he kicked plaintiff in the face and she sustained injuries.

STEWART v. LEVIGNE (1972), 4 N.B.R. (2d) 452 (C.A.).

After a car accident caused by the defendant's negligence, plaintiff got out of the car and slipped while walking on the icy road.

ST. LAWRENCE & OTTAWA RY. v. LETT (1885), 11 S.C.R. 422.

Plaintiff's wife was killed due to defendant's negligence. He recovered for loss of household services and loss to his children of care and moral training.

STORRY v. C.N.R., [1940] S.C.R. 491, 51 C.R.T.C. 161, [1940] 3 D.L.R. 554.

Plaintiff's car stalled while crossing railway tracks. He saw the approaching train and tried to push his car off the tracks. No attempt was made to stop the train. Plaintiff finally ran from the tracks. The train hit the car and threw it against plaintiff.

TATISICH AND HARDING v. EDWARDS, [1931] S.C.R. 167, [1931] 2 D.L.R. 521.

Defendant pulled out of her lane to pass the car in front of her. Edwards swerved off the pavement to avoid a head-on collision and on returning to the pavement collided with plaintiffs' cars.

WEINER v. ZORATTI (1970), 72 W.W.R. 299, 11 D.L.R. (3d) 598 (Man. Q.B.).

The motorist ran into a fire hydrant, causing water to run into plaintiff's basement.

WINNIPEG ELEC. RY. v. CAN. NOR. RY., 59 S.C.R. 352, [1920] 1 W.W.R. 95, 28 C.R.C. 195, 50 D.L.R. 194.

The deceased jumped or fell off a streetcar when it was negligently driven in front of an approaching train.

WOELK v. HALVORSON, [1980] 2 S.C.R. 430, [1981] 1 W.W.R. 289, 14 C.C.L.T. 181, 114 D.L.R. (3d) 385, 24 A.R. 620, 33 N.R. 232.

Plaintiff was injured in a car accident. Wife sought to recover loss of consortium from the negligent driver. The court held that in the modern view of the law, a claim for loss of consortium is entitled only to a minimal award for damages and accordingly awarded her only $100.

Held for Defendant

ANTELL v. SIMONS, [1976] 6 W.W.R. 202 (B.C.S.C.).

A married woman was injured as a result of defendant's negligence. Her husband left her as sexual relations became physically impossible. Eventually, the husband and wife divorced. The husband's desertion was held to be outside the class of foreseeable damage.

SEYMOUR SAWMILLS LTD. v. SINGH (1963), 48 W.W.R. 129 (B.C. Co. Ct.).

Defendant backed his truck into a power pole and caused a short circuit in plaintiff's switch box several miles away, destroying it.

GREAT BRITAIN

Held for Plaintiff

BRADFORD v. ROBINSON RENTALS, [1967] 1 W.C.R. 337, [1967] 1 All E.R. 267.

Plaintiff driver was required by his employers to make a long journey in an unheated motor van in severe winter conditions. He suffered frostbite as a result.

DAVIES v. LIVERPOOL CORP., [1949] 2 All E.R. 175 (C.A.).

While the conductor was on the upper deck collecting fares, a passenger on the tramcar gave the starting signal. Plaintiff was injured when the train started.

DINGWALL v. WALTER ALEXANDER & SONS (MIDLAND) LTD., [1980] S.C. 64 (Outer House).

A bus driver was killed when the bus left the road and overturned as the result of brake failure. The owners of the bus were found negligent in allowing air into the brake system. Plaintiffs, the wife and children of the deceased, recovered compensation for loss of society.

FARRUGIA v. GT. WESTERN RY. CO., [1947] 2 All E.R. 565 (C.A.).

Plaintiff was running behind a truck trying to steal a ride when a container, which had been negligently loaded on the truck, fell off and hit him when the driver attempted to pass under a low bridge.

THE GERTOR (1894), 70 L.T. 703 (Adm.).

A steamship failed to use a tug while getting up anchor in a strong wind and was driven against a pier. When a tug was finally used it could only pull the ship in one direction due to her position on the pier and the effort cause the rope to snap. The ship was driven ashore, damaging plaintiff's property.

GILBERTSON v. RICHARDSON (1848), 5 C.B. 502, 136 E.R. 974 (C.P.).

A collision between a carriage and a chaise threw a person in the chaise against the dashing board which which then fell on the back of the horse. The horse was frightened and began to kick, thereby damaging the chaise.

GREENLAND v. CHAPLIN (1850), 5 Ex. 243, 155 E.R. 104.

Plaintiff, a passenger on a steamboat, was injured by the falling of an anchor onto his leg when defendant's steamboat struck the steamboat plaintiff was on.

HARRISON v. VINCENT, [1982] R.T.R. 8 (C.A.).

Defendant rider in a motorcycle and sidecar combination race missed a gear and failed to negotiate a bend owing to brake failure. The combination struck a recovery vehicle partly on the escape road, causing injury to the sidecar passenger. Plaintiff passenger succeeded in negligence action against the rider and the organizers of the competition. The rider was found negligent in brake installation and inspection. The court found that the organizers should have foreseen that leaving a recovery vehicle protruding partly on the road would be a potential source of danger in circumstances such as had occurred.

ICHARD v. FRANGOULIS, [1977] 1 W.L.R. 566, [1977] 2 All E.R. 461 (Q.B.).

Damages for loss of enjoyment of a holiday resulting from injuries sustained in a car accident, which occurred while plaintiff was on holiday, are recoverable as part of general damages, if the loss is reasonably foreseeable.

JONES v. BOYCE (1816), 1 Stark 493, 171 E.R. 540 (K.B.).

A driver of a coach drove his vehicle in such a negligent manner that it appeared to plaintiff, a passenger, that the coach was about to overturn and he jumped off the coach, thereby breaking his leg.

CITY OF LINCOLN (1889), 15 P.D. 15 (C.A.).

A steamer negligently collided with plaintiff's barque. All navigational equipment was lost due to the collision. The captain of the barque found a compass on board. In an attempt to continue on her way the barque was grounded.

LLOYD'S BANK LTD. v. BUDD (1982), R.T.R. 80 (C.A.).

A lorry driven by the fourth defendant broke down with a burned out clutch on a carriage way. After leaving the lorry overnight in a lay-by, the next morning the fourth defendant tried to move it to a more convenient place for repairs, but the lorry broke down again. Because of poor visibility in the fog a "pile up" of cars occurred behind the lorry. A Granada car ran into the back of another heavy vehicle and then a lorry driven by the first defendant and owned by the second defendant crashed into the Granada killing both the driver and passenger in the car. The administrator of the passenger's estate sued defendants successfully for negligence.

MAYOR OF SHOREDITCH v. BULL (1904), 20 L.T. 254 (H.L.).

Defendant highway and sanitary authority dug a trench under the road for a sewer and let traffic through before the road had settled. Plaintiff drove his cab to the far side of the road to avoid the soft road and ran into a heap of rubbish. The cab turned over, injuring plaintiff.

SLATTER v. BR. RYS. BD., [1966] 2 Lloyd's Rep. 395 (Q.B.).

Defendant's servant made an unnecessary noise during a shunting operation, startling plaintiff and causing him to put his hand on a rail where it was run over by a moving wagon.

SNEESBY v. LANCASHIRE & YORKSHIRE RY. CO. (1875), 1 Q.B.D. 42 (C.A.).

Defendant negligently allowed some trucks to roll down a steep incline into a railway siding, frightening plaintiff's cattle that were being driven across the siding. The cattle then broke through a defective fence and were killed on the railway.

TRUSCOTT v. MCLAREN, [1982] R.T.R. 34 (C.A.).

Second defendant was driving on a major road when, about 50 yards from a crossroad, he saw first defendant's car approaching the crossroad on a minor road. He drove steadily on without paying attention to first defendant's car, which failed to stop at the crossroads, collided with second defendant's car, and injured plaintiff who was sitting by the roadside. Both defendants were found liable in negligence.

Held for Defendant

KNIGHTLEY v. JOHNS, [1982] 1 W.L.R. 349, [1982] 1 All E.R. 851 (C.A.).

Defendant had an accident in a tunnel. A police inspector ordered motorcycle police to ride against oncoming traffic to deter them from entering the tunnel. One of the cyclists was hit by an oncoming car.

S.S. SINGLETON ABBEY v. S.S. PALUDINA, [1927] A.C. 16 (H.L.).

The Paludina dragged anchor and hit the Singleton Abbey breaking her moorings. The Singleton Abbey hit the Sara, breaking her moorings and setting her adrift. These two manoeuvred in the harbour and the propellor of the Singleton Abbey hit the Sara, sinking her and damaging her own propellor.

NEW ZEALAND

Held for Defendant

LAURIE v. GODFREY, [1920] N.Z.L.R. 231, [1920] G.L.R. 181 (S.C.).

Plaintiff had fastened a clothes line across a laneway at right angles to a wire line fastened to a chimney when defendant drove down the lane. She asked defendant to wait until she hoisted the clothes line so that he could drive through. He did not wait but instead drove through, pulling down the wire line and bringing the chimney down on plaintiff.

2. Dangerous Substances and Energy Sources Such as Inflammable Substances, Poisons, Explosions, Fire, and Electricity, and Dangerous Objects such as Knives, Guns, Machinery etc.

AUSTRALIA

Held for Plaintiff

EDWARDS v. MELBOURNE AND METRO. BD. OF WKS. (1893), 19 V.L.R. 432, 15 A.L.T. 96 (S.C.).

Defendants set fire to grass on their land and allowed the fire to spread to plaintiff's land. Plaintiff's wife in endeavouring to put out the fire was blinded by smoke and ran against a piece of iron, suffering injury and shock.

OVERSEAS TANKSHIP (U.K.) v. MILLER S.S. CO. PTY., [1967] A.C. 617, [1966] 3 W.L.R. 498, [1966] 2 All E.R. 709 (P.C.).

Defendant's employees negligently spilled some oil. The oil floated around plaintiff's ships and was ignited by welders on the dock where the ships were moored.

Held for Defendant

OVERSEAS TANKSHIP (U.K.) v. MORTS DOCK & ENRG. CO. (The Wagon Mound), [1961] A.C. 388, [1961] 2 W.L.R. 126, [1961] 1 A.. E.R. 404 (P.C.).

Employees of the charterer, the Wagon Mound, negligently spilt some oil. The oil floated around the plaintiff's dock, ignited, and damaged the wharf and the ships moored there.

CANADA

Held for Plaintiff

AYOUB v. BEAUPRE; McMURTY v. BEAUPRE; EMPIRE WALLPAPER & PAINT LTD. v. BEAUPRE, [1964] S.C.R. 448, 45 D.L.R. (2d) 411.

While draining a gas tank a mechanic dropped a light bulb and the spark started a fire which damaged the surrounding premises of plaintiff.

BOWMAN v. RANKIN (1963), 41 W.W.R. 700 (Sask. Dist. Ct.).

Defendant grocer sold matches to a 6-year-old, being authorized by the child's parents to do so. The child played with the matches and plaintiff's building was destroyed by fire.

BOYANCHUK v. BORGER BROS. LTD. (1964), 48 D.L.R. (2d) 235 (Sask. Q.B.).

Defendant had a contract with the municipality to dig a trench for a water main. Due to defendant's negligence a drainage culvert was broken and surface water forced its way into plaintiff's basement.

CAN. SOUTHERN RY. v. PHELPS (1884), 14 S.C.R. 132.

A fire in defendant's buildings, caused by sparks from defendant's passing train, spread to plaintiff's buildings.

CARMICHAEL v. MAYO LUMBER CO. LTD. (1978), 85 D.L.R. (3d) 538 (B.C.S.C.).

Defendant's employee detonated explosives in such a way that nearby houses were shaken. Plaintiff was about to sit down when the shaking from the blast caused her to lose her balance, fall and injure her back.

DOZOIS v. PURE SPRING CO., [1935] S.C.R. 319, [1935] 3 D.L.R. 384.

Defendant gas company installed a gas furnace in the premises of defendant Pure Spring Co. which were in the same building as plaintiff. Due to either poor installation or poor maintenance, the furnace leaked gas and plaintiff was gassed.

EDWARDS v. SMITH, 56 B.C.R. 53, [1941] 1 D.L.R. 736 (C.A.).

Defendant purchased a spring-gun for his sons' amusement. The parents went out, leaving the children in plaintiff's charge. The gun was left in an unlocked cupboard. One boy removed the gun and shot plaintiff, causing her to lose sight in one eye.

FETHERSTON v. NEILSON, [1944] O.R. 470, [1944] O.W.N. 547, [1944] 4 D.L.R. 292, reversed in part [1944] O.R. 621, [1944] O.W.N. 746, [1945] 1 D.L.R. 98 (C.A.).

A hotel guest knocked over a light stand at a New Year's Eve dance, hitting plaintiff's violin. The hotel was also found liable for leaving such a fixture in a crowded room and for permitting overcrowding.

HOLIAN v. UNITED GRAIN GROWERS LTD., [1980] 3 W.W.R. 632, 11 C.C.L.T. 184, 112 D.L.R. (3d) 611, 2 Man. R. (2d) 374, varied [1980] 5 W.W.R. 501, 13 C.C.L.T. 269, 114 D.L.R. (3d) 449, 4 Man. R. (2d) 253, leave to appeal to S.C.C. refused 114 D.L.R. (3d) 449n (S.C.C.).

Defendant, who had for sale insecticide tablets giving off poisonous gas, failed to store them under lock and key. Some children took the tablets and put them in plaintiff's car. Plaintiff was mildly poisoned and suffered chronic depression as a result. The court held that plaintiff's injury was a reasonably foreseeable consequence of defendant's negligence.

IRVING OIL LTD. v. LUNN'S HAULAWAY LTD. (1978), 24 N.B.R. (2d) 91, 48 A.P.R. 91 (Q.B.).

A gasoline service station owner constructed an enclosed basement area immediately below the gasoline dispensing pumps. A customer's trailer struck a pump resulting in gas flowing into the basement area and causing an explosion which destroyed the gas station and killed five people. Both the customer and the service station owner were held liable. The court found that while the extent of the damage was not foreseeable, the existence of the physical forces which caused the damage were expected.

JEFFREY (F.W.) & SONS LTD. v. COPELAND FLOUR MILLS LTD.; FINLAYSON v. COPELAND FLOUR MILLS LTD., 52 O.L.R. 617, [1923] 4 D.L.R. 1140 (C.A.).

Defendant, in excavating for the foundation of a building, undermined a party wall which settled causing damage to buildings. Damaged building was connected by tie-rods to plaintiff's building which suffered damage.

LEIBEL v. SOUTH QU'APPELLE, [1943] 3 W.W.R. 566; [1944] 1 D.L.R. 369 (Sask. C.A.).

Defendant negligently mixed poison in grasshopper bait and allowed the water in a well near its building to be contaminated. Plaintiff drank some water from the well and became ill.

McKENZIE v. HYDE (1967), 61 W.W.R. 1, 64 D.L.R. (2d) 362, affirmed 63 W.W.R. 128, 66 D.L.R. (2d) 655 (Man. C.A.).

Defendant broke a gas line during a digging operation on plaintiff's land. Gas seeped into plaintiff's basement where it ignited and exploded.

MacMILLAN BLOEDEL (ALBERNI) LTD. v. B.C. HYDRO & POWER AUTHORITY, [1975] 1 S.C.R. 263, [1973] 6 W.W.R. 471, 44 D.L.R. (3d) 767.

Blasting operations resulted in a power line landing on a guy wire. The discharge of electricity through the guy wire produced sparks which caused a forest fire with resulting losses to the plaintiff.

MARTIN v. McNAMARA CONST. CO., [1955] O.R. 523, [1955] 3 D.L.R. 51 (C.A.).

In the process of widening the highway, defendant's workmen felled a tree which struck plaintiff's fence and produced a gap in it. Plaintiff's cows escaped the field and wandered onto the highway where a passing motorist struck one of them.

NOR. WOOD PRESERVERS LTD. v. HALL CORP. (SHIPPING) 1969 LTD., [1972] 3 O.R. 751, 29 D.L.R. (3d) 413 (H.C.).

Ship's officers permitted boiler tubes to be blown. The emission of sparks set the adjacent lumber yard on fire.

OSTASH v. SONNENBERG; OSTASH v. AIELLO (1968), 63 W.W.R. 257, 67 D.L.R. (2d) 311 (Alta. C.A.).

Defendant contracting company converted a coal furnace to natural gas without properly cleaning the chimney. Plaintiff then bought the house. After some time an accumulation of soot fell to the bottom of the chimney as a result of the gas and filled the house with carbon monoxide. Plaintiff's three children died and he was injured.

PRASAD v. PRASAD, [1974] 5 W.W.R. 628 (B.C.S.C.).

Plaintiff, a visitor in defendant's home, was injured when he leaned against a knife that had been left on the sofa by defendant's children.

RY. PASSENGER INS. CO. v. BRODEUR, [1920] 2 W.W.R. 924 (Man. K.B.).

Defendant was carrying a loaded shotgun in a rig when the horse unexpectedly started forward, throwing defendant out of the rig. The shotgun, on hitting the ground, discharged, causing injury to plaintiff.

RICKARD v. RAMSAY, [1936] S.C.R. 302, [1936] 3 D.L.R. 321.

A boy, defendant, was leading a colt along a grassy strip next to the highway when infant plaintiff ran toward the colt after it had passed him. The colt kicked plaintiff.

WKRS. COMP. BD. v. SCHMIDT (1977), 80 D.L.R. (3d) 696 (Man. Q.B.).

Defendant and the deceased were using rags moistened with cleaning fluid to clean machines when defendant's rag caught fire when he lit a cigarette. The deceased tried to put the fire out by throwing wet rags on the fire. The deceased's pants caught fire. He poured the contents of a five-gallon pail over his body and was engulfed in flames. Unbeknownst to him, the rags and pail contained cleaning fluid.

YACHUK v. OLIVER BLAIS CO., [1949] A.C. 386, [1949] 2 W.W.R. 764, [1949] 3 D.L.R. 1, [1949] 2 All E.R. 150 (P.C.).

Defendant sold some gasoline to two small children who told him it was for their mother's car which had stalled. The children played with the gasoline and one was severely burned.

Held for Defendant

BRADFORD v. KANELLOS (1973), 40 D.L.R. (3d) 578 (S.C.C.).

A restaurant owner negligently caused a flash fire. A patron heard the hiss of the extinguisher and mistakenly shouted that gas was escaping. In the stampede which followed, plaintiff was injured.

HARSIM CONST. LTD. v. OLSEN (1972), 29 D.L.R. (3d) 121 (Alta. S.C.).

Defendant, an electrician, negligently caused a short circuit by allowing a screwdriver to touch two power faces simultaneously, A circuit breaker, which should have worked, failed to operate and a fire ensued which damaged plaintiff's building and equipment.

MORRIS v. FRASER (1965), 53 W.W.R. 693, 55 D.L.R. (2d) 93 (B.C. Co. Ct.).

Defendant negligently felled a tree which snapped high voltage wires, causing it to touch lines supplying electricity to plaintiff's house and thus starting a fire. An emergency circuit breaker failed to work for some reason.

GREAT BRITAIN

Held for Plaintiff

BURROWS v. MARCH GAS COKE CO. (1872), L.R. 7 Ex. 96 (Ex. Ch.).

Defendants negligently installed a gas service pipe to plaintiff's premises and allowed gas to leak. One of plaintiff's employees, carrying a lighted candle, went into the room to check the pipe.

HUGHES v. LORD ADVOCATE, [1963] A.C. 837, [1963] 2 W.L.R. 779, [1963] 1 All E.R. 705 (H.L.)

Defendant's employees left paraffin lamps burning beside a manhole. A boy knocked a lamp into the hole which caused an explosion that severely injured him.

MacLENAN v. SEGAR, [1917] 2 K.B. 325.

A fire started on the fourth floor of plaintiff's building. Had she remained in her room she would have been uninjured as the fire brigade put out the fire before it reached her floor. However, in fear, plaintiff tried to escape and sustained injury.

PHILCO RADIO & TELEVISION CORP. OF GR. BRITAIN v. SPURLING LTD., [1949] 2 K.B. 33, [1949] 2 All E.R. 882 (C.A.).

A highly inflammable celluloid film strip was mistakenly and carelessly left on the premises of a factory. It exploded when a typist carelessly approached it with a lighted cigarette.

RE POLEMIS AND FURNESS, WITHY & CO. LTD., [1921] 3 K.B. 560 (C.A.).

A plank, negligently dropped into the hold of a ship, caused a spark which ignited gas vapour and produced an explosion destroying the ship.

SMITH v. LONDON & SOUTHWESTERN RY. (1870), 40 L.J.C.P. 21 (Ex. Ch.).

Workmen of the defendant railway cut the grass and trimmed the hedges near the tracks, piling the cuttings in small heaps near the tracks. A fire started by sparks from defendant's train broke out among the heaps and crossed a dry stubble field, burning plaintiff's cottage.

STEWART v. WEST AFRICAN TERMINALS LTD., [1964] 2 Lloyd's Rep. 371 (C.A.).

Plaintiff's fingers were crushed by a cable in a pulley.

THE TRECARRELL, [1973] 1 Lloyd's Rep. 402 (Adm.).

A ship was being repaired by a coating of highly inflammable vinyl lacquer. While transferring drums of lacquer, one of defendant's employees dropped a drum which then fell on and cut a temporary electric cable. The drum broke, sparks from the short circuit ignited it and fire broke out, damaging the ship and yard.

VACWELL ENRG. CO. LTD. v. B.D.H. CHEMICALS LTD., [1971] 1 Q.B. 111, [1970] 3 W.L.R. 67, [1970] 3 All E.R. 553 (C.A.).

Defendants were liable for a major explosion that occurred where a minor explosion was foreseeable.

Held for Defendant

DOUGHTY v. TURNER MFG. LTD., [1964] 1 Q.B. 518, [1964] 2 W.L.R. 240, [1964] 1 All E.R. 98 (C.A.).

A workman was injured when molten cyanide exploded due to a chemical reaction with an asbestos lid that had been knocked into it.

MACDONALD v. DAVID MACBRAYNE LTD., [1915] S.C. 716, 52 S.L.R. 476.

A merchant climbed onto the roof of his store to put out a fire caused by the negligence of defendant. The roof collapsed, injuring the merchant.

3. Other Kinds of Action.

AUSTRALIA

Held for Plaintiff

DORSETT v. ADELAIDE, [1913] S.A.L.R. 71 (F.C.)

An unattended horse and dray suddenly backed up injuring plaintiff.

CANADA

Held for Plaintiff

CAN. NOR. RY. v. DIPLOCK (1916), 53 S.C.R. 376, 10 W.W.R. 986, 30 D.L.R. 240.

A brakeman attempted to eject a trespasser. Plaintiff was standing behind the trespasser and in the scuffle he fell and sustained injuries.

HOWE v. NIAGARA, ST. CATHARINES ETC. RY., 56 O.L.R. 202, 30 C.R.C. 95, [1925] 2 D.L.R. 115 (C.A.).

Drunken plaintiff was expelled from the train. He wandered down the track, fell on it and was hit by a railcar.

McKELVIN v. LONDON (1892), 22 O.R. 70 (C.A.).

Plaintiff fractured his leg while helping his horse up after it tripped over a stone which had been negligently left on the road by the municipality.

MENOW v. HONSBERGER, [1970] 1 O.R. 54, 7 D.L.R. (3d) 494, affirmed [1971] 1 O.R. 129, 14 D.L.R. (3d) 345, which was affirmed 38 D.L.R. (3d) 105 (sub nom. JORDAN HOUSE LTD. v. MENOW) (S.C.C.).

Intoxicated plaintiff was negligently ejected from a hotel beverage room onto a highway where he was struck by a negligent motorist. The hotel was held liable for his injuries.

OSTAPOWICH v. BENOIT (1982), 14 Sask. R. 233 (Q.B.).

A teenager was driving a motorcycle when the back wheel became entangled in a telephone wire left lying across the road. While he was attempting to untangle the wire, he was hit by an oncoming vehicle. Defendants were held liable in negligence for the boy's injuries and the parents' claim for expenses incurred and services rendered to their son, who had become a paraplegic following the accident.

POWLETT v. UNIVERSITY OF ALTA., [1934] 2 W.W.R. 209 (Alta. C.A.).

Plaintiff, a freshman at a university, underwent common initiation ceremonies undertaken by more senior students, which caused him to have a complete nervous breakdown.

SHERWOOD v. HAMILTON (1875), 37 U.C.Q.B. 410.

Horses bolted through an opening in a fence maintained at the side of the road by defendant municipality, pulling a wagon over a bank and injuring plaintiff. The opening was a defect in the fence.

TORONTO RY. v. GRINSTED (1895), 24 S.C.R. 570.

Plaintiff was wrongfully ejected from a streetcar after an altercation with the conductor. Exposure to the cold in an overheated state caused him to suffer rheumatism and bronchitis.

WINDER'S STORAGE & DISTRIBUTORS LTD. v. SETRAKOV CONST. LTD. (1981), 12 M.V.R. 49, 128 D.L.R. (3d) 301, 11 Sask. R. 286 (C.A.).

Defendant manufacturer of a low-bed trailer knew of its defective suspension before it was sold to plaintiff purchasers, but took no steps to remedy the defect or warn the purchaser. A tractor, carried by plaintiff as a common carrier, was thrown off the trailer and damaged when a bolt in the trailer broke because of the defect. Plaintiff was held absolutely liable in an action brought against it by the third party. The court followed *Rivtow* and held the manufacturer liable on the basis of its breach of a duty to make the trailer safe or give appropriate warning.

Held for Defendant

MELLISH v. CAMPBELL STORAGE, [1946] 3 W.W.R. 157 (B.C. Co. Ct.).

A piano was damaged while being moved. It was taken to an expert for repair. Defendant driver picked up the piano and left it in his van in the warehouse company. The van and the piano were destroyed by fire.

RED RIVER CONST. (1972) LTD. v. MacKENZIE & FEIMANN LTD. (1983), 22 Man. R. (2d) 57 (Q.B.).

Defendant chemical distributor delivered an inherently dangerous mercuric chloride which plaintiff, without sufficient examination, accepted and used in water line to two construction projects. In fact, no chemical was ordered, not even the chlorine required later by plaintiff and believed to be the product delivered. Plaintiff's action in negligence against defendant as dismissed because defendant could not foresee the misdelivery would be accepted and the chemical carelessly used.

GREAT BRITAIN

Held for Plaintiff

ALDHAM v. UNITED DAIRIES LTD., [1940] 1 K.B. 507, [1939] 4 All E.R. 522 (C.A.).

An unattended horse unexpectedly bit and pawed plaintiff.

CARMARTHENSHIRE COUNTY COUNCIL v. LEWIS, [1955] A.C. 549, [1955] 2 W.L.R. 517, [1955] 1 All E.R. 565 (H.L.).

An unsupervised child ran out of a school yard onto a street causing the death of a motorist who swerved to avoid hitting the child.

CONNOLLY (PATRICK) v. SOUTH OF IRELAND ASPHALT CO. LTD., [1977] I.R. 99 Ir. S.C.).

Due to frequent use by occupier's lorries, an adjoining public road was damaged by pot holes, which would fill up with water from time to time. While travelling on the road one evening, a motorcyclist fell off his motorcycle. While he was picking his machine up, he was struck and killed by defendant's car. The widow of the deceased was awarded damages under a settlement of her action against defendant. Defendant claimed contribution from the occupier on the grounds of negligence and public nuisance. The court allowed defendant's claim on the basis that the trial judge had found that the deceased had fallen from his motorcycle because of the potholes or because of the patches of ice that had formed in them, and that the occupier should have foreseen the risk of injury to the motorcyclist in the circumstances accordingly.

HARRIS v. MOBBS (1878), 3 Ex. D. 268.

Defendant left a van and plough unattended. A passing horse became frightened by it and fatally kicked a man.

LYNCH v. NURDIN (1841), 1 Q.B., 29, 113 E.R. 1041.

An unattended cart was set in motion by a child, causing injury to another child.

McKENZIE'S TUTRIX v. EDINBURGH DIST. COUNCIL, [1979] S.L.T. 60 (Sh. Ct.).

Defendant local authority occupied a piece of ground on which there was an entrance to a small, disused tunnel. Children often played there as the ground was open to the public. A child entered the tunnel and struck a match, causing an explosion. The explosion occurred because certain town gas had escaped into the tunnel. The court awarded damages to the child's mother in respect of the injuries suffered by the child as a result of the defendant's negligence. The court noted that the use of naked lights in the hands of young children in the confined space of the tunnel was bound to be attended with the risk that a burning accident of some kind was reasonably foreseeable.

SAYERS v. HARLOW URBAN DIST. COUNCIL, [1958] 1 W.L.R. 623, [1958] 2 All E.R. 342 (C.A.).

A lady was trapped in a public lavatory and was injured while trying to climb out.

THUROGOOD v. VAN DEN BERGHS & JURGENS LTD., [1951] 2 K.B. 537, [1951] 1 All E.R. 682 (C.A.).

Defendant company negligently placed a fan on the floor without a cover. Plaintiff's fingers were caught.

Held for Defendant

GLOVER v. LONDON & SOUTH WESTERN RY. CO. (1867), L.R. 3. Q.B. 25.

Defendant sued for the loss of a pair of racing glasses which he left behind when he was wrongfully ejected from a railway carriage.

LATHALL v. JOYCE & SON, 55 T.L.R. 994, [1939] 3 All E.R. 854 (K.B.).

A bullock being transported to a butcher was allowed to break out of a truck after which it attacked plaintiff.

TREMAIN v. PIKE [1969] 1 W.L.R. 1556, [1969] 3 All E.R. 1303 (Exeter Assizes).

In the course of his employment as a herdsman on defendant's farm, plaintiff contracted Weil's disease, a little-known disease carried by rats but very rarely contracted by humans by reason of their very slight susceptibility to the disease. Plaintiff sought to hold defendants liable on the basis of negligence. The court dismissed plaintiff's action on the grounds that Weil's disease was at best a remote possibility which defendants could not reasonably forcee, and that the damage suffered by plaintiff was accordingly unforeseeable and too remote to be recoverable. Furthermore, defendants did not breach any duty of care owed to plaintiff for which they could be held liable.

B. CLASSES OF DAMAGES WHICH CAN FOLLOW ANY NEGLIGENCE

1. Thin-Skull Cases

AUSTRALIA

Held for Plaintiff

ANTONATOS v. DUNLOP, ALLSOPP & TPT. & GEN. INS. CO. LTD., [1968] Qd. R. 114 (S.C.).
Car accident brought on mental condition.

BARNES v. AUSTRALIA (1937) 54 W.N. 164, 37 S.R.N.S.W. 511 (S.C.).
Plaintiff suffered shock on reading a letter incorrectly informing her that her husband had been committed to a mental asylum.

DALY v. RYS. COMMR. (1906), 8 W.A.L.R. 125 (S.C.).
Plaintiff sustained shock when a train ran into a horse on the track.

DONJERKOVIC v. ADELAIDE S.S. INDUST. PTY. LTD. (1979), 24 S.A.S.R. 347 (S.C.).
A predisposition to neurosis led to trauma when plaintiff was driven roughly over some bad roads.

EDWARDS v. PELVAY, [1961] S.A.S.R. 171 (S.C.).
Plaintiff's left leg was fractured in a car accident. He resumed work, fell, and sustained a second fracture.

GANNON v. GRAY, [1973] Qd. R4. 11 (S.C.).
Plaintiff's predisposition to neurotic depression worsened after a car accident injured her and killed her husband.

GUIFFRE v. SCAFFIDE [1960] W.A.R. 74 (S.C.).
A slight physical injury rendered plaintiff totally disabled due to hysteria.

HABER v. WALKER, [1963] V.R. 339 (S.C.).
A mentally unbalanced man committed suicide after a car accident.

HOFFMUELLER v. COMMONWEALTH (1981), 54 F.L.R. 42 (C.A.).
Plaintiff was involved in an accident and subsequently developed a post-traumatic psycho-neurotic disorder. Plaintiff had an obsessional personality and a predisposition to anxiety. The court allowed recovery on the grounds that mental illness was foreseeable as a possible consequence of the accident and that a predisposition to neurosis was similar to a predisposition to a condition: *Mount Isa Mines v. Pusey* applied.

HUGHES v. STATE OF SOUTH AUSTRALIA (1982), 29 S.A.S.R. 161 (S.C.).

Plaintiff, a nurse attendant at a hospital, suffered a heart attack after lifting a heavy patient from a bath. Plaintiff was suffering from coronary disease at the time. The heart attack was caused by the physical strain of lifting the patient. The hospital authority was found negligent in not providing a hoist for lifting heavy patients from the bath or in failing to give suitable instructions as to bathing such patients. The court further held that it does not matter that a heart attack was a less likely result of unusual exertion than a back injury. The foreseeability of some kind of heart attack was enough.

HOLE v. HOCKING, [1962] S.A.S.R. 128 (S.C.).

A minor bump on the head contributed to a sub-arachnoid hemorrhage that damaged the brain permanently.

MOUNT ISA MINES LTD. v. PUSEY (1970), 45 A.L.J.R. 88 (H.C.).

Plaintiff aided an electrician who had been horribly burned by electrocution. When the electrician later died he suffered nervous shock.

NEWELL v. LUCAS, 82 W.N. (N.S.W.) (Pt. 1) 265, [1964-65] N.S.W.R. 1597 (S.C. (F.C.)).

Injury to plaintiff's back was aggravated by a prior back condition.

PARRY v. YATES, [1963] W.A.R. 42 (S.C.).

The elderly plaintiff was frightened by a nearby accident and thinking she might be injured she ran, fell and injured herself.

SEALY v. COMMR. FOR RYS., [1915] Q.W.N. 1 (Dist. Ct.).

Plaintiff suffered shock when some window glass broken in an accident cut her face.

TAYLOR v. TUESLEY, [1963] 15 (S.C.).

Whiplash suffered in a car accident caused a plaintiff with a precondition of arachnoiditis to lose all coordination.

WATTS v. RAKE (1960), 108 C.L.R. 158 (H.C.).

A car accident caused a condition of quiescent spondylitis to develop rapidly into arthritis.

Held for Defendant

MARTIN v. ISBARD (1946), 48 W.A.L.R. 52 (S.C.).

An accident victim suffered a minor concussion but developed anxiety and litigation neurosis when bad medical advice led her to believe she had a fractured skull.

RICHTERS v. MOTOR TYRE SERVICE PTY. LTD., [1972] Qd. R. 9 (S.C.).

An accident victim became morbidly depressed and committed suicide.

SPENCER v. ASSOCIATED MILK SERVICES PTY. LTD., [1968] Qd. R. 393 (S.C.).

Plaintiff was injured in a car accident and later when informed of his parent's deaths, he suffered neurosis and nervous shock.

CANADA

Held for Plaintiff

BARNABY v. O'LEARY (1956), 5 D.L.R. (2d) 41 (N.S.S.C.).
Plaintiff died after car accident due to a precondition of heart disease.

BATES v. FRASER, [1963] 1 O.R. 539, 38 D.L.R. (2d) 30 (H.C.).
Car accident revived previous symtoms of Parkinson's disease in plaintiff.

BERJIAN v. FORBES (1982), 16 Sask. R. 435 (Q.B.).
Plaintiff suffered a whiplash in a rear-end collision caused by defendant's negligence. The injury aggravated a pre-existing back injury. Plaintiff was awarded $10,000 general damages for non-pecuiary loss.

BIELITZKI v. OBADISK (OBADIAK), 15 Sask. L.R. 153, [1922] 2 W.W.R. 238, 65 D.L.R. 627 (C.A.).
Defendant negligently and falsely reported to a nervous mother that her son had committed suicide. Plaintiff suffered further nervous illness.

BISHOP v. ARTS & LETTERS CLUB OF TORONTO (1978), 18 O.R. (2d) 471, 83 D.L.R. (3d) 107 (H.C.).
Haemophiliac suffered severe injuries from falling out of an unmarked non-working automatic door.

BOOKHALTER v. HODEL (1983), 22 Sask. R. 302 (Q.B.).
Plaintiff, who had advanced degenerative chagnes in the cervical vertebra, sprained his neck in a car accident caused by defendant's negligence. He suffered permanent disabilities as a result of continued neck pain and limited motion plus headaches. Defendant was found liable to plaintiff's injuries on the grounds that a reasonable person ought to have anticipated plaintiff's physical susceptibility as a possibility.

CAN. ATLANTIC RY. v. HENDERSON (1899), 29 S.C.R. 632.
Plaintiff suffered shock when train approached without warning by flagman and caused his horse to bolt.

CANNING v. McFARLAND, [1954] O.W.N. 467 (H.C.).
Precondition to neurosis was exacerbated by road accident.

CHARTERS v. BRUNETTE (1973), 1 O.R. (2d) 131, 39 D.L.R. (3d) 499 (C.A.).
Precondition to nervous shock was exacerbated by injuries and scars.

CORRIE v. GILBERT, [1965] S.C.R. 457, 52 D.L.R. (2d) 1.
Precondition to phlebitis. Actual condition was brought on by road accident.

COTIC v. GRAY (1981), 33 O.R. (2d) 356, 17 C.C.L.T. 138, 124 D.L.R. (3d) 641 (C.A.).
Defendant negligently drove into plaintiff's husband's car, causing the latter severe injuries. The husband's prior neurotic condition degenerated to a phychotic condition after the accident. He subsequently committed suicide.

DIEDERICHS v. METROPOLITAN STORES LTD. (1956), 20 W.W.R. 246, 6 D.L.R. (2d) 751 (Sask. Q.B.).
Injuries suffered in fall on dangerously piled display were increased by precondition of nervous anxiety.

DUWYN v. KAPRIELIAN (1978), 22 O.R. (2d) 736, 7 C.C.L.T. 121, 94 D.L.R. (3d) 424 (C.A.).

Defendant negligently backed his car into a parked car, breaking a window and scattering glass throughout the interior. No one in the parked car was physically injured but a four-month-old baby started to scream. The baby's mother, who arrived on the scene upon hearing the baby scream, became hysterical. The baby suffered a personality change thereafter. Both the mother and the baby sued for damages for nervous shock. The court held that while the nervous shock suffered by the infant was foreseeable, the mother's nervous shock was not reasonably foreseeable.

DVORKIN v. STUART, [1971] 2 W.W.R. 70 (Alta. S.C.)

Plaintiff was not physically injured in car accident, but suffered coronary occlusion and mental anguish as a result of prior traumatic neurosis.

EDMONDS v. ARMSTRONG FUNERAL HOME LTD., [1930] 3 W.W.R. 649, 25 Alta. L.R. 173, [1931] 1 D.L.R. 676 (C.A.).

Husband suffered mental shock when an autopsy was performed on his dead wife's body without his permission.

ELLOWAY v. BOOMARS (1968), 69 D.L.R. (2d) 605 (B.C.S.C.).

Minor injuries suffered in a car accident proved disabling due to predisposition to schizophrenia.

ENGE v. TRERISE (1960), 33 W.W.R. 577, 26 D.L.R. (2d) 529 (B.C.C.A.).

Car accident brought on latent schizophrenia.

FITZPATRICK v. G.W. RY. (1855), 12 U.C.Q.B. 645.

Train accident caused plaintiff to suffer terror and resulted in premature delivery of her child.

GLASGOW v. MILLS (1975), 19 N.S.R. (2d) 119 (T.D.).

Predisposition to degenerative condition of cervical spine greatly aggravated by sprain received in minor car accident.

HAM v. CAN. NOR. RY. (1912), 1 W.W.R. 897, 20 W.L.R. 359, 1 D.L.R. 377, affirmed without written reasons 22 Man. R. 480, 2 W.W.R. 1105, 7 D.L.R. 812.

Minor abrasions received in streetcar accident aggravated a precondition of neurasthenia.

HOLIAN v. UNITED GRAIN GROWERS LTD., [1980] 3 W.W.R. 632, 11 C.C.L.T. 184, 112 D.L.R. (3d) 611, 2 Man. R. (2d) 374, varied [1980] 5 W.W.R. 501, 13 C.C.L.R. 269, 114 D.L.R. (3d) 449, 4 Man. R. (2d) 253, leave to appeal to S.C.C. refused 114 D.L.R. (3d) 449n (S.C.C.).

Plaintiff suffered chronic depression after being poisoned by toxic substance.

HORNE v. NEW GLASGOW, [1954] 1 D.L.R. 832 (N.S.S.C.).

Plaintiff was not physically injured by a runaway car but suffered shock.

KINGSCOTT v. MEGARITIS, [1972] 3 O.R. 37, 27 D.L.R. (3d) 310 (H.C.).

Pre-existing psychoneurotic state was exacerbated by car accident.

KNOSS v. BERGEN MFG. LTD. (1981), 11 Sask. R. 43 (Q.B.).

Plaintiff farmer was injured in a farm accident involving a grain auger purchased from defendant that was negligently manufactured. The injury activated a pre-existing arthritic back condition. Plaintiff was awarded $10,000 non-pecuniary damages.

KIRKPATRICK v. C.P.R. (1902), 35 N.B.R. 598 (C.A.).
Railway accident resulted in nervous shock.

KOVACH v. SMITH, [1972] 4 W.W.R. 677 (B.C.S.C.).
Paranoid condition was worsened by car accident.

LABROSSE v. SASKATOON (1968), 65 W.W.R. 168 (Sask. Q.B.).
Precondition of degenerative arthritis worsened as a result of a fall on a slippery walk.

LENOARD v. B.C. HYDRO & POWER AUTHORITY (1964), 50 W.W.R. 546, 49 D.L.R. (2d) 422 (B.C.S.C.).
Minor fall on bus caused tremendous pain due to psychotic condition of plaintiff.

LEONARD v. KNOTT, [1980] 1 W.W.R. 673 (B.C.C.A.).
Defendant doctor sent a patient to defendant radiologist for an intravenous pyelogram as part of his check-up without seeing the patient first. Defendant radiologist proceeded with the test even though it was unjustified in his opinion. The patient died as a result of an allergic reaction to the pyelogram. It was later found that there was no clinical need for the pyelogram. The patient's widow succeeded in her suit against both doctors in negligence: *Wagon Mound (No. 2)* applied.

MARCONATO v. FRANKLIN, [1974] 6 W.W.R. 676 (B.C.S.C.).
Plaintiff was prone to paranoid tendencies. Minor car accident brought about drastic personality change.

MOROZ v. OLYNYK (1982), 19 Sask. R. 151 (Q.B.).
A 55-year-old farmer, with a pre-existing arthritic back condition, suffered a back and hip injury in a rear-end motor vehicle collision. He suffered permanent partial disability.

MURPHY v. MacADAM (1965), 51 M.P.R. 267 (N.S.C.A.).
Elderly plaintiff was made lame by car accident due to age.

NEGRO v. PIETRO'S BREAD CO., [1933] O.R. 112, [1933] 1 D.L.R. 490 (C.A.).
Plaintiff suffered nervous shock when throat was scratched by glass in bread.

PARENT v. LAPOINTE, [1952] 1 S.C.R. 376, [1952] 3 D.L.R. 18.
Latent tuberculosis was aggravated by car accident.

PEACOCK v. MILLS (1964), 50 W.W.R. 626 (Alta. C.A.).
Precondition of disc degeneration was aggravated by car accident.

PIPER v. BUSSEY, 24 Sask. L.R. 40, [1930] 2 W.W.R. 452, [1930] 4 D.L.R. 722 (C.A.).
Shock to nerves caused by car accident.

REGUISH v. INGLIS (NO. 2) (1962), 38 W.W.R. 245 (B.C.S.C.).
Car accident aggravated state of depression.

SHANE v. LOISELLE (1961), 35 W.W.R. 190 (Man. Q.B.).
Pre-existing spinal condition was worsened by car accident.

SMITH v. CHRISTIE BROWN & CO., [1955] O.R. 301, [1955] I.L.R. 1-181, affirmed [1955] O.W.N. 570, [1955] I.L.R. 1-194 (C.A.).
Predisposition to anxiety led to severe disturbance caused by minor car accident.

SMITH v. MAXIMOVITCH (1968), 68 D.L.R. (2d) 244 (Sask. Q.B.).

Due to a precondition of pyorrhea, all of plaintiff's teeth had to be extracted after an accident.

STRAIN v. TORONTO TRANSPORT COMM., [1945] O.W.N. 870 (H.C.).

Plaintiff suffered nervous shock when two streetcars collided.

SULLIVAN v. RIVERSIDE RENTALS LTD. (1973), 36 D.L.R. (3d0 538, 5 N.S.R. (2d) 318, affirmed 42 D.L.R. (3d) 293, 6 N.S.R. (2d) 642 (C.A.).

Car accident caused damage to mental health due to precondition of nervous state.

TAYLOR v. WESTON BAKERIES LTD. (1976), 1 C.C.L.T. 158 (Sask. Dist. Ct.)

Precondition of emotional depression worsened when plaintiff purchased bread coloured blue by ink.

THOMPSON v. TOORENBURGH (1973), 50 D.L.R. (3d) 717, affirmed without written reasons 50 D.L.R. (3d) 717n (S.C.C.).

Plaintiff, who was suffering from mitral stenois, had a plumonary edema which was triggered by a car accident.

TORONTO RY. v. TOMS (1911), 44 S.C.R. 268, 12 C.R.C. 250.

Mental suffering was caused by a streetcar accident.

UNGER v. STUCKERT (1980), 17 Sask. R. 160 (Q.B.).

In a car accident caused by defendant's negligence, plaintiff was injured. The court allowed recovery in respect of the aggravation of a pre-existing spinal injury.

USHERWOOD v. KEHLER (1980), 1 Sask. R. 262 (Q.B.).

Plaintiff suffered a whiplash type injury in a car accident caused by defendant's negligence. The injury aggravated a pre-existing degenerative spine condition.

VARGA v. JOHN LABATT LTD., [1956] O.R. 1007, 6 D.L.R. (2d) 336 (H.C.).

A nervous plaintiff suffered hysteria when he crank beer contaminated by chlorine.

WINDRIM v. WOOD (1974), 7 O.R. (2d) 211, 54 D.L.R. (3d) 667 (H.C.).

Deceased died very shortly after car accident due to precondition of cirrhosis of the liver and cancer.

WINTERINGHAM v. RAE, [1966] 1 O.R. 727, 55 D.L.R. (2d) 108 (H.C.).

Plaintiff suffered partial paralysis from tetanus injection administered after being bitten by defendant's dog.

Held for Defendant

SWAMI v. LO, [1980] 1 W.W.R. 379, 16 B.C.L.R. 21, 11 C.C.L.T. 210, 105 D.L.R. (3d) 451 (S.C.).

Plaintiff's husband suffered unrelenting pain after being seriously injured in a car accident. As a result he became seriously depressed and committed suicide.

GREAT BRITAIN

Held for Plaintiff

BEISCAK v. NAT. COAL BD., [1965] 1 W.L.R. 518, [1965] 1 All E.R. 895 (Nottingham Assizes).
Plaintiff suffered neurotic pain after a mining accident.

BELL v. G.N.R. (1890), 26 L.R. Ir. 428 (Ex. Div.).
Plaintiff suffered nervous shock when the train she was on rolled backwards down an incline.

BROWN v. GLASGOW CORP., [1922] S.C. 527.
The pregnant plaintiff suffered a miscarriage when she witnessed the negligent driving of a train.

CONSTABLE v. T.F. MALTBY LTD., [1955] 1 Lloyd's Rep. 569 (Q.B.).
Plaintiff suffered nervous trauma after being hit by falling timber.

DULIEU v. WHITE & SONS, [1901] 2 K.B. 669.
Pregnant plaintiff delivered prematurely because of shock suffered when a van was driven into the wall of the building she was in.

GILLIGAN v. ROBB, [1910] S.C. 856, 2 S.L.T. 77.
Plaintiff sustained shock when a frightened cow entered her house.

LINES v. HARLAND & WOLFF LTD., [1966] 2 Lloyd's Rep. 400 (Q.B.).
A fall over a coil of wire exacerbated a pre-existing osteoarthritis condition.

LOVE v. PORT OF LONDON AUTHORITY, [1959] 2 Lloyd's Rep. 541 (Q.B.).
Plaintiff suffered hysterical neurosis after a minor bump due to a "vulnerable personality."

MARRIOT v. MALTBY MAIN COLLIERY CO. (1920), 90 L.J.K.B. 349 (C.A.).
A workman became depressed and finally committed suicide after a mining accident.

OWENS v. LIVERPOOL CORP., [1939] 1 K.B. 394, [1938] 4 All E.R. 727 (C.A.).
Mourners in a funeral procession suffered nervous shock when the coffin was overturned in an accident.

PIGNEY v. POINTERS TPT. SERVICES LTD., [1957] 1 W.L.R. 1121, [1957] 2 All E.R. 807 (Norwich Assizes).
An accident victim suffering from anxiety neurosis hanged himself.

SMITH v. LEECH BRAIN & CO. LTD., [1962] 2 Q.B. 405, [1962] 2 W.L.R. 148, [1961] 3 All E.R. 1159.
A splatter of molten asbestos triggered a pre-malignant cancer condition in the burned tissue.

WARREN v. SCRUTTONS LTD., [1962] 1 Lloyd's Rep. 497 (Q.B.).
A plaintiff with a condition of ulcers on his eye contracted a virus when he cut his finger on a poisoned wire. The virus caused more ulcers to appear.

NEW ZEALAND

Held for Plaintiff

LINKLATER v. MIN. of RYS. (1900), 18 N.Z.L.R. 536, 2 G.L.R. 202 (S.C.).
A woman with ovaries weakened by an operation had to have them replaced after they were injured by the sudden stopping of a train.

MURDOCH v. BR. ISRAEL WORLD FED. (N.Z.) INC., [1942] N.Z.L.R. 600 (C.A.).
The deceased suffered depression and committed suicide after an accident necessitated the amputation of his leg.

STEVENSON v. BASHAM, [1922] N.Z.L.R. 225, [1922] G.L.R. 145 (S.C.).
Pregnant plaintiff miscarried from hysteria when her landlord negligently threatened to evict her.

WILLIAMS v. B.A.L.M. (N.Z.), LTD. (NO. 3), [1951] N.Z.L.R. 893, [1951] G.L.R. 372 (S.C.).
Plaintiff, who had a heart condition, suffered a heart attack when he moved some heavy materials as directed by the defendants.

2. Medical Complication Cases

AUSTRALIA

Held for Plaintiff

ADELAIDE CHEMICAL & FERTILIZER CO. LTD. v. CARLYLE (1940), 64 C.L.R. 514, 47 A.L.R. 10, 14 A.L.J. 334 (H.C.).
Due to a faulty contained, sulphuric acid was spilled on the deceased's leg. Streptococcal septicaemia developed, causing death.

BEAVIS v. APTHORPE, [1963] N.S.W.R. 1176, 80 W.N. (N.S.W.) 852 (S.C.).
Eighteen months after a car accident plaintiff developed tetanus in his leg.

FISHLOCK v. PLUMMER, [1950] S.A.S.R. 176 (S.C.).
Plaintiff broke his leg in a car accident. He broke it again while being helped into the bath and he broke it a third time while crossing a road.

HAVENAAR v. HAVENAAR, [1982] 1 N.S.W.L.R. 626 (C.A.).
Plaintiff was injured as a result of defendant's negligence. In an effort to relieve the pain, plaintiff consumed alcohol to the extent that he developed pancreatitis.

JACQUES v. MATTHEWS, [1961] S.A.S.R. 205 (S.C.).
Plaintiff broke his left leg in a car accident. To unite the fracture a graft was taken from the right leg, weakening it. A year later plaintiff fell and broke the right leg.

MOORE v. A.G.C. (INS.) LTD., [1968] S.A.S.R. 389 (S.C.).
In an operation to remedy injuries caused in a car accident non-absorbal sutures were used which caused an infection and necessitated a second operation.

REA v. BALMAIN NEW FERRY CO. (1896), 17 N.S.W.L.R. 92, 12 W.N. 165.

Shock coupled with an injury to plaintiff's ankle caused by a loose plank developed into a serious disease called ophthalmic goitre.

SAYERS v. PERRIN (NO. 3), [1966] Qd. R. 89 (F.C.).

Plaintiff suffered electric shock due to defendant's negligence. Later, polio set in and he was partially paralyzed.

TUBEMAKERS OF AUSTRALIA LTD. v. FERNANDEZ, [1975] 2 N.S.W.L.R. 190 (C.A.).

Plaintiff's hand was injured in some machinery. He later developed symptoms of a rare disease (Dupuytren's Contraction) of which the patholoical basis is unknown.

WATT v. RAMA, [1972] V.R. 353 (S.C. Full Ct.).

Plaintiff suffered injuries while *en ventre sa mere* and further injuries at birth.

Held for Defendant

McKIERNAN v. MANHIRE (1977), 17 S.A.S.R. 571 (S.C.).

Plaintiff was convalescing in a hospital after a car accident. She was told to take a call in the office and fell over a step that no one had warned her about, thus further injuring herself.

ROWE v. McCARTNEY, [1976] 2 N.S.W.L.R. 72 (C.A.). (Case is on appeal to the High Court).

Plaintiff owner of a car reluctantly agreed to let her friend drive her car but only if he were careful. The friend negligently drove off the road and hit a telegraph pole. He became a quadriplegic and she was less seriously injured. Plaintiff recovered against the driver damages for her injuries but the court denied plaintiff recovery for a depressive neurosis caused by her feelings of guilt at having permitted her friend to drive. The court held that such damage was not reasonably foreseeable.

VON HARTMANN v. KIRK, [1961] V.R. 544 (S.C.).

A car accident caused an occlusion of an artery. A second occlusion resulted because of the first, causing death.

CANADA

Held for Plaintiff

ARMSTRONG v. ARNEIL (1962), 38 W.W.R. 573 (B.C.S.C.).

Thrombosis developed after a car accident and caused plaintiff to become irritable and suffer a personality change.

ARSENEAU v. MILLER (1982), 40 N.B.R. (2d) 91, 105 A.P.R. 91 (T.D.).

Plaintiff suffered whiplash in a car accident caused by defendant's negligence. Although still suffering from its effects, he returned to work. Six months later, the injury was reactivated during the course of his work. Defendant was held liable for this further injury, since it was within the causation of the original accident and there was no *novus actus interveniens*.

BLOCK v. MARTIN, 2 W.W.R. (N.S.) 336, [1951] 4 D.L.R. 121 (Alta. S.C.).

Plaintiff fractured his leg slightly in a car accident. A doctor advised him to walk on the leg. He fell and fractured the leg entirely.

BOSS v. ROBERT SIMPSON EASTERN LTD. (1968), 2 D.L.R. (3d) 114, 2 N.S.R. 412 (S.C.).
Plaintiff injured her leg when she fell in a slight depression in the floor of a store. The weakened condition of the leg caused a series of falls to occur.

DUVAL v. SEGUIN, [1972] 2 O.R. 686, 26 D.L.R. (3d) 418 affirmed (sub nom. DUVAL v. BLAIS) 1 O.R. (2d) 482, 40 D.L.R. (3d) 66 (C.A.).
A pregnant woman was injured in a car accident. Infant plaintiff was later born retarded.

EDDLES v. WINNIPEG SCHOOL BD. (1912), 2 W.W.R. 265 (Man. C.A.).
The deceased suffered a hernia through his work. After an operation to relieve it, blood poisoning set in and the employee died.

GOLDHAWKE v. HARDER (1976), 74 D.L.R. (3d) 721 (B.C.S.C.).
An accident victim walking with crutches was injured again when he fell down some stairs.

LUKASTA v. SAWCHUK, [1975] W.W.D. 98 (Alta. Dist. Ct.).
Chronic asthmatic bronchitis developed several years after plaintiff suffered a lung injury in an accident.

McCARTHY v. CHITTICK (1969), 2 N.B.R. (2d) 24 (C.A.).
After a car accident, plaintiff suffered anxiety which led to a duodenal ulcer.

MERCER v. GRAY, [1941] O.R. 127 [1941] 3 D.L.R. 564 (C.A.).
A child's broken legs grew much worse after doctors mistakenly failed to cut off her cast when cyanosed condition became evidence. Original break occurred in a car accident caused by defendant's negligence.

MORRISON v. PERE MARQUETTE RY. CO. (1913), 28 O.L.R. 319, 15 C.R.C. 406, 12 D.L.R. 344 (C.A.).
Defendant failed to replace a burned railway station. Plaintiff was forced to stand in the open where he caught a cold resulting in further illness.

PAPP v. LECLERC (1977), 16 O.R. (2d) 158, 77 D.L.R. (3d) 536 (C.A.).
Plaintiff suffered injury to his ulnar nerve while he was being treated for injuries suffered in a car accident.

PILUK v. PEAREN (1978), 82 D.L.R. (3d) 605 (Sask. Q.B.).
A knee injury led to degenerative arthritis.

POLLARD v. MAKARCHUK (1958), 26 W.W.R. 22, 16 D.L.R. (2d) 225 (Alta. S.C.).
A mother who suffered nervous shock upon seeing her daughter in a car accident recovered for memory loss caused by electric shock treatment.

PRICE v. MILAWSKI (1978), 18 O.R. (2d) 113, 82 D.L.R. (2d) 130, 1 L.M.Q. 303 (C.A.).
A physician negligently had the foot rather than the ankle of a patient X-rayed for fracture and a specialist continued the wrong treatment resulting in more serious injury.

ROY v. RICHARDSON (1968), 64 W.W.R. 630, 68 D.L.R. (2d) 352 (B.C.S.C.).
Plaintiff was injured in an accident while on her way to the hospital to have a baby. As a result of the injuries received she had to have the baby by caesarian section.

SACCARDO v. HAMILTON, [1971] 2 O.R. 479, 18 D.L.R. (3d) 271 (H.C.)
A decoration fell on the plaintiff injuring his back. His work, which involved manual labour, worsened the back injury.

SMITH v. SELLERS (1982), 17 Sask. R. 246 (Q.B.).

Plaintiff suffered minor injuries in a car accident but had an adverse reaction from the administration of tetanus toxoid which brought on an illness known as systemic vasculitis, an inflammation of the blood vessels.

URZI v. NORTH YORK BD. OF EDUC. (1981), 127 D.L.R. (3d) 768, affirming 30 O.R. (2d) 300, 116 D.L.R. (3d 687 (C.A.).

Plaintiff fractured her left knee when she slipped and fell on defendant's icy sidewalk. Three years later plaintiff's left knee gave way while stepping down a step and plaintiff fell and broke her thigh. The second fall and injury was held attributable to defendant's original negligence.

WATSON v. GRANT (1970), 72 W.W.R. 665 (B.C.S.C.).

After a car accident plaintiff underwent three operations of which two were found to be unnecessary.

Held for Defendant

DAVID v. TORONTO TRANSIT COMM. (1976), 160 O.R. (2d) 248, 77 D.L.R. (3d) 717 (H.C.).

An injury suffered in a car accident was worsened by a doctor's negligence.

GREAT BRITAIN

Held for Plaintiff

WIELAND v. CYRIL LORD CARPETS, LTD., [1969] 3 All E.R. 1006 (Q.B.).

Plaintiff was wearing a neck brace because of injuries suffered on a bus. She could not see properly through her glasses because of the brace, which caused her to fall again.

Held for Defendant

BEST v. SAMUEL FOX & CO. LTD., [1952] A.C. 716, [1952] 2 All E.R. 394 (H.L.).

Plaintiff's husband suffered severe physical injuries resulting in impotency. She claimed damages for partial loss of consortium.

NEW ZEALAND

Held for Plaintiff

STEPHENSON v. WAITE TILEMAN LTD., [1973] 1 N.Z.L.R. 152 (C.A.).

Plaintiff, a steeplejack, was resetting the wire rope system of a crane which had been allowed to become rusty and frayed when the rope sprang out and cut his hand. The hand swelled. Plaintiff became feverish and eventually suffered irrecoverable brain damage from an unknown virus which had entered the wound.

3. Rescue Cases

AUSTRALIA

Held for Plaintiff

CHAPMAN v. HEARSE, [1961] S.A.S.R. 51, affirmed 106 C.L.R. 112 (H.C.).

A doctor was killed on the highway while helping defendant who was injured through his own negligence.

DWYER v. SOUTHERN; CARGILL (THIRD PARTY); HINTON (FOURTH PARTY)., [1961] S.R. (N.S.W.) 896, 78 W.N. 706, [1962] N.S.W.R. 123 (S.C.).

The third party defendant caused a car accident. Plaintiff was struck by first defendant's car while assisting Cargill.

CANADA

Held for Plaintiff

C.N.R. v. BAKTY (1977), 18 O.R. (2d) 481, 82 D.L.R. (3d) 731 (Co. Ct.).

Defendant drove his car into a train. Plaintiff, a conductor, went to his aid and injured his own back trying to rescue defendant.

CONNELL v. PRESCOTT (1892), 20 O.A.R. 498, affirmed 22 S.C.R. 147.

The municipality negligently did blasting work close to some horses, frightening them. Plaintiff attempted to rescue the runaway horses and was injured.

COROTHERS v. SLOBODIAN, [1975] 2 S.C.R. 633, [1975] 3 W.W.R. 142, 51 D.L.R. (3d) 1, 3 N.R. 184.

Plaintiff was signalling traffic to stop after a collision. when a semi-trailer stopped, it jackknifed and injured her.

HAIGH v. G.T.P. RY. (1914), 7 W.W.R. 806, 8 Alta. L.R. 153 (C.A.).

A workman tried to rescue other workers from the danger of an oncoming train and was injured doing so.

HUDSON v. DRYSDALE, [1978] 3 A.C.W.S. 26 (Man. Q.B.).

Plaintiff injured himself exiting from his own vehicle in an attempt to stop an approaching driverless vehicle.

HUTTERLY v. IMPERIAL OIL LTD., [1956] O.W.N. 681, 3 D.L.R. (2d) 719 (H.C.).

Plaintiff was injured while driving his car out of a burning garage.

JONES v. WABIGWAN, [1968] 2 O.R. 837, 1 D.L.R. (3d) 40, reversed [1970] 1 O.R. 366, 8 D.L.R. (3d) 424 (C.A.).

Plaintiff went to assist defendant who had driven his car into a hydro pole. Plaintiff came into contact with live wires and sustained burns.

LOVE.v NEW FAIRVIEW CORP. (1904), 10 B.C.R. 330 (C.A.).

Plaintiff was injured trying to rescue another boarder from a burning building.

MODDEJONGE v. HURON COUNTY BD. OF EDUC., [1972] 2 O.R. 437, 25 D.L.R. (3d) 661 (H.C.).

Defendant took some children swimming and left them unsupervised. One small child died trying to rescue another from drowning.

SCHWAB v. SCHALOSKE (1982), 37 B.C.L.R. 111 (S.C.).

Deceased died when he entered a close silo to rescue the owner and the owner's father from accumulated silage gas. The owner was found negligent in not starting the ventilating blower upon entering the silo. Deceased's wife recovered for loss of support and funeral expenses against the negligent owner.

SEYMOUR v. WINNIPEG ELEC. RY. (1910), 19 Man. R. 412, 13 W.L.R. 566 (C.A.).

Plaintiff was injured trying to rescue a small child, who had fallen on the railroad tracks, from a rapidly approaching train.

TOY v. ARGENTI, [1980] 3 W.R.R. 276, 17 B.C.L.R. 365 (S.C.).

Plaintiff, in attempting to stop defendant's driverless moving car from hitting his own car, suffered a serious leg injury when he was crushed between the two cars. The court held that plaintiff was entitled to recover damages on the basis of being a rescuer of property.

URBANSKI v. PATELS; FIRMAN v. PATEL (1978), 84 D.L.R. (3d) 650, 2 L.M.Q. 54 (Man. Q.B.).

During an operation defendant doctors negligently removed the patient's only kidney. Her father, the plaintiff, volunteered one of his kidneys for transplant in an attempt to save her.

Held for Defendant

DUPUIS v. NEW REGINA TRADING CO., [1943] 2 W.W.R. 593, [1943] 4 D.L.R. 275 (Sask. C.A.).

An employee of the defendant company negligently imperilled herself in an elevator. The deceased went to her rescue, fell down the shaft and was killed.

GREAT BRITAIN

Held for Plaintiff

BAKER v. T.E. HOPKINS & SON LTD.; WARD v. T.E. HOPKINS & SON, LTD., [1958] 1 W.L.R. 993, [1958] 3 All E.R. 147, affirmed [1959] 1 W.L.R. 966, [1959] 3 All E.R. 225 (C.A.).

A doctor was injured while rescuing a negligent mine worker.

BRANDON v. OSBORNE GARRETT & CO. LTD., [1924] 1 K.B. 548.

A wife was injured when she pulled her husband away from the falling glass of a skylight broken by the negligence of a contractor.

CHADWICK v. BR. RY. BD. [1967] 1 W.L.R. 912, [1967] 2 All E.R. 945 (sub nom. CHADWICK v. BR. TPT. COMM.) (Q.B.).

Plaintiff suffered an anxiety attack after helping to rescue victims of a train wreck.

HAYNES v. HARWOOD, [1934] 2 K.B. 240, affirmed [1935] 1 K.B. 146 (C.A.).

A police constable was injured while attempting to push a woman out of the way of a runaway horse that had been negligently allowed to stray.

HYETT v. GREAT WESTERN RY., [1948] 1 K.B. 345, [1947] 2 All E.R. 264 (C.A.).

Plaintiff was injured while trying to extinguish a fire caused by defendant's negligence.

MORGAN v. AYLEN, [1942] 1 All E.R. 489 (K.B.).

A rescuer was injured while trying to save a child from being hit by a speeding motorcycle.

THE OROPESA, [1943] P. 32, [1943] 1 All E.R. 211 (sub nom. LORD v. PAC. STEAM NAVIGATION CO. LTD.; THE OROPESA) (C.A.).

The Oropesa negligently collided at sea with another ship. Some men were sent in a lifeboat from the second ship to rescue others and were drowned when the lifeboat capsized.

OULD v. BUTLER'S WHARF, LTD., [1953] 2 Lloyd's Rep. 44 (Q.B.).

A rescuer mistakenly believed a fellow workman was in danger so he pushed the man who then accidently dropped a crate on the rescuer's foot.

STEEL v. GLASGOW IRON & STEEL CO. LTD., [1944] S.C. 237.

A train collision was imminent due to the negligence of defendant's employees. The deceased attempted to uncouple his employer's trains in order to avoid the damage and was injured.

VIDEAN v. BR. TPT. COMM., [1963] 2 Q.B. 650, [1963] 3 W.L.R. 374, [1963] 2 All E.R. 860 (C.A.).

Compensation was awarded to the rescuer of a child trespasser.

Held for Defendant

CROSSLEY v. RAWLINSON, [1982] 1 W.L.R. 369 (Q.B.).

Plaintiff, a patrolman running to put out a fire on a lorry caused by defendant's negligence, fell before reaching the lorry and was injured. Plaintiff's suit in negligence against defendant was dismissed on the ground that plaintiff's injury was caused by an accident which neither party could reasonably have foreseen, notwithstanding that the fire was caused by defendant's negligence.

NEW ZEALAND

Held for Plaintiff

RUSSELL v. McCABE, [1962] N.Z.L.R. 392 (C.A.).

Plaintiff was injured while helping to extinguish a fire that had been negligently started.

4. Nervous Shock Cases

AUSTRALIA

Held for Plaintiff

ANDREWS v. WILLIAMS, [1967] V.R. 831 (S.C. Full Ct.).

Plaintiff was injured and her mother killed in a car accident. She suffered nervous shock because of her mother's death.

BALL v. WINSLETT; ISAACS (THIRD PARTY) (1957), 58 S.R. (N.S.W.) 149 (H.C.).

Plaintiff succeeded in an action for nervous shock although she was not present at the scene of the accident in which her husband died.

BENSON v. LEE, [1972] V.R. 879 (S.C.).

A mother ran to the scene of an accident in which her child was fatally wounded and she suffered nervous shock.

BROWN v. MOUNT BARKER SOLDIERS' HOSP. INC., [1934] S.A.S.R. 128 (S.C.).
A mother suffered shock when her infant child was burned in the nursery of a hospital.

GANNON v. GRAY, [1973] Qd. R. 411 (S.C.).
Plaintiff suffered nervous shock when she was injured and her husband killed in a car accident.

KOHN v. STATE GOVT. INS. COMM. (1976), 15 S.A.S.R. 255 (S.C.).
Plaintiff suffered severe shock when her friend was killed in an accident in which they were both involved.

RICHARDS v. BAKER, [1943] S.A.S.R. 245 (S.C.).
A mother suffered nervous shock on witnessing her son killed in a car accident.

SCALA v. MAMMOLITTI, 114 C.L.R. 153, [1966] A.L.R. 321 (H.C.).
Plaintiff recovered for nervous and mental shock when her husband was seriously injured in a car accident.

STORM v. GEEVES, [1965] Tas. S.R. 252 (S.C.).
A mother suffered nervous shock when she witnessed her child pinned under the wheels of a truck.

TSANAKTSIDIS v. OULIANOFF (1980), 24 S.A.S.R. 500 (S.C.).
Plaintiff recovered for nervous shock when he was injured and his wife, child and mother were killed in a car accident.

Held for Defendant

BUNYAN v. JORDAN (1937), 57 C.L.R. 1, 43 A.L.R. 204, 10 A.L.J. 463, 54 W.N. 61, 37 S.R. (N.S.W. 119 (H.C.).
Plaintiff suffered shock on hearing the sound of a gunshot after the defendant had threatened to kill himself even though defendant later appeared.

CHESTER v. WAVERLEY MUN. COUNCIL (1938), 62 C.L.R. 1, 45 A.L.R. 294, 13 A.L.J. 129, 56 W.N. 94, 39 S.R. (N.S.W.) 173 (H.C.).
Defendant left a deep trench unattended and plaintiff's son drowned in it. She suffered shock on witnessing his body being recovered from the trench.

PRATT v. PRATT, [1975] V.R. 378 (S.C. Full Ct.).
Plaintiff's daughter was seriously injured in a car accident. Plaintiff was not present at the scene, but suffered shock from seeing her daughter in the hospital.

ROWE v. McCARTNEY, [1976] 2 N.S.W.L.R. 72 (C.A.).
The owner of a car sued for a depressive neurosis caused by feelings of guilt arising from the fact that she lent her friend her car, as a result of which her friend was rendered quadriplegic in an accident.

SHEWAN v. SELLARS (NO. 1), [1963] Q.W.N. 19 (S.C.).
While recovering from an accident plaintiff was informed of the death of his family in the same accident.

SPENCER v. ASSOCIATED MILK SERVICES PTY. LTD., [1968] Qd. R. 393 (S.C.).
Several days after an accident in which plaintiff was injured he was informed while in the hospital of the deaths of his parents in the same accident. The news induced severe trauma.

CANADA

Held for Plaintiff

AUSTIN v. MASCARIN, [1942] O.R. 165, [1942] 2 D.L.R. 316 (M.C.).

A motion to strike out nervous shock as a head of damage where a mother witnessed her son's death in an accident was rejected.

CAMERON v. MARCACCINNI (1978), 87 D.L.R. (3d) 442 (B.C.S.C.).

Plaintiff suffered nervous shock upon witnessing her sister killed and her niece injured in a car accident.

CAN. TRUST CO. v. PORTER (1980), 2 A.C.W.S. (2d) 428 (Ont. C.A.).

Defendant nightclub negligently supplied liquor to a patron to the extent that he drove through a stop sign and killed plaintiff's parents. The child, injured in the same accident, also suffered shock.

FENN v. PETERBOROUGH (1976), 14 O.R. (2d) 137, 1 C.C.L.T. 90, 73 D.L.R. (3d) 177, varied 25 O.R. (2d) 137, 9 C.C.L.T. 1 (C.A.).

Due to defendant's negligence a gas explosion destroyed plaintiff's home and killed his children. He arrived after the accident and searched through the rubble for his family. The ordeal caused him to suffer nervous shock.

HOGAN v. REGINA (CITY), 18 Sask. L.R. 423, [1924] 2 W.W.R. 307, [1924] 2 D.L.R. 1211 (C.A.).

A streetcar backed up into a mother and her two children. The mother was not injured but both children were killed. She suffered severe shock.

McLAUGHLIN v. TORONTO RY. (1916), 9 O.W.N. 407, varied as to amount of damages 10 O.W.N. 135 (C.A.).

While a couple were riding in a streetcar and advertising sign fell on the husband injuring him. His wife suffered shock and miscarried a baby.

McNALLY v. REGINA (CITY), [1924] 2 D.L.R. 1211 (Sask. C.A.).

A mother witnessed her children killed by a streetcar.

MARSHALL v. LIONEL ENTERPRISES INC., [1972] 2 O.R. 177, 25 D.L.R. (3d) 141 (H.C.).

A motion to strike out the statement of claim of a wife who suffered shock when her husband was injured by a defective snowmobile was rejected as this is an acceptable head of damage.

MONTGOMERY v. MURPHY (1982), 37 O.R. (2d) 631, 136 D.L.R. (3d) 525 (H.C.).

Plaintiff suffered a severe depression as a result of an accident in which his wife was killed and he was injured by a negligent driver. The court held that plaintiff could recover damages only for that part of the depression resulting from his injury and nervous shock at being involved in the accident and seeing his wife killed, but *not* that part resulting from grief and sorrow over the loss of his wife.

VANA v. TOSTA, [1968] S.C.R. 71, 66 D.L.R. (2d) 97.

Plaintiff recovered for shock after witnessing his wife's death in a car accident.

WALKER v. BROADFOOT, [1958] O.W.N. 173 (H.C.).

Damages were given in respect of a woman's suicide where it was found that she acted out of severe depression after witnessing her husband's death.

Held for Defendant

ABRAMZIK v. BRENNER (1967), 62 W.W.R. 332, 65 D.L.R. (2d) 651 (Sask. C.A.).

A mother suffered nervous shock on being informed that her children had been killed in a car accident.

BABINEAU v. MacDONALD (1975), 59 D.L.R. (3d) 671, 10 N.B.R. (2d) 715 (C.A.).

A mother and her daughter sustained shock on being told of the death of the husband and father in a car accident.

BOURQUE v. SURETTE (1978), 23 N.B.R. (2d) 357, 44 A.P.R. 357 (Q.B.).

The parents of five men killed in a car accident sued for shock suffered on being informed of the deaths.

BROWN v. HUBAR (1974), 3 O.R. (2d) 448, 45 D.L.R. (3d) 664 (H.C.).

A father went to the scene of an accident to pick up his daughter. He found her condition serious and when he went to the hospital was informed of her death.

DIETALBACH v. PUB. TRUSTEE, [1973] 5 W.W.R. 93, 37 D.L.R. (3d) 621 (B.C.S.C.).

Plaintiff's husband was seriously injured in a car accident. As a result of his injuries and subsequent personality change she suffered nervous shock.

DUWYN v. KAPRIELIAN (1978), 22 O.R. (2d) 736, 7 C.C.L.T. 121, 94 D.L.R. (3d) 424 (C.A.).

Defendant backed into a car and shattered glass on a baby. The child was unhurt but the mother heard it crying and became hysterical. The mother was not present at the time of the accident.

FINBOW v. DOMINO (1957), 65 Man. R. 240, 23 W.W.R. 97, 11 D.L.R. (2d) 493 (Q.B.).

A mother witnessed a traffic accident in which her child was injured and suffered shock.

GRIFFITHS v. C.P.R. (1978), 6 B.C.L.R. 115 (C.A.)

Plaintiff witnessed his wife killed in a car train collision and suffered shock.

GUAY v. SUN PUBLISHING CO., [1953] 2 S.C.R. 216, [1953] 4 D.L.R. 577.

Defendant erroneously published a story that the plaintiff's family had been killed in an accident. Plaintiff read the story and suffered shock.

KERNESTED v. DESORCY, [1978] 3 W.W.R. 623, affirmed [1979] 1 W.W.R. 512 (C.A.).

Plaintiff was injured and her husband and daughter were killed in a car accident. Her claim for compensation for shock was denied.

McMULLIN v. F.W. WOOLWORTH CO. (1974), 9 N.B.R. (2d) 214 (Q.B.).

Plaintiff's children developed salmonella after buying pet turtles from the defendant store. The children suffered no permanent injury, but plaintiff suffered shock.

TAYLOR v. B.C. ELEC. RY. (1911), 16 B.C.R. 109, 17 W.L.R. 470, 13 C.R.C. 400 (C.A.).

Nervous shock caused by train/car accident.

WIPFLI v. BRITTEN (1982), 22 C.C.L.T. 104, supplemental reasons at [1983] 3 W.W.R. 424, 43 B.C.L.R., 145 D.L.R. (3d) 80 (S.C.).

Defendant negligently failed to diagnose twins before plaintiff gave birth. As a result, one of the twins suffered cerebral palsy producing devastating physical disability and partial mental retardation. Defendant doctor was held liable in negligence. However, the parents' claim for nervous shock sustained during the delivery and upon discovering the baby's condition was dismissed, since they had not suffered any proven psychiatric disorder.

YOUNG v. BURGOYNE (1981), 16 C.C.L.T. 100, 122 D.L.R. (3d) 330, 44 N.S.R. (2d) 604, 83 A.P.R. 604 (T.D.).

A young woman was injured in a motor vehicle accident caused by defendant's negligence. Her mother claim for nervous shock suffered some nine months after the accident as a result of seeing her daughter at the scene of the accident. The court denied her claim for nervous shock on the ground that defendant could not be expected to foresee that the mother suffered from an existing nervous condition that would be aggravated by defendant's negligence.

GREAT BRITAIN

Held for Plaintiff

BEHRENS v. BERTRAM MILLS CIRCUS LTD., [1957] 2 Q.B. 1, [1957] 2 W.L.R. 404, [1957] 1 All E.R. 583.

A circus performer suffered shock when he witnessed his wife being trampled by an elephant.

BOARDMAN v. SANDERSON, [1964] 1 W.L.R. 1317 (C.A.).

A father suffered shock when he heard the screams of his child and ran to the scene of the accident in a garage.

CURRIE v. WARDROP, [1927] S.C. 538.

Plaintiff suffered shock when she and her fiance were knocked by a bus. She was uninjured but feared greatly for her finance.

DOOLEY v. CAMMELL LAIRD & CO. LTd., [1951] 1 Lloyd's Rep. 271.

A crane operator suffered nervous shock when some cargo dropped into the hold of a ship because of a defective rope and he feared a workman would be injured.

HAMBROOK v. STOKES BROS., [1925] 1 K.B. 141 (C.A.).

A runaway truck injured a child in the presence of her mother who suffered such severe shock that she ultimately died.

HINZ v. BERRY, [1970] 2 Q.B. 40, [1970] 2 W.L.R. 684, [1970] 1 All E.R. 1074 (C.A.).

A wife suffered shock when she witnessed an accident which killed her husband and injured several of her children.

McCARTHY v. WALSH, [1965] I.R. 246 (S.C.).

Children suffered nervous shock when their sister was killed in a car accident.

McLOUGHLIN v. O'BRIAN, [1982] 2 W.L.R. 982, [1982] 2 All E.R. 298 (H.L.).

A mother rushed to the hospital after her family was injured in a car accident and suffered shock on seeing the condition of her family.

MALCOLM v. BROADHURST, [1970] 3 All E.R. 508 (Q.B.).

After a wife and her husband were injured in a car accident, she suffered severe nervous shock due to his resulting change in behaviour.

S. v. DISTILLERS CO. (BIOCHEMICALS) LTD.; J. v. DISTILLERS CO. (BIO-CHEMICALS) LTD., [1970] 1 W.L.R. 114, [1969] 3 All E.R. 1412 (Q.B.).

A mother recovered for shock from witnessing a thalidomide child being born deformed.

SCHNEIDER v. EISOVITCH, [1960] 2 Q.B. 430, [1960] 2 W.L.R. 169, [1960] 1 All E.R. 169.

A wife suffered nervous shock after she was injured and her husband killed in a car accident.

Held for Defendant

HAY (OR BOURHILL) v. YOUNG, [1943] A.C. 92, [1942] 2 All E.R. 396 (H.L.).

A pregnant woman heard the sounds of an accident and later saw blood on the road. She suffered shock and later miscarried.

KING v. PHILLIPS, [1953] 1 Q.B. 429, [1953] 2 W.L.R. 526, [1953] 1 All E.R. 617 (C.A.).

A taxi backed over the plaintiff's son. She was not present at the scene, but she heard the child's screams and suffered shock.

APPENDIX V

REMOTENESS AND ECONOMIC LOSS

A. ECONOMIC LOSS ARISING FROM PHYSICAL INJURY TO PERSONS AND TO PROPERTY WHICH IS A NECESSARY AND SUFFICIENT CONDITION FOR THE ECONOMIC LOSS TO BE SUFFERED.

TYPES OF LOSS

1. Loss of Income (including loss of profits, earnings, and prospective income).

AUSTRALIA

Held for Plaintiff

FRENCH KNIT SALES PTY. LTD. v. N. GOLD & SONS PTY. LTD., [1972] 2 N.S.W.L.R. 132 (C.A.).

MILLAR v. CANDY (1981), 38 A.L.R. 299 (Fed. Ct.).

O'KEEFE v. SCHLUTER, [1979] Qd. R. 224 (S.C.).

CANADA

Held for Plaintiff

BLAIR'S PLUMBING & HEATING LTD. v. McGRAW (1981), 39 N.B.R. (2d) 356, 103 A.P.R. 356 (C.A.).

COMINCO LTD. v. CAN. GEN. ELEC. CO. (1983), 45 B.C.L.R. 35, 147 D.L.R. (3d) 279, reversing in part 45 B.C.L.R. 26, 127 D.L.R. (3d) 544 (sub nom. COMINCO Ltd. v. WESTINGHOUSE (C.A.).

COURTENAY v. KNUTSON; CLAUSON v. KNUTSON (1957), 32 W.W.R. 481, 26 D.L.R. (2d) 678 (B.C.S.C.).

DUCE v. ROURKE; PEARCE v. ROURKE (1951), 1 W.W.R. (N.S.) 305 (Alta. S.C.).

DULL v. NEUFELD (1980), 4 Sask. R. 94 (Q.B.).

EVERETT v. KING, [1982] 1 W.W.R. 561, 34 B.C.L.R. 27, 20 C.C.L.T. 1 (S.C.).

GOLD v. DE HAVILLAND AIRCRAFT OF CAN. LTD., [1983] 6 W.W.R. 229, 25 C.C.L.T. 180 (B.C.S.C.).

HOPE HDWE. & BLDG. SUPPLY CO. v. FIELDS STORES LTD.; SEARS (CHILLI-WACK) LTD. v. FIELD STORES LTD. (1978), 7 B.C.L.R 321, 7 C.P.C. 321, 90 D.L.R. (3d) 49, varied 137 D.L.R. (3d) 58 (C.A.).

C. W. McLEOD FISHERIES LTD. v. IRVING OIL CO. LTD.; P.A. TRAWLER LTD. v. IRVING OIL CO., 34 N.S.R. (2d) 114, [1980] I.L.R. 91-591 (sub nom. C. W. FISHER-IES v. IRVING OIL, 59 A.P.R. 114 (T.D.).

POBERZNICK v. GOLDSCHMIDT, [1983] A.W.L.D. 117, 18 A.C.W.S. 193 (Q.B.).

RANGER LAKE HELICOPTERS LTD. v. SAUNDERS (1980), 1 A.C.W.S. (2d) 433 (Ont. Dist. Ct.).

R. v. MASON, [1933] S.C.R. 332, [1933] 4 D.L.R. 309.

ROBERT SIMPSON CO. v. FOUNDATION CO. OF CAN. (1982), 36 O.R. (2d) 97, 20 C.C.L.T. 179, 26 C.P.C. 51, 134 D.L.R. (3d) 458 (C.A.).

SCHWARTZ v. HOTEL CORP. OF AMER. (MAN.) LTD., 75 W.W.R. 664, 15 D.L.R. (3d) 764, affirmed [1971] 3 W.W.R. 320, 20 D.L.R. (3d) 759 (Man. C.A.).

SEAWAY HOTELS LTD. v. GRAGG (CAN.) LTD., [1959] O.R. 177, 17 D.L.R. (2d) 292, affirmed [1959] O.R. 581, 21 D.L.R. (2d) 264 (C.A.).

SWEDJA v. MARTIN (1969), 3 D.L.R. (3d) 426 (Sask. Q.B.).

GREAT BRITAIN

Held for Plaintiff

HANNA v. McKIBBEN, [1940] N.I. 120 (K.B.).

BR. CELANESE LTD. v. A. H. HUNT (CAPACITORS) LTD., [1969] 1 W.L.R. 959, [1969] 2 ALl E.R. 1252 (Q.B.).

MORIARTY v. McCARTHY, [1978] 1 W.L.R. 155, [1978] 2 All E.R. 213 (Q.B.).

THE OKEHAMPTON, [1913] P. 173 (C.A.).

S.C.M. v. W. J. WHITTALL & SON, [1971] 1 Q.B. 137, [1970] 3 W.L.R. 694, [1970] 3 All E.R. 245 (C.A.).

SPARTAN STEEL & ALLOYS LTD. v. MARTIN & CO. (CONTRACTORS) LTD., [1973] Q.B. 27, [1972] 3 W.L.R. 502, [1972] 3 All E.R. 557 (C.A.).

NEW ZEALAND

Held for Plaintiff

BEVAN INVT. LTD. v. BLACKHALL & STRUTHERS (NO. 2), [1973] 2 N.Z.L.R. 45 (S.C.).

BOWEN v. PARAMOUNT BLDRS. (HAMILTON) LTD., [1977] 1 N.Z.L.R. 394, reversing [1975] 2 N.Z.L.R. 546 (C.A.).

CERVO v. SWINBURN (FERRETTI, THIRD PARTY), [1939] N.Z.L.R. 430, [1939] G.L.R. 270 (S.C.).

TAUPO BOROUGH COUNCIL v. BIRNIE, [1978] 2 N.Z.L.R. 397 (Wellington C.A.).

2. Cost of Renting Substitute, or Loss of Use

AUSTRALIA

Held for Plaintiff

MILLAR v. CANDY (1981), 38 A.L.R. 299 (Fed. Ct.).

CANADA

Held for Plaintiff

ATHABASKA AIRWAYS LTD. v. SASK. GOVT. AIRWAYS AND HODGINS (1957), 23 W.W.R. 651, 77 C.R.T.C. 65, 12 D.L.R. (2d) 187, varied as to damages 25 W.W.R. 401, 78 C.R.T.C. 246, 14 D.L.R. (2d) 66 (Sask. C.A.).

CAMIONNEURS DU NORD LTÉE v. SEALY (1982), 39 N.B.R. (2d) 272, 103 A.P.R. 272 (C.A.).

EDMONTON v. HABERSTOCK (1982), 40 A.R. 167 (Q.B.).

EGMONT TOWING & SORTING LTD., v. THE TELENDOS (1982), 42 N.R. 220 (Fed. C.A.).

GEMMEL v. DUBE (1983), 1 A.C.W.S. (2d) 494 (Man. Q.B.).

MacGILLIVRAY v. RAM (1982), 52 N.S.R. (2d) 486, 106 A.P.R. 486 (T.D.).

SMITH v. MELANCON, [1976] 4 W.W.R. 9 (B.C.S.C.).

SUMMERS v. MARCH (1982), 37 Nfld. & P.E.I.R. 437, 104 A.P.R. 437 (Nfld. Dist. Ct.).

NEW ZEALAND

Held for Plaintiff

GARDNER v. R., [1933] N.Z.L.R. 730 (C.A.).

3. Cleanup Costs

CANADA

Held for Plaintiff

A.G. ONT. v. CROMPTON (1976), 14 O.R. (2d) 659, 1 C.C.L.T. 81, 74 D.L.R. (3d) 345 (H.C.).

HOPE HDWE. & BLDG. SUPPLY CO. v. FIELDS STORES LTD.; SEARS (CHILLI-WACK) LTD. v. FIELDS STORES LTD. (1978), 7 B.C.L.R. 321, 7 C.P.C. 321, 90 D.L.R. (3d) 49, affirmed 137 D.L.R. (3d) 58 (C.A.).

LYON v. SHELBURNE (1981), 130 D.L.R. (3d) 307 (Ont. Co. Ct.).

POBERZNICK v. GOLDSCHMIDT, [1983] A.W.L.D. 117, 18 A.C.W.S. 193 (Q.B.).

WINDSOR BLDG. SUPPLIES LTD. v. ART HARRISON LTD. (1980), 24 B.C.L.R. 145, 14 C.C.L.T. 129 (S.C.).

4. Reduction in Value

CANADA

Held for Plaintiff

BLACK v. KEYS, RURAL MUN. OF KEYS NO. 303 (1981), 13 Sask. R. 286 (Sask. Q.B.).

DUCE v. ROURKE; PEARCE v. ROURKE (1951), 1 W.W.R. (N.S.) 305 (Alta. S.C.).

GAREAU v. MONTREAL STREET RY. (1901), 31 S.C.R. 463.

GREAT BRITAIN

Held for Plaintiff

BATTY v. METRO. PROPERTY REALISATIONS, [1978] Q.B. 554, [1978] 2 W.L.R. 500, [1978] 2 All E.R. 445 (C.A.).

DUTTON v. BOGNOR REGIS URBAN DIST. COUNCIL, [1972] 1 Q.B. 373, [1972] 2 W.L.R. 299, [1972] 1 All E.R. 462 (C.A.).

NEW ZEALAND

Held for Plaintiff

BOWEN v. PARAMOUNT BLDGS. (HAMILTON) LTD., [1977] 1 N.Z.L.R. 394, reversing [1975] 2 N.Z.L.R. 546 (C.A.).

5. Other Types of Losses

CANADA

Held for Plaintiff

DOM. CHAIN CO. v. EASTERN CONST CO., 12 O.R. (2d) 201, 1 C.P.C. 13, 68 D.L.R. 385, affirmed (sub nom. GIFFELS ASSOCIATES LTD. v. EASTERN CONST. CO.) [1978] 2 S.C.R. 1346, 4 C.C.L.T. 143, 5 C.P.C. 223, 84 D.L.R. (3d) 344, 19 N.R. 298.
Cost of replacing a defective roof and fees paid to engineers and consultants in effecting repairs.

HACKNEY v. CHUBEY; DeKOCK v. H. J. JEFFRIES TRUCK LINE INC. (1981), 13 M.V.R. 84, 12 Sask. R. 19 (Q.B.).
Claim for expenses for hospital visits made by wife of the injured plaintiff (wife resided in another city).

SWEDJA v. MARTIN (1969), 3 D.L.R. (3d) 426 (Sask. Q.B.).
Salary expenditures incurred.

WINDER'S STORAGE & DISTRIBUTORS LTD. v. SETRAKOV CONST. LTD. (1981), 12 M.V.R. 49, 128 D.L.R. (3d) 301, 11 Sask. R. 286 (C.A.).
Plaintiff purchaser and common carrier recovered from the manufacturer the amount of plaintiff's liability to a third party as a result of defendant's negligence in manufacture.

GREAT BRITAIN

Held for Plaintiff

ACREREST LTD. v. W. S. HATTRELL & PARTNERS (A FIRM), [1982] 3 W.L.R. 1076, [1983] 1 All E.R. 17 (C.A.).
Compensation expenditures paid to third party tenants.

C.P.R. v. KELVIN SHIPPING CO. (1928), 138 L.T. 369 (H.L.).
Increased cost of salvage.

MORRISON S. S. CO. v. GREYSTONE CASTLE (CARGO OWNERS), [1947] A.C. 265, [1946] 2 All E.R. 696 (H.L.).
Compensation expenditures paid to third party.

WIMPEY CONSTRUCTION (U.K.) LTD. v. MARTIN BLACK & CO. (WIRE ROPES) LTD., [1982] S.L.T. 239 (Outer House).
Extra overhead incurred as a result of the damaged property.

NEW ZEALAND

Held for Plaintiff

CERVO v. SWINBURN (FERRETTI, THIRD PARTY), [1939] N.Z.L.R. 430, [1939] G.L.R. 270 (S.C.).
Loss of Market in respect of crops.

GABOLINSCY v. HAMILTON CITY CORP., [1975] 1 N.Z.L.R. 150 (S.C.).
Consulting fees paid to engineering firm.

TAUPO BOROUGH COUNCIL v. BIRNIE, [1978] 2 N.Z.L.R. 397 (Wellington C.A.).
Hotel forced to be sold at a loss in an auction, resulting in loss of capital.

B. ECONOMIC LOSS ARISING FROM PHYSICAL INJURY TO PERSONS AND TO PROPERTY WHICH IS NOT A NECESSARY AND SUFFICIENT CONDITION FOR THE ECONOMIC LOSS TO BE SUFFERED.

1. Loss Due to Strikes

CANADA

Held for Plaintiff

PENMAN v. ST. JOHN TOYOTA LTD. (1972), 30 D.L.R. (3d) 88, 5 N.B.R. (2d) 140 (C.A.).

SHULHAN v. PETERSON, HOWELL & HEATHER (CAN.) LTD. (1966), 57 W.W.R. 46, 57 D.L.R. (2d) 491 (Sask. Q.B.).

GREAT BRITAIN

Held for Plaintiff

H.M.S. LONDON, [1914] P. 72.

2. Loss Due to Plaintiff's Pecuniary Position

CANADA

Held for Defendant

ALTA. CATERERS LTD. v. R. VOLLAN (ALTA.) LTD. (1977), 5 Alta. L.R. (2d) 1, 5 C.P.C. 135, 81 D.L.R. (3d) 672, 10 A.R. 501, varied 11 A.R. 181 (T.D.).

BURTON v. DOM. STEEL & COAL CORP. 14 M.P.R. 328, [1940] 1 D.L.R. 476 (N.S.C.A.).

CAMIONNEURS DU NORD LTÉE v. SEALY (1982), 39 N.B.R. (2d) 272, 103 A.P.R. 272 (C.A.).

GREAT BRITAIN

Held for Plaintiff

DREDGER LIESBOSCH v. S.S. EDISON (OWNERS), [1933] A.C. 449 (H.L.).

3. Loss Due to Some Other Causal Factors

AUSTRALIA

Held for Defendant

ANTONATOS v. DUNLOP, ALLSOPP & TPT. & GEN. INS. CO. LTD., [1963] Qd. R. 114 (Brisbane S.C.).
Loss in respect of marriage break up and plaintiff disposing of his share in a partnership at a substantial undervalue were not directly traceable to the tortious act.

MILLAR v. CANDY (1981), 38 A.L.R. 299 (Fed. Ct.).
Additional amount required to be paid by plaintiff to owner of car upon early termination of hire-purchase agreement.

CANADA

Held for Defendant

BLACK v. C.P.R., [1941] 2 W.W.R. 621 (Alta. S.C.).
Loss of expected profit consequent on plaintiff's inability to undertake planned construction project because of poor health.

DUCE v. ROURKE; PEARCE v. ROURKE (1951), 1 W.W.R. (N.S.) 305 (Alta. S.C.).
Loss in respect of tools stolen from plaintiff's car after an accident.

GEMMEL v. DUBE (1983), 18 A.C.W.S. (2d) 494 (Man. Q.B.).
Loss of goodwill resulting from termination of business through plaintiff's choice.

GOLD v. DE HAVILLAND AIRCRAFT OF CAN. LTD., [1983] 6 W.W.R. 229, 25 C.C.L.T. 180 (B.C.S.C.).

Loss of prospective profits traced to factors other than the air crash itself, i.e. increased number of competitors, and poor past performance record.

HELLENS v. PEDERSON, [1977] 3 W.W.R. 372 (B.C.S.C.).

Loss of earnings due to inability to obtain employment was a result of an economic recession.

KERN v. MacDOUGALL (1963), 42 W.W.R. 695 (Alta. S.C.).

Sale of farm at a loss was result of plaintiff's failure to inform himself of its true worth.

KUMMEN v. ALFONSO, 7 W.W.R. at 422, [1953] 1 D.L.R. 637, 60 Man. R. 369 (C.A.).

Travel expense incurred by plaintiff who chose to take a trip south to recover from injuries received in a car accident.

LONDON GUAR. & ACC. CO. v. GIBSON, [1928] 2 W.W.R. 532, 23 Alta. L.R. 518, [1928] 3 D.L.R. 610 (C.A.).

Legal costs incurred as a result of an unsuccessful action taken against the plaintiff by a passenger in another car.

MacGILLIVRAY v. RAM (1982), 52 N.S.R. (2d) 486, 106 A.P.R. 486 (T.D.).

Loss caused by plaintiff's car being disposed of by touring company was due to plaintiff's own failure to pay towing and storage fees.

MONTREAL STREET RY. CO. v. BOUDREAU, [1905] S.C.R. 329.

Loss in respect of future depreciation of value of property too speculative to be recoverable, since other factors may contribute to it.

PRICE v. INTERNAT. HARVESTER CO. (1915), 8 W.W.R. 712, 23 D.L.R. 266, 31 W.L.R. 216 (Alta. S.C.).

Loss from crops destroyed by snowstorm.

SIMMS v. BUTT (1972), 3 Nfld. & P.E.I.R. 537, affirmed 8 Nfld. & P.E.I.R. 14 (Nfld. C.A.).

Loss of earnings due to job being no longer available upon plaintiff's recovery from injury.

SOUTHERN CAN. POWER CO. v. R., [1937] 3 All E.R. 923, 47 C.R.C. 113, [1936] 3 D.L.R. 737, reversing [1936] S.C.R. 4, 44 C.R.C. 129, [1936] 1 D.L.R. 331, varying [1934] Ex. C.R. 142.

Costs of medical and hospital services for injured third parties were incurred as a result of plaintiff's own liability to the third parties.

SULLIVAN v. H.E.P.C. ONT., [1960] O.W.N. 195, 23 D.L.R. (2d) 756 (H.C.).

Loss of profits from anticipated mink breeding were due to plaintiff's own negligence in not installing false bottoms in the cages to prevent kittens from falling through.

WINDSOR BLDG. SUPPLIES LTD. v. ART HARRISON LTD. (1980), 24 B.C.L.R. 145, 14 C.C.L.T. 129 (S.C.).

Increased rental cost of substitute premises was not recoverable, since plaintiffs would have moved into other premises anyway had they known of danger of collapse.

GREAT BRITAIN

Held for Defendant

KIRKHAM v. BOUGHEY, [1958] 2 Q.B. 338, [1957] 3 W.L.R. 626, [1957] 3 All E.R. 153.
Loss of earnings as a result of plaintiff husband voluntarily giving up a lucrative job overseas to be near his injured wife.

THE NOTTING HILL (1884), 9 P.D. 105 (C.A.).
Loss of market caused by delay in arrival of cargo on damaged ship.

SPARTAN STEEL & ALLOYS LTD. v. MARTIN & CO. (CONTRACTORS) LTD., [1973] Q.B. 27, [1972] 3 W.L.R. 502, [1972] 3 ALl E.R. 557, (C.A.).
Loss of profits on other four "melts" which could have been produced were due to power being turned off while the damaged cable was undergoing repairs.

C. ECONOMIC LOSS ARISING FROM PHYSICAL INJURY TO PERSONS AND TO PROPERTY BUT SUFFERED BY PERSONS OTHER THAN THOSE WHO SUFFER THE PHYSICAL INJURY TO THEIR PERSONS AND PROPERTY.

1. Foreseeable in the Particular

AUSTRALIA

Held for Plaintiff

CALTEX OIL (AUSTRALIA) PTY. LTD. v. THE DREDGE WILLEMSTAD (1976), 11 A.L.R. 227, 136 C.L.R. 529, 51 A.L.J.R. 270 (H.C.).
Caltex contracted with company whereby it supplied crude oil to the company's refinery and the company delivered the refined product to Caltex's terminal through the company's underwater pipeline. Through negligent navigation, a dredge broke the pipeline. Caltex then sued the dredge owner for the cost of using alternative means of transporting oil to the terminal while the pipeline was being repaired. The court held that a defendant will be liable for pure economic loss if he knew or ought to have known that plaintiff as a "specific individual," rather than as a member of a "general" or "unascertained" class of persons, would be likely to suffer economic loss as a result of defendant's negligence.

CANADA

Held for Plaintiff

RIVTOW MARINE LTD. v. WASHINGTON IRON WORKS, [1974] S.C.R. 1189, [1973] 6 W.W.R. 692, 40 D.L.R. (3d) 530.
The defendant negligently designed and manufactured a crane used by plaintiff charterers. The defendant failed to warn plaintiff of the danger of collapse even after learning of the defect. The court held that the plaintiff could recover for loss of profits resulting from the loss of use of the crane during the busy season, but not for the cost of repairs (Laskin J. dissenting on the latter point).

YUMEROVSKI v. DANI (1977), 18 O.R. (2d) 704, 4 C.C.L.T. 233, 83 D.L.R. (3d) 558, affirmed 30 O.R. (2d) 288n, 800, 120 D.L.R. (3d) 768 (C.A.).

Plaintiff purchased 12 airline tickets from the defendant travel agent. Defendant promised to take some of plaintiff's family to the airport. En route, he had an accident resulting in the death of plaintiff's father. Plaintiff did not board the charter flight but was unable to recover the cost of the tickets from the airlines. The court held that the plaintiff could recover the ticket costs from the defendant travel agent.

2. Not Forseeable in the Particular

AUSTRALIA

Held for Defendant

FRENCH KNIT SALES PTY. LTD. v. N. GOLD & SONS PTY. LTD., [1972] 2 N.S.W.L.R. 132 (C.A.).

Plaintiff company was associated with another company which acted as its manufacturer and supplier. Both companies occupied the same premises. Plaintiff sued defendant for negligence in permitting water to escape into plaintiff's premises, damaging the companies' stock and equipment. The court denied recovery in respect of plaintiff's loss of profits from its inability to acquire goods from the manufacturer, which was unable to attend to its business for a time after its goods were damaged.

PRATT v. PRATT, [1975] v. R. 378 (S.C. Full Ct.).

Plaintiff, mother of a pregnant woman severly incapacitated in a motor collision, sued for nervous shock induced by seeing the daughter's state after the accident. Plaintiff also claimed for travelling expenses to visit the daughter and loss of earnings due to plaintiff's assistance and own ill health.

CANADA

Held for Plaintiff

DOM. TAPE OF CAN. LTD. v. L.R. McDONALD & SONS LTD., [1971] 3 O.R. 627, 21 D.L.R. (3d) 299 (Co. Ct.).

Several bales fell from defendant's negligently loaded truck and broke a hydro pole, which in turn caused a power failure at plaintiff's factory. Plaintiff's property was not damaged but he sued for lost profits and salary expenditures for the period of the power failure. The court allowed recovery in respect of the salary expenditures on the basis that they were positive outlays which constituted a direct and proximate consequence of defendant's negligence (The case is wrongly decided on this point).

Held for Defendant

A.G. ONT. v. FATEHI (1981), 34 O.R. (2d) 129, 13 M.V.R. 180, 18 C.C.L.T. 97, 127 D.L.R. (3d) 630 (C.A.).

Defendant's negligence caused a motor vehicle accident. The road was strewn with the aftermath of the accident. The fire department was called in to clear the road. The Crown paid the fire department $300 pursuant to an existing agreement and then sued defendant to recover the cost.

BETHLEHEM STEEL CORP. v. ST. LAWRENCE SEAWAY AUTHORITY, [1978] 1 F.C. 464, 79 D.L.R. (3d) 522 (T.D.).

Defendant's ship negligently ran into a bridge over a canal so that shipping through the canal was delayed for several days. One claimant sued for the loss of profits from two ships that could not use the canal, and the other claimed for extra expense in having to ship the overload by truck.

CLARK v. WARRINGTON (1958), 26 W.W.R. 673 (Man. Q.B.).

A child suffered personal injuries in a car accident caused by the defendant. The child's mother claimed special damages for having given up her job from the time of the accident until the time of the child's return to school.

DOM. TAPE OF CAN. LTD. v. L.R. McDONALD & SONS LTD., [1971] 3 O.R. 627, 21 D.L.R. (3d) 299 (Co. Ct.).

Several bales fell from defendant's negligently loaded truck and broke a hydro pole, which in turned caused a power failure at plaintiff's factory. Plaintiff's property was not damaged but he sued for lost profits and salary expenditures for the period of the power failure. The court held that although the plaintiff could recover the salary expenditures, it could not recover its loss of profits.

GYPSUM CARRIER INC. v. R.; C.N.R. v. THE HARRY LUNDEBERG (1977), 78 D.L.R. (3d) 175 (Fed T.D.).

The defendant ship negligently collided with a railway bridge owned by the federal Crown. The bridge was closed for repairs for eight days. The plaintiff railway companies, which had agreements with the Crown permitting then to use the bridge, incurred expenses in re-routing the trains during the time the bridge was closed. Plaintiffs sued defendant to recover the loss in a negligence action.

HUNT v. T.W. JOHNSTONE CO. LTD. (1976), 12 O.R. (2d) 623, 69 D.L.R. (3d) 639 (H.C.).

Plaintiff started a building products business and incorporated H. Co. as his selling agent, and M. Co. as the manufacturer. Defendant negligently caused a fire that partially destroyed some of M. Co.'s goods. Plaintiff sued for the loss of profits from M. Co. not being able to supply H. Co.

MacMILLAN BLOEDEL LTD. v. FOUNDATION CO. [1977] 2 W.W.R. 717, 1 C.C.L.T. 358, 75 D.L.R. (3d) 294 (B.C.S.C.).

Defendant's workmen cut ground cables supplying electricity to plaintiff's building. Plaintiff was forced to dismiss its employees for the day but still had to pay them their wages.

RIVTOW MARINE LTD. v. WASHINGTON IRON WORKS, [1974] S.C.R. 1189, [1973] 6 W.W.R. 692, 40 D.L.R. (3d) 530.

The defendant negligently designed and manufactured a crane used by plaintiff charterers. The defendant failed to warn plaintiff of the danger of collapse even after learning of the defect. The court held that the plaintiff could recover for loss of profits resulting from the loss of use of the crane during the busy season but not for the cost of repairs (Laskin J. dissenting on this point).

SLEEMAN v. FOOTHILLS SCHOOL DIV. NO. 38, [1946] 1 W.W.R. 145 (Alta. S.C.).

Plaintiff, father of a rural school pupil injured in a collision between the school bus and another vehicle, claimed damages for the cost of sending the child to a private school in Calgary on the ground that she was too nervous to go in the school bus again to the rural school.

STAR VILLAGE TAVERN v. NIELD, [1976] 6 W.W.R. 80, 71 D.L.R. (3d) 439 (Man. Q.B.).

Defendant, while driving a motor vehicle negligently, collided with and damaged a bridge, causing economic loss to the plaintiff because of increased travelling distance to plaintiff's place of business while the bridge was being repaired (Many of the plaintiff's customers had suspended their patronage during this time.)

GREAT BRITAIN

Held for Defendant

ANGLO-ALGERIAN S.S. CO. LTD. v. HOULDER LINE LTD., [1908] 1 K.B. 659.

By careless navigation defendant damaged the gates of a dock so that it had to be closed several days for repairs. Plaintiff's ship was detained outside the gates for 2½ days waiting to take on cargo. Plaintiff sought damages for detention.

CATTLE v. STOCKTON WATERWORKS CO. (1875), L.R. 10 Q.B. 453.

Plaintiff builder contracted to build a tunnel under a road. Defendant negligently flooded the tunnel causing plaintiff greater expense to do the job.

DYNAMCO LTD. v. HOLLAND & HANNEN & CUBITTS (SCOTLAND) LTD.; DYNAMCO v. JAMES HARRISON & CO. (BLDRS.), [1971] S.C. 257, [1972] S.L.T. 38 (Outer House).

Estate contractors broke an electric cable carrying power to plaintiff's property while working on adjacent property. The loss of power caused an interruption in production with subsequent loss to the plaintiff.

ELECTROCHROME LTD. v. WELSH PLASTICS LTD., [1968] 2 All E.R. 205.

Defendant's servant negligently drove a truck into a fire hydrant damaging it and causing the main to be shut off for some time. As a result, plaintiff's factory had its water supply shut off, causing loss of a day's work. Plaintiff sought to recover the amount of that loss.

ELLIOTT (TRADING AS ARLINGTON BOOKS) v. SIR ROBERT McALPINE & SONS LTD., [1966] 2 Lloyd's Rep. 482.

One of the plaintiff's telephones was put out of action for three weeks when the defendant, who was engaged in demolition work, dropped concrete on a telephone junction box. Plaintiff alleged that due to lack of a telephone, he lost profits he would otherwise have earned.

SIMPSON & CO. v. THOMSON, BURRELL (1877), 3 A.C. 279 (H.L.).

Two ships owned by the same person collided and the plaintiff insurance company sued the owner of the negligent vessel recover the insurance proceeds that the company had paid in favour of the other ship.

SOCIETE ANONYME DE REMORQUAGE A HELICE v. BENNETTS, [1911] 1 K.B. 243.

Defendant negligently sank a ship that the plaintiff, a tugboat owner, was towing. The tugboat was not damaged but plaintiff claimed for lost profits.

WELLER & CO. v. FOOT AND MOUTH DISEASE RESEARCH INSTITUTE, [1966] 1 Q.B. 569, [1965] 3 All E.R. 560, [1965] 2 Lloyd's Rep. 414.

An escape of virus from research premises led to infection of cattle in the areas and necessitated the closing of the cattle markets. This resulted in economic loss to the plaintiff auctioneers, who did not own the cattle.

WIMPEY CONST. (U.K.) LTD. v. MARTIN BLACK & CO. (WIRE ROPES) LTD., [1982] S.L.T. 239 (Outer House).

Three companies, the plaintiffs, entered into a joint venture for the construction of a tanker terminal. During construction a wire rope sling, supplied by defendant to one of the plaintiff companies, failed. A pile carried by the sling was dropped into the river, the crane and the jackup barge were seriously damaged along with other equipment. The court held that in respect of the economic loss caused by the delay in construction attendant on damage to the barge, only the one plaintiff company which had hired the barge was entitled to recover, since the other plaintiffs had no possessory right in the article damaged.

NEW ZEALAND

Held for Plaintiff

BADHAM v. WILLIAMS, [1968] N.Z.L.R. (Auckland S.C.).

Defendant negligently drove his car into a power pole, cutting electric supply to plaintiff's land. New requirements of the power board required plaintiff to pay £136 for reinstatement under the new regulations as opposed to £20 under the old regulations. Defendant argued that he should not be liable for the entire cost because the new and elaborate installation was not foreseeable. The court held that the damage was foreseeable. (The case is wrongly decided).

SMYTH v. HUGHES, [1974] 2 N.Z.L.R. 573 (S.C.).

The plaintiff wife was injured by a car negligently driven by the defendant. The plaintiff husband took time off from his work to look after his wife and claimed damages for himself for loss of salary. The court allowed recovery. (The case is wrongly decided.)

3. Action "Per Quod Servitium Amisit"

AUSTRALIA

Held for Plaintiff

COMMR. FOR RYS. (N.S.W.) v. SCOTT (1969), 33 A.L.J.R. 126, [1959] A.L.R. 896 (H.C.).

SYDNEY CITY COUNCIL v. BOSNICH, 89 W.N. (Pt. 1) (N.S.W.) 168, [1968] 3 N.S.W.R. 725 (C.A.).

Held for Defendant

A.G.N.S.W. v. PERPETUAL TRUSTEE CO., [1955] A.C. 457, [1955] 2 W.L.R. 707, [1955] 1 All E.R. 846 (P.C.).

CANADA

Held for Plaintiff

BERMANN v. OCCHIPINTI, [1953] O.R. 1035, [1954] 1 D.L.R. 560 (S.C.).

GENEREUX v. PETERSON HOWELL & HEATHER (CAN.) LTD., [1973] 2 O.R. 558, 34 D.L.R. (3d) 614 (C.A.).

KNEESHAW v. LATENDORFF (1965), 53 W.W.R. 672, 54 D.L.R. (2d) 84 (Alta. S.C.).

NYKORAK v. A.G. Can., [1962] S.C.R. 331, 37 W.W.R. 660, 33 D.L.R. (2d) 373.

R. v. BUCHINSKY, [1983] 5 W.W.R. 577, 24 C.C.L.T. 266, 145 D.L.R. (3d) 1, 22 Man. R. (2d) 121, 47 N.R. 208, reversing [1981] 1 W.W.R. 88, 13 C.C.L.T. 98, 114 D.L.R. (3d) 721, 4 Man. R. (2d) 141 (S.C.C.).

R. v. MURRAY, [1967] S.C.R. 262, 59 W.W.R. 214, 60 D.L.R. (2d) 647.

R. v. RICHARDSON, [1948] S.C.R. 57, [1948] 2 D.L.R. 305.

RACICOT v. SAUNDERS (1979), 27 O.R. (2d) 15, 11 C.C.L.T. 228, 103 D.L.R. (3d) 567 (H.C.).

Held for Defendant

A.G. CAN. v. JACKSON, [1946] S.C.R. 489, 59 C.R.T.C. 273, [1946] 2 D.L.R. 481.

BEAULIEU v. RINGUETTE (1979), 26 N.B.R. (2d) 22, 55 A.P.R. 22 (Q.B.).

GENEREUX v. PETERSON, HOWELL & HEATHER (CAN.) LTD., [1973] 2 O.R. 558, 34 D.L.R. (3d) 614 (C.A.).

PAGAN v. LEIFER (1969), 69 W.W.R. 247, 6 D.L.R. (3d) 714 (Man. Q.B.).

RACICOT v. SAUNDERS (1979), 27 O.R. (2d) 15, 11 C.C.L.T. 228, 103 D.L.R. (3d) 567 (H.C.).

R. v. C.P.R., [1947] S.C.R. 185, 61 C.R.T.C. 24, [1947] 2 D.L.R. 1.

SCHWARTZ v. HOTEL CORP. OF AMER. (MAN.) LTD., 75 W.W.R. 664, 15 D.L.R. (3d) 764, affirmed [1971] 3 W.W.R. 320, 20 D.L.R. (3d) 759 (Man. C.A.).

SWIFT CAN. CO. v. BOLDUC (1961), 29 D.L.R. (2d) 651 (N.S.S.C.).

GREAT BRITAIN

Held for Plaintiff

LEE v. SHEARD, [1956] 1 Q.B. 192, [1955] 3 W.L.R. 951, [1955] 3 All E.R. 777 (C.A.).

Held for Defendant

INLAND REVENUE COMMRS. v. HAMBROOK, [1956] 2 Q.B. 641, [1956] 3 W.L.R. 643, [1956] 3 All E.R. 338 (C.A.).

TAYLOR v. NERI (1975), 1 Esp. 385, 170 E.R. 393 (N.P.).

The following cases, even though they raise the issue of remoteness of damages, have not been included in analysis of economic loss cases because liability was denied on the basis of insufficiency of proof of loss:

BARRETT v. METZGAR, [1950] 1 W.W.R. 1044 (Alta. S.C.).

COOK v. FANNING (1976), 10 Nfld. & P.E.I.R. 212 (Nfld. T.D.).

KUMMEN v. ALFONSO, 7 W.W.R. at 422, [1953] 1 D.L.R. 637, 60 Man. R. 369 (C.A.).

PEDERSEN v. McRORRIE (1982), 38 A.R. 67 (Q.B.).

TOMPKINS HARDWARE LTD. v. NORTH WESTERN FLYING SERVICES LTD. (1982), 22 C.C.L.T. 1, 139 D.L.R. (3d) 329 (Ont. H.C.).

WRIGHT v. TORONTO RY. (1910), 20 O.L.R. 498 (C.A.).

INDEX

Stanley Clinton Davis
Berliner
Muhrstrat

Dec   1980

would that de moves
close such purposes
presents — have theatoo

DEBTS OF HONOUR

DEBTS

OF

HONOUR

Michael Foot

DAVIS POYNTER LIMITED

LONDON

First published in 1980 by
Davis-Poynter Limited
20 Garrick Street London WC2E 9BJ

Copyright © 1980 by Michael Foot

ISBN 0 7067 0243 3

Photoset by Photobooks (Bristol) Ltd,
and printed by
R. J. Acford Ltd, Chichester, Sussex

To Jill
the biggest creditor of the lot,
and to the people of Tredegar, Ebbw Vale,
Rhymney and Abertysswg.

Contents

Foreword

Half the pieces in this book have been written especially for it, and the other half were previously published, in a more abbreviated form than appears here, in *Tribune*, the *Evening Standard* or the *Observer*. One of them, the first, on my father, was commissioned for the *Sunday Telegraph* by an old friend of mine, Hugh Massingham, who devised a series in which various present-day politicians wrote about their fathers. It was my first attempt at a portrait of him which I hope at some stage to elaborate into a proper biography, but this sketch, I trust, has the merit of freshness, and certainly no such book as this could be devised by me except under my father's auspices and without his constant instructions and incitements jogging my memory. He loved books and taught me how to read and love them too; not, alas, on his own comprehensive, catholic scale but at least in such a manner that every other activity—politics especially—has become associated with books, and, in particular, with books about books.

It was my father who first introduced me to William Hazlitt; I like to pretend that I can recall the note of scheming resignation in his voice when I finally defended my decision to leave the family's Liberal faith and become a Socialist, and when he in turn recommended me to test my ideas by reading Hazlitt. He could never quite accept the Hazlittean assault on the apostasies of *his* heroes, William Wordsworth and Edmund Burke and a few others. Hazlitt was too much of a flaming radical to suit my father's temperament. But if a son of his was determined to stampede down radical or revolutionary paths, what better guide could there be than Hazlitt?

He also introduced me, for quite different reasons, to Jonathan

Swift. It was his idea to write a book in which the conflict between Swift and the Duke of Marlborough was described in day-by-day detail, and he told the story with so many marvellous dramatic touches that I became captivated. But he himself was always too busy reading to waste time writing; he was happy that I should take over the idea, which I did in *The Pen and the Sword*. However, my notions of Swift were transformed into something quite different from his. Mostly his markings in his books show that he still saw Swift as the great Whig historians and as Sarah, Duchess of Marlborough, had seen him—the furious, vicious, unconscionable enemy of the great Whig captains and statesmen and their theme of English freedom and English greatness. But there was another Swift altogether, the Drapier, the author of *Gulliver's Travels*, the precursor of William Hazlitt. I hope that together, placed at the different ends, they may hold this book together.

Hazlitt may also be invoked to excuse the fact that some sections of this book and some sentences in the other pieces have been printed before. Hazlitt was paid by the page or the word, and, like all good journalists, he therefore regarded the number of words he had to write as a question of some significance. He sometimes had to re-publish what he had written before, in an elaborated or abbreviated form, and good luck to him and good luck to all journalists with similar requirements! Moreover, I recall in this connection a piece of wise advice given me by John Strachey which was based—so he told me—on previous advice which he had received from Arthur Koestler. All writers, especially journalists, find it difficult to cut their own copy, even when style or clarity or the demands of publishers suggest that they should or must. So Koestler, according to Strachey, devised the idea of establishing a special file which he called 'useful bits'. He was able to ease the pain of making necessary cuts in words he had already written by transferring them to the file instead of destroying them altogether, and they—both Koestler and Strachey—did find that the bits could be most usefully revived at a more appropriate time and in a more appropriate context. I recommend the alleged Koestler method to all journalists who aspire to produce books.

One last word: I hope the selection of people to appear in the various chapters in this volume will not be cited to mean that others are excluded from my list of creditors. I think I could easily select at least another fifteen names to compile a new list and threaten to do so if this book meets with any success. I mention two. I wanted to include here Robert Blatchford: among his other claims to fame, he was just about the best writer of books about books there ever was—to be ranked with Montaigne or Disraeli's father or Arnold Bennett or Hazlitt himself. But the more I looked, the more I thought he cried out for separate treatment. And finally, there is Aneurin Bevan; to him I owe the biggest political debt of all, and it is not yet discharged. Since I concluded my biography of him in 1973, some new material has appeared— in particular the claims and accusations contained in Philip Williams's monumental life of Hugh Gaitskell. Then also the Cabinet papers of the 1945–51 period are now becoming available. Meantime, Jennie Lee has written a new volume of autobiography, to be published just at the time this book appears. So perhaps the best time for me to contemplate a fresh contribution to the counter-attack against Gaitskellite revisionism will come a little later.

As with the two volumes on Aneurin Bevan, I must also offer my special thanks to Una Cooze, my secretary, without whom the necessary work could never have been done, and to Elizabeth Thomas who helped so much with those previous volumes.

MICHAEL FOOT
Tredegar, June 1980

ONE

A Rupert for the Roundheads

I recalled a favourite passage from Milton, that, next to the
man who gives wise and intrepid counsels of government, he
places the man who cares for the purity of his mother tongue.

JOHN MORLEY

MY FATHER must have been just about the happiest man who
ever lived. Of course, he had his ailments, irritations, bouts of
testiness, and what might be considered an unfair share of
political disappointments and defeats. But all these and all else,
during his eighty years, were governed by his zest for living and
reading, a seemingly single, unquenchable quality. He was
Wordsworth's happy warrior, the servant of high causes, and yet
he also knew with Wordsworth, maybe learnt from him, that

> *The wise*
> *Have still the keeping of their*
> *   proper peace,*
> *Are guardians of their own*
> *   tranquillity.*

He was, almost from his cradle, a dedicated spirit, yet he could
indulge his vices, if such they were, with the abandon of a Turkish
sultan. He had the best of both worlds, fashioned for himself the
perfect synthesis, or so it seems when I recall him in his
Promethean moments; full days and weeks on end of complete
absorption and exultation, so recurrent and characteristic that
the darker intervals look quite insignificant.

He left school at fourteen, taught himself almost everything he
ever knew, sat for a Civil Service examination in London, but
soon preferred to train as a solicitor in his home town, Plymouth,

and earned every penny he ever acquired. In his early twenties he went on a Wesley Guild excursion and set eyes on one whom only Wordsworth could describe:

> *A perfect woman, nobly*
> *planned*
> *To warn, to comfort and*
> *command:*
> *And yet a Spirit still, and*
> *bright*
> *With something of angelic*
> *light.*

He proposed the day after he saw her, intensified the pursuit week after week in her Cornish home of Callington, swept aside her Scottish caution, brought her back in triumph to Plymouth, reared seven children, and thenceforward bowed to her charm and superior will on almost every question but one. For in those early days, with all the odd sixpences he could spare, he also started to build a library.

Or maybe the trouble had started even earlier, at the Band of Hope of all places. He saw the effects, or the causes, of addiction to alcohol in the crowded, violent back streets of Plymouth. Once he saw a particular carpenter friend of his reeling into the street, fighting drunk, and, when his mother came out to protest, striking her a cruel blow across the face. So Isaac Foot, aged nine, signed the pledge, but at the Band of Hope meetings temperance was not all they preached. At one meeting he heard someone recite the words:

> *Lars Porsena of Clusium*
> *By the Nine Gods he swore*
> *That the great house of*
> *Tarquin*
> *Should suffer wrong no*
> *more . . .*

'I walked home that night on air. A fire was kindled within me which has never ceased to burn.' Lars Porsena's rhetoric was, for my father, more potent than any wine; and certainly no one in his strict nonconformist home had ever sworn by the Nine Gods. Not that that home was oppressive; it was, like so many Puritan households, suffused with music and song, and my father's love for them merged with his new-found taste for declamation.

Macaulay was a chief companion again as he moved back and forth from his lodgings to his work, during his stay as a boy-clerk in London. Since every minute was precious, he acquired the trick of reading and declaiming as he walked. The great passages from Macaulay's essay on Hampden he could recite by heart. 'The nation looked round for a defender. Calmly and unostentatiously the plain Buckinghamshire Esquire placed himself at the head of his countrymen and right before the face and across the path of tyranny.' Soon the little yellow volumes of W. T. Stead's Penny Poets added to his repertoire Milton, Shelley, Keats, Coleridge and, most important of all, an abridged version of Carlyle's Letters and Speeches of Cromwell. He rolled secular words round his tongue as readily as the hymns he learnt at Sunday school, trained himself to wake ever earlier in the mornings to snatch more time for reading, lavished a prodigious proportion of his fourteen shillings a week salary on the second-hand book-shops in the Charing Cross Road. On his return to Plymouth and thereafter, new authors were his milestones. He remembered the 1906 election, not only for the thumping Liberal victory, but for the visiting speaker who mentioned a name he had never heard—Burke, Edmund Burke. Next day he bought the little Temple Classics edition of Burke's American speeches, price one shilling but 'worth a thousand pounds to me.'

Poetry and politics, literature and living, the heritage from the past and the onward march of Christian soldiers; for my father the interweaving never ended. He never talked about commitment, would have been puzzled by the argument. We must fight the good fight and keep the faith. Books were weapons, the most beloved and the sharpest. And there spread out before us were enemies enough for a lifetime: historical figures and their modern counterparts melted into one; brewers, Protectionists, Papists, apologists for Lord North and the Chamberlain family; Spanish tyrants and Stuart kings; Simonites and appeasers, men of

Munich and Suez; sons of Belial or Beelzebub, normally disguised as West Country Tories, an especially reprehensible branch of the species.

In 1910, thirty years old, he crossed the Tamar into Cornwall again on another notable expedition; he just failed to become Liberal M.P. for Bodmin by forty-one votes. In 1919 he fought Lady Astor in Plymouth when Waldorf Astor became a peer, lost his deposit, and the family, all seven of us, or at least all old enough to know what was what, sang in unison:

> *Who's that knocking at the door?*
> *Who's that knocking at the door?*
> *If it's Astor and his wife, we'll stab 'em*
>   *with a knife*
> *And they won't be Tories any more.*

Then in 1922 he returned to Bodmin and won a sensational by-election victory as a Liberal Wee Free Asquithian against the Lloyd George Coalition. Meantime the teetotal Astors became family friends. Lady Astor charmed my father, my mother and the rest, and only in the later Cliveden Set era could we raise a full chorus for our 1919 Marseillaise.

Normally my father fought with the gloves off. When he unmasked Sir Edgar Sanders, director of the Brewers Society, initiating a campaign to make 'the younger customer the mainstay of the public house' and proposing that sportsmen should be recruited to advertise their wares, his pamphlet in reply was called *Blood Money?*, and part of the text insisted:

Footballers, cricketers, prize-fighters, and so on. Why did you stop there? Why not give us poster pictures of the chauffeur or bus driver at the wheel, saying 'I drive on beer', and 'I am the mainstay of the public house?' Would anyone of your brewers trust this gentleman with his lorry or his Rolls Royce?

Sir Edgar did not reply. Sometime later in the House of Commons a spokesman of the brewers or distillers was dilating on the virtues of strong drink. 'Who says it interferes with health? Who says "drink" does anyone any harm? In bygone days

W. G. Grace used to sit up all night drinking and go out next day and make a century.' To which, my father interrupted: 'Yes, that was because the bowlers were up all night.' But usually the rebuke for the brewers was less temperate. 'Your scheme', he told Sir Edgar, 'is concerned with *profit*. Here is a passage on profit: "But who shall cause one of these little ones . . . to stumble, it is profitable for him that a great millstone should be hanged about his neck, and that he should sink in the depth of the sea".'

Such was the tone of controversy down our way in the twenties and thirties, when my father was at his peak. When a fellow candidate in a neighbouring constituency inquired how to deal with some customary Tory trick, he replied: 'Tell them it is a lie. Tell them it is a damned lie. Tell them it is no less a lie because it is uttered by a Tory gentleman of title.' Into every town and village he carried his war, and the Tory agents lamented as he invaded their territories: 'There's Isaac Foot holding another of his bloody little prayer meetings!'

How could they know what Wesleyan revels were afoot? For inside those jam-packed halls where he flayed the Lloyd George Coalition, Churchill's economics, the betrayal of Abyssinia and Spain, the iniquities of the liquor trade or the latest menacing impertinence from the Pope of Rome, laughter always mixed with the righteous fury, whether he spoke from the platform or the pulpit; too fine a distinction, he thought, should not be drawn between the two. Men and women walked for miles and waited hours to witness the phenomenon—a full hour, maybe, of rollicking humour and invective, fifteen minutes of passionate argument and a peroration to take the roof off. On his own ground, where he knew the exact response which every reference, every inflection, could evoke, he was one of the great orators of the century, the last of the few.

He became the best-loved and the best-hated man in Devon and Cornwall, the most dashing champion West Country Nonconformity ever had, a Prince Rupert for the Roundheads. And more zealously than ever—it is hard to blame them—Tory motor-cars and brewers' money and every other resource the forces of darkness could marshal poured into the Bodmin constituency to keep Isaac Foot out. In 1935 they succeeded, with the aid of strange allies. All Liberals were invited to vote *against* my father in the name of true Liberalism, the signatories to the appeal being John Simon, Walter Runciman, and Leslie Hore-Belisha, the three Liberal-National or Simonite members of the National Government, of which my father had briefly been a member before its protectionist policies stuck in his gullet. Simon had been a close friend before the Simonite heresy; the other two he had suckled in their West Country constituencies. However, the ferocity of internal party disputes knows no limit, and my father repaid this scurvy treatment with one of the most selfless odysseys in British political history. After the election he hired halls in Spen Valley, St. Ives and Devonport, the respective constituencies of the three miscreants, and delivered to their electors elaborate, fully-authenticated indictments of their political records, worthy of any trial in Westminster Hall. Never to be forgotten was the climax in Devonport Guildhall, the immaculate timing, the deadly curse drawn from one of my father's unexpected favourites, Lord Alfred Douglas:

> *Cast out, my soul, the broken covenant,*
> *Forget the pitiable masquerade*

And then the final lines:

> *Let him on graves of buried loyalty,*
> *Rise as he may to his desired goal;*
> *Ay and God speed him there, I grudge him not.*
> *And when all men shall sing his praise to me*
> *I'll not gainsay. But I shall know his soul*
> *Lies in the bosom of Iscariot.*

It is satisfactory to recall that, after an interval, the political reputations of all these three victims *did* wither. Several years later, when I had been adopted to fight Hore-Belisha at Devonport as a Labour candidate, I reported to my father that I had met my prospective opponent at some function in London and that he didn't seem so objectionable after all. 'Oh', said my father, with a lighthearted snort; 'you didn't commit yourself to a clean fight, I hope.'

But what of my father's own career? Had that not withered too, even his glorious eloquence being washed away down the gutters of Liberal sectarianism? It may seem so from my account, but the impression is false. Of course his luckless defeat in 1935, like the earlier ones of 1924 and 1910, cheated him of the parliamentary eminence for which he was qualified; no instrument can be more merciless than the electoral guillotine. But, in personal terms, he could usually turn setbacks into conquests. An inscription in a book he gave me (a Swift first edition) indicates his mettle:

> This book (from my library at Pencrebar) is given, with my love, and some reluctance, to my son Michael, as a token of consolation on his defeat at Devonport at the General Election, May 26, 1955. I recall defeats a Totnes, Plymouth, Bodmin, St. Ives and Tavistock in the years 1910, 1918, 1924, 1935, 1937 and 1945. On the whole, these defeats were more honourable than my five victories.

At the toughest, most awkward moments my father was a Titan. He would quote Captain McWhirr from Conrad's *Typhoon*: 'Always facing it, that's the way to get through.' And that was certainly the spirit needed, following 1935, in the most shameful, perilous and epic years in our country's history. Out of office, out of Parliament, with no influence to exert except by personal inspiration and with that so-often-unheeded voice, my father's genius came to its full blossom, or so it seemed to me, since these were the years I knew him best. He grew to be what one of his chief heroes, William Tyndale, was called, an Apostle of England, seeking to rouse his countrymen to face and destroy the Nazi horror. When appeasement was still a respectable word in 1937, he fought a by-election at St. Ives against all it stood for in our age. He hung his head in shame at the news of Munich, and promptly invited a fresh flood of execrations upon it from West Country Tories with a column-long letter to the *Western Morning News* exposing the infamy done in our name. He went back to the villages, where he had once fought the brewers, to fight the Hoares and the Halifaxes, Hitler and Mussolini. His own Plymouth, he said, could suffer the fate of Guernica. Devon and Cornwall—he would never choose between his two loves—were threatened with the same desecration.

His sermon now was England Arise; and England did. As a child, my father had stood on Plymouth Hoe when the statue of Sir Francis Drake was erected, and, like Drake, had looked out across Plymouth Sound a thousand times. Now, when the little ships went to Dunkirk or when the Luftwaffe raided Plymouth, he claimed to hear Drake's Drum and, less credibly, that all other West Countrymen heard it too. Hitler, threatening invasion, standing for nothing but 'brute violence and proud tyrannic power', would have to meet much beyond his understanding; 'the land of William Tyndale and John Hampden and Oliver Cromwell and John Milton—the Britain of Marlborough (another famous Devonshireman) and John Wesley, of Chatham, and Burke and Thomas Paine and Charles James Fox.' That was my father in 1940. In 1945, when he became Lord Mayor of his shattered, bleeding City, he went to every school in the place and told the children how Francis Drake and the people of Plymouth had helped save England and freedom again, as in 1588.

His reading and his mind became even more catholic in the war years and after, as if he wished to embrace the whole of Western civilisation menaced by barbarism. He reached backwards to the Italian Renaissance and the early printers, and outward to our allies across the Atlantic; Abraham Lincoln had always been honoured as the American Cromwell but now the Library of Congress, in our attics, had to be enlarged to equal the Bodleian, down the corridor. Stricken France must be avenged, and Montaigne stepped up onto his proper pedestal. But why list the names thus? Any suggestion that my father's associaton with books was governed by a developing strategy would be a wicked deceit. Apart from my mother and his music, they were the light of his life. They were his meat and drink. They were his bulwark against the world. They became—it is almost impossible to deny—an overpowering disease.

He bought them, read them, marked them, reread them, stored them, reallocated them on the shelves, which spread like erysipelas up every available wall, knew where each precious volume of the countless thousands nestled without the aid of a catalogue. His appetite was gargantuan and insatiable. He was a bibliophilial drunkard—with the difference that the taste never palled and he never had a hangover. The only stab of remorse he ever experienced was the rare recollection of how, at one of Hodgson's sales or in one of the second-hand shops where he spent another of his lifetimes, a temptation had been cravenly resisted. He would tell me over lunch how he had been at the bookshop prompt at nine o'clock that morning to repair some cowardly error of the day before. The treasure was still there on the shelf. Who could want further proof of the intervention of Providence?

Since his house in Cornwall had still to be run as a place of human habitation my mother often found the pressure intolerable. So my father became furtive. He would get up early to waylay the postman or set off for London on a Monday morning with several empty suitcases. When he went on a lecture tour to America he returned with eleven cratefuls. When each member of the family was old enough to leave home, the parting could be borne. Valuable wall space was released. Wordsworth or Napoleon or Montaigne or Dr. Johnson could at last have a room of his own, like John Milton.

More remarkable still was the high proportion of these vast granaries of literary wealth which he had actually consumed in person without bursting. He read everything he could lay his hands on about his favourites; had, like Montaigne, 'a singular curiosity to know the soul and natural judgements of my authors'; compiled several hundreds of his own commonplace books; taught himself Greek and French; and could recite whole plays of Shakespeare and whole books of *Paradise Lost;* could indeed give his own dramatic performance on the family hearth, of Macbeth with the dagger before his eyes, or Jean Valjean escaping through the sewers of Paris, or the murder scene in A. E. W. Mason's *House of the Arrow*, or Fouché and Talleyrand arriving at the court of Louis XVIII, vice leaning on hypocrisy.

His tastes were unrestricted and unpredictable. He knew everything about John Bunyan and Johann Sebastian Bach, about Victor Hugo and Andrew Marvell, about Thomas Hardy and Thomas Carlyle, about the Massacre of St. Bartholomew and the Black Hole of Calcutta, about Blenheim and Gettysburg. He had one room full of Bibles and the next of the French Revolution, one of detective stories and another of modern poetry. He would ask fastidious guests: 'Where would you like to sleep tonight— with Lucrezia Borgia, Dorothy Wordsworth or Josephine Beauharnais?' The specially favoured might find him talking of Joseph Conrad; as my father pronounced it, was there ever such mystery and excitement compressed into a single name as *Nostromo*?

He had a whole shelf full of unwritten books which he had promised himself one day to start and complete. They would, I am sure, have been masterpieces of their own kind, like Isaac Disraeli's compilations, and a few of them did actually reach the stage of publication in the form of brilliant lectures or brief monographs. But, as one of the world's great *readers*, my father could not pause too long for the delays of *writing*; how many irrecoverable hours could be dissipated in this laborious diversion? 'In my father's house there are many mansions'; I remember as a child hearing that from the pulpit, and my father would preach sermons on the text. I never quite knew what it meant; I doubt if I do now, but I would picture in my mind whole lofts and barns and outhouses crowded with histories and autobiographies and collected works, and to each of them he applied and re-applied his Montaigne-like method.

The last time I saw him he was returning with the old zest to Oscar Wilde and Lord Alfred Douglas, the unsuspecting flail of the Simonites, a much better sonnet-writer, said my father, than the world allowed. Sonnets, indeed; they must not be overlooked. He had made his own vast private collection, all written out in his flowing, flamboyant hand. When he died, one could turn over pages of books, heavily marked, which no one would have suspected him of ever reading. How, in heaven's name, did he contrive to lead so many lives? In his seventies, he could still drive from Cornwall to London, to follow with the score that night a rare recital of the St. John Passion at the Festival Hall. He could assure Ralph Richardson from personal recollection that, of all the Macbeths of the century, he had given the best revelation of Macbeth the poet. And somehow too he spent another lifetime securing his proper peace beside his River Lynher in Cornwall; he read of all the rivers in literature, made another private anthology on the subject, knew most of those in the West Country, but loved the Lynher best.

Edmund Burke, I suppose, remained the most revered of all the gods in his teeming Valhalla, and I shall not forget him in one of his procrastinating moods when his library had once again seduced him from his Liberal duties and my mother shook her beautiful head over the dereliction. There he stood before his fireplace, extolling his men-of-action heroes, Cromwell and Lincoln, or declaiming from Burke without a hint of incongruity: 'Public life is a situation of power and energy; he trespasses against his duty who sleeps upon his watch, as well as he that goes over to the enemy.' My father could indeed be wayward in the choice of books as well as other pursuits. Across the river from us in Cornwall, in a nearby mansion, Sir Robert Abdy came as a neighbour, bringing with him a beautiful library and an even more beautiful wife. My father became a frequent visitor. Once, said the observant Lady Astor, 'it was all John Milton and Lady Astor; now its Guy de Maupassant and Lady Abdy.'

Edmund Burke also figured in one splendid scene when my father did step back into the arena of politics, and when his prodigious memory faltered. In 1925, as a leader of the Asquithian Liberals, he went on a mission to Churt to discuss with Lloyd George how to make an end of the ferocious personal quarrels which had torn the Liberal Party to fragments. After a weekend of negotiation, the compact was signed and on the Monday morning Lloyd George bade farewell to his guests with the cheerful appeal: 'Let our slogan be *Measures not Men.*' 'Edmund Burke', replied my father, 'had something to say about that. I think you'll find it on page 500 or thereabouts of that beautiful Beaconsfield edition of Burke I saw on your shelves.' On his return home he looked up his own edition, slightly anxiously, and read about 'the cant of *Not Men, but Measures*: a sort of charm by which many people get loose from every honourable engagement'. In fact, my father lived to fight several battles with Lloyd George as his leader, but he was never sure whether Lloyd George had checked the quotation.

How many battles of long ago had my father refought, and how many of the present day had he watched from his library windows? He preached of Marston Moor, and retreated with Montaigne to his tower. What excuse could a stern Puritan offer for these frivolities? Men of power have no time to read; yet the men who do not read are unfit for power. He was past answering such questions but turned aside to see if Milton or Burke or Wordsworth would answer for him. Wordsworth came nearest, I think. 'We live by admiration, hope and love,' he wrote, and that was my father's creed.

'Hope', he would whisper, and the little Cornish chapel would be utterly still. 'The gospel of hope'; he had the congregation in the hollow of his hand. Within a few sentences the language could become stirring and resonant.

> *Hope, the paramount duty*
> *that Heaven lays,*
> *For its own honour, on man's*
> *suffering heart.*

Outside, the world seemed sharply brighter than when we went in, and we would return to our Sunday dinner, the best of the week, bubbling with an unaccountable optimism, touched no doubt by the beauty of the words, the Bible's, Wordsworth's or his own, all uttered in a voice as rich and memorable as Devonshire cream.

TWO

The Shakespeare Prose Writer

Happy are they who live in the dream of their own existence, and see all things in the light of their own minds; who walk by faith and hope; to whom the guiding star of their youth still shines from afar, and into whom the spirit of the world has not entered! They have not been 'hurt by the archers', nor has the iron entered their souls. The world has no hand on them.

From Hazlitt's essay
Mind and motive, and
occasionally repeated by
him elsewhere.

WILLIAM HAZLITT, in all his glory, at the peak of his powers, still faced a furiously hostile world. Since he would not budge an inch in his opinions, he might have become irredeemably embittered or broken altogether. Instead, he transmuted the way in which he defended his principles into a new serenity.

Born on 10 April, 1778, it was not until he was twenty years old, in the year 1798 ('the figures that compose that date are to me like "the dreaded name of Demogorgon"') that his individual spirit was truly awakened, and not until twenty-five years later again that he described that experience in *My First Acquaintance with Poets*, the greatest essay in the English language.

A year or so later he produced his best book of collected essays, *The Spirit of the Age*. Therein he pinioned, mocked, revalued or extolled some two dozen of his most famous contemporaries with an insight and wit which none of his would-be imitators have ever been able to capture. One after another he chipped away at the pedestals of popular heroes, or bestowed upon them a fresh glow of understanding, often anticipating with precision the verdicts of posterity. He was no respecter of conventional judgements from left, right or centre—crusted Tories might find themselves 'nearly' forgiven; so-called reformers were rebuked when they befuddled themselves with too much of the milk of human kindness; and those who usually came off worst of all were the whiffling moderates in the middle, 'ever strong upon the stronger side', like *The Times* newspaper (yes, even in those days). He hated the inhumanities which his fellow-citizens inflicted upon one another in the world around him; yet he loved the other worlds in which he and they lived, the world of nature, of books, of the theatre, of painting, of music; indeed the whole wide world of the imagination in which he had seen 'the prospect of human happiness and glory ascending like the steps of Jacob's ladder in a bright and never-ending succession'. All these assorted moods and aspirations and freshly-shaped nuances of judgement he poured into *The Spirit of the Age* with a newly-confident profusion.

And yet this masterpiece of a lifetime was abruptly dismissed as too pert and extravagant by the best-known, most genial, Whiggish editor of the day, Francis Jeffrey, and it is impossible to believe that Hazlitt's scorn of the Whigs was not the true cause of a disapprobation so misplaced. (Editors have never been quite the same breed since, for Hazlitt retaliated with an essay which should keep them in their place for eternity—'They are dreadfully afraid there should be anything behind the Editor's chair greater than the Editor's chair. That is a scandal to be prevented at all risk'.) Yet even before Jeffrey had rushed to the defence of his Whig dinner-friends, a printer with a fair enough record for courage thought it judicious at first to publish the volume anonymously, and the suspicion persists that either he or the author or the two together did not wish to risk immediate association on publication day with another volume which had appeared two years before, also published anonymously, but at once unmasked as something too indescribably foul to be mentioned in decent society: Hazlitt's *Liber Amoris*, the product, it was supposed, then and now, of a mind diseased, not to mention a lascivious body and soul.

But let us, for a half-moment at least, leave Hazlitt, the self-confessed fool of love, to return to his unforgettable first acquaintance with poets. Smitten though he still was by the attentions or non-attentions of Sarah Walker, and enfolded in that essay as his customary laments for her cold embraces undoubtedly were ('my heart has never found, nor will it ever find, a heart to speak to'), yet he can recall, with an exhilaration which still tingles in every sentence, all his richest memories, his youth, his father, the first books he read, the first meeting with Coleridge, the visit to Llangollen, 'the cradle of a new existence', the journey to Nether Stowey, the first hearing of the *Lyrical Ballads* from the lips of Wordsworth himself (all in that self-same sacred year of 1798), 'and the sense of a new spirit in poetry came over me'.

No man ever treasured his youth more joyously than Hazlitt did; no man ever honoured his father better; no man ever discharged with such good faith the debts of honour he owed to the favourite authors of his youth—Burke, Rousseau, Cervantes, Montaigne and a legion more. No critic (except perhaps a few fellow poets, and not many of them) ever heard the strange language of a new school of poetry with such an alert sympathy, and certainly no critic ever welcomed the innovation with greater daring and, despite all subsequent political feuds, with more persistence and warmth.

All these claims can be sustained from the evidence offered in this single essay, written when the love-diseased Hazlitt was, on his own testimony, still in a most desperate condition—'I have wanted only one thing to make me happy, but wanting that, have wanted everything!'. There he is again, in the very same essay, bewailing Sarah in one sentence and still in the next quite capable of inflicting one of his most well-considered swipes at Coleridge, and one to be upheld by the scrutiny of modern scholars. It was Hazlitt who first put his finger, without the substantial proof provided since, on Coleridge's addictive plagiarism.

Yet the attempt to rest so heavy a weight on a single essay leaves one wrong impression. It might be truer to say the opposite, as Hazlitt himself said of Burke: that the only specimen of his writing is *all that he wrote.* In literature, Hazlitt relished the old and welcomed the new. He saw how (and was one of the very first to remark how) Shakespeare achieved 'the combination of the greatest extremes'. He himself liked to see all sides of a subject, never for the purpose of searching out some muddled middle ground but rather to force an explosive fusion or an entirely new departure. One of his friends bound Burke's *Reflections on the French Revolution* and Thomas Paine's *Rights of Man* between the same covers and said that together they made a good book. A similar treatment could be applied to Hazlitt's writings. Many of his essays seem to be written in pairs, each presenting opposite aspects of the case, one, maybe, suffused with the romantic spirit unloosed by Rousseau and the other relentlessly reasserting Hazlitt's conviction that men must not only talk and dream, but act. Always he would still strive to extract the effective conclusion from the clash of contrasts. No such dreamer was ever less of a dilettante. No critic was ever more of a self-critic.

Any such claim would have provoked squeals of protest from those apostate politicians or apostate poets whom Hazlitt berated so fiercely in his lifetime. But most of them never had the chance of reading his *Conversations of Northcote* which was published in full only after his death. Many good reasons for reading the *Conversations* may be offered—their sheer readability, the individual charm of the old Plymouth painter, the wonderful assortment of irrelevancies and curiosities which both Northcote and Hazlitt contributed to the pile. But it is hard to escape the belief that Hazlitt had a deeper, if unconscious, purpose. He somehow put into Northcote's mouth most of the current criticisms or condemnations of himself, and then struggled, not always successfully, to find the right retort.

This, unconsciously also perhaps, was what Hazlitt set out to achieve on a much more spacious canvas. Ever since he had carried home in triumph from Shrewsbury to Wem his first book by Edmund Burke, he had been dazzled by that style which he revered more than any other—'His words are the most like things; his style is the most strictly suited to the subject.' Hazlitt's own style owed more to Burke's than to anybody's, but he was never primarily a student of style despite his many apposite remarks upon it. The thing mattered more than the word. Literature was not something removed from life; the two were endlessly intertwined. Books were weapons in the cause of human freedom.

How, then, could Hazlitt, the great rebel, respect Burke, the great apostate? Burke had 'stood at the prow of the vessel of state, and with his glittering, pointed spear *harpooned* the Leviathan of the French Revolution'. How could Hazlitt, the arch-champion of the French Revolution, pay such honour to him? It was not merely the magnanimous gesture of one writer to another across the gulf of politics. The kinship between the two men went much deeper. Hazlitt saw the truth and force of so much that Burke was saying; no man could write like that and tell lies. Burke's understanding of mankind, he said, was 'inexhaustible as the human heart, and various as the sources of nature'. Yet this mighty intellect had somehow been used to persuade the people of England that 'Liberty was an illiberal, hollow sound; that humanity was a barbarous modern invention; that prejudices were the test of truth, that reason was a strumpet and right a fiction'. To explain the phenomenon, the mechanism of politics must be taken to pieces. And somehow Burke must be answered. 'He presents to you', Hazlitt wrote, 'one view of the face of society. Let him who thinks he can, give the reverse side with equal force, beauty and clearness . . .' Hazlitt's life work was his great reply. He gave to the English Left a perspective and philosophy as widely ranging as Burke had given to the English Right.

Hazlitt was not content with the multitude of swift retorts provoked by Burke's *Reflections on the French Revolution*. He was one of the first to recognise that the formidable pamphleteer Thomas Paine, author of *Rights of Man*, the most famous and enduring of all the replies, was a great writer. But neither Paine nor William Godwin, nor the poets with their dreams of Utopia, less still the men of the calibre of Sir James Mackintosh, could prevail against Burke, and not all their defeats were due to the power wielded by authority. The first rebuffs made many of them abandon their creed and go over to the enemy. A tougher fibre was needed, a creed of human freedom more firmly founded on the rock. No one was ever more excited by the soaring hopes unloosed by the French Revolution than Hazlitt; he soaked himself in the romantic prophets; Rousseau's *Confessions* and *La Nouvelle Heloise* made him shed tears. He accepted to the full the reformers' doctrine that 'men do not become what by nature they are meant to be, but what society makes them'. And society could be transformed; the French Revolution looked like romance in action. But the deed would not be done by utopians who would never soil their hands, nor by an arid appeal to reason alone, nor by the economists and utilitarians who inherited the tattered mantle of the revolutionaries.

Thus, Hazlitt was a romantic in revolt against extreme romanticism; he loved the ardour of it and hated the egotism. He was an idealist who knew that present enemies must be fought here and now, tooth and nail, on their own ground; a passionate believer in man's benevolence and his perfectibility, but one who recognised as well as Burke that passion and prejudice could not easily be uprooted from the human heart. Since the passions could be good and the right traditions should be revered, why should they be? They too could be enlisted in the Good Cause. The core of his theory had been worked out in the first *Essay on the Principles of Human Action*. It was vastly illustrated in all his later writings. He tried to separate the wheat from the chaff in the bountiful harvest of new ideas which were sprouting up all around him. He searched for a synthesis between Rousseau and Burke. And they dared call him a bigot!

His politics left their brand on every aspect of his writing, just as they governed or disrupted his personal relationships. Someone said that he took his politics around with him, like a giant mastiff, and love me, love my dog was his motto. (Only Sarah was allowed a special dispensation; it is not recorded that he lectured *her* on the evils of legitimacy, although he did present her with a treasured statuette of Napoleon). But the tide of his political ideas flooded into every cove and inlet of his thought. 1798 was not only the year of the *Lyrical Ballads;* it was also the year of the Reverend Doctor Malthus's *Essay on the Principle of Population as it affects the Future Improvement of Society*. How soon Hazlitt became acquainted and obsessed with this curious literary phenomenon is not clear, but he was certainly the first reader to appreciate to the full the menacing nature of the apparition. Here, it is true, society was offered a philosophy for the rich, an economic textbook for Tories, a faith as firm as a mathematical equation which could salve their conscience and cast the cloak of religion over the whole scene of human wretchedness in the England of his time. 'Malthus,' wrote Hazlitt, 'had given to the principle of population a personal existence, conceiving of it as a sort of infant Hercules, as one of that terrific giant brood, which you can only master by strangling it in its cradle.' And that in turn was how Hazlitt set about Malthus. Without the advantage or encumbrance of expert economic knowledge, with irony and logic and passionate indignation, he exposed the moral consequences of Malthus's infamous clerical decrees.

He thereby anticipated not merely the reply of the economists decades later but the whole temper of nineteenth-century radicalism. He brushed aside the patronising charity of those who would 'take nothing from the rich and give it to the poor', and defended the right to strike with the fervour of a Chartist or a twentieth-century syndicalist. His essays on prison reform and on Benthamism raced beyond the plodding precepts of the utilitarians and came nearer to the ideas of modern psychology. 'Men act from passions, and we can only judge of passions by sympathy.' Criminals, like the world itself, could not be changed by preaching. Somehow the institutions of society must be changed, and men must show the will to do it. There Hazlitt did not differ much from his fellow-reformers, but he added his own ingredient to the reforming creed of his time. The reformers themselves needed to understand the human heart if they were to get men to move, and if they were not themselves, in the face of setbacks, to abandon or betray their cause. So many of the reformers of his time—Robert Owen, for example—who talked so much about the rights of men knew so little about the passions of men. A whole curriculum of schooling for reformers could be compiled from the writings of Hazlitt whom the nervous nineteenth century would have preferred to dismiss as a wayward romantic essayist. In his mind the interaction between words and deeds could never be severed. And the next immediate deed in the struggle, *the one that mattered*, was never long absent from his reckoning. Perhaps the most remarkable of all Hazlitt's feats in imaginative sympathy was the way he, the supreme no-com-promiser, nonetheless understood the exigencies of practical politicians.

He wrote about political ideas and political history, about the immediate controversies of the age, about the motives of politicians, about political parties and the conduct within parties, about the resolute capacity of those who hold power and the chronic failings of the reformers and revolutionaries who would seek to wrest it from them. His themes were as perennial as Burke's. Of course his own heroes both in history and in his own time were the iconoclasts, the intransigents, the rebels who would not bend with the storm or droop in the sunshine; their example suited his own situation and soothed his pride. But his under-standing of the art of politics was not limited by the experience of his own defeats. 'Ambition is in some sort genius', he said. Here is his picture of what a statesman could be. It is rarely quoted: but has it ever been bettered?

> To use means to ends, to set causes in motion, to wield the machine of society, to subject the wills of others to your own, to manage abler men than yourself by means of that which is stronger in them than their wisdom, viz, their weakness and their folly, to calculate the resistance of ignorance and prejudice to your designs, and by obviating to turn them to account, to foresee a long, obscure and complicated train of events, of chances and openings of success, to unwind the web of others' policy, and weave your own out of it, to judge the effects of things not in the abstract but with reference to all their bearings, ramifications and impediments, to understand character thoroughly, to see latent talent and lurking treachery, to know mankind for what they are, and use them as they deserve, to have a purpose steadily in view and to effect it after removing every obstacle, to master others and to be true to yourself, asks power and knowledge, both nerves and brain.

A naïve extremist, unaware of the realities of politics, could not have written that sentence.

It was not only that he could appreciate the politicians of the past—say, Cromwell, with 'his fine, frank, rough, pimply face and wily policy' (Hazlitt was accused of having a pimply face, which doubtless encouraged the show of sympathy); he looked down from the gallery of the House of Commons on the performers below, and had his own list of preferences which can scarcely have accorded with anyone else's, especially those on the left. He preferred Castlereagh to Canning ('One of those spontaneous mechanical sallies of his resembles a *voluntary* played on a barrel organ'), Burdett to Brougham ('He is not a backbone debater. He wants nerve, he wants impetuosity'), the real would-be doers to the self-conscious rhetoricians with all their finical flexibility of purpose and character.

Hazlitt exerted a comparable independence of judgement in every other field too. Naturally he liked to discern the virtues of those whose political views he shared. Not only was he the first to recognise Thomas Paine's literary qualities; he saw also, and won more jeers from fashionable critics, for recognising that William Cobbett's 'plain, broad, down-right English' made him 'one of the best writers in the language'. Of course he paid special honour to the great radical writers of the past, John Milton, Andrew Marvell and many more. But he also wrote more enthusiastically than any previous English critic on a host of others who at first sight might be imagined to have no political hold on him at all—Swift, Pope, Montaigne, Fielding, Cervantes: above all, Shakespeare. Others, like Coleridge, alongside Hazlitt (not anyone hardly *before* him), were encompassing Shakespeare in a new glory. But it was Hazlitt's criticisms which had immediate and lasting impact on two of his greatest contemporaries in Europe, Heinrich Heine and Henri Beyle, alias Stendhal, both of whom came to London and carried the new Shakespearian fashions back across the Channel.

Both Heine and Stendhal acknowledged the debt they owed to Hazlitt, which is more than can be said for Wordsworth or Coleridge. Despite his deepening political quarrels with them, Hazlitt never ceased to honour Wordsworth as the great originating poet of the age, and Coleridge still held the central place in his essay as the man who had opened his understanding, 'till the light of his genius shone into my soul, like the sun's rays glittering in the puddles of the road'.

But intertwined with the tributes—inextricably, as Hazlitt doubtless intended to make sure—were the searing, indelible invectives against those who had deserted the cause of their youth. Wordsworth and Coleridge may be forgiven if they failed to turn their Christian cheeks; what they should never be forgiven—for neither were exactly paragons of sexual virtue— were the Lakeside libels against Hazlitt's alleged sexual antics which they unloosed, not in any sudden fit of outrage at the time, but long after the unspecified exploits had supposedly occurred. However, the point concerns not the Wordsworth-cum-Coleridge intolerance, but Hazlitt's magnanimity. Long after he had plentiful evidence of the venomous gossip with which they had pursued him, even to the point of threatening his most treasured friendships with the Lambs and Leigh Hunt, he still would not be shifted from his recognition of their greatness. Literary cliques are not noted for their generosity. Hazlitt refused to be suffocated even when he had been driven, by the pressures of politics, into a clique of one.

However, for all his readiness to stand alone, for all his gift for solitude, his individuality won him some unexpected or idiosyncratic friends—John Cavanagh, the fives player, or William Bewick, the engraver, or James Northcote, the portrait painter, or William Hone, the allegedly blasphemous bookseller, or the young ex-medical student who came to his lectures, accompanied him on the journeys to Leigh Hunt in the Vale of Health on Hampstead Heath, and who had shown 'the greatest promise of genius of any poet of his day'. Hazlitt, alas, never wrote a full-scale essay on John Keats, but almost every fresh study reinforces Keats's own testimony of how intricate and all-pervasive was the Hazlitt influence upon him. 'The whole cadence of his (Keats's) prose', writes Robert Gittings, 'is that of Hazlitt whose reviews he seems to have had nearly by heart.' It was Hazlitt lecturing at the Institution across Blackfriars Bridge, or Hazlitt talking on the walk to Hampstead, or Hazlitt writing in Leigh Hunt's *Examiner*, who was responsible for most of the introductions which made Keats a poet—to Shakespeare, to Wordsworth and several more. In particular, it was Hazlitt who introduced Keats to his favourite Wordsworthian poem, *The Excursion*, at a time when Wordsworth was still rejected and neglected in fashionable quarters. Here was just another example of Hazlitt's 'disinterestedness' which Keats so much admired and emulated. Keats, of course, shared Hazlitt's political aversions, as he discovered to his disquiet when he called at Wordsworth's home in the Lakes only to find that the poet of cloud and cataract was out canvassing for the Cumberland Tories. Anyhow, thanks to modern scholarship and Mr. Gittings more especially, the truth is now established beyond challenge. Henceforth Keats and Hazlitt climb Parnassus roped together, and a terrible curse of combined Hazlittean-Keatsian power must fall upon anyone who would tear them apart.

What other critic in English literary history, or any other literary history for that matter, ever had such a pupil? And yet poetry was not Hazlitt's first love, and never even at any time his all-consuming passion. He had set out in early youth to become a painter, and he made good use of all he learnt, becoming (in the words of Lord Clark) 'the best English critic before Ruskin'. He was there at the Drury Lane theatre on the night of Edmund Kean's first appearance as Shylock, and the meeting was one of the most memorable in the history of the English theatre. He was, as Professor R. L. Brett has written, 'the first critic to take the novel seriously'. Yet none of these pursuits were the ones which touched him most closely. His pride was that he was a philosopher. In that first essay describing his meeting with the poets he tells of the tears he wept in the long, and at first vain, exertion to get words on to paper. It was nearly six years after the sacred year of 1798 before he finally succeeded in completing his little-read and not-easily-readable *Essay on the Principles of Human Action*. Like other painfully delivered first children, it remained his favourite, especially as no one else showed any liking for the brat.

He finished that first book at the age of twenty-six; he died at the age of fifty-two. What he truly wrote in that bare quarter-of-a-century interval was a vast, rambling, astringent, Montaigne-like autobiography, which abjured all the self-worshipping postures both he and Keats so much detested, but which yet succeeds in telling as much as any man ever told about his convictions, his

tastes, his emotions, his enthusiasms, and how he strove perpetually to subject them to the most severe tests at his command.
It is surely this open invitation to explore the well-nigh
inexhaustible resources, 'the whole compass and circuit of his
mind', which makes the titles 'essayist' or 'critic' such feeble
terms to describe what he sought to accomplish.

Some fine biographers have already made the exploration too,
notably P. P. Howe, the devoted and inspired editor of his
Collected Works, or Herschel Baker, author of the only volume
which deserves to be set alongside Howe's, and, on a lower shelf,
Hesketh Pearson's *The Fool of Love*, and Augustine Birrell's not-
to-be-despised pre-1914 volume. For a real addition to the
existing store of knowledge we shall have to await the forthcoming new biography by the wisest as well as the most thorough
of Hazlitt scholars, Professor Stanley Jones, whose contributions
to the learned journals have already disposed of several anti-
Hazlitt canards.

Meantime, let us return afresh to Hazlitt's evidence against
himself. Very few themes which figured prominently in his life are
left in an unfinished state in his writings. One concerns his
religion, and it is indeed surprising that one born and bred as a
Celtic dissenter, one who shared so eagerly the Puritan vision of
his country's history, one who knew every step in John Bunyan's
pilgrimage, one who would have fought and died for the true
religion's cause at Burford, one who indeed wrote about every
other subject under the sun, hardly ever made any direct reference
to any religious topic, less still any religious conviction. He
mocked the Papists, ('Nothing to be said against their religion
but that it is contrary to reason and common sense'), side-kicked
the Presbyterians ('Weighing their doubts and scruples to the
division of a hair, and shivering on the narrow brink that divides
philosophy from religion'), damned the Methodists ('They
plunge without remorse into hell's flames, soar on the wings of
divine love, are carried away with the motions of the spirit, are
lost in the abyss of unfathomable mysteries—election, repro-
bation, predestination—and revel in a sea of boundless nonsense'),
heaped secular scorn on the Laodicean Anglicans ('Satan lies in
wait for them in a pinch of snuff, in a plate of buttered toast, in

the kidney end of a loin of veal'), and extolled the true Dissenters for keeping their covenant, as the stars keep their courses. But he avoided all deep religious arguments, and one reason may be that he wished to give no open offence to his father. He himself had been intended for the Unitarian Ministry and he knew how his family were disappointed when he was seduced from that vocation by his first dream that one day he would be able to say with Correggio: 'I also am a painter', and, even more, by his later resolve to pursue the wicked trade of Swift, Defoe and such-like infidels. But the tact of father and son, towards each other if towards no one else, was such that no shadow was allowed to fall across their relationship. What would have happened if Sarah Walker had appeared on the scene while his father was still alive, none can tell.

Suddenly, when Sarah did make her first appearance, or rather when 'with a waving air she goes along the corridor', his life was transformed and he became 'the very fool of Love'. It is the only corner of his love life which Hazlitt has revealed, and the evidence has naturally been pursued by scholars with prurient dedication. He himself wrote a classic 'confession'; however, it is his reticence which may first deserve consideration.

Considering how original were Hazlitt's ideas on almost every theme which captivated him, considering how he could race ahead to anticipate the thought, in the field of psychology, say, no less than politics, of the whole ensuing century, it is the more surprising that he never seemed to turn his mind to the great question of the rights of women. He was certainly no feminist, not that the word had yet been invented nor even that the thing itself was common. He was a frequent visitor at the house of William Godwin, and one of his gleaming sentences casts a kindly ray of light across the countenance of Mary Wollstonecraft. Yet the extraordinary fact is that he did not write much more about her; seemingly, he had never read her *Vindication of the Rights of Woman* or it left no mark whatever.

For Hazlitt, as for most of his contemporaries of a similar cast of mind, the great romantic bible was Rousseau's *La Nouvelle Heloise*, which was still also a revolutionary document. Enough for the moment, enough for one century perhaps, to break the love-making conventions of polite, ruling-class society. Hazlitt's ideal of womanhood, I suspect, was Rossini's Rosina whose liberation took the form of enabling her to twist men round her little finger, without them having the foggiest notion what she was up to, and no bad choice either; who in his senses ever could resist her? However, in real life, for Hazlitt, Rosina was transformed into Sarah Walker, and she almost destroyed him with her wiles, her titillations, her prevarications and her treacheries. (Let it not be forgotten, by the way, that no one has ever told Sarah's side of the story: what a find that would be!) Yet despite the absence of the slightest touch of feminism in his make-up, Hazlitt was not a male chauvinist; more like a male pacifist indeed, and his debasement before the idol of his own creation came near to encompassing his ruin then and thereafter.

He could not keep quiet on the subject, stopping to tell everybody about his bewitchment in every tavern from Chancery Lane to Covent Garden. He unloosed a gushing flood upon her fawn-like head and upon his few especial long-suffering friends. Then he turned aside from most other labours to compile and publish anonymously the *New Pygmalion*, the *Liber Amoris*. One of his letters to Sarah—and perhaps even the most presentable—fell into the scurrilous hands of a Tory journal, *John Bull*, and was reproduced, with much sneering and snivelling, to damn him and his politics to eternity. Some of his eminent ex-friends—like Coleridge, for example—to their immortal dishonour, used the occasion to resuscitate an old unproved and unprovable charge that the young Hazlitt had been the villain in some terrible seduction scene (some have even called it 'rape', without a tincture of evidence) twenty years before. He was soon having to publish anonymously also his *Spirit of the Age* essays—some of the greatest in the English language—for fear of inviting too swift an association with 'the impotent sensualist', the lascivious author of *Liber Amoris*.

Fashions, of course, have changed altogether about the *Liber Amoris*. Robert Louis Stevenson was so shocked by it that he gave up the idea of writing Hazlitt's life. Augustine Birrell, whose biography was otherwise intelligently sympathetic, wished to consign the offending volume to 'the realms of things unspeakable, fit only for the midden'. Even the most learned and authoritative of modern biographers, Herschel Baker, turns aside in horror from Hazlitt in love, and even Professor R. L. Brett, a most eminent Coleridgean, invokes the *Liber Amoris* to justify some of the old libels on Hazlitt's youthful sex-life. How Coleridge and Wordsworth would have rubbed their pious hands at the thought. And yet in modern times too Hazlitt has been better enabled to speak for himself. In the excellent Penguin *Selected Writings* (published in 1970 and edited by Ronald Blythe), the *Liber Amoris* is printed in full but also printed where it ought to be, alongside his other writings, and Ronald Blythe also gives proper recognition to two others before him who have helped rescue the book from the midden.

It was indeed only as late as 1948—well over a hundred years after that 'sweet apparition', or, if you wish, that 'slimy, marble varnished fiend' had turned her glance so fatally upon him—that any commentator appreciated to the full the nature of Hazlitt's agony. Charles Morgan wrote in that year an entirely new kind of introduction to the despised volume in which he invoked the case-knowledge of modern psychology, partly to explain Hazlitt but, even more remarkably, to reveal how much of modern discoveries in this field Hazlitt had anticipated. Morgan also made a most discriminating comparison between Hazlitt and Stendhal, Hazlitt's contemporary whom he resembled in so many aspects, although most notably *not* in philandering bravado or technique. Just at the moment when Hazlitt was making obeisance before the statue he had erected, Stendhal was writing his own book of love, *De L'Amour*, in which the Hazlittean trauma, disease, madness, idyll, is immortally diagnosed.

Soon afterwards the two men met in Paris. Stendhal gave his book to Hazlitt who must have read it on his journey onwards towards the two mistresses they shared, Rome and Venice. I have often wondered: how Hazlitt's hair must have stood on end as he turned over those burning pages; how he must have marvelled at this French sympathiser who understood his predicament with Sarah so much better than his own countrymen; (and how he must have concealed the volume from his new sedate wife who was making part of the journey with him). 'She is dead to me, but what she once was to me can never die.' That was Hazlitt's own epitaph on the affair, but perhaps Stendhal and Montaigne even helped finally to soothe his passion. And as Morgan shows, there was one sense in which he carried the investigation further even than these two acknowledged mentors; he 'shows'—in the words of Morgan—'because he is a supreme realist and is unafraid to give himself away, that the crystallising lover is by no means the blind fool that he is traditionally supposed to be. He thus deprives himself of the only romantic defence with which an aloof and self-righteous world might be disposed contemptuously to cover him. The lover, Hazlitt says in effect, is not even a dupe; he is worse, he is a half-dupe, and yet persists'. Hazlitt made himself, again in Morgan's memorable conclusion, 'the sane, unsparing analyst of his own madness'. And yet Stendhal conducted the analysis afresh, and with an even greater clinical precision, and with a sense of humour too (and even with an invocation of the name of Montaigne, sacred to Hazlitt certainly), to recall sexual fiascos as remarkable as his own. Hazlitt surely must have been gratified to be assured, after such painful torture and on such high combined authority, that he was not so abnormal a creature after all.

As for Hazlitt's sanity, so often and interestedly questioned by his political enemies, his friends may take pleasure from the fact that plumb in the middle of the months when he obsessively and vainly waited for a soft word from Sarah, he could still sit down and write a five thousand word letter to his ten-year-old son (suitable for later publication, to be sure), one of the most civilised documents ever written by any father to any son:

> It is a good rule to hope for the best . . . Never anticipate evils . . . Learn never to conceive prejudice against others, because you know nothing of them . . . Never despise anyone for anything he cannot help—least of all for his poverty . . . Never despise anyone at all . . . True equality is the only true morality or true wisdom . . . Believe all the good you can of everyone . . . Envy none, and you need envy no one . . . Never quarrel with tried friends or those whom you wish to continue such . . . Be neither a martyr, nor sycophant . . . Do not gratify the enemies of liberty by putting yourself at their mercy . . .

So the sentences and the elaborations tumble onto the page one after another; no one could doubt the coolness and the reflective wisdom which he had achieved by sheer intellectual exertion, and yet in the midst of it he is well nigh overthrown by the tempestuous nature of his passion. And, a month or two later again, he had governed his temper afresh, and the so-called besotted bigot had returned to his favourite addiction of seeking to explain the other side of the question.

Certainly no condemnation was intended when Hazlitt, the romantic realist, insisted:

> Women have often more of what is called good sense than men. They have fewer pretensions; are less implicated in theories; and judge of objects more from their immediate and involuntary impression on the mind, and therefore more truly and naturally. They cannot reason wrong; for they do not reason at all. They do not think or speak by rule; and they have in general more eloquence and wit, as well as sense, on that account. By their wit, sense and eloquence together, they generally contrive to govern their husbands.

The compliment was barbed, but it was a compliment no less.

With or without the help of psycho-analytical treatment from 'my friend Mr. Beyle', Hazlitt did recover. The period of six or seven years, between his escape from Sarah's listless clutches and his death in 1830, is not by any reckoning a famous one in English history, and for Hazlitt especially it must have seemed craven and squalid. All his soaring political hopes had been shattered; Jacob's ladder had collapsed. No proper acclaim for his literary powers came from most of his fellow-countrymen; he was still an outcast. He embarked on what even his few remaining devoted friends considered to be a chronic wastage of his talents, a monumental Life of Napoleon, which threatened to bury him altogether. Money troubles hit him harder even than ever before; for the first time in his life he spent some months in prison for debt. Yet neither his courage nor his genius were impaired. On the contrary: made ridiculous in love, staring political defeat in the face, libelled by his enemies, harried by creditors, the Hazlitt who was often upbraided for ill-temper wrote with an ever-increasing equilibrium, almost optimism. He reasserted the convictions of his youth with something of the old exhilaration, and not only in the field of politics, and he did it with mellowness but without a hint of retreat, without a jot of weakness or cynicism.

> Really it is wonderful how little the worse I am for fifteen years wear and tear, how I came upon my legs again on the ground of truth and nature, and 'look abroad into universality', forgetting there is any such person as myself in the world.

How little diseased was that mind. T. S. Eliot wrote of Matthew Arnold that 'he had no real serenity, only an impeccable demeanour'. Hazlitt's demeanour could outrage everybody, even the long-suffering Charles Lamb. But, contrary to the impression left by his unfailing pugnacity, he had achieved a real serenity—as the later essays, one after another, prove. It was not that he had become complacent or withdrawn from the battle. He was still in the thick of it, giving blow for blow, whenever the opportunity occurred. But the poets, who in the words of his friend Keats 'pour out a balm upon the world', gave a specially healing dose to Hazlitt. He had fought a good fight; he had kept the faith. 'One source of this unbendingness (which some may call obstinacy)', he wrote in *A Farewell to Essay Writing*,

> is that, though living much alone, I have never worshipped the Echo, I see plainly enough that black is not white, that the grass is green, that kings are not their subjects; and in such self-evident cases do not think it necessary to collate my opinions with the received prejudices.

None could stop him thinking for himself; he was secure in that citadel and could survey the battlefield from its turrets. And he knew too (and who will dare deny the claim?) that 'in seeking for truth I sometimes found beauty'. Above all, he stayed young, 'kept the candid brow and elastic spring of youth'. The iron had not entered his soul although too many folk then and since thought it was uniquely constructed of nothing else.

He is, wrote William Bewick, 'the Shakespeare prose writer of our glorious century; he outdoes all in truth, style and originality'. That was the view expressed by the excited young art student who attended one of Hazlitt's lectures in the company of the equally excited John Keats. Very few agreed with them at the time, and when he died, the political furies which had beaten upon him while he lived did not quickly abate. However, through the influence of his own writings, his literary reputation has steadily increased until now, two hundred odd years after his birth, it stands higher than it ever did. William Bewick's tribute no longer looks like a youthful exaggeration.

THREE

The Good Tory

'The greatest triumph the Conservative Cause has ever had.
And yet,' Lord Buckhurst added, laughing, 'if any fellow
were to ask me what the Conservative Cause is, I am sure I
should not know what to say.'

CONINGSBY

ASK an ambitious young Tory Member of Parliament, at any
time during the past half century, which was his favourite, his
ideal, among all Tory Prime Ministers and the answer would
normally come without hesitation: Disraeli. I once put the
question to eligible candidates in the middle of the Macleod-
Maudling era, and seven out of ten said Disraeli. One said Sir
Robert Peel, but he was soon exiled to the Outer Mongolian
darkness of a provincial university. Sir Robert split his Party, the
most deadly of all political sins: no full Conservative majority in
the House of Commons was secured for twenty-eight years
thereafter. But Benjamin Disraeli was not only granted forgiveness for his part in that affair; he was apotheosised. At the
Oxford of the twenties and thirties, I recall, in the age of Baldwin
and Chamberlain, his was the name which could restore respect
and glamour to their bedraggled creed; every rising hope of the
pliant, appeasing Tories could recite his perorations. Whatever
the true nature of the man, his myth has seemed to possess an
undying magnetism.

Yet in recent times that judgement must be heavily qualified.
Few could have predicted the scale of the latest change in fashion,
and Disraeli himself would have felt most out-of-place in a world
where *laissez-faire* ideas were claimed as the essence of Conservative doctrine. He was the first to use the term 'the school of
Manchester'; it was not intended as a compliment. He satirised

those whose first allegiance was to the principles of free competition in *The Screw and Lever Review*, and would have been aghast to learn that the most likely contributors to such a journal today would be Conservative Cabinet ministers. 'To acquire, to accumulate, to plunder each other by virtue of philosophic phrases, to propose a Utopia to consist only of wealth and toil, this has been the breathless business of enfranchised England . . .' he wrote, and he wrote in derision. But today the worshippers assemble afresh round the altar of Mammon, and the philosophic chorus is conducted by Sir Keith Joseph. Such a transformation must have altered Disraeli's standing in the Tory pantheon. (Who would be the hero of the new Josephite generation? Lord Liverpool, one must suppose.)

However, even before these latest aberrations, the signs of change were detectable. The dethronement of Disraeli had started a full decade before Mrs. Margaret Thatcher was elected leader of the Conservative Party, and the hand which started the fatal work of demolition was that, not of some febrile practising politician, but of a great historian. Books may change the political climate more than politics shape books: Disraeli would at least concur with that proposition. Now, a hundred years after his death, it is a book which has knocked him off his pedestal, perhaps irretrievably.

Lord Blake's masterpiece, his eight hundred-page twentieth-century reassessment of both the man and the myth, was published in 1966, and must have required years of previous preparation and scholarship. It is a legitimate guess that he did not embark upon so prodigious an enterprise with iconoclastic intentions. Much more probably, when he set out on his journey, he too was entranced by the familiar Tory portrait of his hero, and, as publication day loomed, in the dark years of the sixties, when his beloved Party seemed condemned once more to the wilderness of opposition, how enticing it must have been to extol the leader who best taught his followers how to suffer defeat and still to triumph! Who better to reinvigorate modern Toryism than the man who, just a century before—in 1867—had laid the legislative foundation for Tory democracy in his Reform Bills, and who had synthesised word and deed into something worthy to be called a Tory philosophy? The temptation to present the prophet in this garb must have been well-nigh overpowering; a long list of writers, headed by Disraeli himself, had yielded. One measure of Lord Blake's quality as an historian is that he rejected this course, yet the tribute is absurdly insufficient. It is the scale of his renunciation which is breath-taking. No one can write anything further about Disraeli without confronting Lord Blake's lengthy charge sheet.

Disraeli was—on Lord Blake's verdict—an adventurer, impure and complex. He was, for a venial start, a born liar in the sense that he told fantastic tales about his ancestry and heritage, and stuck to them; ever afterwards the gift was vastly developed. He could mislead friends and foes alike, occasionally leaving one by the wayside or dumbfounding the other by his brazenness. He glided more or less successfully out of more verbal scrapes than any other politician of the century; he could be guilty of 'reckless mendacity'. Some of these qualities helped him to become, again to quote Lord Blake, 'the most potent myth-maker in British history,' yet previously Disraeli had used them to fabricate his own version of the past. It is this last monstrous perversion which, one feels, has irremediably offended Lord Blake's professional sense. For politicians to devise myths to help shape the future may be part of their stock-in-trade, and good luck to those who know how to work the trick; for politicians to apply comparable methods to the art of historical writing is to trespass and to vandalise. Anyhow, Disraeli resorted to this brand of devilry in a manner no one has attempted before or since. If the Whig interpretation of history was a caricature, the Disraeli re-interpretation was something much worse, much cruder still, which, apart from its intrinsic evil, has jeopardised the credibility of all subsequent and genuine Conservative essays in the same field. At the time when he did it, the attempt to make a Tory patron-saint-cum-prophet out of the free-thinking roué and rogue, Lord Bolingbroke, deeply and inevitably offended Victorian sentiment. How could anyone so intelligent contrive a theme so implausible? One is almost forced to believe he must have done it for a wager, concocted perhaps after some all-night escapade with his Young England confederates. Serious twentieth-century Tory historians cannot be expected to show patience with these aristocratic carousals.

Moreover, once the tenuous nature of Disraeli's allegiance to fact and truth is appreciated, once the grip of the legend is loosened, so much else falls into place. He was *not* a far-seeing Tory Democrat; he did *not* seek to carry into reality the dreams of Young England and his youth; he did *not* educate his Party in his own romantic ideals. He was never the towering statesman of Tory perorations. He was the inveterate opportunist, the supreme parliamentary practitioner who loved 'the high game' for its own sake, and who would rather outwit Gladstone than gain an empire. He was, as he readily admitted, and claimed every politician to be, 'a creature of his age, the child of circumstances, the creation of his times'; in short, a pragmatist, highly skilled in disguising retreat as an advance. Even when he finally achieved power, with a full parliamentary majority, he did not know what to do with it. Even, and in a sense especially, the great 'imperialist' exertions of his last few years, which previous Tory historians have trumpeted with Elgaresque assurance, may be found on examination (Lord Blake's examination, it must be reiterated) to be built on muddle and misunderstanding. He never quite abandoned the Little Englander leanings of his early years, and the theme of Empire never truly captured his imagination.

Few could discern better than Disraeli himself the test of great men. 'A great man', he wrote in *Coningsby*, 'is one who affects the mind of his generation.' And then again: 'Great minds must trust to great truths and great talents for their rise, and nothing else.' But, of course, Disraeli was never foolhardy enough to rely on his own noble prescription. So Lord Blake has his justification for denying to Disraeli his own title to the highest statesmanship. His victories were always tactical, not strategical; he did not lead, he followed. The age changed him much more than he influenced his age. In *Coningsby*, along with his heroes and heroines, he created the immortal Taper and Tadpole whose perpetual fascination was the way the political wires were pulled. Yet Disraeli lived to acquire that addiction himself. Neither Tadpole nor Taper ever despaired of the Commonwealth, it will be recalled; but Tadpole, it may not be so easily remembered, 'was of a larger grasp of mind than Taper'. And larger still was the grasp of Mr. Rigby who 'hearing that his friends had some hopes, he thought he would just come down to dash them'. Mr. Rigby is the most odious character in the whole Disraelian gallery; but Disraeli had a streak of Rigby in him too.

It would be too severe to conclude that Lord Blake reduces Disraeli to the figure of nineteenth-century Liberal lampoon, the ever-cunning, ever-cynical manipulator of the parliamentary situation, with all loftier flights reduced in proportion, or to Carlyle's 'superlative conjuror, spell-binding all the great Lords, great Parties, great interests of England, to his hand in this manner, and leading them by the nose like helpless, mesmerised somnambulant cattle . . .' But Lord Blake's aim is not so far off that target. He does not seek to withhold—who could?—the meed of praise for Disraeli's charm, his wit, above all, his courage. But how should even this combination of qualities possessed in such abundance dispel what he left behind him everywhere he went, the trail of prevarication, deceit and falsehood? And are those words too severe? They are based on the settled judgement of the man whom no Conservative can dismiss.

> He is an adventurer, and as I have good cause to know, he is without principles and honesty. You will say that I am giving great prominence to a question of mere personal esteem. It is true. But in this matter the personal question is the whole question . . . The worst alternative that can happen is his continuance in power. He is under a temptation to Radical measures to which no other Minister is subject . . . He can forward Radical changes in a way that no other Minister could do—because he alone can silence and paralyse the forces of Conservatism. And in an age of singularly reckless statesmen he is I think beyond question the one who is least restrained by fear or scruple.

Such was Lord Salisbury's (at the time he was still Lord Cranbourne) view of his colleague at a particular moment when their careers jarred, but he claimed to be writing what 'all the country gentlemen were saying in private', and a strong strand of that contempt persisted even after the two men had reached their later accommodation. No reader should suppose that he has taken the proper measure of what personal political hatred within parties can mean until he has read Lady Gwendolen Cecil's classic biography of her father, Lord Salisbury. It is Lord Salisbury's brush which has painted the dark, indelible portrait of the Disraeli whom he first despised, and then vowed never to forgive, only relenting after more than a decade—of course, in the highest interest of the Conservative Party and the English state. But the venom of that earlier time still sears Lady Gwendolen's pages, and Lord Blake does not demur. For Lord Salisbury was, he assures us, 'the most formidable intellectual figure that the Conservative party has ever produced': no mean accolade from the preeminent contemporary Conservative historian. We need be surprised no longer about the lasting injury his book has done to Disraeli's reputation, and might be content to accept the happy conclusion advanced by one of Lord Blake's most enthusiastic reviewers: 'Disraeli's usefulness to the Conservative Central Office can hardly survive this book,' wrote Professor John Vincent.

Leave aside the Central Office: good Conservatives, good Tories (Disraeli made huge exertions to draw a distinction between the two, with no real success), should have reached this conclusion for themselves a hundred years before, and if they had failed before, Lady Gwendolen's book, published in 1921, was there to guide their straying steps back into the path of Tory rectitude. She wrote:

> In all that is disputable in Mr. Disraeli's character—and there are few parts of it which have not been a subject for dispute—his lack of scruple as to the methods which he thought permissible is beyond question . . . He was always making use of convictions that he did not share, pursuing objects which he could not own, manoeuvring his party into alliances which though unobjectionable from his own standpoint were discreditable and indefensible from theirs. It was an atmosphere of pervading falseness which involved his party as well as himself and which culminated in the cynical audacities of 1867.

But could not that stricture be conceivably construed as a particular offence, a passing episode, the exception and not the rule? Not at Hatfield, for sure. Even in the later years, she insists, when 'the older man' had begun to show some glimmering of the elements of 'loyalty', he still revealed his 'inveterate *feather-headedness*', a readiness to pursue contradictory, often self-contradictory courses. 'The failing', she insists again, 'was germane to his genius. Those of his opinions which could claim the permanent quality of principles had their origin in his imagination and not in his reason. He saw visions; he did not draw conclusions.' Altogether—and this it must be repeated was the settled judgement of the brilliant father and the no less brilliant daughter who had known him in his latest and, in the Tory record, his greatest days—there was something deeply alien to the Tory mind in Disraeli's whole outlook and character. Maybe, these features in his make-up were also those which made him un-English no less than un-Tory, but that is another aspect of the tale. Frequently during his life the Tories wished to turn upon their self-appointed saviour: the clash of temperament between leader and followers became almost too painful to be borne. An observer scarcely less perspicacious than Salisbury's biographer wrote:

> No one who lived and mixed with politicians before 1874 or who has read the memoirs of that time can forget the despair and distrust with which Disraeli inspired his followers. Might not salvation be found by shelving or discarding him? by such a combination for example as making the Duke of Somerset Prime Minister, and relegating Disraeli to the serene duties of Chancellor of the Duchy, or even to complete repose? This was the project of Cairns, Disraeli's closest political ally, who nevertheless seems at that time to have had an imperfect conception of the character and aims of his friend. To such straits was the party driven. Anything, they declared, but Disraeli; under him victory was impossible. What a mere adventurer he was! What a fantastic alien! What nonsense he wrote!

Thus wrote Lord Rosebery, a Liberal observer of special acumen; the measure of Tory hatred for Disraeli should never be underrated. And even in this generation, when he was securely in his grave at Hughenden where Queen Victoria's primroses were laid on his coffin, the act of revulsion is re-enacted by his biographer and the reviewers. For Professor Vincent it is almost as if the corpse has been dug up, like Cromwell's, and thrown into a common pit.

One irony of the situation is that we have, and have always had, a better chance of dissecting the mind of Disraeli, alien or not, than that of any other Prime Minister in our history. Winston Churchill is the only conceivable rival in this claim; he poured out his thoughts, in books, letters and writings of every variety in such a superabundant profusion that we may be excused for supposing that no secrets remain. But who else? Only writers themselves, by the way, can be entered in this contest; no secretaries or officials at the great man's elbow, invaluable though their observations may be, can offer the same degree of unconscious no less than conscious revelation. And here, incontestably, Disraeli is in a class of his own. No other leading politician, let alone a Prime Minister, has left a literary treasure to compare with Disraeli's dozen or so novels. What a wonder it would be, to press the point further, if, say, Lloyd George or Charles James Fox had possessed a similar gift; if the one had used the novelist's genius to unmask the Marconi scandal or the other the Fox-North Coalition, or if each had been ready to unleash the dreams and exultations of their youth and the laments and triumphs of old age. A new aspect would be added to their political characters; we should see them full face. The miracle is that Disraeli confronts us in his novels more boldly than any other comparable figure, and yet, all too often, the world, his contemporaries, or his biographers, have turned aside. Constantly, and increasingly in the later years, he urged correspondents to look for his life in his books. A few wise men, Bismarck for one, took the hint, but a host of others resented the invocation or were too disturbed by what they read.

Lord Blake cannot be criticised on this score, for he has woven the evidence from the novels into the life-story as never before; indeed, it would scarcely be too much to say that he finds Disraeli the novelist more attractive than Disraeli the politician. And yet he offers one conclusion with shattering implications and one which he admits Disraeli would have read with incomprehension. Disraeli prided himself on this particular quality, even his enemies vouchsafed it to him, even at Hatfield, as we have seen, it was acknowledged in full measure. Yet Lord Blake dares to assert: 'The truth is that Disraeli lacked imagination.' Lord Blake's comparisons are with the great novelists of the century, and his suggestion is that Disraeli had not the full capacity to design original characters and scenes and situations of his own; he was a copyist and caricaturist, not a creative artist of the first order. Maybe. But the novels—not all, but almost all—have another dimension which has escaped Lord Blake; he has eyes but cannot see. For Disraeli, they offered an escape from the hypocrisies he detested, from Whig and Tory politics alike, from the Conservative Cause and all its squalid inadequacies, from Hatfield and kindred horrors. But let us see; the case has still to be explored. What cannot be in doubt is the gulf which exists between the Tory world, past and present, Lord Salisbury's and Lord Blake's, and the extraordinary assortment of preconceptions and prejudices, wayward hopes and aspirations, realism and romance which made up the mind of Benjamin Disraeli.

It is, paradoxically, the Tory judgement which now denies to Disraeli his greatness, but let the rest of us look afresh and see what was truly there.

Disraeli said that he was born in a library, and part of his attraction was that he never quite escaped. He lived ever afterwards this half-life of romance in his own novels and other people's, saw himself in his youth as a kind of Byronic conqueror who could make a book as great a thing as a battle, and even in his old age, as Prime Minister or ex-Prime Minister, could never resist the temptation to return to his old trade and thereby outrage his sedate contemporaries. (How lucky it was for him, as Carlyle once remarked, that most of his colleagues in the Tory Party never read anything at all.) He had acquired the addiction from his father who, however, quite outdid him in it. Isaac Disraeli never ran the risk of emerging from his library at all, unless it was for the alternative legitimate pursuit of scouring the London bookshops. Morning, noon and night, when all the rest of the candles in the house were extinguished, single or married, for better or worse, he lived, moved and had his being among his favourite authors, and those who love books everywhere (and above all those who love books about books) owe him a debt almost as heavy as the one faithfully discharged by his doting son.

Isaac Disraeli was a Tory of sorts; apart from his highly popular literary compilations which showed no special political preferences, he wrote a few little-read volumes on two Tory heroes, James I and Charles I. But these were scarcely passionate political declarations; they added little to the current orthodoxies. More surprising, for a Tory, were his enthusiasms among eighteenth-century writers. He honoured Voltaire and loved Rousseau; he became a devotee of Gibbon and a friend of William Blake. His own books (not the sycophantic obeisances before Stuart kings) drew glowing tributes from Byron, and Isaac eagerly accepted and repaid all compliments from that quarter. In his old age he contemplated a book on the history of free-thinkers ('a profound and vigorous race', the tutors of Shelley, his son called them). He was surely a dutiful upholder of the wonderful Jewish Montaigne tradition, and he became, not by sudden conversion but by steady gradations, a sceptic and a rationalist. He wished Benjamin would give up novel-writing, not because he did not like the novels but because he sensed better than his braver son how the boy's enemies would rally against him. He had some critical faculties but they were mostly softened when they were turned on Benjamin. 'Imagination only can decide on imagination', he once wrote in an essay on *The Fairie Queen*, and the point might be passed to Lord Blake. From such a father certainly Disraeli received no perceptible guidance about his political future. He was just taught to love books, the best gift of all.

Old Disraeli taught his son to love Byron too, but any paternal instruction here was superfluous. No doubt it was an added enticement that the world-famous poet bestowed such honour on his beloved father but Byron became for a while the very air the young Disraeli breathed. He responded to every various Byronic mood and placed a special Byronic mark of his own on every book he wrote. *Vivian Grey*, published two years after Byron's death, celebrated with full romantic flourish 'the most splendid character which human nature can aspire to', and some side-glances revealed a more individual appreciation: he could celebrate too the great man's 'strong, shrewd commonsense; his pure, unalloyed sagacity'. A year later *The Young Duke* caught 'Byron

bending o'er his shattered lyre, with inspiration in his very rage'.
Contarini Fleming was hailed as 'a *Childe Harolde* in prose', and
so great a fellow-devotee of Byron as Heinrich Heine would not
accept the general verdict that this Disraeli attempt to follow in
the Byronic footsteps was so palpable a failure. Byron and his fate
and his pitiless pursuit by 'the British public in one of its
periodical fits of morality' continued to haunt Disraeli for a
decade or more. True, the phrase and its elaboration were
plagiarised from Macaulay but the theme was no less passionately
felt. Indeed the young Disraeli could write on such themes with a
more intimate knowledge and anxiety than Macaulay; he was
truly a disciple of Byron in deed as well as word. An ambitious
young politician could have been excused if he kept reasonably
quiet on the subject. Instead, he wrote *Venetia*, no literary
masterpiece, but a brave, reckless apologia not only for the
libertine Byron but, for good measure at the same time, for the
atheist and republican Shelley.

Shelley was allowed to summon to his defence a host of
witnesses, Shakespeare, Dante 'and old Montaigne for me', and
one other too, above all the rest, Don Quixote, 'the best man who
ever lived'. Don Quixote, incidentally, was, second only to
Rousseau's classic, *La Nouvelle Heloise*, a Bible among the
romantics, a challenge to Toryism all on its own. 'But what do
you think of the assault on the windmills?' Shelley was asked in
Disraeli's account, and Shelley's answer was firm enough:

> In the outset of his adventures, as in the outset of our lives, he was
> misled by his enthusiasm, without which, after all, we can do nothing.
> But the result is, Don Quixote was a redresser of wrongs, and
> therefore the world esteemed him mad.

Such were the rough lines which the now not-quite-so-young
Disraeli was scratching out at top speed in the winter of 1837.
Venetia was published in May, 1837: one month later he was
elected to the House of Commons as the Tory M.P. for
Maidstone.

Why did he do it? Why become a Tory? Why not let some
woman make him a Whig—as one woman had already boasted she

had succeeded with his hero Byron? He had indeed posed the dilemma wondrously ten years before in *The Young Duke*, so wondrously indeed that the satire was softened and censored by the author in later editions:

> I must be consistent, and not compromise my principles which will never do in England—more than once a year. Let me see: what are they? Am I a Whig or a Tory? I forget. As for the Tories, I admire antiquity, particularly a ruin; even the relics of the Temple of Intolerance have a charm. I think I am a Tory. But then the Whigs give such good dinners, and are the most amusing. I think I am a Whig: but then the Tories are so moral and morality is my forte: I must be a Tory. But the Whigs dress so much better; and an ill-dressed party, like an ill-dressed man, must be wrong. Yes! I am a decided Whig. And yet—I feel like Garrick between Tragedy and Comedy. I think I will be a Whig and a Tory alternate nights, and then both will be pleased: I have no objection, according to the fashion of the day, to take a place under a Tory ministry, provided I may vote against them.

This was not the candid tone of an unprincipled adventurer, as Professor Jerman who first unearthed and displayed them has remarked. And if he was an adventurer, as he further remarks, why not indeed join the Whigs, if not at that precise moment, then soon after?

The answer is: he was a Radical, and *The Young Duke* was the satire of an incipient Radical. The Upper House was put in its subordinate place; the Lower House was patronised; both were warned of what might occur when the young Disraeli turned his oratorical powers in their direction, and meantime the country gentlemen were put in their place too, Sir Chetwode Chetwode of Chetwode, and Sir Tichborne Tichborne of Tichborne:

> Sir Chetwode's hair was straight and white; Sir Tichborne's brown and curly, Sir Chetwode's eyes were blue; Sir Tichborne's grey. Sir Chetwode's nose was perhaps a snub; Sir Tichborne's was certainly a bottle! Sir Chetwode was somewhat garrulous, and was often like a man at play in the wrong box! Sir Tichborne was somewhat taciturn; but when he spoke it was always to the purpose, and made an impression, even if it were not new. Both were kind hearts, but Sir Chetwode was jovial, Sir Tichborne rather stern. Sir Chetwode often broke into a joke; Sir Tichborne sometimes backed into a sneer.

Sir Chetwode and Sir Tichborne were two inoffensive Catholic Baronets and were treated most leniently. A multitude of others in all ranges of the aristocracy he was supposed to revere were given their deserts, astringently or laughingly: the Dukes of Twaddle and Ego and various other exponents of Dukism, those mitred nullities, the Bishops, the Lords Dunderhead, Grubminster and Grouse and Squib, the Lords Fitz-Booby and Fitz-Pompey, the Lords Protest, Content and Proxy, and more besides, not forgetting many who were just content to sink into 'ermined insignificance', or Lord Loraine, in particular, 'a mild, middle-aged, lounging, languid man, who passed his life in crossing from Brooks to Boodles, and from Boodles to Brooks, and testing the comparable intelligence of these two celebrated bodies'. Strong premonitions of Oscar Wilde are evident in many of Disraeli's novels, and this feature has sometimes been noticed; it is the full P. G. Wodehouse strain which has been underestimated. He was, without any rival whatever, the first comic genius who ever installed himself in Downing Street.

However, long before he achieved the feat, this and some kindred gifts of temperament well-nigh crushed him altogether. It was in the decade of the 1830s that by a series of misadventures and misdemeanours, false starts and hair-raising retreats, he imprinted on the mind of his countrymen that reputation for slipperiness, for downright double-dealing, from which he could never quite escape. He fought High Wycombe as a Radical in 1832 and was elected as a Tory for Maidstone in 1837 and for the even safer Tory stronghold of Shrewsbury a year later. Between the two events he twisted and turned and prevaricated and engaged in every form and degree of political tergiversation, to use his own favourite word later hurled at Sir Robert Peel, thereby inviting on his head Daniel O'Connell's famous and terrible curse which traced his ancestry to the impenitent thief on the cross. It was during this period too that his financial and emotional affairs mounted to a climax, or rather a series of overwhelming climaxes which even the most devoted historical inquiries have not finally unravelled. He was thrown ever deeper upon the mercy of the moneylenders, and the last few scenes of his great love-affair with Henrietta are still not finally delineated.

Did he incite or at least encourage his mistress to share her favours with the lascivious ex-Lord Chancellor Lyndhurst and thereby secure the essential backing for his own political advancement? It looks likely. During these years a frenetic, impatient tone creeps into his controversial writings. He wrote a hideous, hopeless poem called *Revolutionary Epick*; and in a strangely rambling diary which he kept at the time he himself noted: 'My mind is a continental mind. It is a revolutionary mind . . .' He had something to say but had not found the means to say it; he could impose no sense of order on the revolutionary passions, the spirit of the age, which stirred within him. So 'without a pang', as he claimed falsely, he 'hurled his lyre to Limbo'. He seems momentarily to have lost his marvellous poise: the combined coolness and courtesy in the teeth of all trials which helped to shape his greatest gift of all, his courage. Perhaps he started to recover this most precious possession in *Henrietta Temple, A Love Story*; it certainly did not tell all, but perhaps it told more than the cynics have allowed and, of course, it concluded with a triumph for the hero. It was written, incredibly, in the hundred odd days of the summer and autumn of 1836 when both his love life and his financial affairs were collapsing into fiasco, but he somehow created for himself a world of hope and composure.

Yet it is another event altogether which truly heralds his recovery from the tribulations of the 1830s, a deed to wipe away all stains. Disraeli's maiden speech in the House of Commons, as every schoolchild is instructed, had been a disaster, and thereafter he was forced to make painful and humiliating efforts to rehabilitate himself in what can be the most unforgiving and ungenerous assembly in the world. But then, at the most unpropitious moment for him, came another test. Outside the walls of Westminster, the great Chartist revolt was mounting to its fullest fury, and inside, all parties, Whigs and Tories alike, Conservatives, Liberals, even several of the self-styled Radicals, huddled together to protect Church and State in panic-stricken unity. Disraeli would not bow to the House of Commons in one of those swelling tempers when it converts itself into a mob. He was one of only three who voted against a Bill advancing money for the Birmingham police where the Chartist Convention was sitting; one of only five who opposed the fierce sentences imposed on Chartist leaders. 'Nobody can deny,' he told the House in that full Petition debate:

> that the Chartists labour under great grievances. Look at the House; it has been sitting now for five months. What has it done for the people? Nothing. The Government sees everything in the brightest colours; everything is the best in the best of worlds. The Government is busy making peers, creating baronets, at the very moment when a social insurrection is at the threshold . . .

He drew upon himself a rebuke from the Chancellor of the Exchequer of the day, and a junior member of the Government rushed in to call him 'an advocate of riot and disorder'. He yielded not an inch to either. It was a proud moment in his life, and he never forgot. When one of the leaders involved in these tumults who had had a spell in Leicester gaol knocked at the door of Disraeli's house in Grosvenor Gate, he was offered exquisite courtesy and excellent advice. Thanks to the guidance received there, the prison-poem, *The Purgatory of Suicides*, by Thomas Cooper, the Chartist, was properly printed. 'Nay Sir', said Cooper to his sceptical publisher, 'I shall not strike "the Chartist" out. Mr. Disraeli advised me not to let anyone persuade me to strike it out, and I mean to abide by his advice.'

Just a few years later again in *Sybil* he was entitled to exult:

> Yes! there was one voice that had sounded in that proud Parliament, that free, from the slang of faction, had dared to express immortal truths . . . that the rights of labour were as sacred as those of property; that if a difference were to be established, the interests of the living ought to be preferred . . .

Years later—in 1870—he wrote that 'the Chartists formed a popular organisation which in its extent and completeness has perhaps never been equalled'. Most of Disraeli's biographers confine the story of his Chartist speeches to a few casual sentences. Disraeli himself saw them in different and wiser proportions. He had no real sense of history, says Lord Blake; he was for ever the propagandist. True, perhaps: but he was the only leading political figure in the Parliament of the 1830s and the 1840s who recognised Chartism for what it was, the stirring of a new class, the movement of the future.

Moreover, Disraeli's sense of history, his comprehension of the revolutionary state of England, so much sharper than that of most of his contemporary politicians, became sharper still when he looked across the Irish sea. A few years later, in February 1844, he delivered in the House of Commons a speech which seems to have compressed into it something of the whole ensuing century of Irish history, a foretaste of the famine, the Fenians, Parnell, 1916, the founding of the Republic and more modern events still:

> I want to see a public man come forward and say what the Irish question is. One says that it is a physical question: another a spiritual. Now it is the absence of the aristocracy; now the absence of railways. It is the Pope one day and potatoes the next . . . A starving population, an alien Church, and in addition the weakest executive in the world. Well, what then would gentlemen say if they were reading of a country in that position? They would say at once, 'The remedy is revolution'. But the Irish could not have a revolution and why? Because Ireland is connected with another and a more powerful country. Then what is the consequence? The connection with England became the cause of the present state of Ireland. If the connection with England prevented a revolution and a revolution was the only remedy, England logically is in the odious position of being the cause of all the misery of Ireland. What then is the duty of an English Minister? To effect by his policy all those changes which a revolution would affect by force. That is the Irish question in its integrity.

No clearer voice than that had ever been addressed to the Irish question. He had never been to Ireland. He relied on his incomparable political imagination, shaken perhaps by the invectives which Daniel O'Connell had directed especially at himself.

When Sir Robert Peel formed his Conservative administration in 1841, he could find no Ministerial place for the young Disraeli, despite the sycophantic, appealing letters which he had demeaned himself to write to his leader. It was an error on Peel's part, as even the most high-minded Peelite might later have been ready to admit. But if the importunate upstart had been given the advancement he craved, would Young England never have been immortalised, would the great contest of the Two Nations never have been unmasked: what would have become of *Coningsby*, *Sybil* and *Tancred*, the trilogy which must certainly form the chief Disraeli claim to literary achievement? The so-called 'ifs' of history can be just tedious. But the whole suggestion that, if the necessary office and cash had been forthcoming, he would never have embarked on these works of imagination, is to depreciate the books themselves. Two of them at least were written long before the Corn Law crisis reached the point of breaking the Peelite administration. None of them, as it happens, ever touched upon the Protectionist issue, except in the most glancing terms. The great themes were quite different which is why the books are so readable—the social disturbances which were threatening all the old landmarks, the argument about what should be cast aside and what preserved, the true place of Parliament in the life of the nation, indeed the future of the two nations, and the role of great and little men within Parliament, but, above all, swallowing up all other themes whatever, the perpetually recurring one of how the world could be reshaped, how England could be saved by the young heroes who understood the age in which they lived. *Contarini Fleming*, Childe Harolde in prose, had already set the tone: 'In imagination I shook thrones and founded empires. I felt myself a being born to breathe in an atmosphere of revolution.' Henry Coningsby and Charles Egremont were Contarini transformed into an English context. Allegedly these characters were intended to portray the now-forgotten figures of the Young England aristocracy but, however true that may be, the words they uttered were drawn from Disraeli's own romantic political philosophy. Bashfulness was never prominent in the author's character; long before the end of each volume he had made himself the hero, and a hero whose whole instinct was to join, indeed to command, the revolt against the existing order.

'I have been of opinion that revolutions are not to be evaded', said Sidonia, and the fact that Disraeli put this remark into the nearly-always wise Rothschild-Solomon figure is the most significant. Not many could be expected to share his wisdom. The more general view of those who so much despised the visionaries was that the great issues could be skirted and sidestepped. *Coningsby* described the unawareness among those inside the Westminster walls: 'they knew as little of the real state of their own country as savages of an approaching eclipse.' *Sybil* described the brewing storm outside. It was no mean or merely egotistical vision. For all the melodrama, even the hero could be pushed aside; it was Sybil who first told Egremont that 'the conquerors will never rescue the conquered'. The salvation of working people would not come from on high, from a supposed superior class. So how was the resistance to be roused and directed? The great Chartist debate, the strategical argument within their own ranks, was not dodged or debased by Disraeli. 'I never heard that moral force won the battle of Waterloo', said Devildust. 'I wish the capitalists would try moral force a little, and see whether it would keep the thing going. If the capitalists will give up the red-coats, I would be a moral force man to-morrow.' Since Julian Harney, the chief spokesman of the physical-force Chartists, lived to pay the highest honour to William Lovett, the chief spokesman of the moral-force Chartists, it is fitting that the author of *Sybil* should have kept the balance between them so delicately. 'The people must have leaders', said one noble Lord. 'And they have found them', replied one Chartist delegate. Disraeli saw that 'the claims of the future are represented by suffering millions', but many others saw that too. He was the first practising parliamentary politician of the age to recognise further that those suffering millions had already found leaders of their own, from their own class, who could speak for them in an accent more authentic and vibrant than any heard before. Sometimes in his pages a false sentiment or nostalgia for ancient times was allowed to mix with the realist assault, but this objection is trivial. His Chartist leader, Walter Gerard, could speak like William Cobbett. 'Half lamentation, half lampoon; half echo of the past; half menace of the future; at times by its witty and incisive criticism, striking the bourgeoisie to the very heart's core . . .' Thus Karl Marx made his comment on the programme of Young England, drawn to Disraeli's design. True, he added (the sentence appears in the Communist Manifesto) that the criticism was always 'ludicrous in its effect through total incapacity to comprehend the march of history', but the first half of the judgement does not thereby lose its force.

But the prophecy was not fulfilled; the march of history took a detour. The revolution did not happen, neither in Ireland nor in England; the Chartist hurricane of 1839 subsided, stirring again a few years later but never recovering its original force. For the next quarter of a century Disraeli concentrated on the necessities and enticements of the parliamentary game: the overthrow of Peel, the outwitting of Lord John Russell, the uneasy alliance with Derby and the mock challenge to Palmerston, the rivalry with Gladstone, above all his own survival among colleagues who could eye him with envy and even hatred. He had descended from the intellectual heights, and that at least helped to put his colleagues more at ease. He finished *Tancred* in 1847 and published no novel until 1870. Like Edmund Burke before him, he could be accused of giving to Party what was meant for mankind. The visionary had become the pragmatist. Certainly Young England and all its romantic imbecilities had been scattered to oblivion, and 'good riddance' muttered many gruff old Tories at the time, with Tory historians more recently renewing the applause. However the outcome was not quite as they may have wished or as we have been latterly assured. Disraeli was resolved to lead the Tories but he was not required to love them. He felt compelled to adopt the Conservative Cause but he retained his private opinion about it, an ineradicable spirit of mockery. Byron's disciple was not dead yet.

One sign of how perpetually irksome he found his captivity within the Conservative hierarchy—self-imposed, but none the less oppressive—was the link he sought to keep with men of other ideas and allegiances—or, more accurately in Disraeli's case, with men and women, or rather, women and men. His strong preference for the society of women grew stronger still, if anything, as he grew older. Women played a major role in most of his novels not only as heroines or lovers but as individual characters differentiated one from another as much or even more meticulously than the men. The Whig ladies were given their chance no less than the Tories (indeed a wittier and more winning lot on the whole), and the Chartists had their individual wives and daughters too who would only flirt with true suffrage men. Not surprisingly at all Disraeli favoured giving women the vote*—while Gladstone was still being denounced by the earliest advocates of votes for women as 'the woman-hater'.

Moncure Conway, the American free-thinker and biographer of Thomas Paine, who came to London, and, incidentally, gave his name to the Conway Hall, Red Lion Square, has left in his autobiography clear evidence of how widely in the 1860s

---

*Indeed, thanks to the recent discovery of the new Disraeli novel, *A Year at Hartlebury or the Election*, (published in 1834, and written, it is supposed, in association with his sister Sarah), his interest in women's questions is found to go back a good deal longer and deeper. That volume has upon it his distinctive literary trade mark: the Disraeli attitude to women, a combination peculiarly his own. The influence, explicit or implicit, of influential women, runs back and forth, but that on its own is not so remarkable. More striking—and much deplored on moral grounds by a contemporary reviewer—are the rousing cheers (and the kindly salutations from the author) accorded the Amazonian Kitty.

'I'll never kiss the lips that don't shout Bohun', cried out a beautiful, bold girl, the leader of those unhappy victims of our virtue who in moments of popular excitement generally distinguish themselves and it is curious are then only treated with consideration.

Defoe might have written that tribute too. But then comes an original scene outside the almshouse where Dame Harrald is 'surrounded by the petticoats.'

'I wish I had a vote,' said Dame Harrald.

'The women have no votes,' said Mrs. Collins mournfully.

'The more's the shame,' said gossip Faddle.

'In this world the men have it all their own way,' remarked Dame Harrald, pensively.

And that was written not quite ninety years before women in Wycombe *did* get the vote. And it was written, too, just a few months after Disraeli recorded in a letter to Sarah on January 29, 1833:

I dined with Bulwer *en famille* on Sunday 'to meet some truffles'—very agreeable company. His mother-in-law, Mrs. Wheeler, was there; not so pleasant, something between Jeremy Bentham and Meg Merrilies, very clever, but awfully revolutionary. She poured forth all her systems upon my novitiate ear, and while she advocated the rights of woman, Bulwer abused system-mongers and the sex, and Rosina played with her dog.

Anna Wheeler looks like the model for a Dame Harrald. (See page 187.)

Disraeli's feminist sympathies were recognised. It was part of his temperament and creed; with Disraeli no sharp distinction could be drawn between the two. 'Talk to women, talk to women as much as you can. This is the best schooling': that had been the advice given to the young Contarini Fleming. Disraeli followed it whenever he could. 'I owe all to women', he wrote to Lady Bradford nearly half a century later; no one could question his consistency on this theme. After some of his parliamentary debating triumphs, rather than waste time celebrating with the Tadpoles and the Tapers he would hasten home to his wife and the champagne supper she had ready. Perhaps he made platonic love to Queen Victoria because in the end he found Tory hosts so boring. He came to detest the society he had conquered, especially male society. Not enough consideration has been accorded to this aspect of the aristocratic world which he loved to inhabit and to delineate and to satirise: a few dashing heroes, several lovely heroines, a good number of scheming politicians of every rank and sex but then also solid phalanxes of bores, intentionally paraded and soon despatched back to the bosoms of their proud and obtuse families. He was supposed to adore the English aristocracy and certainly he gave them a new lease of life in fiction and perhaps in fact. But the whole class, more or less, was, with a show of old-fashioned politeness, put in its place. Once the point was presented to Coningsby in a tone which the author did not entirely disown:

> We owe the English peerage to three sources: the spoliation of the Church; the open and flagrant sale of honours by the elder Stuarts; and the borough-mongering of our own times. Those are the three main sources of the existing peerage of England, and, in my opinion, disgraceful ones.

If necessary Sidonia would make an appearance to remind us that one ancient race had a wisdom which no other could match. How often did Disraeli feel it desirable to mention that he traced his ancestry to Solomon in all his glory and, for better measure still, to the Queen of Sheba too.

However, to descend, alas, from these heights, the House of

Commons offered nothing but male companionship, and perhaps this is one of the reasons why he formed few of his most intimate friendships there. So the one or two exceptions to the rule become the more instructive. For nearly two decades he fostered, across the gulf of party, a special relationship with John Bright which was certainly not due to the enforced proximities of the House of Commons or anything deriving from the fashionable manners of the time. Lord John Russell, Bright's own leader, sometimes found himself in trouble for tolerating the treacherous demagogue at his dinner table. John Bright was the stern upholder of nonconformist morality, the arch-champion of free trade and Little England pacifism; how could he and Disraeli discover any bond of political sympathy? Most of the cultivation of it came from Disraeli's side; he would happily have sought an alliance with Bright and Richard Cobden too, or at least wanted to ensure that this labyrinthine channel was kept open; could they not together get rid of the 'old stagers' and the 'red tapists'? Disraeli did indeed recognise and respect the mighty democratic force in British politics which the two men represented and which Bright clothed in a language never surpassed in the records of English oratory. Disraeli was one of the great listeners in our parliamentary records; he was there all the time. At the supreme moment of crisis in the Second Reform Bill agitation it was the hidden unspoken understanding between them which tipped the balance. Benjamin Disraeli secured the passage of John Bright's Radical conception through the Commons and, more important still, the Lords. Hatfield and the Tory historians are entitled to their scream of outrage. Such consequences, the next great stride forward towards British democracy, could indeed be partly traced to Disraeli's devilry. It was due more to the affinity he would never disown with the radicalism of his youth. Younger Radical members—Professor Fawcett, for example—testified that Disraeli was the first person in the place to extend a hand of welcome. John Bright wrote to his sister in December 1851:

> Disraeli never denies any merit his opponents may possess; speaking of W. J. Fox to me one evening, he said: 'We must go in to hear Fox; I have a great regard for Fox; Fox is a man of genius.'

William Johnson Fox was a famous nonconformist preacher who turned to Radical politics; he was also, a great admirer of Disraeli's novels, and it was to him also that Disraeli confided or boasted: 'I am much misunderstood; my forte is revolution.'

Years later, on what proved to be his deathbed, he was interviewed by, or rather—it must be said, if the authentic atmosphere is to be revived—gave an audience to Henry Mayers Hyndman, then at the top of his influence and powers, as the guiding light of the Social Democratic Federation and the exponent of his own special brand of British Marxism. Maybe Hyndman's detestation of mid-Victorian Liberal hypocrisy established for him a peculiar sense of kinship with Gladstone's great antagonist, and this instinct had been fortified by the views of a Radical friend. Disraeli, he suggested,

> owed something of his success to the fact that he was a foreigner who regarded all the problems of English society from the outside with a detachment of coolness impossible for a native. Thus, said his friend, when he looked round the House of Commons, after he had definitely taken the Conservative side, he saw himself surrounded by men who did not understand him, who were bitterly prejudiced against him, who cordially disliked him indeed as much for his good as for his bad qualities. 'That damned Jew' had therefore a hard time on his way to the leadership, and he needed a set of people who, like himself, were divorced from English politics proper, in order to form a praetorian guard for him, and protect him from the intrigues of the Cecils and the cavils of the Carlton Club.

Alas, due to these supposed necessities, the Conservative leader, despite his instinctive support for Home Rule for Ireland, had allowed himself to fall into the hands of 'the North of Ireland combination'; alas too, 'compelled by the exigencies of an inferior profession', he had been unable to carry further his sympathies with the Chartists. Yet to mark the mood in which the young Hyndman, a man by no means known for his reticence or deference, knocked on the door of Lord Beaconsfield's house in Curzon Street in the year 1881 is to have proof of how startlingly different from the figure revered in Primrose Day perorations was the impression he could leave on an astringent observer. The two men talked for hours, or to be more precise, as Hyndman has the candour to acknowledge, Disraeli listened while he turned to one theme after another, starting with some diplomatically contrived references to Disraeli's recent anti-Russian policy which happened to be partially shared by Hyndman (and Karl Marx, too, for that matter) and moving at last to a grand exposition of the full Hyndman-Marxist case for the damnation of *laissez-faire* and for collective action as the only means to extend and secure democracy itself. 'Why not say Socialist movement? That is what you mean', interposed the old man at one point. And then '. . . private property which you hope to communise, and vested interests which you openly threaten have a great many to speak up for them still.' And then again, 'It is a very difficult country to move, Mr. Hyndman, a very difficult country indeed . . .' But Mr. Hyndman came away believing that he had made a mark, that his audience had been deeply comprehending, that he had in a sense been incited to proceed with all possible speed with his great Socialist campaign. Perhaps the exchange reveals afresh little more than the courtesy of which Disraeli was always capable, but it may be imagined how different would have been the outcome if Mr. Hyndman had had the chance to unleash his eloquence on the head of Lord Salisbury at Hatfield or the Grand Old Man himself at Hawarden. Lord Beaconsfield, like the young Disraeli, was fascinated by political ideas in a way practising politicians usually find to be beyond their grasp.

But the place to look for any clue to Disraeli's inner mind in his old age is not in casual conversations but where he had always offered it before, in his novels. 'My works are my life', he wrote (significantly from No. 10 Downing Street at the reckless age of seventy-one) at the height of his infatuation with Lady Bradford excepting only 'the somewhat puerile frivolity', *Vivian Grey*, which she happened to have hit on first. Her interest in his writing clearly added, if anything could, to her charm. In his last period, he wrote two more novels, one in his sixties, *Lothair*, and another in his seventies, *Endymion*, and left a further fragment, *Falconet*, unfinished when he died. Since he had written no other work of fiction for more than a quarter of a century, since in the interim all his ambitions of political fame had been filled to overflowing, since he had become the revered Prime Minister of his Party and his sovereign, since even the animosities of Hatfield had abated, he might be expected to present an altogether softer, mellower picture of his England and his world. However, the outcome is somewhat different.

One feature common to both *Lothair* and *Endymion*— unwittingly so perhaps, and the more significant on that account —is the transformation to be noted in the character and calibre of his leading figures. Lothair and Endymion are romantic enough names by any reckoning; golden spoons and great estates and glittering political opportunities were at one stage or another in their careers showered upon them; princes and peers and prelates and politicians of every degree were paraded to do their bidding; the general background was more splendid and sumptuous than ever; by every outward sign both of them could be regarded as reincarnations of Disraeli's former Young England heroes. But sharper inspection is required. Neither Lothair nor Endymion had much of Coningsby or Egremont in them, and what was lacking in each was the youthful dynamism, the quick imaginative sympathy, the individual zest to master the world around them, all the special qualities which were the young Disraeli's own.

Less still even were they worthy exponents of Disraeli's dream of love at first sight, the only true love, to which his novel *Henrietta Temple* had been dedicated. True, Lothair did return after much circumambulance and circumspection to the same Corisande upon whom his first tender glance had chanced to fall; but compared with the tempestuous affair with Henrietta Temple it was a marriage of political convenience. As for Endymion, he stifled the first promptings of his passion and never blurted them out thereafter; political caution and sisterly admonitions cut him short at almost every turn. In the end, he, like Lothair, was married off to the most gorgeous and eligible among the great Whig ladies. Not, be it hastily noted, that this was presented as in any sense a slight by the Tory-Prime-Minister-novelist; rather he magnanimously saw them scaling the highest pinnacle and living happily ever after.

Despite their dashing good looks and good manners, despite

the pivotal role in the story which they appeared to be allocated, both Lothair and Endymion were pushed aside to make room for more formidable characters, indeed to let the political world itself assume its rightful, governing pride of place. Byron's heroes would never have tolerated such disrespect, and nor would Disraeli's own Byronic heroes of a quarter of a century earlier. 'You must choose, my lord', he has someone say in *Endymion*, 'I cannot send you out looking like Byron if you mean to be a Canning or a Pitt.' But that, of course, was just how he did send himself and many others out in the 1820s; his wit now made mock obeisance to the different tone of the late 1860s. But it was not just old age which caused the change; by almost any test *Lothair* and *Endymion* were as lively as anything he had ever written. He had new insights, interests and enthusiasms which filled the arena once occupied by the Young England myth, and these required that both Lothair and Endymion should be gracefully put in their subordinate place. So they were both made plastic characters, clay in the hands of the potter or, rather, the potter's wives.

Lothair, it must be noted in passing, was not ostensibly a political novel; its supposed theme was religion. Rome, Canterbury, even Calvinistic Scotland battled for the hero's soul and he finished up, as we have seen, in the Erastian arms of a wonderful Whig beauty and patriot whose faith was embalmed more in the Church of England than the Church of Christ. Considering how deeply religious our Victorian great grandfathers were, it is surprising that the sense of outrage against the book was not expressed infinitely more strongly than it was. Once upon a time he had written of Roman Catholicism with sympathy and appreciation; Sybil after all and her Chartist father were of the old faith. But *Lothair* is a furious and deadly indictment of the Church which set its face against political liberty, of the Scarlet Lady, of a system of sorcery, which 'to save itself would put poison in the Eucharist'.* No comparable invectives are directed

---

*Even sharper is the picture of Cardinal Grandison which Disraeli drew elsewhere:

> The Cardinal was an entire believer in female influence, and a considerable believer in his influence over females; and he had good cause for his

against any other creed, but few Anglican Bishops make even a momentary appearance without receiving a faintly supercilious greeting, whether from the forthright Lord St. Aldegonde ('I do not like Bishops; I think there is no use in them') or his kindred spirit unmasking the celebrated preacher 'who in a sweet, silky voice, quoted Socrates instead of St. Paul.' Even the most devoted of Disraeli's followers had to admit that 'the Church of England was not his strong point'; he never appreciated its spiritual quality. Even in the late 1870s Dean Wellesley was warning Queen Victoria that he just regarded the Church as 'the great state-engine of the Conservatives'. And even when he made his famous pronouncement on the Darwinian theory, professing himself on the side of the angels, not the apes, Conservative congregations, at their prayers, shuddered at his flippancy.

The truth is, Disraeli's mind was rootedly irreligious. He had attempted to frame a religion of his own in *Tancred*, a sort of amalgam of Judaism and Christianity with more than a dash of Mahomet thrown in for makeweight; it was a ridiculous failure, and he privately knew it. He could laugh at others who set out on the same quest and were no more successful than himself—for example, 'Goethe, a Spinozist who did not believe in Spinoza', or 'one of those distinguished divines who do not believe in divinity.' He had found his own resting place in the end, not that the journey had needed to be lengthy, in his father Isaac's free-thinking bosom. 'The time is now ripe for terminating the infidelity of the world', the Cardinal had said to Lothair in Rome. 'I look to the alienation of England as virtually over. I am panting to see you return to the home of your fathers and reconquer it for the Church in the name of the Lord God of Sabaoth. Never was a man in a greater position since Godfrey or Ignatius. The eyes of

---

convictions. The catalogue of his proselytes were numerous and distinguished. He had not only converted a duchess and several countesses, but he had fathered into his fold a real Mary Magdalen.

In the height of her beauty and fame (added Wilfrid Meynell in his book *The Man Disraeli*) 'she had suddenly thrown up her golden whip and jingling reins, and cast herself at the feet of the Cardinal.' This passage offended the taste of the Cardinal.

Christendom are upon you as the most favoured of men, and you stand there like Saint Thomas.' To which Lothair made the reply: 'Perhaps he was as bewildered as I am.' Montaigne himself could not have improved upon it.

But, if *Lothair* has no hero, it has a heroine; as it bows the knee to no particular religion, so it offers the highest honour to a political religion. It is Theodora, 'the divine Theodora' with the look of a Maenad and a voice vibrant with the Marseillaise, the champion of a doctrine which knows that 'the necessities of things are sterner stuff than the hopes of men', who speaks of another Rome, 'that country which first impressed upon the world a general and enduring form of masculine virtue; the land of liberty, and law, and eloquence, and military genius, now garrisoned by monks and governed by a doting priest'. No chink of doubt is left by the author (the sixty-six year old gout-ridden, asthmatic Tory Premier, let it not be forgotten) about Theodora's pre-eminence and glory. She shapes the plot; she directs Lothair's destiny; she stirs from him the ecstatic confession: 'Had it not been for you, I should have remained what I was when we first met, a prejudiced, narrow-minded being, with contracted sympathies and false knowledge, wasting my life on obsolete trifles, and utterly insensible to the privilege of living in this wondrous age of change and progress.' *Lothair*, or *Theodora*, as it might better have been titled, is an anthem of the Roman Republic, not of ancient times, but the Republic of Mazzini and Garibaldi, of the Italian Risorgimento, presented with an exhilaration and richness worthy of Rossini himself:

She spoke to the men in all the dialects of that land of many languages. The men of the Gulf, in general of gigantic stature, dropped their merry Venetian stories and fell down on their knees and kissed the hem of her garment; the Scaramouch forgot his tricks, and wept as he would to the Madonna; Tuscany and Rome made speeches worthy of the Arno and the Forum; and the Corsicans and the islanders unsheathed their poniards and brandished them in the air, which is their mode of denoting affectionate devotion. As the night advanced, the crescent moon glittering above the Apennines, Theodora attended by the whole staff, having visited all the troops, stopped at the chief fire of the camp, and in a voice which might have maddened nations sang the hymn of Roman liberty, the whole army ranged in ranks along the valley joining in the solemn and triumphant chorus.'

And who else would thus have spoken or sung? Who else would have so joyously led that chorus, with Rossini and Verdi? Byron himself, the fellow-conspirator of the Carbonari, the herald of the Risorgimento, the man who wrote of 'a free Italy, the poetry of politics'.

Lothair has other implications too; maybe it contains premonitions of how forces were gathering, strange forces of revolutionary strength, to shake Victorian blandness and power. Apart from the Risorgimento heroes and heroines whom the Tory Disraeli has extolled so incongruously, one other who flitted across the pages was a Fenian leader. Disraeli never lost the imaginative capacity of his youth which enabled him to comprehend the ways and wiles of those who championed political ideas quite different from his own. He would not dismiss them as devils; he wanted instead to explore how their minds worked. So suddenly an Irish cut-throat or terrorist would turn up in his novel as a liberal chieftain, and no one could be more aghast at the apparition than the great Liberal leaders. But *Lothair* laid itself open to much wider misapprehensions. 'It was supposed, on its first appearance', wrote J. A. Froude, 'to be a vulgar glorification of the splendours of the great English nobles into whose society he had been admitted as a *parvenu*, and whose condescension he rewarded by painting them in their indolent magnificence.' But it was nothing of the kind. Froude was one of the few who read and reread the masterpiece, ever more startled by his discoveries. 'The true value of the book', he wrote at the end (in the year 1890, ten years after Disraeli's death):

> is the perfect representation of patrician society in England in the year which was then passing over; the full appreciation of all that was good and noble in it; yet the recognition, also, that it was a society without a purpose, and with no claim to endurance.

But Froude was one of the few of Disraeli's contemporaries who would exert his imagination to understand. Mostly, on the publication of *Lothair*, his political friends trembled and his enemies gloated. Whatever else the book was, it was not the proper work of a Tory Prime Minister, past or present.

Endymion, it seems, was a slighter work altogether; neither on the surface nor beneath did it purport to touch on such mighty themes as those which had befuddled the none-too-brilliant *Lothair*. Disraeli started writing it just before he was launched upon his final Premiership in 1874, laid it aside, supposedly, while distracted by crises ranging from Suez Canal shares to the Congress of Berlin, and returned to complete it a few months after his defeat in the election of 1880. Even a Flaubert might have found his concentration affected by such intrusions; even so friendly a critic as Froude was inclined to depreciate *Endymion*. Yet considering all the circumstances in which he wrote, considering how asthma had finally fixed its grip upon him, considering how he had led his Party to electoral defeat and how the Tory gentlemen, according to their custom, were turning upon their leader, the equable, light-hearted tone of the book is all the more astonishing. A fresh judgement upon it is required, and a hint of *Endymion's* true novelty is forthcoming from the most unlikely quarter. Queen Victoria read it with a rising disquiet: she was not at all amused to discover that it was all about the Whigs. She had been justly dubious about *Lothair* too, and when some Duchess at dinner had asked her whether Theodora was not a divine character, she had looked 'a little perplexed and grave'.

In *Endymion* the Tory Prime Minister set out to describe the parliamentary history of England from the late 1820s when he had first arrived on the scene, and he chose to tell it almost entirely through the eyes of the great Whig houses which were once the victims of his invective and, in particular, through the eyes of Lord Palmerston whom the young Disraeli had variously pilloried as 'the great Apollo of aspiring under-strappers, the Lord Fanny of diplomacy, the Sporus of politics, cajoling France with an airy compliment, and menacing Russia with a perfumed cane'. Lord Palmerston, Lord Roehampton, is, if not the hero, at least the most appealing figure in the whole book. It is a glowing, laughing portrait of the old rapscallion; small wonder Queen

Victoria was outraged. Around him cluster all the adoring Whig beauties of the day—'all the ladies admire him and he admires all the ladies'; indeed, so evidently was he stealing all comers, duchesses and diplomats and dowagers and everyone else, and the book itself, that he had to be struck down before his prime, prematurely and quite unhistorically consigned to an early and chaste grave. Perhaps this was the author's necessary gesture to secure convenient reconciliation with his Queen.

Not, however, let it be insisted at once, that Disraeli would ever allow his women to be reduced to the status of subordinate creatures, even in this extremity and even by the roving Lord Roehampton. 'What women!' exclaimed another of the book's secondary heroes, young Louis Napoleon, 'What women! Not to be rivalled in this city (Paris), and yet quite unlike each other.' It was true enough. Two splendid women mould the book to their design as surely as they moulded Endymion himself. So much so that Froude, so often Disraeli's most perspicacious reader, suggests that Myra, Endymion's sister, may have been intended as the author's attempt to create a female young Disraeli. Endymion himself could never quite screw his courage to the sticking place; Myra always could. 'Power, and power alone, should be your absorbing object', she upbraided him, and when he pathetically protested that he (and she too) was only twenty-five: 'Great men should think of opportunity, and not of time. Time is the excuse of feeble and puzzled spirits.' His Shavian sister knew him so well. 'Give *me* the daggers', was the cry so near her lips. Just as *Lothair* should have been rechristened *Theodora*, so *Endymion* should have given the title of honour to *Myra*. It would have been a just recognition of the role which women played in Disraeli's mind.

However, there is another element in *Endymion*, a strong strand of satire inextricably interwoven in almost every chapter, which must be accorded its pre-eminence in the whole Disraeli saga. One of his most attractive characteristics was his capacity to honour an opponent, his freedom from malice, his readiness to forgive insults and injuries done to himself, his name, his race even. He had plenty to avenge but he would not waste his spirit in such self-destructive pursuits. But he could not be expected to forget, and mockery was an instrument which his good nature did not require him to discard. It is poured forth in *Endymion* in a ceaseless flow on the unsuspecting head of one particular victim. Little doubt is possible about Disraeli's last combined testament of heart and head.

The woman who is given the position of misleading dominance in the early chapters of *Endymion* is not at all one of the upstart Whigs, but Zenobia, the ample, still-utterly-self-confident Queen of London, of fashion, and of the Tory Party, just in those tremulous years when Toryism itself was being ineffably transmuted into the Conservative Cause. 'I shall always think', she said, 'that Lord Liverpool went much too far, though I never said so in his time, for I always uphold my friends.' And she always did. 'I have some good news for you', said one of her young favourites at one of her receptions. 'We have prevented this morning the lighting of Grosvenor Square by gas by a large majority.' 'I felt confident that disgrace would never occur', said Zenobia, triumphant. And her triumphs followed thick and fast, in the last few months before 1830. 'We shall now have a Cabinet of our own. We shall now begin to reign . . . I think now we have got rid of Liberalism for ever.' A little while later the Reform Bill of 1832 was passed over the live body of Zenobia and the House of Lords, and quite contrary to all her expectations and incitements. Momentarily, even she was abashed, yielding to 'that increasing feeling of terror and despair which then was deemed necessary to the advancement of Conservative opinions'. As the years passed, Zenobia recovered a little of her illusive nerve, but it was never a complete rehabilitation, and at the most perilous hour of crisis when the great stake of Church and Constitution had to be defended with every resource which valour and intellect could command, the task was reposed in the hands of an aspiring and newly-respectable Mr. Tadpole. And since Mr. Tadpole did contrive to snatch some temporary electoral success, it was to his towering philosophy that the Tories increasingly turned, in so far as they would ever turn to politics at all. Most of them had other pastimes which they practised more skilfully. Disraeli never ceased to be entranced by the combined phenomenon, the diligence with which the aristocracy he was presumed to adore pursued animals and birds of every size and species, and the determination with which they recounted their feats of the day at interminable, excruciating male dinner tables. 'Jerusalem! What on earth could they go to Jerusalem for?' said Lord Carisbrooke (a real Tory). 'I am told there is no sort of sport there. They say, in the Upper Nile, there is good real shooting.' St. Aldegone (a good Whig) was disappointed. 'I suppose our countrymen have disturbed the crocodiles and frightened away the pelicans?' Then again:

> The general conversation did not flag; they talked of the sport in the morning, and then, by association of ideas, of every other sport. And then from the sports of England they ranged to the sports of every other country. There were several there who had caught salmon in Norway and killed tigers in Bengal, and visited those countries only for that purpose. And then they talked of horses, and then they talked of women.

This, incidentally, was an exchange which occurred in *Lothair*; it was little more than a sideglance. In *Endymion*, the contrast between the Whig and Tory Lords became almost as sharp as that between the Whig and Tory ladies. Lord Roehampton would read French novels, although he happily confessed his inability to spend all his time doing so. Lord Montfort, another Whig, would furtively retreat to his country seat to get back to Don Quixote. But Tory tastes and priorities were inclined not to waver. Lady Beaumaris, inheriting Zenobia's mantle so gracefully, understood: 'It will never do to interfere with my lord's hunting—and when hunting is over there is always something else—Newmarket, or the House of Lords, or rook-shooting.'

Yet *Endymion*, after all, was not quite the last word of Disraeli, the novelist. Perhaps the old man had a slight twitch of alarm lest his Tory colleagues, like Queen Victoria, would understand all too well. So he hastened to make some ostensible amends: not to alter the verdict, but to offer a diversion. Even before *Endymion* was published, he was at work on Joseph Toplady Falconet, what could only be a full-length elaborate portrait of Gladstone. If *Endymion* had bestowed such gratuitous glory on the Whigs, if it had achieved its dangerous object of inflicting sweet vengeance on Hatfield and all such Tory presumptions, might not *Falconet* help to restore him to favour and kill another bird with the same stone? He set to work with a splendid relish and soon everyone was overwhelmed by the Gladstonian rhetoric, even the women, or at any rate one of them, who listened in 'veiled ecstasy as she would to a cataract in the Alps'. Alas, the author had completed only a few chapters of the likely new masterpiece when he died. Alas, too, if reconciliation to the bosom of the Conservative Church and Cause was ever his fleeting aim, the old Byronic scepticism would persist in breaking through. Once religion became the topic, a legion of devils was unloosed within him and he would zestfully return to his old pastime of denouncing all other religions and creating in their place his own secular, humanitarian idols which bore so little likeness to anything in heaven above, or in earth below or in the waters under the earth.

The fragment of *Falconet* left to us suggests that he would have flayed Gladstonian Anglicanism and Non-conformity, all rolled into one evangelical whole, with the same fury with which in *Lothair* he had pursued Rome and the Jesuits. What would be left? 'So they call him a visionary?' one seer-like character says to his disciple in *Falconet*. The word must put us on guard: it was the old charge against the young Disraeli which he took to heart and treasured.

> A visionary! So are you a visionary; so am I; so was Mahomet; so was Columbus. If anything is to be really done in the world, it must be done by visionaries; men who see the future, and make the future because they see it.

It would be tempting to end on that true Disraelian note: that was Disraeli, the revolutionist, as he had claimed to W. J. Fox or half-hinted to Hyndman.

But there are some other words added: 'What I really feared about him (the man damned as "the visionary") was that he had the weakness of believing in politics, of supposing that the pessimism of the universe could be changed or even modified by human arrangements.' Did Disraeli join in delivering that condemnation? If alas so, it must be just about his only utterance which would have won, and deserved, the unqualified approval of Lord Salisbury. But there are other words added too in the same context. 'I heard he was a Communist', interrupts the other party to the conversation, to which the wise man replies: 'He might as well be a Liberal or a Conservative—mere jargon; different names for the same thing . . .' It is not sure from the later exchange in which direction Disraeli's philosophical judgement was moving: was he a Malthusian who did not believe in Malthus, a Marxist who did not believe in Marx, as he had been a Jew who could not worship Jehovah? In his novels at least he always had the courage to follow where his imagination would beckon him, and, whatever else developed, it is legitimate to believe that, if he had been able to complete *Falconet*, the good Tory would have mustered afresh all his derisive strength and left the Conservative Cause, beaten so hard in *Lothair* and *Endymion*, a thing of shreds and tatters. Once, not in a novel, but in his biography of Lord George Bentinck, he wrote of 'the great conservative party that destroyed everything . . .' He knew that party so well; he knew how cold could be its heart and imagination; he had a taste in the last year of his life how defeated Tories can treat a defeated leader, and in his last book he would not have refrained from settling that old score.

Lord Rosebery,* I believe, spoke one last word better than anybody else: 'Disraeli died; and the Tadpoles and Tapers were left wondering what Toryism was next to be. The prophet had vanished and had left not a shred of his mantle behind.' But he had, after all; he had left his shelf-ful of novels to befuddle the Conservative, or the Tory, mind for ever more.

---

*In his essay on Lord Randolph Churchill.

FOUR

The Case for Beelzebub

My son, if thou come to serve the Lord, prepare thy soul for
temptation.

'Ecclesiasticus', quoted by
Arnold Bennett, *Books and
Persons*, 1930

LEGENDS ARE CREATED, as every journalist knows, in the
cuttings libraries at the newspaper offices; no sooner are a man's
or a woman's eccentricities established there than they become
embalmed, and may be disinterred, in every plausible detail, until
the last trump is sounded. But history, against the odds, must
attempt some readjustments.

'You Bollinger Bolshevik, you ritzy Robespierre, you lounge-
lizard Lenin', Brendan Bracken is alleged to have roared, as he
strode up and down the drawing room of Lord Beaverbrook's
Stornoway House, gesturing as he went somewhat in the manner
of a domesticated orang-outang, and his victim was Aneurin
Bevan. 'Look at you, swilling Max's champagne and calling
yourself a Socialist.' The assembled company, including Bevan,
listened with delight. Or so the tale has been recounted by
Brendan Bracken's latest biographer, but his recital is based on a
first report, presumably from Bracken himself, as relayed by
Randolph Churchill in a newspaper article dated 8 August 1958,
and the emphasis must be examined. Certainly Bracken had a gift
of invention, if not of the gab, but his conversational assaults
were rarely delivered with such alliterative polish, and who can
believe that Aneurin Bevan sat silent beneath the downpour? The
story I was told by another eye-witness, Frank Owen, a qualified
reporter, was that Aneurin Bevan claimed his right to like good
wine, adding with the approval of the whole company: 'The best I

ever had from you, by the way, Brendan, I'd call bottom lower-
class *Bolshevik* Bollinger.' The mysterious Brendan was not in the
habit of offering us working journalists liquor of any brand; he
supplied instead a steady flow of fanciful news stories which had
to be laboriously checked the morning after. For the rest,
however, the scene is authentic: the assorted company, the
polemical free-for-all, the deluge of drink and journalism and
politics, the orang-outang manner, the absolute rule that no
holds were barred; indeed, customarily, an incitement from the
host that the more eminent his guests, the more ferocious should
be the cross-examination or the raillery.

I made my timorous entry into this unimaginable world,
thanks to a word to Beaverbrook from Aneurin Bevan. Here was
the origin, or rather in the earlier social exchanges between Bevan
and Beaverbrook was the origin, of all the tales of a sinister
Bevanite-Beaverbrookian conspiracy which historians of the
Nuffield School—notably Mr. Philip Williams, the official
biographer of Hugh Gaitskell—have now sought to erect into a
major theme of vilification. I hope to show that there are more
things in heaven and earth than the Nuffield School may include in
its curriculum. However, back to 1938: at the time Aneurin Bevan
was on the board of the recently founded, but already financially-
ailing weekly *Tribune* where I had worked as assistant-editor and
with whom I had quarrelled over the sacking of its first editor,
William Mellor. I was a journalist-innocent, innocent in most
other ways too, having spent as a journalist only one year of semi-
freelance penury on the *New Statesman* under Kingsley Martin's
critical eye, a few odd months learning typography from the
master, Allen Hutt of the *Daily Worker*, and nearly two years of
elation and occasional dejection on *Tribune*. I was not exactly
equipped with the suit of armour recommended for those
summoned to Lord Beaverbrook's Stornoway House or his
country house, Cherkley, but that is where I turned up one
Saturday evening, after a first peremptory phone-call. I cannot
recall too precisely what happened at the dinner table that night; I
was tongue-tied by the general company and atmosphere but also
by the apparition who sat at my side, an exquisitely beautiful girl
who had some trouble with her English, but who seemed

otherwise at ease and whom I took to be an Hungarian countess or something of that sort. Next day also she was floating through the house; her disturbing presence seemed to be everywhere. But immediately I had other matters pressing for attention. Beaverbrook came downstairs in his riding-attire and asked whether I had read the newspapers. When I replied, 'Yes a few', he insisted: 'Read them *all*. Albert, see that Mr. Foot is supplied with all the newspapers in the library. I will return in an hour or two, Mr. Foot, and perhaps you will be good enough to tell me then what is in the newspapers.' When he did return, he made a bolt for the swimming pool, calling me to follow, and prepared to plunge, naked-ape like, into the water. 'You've brought your notes with you, Mr. Foot; now let me hear what is in *all* those newspapers.' But I had no notes, instead what might have just passed muster as a photographic memory. I had memorised the Sunday newspapers as no one, I trust, has felt required to do before or since. 'Come with me with no delay', he said as the recital concluded, and he led me where the assembled score of house guests, one of his usual congregations of the incongruous, were drinking their pre-lunch drinks on the spacious porch overlooking the Surrey woodlands. 'Mr. Foot will now tell you what most of you no doubt have been too damned lazy to read for yourselves.' I got the offer of a job and started immediately on the *Evening Standard*, at what was then the union minimum of £9 per week which however was exactly double my salary of £4 10s. on *Tribune* (cut from the original figure of £5, to help meet the first of *Tribune's* series of financial crises).

For the next twenty-five years of my life I knew Beaverbrook until the day of his death as well, I believe, as almost any man did (not attempting for the moment to compete with the women), and for all that time, with occasional spasms of fury or hatred and one of four years of something worse, I loved him, not merely as a friend but as a second father, even though throughout I had, as I have earlier indicated, the most excellent of fathers of my own. Many other friends found this friendship absurd, inexplicable, discreditable, scandalous, evil; for, the simple, widely-disseminated view of Beaverbrook was that he was a kind of Dracula, Svengali, Iago and Mephistopheles rolled into one. Anyone who crossed his threshold, anyone who took his shilling or the larger sums soon on offer (my £9 was increased to a munificent £12 within months and much more later on) was jeopardising his immortal soul. 'Well, how was it in the House of Rimmon?' my real father would ask when I returned to his chaste, puritan, teetotal hearth. He at least cheerfully accepted my discriminating reports.

When I first set eyes on the monster he was sixty years old; everyone working at close quarters talked of 'the old man' (no one called him 'the Beaver'), but, apart from lapses into hypochondria, chiefly on account of his asthma, he showed no signs of age or decline in any of his faculties. Mind and body could move with an electric alertness. The first impression also was sharply different from that conveyed by the cartoonists, Low and Strube and Vicky, who, doubtless for their own good reasons, made him gnomelike, too squat, too much dominated by the big head and the big smile. He liked to dress with a careless elegance and was positively vain about the delicacy of his hands and the meticulously-well-shod feet. His strong Canadian accent which he himself fostered and exploited, and which so many who came in contact with him found it tempting to imitate, was more likely to surprise by its softness than the calculated bursts of power. And most remarkable of all, in this general physiognomy which was somehow shifted from the expected focus, were his ears, and the purpose to which he put them. He *listened*. He took in everything said to him, everything he overheard. No use to give *him* false scents, misleading hints, half-baked suggestions; he could always remember. Nothing but candour could survive his sensitive powers of cross-examination and recollection. Yet on this same level of personal exchange there was no cant, no personal pretension, no side, no snobbery, not the smallest tincture of it. I soon discovered I could say anything to him. No sacred topics, political or otherwise, had to be skirted. Indeed, many of the public crusades which he espoused could be quite safely derided in private, and he had quite unexpected sympathies in personal dealings and a political imagination which could be convulsively stirred. The private 'old man' I met in the autumn of 1938 remained for me ever afterwards a figure of bewitching interest.

Nothing the public man did could kill it, and truly the public Beaverbrook, I believe, has not received his due honour.

One partial explanation of the devotion he could excite in the most unlikely quarters derived from the nature and scale of his emotional radicalism. Observers whose first or lasting impression of him was imprinted by the *Daily Express* of the thirties ('No war this year or next') or even by that journal in its last great decade of the fifties may rub their eyes in bewilderment at any such claim; but here was always one clue to the mystery, evident to anyone who saw the man himself instead of the varying portraits which, for whatever recondite purpose, he sought to present to the outside world. When he had arrived in London in 1910 he had at once become encoiled in the dismal politics of the Conservative Party, and the rest of his life might be construed as a prolonged exertion to break loose. He was a rampaging individualist—no one could ever question that—and he always favoured the rumbustious, marauding private enterprise system which had enabled him to become a multi- or, as he would call it, a Maxi-millionaire.

But he brought with him too, in those pre-1914 days, inherited from his Covenanting Scottish ancestors or blown across to him in the continent of his birth from the tradition of American populism, a detestation for the stuffiness and stupidities and snobberies of the English Establishment. He was an instinctive radical—not as the word may be risibly applied nowadays, say to Mr. Jo Grimond or Mr. Roy Jenkins—but in the true sense that he had an urge to get to the roots of the question and the will to wrench them up with both hands. This is what he did at his greatest moments, in 1916 and 1940, and at several other dates less famous in our history. His paradox-loving biographer, A. J. P. Taylor, has even gone so far to see Beaverbrook as a reincarnation of another radical hero, Richard Cobden, but that cap will never fit on this unique skull. For Beaverbrook was interested in political moods and intrigues, not theories or principles, and Cobden, unlike Beaverbrook, was a born and dedicated leader and organiser. Nonetheless, Beaverbrook's radicalism was deep and abiding and would break out when least expected, and was often active behind the scenes, it appeared to me, in his approach to journalism and indeed to politics too. Seemingly, and according to his own later reiterations, the rich, young pre-1914 Max Aitken-on-the-make had selected Bonar Law as his man of destiny. But, of course, that was ridiculous; it was a simple case of mistaken identity. Lloyd George was his true and natural hero, and nor was it a matter of mere temperamental affinity. Beaverbrook engaged in 'the honest intrigue' to make Lloyd George Prime Minister in 1916 and to sustain him thereafter since he was convinced that incompetent generals and an irresponsible War Office, shielded by the monarchy, must be brought under masterful civilian control. To tackle that root question was necessary for victory. Doubtless too he was dazzled by the sheer power and glory of Lloyd George at the peak; Lloyd George in 1918 was a spectacle which entranced him then and thereafter:

> He dictated to Europe; he flung out great dynasties with a gesture; he parcelled out the frontiers of races; everything was in his hands and his hands showed that they had the power to use everything.

And yet with a subtlety of perception for which his contemporaries rarely gave him credit, Beaverbrook also saw the weakness of his idol—'the glitter of his supreme office held him in chains'. Certainly it was the native radicalism of the two men which provided the blood bond, and was, incidentally, one of the reasons why neither could establish the same intellectual intimacy with the traditionalist Churchill.

　　Together, too, this couple of prophetic adventurers, Lloyd George and Beaverbrook, joined in vehement protest—and again with no assistance from the orthodox Churchill—against the long agonies which the bankers and the City inflicted on their fellow countrymen but here the primacy could be claimed for Beaverbrook (—'when it comes to Finance, I am a tub which stands on its own bottom'; he could teach both Lloyd George and Churchill how to keep out of financial scrapes). 'The power of the bankers must be wiped out', he wrote in 1932, although the same theme might be quoted from his utterances consistently, from the deflationist twenties to the squeezes of the sixties. 'They have used their powers so badly that they have shown they are not safe custodians of the money and credit of the country.' That was the flavour of Beaverbrook's iconoclasm which could make his judgements truly original. Since 1918 he had favoured the Government controlling the banks and not the other way round. The radical temper of the man had sure foundations.

Constantly through his life he sought friendships which seemed to conflict with his public professions or allegiances, and once formed they were not easily broken. The case of Lloyd George was only the most spectacular; more acutely than almost any other associate he saw the nature of Ll. G.'s genius and the moment when he must strike; that was 1916. But there was another date and another drama of personal perception with immense consequences a few years later. Incongruously again the up-and-thrusting Canadian adventurer had formed one of his closest friendships in the House of Commons with Tim Healy, the wily Catholic spokesman of Irish independence, once the flail of Parnell. The friendship governed him so powerfully that in 1920, when the Treaty to establish the Irish Republic was being negotiated, he used all his influence to reach the settlement which some have said since, and some suggested at the time, led to the eventual break-up of the British Empire; yet in 1920 Beaverbrook broke one friendship with Rudyard Kipling, risked another even with Bonar Law and successfully beguiled the arch-beguiler, Lloyd George. The radical recognised the roots of that question too.

Yet were these not battles fought and victories won long since? In the autumn of 1938, just after Munich, when I arrived on Beaverbrook's scene, had he not become an arch-appeaser, the prophet of peace when there was no peace, the defender of Neville Chamberlain and Samuel Hoare, even enduring their presence at his dinner table? He had indeed, and may his Presbyterian God forgive him this sin more scarlet than all the others. But the Cherkley atmosphere, or Stornoway House where the rhetorical prize-fights were staged throughout the week, bore, I swear, little relation to the suffocations perpetrated in Fleet Street and beyond. Robert Vansittart would be there to put his case and he could charm and persuade in the same sentence; Randolph Churchill lashed out at any Munichite in range; Brendan Bracken would aver that Hitler was bluffing and that the bluff must be called; Aneurin Bevan was not likely to be silent for long, and most of Beaverbrook's leading journalists, headed by Frank Owen, were moving into the anti-Munich camp. Beaverbrook remained unconvinced; he still clung wretchedly to his dream of splendid isolation, but he would never bring the shutters down on the debate. And he listened; always listened.

He loved good talkers, good reporters, keeping a strict ration on the monologuists, even if the offender happened to be Winston Churchill. Beaverbrook was a good talker himself; Arnold Bennett, no mean judge surely, called him the best dramatic raconteur he ever heard. Exaggerated or not, he certainly knew what good talk was, and had assembled around him no conventional crew. Viscount Castlerosse could talk; no one who ever heard him doubted that he was one of the real wits, but the difficulty of proving the claim is that he relied very little on his considerable powers as a story-teller; his forte was the sudden audacious blow between the wind and the water which could convulse the whole company and send his victim—usually one who richly deserved it—reeling through the ropes. Everything depended on his exquisite timing, or rather the timing plus the presence; it was incomprehensible how this grotesque elephant of a man could deliver his thrusts with such feline precision. As a ne'er-do-well Irish Catholic peer, dependent on the Calvinist Beaverbrook to keep him in cigars and mistresses, he might have cut a pitiful as well as a ridiculous figure, but by sheer nerve and talk he carried off the whole performance. 'And how is the old bucket shop today?' he was reputed to have asked as he entered the banking sanctum of his Baring-Brothers relation, Lord Revelstoke, who had tried to find him a niche in the city. That stroke helped to end his career as a financier, and he was soon back at Beaverbrook's for board and bed.

Robert Bruce-Lockhart was another in the company, the dashing, handsome author of the *Memoirs of a British Agent*, once the friend of Trotsky and the suitor of 'the big-minded, big-hearted', wise and beautiful Moura Budberg who had understood him so well and some others too, from Maxim Gorky to H. G. Wells. 'Moura says', Bruce faithfully reported, 'I am a little strong but not strong enough, a little clever, but not clever enough, and a little weak but not weak enough.' Moura knew. And Moura also was there on one of the very first weekends I spent at the house of ill-fame, not with Bruce or Gorky or even Budberg, but with her later lover, H. G. Wells, and I heard H. G. in person protesting against the playing of the national anthem 'and all that Hanoverian stuff' in a fine republican squeak which the near-republican Beaverbrook was happy to applaud.

H. G. Wells had the distinction of being re-invited even though he had committed the unforgivable solecism of satirising in a book 'one of those crude plutocrats with whom men of commanding intelligence, if they have the slightest ambition to be more than lookers-on at the spectacle of life, are obliged to associate nowadays'. Of course, the villain of *The Autocracy of Mr. Parham*, Sir Blasted Bussy Bussy Buy-up-the-Universe Woodcock, was a composite figure:

> He's the sort of man who buys up everything. Shops and houses and factories. Estates and pot houses. Quarries. Whole trades. Buys things on the way to you. Fiddles about with them a bit before you get 'em. You can't eat a pat of butter now in London before he's bought and sold it. Railways he buys, hotels, cinemas and suburbs, men and women, soul and body. Mind he doesn't buy you.

Beaverbrook was not quite engaged in that scale of business, but there was the popular suspicion, and Sir Bussy was also 'a short ruddy man', with 'a mouth like a careless gash', and, more precisely incriminating still, the book also contained a cartoon by David Low in which the Cherkley luncheon party was indelibly portrayed. There, in the corner, was Castlerosse, flirting with two flappers of the thirties; 'hangers on and parasites of the worst description', calling Sir Bussy Woodcock, 'Bussy dear'. The whole scene could have ensured that neither H. G. Wells himself nor David Low nor even the still radiantly composed Moura Budberg would ever darken his doors again. But there they all were, graciously invited back for more; the magnet was irresistible. And H. G. Wells was one of the heroes of my youth. I had devoured *Kipps* and *Mr. Polly* and *Marriage* and all the rest, and when it came to *Tono-Bungay* had rationed the reading to twenty pages a day so that paradise should not come to an end too abruptly. Beaverbrook had devoured those same pages too twenty years before, not quite in the same spirit of Socialist excitement, but with all his own discernment. So he managed his *ménage* not quite in the manner of Sir Bussy Woodcock after all. Souls and bodies might be in peril in his household; but the atmosphere was subtler than any caricature.

The morning after my own Cherkley hiring, I was instructed to report to Frank Owen, editor of the *Evening Standard*; we became from that moment onwards bosom companions, night and day, if such terms may be used without giving any misleading notion about one so spectacularly heterosexual. During those next months, indeed the next year or two, he gave me an intensive pressure-course introduction to the world, the flesh, the devil, and his notion of Beaverbrook, not troubling always to draw too sharp a distinction between the last two on the list. He was himself a superlative journalist and editor, being capable of enlisting an incomparable allegiance from those who worked for him. But the man was even more appealing than the journalist. His high spirits had a God-like quality. His physical capacity was such that he could drink all night everything and anything set before him, and be hard at work at his desk, after a couple of Coca-Colas, at seven o'clock next morning; so he continued for some twenty years, with suitable recuperations at weekends, until tragically that physical apparatus suddenly snapped, never to be restored to full working order again. Women fell for him in droves, at a glance; no one else I ever saw was ever in the same competition. Yet he did not treat the matter offensively or vaingloriously but rather as if this triumphant promiscuity had been the natural lot of man (and woman) since Adam or soon after. More than any other human specimen I have ever known, he was utterly absorbed by the pressing moment. He could forget everything except the article he was writing, the next edition to catch, the next round of drinks, the girl in hand. He had a first-rate mind, according to the tests they make at Cambridge University, and would sit up all night devouring some new book when not otherwise preoccupied. He liked to call himself a Trotskyite, partly because he was steeped in Trotsky's writing but partly also to disown the current Stalinite vogue which he abhorred. He was then (as he had been as the youngest M.P. in the 1929–31 Parliament) a Lloyd George Liberal, and he remained such till his dying day. He had already experienced eight years of Beaverbrook, and had touched the heights and the depths. When in the first year or so of their acquaintance, Frank's lover had literally died in his arms, it was Beaverbrook who knew best how to help him at the moment of human crisis, and when six years later he went off in pursuit of Grace who became his wife, it was the possessive Beaverbrook who—along with several others—felt himself to be mistakenly abandoned. Frank viewed Beaverbrook with a finely balanced scepticism and admiration, a kind of adoring fury; it lasted for nearly two decades.

Anyhow, in the autumn of 1938 he was just the man who might be expected to take the *Evening Standard* by the scruff of the neck, and transform it from what it was, the house-journal of the exclusive London West End, into a real rival of the *Star* and the *Evening News* with their larger circulations. Not that the characters of newspapers can be subjected successfully to such revolutionary seizures, to coups-d'état. They must be moulded, re-shaped by organic methods and loving hands, applied softly day by day. That autumn, it was Frank more than most rivals who discovered first how Hitler's awful name sold newspapers. He started, just for one week at first, to write a serial on Hitler's *Mein Kampf*, a work little studied before in the England of the Chamberlain appeasement epoch. Then, when sales soared, he continued the enterprise for weeks on end. Two or three times a week each night, after the paper had been put to bed, he would attend a session at Stornoway House where the successes and failures of the day and the prospects for the next day were compared with those of our rivals by our most relentless reader. Soon I was attending these meetings too, and would sit enthralled as managerial and editorial heads were knocked together. Why did the *News* and the *Star* seem to have more space available for real news? One answer supplied by Frank, much to the horror of Captain Wardell, the manager, was suggested by the columns of advertising puffs, 'musts' which the management required to be printed. One night Frank supplied a stack of this scandalous material to prove his charges; Captain Wardell received his instructions; and the victory was celebrated long before we returned to Shoe Lane.

Not so long after my arrival at the *Standard* I was whisked away on a travel jaunt with Beaverbook himself alone, apart from valets and secretaries, on the blue train to Cannes, to Monte Carlo, and back to the Ritz in Paris; I could hardly have been more surprised if Aladdin had turned up with his lamp and put me on a magic carpet to Baghdad. The idea was, apart from telling him what was in the newspapers, that I should be instructed in the business or art of writing a column. I was told to study the modern American masters of the craft, Arthur Brisbane, Heywood Broun and Westbrook Pegler. Soon some specimens were being despatched back to the *Standard* office and the row which one of them provoked started to endear my new master to me more even than the introduction to the delights of Heywood Broun. In pursuit of our belated aim of transforming the *Standard*, one idea was to provide a real *London* paper, and our leader column was to be freshly directed to that purpose. 'PULL DOWN THE RAIL-INGS', was the headline I had produced for a column and the proposed text began:

> Henry VIII built a fence round Hyde Park. The fence was changed to a wall and the wall to railings. And there those railings stand to-day, ugly iron monuments to the tyranny of a rapacious monarch. Someone ought to pull them down.

But, in the sedate Shoe Lane of those times, this smacked of the tumbrils. Captain Wardell, a constant attender at Cherkley, a passionate Munichite, and a scarcely less passionate philanderer, an admirer even of 'Tom' Mosley, a stern protector of the *Standard*'s elitist appeal but no equally successful protector of its finances, was shocked, deeply shocked. He knew, and also took the precaution to check, the long-standing objection of the police to the removal of Hyde Park railings; it was hard enough to guard against the spread of vice in any case, but, with the railings down, the task would become hopeless. However, Beaverbrook would have none of it, and his message was conveyed to the pious and passionate Captain in his presence and in a manner not calculated to advance my popularity in the office. 'No more of it, Captain Wardell; you have beautiful beds in Claridges and all over London where you can do your fucking; what about the rest of us?' The column was printed without amendment, and indeed with a mischievous reference to the expected protests from the moralists, on 2 March, 1939.

Within a year or so, I had become, I suppose, one of the family, a favoured son, and the real sons and daughter showed not a twinge of enmity or jealousy. Max and Janet and Peter all had strong streaks of the Beaverbrook charm but none of them possessed their father's devotion to politics and journalism, the two inextricably mixed together in one tempestuous passion. Each had other pursuits: apart from romantic explorations, Max was off driving passenger planes in America or delivering war planes to Republican Spain and acquiring the exceptional experience which made him the best-equipped pilot in the world when the catastrophe finally came. He was handsome as Apollo, as swiftly-moving as Mercury, but newspapers would have to wait for his attention until after he had helped win the Second World War. Janet had a streak too of the old man's guile to add to the charm, but she was still no politician. Only one member of the family, so far, has inherited the golden journalistic talent. She was Jean Campbell, daughter of Janet, and when I first went to Cherkley she and her brother were seven and five years old respectively, and I played with them around the porch where I had once recapitulated the contents of the Sunday newspapers; her Beaverbrook smile was already the most bewitching of the lot. (Read the Jean Campbell reports from Chippaquidick, 1969, if anyone wants to know how a true Beaverbrook can report.)

The word *charm* keeps intruding, and may seem quite out of place in the light, say, of the H. G. Wells caricature and many others besides. But, as with Charles James Fox, it is his charm that lives even if the debased word is insufficient for the purpose. Beaverbrook's charm was more like the secret potions used in *A Midsummer Night's Dream*, and he could apply them, seemingly at will, to men and women alike. So, sharply contrasting with the harsh or even crude appearance which readers of his newspapers might deduce, he fitted regularly into no definable category, political or personal. He was wary, high-spirited, erratic, cunning, calculating, passionate, sentimental, restless, impulsive; he could be mean and magnanimous; he had the most perfect manners, and he could turn savage. If intuition is a feminine characteristic, he was at least half feminine. It was the perpetual interplay of temperament and character all around him, in politics, in Fleet Street, and in his own circle which fascinated him and which doubtless gave rise to the notion that he was engaged in some vast Faustian conspiracy against the human race. But most of his critics knew barely one per cent of the story, and the nearer one approaches the whole truth, the more necessary it is to speak in nuances and to search for qualified judgements. He could combine—almost in the same deed, on the same day—the most staggering misjudgements and the most piercing insights. He had many of the visions or far-seeing appreciations of greatness but he could also feel his way round the furniture of the English political workshop like a blind man.

So the respectable Stanley Baldwin outmanoeuvred this would-be master manoeuvrerer, once in the battle over Empire Free Trade and once again in the Abdication crisis. In the late thirties, it might seem his star, especially any radical star, had set for ever. He became for a moment an aggressive defender of Munich and all it stood for, and it would have been a wretched irony indeed if his fame had come to rest on his championship of the Chamberlains and the Halifaxes, the Simons and the Hoares, the English Establishment which he despised, at its most ignoble and defeatist. But, fortunately for his adopted England, which he loved but never comprehended, he would not break his other associations. He kept open his line with the Churchillites, I felt, in much the same way he retained his interest in the hereafter; it might be true after all. How foolish to foreclose the chance of reversion in the skies by some premature and quite uncharacteristic descent into dogma.

Yet the truth, or rather another truth, was that nothing could subdue him for long. Night and day, day and night, there were editions to be caught, stories to be pursued, editors to be whipped from their conjugal relaxations, fellow proprietors to be baited, fresh young talent to be hired, a world to be ransacked for every curious proof of human frailty and courage. He was truly a born editor, and not a manager or financier; for each hour he devoted to his business interests he would give ten to every detail of each issue of every paper, stopping only at the sports pages in which he had no interest whatever; there the Christiansens and John Gordons were free to print what they liked. I went on many strange expeditions with him in those years, apart from the trips on the magic carpet; to a theatre in Brighton, for example, where he had been told how, in the interval between acts, a young man called Godfrey Winn could hold the audience spell-bound, just talking. The report was true, and Godfrey Winn was soon on the pay-roll. But, wherever we went, some of the best explorations were into his peculiar realm of books, starting where he had started at his father's knee. If you wanted Bible stories you'd never heard before, Beaverbrook was the man. He had a full repertoire of the greatest of them, a kind of Old Testament in modern dress, a blood-soaked Calvinistic horror comic, and of course the undoubted hero who fascinated him most was David, master of word and deed, of daring and subterfuge, the man of power and propaganda, the gangster-politician. And David, be it noted again, could sing and talk as well as act.

Apart from his own prodigious reading in the first years of his arrival in Britain, it was Arnold Bennett who guided or kept pace with his enthusiasms either in person or in the *Evening Standard* 'Books & Persons' column. Always thereafter Beaverbrook wanted to recapture the exhilaration of that book column, the best that ever was, and always he would be berating his barbarian editors who failed to comprehend that all wisdom could be found in books and that at that precise moment all over the planet authors in their solitude were producing the stories which each intelligent editor should seek to purvey first to his readers. Arnold Bennett said that his own curiosity about new books was unappeasable and divine; Beaverbrook's was not quite in that class, but almost. His own library, like that of other rich men, had been partly bought for show; but some authors, apart from the Psalmist, he knew intimately and could summon to his aid at will. The interaction between his mind and Arnold Bennett's offers sidelights into both. His first interest had been excited by the author, before he ever met him, not by any Five Towns' saga, but by the much slighter and lesser-known *The Pretty Lady* which no doubt started with the advantage, with Beaverbrook, of its semi-salacious appeal. But no doubt is possible also about their shared instincts and cast of mind. They had the same down-to-earthiness, the same idolatry of commonsense, the same streak of radicalism, the same taste for champagne and the sybaritic life, and the same lack of cant in avowing it; above all, the same faith in life itself sometimes and in books *always*, the same sacred gift of enthusiasm, Hazlitt's gusto. It was Beaverbrook who prompted, cajoled, bribed Arnold Bennett into writing that famous book column in the *Evening Standard*—just another proof of his inspiration as an editor. The whole collection (not republished, amazingly, until 1974) shows what a bursting storehouse of literary intelligence, knowledge, generosity and discrimination Arnold Bennett's mind truly was. Without Beaverbrook, this last particular display of Bennett's genius would never have happened; without Beaverbrook, the forthcoming Bennett revival would have to wait a few more decades. Once Rebecca West wrote a piece in which she referred to the four 'uncles' of her youth, Shaw, Bennett, Galsworthy and Wells; the iconoclastic Rebecca being capable of worshipping four literary uncles in place of gods. Three of those four were my uncles too, as they were for the whole of our Socialist generation, and here, lo and behold, before my eyes, was a fellow who certainly knew Arnold Bennett, knew him indeed as few others ever knew him.

So I soon discovered that, along with the political-cum-journalistic obsession, I shared with Beaverbrook other oddities or interests: a firm Biblical grounding, if a lapsed Methodist may make the generous concession to a lapsed Presbyterian; a taste for films and pop music perpetually on tap; an asthma affliction, both real and exploitable; and an eye for the same girl—but more of that in a moment. When I had a bout of asthma, Dan Davies (not yet Sir Daniel and physician to the Queen, but already Aneurin Bevan's friend) was despatched to my bedside. He brought no cure but all the mitigating potions without which asthma can be hellish and to which Beaverbrook was perpetually resorting. My brand, I believed, was at that time considerably more chronic than his but the claim was not pressed too hard. As for the pop music, the place shunted when I first went there, to the rhythm of 'A tisket, A tasket, my little yellow basket', and since that was my current favourite too, I took it as an augury. His favourite of all time was, 'See what the boys in the backroom will have, and tell 'em I'm having the same', sung by Marlene Dietrich as she danced along the bar counter in *Destry Rides Again*. A topic never to be mentioned was Orson Welles's *Citizen Kane*. No one could deny it: there was just an element of Citizen Kane in him, and he could be furious with any reference which exposed it; for instance, the speech in the classic film did give a flash of Beaverbrook on the hustings, and there are other glimpses too. It was deeply sad that he never appreciated Orson Welles who could worthily have taken a place alongside his Edward G. Robinson. However, there was never any danger, as enemies suggested, that Beaverbrook might lapse into the paranoiac condition of a Hearst or a Northcliffe. His sense of humour remained his life-line to sanity.

He was saved, moreover, by the war which he had said would not or should not come. Deeply shaken as doubtless he should have been by the collapse of the appeasement policy, he scarcely emerged, in the first few months of the so-called phoney war, from the worst bout of surliness which he—and we—ever experienced. But the release and rejuvenation when they came were all the more spectacular. Long before the Norway fiasco, he and we and most of the nation besides (there was nothing perspicacious in the observation) had been coming to recognise that a dramatic change in the constitution of the British Government would have to be engineered. Who better to conduct the conspiracy than the arch-conspirator of 1916? As it happened, his hand was not required for that purpose, but he was emotionally prepared to play his decisive role in the greatest crisis in British history, the moment when we could have become the victims of a Nazi conquest and when we saved ourselves by our exertions, with Beaverbrook's among them.

Nothing can ever take from him what he accomplished then, and indeed the achievement grows in retrospect. He had an original grasp of the necessities of the Battle of Britain four precious months before it happened, and his essential conclusions were not the result of inspiration alone. Nor were they due only to his obvious qualities of energy and daring. They were the fruit also of that extraordinary faculty for *listening*, for extracting the facts of a novel situation, for making himself the best informed person in the land—or the War Cabinet—on the immediate matter in hand. In those hectic months of 1940 he picked the Hennesseys and the Westbrooks who came from the factories and were capable of withstanding his deadly verbal scrutinies, and discarded the Nuffields who could not. He listened to Sir Hugh Dowding and preferred his still small voice to the massed chorus of all the other assembled Air Marshals. And he listened too, while pretending that his ministerial position forbade him to do anything of the kind, to the first-hand reports which Max Aitken brought back from the skies. 'Tell an old man what young men are thinking', he said to his secretary, David Farrer. Night and day that ceaseless curiosity never deserted him, and it helped him to ride the whirlwind when the men of the old Treasury Establishment held up their hands in defeatist horror at Ministers determined to command events.

Yes, he truly played his part in our finest hour, preparing for it and at the moment itself, and in the *Evening Standard* office we naturally watched the performance with some pride. In those first weeks we had another interest too. Right up till the moment when Hitler's tanks smashed through the Ardennes, Beaverbrook had continued to exercise his perpetual, erratic, inescapable surveillance over the newspaper; he was the editor-in-chief and everyone inside the office knew it. Then, one fine memorable morning, peace descended. The blitz was just about to burst upon us in all its fury. All Beaverbrook's improvising energies were devoted to the task, night after night, for weeks on end. So, led by Frank Owen, we on the *Evening Standard* went about our task all the more zestfully, producing the best paper sold on the streets of our beleaguered city. Day after day, I dare say, our tone become more exhilarated and revolutionary—that was the mood of the time. And one fine morning I embroidered a leading article with a quotation from Cromwell on the eve of the battle of Dunbar: 'We are upon an Engagement very difficult . . . But the

only wise God knows what is best. All shall work for Good . . .'
that and more. Within a few hours, it seemed more like minutes,
of that paper reaching our street-sellers, the blitz-laden peace of
the previous weeks was broken by a thunder-clap. It was
Beaverbrook back on the telephone:

> How dare you, Mr. Foot, how dare you use the columns of the
> *Evening Standard* to attack the Presbyterians. The tale is spread in
> Westminster and Whitehall that Beaverbrook no longer takes an
> interest in his newspapers. I would have you understand, Mr. Foot,
> that his newly-developed good nature does not extend to some
> damned dispensation permitting attacks on Presbyterians. And
> Cromwell at Dunbar, I would have you know, had no title to pray to
> the god of battles to destroy his Presbyterians.

So the tirade continued, and I had no courage left at the end to
remark that Cromwell's prayers at Dunbar were in fact answered.
Still, it was good to know that our most regular reader was still
reading the newspaper.

Most close observers of the spectacle, even those at the
Treasury, were willing to admit, once the assault course was over,
that Beaverbrook was an inspired improviser. As Carlyle replied
to the philosopher who said he'd accept the universe, they'd
better: without him the famous few would have had even fewer
aeroplanes with which to fight the battle. But the admission,
ready or grudging, was also used to imply that he was not much
good at anything else. He was the great disorganiser, the
untrained, disorderly mind, the inveterate intriguer, the evil
spirit with circuitous access to Churchill's ear. Whitehall and
Westminster overflowed with interested individuals and groups
who would join in this denigration: Sir Archibald Sinclair and the
outraged Air Marshals, Labour Cabinet Ministers who could not
see what right the buccaneer Beaverbrook had to be in the War
Cabinet at all, civil servants who might still imagine that wars
could be conducted according to rules, fellow newspaper proprietors who felt towards him no spirit of fellowship, above all,
the old Conservative Establishment in the House of Commons
and the Carlton Club which had still commanded a considerable
numerical majority in the House of Commons at the end of the

fatal Norway debate and which indeed still retained a large number of plum places in the Churchill Cabinet. Beaverbrook, for all his pro-Chamberlainism, had never been a favourite even with the Chamberlainites, and their sensitivities were ruffled when a few weeks after the retreat from Dunkirk a book was published called *Guilty Men* in which the leading figures of the Chamberlain set figured prominently and specifically in the cast. The pamphlet touched the temper of the times, epitomised in the two quotations which appeared as the preface, one from the Winston Churchill of 1936, now Prime Minister—'the use of recriminations about the past is to enforce effective action at the present'—and the other recalling the far-off spring day in 1793 when an angry crowd had burst their way into the assembly room of the French Convention and demanded 'not a lot of phrases', but 'a dozen guilty men'. What had that to do with Beaverbrook? Nothing which could be proved but much to be suspected. Occasionally the pseudonymous author 'Cato' seemed to lapse into a pseudo-Beaverbrook jargon, and at the end, when a sharp revolutionary distinction was drawn between sheep and goats, between those led to the slaughter and those who did the leading, between the new potential saviours of the nation and the guilty men, Beaverbrook was safely shielded in the first category. Enticing rumours spread about the identity of Cato. Who could it be: Duff Cooper? Randolph Churchill? Beaverbrook himself? The man would stoop to any gutter.

The idea of *Guilty Men* was in fact concocted on the roof of Beaverbrook's *Evening Standard* where Frank Owen and I and a few others might assemble, after the last edition had gone and before The Two Brewers opened across the road. Peter Howard, then the political columnist on the *Sunday Express* and not yet a convert to Buchmanism, was a frequent fellow-conspirator and imbiber. One Thursday or Friday night in that summer of 1940, as the reporters were returning to Fleet Street with their first batches of first-hand interviews with those saved from the beaches of Dunkirk, we had the idea. I suggested the title, taken from a story in J. B. Morton's *Saint-Just*. What we needed was a publisher and speedy action, and next day Frank had summoned one, Pinker, from the famous firm of literary agents, to our secret roof top. He swiftly made arrangements with a slightly hesitant Victor Gollancz; after all, the book at first hearing might sound like a seditious attack on the new Government, and who wanted or would tolerate that? However, we divided up the work between the three of us and literally produced it over that weekend. Three weeks later it was published. Victor Gollancz had insisted, with good reason, on a softening of the final pages; even so some thought it too hot to handle. An early ban by W. H. Smith proved marvellously counter-productive and we made arrangements to sell copies from barrows round Ludgate Circus and Charing Cross. That enticing title also had a special appeal for the bookshops in Leicester Square.

However, the bashful, breathless authors were not concerned with the mass sales which might come later; we were more interested in the reactions of one particular critic. He was puzzled and gratified and circumspect. Maybe some of his Cabinet colleagues were aggrieved, but since he could sincerely disown any knowledge of the authorship, must he share their grief? He himself emerged from the whole story better than he might have dreamed and deserved; how much more deadly the indictment could have been? And Churchill was lauded to the heavens; he might growl a momentary resentment, but had other matters on his mind. Beaverbrook hated not to be the best-informed man in London on matters of disputed gossip, and the more so, naturally enough, if he was alleged to be personally implicated. During the early weeks when he might have reached an adverse verdict on the whole affair, it was the three-way split in the authorship which put him off the scent, assisted by a justly critical review of the book under my name in the *Standard* itself. Anyhow, and for whatever reason, he never put to me the direct question. Within a couple of months, *Guilty Men* was a roaring success, and one by one, by one route or another, the guilty men did disappear from the central stage. Later still, the story circulated that Lord Halifax (one of the guilty men, for sure) had condescendingly remarked to his fellow-Cabinet Minister, Beaverbrook: 'You must find it hard to live on your Cabinet salary of £5,000 a year', to which Beaverbrook allegedly replied: 'Ah, but I've always got my royalties from *Guilty Men*.' Whether he actually said it, to Halifax's face, I know not; even if he fabricated the whole exchange, it is hardly less endearing. What could be done with a boss like that?

However, before they were finally removed, the guilty men were among the most prominent who joined others with better credentials to deny to Beaverbrook his true worth amid the tests of the greatest war in history. For allied with his virtue as an improviser went another quality scarcely less precious at such a time. His thought-process was entirely different from that of most English politicians; he understood the Americans better than many who sat round the Cabinet table. He had few of the prejudices of English Conservatism; so he could conceivably understand the Russians better too, and this last advantage applied in comparison with some of the Labour Ministers hardly less than the Tories; with Ernest Bevin, for example, of whom, according to the old instructive joke, it was said that he never ceased to regard the Soviet Union as a breakaway organisation from the Transport & General Workers' Union. Beaverbrook, the splendid isolationist, had never favoured the Polish alliance which had helped, at a fatal moment, to block any chance of establishing an Anglo-Soviet alliance. He had been implacably opposed, at the time of the Russo-Finnish war, to those who were ready to invite conflict with the Soviet Union as well as Nazi Germany. And all through the period of the phoney war and the period of Hitler's conquest of France, he had kept alive his link with another in the company of his incongruous friends, Ivan Maisky, the Soviet Ambassador in London, an old Bolshevik and an old Anglophile. Beaverbrook's *Evening Standard* was the one paper in London which, along with Aneurin Bevan's *Tribune*, all through 1939 and 1940 and the early months of 1941, returned persistently to the theme of how the world-shaking catastrophe of a full-scale Nazi-Soviet military alliance might be avoided, might at the very least not be encouraged. Maisky sent back reports to Moscow that the Britain of 1940 would survive; they may have had some minute marginal influence on events, and certainly they owed something to Beaverbrook's association with Maisky. He tried, and alas failed, through those same months, in our finest hour, to exorcise any tendency toward defeatism at the

United States Embassy—then conducted by Joseph Kennedy—
in London.

So, with no thanks whatever from orthodox or Establishment
opinion, Beaverbrook had equipped himself to exploit, when it
came, a new emergency and the new magnificent hope of national
deliverance. The news arrived on the morning of 22 June 1941. Of
course there had been rumours before then, even reports brought
back by Stafford Cripps from Moscow and re-despatched by
Churchill to an incredulous Stalin. But when the Cherkley house
party retired late on the night of Saturday 21st, the talk was on
quite other themes. I heard the news first on the early morning
radio, and then I heard it again, and then I ran down the stairs and
ransacked from the gramophone cupboard the record I knew was
there of the *Internationale*, and turned it on full blast. The whole
place was awakened, and as they poured downstairs, I was happy
to inform Beaverbrook's bleary-eyed household, guests and
butlers alike, that they were now allies of the Soviet Union. No
one seized the moment more exuberantly and imaginatively than
Beaverbrook. That morning he went to Chequers; all day he
assisted in preparation of Churchill's famous broadcast, and a
reception committee awaited at Cherkley for his return.

Our chance of survival was fortified; a hope of victory was
reborn; the whole world-prospect was revolutionised if, and *only*
if, the new great ally could be sustained. So much was obvious to
us, obvious to Beaverbrook, obvious to the mass of the British
people, obvious to babes and sucklings, and, so it must appear to
the historians, obvious to all. But, incredibly, it was not so at the
time. The military vision of Churchill and his chief advisers was
still fixed on other and lesser objectives, and it was Beaverbrook
who, within the Cabinet, within the Government machine, seized
and sustained the initiative to turn the national energies along the
road of commonsense. He feared with much justice that the
orthodox military mind, granted plenary command, could lose
the Second World War as it had come so near to losing the First.
But thanks to those old memories too, he knew perhaps that he
was the only man who could argue with Churchill as an equal.
Since he had sustained his leader at one desperate hour, he was the
better entitled to debate with him about the next necessities, and

in public, if need be. The scurryings of the guilty men contrast somewhat sharply at such a moment with the independence of Beaverbrook's mind and action. When the test came, how different a creature from them he truly was.

Yet a qualifying judgement must even now be added, since any portrait of Beaverbrook, even in the war, which stressed too insistently his assiduity, his consistency, his fiendish powers of application for himself or others, would be a travesty. He could also be wayward, quickly bored, moved by whims, and for all his dogmatic manner of expression, he often lacked an inner confidence. This facet of his character, about which everyone who knew him best could testify, made his periods of resolution —as on the aid to Russia issue—the more remarkable and honourable, but it is the clue to his comparative failures in politics. He was regarded, and often regarded himself, as the master of backstairs manoeuvre, and yet I have often imagined that he printed the verse at the beginning of his book, *Men and Power*, with a touch of envy, as a rebuke to himself. Churchill and Lloyd George might possess the unfaltering diligence which high politics demanded, but not, alas, he.

> *The heights by great men reached and kept*
> *Were not attained by sudden flight,*
> *But they, while their companions slept,*
> *Were toiling upward in the night.*

Beaverbrook did not pass that test. He revelled in the excitement and crises of politics but had no taste for the slow grind, without scorning those who had. He could feed the resolution of others so much better than his own. Besides, he had other nocturnal preoccupations.

Apart from that most memorable feast of celebration on 22 June 1941, Cherkley at the weekends in wartime offers such crowded recollections of Beaverbrook in action and Beaverbrook in manoeuvre that it is hard to disentangle one from another. The most regular attendants were no longer the journalists, apart from a very few, but the aircraft factory managers, the civil servants and visiting firemen from across the Atlantic and the world. Cabinet Ministers, Ministers, ex-Ministers and would-be

Ministers jostled one another, and it was pleasant to watch the various means they might employ to parry the Beaverbrook seduction or persiflage: Herbert Morrison, chirpy, well-informed, eager for good publicity and often getting it; A. V. Alexander, handy to have for strumming at the piano, and handy to have at the Admiralty too; Ernest Bevin, dignified, opinionated, utterly unseducible by Beaverbrook, monologuist and not invited a third time. I recall too Leslie Hore-Belisha, out-of-office and out-of-temper, sitting up in bed one Sunday morning with all the newspapers scattered around him on the day after Stafford Cripps had just returned from Moscow, trailing stolen clouds of glory as the man who had shaped the Anglo-Soviet alliance and who could even very soon step into Churchill's shoes. 'How does he do it!' I pretend I can still hear poor Leslie's baffled lament. Or one night, bursting into what was called the saloon where visitors might be offered a fortifying but watery whisky before moving to their appointment with Beaverbrook in the library, I saw, sitting bolt upright in his chair, a Wodehousian figure, at least on the evidence of his accent and moustachios, who at once launched into a fulsome tribute to the varied and matchless talents of the Max Beaverbrook to whose office at the Ministry of Supply he had just been appointed as Parliamentary Secretary. The point of the over-rehearsed oration, I supposed, was that he wanted his perceptive verdict on England's man of destiny, second only to Churchill, passed on, quite casually of course, to the proper quarter which I faithfully, but not quite so casually, did. Beaverbrook adored praise but he could, usually, detect sycophancy. It was Harold Macmillan; I could never quite take him seriously thereafter; an error no doubt.

However, colliding and colluding with one another in that saloon were the press lords and ladies of the Western World: Clare Boothe Luce who wrote *The Women* and was reputed next day to have said that hers was kindergarten stuff compared with what she had heard round the Cherkley dinner table, or her husband, Henry Luce, creator of *Time, Life* and *Fortune* who saw Fleet Street surrendered, hook-line-sinker, to a bunch of Russian-loving Reds, or our own domestic breed, headed by Esmond Harmsworth, treated most politely while the later Mrs. Fleming was in tow but whipped unconscionably when she was out of the room. One of these, Lord Kemsley, was never, so far as I recall, seen on the premises, yet he was raised from Baron to Viscount in one of Churchill's first Honours Lists. Lloyd George could not resist telephoning that Sunday morning to ask what had happened and offer commiserations, but Beaverbrook was not so easily nettled, and his reply came pat: 'Better a Lloyd George Baron than a Churchill Viscount.' It was one of his last tributes to his old master.

A little earlier Frank Owen and I had been despatched by Beaverbrook on a private mission to see Lloyd George at Churt to feel out the ground and discover how much he might be interested in joining the Churchill Government. Whether we were sent with Churchill's connivance, who knows? More conceivably, Beaverbrook saw Lloyd George as a potential ally in a War Cabinet where he so often acted in isolation and one like himself who had kept open the line of friendly communication with Maisky and the Russians. Anyhow, naturally enough, Frank and I leapt at the suggestion. Frank, as the one surviving member of the rank-and-file of the old 1931 Lloyd George Liberal Party rump, was always welcomed there as a brilliant disciple, and I had written a recent editorial in the *Standard* comparing a Lloyd George return to the House of Commons with that of Chatham in 1761. I had heard Ll. G. many times on the platform and most memorably of all from the House of Commons press gallery in the Norway debate when it was his speech which stabbed Neville Chamberlain to death in the open forum. By the time Frank and I went to Churt, Lloyd George was still in full control of his incomparable faculties but he was also, in his heart of hearts, defeatist. He did not see how we could win the war, and he did not see, in particular, how Churchill could lead us to the victory. He was deeply offended by a remark Churchill had made in a debate a few weeks earlier comparing one of his own sombre wartime speeches to the kind of speech with which Marshal Petain might have sought to enliven one of the last French Cabinet meetings, before his surrender to Hitler. So when we talked of our mission, he brushed the suggestion aside with the inquiry: 'What me? Old Papa Petain?' And as he talked, he resorted to mimicry, and soon cheered himself and the company by the malicious impersonation of one political character after another. He professed to be shocked by the subservience shown by members of Churchill's War Cabinet and the high-handed manner which Churchill displayed towards them. 'Now my War Cabinet was different', he insisted. 'They were all big men. I was never able to treat *any* of my colleagues the way Churchill treats *all* of his.' Then the old man paused, and his eye twinkled. 'Oh yes, there was one I treated that way—Curzon.' Beaverbrook at least could never be treated by Churchill the way Lloyd George treated Curzon.

Like Beaverbrook himself, I could not live by politics alone, and Cherkley for me in those years had one special irrepressible attraction. Making a pass, however shyly or ineffectually, at the boss's girl may not normally be recommended as the road to fortune, but I never lived to repent it and I never quite knew how he viewed the matter. I had had my first glimpse of Lili Ernst on the very first night I had arrived at Cherkley in the autumn of 1938; it was a stunning glimpse too, but then she vanished before I knew who or what she was. She was the Hungarian countess who in reality was neither Hungarian nor a countess but a much more exciting combination. Many months later, after the war had started, I wrote an article about the civilised treatment which should be offered to refugees from Hitler's Europe, and she wrote to me. I met her again, and she told me part of her story, and no one in his senses could fail to be captivated. She was a Yugoslav Jewess, a ballet dancer attached to a famous Viennese opera company, beautiful and delicate and fragile, and Beaverbrook had met her when she was dancing in Cannes, and had told her to communicate with him if she was ever in trouble. Thanks to his intervention, she was smuggled out of Vienna a few weeks after Hitler's troops had occupied the city; thanks to his assistance, she had what proved to be a last, fleeting glimpse of her parents on a holiday in Switzerland. Beaverbrook had fallen for her; no possible doubt about that, and one day, just about the time when I was having troubles with Captain Wardell, I wrote, on Beaverbrook's incitement, a full length leading article in the *Daily Express*, not the *Evening Standard*, on the Jewish Feast of Purim, on how Haman was hanged in place of Mordecai, on how the

Nazis would never be able to execute their monstrous programme for the final extermination of the Jews. Readers of the
Express must have rubbed their eyes in some amazement; never
before had the paper shown itself so passionately pro-Jewish.
Readers of the Bible must have rubbed their eyes too, for
although the story was retold, I trust, well-enough and reverently
in the space available, it was the story of Haman and Mordecai
without Esther, a serious, a most unconscionable omission. When
Beaverbrook had recited to each of us, Lili and myself, that Bible
story, Esther had certainly not been overlooked; she is, and was,
and always will be, the heroine. However, the leading article did
serve its purpose. Lili was pleased, and he was pleased, and the
readers of the *Express* could lump it. Thereafter, I took leaves,
whole chapters, from his book, and wrote in the *Evening
Standard* on Jewish themes and Yugoslav themes and sometimes
the two together (we became, at a somewhat later date, enthusiastic supporters of Tito) at every available opportunity and
thereby helped to win her friendship but not her heart. Then
came graver, terrible complications. What happened to Lili's
family and friends in Yugoslavia when it was overrun by the Nazis,
no one could know; the assumption was that they had been
hauled off to Auschwitz. Her home in Yugoslavia was gone;
never to be revisited. She loved Beaverbrook, and he loved her,
but doubtless he could be hard and demanding as well as sensitive,
possessive and wayward by turns, as he was in politics. Her health
broke and the doctors, including the expert Dan Davies,
diagnosed the disease as incurable. She moved from hospital to
hospital, from doctor to doctor, and then finally devised her own
cure. She made her escape from him and lived (and still lives)
happily ever after. She was lovely, zestful, affectionate, independent, inquisitive, a passionate Maccabean upholder of the rights of
the Jewish people, just like Esther. And the best thing I ever knew
about Max Beaverbrook was that Lili Ernst had truly loved him.

To set the chronology straight, I left him about three years
before she did, and I took what I thought was the proper course of
doing it without a row. For two years, since the departure of
Frank Owen for the forces, I had had the enthralling job of
editing the paper which he above all others had created, the war-

time *Evening Standard*, the *Standard* in its very greatest days I naturally contend, although it has had some other great ones since.

The war, as one of its minor by-products, raised the quality of British journalism as a whole and especially London journalism in a manner which has never been properly and collectively acclaimed. For one thing, the profit test, advertising pressures, were overnight tossed out of Fleet Street's bomb-threatened windows, and there prevailed instead a genuine competition of merit to use the precious supplies of newsprint to serve the supreme common interest of the hour. We believed on the *Standard* that we changed to meet the new conditions and caught the new atmosphere better than any rival. For a start, we reported the new kind of war itself more freshly, analysed strategy more contentiously. For this, Frank Owen, an inspired military reporter himself, was chiefly responsible, but he hired a remarkable and strange company to help him. During the pitiful period of the phoney war, Liddell Hart had been the principal military writer on the paper, but his reputation, somewhat unjustly and only temporarily, was knocked through the ropes by the same Nazi tanks which smashed through the Ardennes. By a similar reckoning, Major-General J. F. C. Fuller, the so-called father of the tank, disinherited by the British War Office, saw his reputation suddenly restored. In his bitter frustration, he had even dabbled with Fascism itself, and it would have been easy to outlaw him from our democrat columns on that ground alone. But Frank would tolerate no such nonsense; he knew, and the *Evening Standard* readers came to know, that Fuller was the best professional military writer in the business. Yet Fuller was never '*the* military correspondent of the *Evening Standard*'; *his* identity, much to the fury of the War Office, was itself preserved as a military secret. Either it was Frank himself or it was our newfound independent monitor of the Western war. Down towards Ludgate Circus was a little I. L. P. bookshop where Frank and I made purchases of such essential topical documents as the writings of Leon Trotsky or Tom Wintringham and which was run by a Swiss Socialist called Jon Kimche. He listened to the babel of Europe's battling radio stations in God-knows how many languages, and out of it distilled another original approach to the new kind of war, and a new profession for himself. Another independent voice which caught Frank's ear was Polish. He could not speak much English as yet—although, as Lenin said of Rosa Luxemburg, he already spoke excellent Marxism: his name was Isaac Deutscher, and he lived to write, in English, the best biography of the century. All kinds of degrees of independent persons were drawn to Shoe Lane or to the surrounding consulting rooms. Wilfrid Macartney, author of the prison best seller, *Walls Have Mouths*, having served a sentence in Dartmoor for giving secrets to the Russians, was now happy to discover that he had been assisting our allies all along; he came to propose a series of Second-Front-Aid-to-Russia meetings, to be organised by the front organisation, the Russia Today Society. We agreed, and at the Stoll Theatre the first of the great mass meetings of wartime was held with the following speakers: Aneurin Bevan, Frank Owen, Harry Pollitt, and myself. Harry Pollitt, leader of the Communist Party, removed from that post for his patriotic defection in September 1939, had indeed been a frequent, frustrated, drinking companion of those wretched months; he deeply believed that another kind of opportunity would develop, and so did we. So did a young soldier called Orde Wingate, as frustrated as Harry Pollitt, who much to my amazement sat up through one whole night at Frank's flat in Lincoln's Inn and drank even Frank under the table. He told us how he had trained Jewish boys in Palestine to fight the Arabs at their own guerilla game; how the War Office had never quite favoured his politics or his new notions of partisan war; how he was exiled at that precise moment to some training backwater on Salisbury plain; how he saw the war as one directed by Jehovah-Nemesis and designed to expunge all the wickedness of the appeasement years. The Jews, the Czechs, the Spaniards, the Ethiopians, all would be avenged. He himself intended to walk through the streets of Addis Ababa by the side of Haile Selassie. At five o'clock in the morning, with Frank's last bottle of sparkling Burgundy deflated and dead, all seemed possible—and two years later he did it.

Not everyone attracted by our *Evening Standard* magnet could quite equal that. Seaman Frank came to see us or rather we went in search of him, having heard the ever-memorable broadcast in which he described how he had lost his leg in the world-famous wreck of the *San Demetrio*; how when the torpedo had hit the ship it had made a noise like the opening of the gates of hell; how he had run across 'a gruel of men's bodies', to the life boats; how the shark had taken his leg; how he had made the miraculous return-journey to his native Liverpool. Seaman Frank could talk like that at will; he was soaked in Joseph Conrad, if not the *San Demetrio* waters. I wrote a leading article called 'English Seaman' with many overtones of Froude. For a few weeks we placarded his name all over our delivery vans and even started to remind him how splendid it would be for our sales when he went to sea again. However, a few had had doubts from the beginning, and when we heard that a reporter from the *Evening News* was allegedly being despatched to make some first-hand inquiries in Liverpool, we sent our best reporter, Leslie Randall, on the same trail and to get there first. Seaman Frank had never been nearer to the sea than Birkenhead ferry; he had lost his leg in a tram accident. He *was* an admirer of Conrad, long before Professor Leavis. But we hardly believed that Beaverbrook, for all his special interest, would be concerned with these distinctions, and Seaman Frank was allowed to withdraw quietly from the literary scene.

With or without Seaman Frank's inspiration, we did transform the political tone of the *Evening Standard*. (We also just about overhauled the *Star* in circulation figures for the first time in history.) Some long-standing readers were naturally offended. I had written some editorial which concluded with the claim that 'we are fighting this war to uphold the principles of the French Revolution', whereupon I received the most treasured protest ever to come my way. The writer was Lord Alfred Douglas, the same whose sonnets my father had so justly taught me to revere. Whatever his other delinquencies, Lord Alfred had mastered the form of the sonnet to place him among the masters. This is what he sent in reply to my editorial:

Not by Beelzebub is Satan cast
Out of the mind possessed; darkness abides
Unexorcised by darkness. Who that rides

In Error's dismal train can face the blast
Which Error's self engenders and stand fast?
You challenge Hitler, but your dullness sides
With Hitler's blackness, and plain sense derides
An idol-worshipping iconoclast.
Sinistral sheep, poor mass-suggestioned dupe
Parrot your catchwords, crook your governed knee
Before your goatish god; your little span
Will not endure, and we will never stoop
To make a fetish of Democracy
Or worship at the shrine of Caliban.

Of course, the protest was prominently printed; indeed it supplied the distinction for a regular page of protest on which we encouraged old or new readers to try their hand at invective. Once I had expressed my admiration for his poetry, Lord Alfred and I became pen pals. Another of the sonnets he wrote at this time was dedicated to Winston Churchill, a magnanimous gesture since it was Churchill who had once despatched Lord Alfred to serve a prison sentence for criminal libel. However, we, the sinistral sheep, could not quite follow him there, and, to say all we wished, we looked for other pastures to combine with those which the *Standard* offered.

Another pseudonym provoked a real stir. On 1 May, 1942, *Tribune* started publishing under the title 'Why Churchill?' a series of articles written, so they claimed, by a brilliant and unusually well-informed writer who had adopted the name of Thomas Rainsboro', the Leveller captain in Cromwell's army. No such attack on Churchill himself, no comparable and comprehensive critique of the general war strategy, had been published anywhere in any wartime newspaper before, and quite a number of well-informed readers did accept the general critique. The disguise was successful; Aneurin Bevan or Jon Kimche who was now working full-time for *Tribune* had to carry and share the blame or glory. But, of course, the real author was Frank Owen, then established for his tank training in a barracks near Andover. Once War Office or MI5 agents had accompanied us over most of the country, at our Second Front Campaign meetings, vainly in pursuit of treasonable utterances; but everything said from those

platforms was patriotic to the finger tips, as royal and loyal as the
Russians themselves. But highly well-informed articles on issues
of military strategy, all too redolent of the very criticisms which
were now being uttered in army messes, were another matter. It
was Beaverbrook who gave me the tip. 'When's the next article
due from Frank?' he asked without any preliminary discussion on
the point. 'This week,' I replied. 'You'd better stop it—tonight'.
So I raced off to Andover, scoured the pubs, found Frank, took
the copy off him, started to race back to London, crashed the car
on the humped bridge on the London road outside Andover, and
was taken off for repairs to the nearby Army camp who put me on
the road next morning. It was one of the few occasions when
Frank, the professional journalist, was ever late with his copy, and
one of the few occasions when Beaverbrook probed a little more
closely than he himself, a member of the War Cabinet, might have
thought prudent into those tender relationships between the
Evening Standard and *Tribune*.

However, the wartime *Evening Standard* was concerned also
with more than these mere military matters. I think we did
capture something of the special flavour of what London was like
amid the greatest war for freedom ever fought. The people of
London did truly play an heroic role, and the *Standard* reported
their daily and nightly ardours, gave voice to their protests
against blind or tardy bureaucracy, and endlessly argued about
the way in which the supreme common objective could be
achieved. For London was also the nerve-centre of the whole
world-wide struggle against Nazism, and, for all our love of our
precious city and our precious island, no insular imagination
could express fully the spirit of the age. When officialdom started
the momentary madness of locking up all aliens, many of them to
be counted amongst our most devoted allies, we helped to put a
stop to it with an article: *Why Not Lock Up General de Gaulle?*
When a handful of twentieth-century French revolutionaries
aided our cause by blowing up French battleships in Toulon
harbour, we printed several verses of the *Marseillaise* on the front
page. And when we got the news late one evening that Mussolini
had been overthrown by a handful of brave Italians, we sat up all
night to produce a souvenir edition, telling his whole life story

from the march on Rome to Abyssinia and to Spain, embellished with Low cartoons, and all designed together, to carve him at last as 'a carcase fit for hounds'. I had always had what I presumed to regard as a proprietary interest in the overthrow of Mussolini ever since I had been instructed in the matter by Ignazio Silone in his *School for Dictators*. So I wrote a swift sequel to *Guilty Men* called *The Trial of Mussolini* by Cassius, in which I hoped that the truly Socialist and internationalist issues at stake were properly celebrated. This time any mystery of authorship lasted little more than a few hours, and Beaverbrook with whom I'd been arguing on other political topics made the legitimate point that I could be an editor or a pamphleteer but not both at the same time. And, incidentally, what had happened to the form, circulated in the *Guilty Men* aftermath, requiring all Beaverbrook employees to inform the management about prospective books they had in mind? No I had not signed it; I had put it in the wastepaper basket where indeed, after a suitable interval, we would assign all the awkward messages from the Beaverbrook dictaphone which we hoped would not stir future animosities. There had been trouble, too, about the Beveridge Report about which the *Evening Standard* had secured an excellent scoop and we had stepped in to welcome the document itself. For a while, having left the *Standard* editorship, I was in a ridiculous limbo on the *Daily Express*, and then in June I wrote him a long letter. 'Your views and mine are bound to become more and more irreconcilable. As far as this Socialist business is concerned my views are unshakable. For me it is the Klondyke or bust, and at the moment I am not sure I am going the right way to Klondyke . . .' and much more to the same effect. So I took the offer from an old friend and fellow-Beaverbrook spotter, Percy Cudlipp, to join the *Daily Herald*— whether that Long Acre route was the right way to Klondyke is another matter.

But back to Beaverbrook: during the next few years my association with the old man became bruised almost beyond recognition or repair. Beaverbrook in the distance looked a very much less enchanting figure than he had done at close quarters. All through the period towards the ending of the war, the election of 1945, the overthrow of Churchill, the instalment of the Labour

Government, my own election in Devonport, every public issue seemed likely to inflict fresh wounds on any private feeling which remained. Perhaps also there were jangled jealousies left over from the Lili Ernst days. Many who had worked for Beaverbrook· would devote a considerable part of the rest of their days to his vilification, and perhaps I had started down that same path when I said in a Commons debate on the Royal Commission on the Press, instituted by the Labour Government, that the occupational disease among newspaper proprietors was megalomania. Many a true word is spoken in venom; and yet for me to have wasted much time on that theme in dealing with Beaverbrook would have been dust and ashes.

Providentially, an occasion occurred which set matters aright. Someone invited me to a dinner to celebrate Beaverbrook's seventieth birthday at the Savoy Hotel on 28 April 1948; and the chairman asked me to speak. It was natural to recall the finest hour when he had waited each night for Max's return from the skies where London was saved and when he himself had seemed to be translated into another being. I quoted Milton:

> . . . *with grave*
> *Aspect he rose, and in his rising seemed*
> *A pillar of state; deep on his front engraven*
> *Deliberation sat, and public care;*
> *And princely counsel in his face yet shone,*
> *Majestic, though in ruin: sage he stood,*
> *With Atlantean shoulders, fit to bear*
> *The weight of mightiest monarchies; his look*
> *Drew audience and attention still as night*
> *Or summer's noontide air.*

The diners were properly hushed and impressed, and then I had to remind the ignorant bunch that they were that, of course, those famous lines had been written about Beelzebub. It was a trick purloined straight from my father but I doubt whether he had ever had a more apposite occasion for working it. Beaverbrook was overcome; he sent me next day a touched and touching letter, scrawled in his barely legible hand. Our friendship was renewed, and never collapsed thereafter. Destry rode again.

I think I was as well placed as anyone to see what Beaverbrook did for all of us in those supreme years, and I am prepared to repeat the testimony anywhere and at any time, including the Day of Judgement, where possibly, now the thought occurs, I may have a chance of giving evidence before he does. But at that higher tribunal, I suppose, one would have to be careful about quoting Milton with effect: there it may not so readily be appreciated that Beelzebub had a better side to his nature.

Two other improbable friendships contributed to mine with Beaverbrook. First and foremost, Jill, my wife, knew how to deal with him from the very first meeting, how to awaken and sustain his curiosity, how to keep his eyes on today and tomorrow and not the past, how to appreciate all those human sides of him which the outside world believed not to exist. Mostly Beaverbrook was on uneasy terms with the wives of the journalists who worked for him; he wanted exclusive rights. Many quarrelled with him because of their wives, and some of the wives he preferred were already on bad terms with their husbands. But Jill was one of the very few who knew best how to deal with him in every mood and extremity. And it was with her blessing that I went off one hazardous morning to get £3,000 from him when *Tribune* was faced with extinction in 1951. Without it, we would not have survived and I felt I could argue that the *Express* newspapers had not paid me a penny when I left in June 1944. However, that was really beside the point. At the time no one except Jill knew where the money had come from, but when Alan Taylor was writing Beaverbrook's biography, he wrote me a personal letter as follows, on 6 May 1970:

Here is a little query to take your mind off greater things. You told me that Max gave *Tribune* £3,000 in 1951. I decided to forget it. Now I find from the letters that Max told Robertson to charge this to the *Daily Express* and added: 'What would we do for recruits without *Tribune*?' My rule is everything about Max good or bad. Like all rules it has an exception which I know Max would have approved of: nothing to hurt Mike. So if you ask me to forget it again, I will do. Otherwise I'll put it in. It is for you to decide. A Yes or a No on a postcard is all I want.

I said, and Jill said: 'Put it in', and quite right too.

How deeply corrupted *Tribune* was by Beaverbrook gold is a research-subject not yet completed by the Nuffield School, but one affair, awkward perhaps for their verdict of damnation, ran concurrently with my rapprochement with the old friend and new benefactor. On 2 March 1950, the *Evening Standard* produced a scandalous front page under the headlines 'FUCHS AND STRACHEY: A GREAT NEW CRISIS. War Minister has never disavowed Communism. Now involved in MI5 efficiency probe.' *Tribune* hit back harder than anyone else in Strachey's defence. When I'd written the article, someone in the office suggested the title: 'Prostitutes of the Press.' I thought that too banal and too defamatory, and we therefore substituted what I thought to be the more anodyne, but equally accurate and insulting: 'Lower than Kemsley'—Lord Kemsley, proprietor at that time of the *Daily Sketch* and the *Sunday Times* and held to be in our estimation the criterion of low Tory journalism. Kemsley instituted libel proceedings against us, and the case which dragged on for the next three years, and which could have landed *Tribune* and myself and all my fellow directors in the bankruptcy court, had many legal and political aspects of lasting fascination. Eventually the cause of Right prevailed—and in the House of Lords of all places. There for five long days our fate was in the balance while lawyers argued, the costs mounted and the Lord Chief Justice, Lord Goddard (who happened to be the victim of another of *Tribune's* onslaughts in the very same issue of the paper where the alleged defamation had occurred), probed and ransacked the mysteries of libel precedent. But there were no precedents; so the point had much significance for others besides ourselves. To plead 'fair comment' in a libel action it is necessary that the facts on which the comment is based should be 'truly stated'. In the offending *Tribune* article, *Tribune* with its customary respect for the quick awareness of its readers, had stated none of the facts on which the comment was based. Was the defence of 'fair comment' still available to us? The Master in Chambers said 'No'. The court of Appeal said 'Yes'. Eventually, the House of Lords agreed with the learned legal interpretation reached without all that expense in *Tribune's* office three years before.

Beaverbrook followed each twist and turn in the affair with his customary solicitude. He was not at all eager to see his secret £3,000 finish up in Lord Kemsley's clutches. As a journalist, he was on *Tribune*'s side in the fight to prevent any tightening of the libel laws. And behind the scenes too, although in deference to his existing editors he would not admit as much to me, he believed the original *Evening Standard* headline was an outrage and a blunder. The editor concerned did not last long thereafter.

Thus, absurdly in a sense, the 'Lower than Kemsley' episode proved more of a new bond between us than anything else. However, that the *Standard* of all papers should have indulged in such scurrility-cum-hysteria gives a forgotten hint about the political climate of the time. It was the age of the spy scares, of Burgess and Maclean, of the renewed cold war, of the sudden mounting fear, on both sides of the Atlantic, that it might break out into a hot one. Beaverbrook, whatever his paper might say in public, never surrendered to the hysteria in private. One evening he was somehow stirred into describing to the astonished company how the cold war had started, or rather how the Russians might reasonably imagine it had started, and he went back to the fateful months of 1945 and 1946, and recited the individual events of the time in a novel sequence. It was not his verdict on the whole business; it was his imaginative flight, assisted by a considerable quantity of hard fact, to see how his old wartime associate Stalin and the others in the Kremlin might intelligently view the scene. The dinner party was overwhelmed. Some Canadian banker or American newspaper proprietor, sitting next to Jill, muttered under his breath 'He's a Commie!' It was the first time Jill had seen his imaginative side in action; and that formed one part of the quality which had made Arnold Bennett say he was the best dramatic raconteur he ever heard.

One other scene of corruption at the hands of the old man cannot be omitted from the record. Round about the year 1954 we had to leave our house in Rosslyn Hill, Hampstead, in a hurry since the ecclesiastical Commissioners who owned the place would not renew the lease on acceptable terms. For about six months on end, we were gipsies, driving around in two cars, one which took Jill to her work and the other which took me. We cadged odd nights off friends while we looked for a new house, and one day Beaverbrook, hearing of our plight, rang up to say that he could offer us a roof for our heads; he had especial sympathy for refugees from the English Church. So we turned up at Cherkley in the late afternoon, supposing we had been offered a bed for the night. Instead we were taken on a tour of four derelict cottages on his estate, each more dilapidated than the other and none of them conceivably habitable on the spot. His eye normally so observant, was averted from our car-cum-caravan; the procession plunged deeper across the fields and darkness descended. 'Well, choose which you like', he said, and 'let me know', and he waved us goodbye. We hastened off that night to find a bed at the house of Curly and Rita Mallalieu where we asked to stay for one night and in fact stayed for six months. But the picture of Paddock Cottage, stuck in the middle of one of the Cherkley fields, stuck in our minds too and, more especially, in Jill's imagination. She could see what it could be and what she could make of it. But there was also the moral question, if indeed, as it seemed, he was offering us it on a peppercorn rent? We consulted Aneurin Bevan and he replied: 'It isn't what you take, it's what you give.' And Jill consulted my father whom she justly regarded as an expert on such questions. Anyhow, with his blessing, she took the whole project in hand, painted the cottage white, introduced calor gas, and made it into a marvellously convenient hide-out for a writer. Both the old man and young Max to whom great stretches of the estate had been handed over marvelled at the transformation. Max promptly decided to follow Jill's example with the other cottages, and when the old man died, told us we could keep it as long as we wanted, but Jill was already working a similar miracle with an old miners' cottage in Tredegar; so Paddock Cottage was handed back to the Cherkley estate. It had only had one snag. Remote from the road and most other signs of human association, there was however a path nearby which led soon to the neighbouring Rowton House. When we were absent, the temptation for the Rowton House population to have a night out in the cottage was overpowering. The police could never track them. The visits became so frequent that we almost had a sense of communal living. And the real risk was fire; not all our visitors had made themselves experts in dealing with the calor gas apparatus. On a winter's night they were inclined to use the furniture for firewood. Jill feared she might have to confront Max one morning with the old greeting from the P. G. Wodehouse story: 'I fear you're a cottage short, old boy.'

Alan Taylor's friendship was the other unlikely one which shaped and enlivened Beaverbrook's life in the last decade, and it all started because Alan read Beaverbrook's books with fresh eyes. His style, in any case, had a kinship with Alan Taylor's own; the taste of the two men for brevity, clarity and mischief was similar. But Alan also set aside the preconceived assumption that Beaverbrook must be a second-rate journalist writing for the hour or the day or for the immediate sensation. He wrote a review in the *Observer* in which, incredibly in the light of all previous academic judgements, he compared Beaverbrook with Tacitus.

I was present in the room when he read that review, and his life took on a new exhilaration. He had truly always been most modest about his own writings, never expecting to be regarded as anything more than a chronicler, the good teller of a tale which he knew himself to be and had every right to accept as a fair assessment. As for the comparison with Tacitus, utterly flattering as he believed it was, it meant that a new world and a new friendship had opened before him. Alan Taylor became his intimate confidante on all these questions, his biographer and his friend indeed. Certainly the public judgement on Beaverbrook as a writer was revolutionised by that single verdict. Not all his writings, of course, are in any sense in the same class. Most of them were sheer journalism, good or bad. But the three or four main books on politics *are* masterpieces of political writing, and it took Alan Taylor's discernment to make the discovery in full measure. Moreover, as with Taylor's own style, there are no adventitious aids to conceal the quality. Dubieties are made as hard as diamonds. The high, bold, bald claims can be put to the test; he is never seeking to dodge or prevaricate. Beaverbrook, the historian, is always giving the evidence, if it is there, against his own pre-conception, against his own Party, even against his own heroes. Who could ever have believed that he of all people would have assumed the mantle of historian? Yet, it is true, and, in the case of his Conservative Party, he plays the part with a special relish and glee.

It is there, to his humour, we must always return. 'If Max gets to heaven', wrote H. G. Wells, 'he won't last long. He'll be chucked out for trying to pull off a merger between Heaven and Hell . . . after having secured a controlling interest in key subsidiary companies in both places, of course.' But the merger had already taken place under his roof; a mixture of Heaven and Hell was what it could be like but, after some moments of Miltonic doubt about the outcome, it was usually heaven which triumphed in that combat, and a heaven too which no Calvinist could recognise, one which was always liable to dissolve in laughter. Even at the gravest moment the chance of such a beneficent explosion would reappear, and the House of Rimmon might resound to the healing strains of *The Red Flag*, led, say, by another companion treasured for his company alone, Stanley Morison of *The Times*, ex-jailbird, ex-pacifist, militant Catholic, and, as far as I can recall, a light baritone. 'Stanley,' said Beaverbrook, 'does not make the mistake of pouring old wine into new bottles. If the wine is old and really good, he has another use for it.' Truly, it was his humour which had a special all-encompassing dimension. This was more part of him, I believe, even than the ceaseless energy with which he could whip everyone in sight, the furious yet fitful zeal for the great causes and the others, strange and terrible, in which he believed. Not all the paroxysms of anger, of urgency, of frustration could shake those walls as the laughter did, and there was in it no vein of pretence or hysteria but rather a rich comic view of the human species. It could be called Dickensian or Chaplinesque were it not for the fact that Dickens and Chaplin, along with the Co-op or Covent Garden or the British Council, were listed among his absurd *bêtes noires*, and were it not that he lacked the last full measure of compassion which only the greatest comedians have. Anyhow, Beaverbrook's was a volcano of laughter which went on erupting till the end. No one who ever lodged for a while beneath that Vesuvius will ever forget.

FIVE

Hyde Park Sceptic

England must remember that the Keltic fringe has been a
bulwark of gay and lively steel around these islands.

SEAN O'CASEY

OF ALL THE SIGHTS and sounds which attracted me on my first
arrival to live in London in the mid-thirties, one combined
operation left a lingering, individual spell. I naturally went to
Hyde Park to hear the orators, the best of the many free
entertainments on offer in the capital. I heard the purest milk of
the word flowing, then as now, from the platform of the Socialist
Party of Great Britain. I heard at the May Day meetings some of
the old masters, not at their greatest but still magical in their
presence and presentation—Ben Tillett, Tom Mann, George
Lansbury, Jimmy Maxton. I heard a striking and handsome
young Methodist preacher who insisted on dressing in a strange
costume which my father would have doubtless described as
Popish but who advocated Socialism and pacifism in ever-fluent
classical English; my mother was the one who urged that I should
hear Donald Soper, hoping, and I'm sure praying, that he might
be the divine agent to reconvert me, via Socialism, to the family
creed. I heard the whole range of religious crusaders, including
the unsuccessful pugilist who had taken to evangelism; pug-
nosed, black-eyed and cauliflower-eared, he was still singing:
'Jesus wants me for a sunbeam'. However, in defiance of all my
mother's prayers, I heard, most potent and perilous of all, Bonar
Thompson, the one-man satirist of the universe, this world and
the next.

I quickly became an addict. Twice or thrice every Sunday,
weather permitting, he gave his review of what had happened the

week before. He knew what had passed or been perpetrated in Buckingham Palace, the Cabinet, the Kremlin, the Vatican, and the Stock Exchange, and he didn't think much of it. All the stridencies of the thirties were at their highest pitch, and all the religious wars, for a start, were being refought across the same ground in Hyde Park. Bonar Thompson's scepticism was, I suppose, the sanest thing in the land. Certainly he was the most innocent citizen of the whole metropolis; he never did anybody any harm and did nameless, countless multitudes plenty of good.

I learnt from him much useful or, better still, useless knowledge which, as they say, stood me in good stead ever after. I learnt, for example, the secret of Anthony Eden; it was not so easy to spot then. He was, said Bonar Thompson, 'the best advertisement the Fifty Shilling Tailors ever had'. I learnt an elementary suspicion of policemen, particularly the plain clothes type. 'By their boots ye shall know them', Bonar would gravely announce from the platform, and the whole audience would automatically look down at their feet and at their neighbour's feet too, much to the embarrassment of the few plain clothes spectators who naturally preferred his platform to all others. I learnt some other knowledge quite unavailable elsewhere: 'On the London buses a notice says *Spitting Prohibited: Penalty 40/-*. In the British Museum a notice says *Spitting Prohibited: penalty 20/-*. What's the moral? If you must spit, spit in the British Museum.'

Bonar Thompson was, of course, an anarchist, although even this most honourable title gives too feeble an indication of his comprehensive iconoclasm. Freedom meant more to him than to anyone else I ever met; a kind of added dimension. He had talents enough to have gained an agreeable income as an actor or a writer; but the very idea of any form of regular employment offended his heart and soul. He would not soil his hands or his faith with actual work. He had had nothing whatever to do with authority ever since, as he told us, he had refused to join the Army in the First World War because he wasn't approached in the right manner. Yet his attitude, his whole life-story, had a quality more all-embracing than anything suggested by the customary revolt of the young against authority, military or civil. He loved the good things of life: food, drink, love-making, the countryside, waywardness, ease; above all, the theatre, literature, the English language. Yet he would sacrifice any and all of these delights in the last extremity, to preserve his precious independence, or, perhaps it might be truer to say, to preserve his right to make the enjoyment of literature literally a full-time occupation. He knew Shakespeare and Dickens and Yeats and Sean O'Casey and a few others besides, as well as any man ever knew them. It was from him that I learnt that the fellow called Yeats, of whom I'd never heard, was destined to be the poet of the century. He could extract from all these favourites a pleasure which was sensual as much as artistic; he could not waste time on trivialities or diversions, or so he appeared, at the height of his powers, in the thirties and the early forties. His immaculate independence and all its outward manifestations were glories to behold. Yet the means by which it was established and sustained surely make the achievement the more remarkable.

He wrote an autobiography, *Hyde Park Orator*, which unfortunately did injury to his reputation, since running through it was a strand of sourness quite uncharacteristic of the public or, indeed, the private man. Sean O'Casey, the most generous of comrades, felt obliged to remark upon these political and other delinquencies in his preface; rarely has a book been presented to the world under such damning auspices, and Sean O'Casey had an excuse; repeatedly in those pages the author reveals a spleen, especially against political enemies in the mass, which he rarely showed in real life and never against individuals. Yet the book's inherent virtues should surely have been sufficient to subdue all such criticisms from O'Casey or anyone else. The bareness of the combined effect of poverty and Puritanism in the Ulster where he was born is there for all to see and feel; the road from the glens of Antrim is more sharply marked than Orwell's road to Wigan Pier. Indeed, the poverty of Edwardian Ireland and Edwardian England, Edwardian Manchester and Edwardian London, was, as Bonar Thompson knew, in his own aching bones and bleeding feet, a physical pain for multitudes of our people which by comparison even the thirties never experienced.

Bonar's humour was a triumph of the human spirit over all these conditions. It was not part of some indictment against him, as several of his humourless ex-comrades alleged; it was rather part of the counter-attack against the capitalist system. Bonar Thompson could at least boast—how many other Socialist propagandists could say the same?—that he had never helped to sustain that system with so much as a single movement of his hand or finger. To that particular article of his faith he never found it too difficult to remain true. But he had other tests and trials, and some of them were traceable to the overflowing appearance of good nature which he brought along with all the horrific memories of Ulster and of the north and industrial England.

'Good God!' he once wrote to me when quite unconsciously I had apologised for not having replied to some earlier letter. 'Good God! The most exemplary heaping of coals of fire on an offender's head I have ever known in the course of a long-suffering career of default and procrastination by land, sea and air! It is an open secret that I am not only an habitual and inveterate procrastinator but a confirmed and case-hardened prognosticator as well.' But how he suffered:

> My appearance and manner are deceptive in every way. I generally look in good health and the truth is I'm nearly always very far from well. I look fairly prosperous and am almost always on the verge of destitution, and often over the precipice into the deep abysses of penury. I look stout and even plump as a rule and am a walking skeleton . . . As to age, I looked about thirty-five until recently, while actually I have been an old man tottering towards senility for over five years . . . And then I appear to be a merry fellow when in reality I'm a melancholy brooder on death and the meaningless futility of life. I could furnish a fuller list of ironical contradictions, tending to prove me the most deceptive entity now extant upon the surface of this strange and tragic planet. Arrogant and bombastic on the platform and in private the most hopeless embodiment of diffidence, timidity and self-obliterating nullity it has ever been my misfortune to meet. A robust invalid who has been masquerading for years as a living being when actually a member of that grey company of human simulacra that I've made fun of so often in days gone by—the Unburied Dead . . . In justice to myself it is only fair to say that all this is no more than 20 per cent my fault. My birth was a *faux-pas*, the tragedy, not of being born *out of wedlock* but being born *out of*

pocket. My continued stay in the world has been a lamentable solecism and the whole affair a regrettable lapse on the part of Fortuity.

(You may not know that word existed, but he knew) . . . And then, after much more he added, a typical postscript:

> If you see Frank Horrabin, please give him my kind regards. He flabbergasted me when he spoke at the Conway Hall last winter. I had dropped in to hear him speaking on Socialism and Art. Suddenly and without having given me notice of the question he launched into a glowing tribute to my acting in *St. Joan.* He had seen me in the play at Brighton in the summer. Naturally I demanded an apology for his daring to find merit in a performance where I had never been able to detect any myself. A good chap—and speaking more seriously—a penetrating and illuminating critic of the art of acting, for I can say in all humility that my performance in *St. Joan* was a *tour-de-force,* worthy of Edmund Kean at his very best. *Bon Voyage*, as Sam Goldwyn would say.

How many times did he pick himself up from the dust so bravely, and stagger to his feet and to his own independent pulpit in Hyde Park. There, for most of his years, instead of genuinely seeking work, he made collections from his fans and cheerfully condemned those who listened without paying to an endless, excruciating inferno of his own making. He did not believe in an after-life, but for those who habitually offended in respect of the collection he was prepared to make an exception. Then, at one stage in his career, bumbledum contrived the by-law—no collections within the Hyde Park gates, a piece of gratuitous tyranny if ever there was one. Bonar Thompson bore it all with the sweetest of smiles, and he managed to convert this blow to his fortunes into the most admired of all his perorations. Though he preached no cause, though he offered no remedy, though he would countenance no hint of a conceivable improvement in the human condition here or, more especially, hereafter, yet he was still persuaded that his vast heaving audience, the most upright and farseeing which he had ever seen assembled in his long memory of the Park's history, would march, shoulder to shoulder, twenty abreast if need be, in one mighty all-conquering phalanx, TO THE GATES—in such accents had the people of Paris been roused by the *ça ira* and sent to storm the Bastille. There, outside the gates, beyond the eye of any prying policeman and beyond the range of their thumping boots, where authority could still be successfully defied, he would be prepared to discuss in the strictest confidence with any curious client either the Swedish banking system or the likely fall in the value of the rupee or any other convenient financial topic 'under the blue canopy of heaven'. All the accumulated knowledge of the House of Rothschild would be at the disposal of the favoured few, the tramping masses, who would march with him, 'to the great rosy dawn', TO THE GATES, to death or glory.

As it happened, he lived, rickety and rosy to the end, to the age of seventy-five and died, as he was born, out of pocket. He himself once wrote: 'Most people, says a brilliant writer, are other people. I have never had any difficulty in remaining myself.' It had not been quite as easy as that; all manner of circumstances combined to prevent him from succeeding. But he did seem to create himself more than any other human specimen, and in the process he became the best one-man act London ever saw in his own time at least, a priceless piece of England's endless loot from across the Irish sea.

SIX

Philosopher-Englishman

'He was a warm friend, not to liberty merely, but to English liberty.'

LORD JOHN RUSSELL, grandfather of Bertrand Russell, writing of his ancestor, William Lord Russell, executed by Charles II on 21, July 1683.

MY FIRST INTRODUCTION TO Bertrand Russell occurred when someone at Oxford gave me a copy of his book, *The Conquest of Happiness*. Then, a few weeks later, he turned up in person for a University meeting of some sort, spreading his own special blend of wit and wisdom and beaming with happiness. Who could resist so radiant a practitioner of his own theories?

I reread that volume recently, exactly fifty years after its first publication, and, amid the modern Muggeridgean gloom, it is a light from another world. Bertrand Russell himself acknowledged that the light of nature shone more brightly in a past age, and in almost everything he ever wrote he strove to recover that particular translucent quality. It is the liberal glow of the eighteenth-century enlightenment which he transmuted into twentieth-century terms more intrepidly than anyone else: the spirit which Thomas Jefferson, with the assistance of Thomas Paine, instilled into the American Declaration of Independence, and which provoked Saint-Just, the twenty-four year old French revolutionary, to declare: 'Happiness is a new idea in Europe.' But it is Bertrand Russell who gave, and can still give, to the word its special English accent. *The Conquest of Happiness* itself was little more than a footnote to his larger philosophical theses, a practical manual not merely worth reading but ready for immediate application in everyday life. It works; contrary to Shakespeare's verdict, here at last a philosopher had appeared who could cure the toothache or at least the slightly less formidable ailments with which psychoanalysts claim to contend.

However, both before and after that little textbook was published, the conquest was carried into many other territories, by taunts, witticisms, light-hearted forays and full-scale philosophical assaults. 'Really high-minded people', he said, 'are indifferent to happiness, especially other people's.' Or again, 'If you wish to be happy yourself, you must resign yourself to seeing others also happy.' Or more aggressively:

There have been morbid miseries fostered by gloomy creeds, which have led men into profound inner discords that made all outward prosperity of no avail. All these are unnecessary. In regard to all of them, means are known by which they can be overcome. In the modern world, if communities are unhappy, it is because they choose to be so. Or, to speak more precisely, because they have ignorances, habits, beliefs, and passions, which are dearer to them than happiness or even life. I find many men in our dangerous age who seem to be in love with misery and death, and who grow angry when hopes are suggested to them.

That is an extract from *Portraits from Memory*, published nearly thirty years after *The Conquest of Happiness*. It was not, heaven forgive us for even mentioning the term in such a connection, the consistency of a feeble mind. It was all part of the spacious liberating doctrine of one who—more than any great man of his century, as I shall try to hint later—never sought to dodge the realities, bitter, tragic or whatever else they might be, which most directly challenged his creed. He could after all put Malcolm Muggeridgism or Christopher Bookerism or Bernard Levinism or whatever label may be attached to the latest outbursts of mystical reaction in some perspective. He wrote in that same *Portraits from Memory*:

For over two thousand years it has been the custom among earnest moralists to decry happiness as something degraded and unworthy. The Stoics, for centuries, attacked Epicurus who preached happiness;

they said that his was a pig's philosophy, and showed their superior virtue by inventing scandalous lies about him. One of them, Cleanthes, wanted Aristarchus persecuted for advocating the Copernican system of astronomy; another, Marcus Aurelius, persecuted the Christians; one of the most famous of them, Seneca, abetted Nero's abominations, amassed a vast fortune, and lent money to Boadicea at such an exorbitant rate of interest that she was driven into rebellion.

Our English Epicurus was the target, throughout most of his life, of lies hardly less scandalous, but fortunately he devised for himself a shield which will never be penetrated. He translated the word freedom from Greek and Roman and any other language into the purest English, or rather he saw how the English people and so many English writers had been engaged in this work before him, and not merely those directly in the liberal or revolutionary tradition but, hardly less, men like Francis Bacon, Thomas Hobbes, David Hume; all these too are enfolded into the great Bertrand Russell synthesis and help to make that shield irrefragable.

One part of the debt, his and ours, must be accorded to an English phenomenon, the Whig aristocracy which somehow made a most appealing virtue of not caring a damn for anybody. Hard, self-centred, materialist, pleasure-loving, it still offered, against all the odds, and in contra-distinction to what was happening in almost every other country at the time, the essential protection for scepticism and the thought of the future. Bertrand Russell was born into the bosom of it and never wanted to disown his heritage although he came to appreciate its insufficiency. Daring and eccentric thought was encouraged at his fearless old grandmother's knee. 'Thou shalt not follow a multitude to do evil' was her favourite text. At the age of two, young Bertie rebuked a garrulous Robert Browning: 'I do wish that man would stop talking.' And the famous poet did. He could remember his grandfather recalling a visit to Napoleon in exile on Elba and a niece of Talleyrand giving him chocolates. He went to church with Sir Charles Dilke and often wondered what the Liberal statesman's thought must have been when he heard the Seventh Commandment. He shook hands with Parnell and Michael

Davitt, and recollected, still with a tremor, how the hawk's eye of Mr. Gladstone had quelled even his formidable grandparents. He wrote a loving essay on that grandfather, one which can help us to understand better than the historians why Lord John Russell had such a hold on the affections of his countrymen, yet the essay too, has its hints of criticism.

> My grandfather belonged to a type which is now extinct, the type of the aristocratic reformer whose zeal is derived from the classics, from Demosthenes and Tacitus, rather than from any more recent source. They worshipped a goddess called Liberty, but her lineaments were rather vague.

But was that quite fair to one who, after the true English style, battled for so many particular liberties? Moreover, Lord John Russell was more fascinated by the name and superscription of his ancestor Lord William Russell than by any Roman—the same of whom Bertrand Russell wrote: 'Of remote ancestors I can only discover one who did not live to a great age, and he died of a disease which is now rare, namely, having his head cut off.' No other family in English history can claim to have worshipped the Whig goddess so long and so nobly, and in the process they reshaped her limbs to match the modern age.

But it was not achieved, in Bertie's own case, without much pain and trial. Due perhaps to the death of his mother and father in his infancy, he was inexpressibly lonely and shy and awkward. He was blessed or cursed by a Puritan soul, weighed down by a sense of sin and the wickedness of sex. To achieve his own liberation from this encircling darkness was a Herculean labour, and doubtless this is the reason why in his books he could so well strike off the chains of others. But the feat in his own case was accomplished by the most original means. His introduction to Euclid—at the age of eleven—was 'one of the great events in my life, as dazzling as first love'. He rejected suicide 'because I wished to know more of mathematics'. And scarcely less excruciating was the story of the young man who fell disastrously in love with the Quaker girl, who thought sex was not merely wicked but beastly: the two condemned by the general ignorance of the time

to endure the most haunting Victorian terrors. Poor Bertie had
indeed to find his own way to the conquest of each particular
happiness—even drink:

> I did not take to drink until the king took the pledge during the first
> war. His motive was to facilitate the killing of Germans, and it
> therefore seemed as if there must be some connection between
> pacifism and alcohol.

As usual, he saw the comedy of his situation, but he could,
without histrionics, be truly noble too.

The picture of what Bertrand Russell meant to those, young
and old, who refused to fight in the 1914–1918 war is presented
best of all by Lytton Strachey. Lord Russell, on the scaffold in
1683, could not offer a braver example:

> Bertie's lectures help one. They are a wonderful solace and refresh-
> ment. One hangs upon his words, and looks forward to them from
> week to week, and I can't bear the idea of missing one. I dragged
> myself to that ghastly Caxton Hall yesterday . . . It is splendid the
> way he sticks at nothing—governments, religions, laws, property,
> even Good Form itself—down they go like ninepins—it is a charming
> sight! And then his constructive ideas are very grand; one feels one
> has always thought something like that—but vaguely and incon-
> clusively; and he puts it all together and builds it up, and plants it
> down solid and shining before one's mind. I don't believe there's
> anyone quite so formidable to be found just now upon this
> earth.

That was in February 1916. Throughout that war, he hurled his
whole fragile frame against established institutions until, happily,
they put him safely behind bars and lifted the anxiety that he
might not be resisting ardently enough. ('Prison has some of the
advantages of the Catholic Church.')

Yet if any might consider that his finest hour, a finer one
quickly followed. The months which marked the ending of that
war and the year or two which followed were among the most
tumultuous and seminal in the history of modern Socialism. They

were the years of the Russian revolution, of a moment of European opportunity which was lost, of a moment for England too. Bertrand Russell wrote in March 1918, while the tumult was all around him, a book, *Roads to Freedom*, which showed how deep were the sources of his democratic Socialism, how much he respected the Marxist tradition but how much he feared and hated its totalitarian potentialities. What other Socialist, writing at that hour, could so readily and appositely see his books republished today? And it was not merely his deliberate, published works. 'I am troubled at every moment by fundamental questions, the terrible, insoluble questions that wise men never ask'—so he wrote from Petrograd in May 1920, but the place and time could be endlessly multiplied. He was always ready to pose the truly awkward dilemmas, and time and again he swam against the stream, risked reputation and livelihood to state and act upon his arduously-discovered opinions. Few figures in history can match his persistent intellectual courage. He was the twentieth-century Voltaire, and one, moreover, who never bowed to any power and principality whatever. Here again, just to select one glance from a hundred equally penetrating, is his 1920 view of the world, on the eve of his departure for revolutionary Russia. How freshly the words still read; how closely interwoven his story appears to be with that of the human race itself:

Reason and emotion fight a deadly war within me, and leave me no energy for outward action. I know that no good thing is achieved without fighting, without ruthlessness and organisation and discipline. I know that for collective action the individual must be turned into a machine. But in these things, though my reason may force me to believe them, I can find no inspiration. It is the individual human soul that I love—in its loneliness, its hopes and fears, its quick impulses and sudden devotions. It is such a long journey from this to armies and states and officials, and yet it is only by making this long journey that one can avoid a useless sentimentalism.

That was Bertrand Russell in 1920; he kept his balance, amid all the storms that blew. Thanks to his scepticism about the Soviet revolution, thanks to his boldness in declaring his doubts, it might have been expected that the Establishment would rush to embrace him. But no; he was more untouchable than ever. For it was during the twenties and early thirties that he expounded his views on marriage and morals in a manner which outraged Christian and kindred orthodoxies. He did it with a ferocious deliberation. Nothing angered him more than the way the English law or legal system seemed to operate. Books about sex which could be understood only by the middle or upper classes were not prosecuted; books about sex, which could be understood by working people and which might spare them endless, needless misery, were to be tracked down and suppressed by policemen who did not know what they were doing and magistrates and legislators who presumably did. *Marriage and Morals*, published in 1929, contained pages of divine, or rather, I suppose we should better call it, human, fury. It was written in a language every single word of which could be understood by everybody; it is, I suppose, the book which more than any other opened the gates to the truly liberating aspects of the permissive age which came two or three generations later. He said what others said, but he said it more gaily, more mercilessly, as well as more clearly. I once wrote to him, as editor of *Tribune*, asking him to review a book on the subject and received in reply this treasure:

Dear Michael Foot,
I have read the document on Sexual Offenders and Social Punishment with great interest and surprised approval. I should be very glad if homosexuality between adults ceased to be a crime, and if I thought that I could hasten reform in this matter by expressing approval of the report, I would certainly do so. But, in view of the fact that I have been judicially pronounced 'lewd, lecherous, lascivious and obscene', I fear that my support might do more harm than good. The comment on my book *Marriage and Morals* which is made in the report concerns only sacred prostitution in antiquity, and does not seem to me sufficiently important to need a reply.
Yours sincerely,
Russell.

But let me set beside that masterpiece another burst of astringency. Just after that visit to Oxford recorded earlier I was engaged in organising an all-party anti-Nazi demonstration, and received the following from the Deudraeth Castle Hotel, in North Wales, on 14 November 1933:

> I am sorry to inconvenience you in arranging your meeting, but I can't speak with Pollitt. I was at an anti-Fascist meeting in London when, after Ellen Wilkinson had shown implements of torture used by the Nazis, Pollitt made a speech saying 'we' would do all the same things to them when 'our' turn came. One was forced to consider that if he had his way he would be just as bad as they are. I know and admire Toller, and I know Pollitt.
> Yours very truly.

The reference to judicial proceedings was to the New York Court where the pronouncement of prosecuting counsel was indeed even more elaborate than this letter records. He called Russell's writings as a whole 'lecherous, libidinous, lustful, venereous, erotomaniac, aphrodisiac, irreverent, narrowminded, untruthful, and bereft of moral fibre', to which Russell modestly retorted that the point was somewhat simpler. 'It is', he said, 'the principle of free speech. It appears to be little known. If therefore anyone should require any further information about it I refer him to the United States Constitution and to the works of the founders thereof.' No one was better qualified than himself to make that reference, and especially to Thomas Jefferson, the nearest thing to an English Whig who had ever held high office beyond our English shores, one qualified to take his place at the side of the Russells and one of whom Bertrand Russell had taken the precaution of writing a suitable encomium.

Sometimes friends would plead with the philosopher-Englishman to return to the academic studies from which he had been expelled by universities on both sides of the Atlantic. 'The fact is', he replied once, 'I am too busy to have any ideas worth having, like Mrs. Eddy who told a friend of mine that she was too busy to become the second incarnation.' Or he would offer his view on philosophers generally and their chronic timidity, or their particular vices—'I disapprove of Plato because he wanted to prohibit all music except Rule Britannia and The British

Grenadiers. Moreover, he invented the Pecksniffian style of *The Times* leading articles.' At that, one can perhaps hear from many quarters the rising mutter of protest against the 1914 pacifist, the 1940 emigré, the father of our permissive, decadent society, the friend of every country but his own, the scoffer at every British institution, not to mention still more heavenly bodies. How swiftly the features can be twisted to fit the caricature which made him so often the butt of respectable, diehard xenophobic fury. But how sure, if unexpected, was his own answer to all such slanders. 'Love of England is very nearly the strongest emotion I possess . . . the history of England for the last four hundred years is in my blood . . . I simply cannot bear to think that England is entering on its autumn of life—it is too much anguish . . .' It was in such a mood that he returned to England having barely survived years of suffocating exile in the United States. Not merely did he rejoice in the feeling of home; not merely was it agreeable no longer to be treated as a malefactor. Not so long afterwards, honours were on the way, and the only one worth having and probably the only one he would ever have accepted. Thanks to his opposition to communism, maybe, or thanks to some ill-advised but much-misinterpreted words about dropping the atom-bomb on Russia, the English Establishment felt the time had come to fold this eighty-year old rebel to its bosom. Anyhow, a scene of matchless combined irony and comedy followed. Bertrand Russell went to Buckingham Palace to receive the Order of Merit from an affable but somewhat embarrassed George VI. How could the King behave towards 'so queer a fellow, a convict to boot'? In fact, he remarked: 'You have sometimes behaved in a way which would not do if generally adopted.' The instant reply which sprang to Russell's mind was: 'Like your brother.' But he refrained from uttering the words and was always glad that he did so. Instead, knowing that the King must be referring to such matters as his record as a conscientious objector and feeling that the remark could not be left to pass in silence, he said: 'How a man should behave depends upon his profession. A postman, for instance, should knock at all the doors in a street at which he has letters to deliver, but if anyone else knocked on all doors, he would be considered a public nuisance.' It is not clear whether the point was appreciated and, in any case, everyone probably thought that Bertrand Russell's 'public nuisance' days were over. Receiving a Nobel Prize to set alongside his OM, he himself felt the onset of an incipient mellow orthodoxy. 'I have always held that no one can be respectable without being wicked, but so blunted was my moral sense that I could not see in what way I had sinned.'

But in fact he was just stopping to get his iconoclastic breath back in the exhilarating English air. Ahead of him was another lifetime, another marriage, nearly two more decades of campaigning in which he would become the great prophet of the nuclear age, with his gospel that life and joy are better than dusty death. I had the good luck to be present at the meeting in Canon Collins' home in 2 Amen Court when the effective decision which launched the Campaign for Nuclear Disarmament was taken. Bertrand Russell and J. B. Priestley were the two men who above all others gave to the movement its imaginative appeal, its passionate impetus, its intellectual distinction and force. Russell himself had not come to the meeting prepared to advocate a British *unilateral* repudiation of nuclear weapons. He had just written a most powerful declaration—*Commonsense about Nuclear Weapons*—which advocated multi-national nuclear disarmament as the only safe and proper course for mankind as a whole, but he had also just written a scarcely less powerful article which condemned the British bomb as 'a frivolous exercise in national prestige'. It was the decision to demand *unilateral* action by Britain which gave to the Campaign its originality, its fire, its inspiration. Gradually at that meeting, he concurred with the majority opinion, and became the most passionate advocate of the lot. In that very same year when he staked the prestige of his life afresh in such a cause, the Bishop of Rochester was telling him how, in his book *Marriage and Morals*, 'the cloven hoof of the lecher cannot be disguised; it is lechery that has been your Achilles heel'. Things were back to normal.

Of course the old man was not deterred. He was not cowed by the epoch of the cold war when freedom came to be thought of as weakness, and tolerance was compelled to wear the garb of treachery. He continued to rephrase his old liberal creed in a new idiom:

> There are certain things that an age needs, and certain things that it should avoid. It needs compassion and a wish that mankind should be happy; it needs the desire for knowledge and the determination to eschew pleasant myths; it needs, above all, courageous hope and the impulse to creativeness. The things that it must avoid and that have brought it to the brink of catastrophe are cruelty, envy, greed, competitiveness, search for irrational subjective certainty, and what Freudians call the death wish.

Occasionally he did despair and would announce his shame at belonging to the species *Homo Sapiens*, and yet it was at those moments in particular, surely, that his English pride, his love of England's literature, history, language and beauty helped him to recover; helped him to proclaim at the end of his autobiography, one of the truly great autobiographies of all time: 'These things I believe, and the world, for all its terrors, has left me unshaken.'

He became one of the chief glories of our nation and people, and I defy anyone who loves the English language and the English heritage to think of him without a glow of patriotism. The world-famous philosopher, the international publicist, the critic of all principalities and powers, the incorrigible dissenter, the foremost sceptic and exponent of free thought throughout the last half-dozen decades was English to the core, as uniquely English as the free-thinking Whiggery in which he was reared and against whose complacencies and limitations he revolted.

Yet the old Whig or the young Whig, whichever he was, should not quite have the last word. One of his last writings was an article which appeared in *The Times* a few days before men landed on the moon. He argued the issue of whether it was right and intelligent for us to seek to do so with his usual fairness and readiness to see both sides of the question. But there could be little doubt about his verdict, and in the course of the article, which bears the stamp of Bertrand Russell at his greatest, comes the sentence which nobody else could have written: 'It is not by bustle that men become enlightened. Spinoza was content with The Hague, Kant, who is generally regarded as the wisest of

Germans, never travelled more than ten miles from Konigsberg.' Our philosopher loved his home and his country too. He was a passionate patriot. In his nineties, he had caught the ear of the whole wide world as well as his countrymen, and my guess is that his last, almost his everlasting, service to the British people will be that, now and hereafter, countless millions of the world's inhabitants will learn to speak the international language in the pure English of Bertrand Russell.

SEVEN

Knight Errant of Socialism

Brave to the point of folly, and as humane as he was brave, no
man in his generation preached republican virtue in better
English, nor lived it with a finer disregard of self.

H. N. BRAILSFORD, in his
essay on Thomas Paine.

HIGH UP ON ANY LIST of classics in Socialist literature, I would
include a modest little volume in the Home University Library,
first published in 1913, called *Shelley, Godwin and Their Circle* by
H. N. Brailsford. Brailsford himself once told me that it was
Shelley who made him a Socialist, and here is the proof. Here in
this volume is fittingly portrayed the ferment which the French
Revolution produced in the English mind, and which later found
expression in Chartism and in the revolt against the savageries of
nineteenth-century industrialism and modern imperialism, and in
the ideals of twentieth-century democratic Socialism.

The book is well-nigh perfect. Every sentence rings true. Every
page glows with a splendid ardour. Is there, for example, in the
whole range of English literature a better tribute by one liberal
spirit to another than Brailsford's twenty-page essay on Thomas
Paine? The opening paragraph sounds like a tocsin:

'Where Liberty is, there is my country.' The sentiment has a Latin
ring; one can imagine an early Stoic as its author. It was spoken by
Benjamin Franklin, and no saying better expresses the spirit of
eighteenth-century humanity. 'Where is not Liberty, there is mine.'
The answer is Thomas Paine's. It is the watchword of the knight
errant, the marching music that sent Lafayette to America and Byron
to Greece, the motto of every man who prizes striving above
enjoyment, honours comradeship above patriotism, and follows an
idea that no frontier can arrest.

It was that same watchword which sent Brailsford himself to enlist in the Greek forces in the war with Turkey in the 1890s. He was always a knight errant in Socialist politics, whether the battlefields were real or imagined. Never did a man so completely subordinate his own personal interests to the cause in which he believed. Rarely has anyone striven so persistently and so passionately to translate word into deed, to make the one inextricable from the other.

He was, and remains, the greatest Socialist journalist of the century, or at least, the greatest of those who wrote in the English language. His only competing claimant for the title is Robert Blatchford, and perhaps the fair way to apportion glory between the two is to invent two different competitions. Blatchford doubtless made more Socialists than Brailsford; indeed my guess is that he probably made more than all the other Socialist propagandists rolled into one. He spoke more directly to the heart of his English working-class readers than anyone has done since, and, in his spare time, or rather as a principal accompanying preoccupation, he was an unrivalled popular educator. How many millions did he teach to read, to love books, to imbibe their Socialism, almost unconsciously, between the lines? Brailsford did not have that gift, at least not in Blatchford's overflowing measure. He had not the common touch of unfailing readability, the quality of Blatchford or, say, Daniel Defoe, or William Cobbett, or Thomas Paine himself. But in most other qualities he was supreme. He had an intellectual passion to which Blatchford never aspired; a determination to ransack the truth from any situation and to tell it with all the power at his command; a combination of honesty and courage and astringency which put all rivals in the shade; an individual streak of mordancy which gave his own character to everything he wrote. Shamefully, his journalism or substantial sections of it have never been properly collected and republished as it should be. However, his books, a few of them masterpieces, do convey the same sense of urgency and exhilaration with which his journalism was impregnated. He could write about Shelley or Thomas Paine or the Levellers as if they were his own living comrades. He could turn the pages of history into modern battlecries. Within him the past and the present were fused into a single revolutionary force.

And yet, before these high claims may be accepted, it is necessary to remove some legitimate objections or misapprehensions. Hardly ever in his life did he receive unqualified acclaim. He was always just out of step, even with his closest associates. He was rarely, if ever, the foremost spokesman of a particular campaign. He repeatedly devoted his whole soul to lost causes. Such features of his political record may give the momentary impression that he must have been argumentative, priggish even, too fastidious in his choice of means and allies, and ready to set sectarian purity above rough victory for the ideals he cherished. Did he not even perhaps have a taste for martyrdom? But any such suggestions must be swept aside at once and for ever. In personal dealings he was diffident, modest, and exquisitely gentle. He had a soft, precise, insistently courteous manner of speech which made the epigrammatic flashes all the more startling. His scruple about forms of political action had a peculiar combined derivation; he had a non-conformist conscience and a Marxist imagination and a romantic Shelleyan faith in the perfectibility of man and, more especially, woman.

When I first encountered him, at the time the Socialist League was formed in the early thirties or a few years later when *Tribune* was first published, the individuality of his political stance was marked with especial sharpness. He had only recently broken with his old friends of the Independent Labour Party, whose paper the *New Leader* he had once edited with a distinction which made it nationally, indeed internationally, famous. His breach with them was not due to any new-found respect for what he derided as 'the slouching leadership' of the official Labour Party. He, like most other Socialists of the time, had had to pick their path between the Right-wing of the Party which had only escaped from 'MacDonaldism' by the narrowest of margins and a variety of Left-wing lurches towards sectarian impotence or the Communist Party. As the horrors, and the opportunities, of the decade unfolded—the rise of Fascism, and the rise too, as is customarily and conveniently forgotten, of a predominantly Socialist opposition to the assault on the most elementary standards of human decency—Brailsford with his boundless romantic faith in Socialism as an international creed was better qualified than anyone to give the necessary summons to resistance. He did so, with all his eloquence and courage, as the European crisis mounted to each fresh climax; when, for example, Dollfuss machine-gunned the Socialists in Vienna, when Mussolini invaded Abyssinia, when Franco invaded Spain. Yet all through these years of agony he conducted, single-handed in the British Left-wing press, a persistent criticism of the Stalin show trials in the Soviet Union.

Almost the entire Labour movement in Britain, Left, Right and Centre, was blindly, vehemently eager to be pro-Russian and pro-Stalin. Brailsford himself had written tens of thousands of words defending the Russian Revolution; more than almost any other Western Socialist journalist he had seen the early years of the Soviet Revolution with his own eyes and his own faith. The moment of the thirties was not inviting for anyone to step out of the popular Left line, particularly after the spring of 1936 when Spain was afire, and the flames might engulf all Europe. Militant Socialism moved to the tramp of the International Brigade. How deeply the Left craved to give the benefit of all the doubts to Moscow! No one who did not live through that decade can quite appreciate how overwhelming that craving was. If Juan Negrin, the valiant, inspired, highly discriminating leader of Spanish democracy knew the necessity of embracing his Soviet ally, who were the rest of us to cavil?

But Brailsford would not be budged from his allegiance to his own first principles. He had been the friend of many of those called 'the traitors and the wreckers', Radek, Bukharin, and many more. He would not betray them and the finest ideals of the Soviet Revolution itself. 'One begins by suppressing Mensheviks, one ends by suppressing Trotsky', he wrote. Week by week in his articles in *Reynolds News*, he struggled against the flood, and the Socialist defence of freedom which he asserted more bravely than anyone else had a significance for the whole future of Socialism. A Socialism which did not embrace freedom as it most precious strand was for him no Socialism at all. In him, the best and only the best of the liberal heritage became intertwined with the exposure of capitalist economics. Voltaire stood beside Marx in his gallery. (His *Voltaire*, also in the Home University Library, is another classic).

Brailsford drew his richest inspiration from English sources, but, unlike so many English Socialists, he never weakened in his appreciation of the greatness of Marx. Rather, he saw him, like his other heroes, in a spacious international context. He wrote in *Property or Peace?* (published in 1934):

> The world may one day come to join in the honour that Russia pays to Marx. But the world will then be a medieval monastery, unless, while it honours him, it is free to doubt and deny every word he uttered. On no other terms can the human reason live. Religious faith is vital just in so far as it dare listen to an atheist. Socialist conviction is genuine, only in so far as it will open its ears to the classical economists. In so far as any society departs from this principle, it lessens its own intellectual vigour and betrays the spirit of science.

The extreme terms in which Brailsford stated his intellectual allegiance to Marxism should be constantly reiterated: thus, beneath the darkening shadows of Nazism and Stalinism, he contributed something of the purest nobility to Socialist thought and history. In a sense, it was his finest hour. He was almost alone in combining such a perception of all the monstrous horrors of the age with an unwavering determination still to act—alone certainly in the eloquence with which he both analysed the scene and issued the call to action. Yet, thanks to that perception, to which no power on earth could prevent him from giving utterance, it is *his* writings on those mighty themes which can better endure scrutiny three-quarters of a century later than those of any other Socialist of the age. It was not his last service to the cause of Socialism, but it is one that still shines with a matchless splendour.

Yet it may be objected: Brailsford's critique of Stalinism, indispensable, courageous and far-seeing though it may be, was still a by-product of his thought and of events. What of a larger Socialist theme which necessarily figures more prominently in his writings, and which he had made peculiarly his own, and where his power of prophecy, his interpretation of Marxism, can be exposed as a most misleading instrument and guide? The question cannot be dodged. As a journalist—for many years, for example, the editor of the Independent Labour Party's weekly the *New Leader*—he was required, as Socialist editors always are, to write on every subject under the sun and moon. Long before Keynes and Beveridge and with much more acknowledgement to his tutor, he had grasped and applied J. A. Hobson's analysis of the causes of capitalist slump, deduced no doubt from Marx's *Das Kapital*. But he also learnt from Hobson (Lenin also was not too proud to do), how Marxist economics could and should be extended to establish a full-scale critique of imperialism—a thesis developed most famously in *The War of Steel and Gold*, published first of all a few months before the outbreak of the 1914 war, and then in the later years in such volumes as *Rebel India* or *Property or Peace?*, and it merged too into his frequent articles and pamphlets on the origins of the 1914–1918 war and on the role of Germany both in those pre-1914 years and thereafter. He was not, and he never became, as some of his pamphleteering opponents at the time had alleged, an apologist for German policy and German imperialism; that was merely the vicious taunt to which he exposed himself by his persistence in attacking the policies of the Entente powers before 1914 or the Versailles powers after 1918. Maybe, in striving to adjust the balance, he did trap himself into an illegitimate pro-German sentiment. But that is not the core of the controversy. The question is: did his neo-Marxism, his neo-Hobsonism, his elevation of imperialism into the central place in his theory, lead him and others into a false appreciation of the causes of the two world wars of the century—no trifling criticism for sure, if indeed the charge can be driven home?

The criticism has been delivered most formidably by A. J. P. Taylor, once in his volume on the pre-1914 years* and again in his lectures, *The Troublemakers*, and in one of these the contest seems to be initiated with a knock-out. There, a conclusion from *The War of Steel and Gold*, published in March 1914, is quoted:

> The dangers which forced our ancestors into European coalitions and Continental wars have gone never to return . . . It is as certain as

---

*The Struggle for Mastery in Europe 1848–1918, Oxford.

anything can be, that the frontiers of our modern national states are finally drawn. My own belief is that there will be no more wars among the Six Great Powers.

Clearly, when the next edition of the same book appeared in 1915, some modification was called for. The last sentence quoted above was omitted, but another was inserted in a preface thus:

> It seems to me doubtful whether [questions of nationality] could have made a general war, had not colonial and economic issues supplied a wider motive for the use of force.

And then again in the postscript:

> War could never have come about save for these sordid colonial and economic issues . . . France is defending the colonies and especially Morocco. Germany is attacking and the Allies are maintaining the present distribution of colonies and dependencies. The stakes lie outside Europe, though the war is fought on its soil.

By contrast, it is hardly overstating the case to say that A. J. P. Taylor's historical verdict, after the most scrupulous, modern and original examination of the evidence, reaches the exactly opposite conclusion. The decisions of the great powers were shaped not by any estimate of the stakes outside Europe but by calculations or miscalculations about the balance of power in Europe itself. Marxism, for all its much-trumpeted world-vision, or Marxism as interpreted by Brailsford, attributed too much discernment and rationality to the leaders of 'finance capitalism' who controlled events. Strategy, not economics, governed diplomacy, and the strategy might have no more decipherable aim than diplomatic gain in 'the perpetual quadrille of the balance of powers'. So fears, often unfounded, bred wars. Taylor insisted:

> The war of 1866, like the war of 1859 before it and the wars of 1870 and 1914 after it, was launched by the conservative power, the power standing on the defensive, which, baited beyond endurance, broke out on its tormentors. Every war between great powers [between 1866 and 1914] started as a preventive war, not as a war of conquest.

No fair-minded student of this controversy can deny that Alan Taylor does make a considerable dent in the Brailsford case; but does that admission also mean that his many books on this subject are robbed of their potency and appeal? If this theoretical heart is knocked out, what life can possibly remain in the rest of the work? The curious answer is, I believe, that, thanks to the fact that Brailsford was only superficially writing in strict economic terms, the value of his books is scarcely touched. He was never much attracted by the supposed inexorable necessities of Marxism. He was never entranced by the all-consuming dominance of economics, Marxist or any other. He was much more concerned with the victors and the victims in the class war; no one could doubt *that* reality. He was outraged by all the indecencies and savageries inflicted on human beings in the name of Empire and its trappings, and no Marxist theory was needed to instil that sense in his mind and heart. Whenever he wrote about imperialism his words scorched. 'Property must go armed', he said, and the aphorism ranks with the greatest of Marxist revelations. The spectacle of imperialist oppression in every guise or disguise unloosed within him a scorn, a fury, a passion which no soft excuses could ever abate. If his theory and nature did not accord due weight to the calculations of diplomacy in the pre-1914 or the pre-1939 periods, the balance is much more than restored by his deeper imaginative understanding of the spirit of revolt which in this century has shaken to their ruin all the old empires, and a few of the new ones too. When he set out on his first anti-imperialist odyssey in 1897, almost all those old elaborate imperial courts and structures, even the Turkish one, looked strong, well-nigh invincible; when he died in 1958, they had all, without exception, vanished from the world stage. And his pen was one of the weapons which had assisted in their disappearance. Revolutionaries in every continent where the English language prevailed—in India, above all—read Brailsford. He had translated Shelley and Voltaire and Karl Marx into sentences they could all understand.

Impossible indeed to write about any aspect of Brailsford's life without invoking his inheritance from the past; it was his constant, treasured companion. And here was one reason why he, in the service of another of his great causes, the pre-1914 fight for women's suffrage, could set the struggle in its proper setting. The suffragette movement was looked upon by some at the time, and much less excusably has been treated by some historians since, as a distraction from the great historical mainstream of democratic emancipation. Brailsford knew better; he was steeped in the writings of John Stuart Mill and Mary Wollstonecraft, and indeed of Shelley and Thomas Paine who had been pioneers of this cause along with the others. Hurling himself into the struggle with all his customary zest, he was soon horrified to discover that he was thrust into controversy with some of his closest liberal associates. He was working at the time on the *Daily News*; a Liberal newspaper then in its greatest days, edited by a great Liberal editor, A. G. Gardiner. But when Brailsford, with his colleague, H. W. Nevinson, was confronted at last with the fact that their newspaper was ready to condone the forcible feeding of suffragettes in prison, they wrote to *The Times*—on 5 October 1909—a letter which concluded with these paragraphs:

> At the outset the Government treated the movement with blind contempt. The movement grew under persecution. Exasperation begat violence, and with suffering came a bravery and a spirit of self-sacrifice which no penalty can crush. The weeks as they pass are bringing us nearer to the phase of mortal tragedy. To our minds the graver responsibility will fall on the members of a nominally democratic party who have turned their backs upon a gallant movement of emancipation, and, above all, on 'the great leader', (that is, the Prime Minister, Asquith) whose obstinate refusal to the appeals even of the constitutional women has made at each repetition a multitude of converts to violence. Lest we should seem in our strictures on Liberalism and its organs in the Press to be guilty of inconsistency, we wish to take this opportunity of stating that, despite our warm approval of the Budget [Lloyd George's People's Budget, of course], we have resigned our positions as leader-writers on the *Daily News*. We cannot denounce torture in Russia and support it in England, nor can we advocate democratic principles in the name of a party which confines them to a single sex.

Thereafter Don Quixote turned his energies, without a moment's delay or relaxation, to the pursuit of the cause. He campaigned on suffragette platforms. He crossed lances with the new Home

Secretary, Winston Churchill, and won the contest so unmercifully that more than half a century later Churchill's biographer, Randolph, was still wisely unwilling to risk renewing the argument. He worked mightily behind the scenes to replace the danger of fresh violence with conciliation. He became secretary of the so-called Conciliation Committee. And the cause came so near to victory. On 12 May 1912, at the Connaught Rooms in London, Brailsford made the speech celebrating the 'Second Reading Majority' of a few days before:

> I am not nervous about the result. And that is not because I am naturally of a sanguine disposition. I think, in point of fact, that the only service I may have been able to render to this cause came from a certain cynicism of disposition which taught me to see that while you were talking about your emancipation, the only thing that concerned the House of Commons was not your freedom, not your elevation, not the future of the human race, but simply, solely their own constituencies, their own fortunes, their own party calculations.

And that, be it not forgotten, was the great pre-war Liberal House of Commons, but Brailsford continued:

> The honour has fallen to me of proposing the toast of 'Votes for Women' but I am not going to identify that toast with the Bill before the House of Commons. It is a compromise. It has the greyness and inadequacy of every compromise. I listened throughout the debate last week to the discussion on the political status of women, and as it went on I asked myself whether you and I and all of us had not been perpetuating a sort of practical joke. We have dreamed our dreams while we have talked about something so relatively small as this matter of parliamentary voting, so modest in this Conciliation Bill. But I question if the men on whose decision your fortunes rest fully realise that what is at stake is anything larger than their own future and the fortunes of their party. I do not think it has yet dawned upon them that what is really at issue is nothing less than a revolution in European civilisation. It will be achieved half-consciously amid the pettiness of partisan debates. But we at least know what it means. We know what it means for the cause of the poor and the sweated, for the widows and the women of the slums. But above all we know that it means a transformation in the mind and spirit of every human soul which comes into the world a woman. It means the removal from

every growing mind and every developing spirit of the shackles which would otherwise have bound her brain, fettered her limbs. It is a mental emancipation and a moral awakening that lie at the root of this great cause of ours.

And so it was—after a few more years of unconscionable delay. Even the compromising Conciliation Bill, despite its Second Reading victory, was still blocked by male obstinacy, fear and stunted imagination, and perhaps even more by Asquithian double-talk and double-dealing. The romantic Brailsford had foreseen the future so much more clearly than the foremost Liberal statesmen of his time.

Brailsford's magnificent gesture of resignation from the *Daily News* was made when he was thirty-six years old; he never secured a regular job on a daily newspaper again. That was another of his finest hours; they were constantly recurring. Perhaps he later had doubts, or at least it became clear how painful were some of the choices he did make. For, thirty years later, on 6 August, 1938, he wrote me a most generous letter about a quarrel I was having with *Tribune*, and here are a few extracts which recalled his own experience:

> [I had to resign] three times in my journalistic career, and each time was in some difficulty until I found other work. So I know it has to be done sometimes, and may cost a lot . . . I had to face a motion demanding my resignation at almost every Board meeting through four years, when I edited the *New Leader*. It wasn't pleasant and in the end I was defeated. But I had the satisfaction of making what I, anyhow, thought a pretty good paper. One may be too subjective— that's in the Liberal-Non-conformist tradition— and forget that to run a good paper matters more than to perform prodigies of conscience. (I too came out of that tradition, and it has poisoned most of my life. One never wholly liberates oneself. It is a great inheritance—to throw away).

Startling sentences indeed, and they still leap from the faded manuscript when I read them. Did he truly mean it? I knew nothing of his personal life, and it was to this I believe he must have been referring. Anyhow, the Brailsford who so brazenly suggested that he had tossed aside his non-conformist conscience, presumably in deference to the masterful, objective Marxist voice overpowering him, was at that very moment defying all the popular storms and temptations on the Left to instruct Socialists on the historic evils of Stalinism—in the years 1937 and 1938, I repeat, long before most of us had heard of Koestler or Orwell or Silone.

However, whatever crises of conscience may have afflicted him in other fields, he never wavered an inch in his allegiance to the cause of women's rights. It was not just a question of a desirable reform; it was a democratic necessity. The dominant sex, he would insinuate, always had some other dominant issue which should be allowed to push the campaign for equality off the agenda altogether. For him, 'Votes for Women' had never been an odd Edwardian affair suddenly blazing across the skies and then vanishing to leave no mark on the politics of the century. It was a major campaign in the great war of liberation in which he never ceased to enlist, and it was fitting that his last service of all took the form of an adventure into the origins of English democracy itself. For long he had contemplated the task, and during the last decade of his life he applied himself devotedly to it. Two years after his death, the wonder appeared: *The Levellers and the English Revolution* by H. N. Brailsford. Edited by Christopher Hill. Cresset Press. Brailsford himself had not been able to apply the finishing touches, and, since he was such a perfectionist in points of literary style, we cannot be sure that the text is all he would have wished. But it speaks for itself.

Who *were* the Levellers? All the great Whig historians, including the last of them, G. M. Trevelyan, had been content to dismiss them in a paragraph or a footnote. 'A few visionaries' was S. R. Gardiner's phrase. Even those sympathetic to their ideas had found it difficult not to be influenced by these serried judgements. John Lilburne had often been regarded more as a brave and endearing eccentric than a figure of historical significance. The ancient sneers of the Royalist writers helped to fortify the usual portrait of a bunch of cranks, men centuries ahead of their time who intruded upon no more than the fringe of great affairs. 'The name of the Levellers', one wrote:

a most apt title for such a despicable and desperate lot to be known by, that endeavour to cast down and level the enclosures of nobility, gentry and propriety, to make us all even, so that even Jack shall vie with a gentleman and every gentleman be made a Jack.

How inconsiderable must these men have been in the stupendous struggle between Roundhead and Cavalier! What dwarfs in the shadow of a Cromwell!

The first big achievement of Brailsford's book was that it shattered this assumption for ever. Never again could the history of the Civil War and the Commonwealth be written in the old terms. 'Enough has come to light in recent years', said Brailsford, 'to compel a revision of the classical story of the Revolution. Not in ideas only but in action, the initiative during this critical phase came from the Levellers. They led the struggle against clericalism and intolerance; they challenged the ascendancy of Holles and his class; they set the Army marching.' Modestly Brailsford did not claim the credit for the discovery; but the beauty of his mind, the sweep of his narrative, the detailed, scrupulous proof he offered in seven hundred massive pages carry conviction for his high claims. What Clarendon did for the Cavaliers, and what Carlyle did for Cromwell, Brailsford did for the Levellers and their associates, and in any proper English library the volumes of these three should be placed on the same shelf.

Of course, a few objections may be heard. In particular, as the devoted editor of Brailsford's volume, Christopher Hill, pointed out, Brailsford may have been wrong in his assertions that the Levellers were demanding *manhood* suffrage; the full democratic claim had not yet been tabled. Alas, too, not even for Brailsford's benefit, could it be claimed that they were demanding *womanhood* suffrage, and yet he did place special emphasis on the fact— which other historian had ever stopped to do so?—that in 1849 ten thousand women had signed one of the first Leveller petitions and that one thousand of their number had presented it to the House of Commons insisting:

> Have we not an equal interest with the men of this nation in those liberties and securities contained in the *Petition of Right*, and the other good laws of the land?

Certainly no qualifications can alter or injure Brailsford's two main themes. First he showed how much more formidable than anyone had conceived before was the Leveller organisation; how deeply the Army was infected by the doctrine that 'our being soldiers hath not deprived us of our rights as commoners'; how at so many moments of crisis Cromwell was more their servant than their master. And secondly, and more expectedly, in the realm of ideas, he showed how various, how humane and far-seeing, were the anthems which Lilburne and his colleagues could play on their 'eternal trumpet of defiance to all the men and devils in earth and hell'. If he exaggerated the all-embracing nature of their democratic faith, it is still true that they were the first organisers of a democratic party and a citizen army, the first advocates of a secular democratic Republic, the first consistent champions of a genuine tolerance for everyone, for Catholics and Jews no less than good Puritans. 'What is done to anyone may be done to everyone', said Lilburne, and upon that rock he built a programme of reform which most of the free world still has not shown the will to execute. And, bless their revolutionary souls, they called their weekly newspaper, the first of its type, the ancestor of the *New Leader* or *Tribune*, *The Moderate*, to put all future moderates in their place.

These despised, irresponsible moderates were seeking to pierce the mysteries of the universe as daringly as they argued about society and strategy with their officers in Putney Church. 'They were freemen of the century of Galileo, Harvey and Newton.' Who but Brailsford could have made that claim? It is hardly less bold than his insistence on their direct week-by-week political influence. But the proof was offered in the most perceptive examination of the Levellers' writings ever undertaken; Brailsford knew what qualities weekly immoderate journalism could require. In the end they were crushed. But their sea green ribbons were never trailed through the mud. When Cromwell set out on his terrible mission to Ireland, they would have no part of it. They raised the first English banner against the crime of imperialism as they had set the fashion in so much else. 'It will be no satisfaction to God's Justice', wrote William Walwyn, 'to plead that you murdered men in obedience to your

General.' Here indeed, deeper than in his Marxism, was Brailsford's fury against imperialist oppression traced to its source.

The Levellers is a glorious book. Not only did Brailsford add a new dimension to seventeenth-century history; presented in this context, a whole long list of men acquire a new stature and step forward to enrich still further the richest pages in our history. Richard Overton ('A wit always pays a heavy penalty for amusing Anglo Saxons; he is classed among the not quite respectable'), William Walwyn, Edward Sexby, Henry Marten, Thomas Rainsborough, John Lilburne himself and many more, not overlooking Elizabeth Lilburne or Katherine Chidley and her 'practised pen'. Brailsford would not look upon any scene in our history without asking what the women were doing; the habit started opening before him archives still scarcely scratched by others. Altogether, at last, after three centuries these names begin to get their due and should recover in the eyes of their countrymen the place of honour they once held among 'the plain men' of Cromwell's armies and the London mob. Henry Noel Brailsford was their truest descendant, a knight errant fit to take his place in their company. When he died his friends talked of a monument for him. Here with *The Levellers* it is, an imperishable work of passion, scholarship and art.

EIGHT

The New Machiavelli

He loved Italy as the saints love God.

G. M. TREVELYAN on Garibaldi.

WHEN IGNAZIO SILONE DIED at the age of seventy-eight in a Geneva hospital, in the year 1978, he was given respectful English tributes in a few, a very few, obituary columns. Naturally in Italy more was said and written, although for some reason not easily discernible he is one of the prophets who was never accorded proper honour in his native land. Yet taking the man and his books together, and they can never be separated, he is one of the great men of the last half-century, of the whole Fascist-Communist epoch in human history. Machiavelli died penniless, was condemned to do most of his work in exile and never saw his great writing published in his lifetime; and yet his became a household name the world over. Ignazio Silone may achieve a similar posthumous conquest in Italy and beyond; his greatness, I believe, is on the same scale. He shows a comparable combination of insight into the tumult of his own age, together with an enduring vision of the heights and depths which human nature can attain, and he combines with it too a splendour and fortitude in his own character which, in some degree, Machiavelli had too.

Silone's first novel, scarcely more than a short story, *Fontamara*, published in 1934, told how Mussolini's Fascism came to a medieval Christian village in the Abruzzi, the scene of all his writings from which he never wished or sought to escape. The plain picture of poverty and cruelty, of the heroism of the rebel and how resistance is born, survives better than most of the rhetoric and poetry of the thirties. Unlike loftier exponents of the anti-Fascist case, Silone never had anything, not a single syllable, to qualify or retract. He never forgot what poverty meant in humiliation of the individual. Years later he was still asserting, with all the passion at his command, that the claptrap about the virtues of poverty is an odious falsehood. In any case, there were no words to spare in *Fontamara*. Only a great mind dares to express itself simply, said Stendhal, and Silone, himself a student of Stendhal, is the best modern exponent of the latter's practice and precept.

The same lack of any necessity to disavow his earlier words and deeds applies to Silone's disillusion with Communism, which he explored in his later novels and expounded best of all in that little-known classic, *The School for Dictators*, the one among his writings which truly deserves its place alongside Machiavelli's *Prince*. Silone at least did see his masterpiece published, but the precise moment and method of publication were wretchedly devised. *The School for Dictators* first made its appearance in 1939, just after a British Prime Minister had been toasting Mussolini in Rome, and just before Stalin made his Pact with Hitler. Most political leaders of that pusillanimous age did not want to learn the truth from anybody, least of all from an Italian exile, an ex-Communist denied entry into Britain.

Moreover, Silone fitted easily into no party or definable group; his every sentence bristled with his own brand of independence. Most members of the legion of literary ex-Communists beat their breasts, and deserted the revolutionary camp altogether, following a well-smoothed track to comfort and complacency. Silone instead purified his Socialist faith, made it an instrument of sharper metal and never lost the dignity and ardour which he had seen in his peasant heroes. Indeed, even in this restricted category of anti-Communist literature, it is too easy to forget what an originator he was. He first found the path which writers like George Orwell and Arthur Koestler were to follow later, and both of them, to their credit it should be quickly added, were later to acknowledge his example.

None of Silone's anti-Communist writings, taken singly, ever achieved the success of Orwell's *Animal Farm* or Koestler's *Darkness at Noon*; none of them could lay claim to the same artistic triumph. But taken together they stated, no less effectively the Socialist answer to Stalinism, and some of the scenes he has described will never fade from the history books.

It was, according to his own description, way back in 1922, as he was leaving Moscow on one occasion, that Alexandra Kollontai had jokingly warned him: 'If you should read in the papers that Lenin has had me arrested for stealing the Kremlin's silverware, it will mean simply that I have not been in full agreement with him on some problem of agricultural or industrial policy.' And it was a year or two later again that another ineffable exchange occurred in Moscow which should surely have shaken the universe. Confronted with a dilemma of tactics posed by the British Communist Party, a Russian expert offered a simple if Jesuitical solution, whereupon the British Communist delegate interrupted: 'But that would be a lie.' Then follows Silone's great scene—'This naïve objection,' he wrote,

> was greeted with a burst of laughter, frank, warm, interminable laughter, the like of which the gloomy offices of the Communist International had certainly never heard, laughter which rapidly spread all over Moscow, since the Englishman's incredibly funny answer was immediately telephoned to Stalin and the most important offices of State, leaving new waves of astonishment and hilarity in its wake, as we learned later. 'In judging a regime it is very important to know what it finds amusing', said Togliatti, who was with me.

But why and how, after moments such as that, did it take so long for the world to unearth the truth? Silone was the most incorruptible of witnesses. Togliatti was a politician of genius. And both, incidentally, had been trained on Machiavelli and Mazzini as well as Marx. A host of the most intelligent and selfless men and women of that age or any other saw what happened in the Kremlin—until, for example, Silone was prompted to ask Togliatti: 'Do you suppose that's the way they do things in the Sacred College of Cardinals? Or in the Fascist Grand Council?' How could Stalinism survive such an inquisition, pressed at a time, be it noted, when Trotsky was still alive and kicking in Moscow?

Silone's simple answers ring truer than any elaborate treatise. He understood why the Communist Party was 'school, church, barracks, family'; he knew that 'consciences are not synchronised like traffic signals'. And he knew why his own brother, tortured to death by the Fascists, proclaimed himself, falsely, a Communist, to honour the creed of defiance, learnt in the Abruzzi. Even when he was risking his life to swear eternal war on the monstrous evil unmasked before him, Silone could not or would not forget the human face of Communism which had first inspired himself and his young comrades.

He once wrote a fierce criticism of modern British writers, accusing them of shirking the great themes, and whether that stone was well-aimed or not, no one can reply that it was thrown from a glasshouse. Silone himself could breathe only on the highest altitudes. He was obsessed by the perpetual interaction of morals and politics, thought and action, ends and means, the flesh and the spirit. He could not stoop. He would castigate not only the gaolers and executioners of totalitarian states, but the literary tradesmen who pandered to the lowest tastes, particularly those who trafficked in eroticism in the name of liberty. For the liberty he treasured, in his work and with his life, was something inexpressibly richer and nobler. Since it had had to be wrested from Fascist thugs and Communist dogmatists, how could it not be? It was not a word but a thing. Indeed, in Silone's hands, many other dusty abstractions regain, like polished silver, a gleaming brightness and purity: honour, conscience, courage, faith. And on a similar reckoning, he saw, as Orwell saw, how human misery can derive from the debasement of language, what stark horror can breed beneath Byzantine pomposity, how words like poverty and slavery must not be allowed soft edges, just as freedom must keep its revolutionary force.

The words and the man perpetually merge; every Silone aphorism seems sharpened by his personality. He was truly a saint, and yet saints who devote their lives to politics can prove to be the most dangerous persecutors of all. Silone knew that better than any of his potential critics, and had devoted his wit to expose the peril. 'This ordinary man', he wrote in *The School for Dictators*,

is a hotch-potch of desires. He likes eating, drinking, smoking, sleeping, keeping a canary, playing tennis, going to the theatre, being well-dressed, having children, stamp-collecting, doing his job, and many other things besides. This is the reason he remains a nobody; he spreads himself over so many little things. But the born politician wants nothing but power and lives for nothing but power. It is his bread, his meat, his work, his hobby, his lover, his canary, his theatre, his stamp album, his life-sentence. The fact that all his powers and energies are concentrated upon one thing makes it easy for him to appear extraordinary in the eyes of the masses and thus become a leader, in the same way as those who really concentrate on God become saints and those who live only for money become millionaires.

Fortunately, this man who guarded his cherished ideas from all assaults with such saint-like fanaticism also possessed the mordancy of a Machiavelli, and he brought this quality to its peak in *The School for Dictators*. Here Thomas the Cynic explained to an aspirant from the United States how to establish a dictatorship in that country ('How can I save America from the Red Menace, if the menace doesn't exist?'). The aphoristic arrows are fired off in all directions and few escaped unscathed: no dictator has ever had trouble finding Civil Servants; if a party calls itself 'radical' it's bound to be moderate; the height of the art of government for our contemporary democratic statesmen (1939, don't forget) seems to consist in accepting smacks in the face to avoid having their posteriors kicked; America, as you know, never had an Age of Enlightenment, and was therefore spared Socialism and the struggles of political ideologies; a sincere orator only feels inconsistent when he is silent.

And yet it is his imagination and his courage, even more than his wit, which will make him so powerful a voice in the years to come: especially for Socialists, to whom he continued to the end to address his strictures, his warnings, his invocations, and his hopes. Socialism, he was convinced, would outlive Marxism, and he said that as one who knew how human and inspiring, no less than corrupting and explosive, Marxism could be:

I cannot conceive of Socialism tied to any particular theory, only to a faith. The more Socialist theories claim to be 'scientific', the more transitory they are. But Socialist values are permanent. The distinction between theories and values is still not clearly enough understood by those who ponder these problems, but it is fundamental. A school or a system of propaganda may be founded on a collection of theories. But only a system of values can construct a culture, a civilisation, a new way of living together as men.

A few have sought, like Silone, to remodel their faith in democratic Socialism in the light of the experience of Soviet Communism which has afflicted the East and what Silone calls 'the leprosy of nihilism' which has afflicted the West. But no other Socialist writer has refashioned the call to action so nobly as Silone. He never allowed himself to be overwhelmed by cynicism or lassitude; he kept to the end just as he had infused all his writings with the spirit of resistance he had learned in the Abruzzi. 'I don't believe', he said, 'that the honest man is forced to submit to history,' or, again: 'No predicament, however desperate, can deprive us of the power to act.' The kinship between the old Machiavelli and the new one looks closer still. The old Machiavelli refused to submit to history, much in accordance with Ignazio Silone's admonition, and yet his books survived to play a foremost part in reshaping the Italy he loved.

NINE

Vicky

Cold and shrewd philosophers! How compassionately they
smile down at the self-tortures and crazy illusions of poor
Don Quixote; and in all their school-room wisdom they do
not mark that this very Don Quixotism is the most precious
thing in life—that it is life itself—and that Don Quixotism
lends wings to the whole world, and to all in it who
philosophise, make music, plough and yawn!

HEINRICH HEINE.

OVER A PERIOD of some fifteen years up till two days before his
death I met Vicky more and more frequently; he became, I
supposed, just about the closest friend I had. We had fixed a
standing Monday lunch date and often met in the evenings too.
We could resume an argument in the middle of a sentence; I
thought I really knew him. Then one cold afternoon, Charles
Wintour, editor of the *Evening Standard*, rang up and told me he
was dead. I had barely understood at all. Despite persistent
conversations on the fringes of the subject, I had no comprehension of how near his mind was to the end of its tether.

One person at least did comprehend—James Cameron, truly
Vicky's closest associate over a few decades. Their response to
events was continuously and uncannily the same. They often
found themselves, in Cameron's phrase, 'poised between hilarity
and despair'. Incredibly for two such complicated anatomies,
their hearts beat as one. Moreover, for Vicky, James Cameron
always was, as for many of us he remains, the prince of modern
journalists, the reporter who can best place each individual scene
and spectacle in the world-wide drama. He could place Vicky's
death amid that drama too; for Vicky was a casualty of the
Vietnam war and its kindred enormities, not forgetting the

sophistries with which those much nearer home, within his own adopted country and his beloved, wayward Labour movement, excused their part in the holocaust. And if he had lived, which of us would have escaped the lash?

He was a twentieth-century Don Quixote and honoured the mournful knight just as his adored Heinrich Heine, fellow artist, fellow Jew, and kindred spirit, had done before him. Heine wrote:

> My colleague mistook windmills for giants; I, on the contrary, see in our giants of today only ranting windmills . . . I must constantly fight duels, battle my way through untold misery, and I gain no victory which has not cost me something of my heart's blood. Night and day I am sorely beset, for my foes are so insidious that many of them, whom I have dealt a death-blow, still show the semblance of life and appear in all shapes and molest me day and night. What agonies I already have had to endure from these perfidious ghosts!

And that was Vicky too. He had painted a Daumier-like painting of his knight-errant hero, and was justly proud of the technical skill it displayed; wherever he moved, it was given the pride of place on his wall. No doubt was possible; his Don Quixote was a tragic figure. Yet, naturally enough at those lunches, the hilarity quickly subdued the despair, and it was not until after his death that a conversation with his wife, Inge, cast a most curious retrospective glance on their therapeutic effects. Whenever I had sought, born, blind, boneheaded optimist that I was, to cheer him in his most despondent moments, he would come home to dinner more despondent than ever. But when Jimmy had been there, to deepen the darkness from the outset and at every turn in the argument, the balm would take effect and he would return with a renewed light in his eye, the same indeed which, if only I had had the sensitivity to see it, had helped to shed a few gleams into Jimmy's hell. James Cameron, like Vicky, was sometimes derided for his Don Quixotism. Perhaps this was the only form of journalism fully suitable for the age of Auschwitz, and Hiroshima, and Vietnam, and Afghanistan and all such horrors. Together, the two of them, Vicky and Cameron, lifted the old trade to a new level.

Vicky made himself the best cartoonist in the world, the one proper successor of David Low, a student and example of the greatest tradition of caricature. It could be argued that others might equal or occasionally surpass him in draughtsmanship. He more than restored his pre-eminence with his humour, his fertility, his diligence, his political insight and instinct. Few observers have ever studied the English political scene with more persistence and acumen. He knew every corner of the workshop, every twist in the game, every shade of character. In this sense his equipment as a cartoonist was unique. It is hard to believe that any of his famous predecessors, Gillray, Rowlandson and the rest, understood the internal operations of British politics as Vicky made it his business to comprehend them.

And, of course, this extraordinary knowledge was not easily acquired. If he had not been a genius anyhow, he would have become one by taking pains. When he arrived in London in the thirties and got a job on the *News Chronicle* he had none of the uncanny understanding of English habits, pastimes and idioms which became one of his strengths. He set about learning them, by reading, listening and the range of his all-perceptive eye. Gerald Barry was his first editor and mentor, and Vicky was always eager to acknowledge the debt. Richard Winnington, and later James Cameron and Tom Baistow, were his intimate journalistic confederates. Somehow the greatest days of the *News Chronicle* were associated with Vicky, and when he left—after some of his cartoons had been refused publication by Barry's successors—the Liberal journal seemed preparing for its own doom.

Then came more strained and strenuous years on the *Daily Mirror*. Here freedom was complete. Vicky had won the opportunity to say exactly what he wished to a vast national audience. But year by year his own doubts and anxieties tortured him, to the amazement of his employers and friends. Somehow he needed to preach to the unconverted. Somehow he needed to awaken his enemies. He sought a new context for his message, and found it in the *Evening Standard*, signing a contract guaranteeing his freedom more secure than any cartoonist before him, even Low, had ever had. Little Vicky had become an independent power, almost the Fifth Estate of the Realm.

Most men who wield such power become corrupted, but here was one of his secrets. He was incorruptible, the most incorruptible man I ever knew. Neither money nor other material offerings could sway him from what he considered the course his conscience dictated. All the other more subtle seductions were equally pushed aside, rejected without reckoning. He could not be bought, browbeaten, or bulldozed. He stood against the world, the proud unshakable anarchist who knew there was a force more explosive than bombs and who, knowing so well how power corrupted others, stayed miraculously immune himself. Above all, he had an abiding compassion, drawn from his heart and nurtured by his love of music, literature and beauty. Some of his victims may find the claim baffling, but if ever they dare breathe a word of dissent, a host of *their* victims from the underworld of the defeated, the forgotten and the maligned, could rally from the depths to defend their champion. Vicky felt for those who suffered, the casualties of war, poverty and persecution, as if the strokes fell across his own back. 'No one ever lost an inch of sleep from any public worry', said Dr. Johnson. Vicky utterly disproved the thesis. He hardly had a full night's rest for most of his adult life, and one cause of his unsettled mind was undoubtedly that he felt more sharply than most of the rest of the human race. He had no armour to protect himself against the twentieth-century horrors.

It was a good day for Britain when he came to these shores. It was even better, the day after and thenceforward, when he resolved to take us at our best liberal word—when he assumed that he would have the right to say what he thought, though the heavens fell and however much all the undercover totalitarians and skin-deep democrats might scream. Curiously, the little Hungarian became a great English patriot, upholding the finest traditions of this land, our most precious treasures of free speech, free thought, the right to laugh at the mighty, the duty to appease the pains of the weak.

When he died tributes flowed in from all over the world to Vicky the artist, the incomparable master of political humour, and some of us in Fleet Street bowed our heads in remembrance of the most lovable companion we ever knew. But the proper epitaph for Vicky was that which Heinrich Heine, whom Vicky so greatly honoured, had asked to be accorded him when he died. He wrote:

I doubt that I deserve the laurel wreath, for poetry has always been merely an instrument with me, a sort of divine plaything. If you would honour me, lay a sword rather than a wreath upon my coffin; for I was, first of all, a soldier in the war for the liberation of humanity.

Vicky and Heine, divinely gifted, lovers of peace, haters of tyranny, belonged to the same army.

TEN

Randolph

It doesn't matter what you do as long as you don't do it in the street and frighten the horses.

> MRS. PAT CAMPBELL, whose comments on many matters were recited with much relish by Randolph Churchill. She was the heroine of another of his favourite tales; how, having safely transformed one of her innumerable suitors from a lover into a husband, she remarked, 'Ah, the peace of the double-bed after the hurly-burly of the *chaise longue*.'

RANDOLPH CHURCHILL and I would wake up every morning, for several weeks on end, polishing the thunderbolts which each hoped to unloose on the unbowed head of the other before the night was done. I was the Labour candidate for Devonport, dourly defending my home town against a Churchillian carpet-bagger. He bustled in like something not merely from another world, but another century, talking as if the place belonged to him, as the Churchills have often done, from the great Marlborough and his Duchess onwards. The brilliant cascade of abuse poured forth in all directions, sometimes drenching his own supporters. They say that the joists and beams of Conservative clubs in Devonport still quiver at the name of Randolph.

Then suddenly, when he learned that he had lost, in the agonising seconds which only parliamentary candidates can appreciate, the storm subsided and all was sweetness and charm. 'I thought you took that marvellously', I felt compelled to acknowledge. 'Yes', he replied, 'I've had plenty of practice.' He had indeed. He lost all the parliamentary contests he ever fought.

(When he actually got in he was unopposed).* Considering his boast at the age of twenty that he might emulate William Pitt and become Prime Minister at twenty-four, considering the family background and the expectations of his doting father, his whole political life might be seen as a crushing defeat.

He did not bury his talents; rather he scattered them in a riot of political profligacy. Way back in the early thirties he tried to batter his path into Parliament *against* the massed power of the Conservative Party machine. He turned up at a famous by-election in Wavertree, Liverpool, as an Independent Conservative. I happened to be present at one of his packed meetings when, mimicking his father, he perorated on the menace of Baldwin's India policy to the Lancashire cotton trade. The periods soared until he was shot down in mid-flight. 'And who is responsible for putting Liverpool where she is today?' he cried, whereupon a voice from the back recalled the devastating blow inflicted upon

---

*I had, during the war, taken the liberty of celebrating these events in a blasphemous document which was designed only for private circulation; here it is:

The Apostles' Creed

Then shall be sung or said the Apostles' Creed by the Minister, and the people standing . . .

I believe in Churchill the Father Almighty, Dictator of Heaven and earth; And in Randolph, his only Son, Who entered politics at Wavertree, Contested the Toxteth division of Liverpool, Fought at Ross and Cromarty, Was roundly defeated, rejected and forgotten: He descended into the Army; The third day he rose again from obscurity; He was returned unopposed for Preston, And sitteth on the right hand of Churchill the Father Almighty; From thence he and his descendants shall continue to govern us through eternity.

I believe in Bracken the Holy Ghost; the Holy Ministry of Information; the Communion of Yes-Men; The Forgiveness of all Churchill's sins; The Resurrection of the Conservative Party, And the tenure of office everlasting. Amen.

And after that these Prayers following, all devoutly kneeling: the Minister first pronouncing with a loud voice,

	The Lord be with you
ANSWER:	*And with thy spirit*
MINISTER:	*Let us pray. Lord, have mercy upon us.*
	Christ, have mercy upon us. Lord, have mercy upon us.

the city on the previous Saturday; 'Blackburn Rovers!' It almost seemed that the campaign floundered from that moment. But Randolph's achievement was truly amazing. He collected 10,000 Independent votes in a few days and handed the seat on a platter to the Labour Party. And the machine never forgot or forgave, even when his father had helped lead the nation and, more especially, the Conservative Party, cowering beneath his shield, through the valley of the shadow of death.

Not that Randolph never contributed to his own misfortunes, the ostracism, the constantly repeated thud of blackballs; no one could ever say *that*. At Eton he was beaten for some crime he had never committed. When he protested his innocence with customary volubility, the Captain of Games refused to relent: 'Anyway, you have been bloody awful all round—bend down, you're going to have six up.' The words have an authentic ring. 'Bloody awful all round' is the kind of comprehensive verdict which others who had dealings with him were always searching for—politicians, newspaper proprietors, editors, reporters, TV interviewers and, alas, some less able to answer back. Often in Fleet Street I have heard a fellow-journalist, still reeling from the impact, recall how Randolph had set the Thames, the Hudson, the Tiber or the Danube on fire with his boiling intoxicant invective. In how many places, in how many hemispheres, I wonder, did he stand there, unterrified and untameable, while the insults and the champagne bottles hurtled all around?

There were those days in 1938 and 1939, at Beaverbrook's house when he metaphorically coshed any Munichite Minister whom his host had been ill-advised enough to invite to the party. Or the splendid occasion when he turned the Foyle's luncheon table at the Dorchester upside down, knocked Hugh Cudlipp's and Lord Rothermere's heads together, gave his own award to the Pornographer Royal, and launched a one-man campaign to stop newspaper bosses from selling the equivalent of filthy postcards on the street corner. Sunday journalism has never quite been the same since, or rather it was only quite a number of years after he was safely in his grave that the Murdochs and his craven imitators dared to creep out again so brazenly from beneath the stones. Randolph would have stamped upon them.

Invective was his strongest suit but he had real wit too. When an editor of the *Evening Standard* spiked one of his articles on the grounds that it was 'obscure', Randolph replied: 'To the obscure all things are obscure.' When Lord Beaverbrook's valet, who normally referred to his master as 'The Lord', informed Randolph that 'The Lord was walking in St. James's Park,' he insisted: 'On the water, I presume?' Then there was the early hours session in the startled salon in the Marrakesh Hotel when, half-dead, he poured scorn on all the bronzed weaklings who escaped from his entrancing monologue to their beds. A couple of days later after he had been operated upon in London for cancer, my wife found him sitting up, smoking, drinking and protesting to one of the most eminent physicians in the land: 'Stop treating me like an invalid.'

Somehow it is such incidents, senseless or grotesque, which stick in the memory. Somehow his character compensates for all offences and explosions. One feels it was all his own work, achieved against hopeless odds; the spoilt child, the staggeringly handsome adolescent; the illusion that this Adonis could also talk as sparklingly as his father's beloved F. E. Smith, or write as readily as his father's model, Macaulay.

By the age of thirty or earlier, all his juvenile ambitions were shattered. Every time he attempted a political comeback he met fresh rebuffs. Every way he turned he faced the jibe that when nature makes a genius she breaks the mould. But he would not be beaten. He would retire to the garden he loved. He made himself a most formidable journalist, the trade he had never bothered to learn before. He made himself the biographer of his father and set the style for a great book; the father with whom he could quarrel but whose political cause he served with selfless loyalty.

He was outrageous and endearing, impossible and unforgettable, a Churchill who scarcely ever tasted victory, and what super-Churchillian courage that must have called for. Along with his honesty ('Lies are so dull', he would say) and his streaks of kindness, it was this reckless courage which shone most brightly. It could make him magnificent in political controversy, as he had once shown himself on the battlefield.

Friends and enemies would look on, admiring or aghast. Both

enjoyed the witticism when someone said that he was the kind of person who should not be allowed out in private. But it was the private Randolph whose memory many of us treasured. He was a friend and enemy worth having.

ELEVEN

The Greatest Exile

His pen continued an overmatch for the whole brood . . .

RICHARD CARLILE,
imprisoned in 1823 for selling
Paine's *Rights of Man*.

WHEN THOMAS PAINE died in New York on 8 June, in the year 1809, no one took much notice. A Quaker watchmaker, an old Frenchwoman alleged (falsely, as far as we know) to be Paine's mistress, her two little boys and two Negro pall-bearers were the only people at the graveside. Next day the leading New York newspaper supplied an epitaph: 'Paine had lived long (he was seventy-two), done some good, and much harm.'

Few of his legion of enemies spoke in so temperate a tone. Since his return to America in 1802 he had been denounced from the pulpits as the most wanton of blasphemers. Shortly after his death a full-length biography appeared in which accusations of drunkenness, lechery and dirtiness in all his personal habits were added to the charge-sheet. 'He had no country in the world, and it may truly be said that he had not a friend. Was ever man so wretched? Was ever enormous sinner so justly punished?' Three years before his death he was stopped at the polling booth when he went to cast his vote; the men in power chose to deny his claim to be a citizen of the Republic—he who had first dared to use the words 'the United States of America'. So he died in contempt, poverty and squalor.

It has taken generations to wipe away the mud. For years, on both sides of the Atlantic, publishers went to prison for attempting to reprint his books. By some inscrutable Stalinite censorship, whole histories of the American Revolution were written without mentioning the American Trotsky. A century after his death Theodore Roosevelt could still dismiss him as a 'filthy, little atheist'. Even now he is sometimes written down as a crank, a busybody, a third-rate taproom philosopher. And yet, judged by the test of his impact on his own generation and many since, Thomas Paine was the most far-seeing Englishman of the eighteenth century. He was the greatest exile ever driven from these shores. In the teeth of all the slanders and the libels, he remains the major prophet of democracy and representative government, the much-vaunted creed of our Western world. Today, Presidents and Prime Ministers, even Queens on Christmas Day, make obeisance before the central theory of Thomas Paine, the English outlaw and the outcast in the land of his adoption.

In all history, there is no more curious story than that of Paine's blaze to fame, his pitiable fall, and then the slow but assured recovery in his reputation. Strangely, that recovery itself is chiefly his own achievement; it is due to the persistent potency of his pen. No master of the English language—with the exception of H. N. Brailsford in one brief, classic essay—has written his biography.* It is Paine's own writings which have made his name survive while the forgotten historians were busy expurgating it from the records; almost every great democratic statesman or writer has found his way back to the source books.

---

*This sentence is not intended as a reflection on Moncure Conway's excellent and well-researched two-volume work which, published in 1892, started the work of rehabilitation, after Paine and the Painites had had to endure nearly a century of defamation on both sides of the Atlantic. And here for sure was an attempt by an American to repay the debt to 'the Englishman', who wrote *Common Sense* and so described himself on the front page of the first edition. But Conway's book, for all its many virtues, does not place Thomas Paine's life in its full world-wide setting, and none of the others who have written about him would claim to have achieved that spacious feat. He has not received the historical treatment accorded to all the other founders of the American Republic. Neither the United States nor the other country of his adoption nor his England have given him his due. No single country and no exclusive creed can claim him as their own; that is part of his greatness.

And yet even on this reckoning, as a writer, Paine has seldom had his due. American Tories who disliked his arguments found fault with his grammar. Hazlitt was scoffed at for calling him a great writer. More often than not since then, any reference to his literary claims is compressed into a few patronising paragraphs. While he lived his pamphlets probably had a bigger sale than anything published since the invention of the printing press, second only to the Bible. Since his death they have been reprinted and reprinted again in almost every language. Momentary bestsellers can be dismissed; but how can the critics deride the verdict of so mammoth an electorate?

Certainly, his pamphlets sometimes seem ill-constructed and uneven. There is none of the smooth perfection of Swift, although Paine, like Hazlitt and Cobbett, had obviously soaked himself in Swift. There is indeed a grating, metallic flavour in some of his writing. All the mysteries of the universe are quickly made to fit into his mechanical symmetrical system. The lack of subtlety and colour can begin to pall. But then, suddenly, the whole surrounding landscape is lit up by another streak of lightning. These are the real riches of Paine's prose, the abundance of his aphorisms, sharp, hard and glittering, like diamonds. How the gorgeous eloquence of Edmund Burke on the tragedy of Marie Antoinette withers before Paine's most famous epigram: *he pities the plumage, but forgets the dying bird*. More perhaps than all the others who revolted against the English prose style of the eighteenth century, Paine changed the fashion. He is still read because he is still modern. He is, therefore, also, a foremost figure in the history of English literature.

The curiosity is that his immortality could so easily have been foreseen. All the historians had to do was to let his contemporaries bear witness. In an age when it took weeks to cross the Atlantic, he gained an international notoriety such as only pop stars have today. News of the spirit he had aroused around the American campfires spread fast across the civilised world. Little children in Philadelphia and New York knew the name of 'Mr. Common Sense'. A song specially composed in his honour—'He comes, the great Reformer comes'—was sung in the London taverns. He was appointed an honorary member of the French

Convention. When he set foot at Calais the whole town turned out to see him, and pretty girls presented him with cockades all the way to Paris. Hazlitt wrote:

> In 1792 Paine was so great, or so popular an author, and so much read and admired, that the Government was obliged to suspend the Constitution, and to go to war to counteract the effects of his popularity.

Of course the exaggeration was intended, but was it really so wide of the mark? The real crime of Thomas Muir, sentenced to Botany Bay for fourteen years, was the circulation he had given to Paine's *Rights of Man*; twenty-six years later Richard Carlile was put away to solitary confinement in Dorchester gaol for a similar offence. And even today no historian has fully unravelled how large a part was played by fear of the English Jacobins—with Paine as their most effective spokesman—in sending the England of William Pitt to war with revolutionary France. 'A statue of gold ought to be erected to you in every city of the universe', said Napoleon who searched out the old rebel in some Paris back-street. Napoleon claimed, no doubt lyingly, that he slept with the *Rights of Man* under his pillow. Paine was not deceived by the flattering 'French charlatan', but Napoleon's measure of the man and his influence surely offers some proof of his significance.

Finally, the greatest American of the age never wavered in his opinion. Thomas Jefferson always paid honour to Thomas Paine. He knew how Paine had shaped and captured—and refused to betray—the spirit of 1776. That was his supreme moment. Paine was not the very first to use the word but he more than any other had made the Americans unafraid to declare their *independence*. 'The debate is ended', he insisted; America must fight. It was as if in the Britain of 1940 the Churchill resistance speeches had been made not by a national leader but by an unknown journalist who suddenly forced his way to the centre of the stage.

Indeed, in another sense, it was so much more difficult for Paine to give the summons to battle. It was not merely that he made Americans see the prize of independence as something within their grasp; not merely that he personified their frustrations in his picture of George III, the 'Royal Brute of England', the 'hardened, sullen-tempered Pharaoh'. He had also to persuade the aristocratic experts and fainthearts that an upstart pamphleteer understood the English political system better than they. It was not true that the King was the unwilling prisoner of his Ministers, that a message of magnanimous reprieve and reconciliation would miraculously arrive by the next boat. Paine never had the advantage of studying Namier, but he knew how the structure of politics in the reign of George III really worked. He explained how the King and his Ministers distributed their *loaves and fishes*. He knew the contempt in which 'the colonists' were held. He knew, while most Americans would not face it, that America must fight. Jefferson was only nineteen at the time, but he never forgot the man who performed this service to his country.

How grotesque, then, in the face of all these contemporary tributes is the tale that Paine's reputation was something of a bubble. His strength was that he saw with shining clarity the forces changing his world. History offers few examples of such confident and breathtaking foresight. He always believed that the words he had written in some desperate garret forecast the shape of things to come. No cloud of uncertainty crossed his horizon—neither when he walked amid Washington's bedraggled and beaten armies nor when he was being hunted out of England for his high treason with William Pitt's policemen on his heels, nor even, on that most macabre occasion, when he waited in one of Robespierre's prisons to be taken to the guillotine. That was an hour of disillusion and despair if ever there was one. He, the most merciless exposer of monarchy, had pleaded for the King's life in the name of mercy; and when his own life was at stake even his beloved America would not breathe a word to rescue him. Yet with his great argument on earth gone temporarily awry, Paine turned to put heaven to rights. He settled down in his overcrowded cell to write *The Age of Reason*.

Of course, such faith was fanaticism, but it was the fanaticism of genius. Always, once he had become a public figure, Paine was proud, cocksure, incorrigibly combative and vain; vain, in particular, about his writings. (Who wouldn't be when all his major works sold at least 100,000 copies within a matter of months?) Nothing could shake his conviction that within his own lifetime or shortly afterwards—and thanks largely to his own Atlas-like exertions—the world would be turned upside down. He knew he possessed the implement which could work the miracle—the power of free speech, free writing and free thought. Nothing could induce in him a hairsbreadth of doubt; the bigger the bonfires they made of his books, the bigger would be the sales. No other figure in history can ever have believed in the *power* of freedom—and not merely its virtue—with Paine's single-minded intensity. That was his secret. 'Mankind', he said with his grand simplicity, 'are not now to be told they shall not think, or they shall not read.' And, incredibly, he was proved right, as near as mortal man can be.

Thus if the historians malign Paine himself, they are still forced to acknowledge the victory of his opinions. Our modern spacious histories of his times, written with all the advantages of hindsight, portray the American Revolution, the French Revolution and the movement which led to the English Reform Bill as three parts of the same whole. Each reacted on the other and each is incomprehensible without the other. A few Englishmen realised that the cause of English freedom was at stake in the American revolt. A few Englishmen realised that English freedom might be forfeited in the war against revolutionary France. A few Americans realised America's interest in the triumph of the French Revolution. Paine had seen that the same battle was being fought in all three countries. He was the link between the three convulsions. He, an Englishman (and thus he signed anonymously his great American pamphlet, *Common Sense*) was given the key of the Bastille by Lafayette to take across the Atlantic and lay on Washington's table. He wrote:

That the principles of America opened the Bastille is not to be doubted, and therefore the key comes to the right place. I am returned from France to London, and am engaged to return to Paris when the Constitution shall be proclaimed and to carry the American flag in the procession. I have not the least doubt of the final and complete success of the French Revolution. Little ebbings and flowings, for and against, the natural companions of revolution, sometimes appear; but the full current of it is, in my opinion, as fixed as the Gulf Stream.

The England which had denounced Paine as a traitor could not remain immune; it was washed by the same sea. William Blake had helped him to escape from London. William Cobbett, once his most ferocious assailant, admitted: 'at his expiring flambeau I lighted my taper'. All the other English rebels who raised the ferment which led to the Reform Bill pored over his forbidden pages. 'Government is for the living not for the dead', had been Paine's reply to Burke in 1791; forty years later, England marched on, in company with France and America, along the road which Paine, not Burke, had mapped out for her.

Enough of achievement for one man, surely—to understand the three great revolutions of his age before they happened, to bring politics home to the common people, to build a bridge of common idealism across the Atlantic and the English Channel (as firm as the real iron bridge which he invented in his spare time). Yet this was not all. Scattered through his writings we can find hints, often much more than hints, of the other ideas which have given vitality to the democratic movement for the past hundred and fifty years.

Almost a century before Lincoln he sought to write into the American Constitution a clause against slavery. Long before even John Stuart Mill, he championed the rights of women. He was among the very first of English writers to espouse the cause of Indian freedom. Well ahead of my old friends, Dick Crossman or Barbara Castle, he had a good plan for old age pensions. And how men in all our modern parties might tremble at his proposals for land nationalisation; he wanted new laws for marriage and divorce. International arbitration, family allowances, maternity benefits, free education, prison reform, full employment—yes much of the future the Labour Party has offered was previously on offer, in even better English, from Thomas Paine. Note how true these single syllables ring with the triumphant organ note of that last final word: 'It is wrong to say God made *rich* and *poor*;

He made only *male* and *female*; and He gave them the earth for their inheritance.'

It was not until more than 150 years after his death that a statue to Thomas Paine was erected in England. (After a protest, in the year 1963, from a Thetford Conservative Councillor: 'A monument to Thomas Paine on the Market Place would be an insult to the town'). The French and the Americans were less churlish. Paine himself, for all his vanity, would probably agree with Cato who said he would prefer people should ask why he had *not* a monument erected to him than why he had. Even so, surely it is time to make amends. Or can it be that our Establishment, meticulously ticking off those items in his programme still unachieved, feel that no unnecessary chances can be taken? The man still lives. *Rights of Man* still sells some 5,000 copies a year and even that 'Devil's Prayer Book', *The Age of Reason*, can still be read, if not to bring down thunderbolts from heaven, at least to prove that the 'filthy little atheist' was not an atheist at all.

TWELVE

Daniel Defoe, Feminist

> On any monument worthy the name of monument the
> names of *Moll Flanders* and *Roxana*, at least, should be
> carved as deeply as the name of Defoe. They stand among
> the few English novels which we can call indisputably great.
>
> VIRGINIA WOOLF

SOMETIME IN THE SUMMER of the year 1660 (the exact date is
unknown) a Cripplegate butcher and his wife brought forth a
prodigy—Daniel Defoe, author of almost the first and still the
most famous novel ever written. But the world had still to wait
more than half a century for *The Life and Strange Surprising
Adventures of Robinson Crusoe, of York, Mariner*. It was not until
his fifty-ninth year—in 1719—that Defoe turned his aching hand
from journalism and sat down in his Stoke Newington retreat to
produce his masterpiece.

Success was instantaneous. 'There is not an old woman',
wrote one jealous competitor, 'that can go to the price of it, but
buys the "Life and Adventures," and leaves it as legacy with the
"Pilgrim's Progress," the "Practice of Piety" and "God's Revenge
Against Murther" to her posterity.' Everybody was snatching for
it, even those who sneered. So Defoe swiftly scribbled off a
sequel. He went on scribbling at an unaccountable pace for the
remaining ten years of his life, churning out newspaper articles,
manuals on manners, marriage, economics and every conceivable
topic, with a new novel roughly every twelve months. Three more
at least—*Moll Flanders, Roxana, A Journal of the Plague Year*—
must be classed as masterpieces alongside *Robinson Crusoe*. During
that last decade, indeed—particularly between the years 1719 and
1722—the genius of Defoe suddenly sprouted into a winter
blossom unexampled in the whole range of literature.

No one at the time foresaw his immortality. Alexander Pope recognised the excellence of *Robinson Crusoe*, but his tribute had a touch of patronage. No one believed that Defoe would surpass in fame all the other great men of the age, the Addisons and the Steeles, with Swift alone surviving as his one acknowledged master. Defoe, to his contemporaries, was a Grub Street hack who could never aspire to real literary eminence. And Defoe himself, despite his abounding vanity, half shared the general opinion. The erratic promptings of his old Puritan conscience made him apologise for writing 'mere fiction'. *Robinson Crusoe* and *Moll Flanders*, he claimed, were moral tracts, like so much else he had written. He was prouder of his *True-Born Englishman*, the doggerel verse he had produced twenty years earlier. The fact was he wrote for bread, and the *True-Born Englishman* had sold 40,000 copies, making him for a moment the most widely read poet in the English language.

Even when he died—he was still on the run from his creditors whom all the royalties from *Crusoe* could not fend off—none of the obituaries mourned the founder of the English novel. On the burial register they got his name wrong: 'Mr. Dubow.' And the register of St. Giles, Cripplegate, recorded quite simply and falsely: 'Mr. Defoe, Gentleman.'

Whatever else he was, he was never that. He was by turns a tradesman, an adventurer, a radical pamphleteer and agitator, a reporter, a spy, a gallant crusader, a crawling sycophant, a man accepted in court circles and once the confidant of the King and then able to plunge with equal zest into the lowest life of London; for months or even years on end, his diligent biographers cannot track him down through those murky, labyrinthine lairs. Half his life he seemed to be bombarding Ministers with far-seeing schemes for new trading projects, for founding new colonies, for military expeditions, for old-age pensions and marine insurance, for establishing academies for education or asylums for the insane. Through the other half he was getting practical acquaintance with 'that worst of devils, poverty'.

He was a preacher and a moraliser, too, obsessed with the religious controversies of his time. Often he reads like an eighteenth-century Samuel Smiles. But often again all the smugness is shattered with one sharp blow from the Defoean hammer for hypocrisy.

> To be reduced to necessity is to be wicked; for necessity is not only the temptation, but it is such a temptation as human nature is not empowered to resist.

Who could believe, after this, that some of his biographers would strive to reduce him to a plaster saint, a little bourgeois Bunyan?

Even those two halves of his life were nothing more than fragments; so many other lives as well remain to be explained. Apart from the great merchant sailors themselves, he was the foremost traveller of his age; searching out, as he claimed, every nook and corner of England, the first English writer to discover Scotland, knowing Italy, France and Spain besides and still, with it all, staying the most obvious and knowledgeable of Londoners. He called himself a native of the universe; and he explored his own city as ruthlessly as Hogarth or Dickens.

He was, too, the most prolific writer of his age, and perhaps of any other. Only when forty years old did he set out on his full career as a journalist, but then he went to work with a stupendous will and energy. He devised his own shorthand. He established some sixty correspondents or agents all over the country. For nine years he ran his own *Review*, producing the whole of it two or three times a week and still finding time to write for other journals (not omitting to commend their most percipient articles from his own anonymous hand in his own *Review*) and pour forth a deluge of pamphlets and satirical poems interspersed with full-length histories and biographies. Every night of those hectic years, after his day in the saddle, Defoe must have been writing several thousands of words.

He wrote:

> The unhappy People are deluded, are impos'd upon, are fermented, their Spirits disorder'd, *and how?* By raising false Reports, affirming forg'd and barbarous Allegations, raising Scandalous Surmises, and

pushing about absurd, ridiculous and incongruous Whymsies among the well-meaning but ignorant People.

Daniel Defoe undertook to turn back the flood single-handed. The father of English journalism, like the later founder of the English novel, did not care a straw for academic theories about his art. He had to feed his wife and eight children.

Above all, he was at war. He was himself, of course, 'a man of peace and reason', set upon from every quarter by devils. How wrathfully he insisted on liberty for himself and how complacently he watched restraints imposed on his licentious competitors. Apart from his clear distinction, he never worried his head about drawing the ineffable line between liberty and licence. Doubtless he was right; no one since has discovered where to draw it, either. For thirty years Defoe was in the thick of the journalistic hurly-burly at a time when it raged with more ferocity than in almost any other epoch. In one sense the struggle must have been more wearing for him than most of the others; for he was alone, a member of no party at a time when party affiliations were being drawn as sharply as battle lines. Although a life-long supporter of the Protestant settlement of 1688, Defoe was never able to enlist wholeheartedly under the flag of its most loyal upholders, the Whigs. Always his unfailing curiosity, ingenuity and inventiveness were forcing him to stray from the beaten track. All he would be able to claim with certainty on the Day of Judgement, in extenuation of his twists and turns, was that he had never actually been a Tory; was he not one of the first of English writers to explain the origin of those party labels and had he not further gleefully explained how the nicknames served their purpose 'till at last the word Tory became popular, and it stuck so close to the party in all their bloody proceedings, that they had no way to get it off?'

Defoe was, in fact, sent to Newgate Prison and made to stand in the pillory by the highest of high Tory Ministers for his satirical pamphlet, *The Shortest Way With Dissenters*, which outraged the bishops without comforting the dissenters. But then, within a few years, it seemed that, for all his disavowals of the horrific charge, he was content to do the bidding of a Tory Ministry. The suspicion grew that he was not merely a hack, but a treacherous paid hack at that. The suspicion was well-founded, although we have had to wait until the archives were opened to clinch it. In Newgate, Defoe's spirit wilted.

> I agreed to give the Court No Trouble but to plead Guilty to the Indictment, Even to all the Adverbs, the Seditiously's, the Maliciously's and a Long Rhapsody of the Lawyers et Ceteras; and all this upon promises of being used Tenderly.

The man who got him out was Robert Harley. Harley, like Defoe, was a middle-of-the roader, but he became more and more encoiled in the manoeuvres of the Tories and lived to be the head of the most explicitly Tory Administration which Britain had yet known; indeed, the first man in history to be called Prime Minister in the parlance of the day. This was another piece of English history which Defoe helped to make; the term had first been used in one of his letters to Harley. Defoe was ready to serve his hero with uncritical devotion. 'Intelligence', he wrote, 'is the Soul of all Publick Business.' He showed an incredible assiduity in supplying it. 'If you'll allow the Vanity of the Expression, *If I were a Public Minister*, I would if Possible kno'what Every body said of me.' Harley, it seems, was the first politician who, with Defoe's help, paid proper attention to his press cuttings.

It might have been thought that all Defoe's other multitudinous activities were enough. He was a merchant as well as a journalist, dealing at one time and another in bricks, tiles, hosiery, cheese, oysters, and heaven knows what else and bankrupting himself to the tune of £17,000 at the age of thirty. But in his busiest decade, when he worked for Harley and wrote his *Review*, he was also secret agent and propagandist-in-chief for the man who had saved him from prison and might still save him from his creditors. For his chosen Prime Minister he performed all the duties now severally discharged by Downing Street Public Relations Officers, Durrant's press cutting agency, the research students of the Conservative Central Office and the leader writers of the *Daily Telegraph*.

Small wonder that his fellow practitioners in Grub Street

pursued him with a special venom. One of the ablest, Abel Boyer—as a journalist and historian quite a match for Defoe himself—ripped aside the mask at every available opportunity. Defoe, the man of moderation, retaliated by calling Boyer a sodomite. The daggers were out in those last years of the Queen and the early years of the new King.

Defoe stooped or was driven to the depths. Switching back his allegiance to the Whigs, he was ready to be assigned by the government spies to a Tory newspaper, there to pass himself off as a Jacobite, doctor the editorials in the government interest and play the informer against his unsuspecting editor. 'Thus I bow in the House of Rimmon', said the man who had once so bravely, in his dissenting youth, marched out to fight under the green banners of 'King Monmouth' at Sedgemoor, challenged the silly boasts of racial superiority with his satire *The True Born Englishman*, and paid for his detestation of religious persecution in the pillory. It seemed a pitiable end but the end had not quite come.

Those biographers of Defoe who try to wipe away the dirt from his political apostasies and subterfuges cannot adequately explain the glorious flowering of his final years. The miracle of Defoe remains his sudden and belated mastery of a new form of writing in *Robinson Crusoe* and *Moll Flanders*. The world would not have had either if their creator had not been forced by the screw of money and politics from desperation to dishonour. If Swift had never descended into the mire of English politics *Gulliver's Travels* would never have been written. Defoe never achieved Swift's corrosive indignation and contempt for the conventional thought of his day. But he learnt enough to take the edge off his complacency and transform the self-righteous polemicist into a great novelist.

The jaunty, inquisitive, bubbling, so self-confident, moralising bourgeois adventurer, which is the face Defoe so often presents, had also seen with his own eyes and knew in his own heart how relentless the devil of poverty could be. Like Moll, if not so frequently, he had yielded to temptation. Once he turned to fiction he could tell the whole truth; all the half-lies and the devious cheatings and devices he had felt compelled to employ in his journalistic career enabled him to do it with a special relish.

Robinson Crusoe was a moral tract in a way, but not in the way that Defoe tried to commend it to his prudish public. If anyone wants to see how an incipient agnostic in a religious age tries not to shirk while still camouflaging his doubts, let him study Crusoe's lame efforts to make Man Friday a good Protestant. And yet *Robinson Crusoe*, despite all its marvellous invention and suspense, is not the finest of his works. As the best of his biographers, Mr. James Sutherland, has suggested, there is more of Defoe in Moll Flanders than in any other of his characters. Here he returns to the radicalism of his youth. Once in his young days he wrote a pamphlet called *The Poor Man's Plea*, some passages of which could have been written by a Leveller around the camp-fires of Cromwell's army. Here, in *Moll Flanders*, the Poor Man's Plea is heard again; even more the Poor Woman's Plea, for *Moll Flanders* is also a feminist tract, justifying the ways of woman to God and man.

'There are more thieves and rogues made by that prison of Newgate, than by all the clubs and societies of villains in the nation.' Moll was born in Newgate; she ought to know. She knows much else besides:

> She is always married too soon who gets a bad husband and she is never married too late who gets a good one; in a word, there is no woman, deformity or bad reputation excepted, but if she manages well may be married safely one time or another; but if she precipitates herself, it is ten thousand to one she is undone.

If anyone could doubt that moral embedded in this most immoral of tracts, *Roxana* came a few years later to clinch the case even more impudently.

But, most of all, *Moll Flanders* displays the art, the insight, the mind, the humour—a quality which he shows only in occasional flashes—the unquenchable optimism amid despair and disgrace of Defoe himself. We are told in the Preface:

> When a woman, debauched from youth, nay, even being the offspring of debauchery and vice, comes to give an account of all her vicious practices, and even to descend to the particular occasions and

circumstances by which she first became wicked, and of all the progressions of crime which she ran through in three score years, an author must be hard put to it to wrap it up so clean as not to give room, especially for vicious readers, to turn it to his disadvantage.

However, the fact underlined in that superb Defoean sentence is that at last Defoe did not feel the need to wrap it all up. The truth he had bottled up within himself for so long poured out in golden spate.

POSTSCRIPT

In August 1959, the House of Commons passed a so-called Street Offences Act designed to fulfil that part of a Committee of Inquiry which proposed means of moving prostitutes off the streets.

Daniel Defoe had always been fascinated by this subject. Hence *Moll Flanders, Roxana* and many other references throughout his writing. Here is how he, or rather Moll Flanders, his favourite creation, might have viewed the 1959 Act.

AN INCIDENT WITH A CONSTABLE

I was walking down one of those streets near Soho fields as cool and jaunty as can be imagined, decked in some finery and with my head held high but with at least one eye well cocked to study what might befall, when a young constable (he could not have been above twenty years and was handsome enough, I swear, to be my own son by my Lancashire husband) approached me in a manner too insolent to be mentioned.

'You're a common whore,' he said without so much as a by-your-leave; 'and I'll have you in front of the magistrate and into Newgate prison before you can say Robinson Crusoe.'

My distress, you may suppose, was something considerable. Never before had I been confronted in such a manner in a public place, not to say privately.

Readers of my earlier misfortunes will recall that never once had I been so indelicate to transact my business on the streets;

except on that one occasion when I went to Bartholomew Fair and met the gentleman extremely well dressed and very rich whose name I was mannerly enough not to record; and, then, you may agree, something must be allowed for the quality of the gentleman, the quantity of drink he had taken and the merry time of year: not that any of these matters are advanced to reduce the fervour of my penitentials. I offer no opinions and recite only facts.

'Indeed,' says I to the constable with as much spirit as you may guess; 'and what gives you the right to accost honest gentle-women in this style? Save your insults for your own sex and save your daring to deal with those thieves and pickpockets who, with so little to fear from the bold guardians of the law, threaten and terrify hard-toiling traders. Begone, you dog, before I must report you for your pranks to your grieving mother.'

'Not so fast, Mrs. Flanders,' says he, with a scoff. 'Not so hasty, Moll.' This was indeed a strange address. Few knew my name, at least in those outlying villages. But I was granted no time for cautious reflection. Did I not read the public prints? Did I not know the new law? 'Madam,' says he, affecting the stiffest decorum, 'I find you don't know what it is to be a constable now; I beg of you, don't oblige me to be rude to you.'

In short, the whole tale came out. He had the power, so he insisted, to clear the streets and bundle us all into Newgate.

I had a mind to tell him, and had already started, of my own mother and how she had only escaped from that terrible place by pleading her belly; how Newgate was a house to make whores, not to cure them; how in that roaring, swearing clamour, amid that stench and nastiness, thieves and murderers, let alone women sadly neglectful of their virtue, were bred in legions too vast to be apprehended by all the constables in Christendom; and such like and so forth and much more.

But by now a considerable company had assembled. 'They've got you now, Molly,' jeered one who could not have known me from Eve. 'Take her away,' said another. The rest were not so churlish. 'Leave her alone; what's she done to you?' they cried.

And so the buzz became louder every minute. However, as luck would have it, the press was so great, that several sturdy citizens of Soho had wedged themselves between myself and the constable. I decided to run for it, never stopping until I had reached my governess's house and slammed the door behind me.

My governess had always acted the true mother. She cried with me and for me. She put me to bed. And then, with my breath recovered, she told me to tell her plainly all that had happened and everything the constable had said. She followed all I had to recount with many an 'indeed,' many 'Oh Fies!' and such-like expressions.

I did not refrain from appealing to her with the woman's rhetoric of tears. But now my governess who, as I have told you, had treated me more amiably than anyone else in my life, showed a mood more curious than anything I had ever known. At first, I thought she was sobbing at the affront offered to her comrade in so many adventures. But no; these were not sobs. She was shaking with mirth and not so long after she broke into peals of laughter.

'Mrs. Flanders,' says she. 'We shall help your handsome brave constable to clear the streets. We shall do it for him. I did not tell you, dear Moll, when first you came to entrust yourself to my care, what was the exact nature of my calling or profession. But now that it is blessed by the Secretary of State, by the House of Commons, by the House of Lords, by the full bench of Bishops and high society, I need blush no longer.

'Others, I fear, may not treat you as gently as I. We shall have every rogue and escaped felon fit for Tyburn competing in our trade. But then, consider the gain for honest folk too fastidious to believe their own eyes; you always had the tenderest thoughts for gentlemen and gentlewomen, never reckoning your affairs so different from theirs, since all you ever did (apart from that visit to Bartholomew Fair in the Springtime) was to make matrimony a matter of fortune.

'Sleep soundly, dearest Moll. Spare yourself, if you can, any nightmares about Newgate. Tomorrow or the day after both of us shall be rich beyond our dreams; and, along with us, every lord and lady, every gentleman and gentlewoman in the land, may give praise to the authors of the Brothel Keepers' Charter.'

THIRTEEN

In Defence
of the Duchess

> 'I am afraid that we must expect things to go from bad to
> worse in England so long as a woman is in charge. She lets
> herself be led by many wrong-headed people . . .'
>
> Prince Eugen of Savoy, to the
> Imperial representative in The
> Hague, January 1710.

'A BOOK WITHOUT A WOMAN', said Jill, my wife, more on a note
of scorn than anything else, and in our household the offence, if
true, was especially reprehensible. The room of her own, the
room where she works, when she is not cooking, gardening,
shopping, cleaning, making beds, entertaining and the rest, is a
feminist temple, a shrine dedicated to the cause of women's
rights. Every book on every shelf, every picture, every inch of wall
space helps to tell the story of how, mostly, women had to
liberate themselves, what mountains of male tyranny and
imbecility they had to move to achieve it, what agonies of
subjection they endured; how indeed the true role of women in
history and in literature has been twisted and bowdlerised
beyond all reckoning, and how only now, and still most
diffidently, has the task of discovering the truth begun; and yet,
with it all, how the liberation of women is always properly to be
seen as part of the wider liberation of mankind and womankind in
general: a splendid, spacious theme, if ever there was one, with
endless permutations.

An error, then, not to have included even one woman in a title
role in the original cast, and I thought for one swift moment that

an easy riposte might be found by adding up the number of males and females which Virginia Woolf, the princess of modern feminists, includes in her two volumes of one of our favourite companions, *The Common Reader*, but that argument does not quite hold. (The figure, if anyone still wants to know, is seventeen women subjects out of the full list of thirty-eight.) So I was driven back on the fragile defence that women of one kind and another, conspicuous if not actually liberated, played their part in the lives of all the chosen heroes, and a brief backward glance at the list may reveal how the original error was merely compounded.

My mother ruled every roost where she and my father ever alighted; she knew something of women's rights, but still had little enough time to enjoy them, having to rear seven children, five of them males, each with his streak of armour-plated male aggressiveness which she condemned in theory and unwittingly encouraged in practice: so no sign of rescue appeared there, and, thereafter, the case seems to weaken further. William Hazlitt deserted two wives, or two wives deserted him, and his affair with Sarah was, from the woman's point of view, a romantic fiasco. Thomas Paine left, or was left by, only one actual wife, but mostly over his relations with women a veil is drawn, and by his own hand. Bertrand Russell left several and, as one of them, Dora, has explained, he was not quite, as he appeared to outside admirers like myself, the strict practitioner of his own precepts. Bonar Thompson, it must be sadly admitted, although happily married, was a fierce, explicit enemy of the women's movement in his time. As for Max Beaverbrook and Randolph Churchill, they were raging, rampaging male chauvinists long before the term had ever been considered sexually apposite. And even little, endearing Vicky had his marital and sexual disasters; not that they, by themselves or in any combination, can clinch the feminist case, but he can hardly be listed as a firm recruit in the opposite camp.

So where does that leave us—or me? Has some revealing manual been unwittingly compiled by a series of Freudian slips, by this time almost a Freudian avalanche? Can the others come to the rescue? The sex life of Jonathan Swift, the mystery of his relationship with Stella and Vanessa, has been for years a prime subject of scholarly studies; but here too there is an awkward case to answer. James Joyce was a devoted Swiftian, honouring his writing by every form of allusion, imitation and assimilation. But he also made a direct attack on Swift's character. Once he and Frank Budgen engaged in a conversation about Swift's 'secret grief'.

'I suppose', said Budgen, 'that the proud, sensitive man needed love but that pride robbed him of the power of self-surrender that love demands of man or woman.'

'Maybe', said Joyce, 'but that isn't enough. The reason must be not latent but manifest. Anyway, the man was a strong and stingy sentimentalist. He meddled with and muddled up two women's lives.'

Let that terrible indictment stand for just a moment. Three at least out of the full complement here can be impregnably registered as champions of women's rights without any question or qualification whatever. One is Daniel Defoe, almost the first, if not *the* first, male spokesman in the cause. The second is H. N. Brailsford, the most eloquent male spokesman in the pre-1914 struggle, with his friend, H. W. Nevinson, as his only rival claimant to the title. The third is Benjamin Disraeli who expressed his feminism, to use the word anachronistically, more in thought and word than in deed, but whose long allegiance to the idea is all the more remarkable in the light of his other political interests and affiliations.

Where did he learn it? The newly discovered Disraeli novel, *A Year at Hartlebury or The Election*, published in March 1834, contains a passage in which a fine old Dame, Dame Harrald, laments outside some almshouse door the fact that women have not the vote. 'In this world', she protests, 'the men have it all their own way.' Here is an early suffragist or suffragette demand, it might be thought, considering that women did not get the vote until ninety-odd years later, and considering that even the Chartists in their confabulations at the time, in that very same decade, could not finally agree to include votes for women in their demand for parliamentary reform. Yet the idea was not so entirely novel. 'I dined with Bulwer *en famille* on Sunday, "To meet some truffles"—very agreeable company,' wrote Disraeli to his sister Sarah in 29 January, 1833. 'His mother-in-law, Mrs.

Wheeler, was there; not so pleasant, something between Jeremy Bentham and Meg Merrilies, very clever, but awfully revolutionary. She poured forth all her systems upon my novitiate ear, and while she advocated the rights of women, Bulwer abused system-mongers and the sex, and Rosina played with her dog.'

Anna Wheeler's political assault upon, or seduction of, the young Disraeli—she looks very much like the model for Dame Harrald in *Hartlebury*—was just one of her minor casual triumphs. More serious and significant was her association with the early Socialist writer, William Thompson, who wrote in 1825 and dedicated to her his *Appeal of One Half of the Human Race, Women, against the Pretensions of the Other Half, Men, to restrain them in Political and thence in Civil and Domestic Slavery*. Anna has some claim to be the biggest woman figure in the movement of woman's emancipation between Mary Wollstonecraft and Emmeline Pankhurst. But who knows anything about her? Who writes about her? Where can we read of her? She finds no place in the Dictionary of National Biography. Her name and fame are suppressed, forgotten, hard now to disinter from the man-made mausoleum of history.

The monstrous suppression will not last for ever, and mostly of course the women achieve their own historical and literary discoveries. But sometimes the men assist in rolling away the boulders. 'When I read history, and am impressed by any deed or occurrence', wrote Heinrich Heine, 'I often feel as if I should like to see the woman concealed behind it, as the secret spring. The women govern, although the *Moniteur* only mentions men: they make history, although the historians know only the names of men.' And lest anyone imagines that Heine, writing a century and a half ago on the subject, was soon to be overtaken by the modern age or modern historians, let us recall the verdict of one of the most eminent of modern English historians, Professor J. H. Plumb, Professor of Modern English history at Cambridge University:

How very few women have left an indelible mark on English history—a queen or two, a novelist or two, a couple of nurses, maybe a brace of actresses, but the list is a short one, and perhaps only Sarah,

Duchess of Marlborough gets into it by sheer flaming temperament. What a virago she was!*

The word *virago* is now being transmuted by a most excellent publishing firm into a term of approbation and honour, like *Leveller* or *Suffragette* itself; but it was not always so, and certainly it was never so intended by Professor Plumb. And how mean and miserable is his fiercely truncated list of the names which are known, and how aggressively oblivious he is of the legions who are unknown or half-known, and how wretched are the conditions upon which Sarah is admitted to the English pantheon inhabited well-nigh exclusively by males. Nothing much but her screaming tantrums to recommend her! Thus history is reduced to the level of something concocted by gossip columnists.

The only excuse for such churlishness in the estimate of Sarah's character at this late date is that the same misapprehension has occasionally been shown, not only by her sworn enemies but even across the centuries by the supposedly magnanimous Churchills. The first Duke of Marlborough loved the Duchess and, probably, never wavered in his affections, despite her furious allegations to the contrary. Yet the extraordinary fact is that he never grasped the scale of her political intelligence. Not all her huge progeny of sons, daughters, sons-in-law, daughters-in-law, grandsons and granddaughters, shared that devotion; indeed if the tally is properly made she quarrelled with them all. Yet politics lay at the root of much of this dissension, and if the first great Duke could not see the wisdom of her prescriptions, why should these lesser figures in the family show a greater perspicacity? All through her long, cantankerous widowhood—she survived the Duke by twenty-two years—she unloosed what looked like spleen on almost everyone within range, with a special spatter of venom for

---

*Professor Plumb's words are taken from his review of two books on the Duchess published a few years ago, one *Sarah, Duchess of Marlborough* by David Green (Collins, 1967) and the other *Rule of Three: Sarah, Duchess of Marlborough and her Companions in Power* by Iris Butler (Hodder, 1967). Both are reasonably friendly to the Duchess; both are well worth reading; but neither succeeded in altering the assumptions about the Duchess, of which Professor Plumb's comment was all too typical.

members of the family. Most of Marlborough's biographers, including Sir Winston Churchill, felt little obligation to come to her rescue. Rather, she can be made the scapegoat for the Duke's political setbacks. Most of his letters to her are preserved; most of hers to him are gone. So it is his case which is readily available to historians. Moreover, despite that deep love between them, there is the ugly fact, which obviously stuck in Sir Winston's gullet, that her charge of infidelity against him was made just at the moment when he was preparing to march across Europe to Blenheim and eternal fame. How can her reputation ever blossom beneath his shadow—even if we may dare to whisper that he was not actually put off the march or the glory? Finally, to descend from these heights, I may be permitted to recall that the Winstonian view of Sarah was adopted by Randolph (*our* Randolph, of this century) in an extreme form. He could not sit silent and hear Sarah praised. Nothing else mattered but military victory, and her single womanly duty in life was to protect the Duke's interest at Queen Anne's court. This influence, for whatever reason, she had forfeited, and judgement upon her must be pronounced accordingly—which final rite Randolph performed with mounting wrath, thus proving, as I believed, before our eyes that Sarah's sulphurous blood still ran in his veins.

Could it be, can it be, that the Plumb portrait is accurate after all? Contemporary pamphleteers saw her villainous profile:

On the Right Hand an oldish woman, of a fair countenance, in youthfull Dress; her chin and nose turning up, her Eyes glowing like Lightning; blasted all she had power over with strange Diseases—Out of her nostrils came a Sulphurous Smoak, and out of her Mouth Flames of Fire. Her hair was grisled and adorn'd with Spoils of ruined People. Her neck bare, with Chains about it of Dice, mixed with Pieces of Gold, which rattling, made a horrid noise; for her Motions were all fierce and violent. Her garment was all stained with Tears and Blood.

And another pamphleteer, not so anonymous then and not at all since, Jonathan Swift, compiled a whole anthology of abuse designed to deluge this single head 'Three Furies', he said to summarise, 'reigned in her breast, the most mortal enemies of all softer passions, which were sordid Avarice, disdainful Pride and ungovernable Rage.'

But let judgement be reserved. One of the strongest strands in Sarah's character, the one I suspect which especially provoked the blindest fury from her legion of enemies, was that she mastered many of the arts in which women were not supposed to dabble. She despised the backstairs ('I think anyone that has common sense or honesty must needs be very weary of every thing that one meets with in courts'), and wanted to capture other arenas altogether. She conducted, even apart from her battles on behalf of Marlborough, a one-woman liberation.

She made herself, as she herself said, 'a kind of author'. It is hard to know which to marvel at the more, the modesty of the claim from one not normally modest or its truth—especially since in her early years she had accepted the orthodox doctrine of the time about the non-education of girls. 'I am no scholar', she came near to boasting, 'nor a wit, thank God', or on another occasion: 'An ounce of mother wit is better than a pound of clargy.' Her mother wit and her other charms were quite sufficient to enable her to capture young Churchill at the time of her choosing; she needed no assistance from any other art. True, women authors were beginning, just at that time and soon after, to make something of a name in Grub Street or elsewhere: Mary Astell, for example, a true pioneer among woman writers or Mrs. Riviere Manley who was there to prove that the malice would not be left to the men. But why should radiant court beauties who had already set out, with the aid of other gifts, on the path to fame, fortune, and great estates, worry their pretty heads about learning how to use pens? Sarah soon did, and what she must have absorbed for the purpose is a wonder in itself. 'I am of the simple sex', she once said, incredibly, 'and I tumble my mind out on paper without any disguise.' Who will believe it was just quite like that? Mostly she would scorn any disguise in any situation anywhere, but her downright simplicity of style was not so easily acquired. The books on the shelves in her libraries at Blenheim or later St. Albans included Burton, Burnet, Clarendon, Milton, Cowper, Dryden, Spencer, Shakespeare, Ben Jonson, *Don Quixote*, Montaigne, Cowley, Waller, St. Egremont, Plutarch and Epictetus in translation, several volumes on medicine, architecture and theology, with Swift and Addison to add the final contemporary touch. No doubt most of these shelf-fuls in great houses, even in those days, were intended for display, and Sarah herself would not allow that she was deeply read; but she did take one or two favourites to her heart, notably *Don Quixote* and Montaigne, and one of her correspondents was driven to remark: 'In your letter that lyes now before me, one part is written exactly after Montaigne's manner, so much has your Grace profited by those few Books which you say you have read.' No bookworm, for sure: what she wanted was action, but that she did read is proved in her own writing. Anyhow, she had plenty to divert her from Queen Anne's royal 'twitell-twatell'.

Alas, huge stacks of what she wrote herself, in her correspondence to Marlborough in particular but to many others besides, were destroyed on her own orders. Yet mountains remain—some six hundred volumes have recently arrived from Blenheim at the British Library, and out of it all a new vindication of Sarah may come. Yet for some reason her published writing, her own book *The Conduct**, together with the portraits of some of her contemporaries, has rarely received the credit it deserves. Horace Walpole condemned it, at the time of publication, as 'the annals of a wardrobe rather than a reign', and neither she nor her admirers have ever been able quite to remove the effects of that sneer. It is true that she managed to recount the events of that age, including even how King William would gobble his dish of peas, without even mentioning the Battle of Blenheim. Must she not be convicted, then, from her own mouth, as a woman of constricted mind, an incorrigible gossip herself, confined by the Horace Walpole sense of proportion? Maybe; and who is Horace Walpole to complain? It is hard not to suppose that in dealing with the Duchess he was just avenging his father for her ancient feud against him. But *The Conduct* is truly a much better book than that. It is fresh, glowing with life, lit up by the political

---

*An Account of the Conduct of the Dowager Duchess of Marlborough. From her first coming to Court to the Year 1710 In a letter from Herself to MYLORD published in 1842.

flames of party strife which rose so high in Queen Anne's time but which scarcely still smouldered when the book was published thirty years later. The language in which it is written has a force and fury of its own; sharp, hard, belligerent, immediately intelligible, and yet not in any sense naive. She wanted everyone to know—a good reason for writing.

And she always had the sense to realise there was a battle on. Never had she had any patience with those, her husband included, who hankered always for some uneasy accommodation above party strife. The facts could not be altered; the beginning of wisdom was to face them. From her earliest days of introduction to the political scene she had imbibed Whig principles, a hatred of 'the gibberish' of the Tories 'about non-resistance and passive obedience and hereditary right', a splendid contempt for 'the High Church nonsense of promoting religion by persecution'. As it happened, when King William III first arrived he heaped hardship on the Marlborough family, but that could not drive Sarah into the opposite camp:

> As I was perfectly convinced that a Roman Catholic is not to be trusted with the liberties of England, I never once repined at the change of government, no, not in all the time of that long persecution I went through.

When William had sent Marlborough to the Tower, she still did not waver. To a friend who offered bail she replied that 'one of his best friends was a paper that lay upon the table which I had often kissed, the Act of Habeas Corpus'—and Sarah, be it not forgotten, was only then nine years old when Habeas Corpus was enacted. England was at that time the only country in the world where such a protection for individual rights existed; how much of English liberty do we owe to those who treasured it as Sarah did. Marlborough would go off and fight, and win, the wars; no one appreciated that necessity better than Sarah. But there were other unavoidable battles to be fought and indispensable victories to be won here at home, where Sarah grasped the reality so much more firmly than Marlborough himself, and how infuriating it must have been when the doors were slammed in her face. 'I am confident', she asserted (and who would ever doubt it?), 'that I would have been the greatest hero that was ever known in the Parliament House, if I had been so happy as to have been a man.'

How nearly the men on the larger stage, in the Parliament House without her assistance and outside, came to casting aside all that had been won at home and abroad. How foolish they were not to recognise her simple proposition. If English and European liberties depended on victory, Marlborough would need to make terms with the men who truly believed in them, the party which had burnt its boats and staked its whole future on the Protestant succession. This was the gospel which she preached in season and out of season, to the Queen, to the Duke and to the whole of her entourage. And who can say that she was wrong? Terribly late and by *force majeure* Marlborough himself was brought to the same conclusion. At last he too realised that his fate was interlocked with that of the great Whig Lords. But how much safer his base at home would have been if he had recognised the fact earlier, and had pursued the aim of an alliance with the Whigs from the beginning of the reign with something of Sarah's rock-like determination.

Sarah foresaw the future more plainly than most of her contemporaries, especially those of her own class. She recognised that the Whig grandees, denounced by Anne and Marlborough as factious self-seekers, were the real custodians of the spirit of the age, the unwitting protectors of the English liberty she loved. They alone could safeguard the achievements of the English Revolution against Stuart counter-revolution. She strove to rally all her friends, including her husband, to this cause, and everyone would have been saved a lot of trouble if her advice had been accepted sooner. She was a modern, independent woman, and, judged by her ideas and manners, the citizen of a new century into which Marlborough, with his fear of public opinion and open debate, survived only as an anachronism.

So there was a political clash of temperament between them, arising partly from her feminism, to use the word even more anachronistically than in the case of Disraeli, and how little it has been allowed for by even the greatest of the Duke's biographers may be seen in the famous story of her retort to the Duke of Somerset's proposal of marriage delivered, of course, long after

Marlborough was dead and when she was a ripe but still devastatingly beautiful sixty-three. The historian William Coxe, a near-contemporary, had one majestic version which Sir Winston grandiloquently and excusably reiterated:

> If I were young and handsome as I was instead of old and faded as I am, and you could lay the empire of the world at my feet, you should never share the heart and hand that once belonged to John, Duke of Marlborough.

Magnificent, but not Sarah! In more recent times a copy of the actual letter of refusal was discovered in the Blenheim archives and a review in *The Times Literary Supplement* described it as 'more prosaic and more probable'. More probable and less romantic, for sure: but prosaic is not precisely the term to describe this declaration of independence which was surely directed not to the Duke but to mankind in general:

> I am confident that there is very few women (if any) that would not be extremely pleased with what your grace proposes to me; but I am resolved never to change my condition, and if I know anything of myself I would not marry the Emperor of the world tho I were but thirty years old . . .

Such was the woman to whom Professor Plumb will attribute greatness only on account of her viragoish temperament. What great men could survive similar discrimination—to see all their political aims and accomplishments submerged beneath domestic embroilments and vanities. What would happen, on such a condition, to Lloyd George's fame or Lord Palmerston's, and how many more? Even Henry VIII managed to pass himself off as a Renaissance prince, a Protestant hero, a Tudor statesman, and that, moreover, at the hands of Victorian historians. How pitiful by comparison is the dispensation customarily allowed poor Sarah, and the caricature largely sketched by Professor Plumb would not have been recognised, even in her rancorous old age, by some of her bitterest critics and former enemies. For, strangest of all, this Lady Macbeth *manqué* had a sense of humour which kept on breaking out at the most unlikely moments and right to her dying day. Voltaire came to call on her, wanting to see her Memoirs before publication, but she insisted: 'Wait a little; I am altering my account of Queen Anne's character. I have come to love her again since the present lot have become our governors.'* At the age of eighty-one she exchanged enchanting letters, part flirtatious, part remonstrative, with Alexander Pope who had once attacked her and her Duke almost as furiously as Swift but who became so captivated that, enfolded in a character-sketch of her of excruciating perception, were his last words, almost: 'What a girl you are!' Almost, but not quite. Pope, allegedly, lampooned her as Atossa in his *Moral Essays*. Almost certainly the allegation was false; he had another beauty on his list. Enough damage had been done, in her estimate, however, to restore him to the status of 'that crooked, perverse little wretch at Twickenham'—quite a kindly rebuke in the circumstances. And happily no such last-minute cloud befell an even more remarkable literary reconciliation. She was 'in raptures' over *Gulliver's Travels*, and sat up in bed lamenting—if only *he* had been on our side in the old battles of Queen Anne's time. She 'grew prodigiously fond of him', and 'could easily forgive him all the slaps he has given me and the Duke of Marlborough'. And she could flick aside anyone she wanted with the lightest touch of one of those old arthritic fingers. I like this epitaph on a great man otherwise quite forgotten:

> Lord Scarborough voted with the minority, and spoke, though he has something so very particular, that I can't be sure he will go on, for he is always splitting a hair; but there is now, I think, no hair to split.

One of the great questions of politics which politicians do not always appreciate is to discern the moments when there are no more hairs to split. In the great age of Queen Anne, Sarah knew

---

*A recent, most substantial and perhaps definitive life of Queen Anne—*Queen Anne* by Edward Gregg (Routledge, Kegan Paul, 1980) has rehabilitated the Queen at the expense of the Duchess, and some reviewers have rushed in to damn the Duchess afresh. But it is pleasant to note here how Sarah had anticipated them.

that better than anyone else. It was the men, *pace* Prince Eugen at the head of this chapter, who had allowed things in England to go from bad to worse, and Sarah, given her magnificent head, could have saved it all.

FOURTEEN

Round the next corner: the pursuit of Jonathan Swift

Oh, when shall we have such another Rector of Laracor!
—William Hazlitt

JONATHAN SWIFT was born in Dublin in the year 1667 (the exact circumstances and the details of parentage are all part of the endless mystification which still surrounds his name), and three hundred years later proper and lavish tercentenary celebrations were conducted in Trinity College, Dublin, where he was educated and which he had left in the year 1686, not exactly 'under a cloud', yet without the slightest hint of the world-wide fame which was one day to be his. Any writer anywhere who had shown any interest in Swift was invited to the occasion, and this was already a guarantee of a mass attendance. At the opening ceremony in the Public Theatre the Roman Catholic Bishop from University College talked as if Swift, with a few nods and adjustments, might almost have been a Catholic, and the Presbyterian Provost from Trinity itself managed to make no embarrassing reference to Swift's unprintable views about Presbyterianism. The only speaker who attempted to attain Swift's own standard of candour, renouncing all traces of hypocrisy whatever, was the President of the Irish Republic at that moment, Eamon De Valera. It was wonderful to see him in his eighties, almost blind, being guided to the rostrum, to put the assembled worlds of scholarship, literature and religion in their respective places. He explained his own difficulties in accepting Swift as a true Irish patriot. He described how the snatches of information which he had learned about Swift in his childhood had not originally been convincing; and how hard it was to suppose that any good thing could come out of such a stronghold of the English ascendancy as Trinity College. A whiff of Easter, 1916, wafted through the hall. And yet it was Swift's slogan, we were told at last, which had touched the heart of Mr. De Valera: 'Burn everything English but their coal'—the most successful example of sanctions in history, enforced by the Irish against the English, according to the directions of a disappointed would-be Anglican bishop turned revolutionary.

We must go to Ireland to appreciate Swift in the fullest measure. There he was born, there he was exiled or self-exiled, there he died, but there he scaled the highest peaks of his greatness, and there he was rescued during his lifetime, and on numerous notable occasions thereafter, from his English defamers. There the true Swift is still guarded today. In England he is a great writer; in Ireland he is part of the folklore. You can walk beside St. Patrick's Cathedral and imagine, as Yeats said, that you see him round the next corner, being cheered through the streets by the people, riding respectably in his carriage with Stella and Mrs. Dingley or sneaking off to an assignation with Vanessa. In Dublin, for some twenty years during his lifetime, they lit bonfires to celebrate his birthday, and three hundred years later not a single one from the host of critics, for all their other controversies on every other aspect of his life and work, could question his devotion to the cause of Irish freedom. And it was at the height of his Irish popularity, let it never be forgotten, that he wrote *Gulliver's Travels* and unloosed within the human mind a tumult which has never since subsided.

Gulliver's Travels, like most of the other great books of the world, has been freshly interpreted from age to age. Cherished alongside *Robinson Crusoe* as a children's book, it has, quite unlike *Crusoe*, been the subject of furious debate among historians, philosophers and literary critics. Many of its pages are devoted to direct political satire, but we may safely guess that not one in ten thousand of its appreciative readers is aware of even the most patent particular references. Writers claiming to do no more than appraise its philosophical content have been driven to paroxysms of denunciation. Somehow the foremost exponent of lucidity in the English language has left as his chief legacy a grotesque enigma.

The author protests at the outset that 'the style is very plain and simple'. And so it is. In accordance with his custom, Swift read large chunks aloud to his servants, to make sure that every sentence attained his rigorous standard of simplicity. It is possible, with much enjoyment, to skate over the surface, most of it as smooth as ice, without noticing the dark chasms underneath, and this no doubt is what children do with their expurgated editions. But no one can deceive himself for long. Gentleness, playfulness, irony, finely-poised argument and lacerating invectives are so carefully enfolded one within another that it is evident Jonathan Swift created the endless mystery on purpose.

Part One, A Voyage to Lilliput, is the fantasy about the giant in the land of midgets told in such unchallengeable, precise, matter-of-fact terms that it has become a household word and idea in every civilised tongue throughout the world. Yet through this section in particular runs a long, weaving stream of topical innuendo about the forgotten politics of the reign of Queen Anne. Part Two, A Voyage to Brobdingnag, is Lilliput in reverse, but it also offers some of Swift's fiercest assaults upon the behaviour of his fellow countrymen and the nearest effort he ever made to describe his own notion of an ideal state. Part Three, A Voyage to Laputa, etc., is evidently directed against the scientists and philosophers of his own age, but how up to date these gentlemen appear. Part Four, A Voyage to the Houyhnhnms, has been regarded as a vile or corrective satire on human nature itself, but any attempt to compress its meaning into a sentence becomes an absurdity. In the country of the Houyhnhnms, the ground trembles beneath our feet; a storm beats about our heads; terrifying shafts of light and darkness are thrown backwards across the rest of the book, into every corner of the human mind.

Gulliver's Travels is a perpetual, unfinished argument, one from which flatly contradictory morals have been and still can be extracted. And, wondrously, no reader need be deterred by the experts from forming his own judgement. On this subject, some of the most eminent authorities have made the most eminent asses of themselves, a development which Swift foresaw and invited. He says in the last chapter that he hopes he may pronounce himself 'an author perfectly blameless, against whom the tribe of answerers, considerers, observers, reflecters, detecters, remarkers, will never be able to find matter for exercising their talents'. By which, of course, he meant the opposite. One of the fascinations of *Gulliver's Travels* is that, although every phrase seems immediately comprehensible, the whole subject matter is endlessly complex.

When the book was published, anonymously, on 28 October 1726, success was instantaneous. One report said that ten thousand copies were sold in three weeks. Immediate translations were made into French and Dutch, weekly journals started printing pirated extracts, and Swift's friends in London competed with one another in dispatching glowing reports to the author in Dublin. Dr. John Arbuthnot, the closest friend of all, wrote:

> I will make over all my profits to you for the property of Gulliver's Travels; which, I believe, will have as great a run as John Bunyan. Gulliver is a happy man, that, at his age [Swift was fifty-nine], can write such a merry book.

Alexander Pope and John Gay wrote jointly: 'From the highest to the lowest it is universally read, from the cabinet council to the nursery.' Thus soon was the volume accepted as a classic simultaneously from the cradle to the corridors of power. The old Duchess of Marlborough, once the victim of Swift's harshest abuse, was said to be 'in raptures at it; she says she can dream of nothing else since she read it'. And Swift's own fears were set at rest. He had told Pope a year before that publication would have to wait until 'a printer shall be found brave enough to venture his ears'; in those days authors at odds with the authorities risked the pillory or imprisonment as well as mere poverty. He had warned the publisher, to whom the manuscript was deviously delivered, that some parts of what he had written 'may be thought in one or two places to be a little satirical'. But all was well. No hint of a prosecution, such as had often threatened Swift before in his pamphleteering career, was heard. 'It has passed Lords and Common's *nemine contradicente*, and the whole town, men, women and children are full of it', was Pope's reassurance. One of the few expressions of protest at the time, heralding what was to follow later, came, curiously, from a member of Swift's intimate circle, Lord Bolingbroke; 'he is the person', continued Pope, 'who least approves it, blaming it as a design of evil consequence to depreciate human nature.' But this might have been no more than a joke at Bolingbroke's expense, comparable with that told of the old gentleman who, when lent the book, was alleged to have gone immediately to his map to search for Lilliput, or of the Bishop who said it was 'full of improbable lies, and, for his part, he hardly believed a word of it'. Pope, the Roman Catholic, and Swift, the militant Church of England or Church of Ireland man, needed no excuse to poke fun at Bolingbroke and his deistical, or even atheistical, deviations from the Christian faith. 'A merry book' by a man gay-spirited and greatly loved as well as feared—that was the general view of Swift's contemporaries. Stomachs were stronger in the reigns of Queen Anne and George I.

Fifty years later, in his *Lives of the English Poets*, Dr. Johnson gravely recalled the publication of the already famous volume:

> A production so new and strange that it filled the reader with a mingled emotion of merriment and amazement. It was received with such avidity, that the price of the first edition was raised before the second could be made; it was read by high and low, the learned and illiterate. Criticism was for a while lost in wonder; no rules of judgement were applied to a book written in open defiance of truth and regularity.

Thereafter, Johnson applied his own rules. Boswell tells how the assault upon Swift was renewed on all available occasions, despite his own valiant efforts to withstand the deluge of nonsense. Johnson thought that Swift's political writings were inferior to Addison's, that his most brilliant pamphlet, *The Conduct of the Allies*, was a mere bundle of facts, that *Gulliver's Travels* might be assigned to its proper place thus: 'when once you have thought of the big men and the little men, it is very easy to do all the rest.' A good Johnsonian joke, maybe, but it still leaves us wondering whether, apart even from his critical judgement, he ever got past the first two books and the disappearance of the big men and the little men from the scene.

More insidiously effective, however, than the criticism of Swift's talents was the denigration of his demeanour and character. A man of muddy complexion, of sour and severe countenance, deficient in both wit and humour, one 'who stubbornly resisted any tendency to laughter', was Johnson's summary. The beloved friend of Arbuthnot and Pope, the drinking companion of Addison and Steele, recedes, and a grim twisted specimen begins to take his place. Dr. Johnson even recalls, with some relish and too faint repudiation, the false tale that Pope entrusted to his executors a defamatory Life of Swift which he had prepared in advance as an instrument of vengeance to be drawn from its scabbard if provocation arose; the implication being, presumably, that Swift might have savaged Pope or at least that Pope considered him capable of it. The historical evidence is different. Never in our literary annals has there existed between two prominent figures a purer friendship and one so untinged by the slightest strain of jealousy or envy as that which prevailed between Pope and Swift. All Pope's superabundant venom subsided in the presence of Swift, and Swift's devotion, in particular it could be said, never wavered or weakened to the end of his days. Yet the tale-bearers spread lies about Swift's disloyalties, his eccentricities, his furies, his diseased nature, his madness. 'The merry book' was quite forgotten; it had become something sinister. Indeed, the strangest fate overtook Swift's general reputation. When he died in 1745, he had already, in the words of a recent critic, Professor Ricardo Quintana, 'ceased to be understood by the eighteenth century . . . No English writer of corresponding stature has been repudiated so persistently and so fiercely by immediately succeeding generations'.

How the change occurred, from the first exultation that the human mind had produced a delight and a marvel to such frantic fear or hate, is not easy to discern. Some responsibility may rest with the ineffectualness of Swift's early biographers who purveyed silly gossip about him with ponderous assiduity. But the heaviest burden of guilt must still rest on Dr. Johnson. True, ever-growing multitudes of readers continued to read Swift despite Johnson's condemnation of his manners and his morals. True, some years later, a few stray voices were raised openly in defence—William Godwin, William Cobbett, William Hazlitt. But these were literary no less than political outcasts, quite beyond the pale of the early nineteenth-century literary Establishment, rabid apologists for, if not actual advocates of, revolution after the French style. Defence from that quarter damned Swift more than ever.

And who truly wished to defend him? Sir Walter Scott, a kindred Tory and fellow spirit, it might be thought, made the effort valiantly. He produced a collected edition of Swift's works, greatly admired his poems, read the *Journal to Stella* with a fresh, sympathetic eye, and wrote a compassionate, intelligent Life. Yet he recoiled from *Gulliver's Travels*:

> Severe, unjust and degrading as this satire is, it was hailed with malignant triumph by those whose disappointed hopes had thrown them into the same state of gloomy misanthropy which it argues in its author.

If this was how Swift was to be defended by his political friends, what could he expect from his enemies? Francis Jeffrey, in his *Edinburgh Review* article on Scott's book, made a momentary effort to distinguish between the literary achievement and the character, and then launched into a brilliant libel in which the victim might have been a composite Tory figure of Jeffrey's own age. Macaulay, in 1833, went much further. He conjured up in one ferocious sentence a vision hard to dispel:

> the apostate politician, the ribald priest, the perjured lover, a heart burning with hatred against the whole human race, a mind richly stored with images from the dunghill and the lazar house.

The portrait of the monster was now widely accepted, and, in 1851, Thackeray unloosed an invective which, even when its more flamboyant passages are dismissed as hysterical, leaves no doubt about what had become the settled verdict of Victorian opinion.

Dr. Johnson, wrote Thackeray (it was always safe to ride into battle behind that shield),

> could not give the Dean that honest hand of his; the stout old man puts it into his breast, and moves off from him . . . As fierce a beak and talon as ever struck, as strong as ever beat, belonged to Swift. . . One can gaze, and not without awe and pity, at the lonely eagle chained behind bars . . . The 'saeva indignatio' of which he spoke as lacerating his heart, and which he dares to inscribe on his tombstone—as if the wretch who lay under that stone waiting God's Judgement had a right to be angry—breaks out from him in a thousand pages of his writing, and tears and rends him . . .

Thus the prelude on Swift's character has prepared the way for the cool appraisal of his book:

> Mr. Dean has no softness, and enters the nursery with the tread and gaiety of an ogre . . . Our great satirist was of the opinion that conjugal love was inadvisable, and illustrated the theory by his own practice and example—God help him—which made him about the most wretched being in God's world . . . As for the humour and conduct of this famous fable, I suppose there is no person who reads but must admire; as for the moral, I think it horrible, shameful, unmanly, blasphemous; and giant and great as this Dean is, I say we should hoot him . . . It [the fourth book of Gulliver] is Yahoo language; a monster, gibbering shrieks and gnashing imprecations against mankind—tearing down all shreds of modesty, past all sense of manliness and shame; filthy in word, filthy in thought, furious, raging, obscene.

And thus—but there is much more of it—in the name of everything the nineteenth century considered holy, Thackeray anticipated the Day of Judgement. The merry book had become a work of the devil.

A few decades later, some lesser figures than Macaulay and Thackeray struggled to retrieve the century's critical reputation. A series of writers attempted the serious work of biography previously neglected and the more they assembled facts in their proper context the more the picture of Swift, the ogre, began to dissolve. Leslie Stephen in his volume (1882) and Churton

Collins in his (1893) surveyed the work already done in rectifying glaring injustices, but even so, both quailed before the later sections of *Gulliver's Travels*. Leslie Stephen called them 'painful and repulsive' and 'a ghastly caricature':

> Readers who wish to indulge in a harmless play of fancy will do well to omit the last two voyages; for the strain of misanthropy which breathes in them is simply oppressive. They are probably the sources from which the popular impression of Swift's character is often derived. It is important therefore to remember that they were wrung from him in later years, after a life tormented by constant disappointment and disease.

Churton Collins's reactions were similar:

> It [*Gulliver's Travels*, he wrote] has no moral, no social, no philosophical purpose. It was the mere ebullition of cynicism and misanthrophy. A savage *jeu d'esprit*. And as such wise men will regard it . . . At no period distinguished by generosity of sentiment, by humanity, by decency, could such satire have been universally applauded. Yet so it was. The men and women of those times appear to have seen nothing objectionable in an apologue which would scarcely have passed without protest in the Rome of Petronius.

So even strong Swift defenders seemed unable to repel the weight of the attack. Augustine Birrell, reviewing Churton Collins's biography in the 1890s, could write:

> It is a question not of morality, but of decency, whether it is becoming to sit in the same room with the works of this divine . . . Thackeray's criticism is severe, but is it not just? Are we to stand by and hear our nature libelled, and our purest affections beslimed, without a word of protest?

Somehow *Gulliver* could not be treated as a book at all; it was unfit for human consumption.

Twenty-five years later, to his credit, Birrell had recovered a sense of proportion. Partly he had been studying Swift's new biographers, although these, as we have seen, were still on the defensive about *Gulliver*. Partly he attributed the conversion to a warm-hearted lecture in defence of Swift, as the enemy of injustice and oppression, delivered by Charles Whibley at Cambridge in 1917. But, more obviously, he himself had been reading—and writing a Life of—William Hazlitt, and Hazlitt could have saved all concerned a century of trouble and defamation. For in the year 1817—exactly a century before Whibley's apologia—Hazlitt had delivered a lecture which both replied to Dr. Johnson and leaped forward to adopt a modern view of *Gulliver's Travels*. Little notice was taken of it at the time, except by an unknown John Keats, then twenty-two years old. Leslie Stephen and Churton Collins, disintering Hazlitt's case as if they had made some recondite discoveries, both acknowledged its force, but found it too extreme for acceptance. It must be pardonable to quote a part of the passage at length and to marvel that Hazlitt, Macaulay, Thackeray and the rest were supposedly talking about the same man and the same book.

Whether the excellence of *Gulliver's Travels* is in the conception or the execution, [wrote Hazlitt] is of little consequence; the power is somewhere, and it is a power that has moved the world. The power is not that of big words and vaunting common places. Swift left these to those who wanted them; and has done what his acuteness and intensity of mind alone could enable any one to conceive or to perform. His object was to strip empty pride and grandeur of the imposing air which external circumstances throw around them; and for this purpose he has cheated the imagination of the illusions which the prejudices of sense and of the world put upon it, by reducing everything to the abstract predicament of size. He enlarges or diminishes the scale, as he wishes, to shew the insignificance or the grossness of our overweening self-love. That he has done this with mathematical precision, with complete presence of mind and perfect keeping, in a manner that comes equally home to the understanding of the man and of the child, does not take away from the merit of the work or the genius of the author. He has taken a new view of human nature, such as a being of a higher sphere might take of it; he has torn the scales from off his moral vision; he has tried an experiment with human life, and sifted its pretensions from the alloy of circumstances; he has measured it with a rule, has weighed it in a balance, and found it, for the most part, wanting and worthless—in substance and in shew. Nothing solid, nothing valuable is left in his system but virtue and wisdom. What a libel is this upon mankind! What a convincing proof of misanthrophy! What presumptions and what *malice prepense*, to shew men what they are, and to teach them what they ought to be! What a mortifying stroke aimed at national glory, is that unlucky incident of Gulliver's wading across the channel and carrying off the whole fleet of Blefuscu! After that, we have only to consider which of the contending parties was in the right. What a shock to personal vanity is given in the account of Gulliver's nurse Glumdalclitch! Still, notwithstanding the disparagement of her personal charms, her good-nature remains the same amiable quality as before. I cannot see the harm, the misanthrophy, the immoral and degrading tendency of this. The moral lesson is as fine as the intellectual exhibition is amusing. It is an attempt to tear off the mask of imposture from the world; and nothing but imposture has a right to complain of it.

There! Swift, one feels, would have cheered. At last someone had understood. In the next paragraph, Hazlitt, at the distance of a century, took it upon himself to forgive Swift for having been a Tory, and Swift, if he had read this encomium, would surely have repaid the compliment and forgiven Hazlitt for a lifetime's dedication to his rebel faith. Across the gulf of time and politics, there was a kinship between their spirits, and the common strand runs through *Gulliver's Travels*.

It is curious that Augustine Birrell, the biographer of Hazlitt, did not record his debt to that passage, and curious too that, in the period of the so-called Whibley revaluation, he did not take into account an essay by H. W. Nevinson far more telling than Whibley's and written some years earlier. Nevinson, the rebel and the intimate friend of rebels, like Hazlitt, recognised Swift as one of the same tribe. The rebel streak was not the whole of Swift, but it was part of him.

It was not [wrote Nevinson] any spirit of hatred or cruelty but an intensely personal sympathy with suffering, that tore his heart and kindled that furnace of indignation against the stupid, the hateful and the cruel to whom most suffering is due; and it was a furnace in which he himself was consumed. Writing while he was still a youth in *A Tale of a Tub*, he composed a terrible sentence, in which all his rage and pity and ironical bareness of style seem foretold: 'Last week,' he says, 'I saw a woman flayed, and you will hardly believe how much it altered her person for the worse.'

How has it ever been possible to think that the man who wrote those words lacked a heart, and could anyone but the author of *Gulliver* have written them?

The man and the book; the two become inextricable, however open to objection such a method of judgement may be. It is peculiarly difficult to discuss Swift's writings, insisted F. R. Leavis, without shifting the focus of discussion to the kind of man that Swift was:

> For instance, one may (it appears), having offered to discuss the nature and import of Swift's satire, find oneself countering imputations of misanthrophy with the argument that Swift earned the love of Pope, Arbuthnot, Gay, several other men and two women; this should not be found necessary by the literary critic.

Yet did Dr. Leavis abide by his own rule? Having reached the conclusion that Swift's greatness 'is no matter of moral grandeur or human centrality: our sense is merely a sense of great force', he added: 'And this force, as we feel it, is conditioned by frustration and constriction: the channels of life have been blocked and perverted.' The man-monster peeps out again, and before proceeding farther it must be discovered how valid the apparition may be.

Was *Gulliver's Travels*, or at least the Voyage to the Houyhnhnms, the product of a perverted, diseased mind? Was Swift a gloomy misanthrope who never laughed, a tormented hater of all men and, more particularly, all women, consumed at last in the furnace of his own fury? Did he, in short, go mad? Altogether, the charge of madness has been made by the following, among others: Dr. Johnson, Walter Scott, Macaulay, Thackeray, Aldous Huxley, W. B. Yeats possibly, D. H. Lawrence probably, George Orwell, Malcolm Muggeridge and A. L. Rowse. A reviewer of Professor Rowse's major book, *Jonathan Swift: Major Prophet** Mr. Michael Gearing Tosh in the *Sunday Times* in January 1976 wrote: 'Swift was a Christian who hated mankind. This must have created a fierce tension whose outcome,

---

*Published by Thames & Hudson, 1975.

if suicide were excluded by faith, could hardly have been other than madness. And Swift became insane.' Q.E.D. 'The odds are', we were coolly told a few years earlier, on the combined medical and scholarly authority of Malcolm Muggeridge, a delighted and delightful admirer of Swift, 'that the illness which struck him down was GPI, doubtless due to syphilis, contracted when he was young and addicted to what he called low company.' Maybe literary critics should not be concerned with such trifles. But if the author did in truth go mad, it would be hard to deny that some support is given to the Johnson, even the Thackeray, view of the book. Moreover, in the list of accusers tabulated above appears the potent name of Yeats. If he, the great Irish poet of the twentieth century, was willing to pass such a judgement on his great Irish predecessor, must not others be excused? Yeats wrote a play in which the subject was Swift's supposed premonition of madness, and he had a vision of

> *Swift beating on his breast in sibylline frenzy blind*
> *Because the heart in his blood-sodden breast had dragged him down*
>   *into mankind*

True, Yeats also turned into poetic form Swift's epitaph which he called the greatest ever written, and there is no element of madness to be discerned there. Yet it is hard, once the phrase is uttered, ever to expunge the thought of that sibylline frenzy.

Swift, it must be acknowledged too, has offered much testimony against himself. Someone called him, justly, an inverted hypocrite because he often seemed to paint himself in undeservedly harsh colours. 'I shall be like that tree, I shall die at the top', he said and the prophecy has been quoted a hundred times, out of context, as a key to his personality. 'Principally I hate and detest that animal called man . . .' runs another half-sentence of self-conviction. He bequeathed his small fortune to found an asylum in Dublin and wrote the famous lines on his own death:

> *He gave the little wealth he had*
> *To build a House for Fools and Mad.*
> *And shew'd by one Satyric Touch,*
> *No nation needed it so much.*

Have we not here intimations of his sympathy for those who suffered his own fate? He resented his enforced exile in Ireland and talked of dying 'in a rage, like a poisoned rat in a hole'. There is, alas, plentiful evidence from various witnesses of the scarcely endurable pains and miseries which bore him to the grave. Is all this, then, plus the horrific passages of *Gulliver's Travels*, not enough to clinch the case?

It is not, and nothing like it. Most of the real evidence available strongly suggests that Swift did not go mad, and that the story of an appalling end compounded of rage, violence and fatuity was a myth at first maliciously spread and then much too readily adopted and disseminated by Dr. Johnson, who rounded off a verse with the charge that Swift became, in his last years, 'a driviller and a show'. The medical case was examined a couple of decades ago by one of Britain's most distinguished brain neurologists, Lord Brain, who confirmed that most of his life Swift must have suffered from what is defined as Bilateral Meniere's disease, and that this would have accounted for his bursts of giddiness, vomiting and deafness. Eventually he also suffered from senile decay, as most of his accusers have or will. All these matters were properly surveyed by Professor Irvin Ehrenpreis in his book *The Personality of Jonathan Swift* (published in 1958, Methuen), and there is no reason to dissent, or rather there can be no means of escape, from his conclusion:

> Swift, from birth to death, was insane by no medical definition. He was no more eccentric or neurotic than Pope or Johnson, and probably less so. The tradition of his madness has been rejected for forty years by every qualified scholar who has bothered to look into the question.

As for the verses on his own death now cited as an illustration of Swift's awareness of his own fate, no claim could be more ludicrous. They were written some thirteen years before his death, long before the first time when the most virulent of his enemies has thought to suggest that he showed signs of insanity. To argue, even to hint, that they reveal a premonition of madness is to wrench four from the 486 most cheerful lines Swift ever wrote. It might indeed be the shortest cure for those who still talk of Swift's madness—better even than Lord Brain's diagnosis or Dr. Ehrenpreis's scholarship—to compel them to read the verses on the Death of Dr. Swift right through. They have some claim to be the gayest poem in the English language.

And what, we may wonder, was Yeats's verdict on this poem and this whole spacious arena of Swift's mind which they represent? He never attempted to tell us. Moreover, Yeats, when he talks or writes of Swift, must always be treated with some circumspection, to use no harsher word. He himself has described how, at some Irish Literary Society meeting in London in the 1890s, he in turn would attack 'the dishonest figures of Swift's attack on Wood's halfpence, and, making that my text, had argued that, because no sane man is permitted to lie knowingly, God made certain men mad, and that it was these men—daimon possessed as I said—who, possessing truths of passion that were intellectual falsehoods, had created nations',* An astonishing passage indeed; why, two hundred years and more after the event, should Yeats be so eager to reopen in dubious terms, it must be said, the arithmetical argument about Wood's halfpence? And Yeats must be surely the first person, certainly the first Irishman, who would attempt to trace such a direct, unbreakable connection between insanity and patriotism. Maybe Swift was 'dragged down into mankind' more readily than Yeats himself.

However, the case of Swift's madness, or rather of the determination of some of his enemies or critics or admirers to believe in it in the teeth of all the evidence, has a glaring feature all its own. His rescue from the charge does not depend solely on the latest neurological knowledge, valuable though that may be. Way back in the year 1846, a Dr. Mackenzie of Glasgow wrote to his medical friend W. R. Wilde, FRIA, FRCS of Dublin—later Sir William and later too the father of Oscar Wilde—suggesting that some of the medical assumptions of Swift's biographers were questionable, to say the least. Sir William obliged with three years of intelligent research and reached the firm conclusion:

---

*W. B. Yeats, *Memoirs* Macmillan 1972.

as we trust a fair examination of his case will show, Swift was not, at any period of his life, not even in his last illness, what is understood as mad.

The first edition of the book, *The Closing Years of Dean Swift's Life*, was published in Dublin in 1849 and received widespread and justified critical acclaim in Ireland principally but in some degree in England too. A second enlarged edition—with the epigraph added on the title page, 'I am not mad, most noble Festus'—was published in the same year. It contains a detailed examination of the evidence available, including of course Swift's own comments on his own health:

> Neither in his expression, nor the tone of his writings, nor from any examination of any of his acts, have we been able to discover a single symptom of insanity, nor aught but the effects of physical disease, and the natural wearing and decay of a mind such as Swift's . . .

The examination continued, as best the scrupulous Doctor could continue it, throughout the period when guardians had to be appointed to protect Swift in his senility, as has been required in the case of many others with no charge of insanity being preferred. Only at the end did the Doctor seek his revenge. He had given a glancing rebuke to Dr. Johnson, 'the most malevolent of all Swift's biographers', but even the more kindly Walter Scott could not be spared altogether:

> Sir Walter Scott's edition of Swift's works, [wrote Wilde] contains the following notice of his last poetical effusion. The exact date of the circumstance has not been recorded, but it appears to have been subsequent to the appointment of guardians of his person. 'The Dean in his lunacy had some intervals of sense, at which his guardians or physicians took him out for the air. On one of these days, when they came to the Park, Swift remarked a new building which he had never seen, and asked what it was designed for? to which Dr. Kingsbury answered "that Mr. Dean, is the magazine for arms and powder for the security of the city"—"Oh! Oh!" says the Dean, pulling out his pocket-book, "let me take an item of that. This is worth remarking: 'My tablets', as Hamlet says, 'my tablets—memory put down that!' "

Which produced these lines, said to be the last he ever wrote:

> *Behold! a proof of Irish sense;*
> *Here Irish wit is seen!*
> *When nothing's left that's worth defence,*
> *We build a magazine.*

Now if this proves the insanity of its author the reader is to judge.

And we may add: nothing frenzied could be detected in such an attitude, sibylline or otherwise.

It is insufferable that any subsequent biography of Swift should have been written without account being taken of William Wilde's examination, especially since a few of the latter-day nineteenth-century biographers did recognise its significance. Yet this has been the treatment in many twentieth-century biographies, including Professor Rowse's. Time and again Dr. Wilde's findings are neglected or overturned without a scrap of fresh evidence being offered. And what in any case has this two-and-a-half-century old debate about the last few years of Swift's life to do with *Gulliver's Travels*? 'A man's life', wrote Hazlitt in another connection, 'is his whole life, not the last glimmering snuff of the candle.' If Swift had gone mad in the last years, here would have been a sufficient retort. For *Gulliver's Travels* was published about twenty years before Swift's death; it was mostly written earlier still; the especially offensive voyage to the Houyhnhnms, the scholars reckon, was not the last part of the book to be compiled. It is just not true, as even the appreciative Leslie Stephen had inferred, that the last chapters were the outpouring of 'a diseased condition of his mind, perhaps of actual mental decay'. It is just not true, as Scott asserted, that when he wrote of the Yahoos he was suffering from 'incipient mental disease'. When he finished the book Swift was fifty-nine years old, still fully active, in complete possession of his faculties. If what he produced then, by far the most ambitious literary achievement of his life, was morbid and demonic, then the whole man was morbid and demonic. And such is often still the claim which must be considered.

Yet before attempting the ascent to this higher philosophic

ground, it is impossible to avoid the other personal questions. What of the perjured, syphilitic lover; the treacherous or impotent suitor of Stella and Vanessa, not to mention those more shadowy beauties, Varina and Betty Jones, and not to forget Mr. Muggeridge's low company? It is the seemingly inescapable conjecture about his treatment of Stella and Vanessa which leave so sickening a taste on the palate; the most formidable charge, in the words delivered by James Joyce, that he had destroyed two lives with his sentimental muddling. Biographers at one stage tended to divide themselves into Vanessa-ites and Stella-ites, but in the tercentenary year of 1967, at the hands of Mrs. Le Brocquy, an assault was made upon him on behalf of Vanessa *and* Stella, a most formidable combination, and a heavy blow for a man to receive as a tercentenary birthday present. Moreover, even these accusations may be considered mild in comparison with some others. D. H. Lawrence deduced from the scatological poems that the fellow suffered from 'a terror of the body', and Aldous Huxley was no less excited by the discovery that he hated the word *bowels*—'It was unbearable to him that men (and women even more, no doubt) should go through life with guts and sweetbreads, with liver and lights, spleens and kidneys'; he was an incurable romantic, one who resented the world of reality and would never dare face it. After such stuff, it is a relief even to arrive at Dr. Rowse. Professor John Kenyon, reviewing Dr. Rowse's book in the *Observer* wrote: 'All the evidence suggests that Swift was a latent homosexual, deeply frightened of women . . .', but 'all the evidence', not even Dr. Rowse's, suggests nothing of the sort. Dr. Rowse himself, having informed us at the start, without even a pretence at hinting at any substantiating evidence whatever, that the young Swift suffered from 'complete sexual repression', later excuses what may be supposed to be the outward expression of this disability by the difficulties all males must encounter from 'typical female unreason'. Later we are told, again without a shred of evidence, that the iron control which he sought vainly to impose on his sexual nature broke out in a reeking self-pity, 'as it did in the comparable exemplar of self-repression in our time, Lawrence of Arabia'. And, finally, to win sympathy for Swift (or, more likely, his biographer) which, in defiance of all self-pitying allegations, Swift himself never invited, Vanessa is dismissed as an importunate, infatuated bore, 'a hopeless case'. Vanessa, the twin subject of Swift's most delightful poem, 'a hopeless case'! Stella had every excuse for her deadly comment: that Dr. Swift had been known to write matchlessly on any subject, even a broomstick. But not even the most sexaddicted author should be allowed the same licence. And Swift had his own final word on the point:

> *For who could such a Nymph forsake*
> *Except a Blockhead or a Rake?*

The best cure is to read Swift himself, to return afresh and in particular to the seemingly inexhaustible sources of his comic invention. He could make any company he was in laugh or smile; he could lash any opponent, worthy or unworthy, with his wit; and most of both the humour and the wit can still work their magic today when the audience and the victims are no more. One from that array of beautiful women was Mrs. Finch who, under the more bewitching title of Ardeliah, was lauded for her prowess in outwitting Apollo.

> *The Nymph who oft had read in Books*
> *Of that Bright God whom Gods invoke,*
> *Soon knew Apollo by his looks*
> *And Guest his Business ere he Spoke*
>
> *He in the old Celestial Cant,*
> *Confest his Flame, and Swore by Styx,*
> *What e're she would desire, to Grant,*
> *But wise Ardeliah knew his Tricks.*
>
> *Ovid had warn'd her to beware,*
> *Of Stroling Gods, whose usual Trade is,*
> *Under pretence of Taking Air,*
> *To pick up Sublunary Ladies.*

Apollo might be resistible, but not the irreverent Vicar in such a mood. It is hard to believe that such faculties could be invoked at will by a monster scarcely fit to associate with the rest of human kind. However, a few more particular replies to the charges listed above may be offered, not in the hope that the whole case may be clinched but rather to illustrate how wretched is the attempt to constrict Swift's genius in any narrow limits whatever. 'To discuss the colossal mind of the great Dean of St. Patrick's', wrote Lytton Strachey, 'would be no unworthy task for a Shakespeare. Less powerful spirits can only prostrate themselves in dumb worship, like Egyptian priests before the enormous effigies of their gods.' But the Swift-haters or the Swift-detractors have no such humility. His personal life, the scatalogical poems, the Stella-Vanessa imbroglio in particular, provide them with material which has been digested and regurgitated, from Dr. Johnson's day to Dr. Rowse's. No great writer, except Shakespeare himself, has had to endure more from the biographers or critics who would fasten on their subject their own vices or supposed virtues.

Nothing, for example, could be more pitiful than Dr. Rowse's attempt to foist upon Swift his own contempt for women. Poor Swift, of all people in his generation, would have squirmed to be defended thus, and Stella and Vanessa would have arisen, united in this if nothing else, and sustained by a vast assembly of their women contemporaries, to repudiate the indictment. He adored the company of women and they adored his; he was one of the very first to insist that women should have the same education as men ('my Master among the Houyhnhnms thought it monstrous for us to give the Females a different Education from the Males'); he could deride the notion of male superiority; by the cramped standards of his time he was almost a women's liberator. And similarly, and scarcely less conclusively, we can dismiss all the downright charges of perversion. One of the great Swiftian scholars dealt with at least two of these—the Huxley theory and the Lawrence theory—several decades ago, and no good reasons exist for reviving them. Herbert Davis explained how Huxley had stumbled on a Swiftian phrase in a letter to Stella—'I hate the word bowels'—and then attempted to construct upon it his notion of how Swift also hated the bodily functions. But Huxley had failed to notice that the word bowels, in its seventeenth or early eighteenth-century sense, meant something quite different from his assumption. And Lawrence's charges too may be equally discarded. He had argued that Swift's prudery had arisen partly from 'having taboo words'. Yet whatever other crimes he may have committed, Swift was guiltless on that count; he used all the words which Lawrence dared to utter a few centuries later. 'The whole significance of these poems (the ones selected by Lawrence and Huxley for attack)', wrote Herbert Davis, 'lies in the fact that Swift hated the ordinary romantic love-stuff.' It is scarcely credible that sentimentality should still figure on the charge-sheet. Indeed, in a sense the assault can be carried into the opposite camp. The best modern essay on Swift's scatalogical propensities is Norman O. Brown's *The Excremental Vision*, in which he expounds how 'if we are willing to listen to Swift we will find startling anticipations of Freudian theories about anality, about sublimation, and about the universal neuroses of mankind'. The thesis is driven home with Swiftian force. No longer is it necessary to consign the extensive excursions of Swift into scatalogy to some bluebeard's chamber. Norman Brown has nothing but contempt for those who would 'domesticate and housebreak this tiger of English literature'. He never commits the same error himself. But his tiger is a real live animal, not some figure of evil and of shadowy omen.

So with all idea of perversion, mild or monstrous, set aside, let us return to the Vanessa-Stella mystery. No solution is offered here—except the simplest: that is, that he loved them both and that his heart was torn between the two. It is hard to read of his long years with Stella, the poems he wrote to her, and the *Journal*, without believing he loved her; and if it wasn't love, it was something of his own invention very like it. As for Vanessa, it is impossible to read the poem to her without believing it was love, and that he must in some way have avowed it. If not, the last famous lines were too tantalisingly cruel to be imagined, and there is not even the faintest tinge of cruelty in the rest of the poem, and no sign indeed that Swift was ever cruel to his friends; he saved that for his assortment of well-chosen enemies. And why should it be difficult to accept the simplest explanation? Swift, for all his devotion to truth, could be defensive and secretive. He insisted upon his independence and privacy, even to his life-long companion, Stella. The nearest we can come to intimacy with him appears to be through his letters to her ('diurnal trifles', as Dr. Johnson fatheadedly called them), and yet these cover only a few years of his life and all but the most oblique reference to Vanessa is excluded from them. If he had *not* loved Vanessa, Stella and Mrs. Dingley back in Laracor, and the world at large ever since, would have been told much more about her. But we would never have had the love poem: *Cadenus and Vanessa* would never have enfolded its riveting mysteries in the language of grace and tenderness.

The most plausible elaboration of the simplest conclusion—not proof, of course: that will surely never be available—was supplied in Denis Johnston's *In Search of Swift* (published in 1959 and based on an article which he had written in *The Dublin Historical Record,* in June 1941). This is no place to recite the complicated details; but if it is true, as Johnston argues, that Swift was Stella's uncle, and that he discovered this at some date we do not know, then so much in his relation with Stella is explained. It explains the strange business whereby they were never known to meet alone in the same room and the terrible story of Swift demanding Stella's removal from the Deanery before she died. He could not live with Stella as man and wife, if those were the facts, without provoking or risking an intolerable scandal—intolerable for her as well as himself. As for Vanessa's endearing importunities, in Mr. Johnston's words: 'When cruelty was the only thing that could have saved her, he should have been cruel. She was wronged through the demonic pity that was the keystone of his character.' But that does not make him any form of monster or sex maniac or even Joyce's muddled sentimentalist. Denis Johnston concludes: 'He was a perfectly normal man, of colossal proportions, motivated by two of the most universal, the most lovable and the most dangerous of all human emotions—Pride and Pity.' It is intolerable at least that anyone should still write, as many have done, about Swift's life without considering Denis Johnston's formidable theory; intolerable too—even if the precise details of the Johnston theory are not accepted—that the shades of Stella and Vanessa should still be summoned from the grave to bring fresh damnation upon him. Thackeray talked as if it were Swift's treatment of the divine

Stella which stirred him to his highest pitch of fury; surely a combined piece of impertinence and vanity if ever there was one, since he, like the rest of us, did not know the intimate detail of Swift's relationship with the apparently uncomplaining Stella and since we are obviously intended to admire the gallantry with which Thackeray rushes to her aid. But Stella or Vanessa or anyone else, male or female, whom Swift is alleged to have used badly, serves the same purpose—to feed the insensate hostility which he beyond all other great writers seems to provoke. The reason must lie deeper in the doctrines he made peculiarly his own.

However, let us draw back again from any such ascent or descent. Let us glance at a few other items on the charge sheet. He spent a large part of his time—much more than a man of genius ought to waste—in seeking, scheming for, preferment in the Church, and that in turn meant toadying to politicians. It is, alas, true; that is what he did do, for a considerable part of his life. He devoted himself to becoming what he called that 'apt conjunction of lawn and black satin we entitle a Bishop'. He learnt the tricks and necessities of politicians in his own soul. In that world he noted that 'climbing is done in the same posture as creeping'. And some people tend to deplore the whole of this part of his career, but quite wrongly. If he had never descended into Grub Street, *Gulliver's Travels* could never have been written. And not only in *Gulliver's Travels*, but in many of his writings, he offers excellent advice for the treatment of politicians. He said, when he wrote to Stella: 'If we let these Ministers pretend too much, there will be no governing them.' And yet, at the same time when he said that, he also wrote a great defence of Grub Street and the journalists, which must be quoted at rather greater length. Maybe there are journals of the present age, possibly *Private Eye*, which would find comfort in painting these words on their walls.

In the Attic Commonwealth, [he wrote] it was the privilege and birthright of every citizen and poet to rail aloud, and in public, or to expose upon the stage, by name any person they pleased, though of the greatest figure whether a Creon, an Hyperbolus, an Alcibiades, or a Demosthenes; but, on the other side, the least reflecting word let fall against the people in general, was immediately caught up, and revenged upon the authors, however considerable for their quality or merits. Whereas in England it is just the reverse of all this. Here you may securely display your utmost rhetoric against mankind, in the face of the world . . . And when you have done, the whole audience, far from being offended, shall return you thanks, as a deliverer of precious and useful truths. Nay, farther, it is but to venture your lungs, and you may preach it in Covent Garden against foppery and fornication, and something else: against pride, and dissimulation, and bribery, at Whitehall: you may expose rapine and injustice in the Inns of Court Chapel: and in the city pulpit, be as fierce as you please against avarice, hypocrisy and extortion. 'Tis but a ball bandied to and fro and every man carries a racket about him, to strike it from himself, among the rest of the company. But on the other side, whoever should mistake the nature of things so far, as to drop but a single hint in public, how such a one starved half the fleet, and half poisoned the rest; how such a one, from a true principle of love and honour, pays no debt but for wenches and play; how such a one has got clap, and runs out of his estate; how Paris, bribed by Juno and Venus, loth to defend either party, slept out the whole cause on the bench; or how such an author makes long speeches in the senate, with much thought, little sense, and to no purpose; whoever, I say, should venture to be this particular, must expect to be imprisoned for *scandalum magnatum*; to have challenges sent to him; to be sued for defamation; and to be brought to the bar of the House of Commons.

No better defence of the journalistic craft has been written since that day.

Yet Swift's politics—the truth can no longer be blurred—left much to be desired. He himself made the confession playfully:

> *He was an Honest Man, I'll swear—*
> *Why, Sir, I differ from you there.*
> *For, I have heard another Story,*
> *He was a most confounded Tory.*

It is true. Search as we may, it is impossible to refute it. He did believe in a form of static society. He ranged himself against the moderns. He sneered at scientists. And what he would have said of the white heat or the black heart of the technological age passes comprehension. He believed that the hierarchical forms

of society should be left untouched. Walter Scott, certainly
no advanced thinker himself, talked of the antiquated and
unpopular nature of Swift's politics. Indeed Swift was inclined to
curse *all* politics. He put his verdict into the mouth of the King of
Brobdingnag. When Gulliver was in Brobdingnag, he explained to
the King how politics worked in England, and Swift wrote:

> The prejudices of his education prevailed so far, that he could not
> forbear from taking me up in his right hand, and stroking me gently
> with the other, after an hearty fit of laughing, asked me, whether I
> were a Whig or a Tory.

He was opposed to the idea of progress. He was inclined to be
extremely pessimistic about human nature. Which brings us to
the even more familiar charge: that he was a misanthrope; that he
was anti-life; that *Gulliver's Travels*, and especially the last book
and the picture of the Yahoos, is a vile satire on the whole human
race; almost the most terrifying ever written. That is the charge
which has been sustained over centuries. Before seeking to answer
it, however, it is necessary to pose the other side of the mystery.

If Swift was such a Tory, if he was so dedicated a champion of
the doctrines of original sin, why has he commanded such interest
and allegiance on the Left in British politics, and from the
romantic revolutionaries of later times who believed in the
perfectibility of man? It is no exaggeration to say that, for
considerable periods since Swift's death, the protection of his
reputation has rested almost entirely with people on the Left.
Tories and Whigs have reviled him, Dr. Johnson, the greatest of
the Tories, and Lord Macaulay, the greatest of the Whigs. But the
extreme radicals rallied to his defence. Before asking why they did
it, let us substantiate the claim.

Swift's defence of 'the whole people of Ireland' naturally made
him the enemy of the English Establishment, and he became a
great popular writer and a popular symbol. During John Wilkes's
fight on behalf of the free press against the King and the House of
Commons, there were riots and political demonstrations throughout London. One of them occurred outside the Rose and Crown
in Wapping, and it is recorded that an Irish voice above the

tumult was heard to greet Wilkes thus: 'By Jasus, he's a liberty
boy—like Dean Swift.' And coming a little later, to the epoch of
the French Revolution and its aftermath, when England was near
revolution too, evidence of how influential was the liberty boy is
startling. William Godwin, father of English anarchism, and
husband of Mary Wollstonecraft, mother of English feminism,
was a devotee of *Gulliver's Travels*. So was Thomas Holcroft,
tried in 1794 at the famous Treason Trial. When Edmund Burke
denounced all would-be revolutionaries as the 'swinish multitude', a penny news-sheet was produced by Thomas Spence called
Pig's Meat. It was stuffed with Swift; whenever the editor had a
hole to fill, more Swift was used to plug it. When Leigh Hunt
wanted a name for his radical newspaper, he called it after Swift's
old paper, *The Examiner*. And William Cobbett, as a boy, bought
for threepence a copy of *A Tale of a Tub* and kept it as his Bible.
Swift has told us, he said, not to chop blocks with razors. Swift
was Cobbett's tutor. Cobbett understood Swift's dictum which
should be inscribed on the wall of every political journalist: 'Use
the point of the pen, not the feather.'

It was people on the Left in English politics who came to the
aid of Swift, when he was being attacked from quarters where he
might have expected defence, and most significant and comprehensive was the defence of Swift against all comers by William
Hazlitt in his 1818 London lecture delivered at the Surrey
Institution, just across from Blackfriars. That, as we have seen,
was a literary occasion. There he defended Swift as a writer,
became the first critic to recognise his greatness as a poet, and was
even prepared to forgive him for having been a Tory. Yet how
well he knew what he was doing; how safe, from the viewpoint of
his own political dreams, the encouragement might be. Hazlitt
was addressing the stolid English; in Ireland they had seized the
point more quickly and partly no doubt because Swift's style was
sharpened for the purpose. It became colder, clearer, harder still.
The common people—a phrase Swift would use himself as a
compliment—understood. In Dublin he became an even more
popular writer than he had ever been in London. Irishmen read
him even more eagerly than the English. Henry Grattan and
Thomas Davis hailed him as their patriotic guide; Wolfe Tone

and James Fintan Lalor sought to adopt his pamphleteering style, and Michael Davitt, the truest patriot and wisest and most selfless leader of them all, saw him as the prophet of the land war and the supremacy of moral force. John Redmond declared: 'He did as much as any man in history to lift Ireland into the position of a nation.' In Ireland throughout the whole nineteenth century and beyond he was overtly and effectively a revolutionary figure. And yet he rarely addressed his words to the Irish alone. He wrote, as he often laughingly said, for the universal improvement of mankind.

Some of his more recent and reputable critics can admit his qualities, as if they were making a grudging confession, or accuse him of vices which seem the exact opposite of those which could ever be attributed to him. George Orwell, for example, accepts that Swift was 'a diseased writer' and that he solved his dilemmas by blowing everything to pieces in the only way open to him, that is, by going mad, and then cudgels his brain to discover how a man with 'a world view which only just passes the test of sanity' can still have such appeal to so many, himself included. He offers no sufficient answer, and given the diseased mind as the unalterable factor in the situation, the failure is not surprising; men do not gather grapes of thorns and figs of thistles. Aldous Huxley, as we have seen, is even more startling, with his accusations about Swift being an incurable sentimentalist and romantic, one who resented the world of reality and would never dare face it. And Dr. Leavis concluded that 'he certainly does not impress us as a mind in possession of its experience'. These, from three such powerful and independent minds, seem the oddest conclusions. Surely the author of *Gulliver*, whatever else he was doing, was consciously compressing his whole life into one book and stripping aside all sentimental impurities.

George Orwell's essay, however, offers some useful signposts to other conclusions. 'Why is it', he asks, 'that we don't mind being called Yahoos although firmly convinced that we are not Yahoos?' His own reply is unconvincing, and perhaps a better one is that Swift does *not* call us Yahoos; Lemuel Gulliver does, but he is not Swift. Orwell also remarks, as others have done, how dreary is the ideal world of the Houyhnhnms. 'Swift did his best for the Houyhnhnms', says Dr. Leavis, 'and they may have all the reason, but the Yahoos have all the life.' This undeniable effect of the last book in *Gulliver* is commonly attributed to the failure of all writers to produce a tolerable ideal. All Utopias are too dull to be lived in; the perfection, the immobility, become suffocating. But suppose Swift knew that as well as, or better than, we. Suppose he intended the ideal world to be dreary, its inhabitants too good to be true. Suppose he wanted those who might rise above that brutish Yahoo level to be quite endearing creatures, despite their assortment of obvious defects. Suppose it was his purpose to expose the insufficiency and the insipidity of the Augustan virtues of Reason, Truth and Nature which the Houyhnhnms allegedly exemplify. Suppose the Houyhnhnms are not the heroes and heroines of the book. Suppose (and a fair hint of it is given in the last chapter of the Voyage to the Houyhnhnms) it is the wise and humane and 'least corrupted' Brobdingnagians and their kind-hearted king who represent Swift's positive standard for erring man. Suppose, in short, that *Gulliver's Travels* is not the work of some indefinable demon operating in the decaying carcase of the infamous Dean of St. Patrick's but the deliberate contrivance of his intense, luminous, compassionate mind.

The view crudely summarised in these suppositions is expounded at length with something approaching Swiftian grace and lucidity in the book *Jonathan Swift and the Age of Compromise* by Kathleen Williams (Constable 1959). It is fortified in the conclusions reached by Professor Irvin Ehrenpreis in *The Personality of Jonathan Swift* and the three-volume Life on which he has been engaged. Swift, insists Miss Williams, refused to simplify; as a moral being and a political being, man is a complex creature, and only a process of compromise can produce in any sphere a state of things which will do justice to his complexity. She makes a startling comparison between Swift and Montaigne, and at first thought any alleged common characteristics between the two may seem absurd. How can the meandering ruminations of Montaigne be likened to Swift's fierce polemical thrust? But she notes how Montaigne must have been one of Swift's favourites; 'your old prating friend' was Bolingbroke's taunt.

And there is another fact more clinching than any literary allusion. Swift gave a copy of Montaigne to Vanessa.

'Both [that is Swift and Montaigne] search among ideas, rather than assert ideas', writes Miss Williams, 'feeling their way among a multiplicity of conflicting and assertive doctrines . . . but for Swift the search is a thing of urgency, and he cannot exist calmly in the life of suspense.' It is tempting to lift one quotation after another from her book, especially as she sees the Voyage of the Houyhnhnms as summing up all Swift's writing, the most complete expression of his moral, political and social outlook. But since her views are complex to match Swift's, quotations impair the complete effect. One may be given, since it offers a fresh approach to the perpetually changing interpretation of *Gulliver's Travels*:

> Our first impression, in Swift's work [she writes] is of the elusive brilliance of the attack; a glancing, dazzling mind appears to be concerned solely with the presentation of absurdity or of evil, shifting its point of view constantly the better to perform its task. But as we grow accustomed to his ways of thinking and feeling we become aware that at the heart of Swift's work are unity and consistency, and we see that the attack is also a defence, that tools of destruction are being employed for a positive and constructive purpose. The inventiveness and resourcefulness of his satiric method is seen as arising directly out of the necessities of his mind and of his age: the changing complications of his irony are the necessary expression of an untiring devotion to the few certainties that life affords. For all his elusiveness and indirection, his readiness to compromise or change his ground, few writers have been more essentially consistent than Swift, but for him consistency could be sustained only by such methods as these. Balance in the state or in the individual mind could be kept only by an agile shifting of weights.

It may be added that there was nothing accidental in Miss Williams's return to the estimate Swift's contemporaries made of him, for her method is to discover and describe the exact context in which he wrote.

Swift, then, as a militant Montaigne! One can almost hear the snort of derision from Dr. Johnson or Dr. Leavis. Pope, Gay,

Arbuthnot and Bolingbroke might have found it easier to recognise the likeness. They knew how sane he was and how cheerful he could be, and did he not write to them about *Gulliver* and say:

> I desire you and all my friends will take a special care that my disaffection to the world may not be imputed to my age . . . I tell you after all, that I do not hate mankind: it is *vous autres* who hate them, because you would have them reasonable animals, and are angry for being disappointed.

Swift's scepticism never went so far as Montaigne's. His pessimism about man and his sinful nature and the possibilities of improvement by human effort stayed close to that of orthodox Christianity. But it did not reach the depths of black despair which is supposed to have issued in his madness, nor did it prevent him from declaiming, denouncing, preaching and exhorting with all his skill and might—occupations which certainly would have been senseless if man's condition were incurable.

No one indeed has ever lashed the brutalities and bestialities which men inflict upon one another with a greater intensity. He had a horror of state tyranny and, as George Orwell has underlined, an uncanny presentiment of totalitarianism and all the torture it would brand on body and mind. He loathed cruelty. He was enraged by the attempts of one nation to impose its will on another which we call imperialism. He exposed, as never before or since, the crimes committed in the name of a strutting, shouting patriotism. Gulliver doubts whether our 'conquests in the countries I treat of, would be as easy as those of Ferdinando Cortez over the naked Americans' (where did he learn that, except from Montaigne?), and then comes an outburst as topical as the news from Cambodia or Kabul in the year 1980:

> But I had another Reason which made me less forward to enlarge his Majesty's dominions by my discoveries. To say the truth, I had conceived a few scruples with relation to the distributive justice of princes upon those occasions. For instance, a crew of pirates are

driven by a storm they know not whither; at length a boy discovers
land from the top-mast; they go on shore to rob and plunder; they see
an harmless people, are entertained with kindness, they give the
country a new name, they take formal possession of it for the King,
they set up a rotten plank or a stone for a memorial, they murder two
or three dozen of the natives, bring away a couple more by force for a
sample, return home, and get their pardon. Here commences a new
dominion acquired with a title by *divine right*. Ships are sent with the
first opportunity; the natives driven out or destroyed, their princes
tortured to discover their gold; a free licence given to all acts of
inhumanity and lust, the earth reeking with the blood of its
inhabitants: and this execrable crew of butchers employed in so pious
an expedition, is a *modern colony* sent to convert and civilise an
idolatrous and barbarous people.

Above all, he hated war and the barbarisms it let loose. War, for
him, embraced all other forms of agony and wickedness. *Gulliver's
Travels* is still the most powerful of pacifist pamphlets. And, of
course, it is these aspects of his iconoclasm which have won for
him such persistent allegiance on the Left. It is not surprising that
Hazlitt, Cobbett, Leigh Hunt and Godwin, in the midst of
another great war when spies and informers were at work in the
interests of exorbitant authority, in the age of the press gang and
Peterloo, treasured *Gulliver's Travels* as a seditious tract. It
spoke the truth at that hour called high treason. It sounded the
trumpet of anarchistic revolt when others who did so were being
dispatched to Botany Bay. It assailed the Establishment, Whig
and Tory (what Cobbett called 'The Thing'), and reduced the
whole pretentious bunch to their proper stature. Small wonder
that stout patriots like Dr. Johnson, Sir Walter Scott, Macaulay
and the rest, found the meat too strong for them. But they might,
in their various epochs, have hit upon a more creditable retort
than merely to call the man mad. Not even we today, in the
twentieth century, regard a hatred of slavery, oppression and war
as infallible signs of insanity.

Enough, by any reckoning, to have established Swift's claim as
a revolutionary figure—to have assailed in frontal attack the war-
makers and the empire-builders at the supreme moment of their
power, in England and in Ireland: the first voice to be raised in
this ferocious tone. Yet, miraculously, there is more, and much

more. He marked the clash between 'the common people' and their rulers, their landlords, their oppressors. He saw that 'Freedom consists in a People being governed by Laws made with their own Consent; and Slavery on the contrary'. He saw that 'Poor Nations are hungry and rich Nations are proud', and Pride and Hunger will ever be at variance. He saw what real politics are about. He prophesied what would happen if the new moneyed class, the new economic man, should rule the community. 'Swift's special distinction'—the words of F. W. Bateson—'is that he exposed *laissez-faire* capitalism, and all that it stood for, while it was still no bigger than a cloud the size of a man's hand.' *The Modest Proposal for Preventing the Children of Ireland from being a Burden to their Parents or Country* was not solely addressed to the Irish. It was 'the actual language of Cheapside and Threadneedle Street'. It was the most tremendous curse on the money lenders since Jesus of Nazareth drove them from the temple.

Hazlitt had noted, earlier than anyone else, earlier than such excellent modern critics as Bateson, what service Swift, properly invoked, could do for the cause of the people against their rulers. He wrote a letter to *The Examiner* on 25 August, 1816, which shows how closely Swift always stood at his side:

> Sir,—One reason that the world does not grow wiser is, that we forget what we have learned. While we are making new discoveries we neglect old ones. Mr. Burke had certainly read *Gulliver's Travels*, yet in his invidious paradox, that 'if the poor were to cut the throats of the rich, they would not get a meal the more for it', he seems not to have recollected what that very popular Author says on this subject. In the sixth chapter of the Voyage to the Houyhnhnms, is the following passage, which may show that Swift's Toryism did not, like Mr. Burke's Anti-Jacobinism deprive him of common sense. . .

And then, under the simple class war title, *Rich and Poor*, the great passage followed, showing that the last Voyage is not solely concerned with high philosophical themes:

> My master was yet wholly at a loss to understand what motives could incite this race of lawyers to perplex, disquiet, and weary themselves by engaging in a confederacy of injustice, merely for the sake of

injuring their fellow-animals; neither could he comprehend what I meant in saying they did it for *hire*. Whereupon I was at much pains to describe to him the use of *money*, the materials it was made of, and the value of the metals; that when a Yahoo had got a great store of this precious substance, he was able to purchase whatever he had a mind to, the finest clothing, the noblest houses, great tracts of land, the most costly meats and drinks, and have his choice of the most beautiful females. Therefore since *money* alone was able to perform all these feats, our Yahoos thought they could never have enough of it to spend or to save, as they found themselves inclined from their natural bent either to profusion or avarice. That the rich man enjoyed the fruit of the poor man's labour, and the latter were a thousand to one in proportion to the former. That the bulk of our people was forced to live miserably, by labouring every day for small wages to make a few live plentifully. I enlarged myself much on these and many other particulars to the same purpose: but his Honour was still to seek: for he went upon a supposition that all animals had a title to their share in the productions of the earth, and especially those who presided over the rest. Therefore he desired I would let him know, what these costly meats were, and how any of us happened to want them. Whereupon I enumerated as many sorts as came into my head, with the various methods of dressing them, which could not be done without sending vessels by sea to every part of the world, as well for liquors to drink, as for sauces, and innumerable other conveniences. I assured him, that this whole globe of earth must be at least three times gone round, before one of our better female Yahoos could get her breakfast, or a cup to put it in. He said, That must needs be a miserable country which cannot furnish food for its own inhabitants. But what he chiefly wondered at was how such vast tracts of ground as I described should be wholly without *fresh water*, and the people put to the necessity of sending over the sea for drink. I replied, that England (the dear place of my nativity) was computed to produce three times the quantity of food more than its inhabitants are able to consume, as well as liquors extracted from grain, or pressed out of the fruit of certain trees, which made excellent drink, and the same proportion in every other convenience of life. But in order to feed the luxury and intemperance of the males, and the vanity of the females, we sent away the greatest part of our necessary things to other countries, from whence in return we brought the materials of diseases, folly, and vice, to spend among ourselves. Hence it follows of necessity, that vast numbers of our people are compelled to seek their livelihood by begging, robbing, stealing, cheating, pimping, forswearing, flattering, suborning, forging, gaming, lying, fawning,

hectoring, voting, scribbling, star-gazing, poisoning, whoring, cant-
ing, libelling, free-thinking, and the like occupations. But besides all
this, the bulk of our people supported themselves by furnishing the
necessities or conveniences of life to the rich, and to each other. For
instance, when I am at home and dressed as I ought to be, I carry on
my body the workmanship of an hundred tradesmen; the building
and furniture of my house employs as many more, and five times the
number to adorn my wife.

Sometimes the voice of Swift rose thus in mockery or invective,
and sometimes it subsided into something softer but no less
piercing:

The Scriptures tells us that *oppression makes a wise man mad*:
therefore, consequently speaking, the reason why some men are not
mad, is because they are not wise; however, it was to be wished that
oppression would, in time, teach a little *wisdom to fools*.

No doubt there about his sanity or his astringency; what about
his faith? Most modern scholars insist, and they have substantial
evidence on their side, that Swift's religious convictions cannot
be questioned. They show that he was a most diligent parson.
They show that he served the Anglican church with a fighting
spirit. Nobody can deny that. They show that he was careful not
to reveal the evidence of his scepticism, if indeed he had it. The
case is not argued here, but some of his contemporaries, it may be
noted, were not so certain as some of the modern scholars. There
was the famous rhyme, pinned to the door of St. Patrick's
Cathedral when Swift arrived there:

Look down, St. Patrick, look we pray,
On thine own Church and Steeple.
Convert the Dean on this great day
Or else God help the People.

Despite the strong evidence to the contrary, it is not so easy to
abandon the suspicion that Swift wrote those lines himself. And
he was the author of a sentence which seems to disavow all pretensions to piety. Life is not a farce he explained: 'it is a
ridiculous tragedy, which is the worst form of composition.'

He certainly did write, too, the greatest epitaph a man ever had, as Yeats called it, and in that epitaph there is not a tincture of Christianity, just as there is no trace of madness. He was, for about two centuries, confidently consigned to hell-fire, but now, under the power of modern scholarship, he almost joins the angels. The Church has claimed him, but so did Voltaire. He loved England, but it was Ireland which inspired him. He knew what crawling self-seekers politicians could be, but he knew too that politics was concerned with the great question of rich and poor. He saw how human nature could be rootedly conservative yet he saw too how common decency so often required that it should be convulsively revolutionary. He served human liberty. That was his own secular boast. He did, and still does.

And he was something else besides. He was, after all, a comic genius, like Rabelais or Cervantes or Charles Dickens or Benjamin Disraeli or Charlie Chaplin or Groucho Marx or Spike Milligan; along with all his other attributes, he belonged to that exclusive company. A few (or, if you like, not so few), like Alexander Pope or Henry Fielding or John Gay or Dr. Arbuthnot or Patrick Delany or Thomas Sheridan or Stella or Vanessa were clever or lucky enough to be able to see for themselves from the start. The flow of satire, soft and savage, poured forth in verse and prose in an endless flood. The invectives can still turn the stomach; yet it was he who described how mankind could be furnished with 'the two noblest of things, sweetness and light'. Nothing could hold his humour and his wit in check for long. Let attention be addressed at last to the Voyage of Laputa, the merit of which, by the way, has sometimes been shamefully depreciated, the bad fashion having been set by Dr. Arbuthnot, who, despite his love for Swift, possibly found the attack on the medical profession within it too near the bone. Anyhow, Laputa contains many varied treasures, such as these two sentences:

He had been eight years upon a project for extracting sunbeams out of cucumbers, which were to be put into vials hermetically sealed and let out to warm the air in raw inclement summers. He told me, he did not doubt in eight years more, that he should be able to supply the Governor's gardens with sunshine at a reasonable rate; but he complained that his stock was low, and entreated me to give him something as an encouragement to ingenuity, especially since this had been a very dear season for cucumbers.

According to Dr. Johnson, the man who wrote that was deficient in both wit and humour, and could not conceivably be related to the author of the vastly superior work, *A Tale of a Tub*. Thus the greatest of English critics or, at least, the greatest of English Tories would have banished Jonathan Swift to damnation and oblivion. It was fortunate that the magnanimous English Left, led as usual by the Irish, was able to come to his rescue.

Index